Human Development in the
Indian Context

Human Development in the Indian Context

A Socio-cultural Focus

Volume I

Margaret Khalakdina

SAGE Los Angeles • London • New Delhi • Singapore
www.sagepublications.com

First published in 2008 by

 SAGE Publications India Pvt Ltd
B1/I-1 Mohan Cooperative Industrial Area
Mathura Road, New Delhi 110 044, India
www.sagepub.in

SAGE Publications Inc
2455 Teller Road
Thousand Oaks, California 91320, USA

SAGE Publications Ltd
1 Oliver's Yard
55 City Road
London EC1Y 1SP, UK

SAGE Publications Asia-Pacific Pte Ltd
33 Pekin Street
#02-01 Far East Square
Singapore 048763

Published by Vivek Mehra for SAGE Publications India Pvt Ltd, typeset in 10/13 pt Palatino by Star Compugraphics Private Limited, Delhi and printed at Chaman Enterprises, New Delhi.

Library of Congress Cataloging-in-Publication Data
Khalakdina, Margaret.
    Human development in the Indian context: a socio-cultural focus/Margaret Khalakdina.
      v. cm.
    Includes index.
    Contents: Preface—Acknowledgements—Introduction—The hexagon of human development: the Indian setting—Human development: bases and processes—Origins of knowledge on human development—Sources of knowledge on human development—The methodological study of human development—Research concerns—Identity and interpersonal competence—The development of critical skills—Societal mores: their implications for human development—A concluding view—Appendices—Glossary—Index—About the author.
    1. India—Social conditions. 2. Social psychology—India. 3. India—Civilization. I. Title.

| HN683.5.K413 | 303.440954—dc22 | 2008 | 2007052672 |

ISBN: 978-0-7619-3610-7 (HB)   978-81-7829-773-6 (India-HB)

The SAGE Team: Sugata Ghosh, Ankur Agarwal, Amrita Saha and Trinankur Banerjee

To my husband Nazeem A. Khalakdina
and
our grandchildren Isabella and Alessia

Contents

Foreword

I T IS with great pleasure that I write a Foreword for *Human Development in the Indian Context: A Socio-cultural Focus, Volume I* by Margaret Khalakdina.

Amartya Sen has pointed out that people have multiple identities. India is a country with myriad regions, dialects and subcultures. It is compounded by many fissioned sects or religions in differing terrains. In India's multicultural society, these identities become more complex and nuanced. Also, the identities are not static; they evolve over time as a society develops. If economic development is to improve human well-being, we need to understand how such identities are formed and how their expectations can be met.

Some decades or so ago, India, perhaps, was at the crossroads betwixt and between modernity, with its age-old anchored systems of traditional ways and its own unique ethos. India is now fast learning to straddle both the worlds. Indians are dynamically traditional in context, and at the same time moving along a fast modernising track, especially the economic one. As in all spheres, 'there is a human face'. It is this face and its changing contours that need to be intensely and incisively analysed in the Indian context.

The author of this volume, Margaret Khalakdina, in this scholarly and exhaustive treatise, amply illustrates the psychology and sociology of the human face in its cultural milieu. Using data, both discussive and empirical, that exists on the psychological, sociological and cultural development of the Indian, she argues that even though Indians have generic phylogenetic qualities which are similar to other races, they develop their ontogenetic skills into being a uniquely different psyche from that of others. The stress is on giving the reader a framework which is theoretical. The author has illustrated these differences in a way that it gives a balanced intertwining between the homogeneity of being an Indian and also the heterogeneity of being a tribal, an urbanite or a peasant, from different regions of the country. This gives the Indian his resilient ability to adapt and adjust, especially in those who are economically deprived, but not necessarily socially or emotionally deprived.

It is my sincere hope that this task of looking at the Indian holistically in the developmental process will continue in the writing of such useful treatises as this volume.

Kirit Parikh
Member, Planning Commission

Preface

Human beings develop and behave in a generally homogeneous manner, whether in the developing nations of Asia or Africa, or the economically developed nations of the West. As such, the basic principles of human growth and development are the same the world over. These are known general concepts and forms of behaviour. However, there is growing concern among experts in India that the content of knowledge should also incorporate dynamic cultural concepts that have social relevance in the Indian milieu.

A popular notion exists that we can reliably compare an individual from the West with an individual from the East, because of the homogeneity of general or phylogenetic characteristics. Often clichés about the Indian are used, such as: 'The behaviour of the average child in the West is more enquiring than the average child in India', or 'The Indian child is submissive, non-aggressive and dependent, unlike the child from the West'. Equally common are clichés that describe the Western child as 'aggressive, independent and risk-taking'.

These statements are based on symptomatic behaviour, without much analysis of the deeper causes and correlates of such behaviour, given the particular milieu in which the child/adult lives. One should rather ask: what makes the environment of the individual from the East different from the individual in the West?

To understand the development of the Indian individual, it must be realised that the Indian lives in an *in situ* environment, different from other societies. Such environments mediate the development processes in a relatively indigenous manner. This is not to say that this phenomenon is unique to India. Individuals from other societies also exhibit traits unique to their own relevant environments. These traits are sufficiently discrete as to warrant contrasts rather than comparisons as the platforms for analysis are different. One such concept meriting contrast is that the child in the East is inaccurately said to live in a relatively deprived environment. Deprivation may be of many kinds: physical, emotional, economic or social. One can say with conviction that the Indian individual is normally not emotionally deprived. He may have fewer economic goods, but then one can ask a further question: does only possession of material goods make for a better quality of life? Such issues are also looked at in this volume from the foundations of social science philosophies, especially the Indian aspect, and from the perspectives of experts who document such information. It must be said that there are noteworthy attempts of Indian social scientists to brave the winds and discuss cultural differences as systemic, discriminatory variations.

These are discussed within the generic cultures and even within subdivisions of the generic culture. In India, for instance, these discriminatory variables tend to be classificatory, such as ethnicity/religion/region/caste. These differential concepts also emerge from the writings of cultural sociologists, cultural psychologists and cultural anthropologists. A noteworthy direction is the progress made in the disciplines of psychology and sociology to view culture specifics using indigenous interpretations of concepts. Wherever possible, in this volume, there is a judicious mix of empirical data and discursive philosophies applicable to the Indian psyche.

Given that India is composed of many little communities, it is necessary to look at permutations and combinations of influencing factors. These factors cause shifts to appear dynamically as if through a kaleidoscope, which then affect the understanding as one moves from one lifestyle to another, such as the nomad, the tribal, the rural peasant, the urban slum dweller, the striving middle class and the swiftly moving, upwardly mobile elite who live in proximity.

The ecological environments of the West are more cohesive and more homogeneous than those in India. A great deal of similarity exists among them from one ecological area to another. Most of their environments are technologically oriented. Their festivities and socio-religious customs are similarly celebrated within their societies. In the USA, for instance, everyone celebrates Thanksgiving. Almost all, barring a few, participate in Easter and Christmas. Apple pie and doughnuts are similarly available everywhere, even in the most remote villages. The dominant ethos of Anglo-Saxon Protestantism prevails in all walks of life in the western world just as Hinduism is the dominant ethos prevalent in India. Yet in India, at the same time, there are norms of discrimination. For instance, among the different ethnic groups there exist differences in eating patterns, marriage alliances, attitudes of upper castes towards the lower, religious differences and other forms of behaviour. Even the lifestyles in various ecologies differ and, whether in rural subsistence economies or in affluent urban areas, the hiatus between the well-to-do and the not-so-well-to-do continues to exist. The tribal, for example, lives in a subsistence economy and his lifestyle is basic and primary to existence, whereas the urbanite is fast becoming accustomed to technologically-oriented patterns of living.

Nevertheless, it is important to state that no one environmental system or its subsystems is either static or exclusive of the other. In India there are forces that move subsocieties to change or to find another state of homeostasis. When this state becomes destabilised, a rearrangement through adaptation occurs to the environment for another level of equilibrium. A decade ago it was television, which spread all over the urban areas, now it is the cellular phone and the Internet. A rural child, for instance, moves ecologically from a subsistence village economy to an urban slum with his migrant family, and from his village primary school to an urban college, and so on. Such changes in adapting to different environments are occurring within India's subsocieties, as the country moves in fits and starts towards modernisation, more in one group than another. For instance, in some remote tribal hills in dense forests, hardly any transformation in lifestyles is apparent. In villages on the periphery of large cities, cow-dung cakes are still prepared for cooking purposes, often alongside with electricity for lighting houses. Such is the jostling of traditional with modern ways in the Indian scenario.

The study of human development is based mainly on the discipline of developmental psychology when describing motor, mental, emotional and social development. It borrows concepts from social psychology, anthropology and other socio-economic sciences to explain societal and familial factors influencing development. Human development is therefore a hybrid and an amalgam of several strands of social sciences. In the Indian environment, interdisciplinary dimensions are therefore extremely relevant for a pluralistic, multicultural, multilingual society.

Human development specialists, cognisant of the relationships stated above, view human development holistically. In the use of such an approach, development is explained through multidisciplinary thematic constructs. As such, wherever concepts from other supporting disciplines are incorporated in the writing of this volume, they are intended to enhance understanding of human development in the Indian context. For instance, the economic environment is a high-profiled factor when describing the growth in economically underprivileged environments. Therefore, economic considerations will be introduced when discussing ecology and habitat.

Experts have urged the use of contextual and culture-specific variables in describing the whole process of development. For instance, in the Indian context, toilet training is not such an intense parenting practice as in the West, or the expression of frustration. True, a frustrated child may create a tantrum. Indian parents, however, try to appease the child or just ignore the behaviour till it dies down, and do not go into intense analysis of the behaviour themselves as parenting individuals or seek the help of a psychiatrist. Frustration, interestingly, in the Indian context, may also lead to a variety of consequent behaviours such as aggression, regression or apathy, resignation or even sublimation if philosophically oriented, whereas American studies describe this behaviour mainly in the dimensions of frustration–aggression. There is no straight one-to-one relationship. Resignation might arise from a sense of being used to deprivation, or a sense of tolerance of differences. For instance, if the rich are born rich, it is traditionally believed to be a part of one's *karma*, leading to a sense of tolerance by the not-so-rich neighbour. In fact, such tolerance might accrue to one's *dharma* for the next life. It is essential, however, to know what factors bring about these overt behaviours. Is apathy an outcome of resilience to economic deprivation, or an innate tendency, or a socially reinforced habit? We honestly cannot say. How is it that a deprived environment for a particular individual leads him to become a respected leader in adult life?

The task of conceptualisation is to offer logically derived premises. For instance, how do we account for the potter's child's better skills in perception of mass and weight (Anandalakshmy and Bajaj, 1981) as compared to a bureaucrat's child in the same geoecological area? Or how do we account for the urban child's familiarity with the clock and the concept of time, as contrasted with the tribal child's skills for discerning the impact of natural occurrences like sowing time, direction of the wind, impending rain, and so on? Do they relate to general intelligence levels or is there some specific stimulating process operating? How do we account for the ordinary young engineer educated in India becoming a successful tycoon in the West? To what extent, if any, are these skills related to innate development potentials, or the influences surrounding the developing Indian individual, or both? While there is not much empirical data in these areas, we do know that development is modified by many interacting influences in the environment: by religion or lack of it, by social norms, economic status and types of parenting. In India, traditionality cohabits with modernity in varying degrees. We have, therefore, many discrete, miniature Indias. In this context it is necessary to stress that time is perhaps one of the more powerful variables that influences or facilitates opportunities to develop skills, whether in a traditional or a modernising environment. Time is used as a medium of social transformation in concepts of tradition and modernity (time is linear and standardised), associated with capitalist market economy. On the other hand, a traditional perspective sees time as being cyclic, continuous and repetitive (Ostor, 1993). In understanding development in a contextual manner we cannot ignore the world of reality where a child is traditionally socialised and yet exposed to the modern world of science and technology. There are few Indian children of today who do not know items of modern consumption, such as soft drinks and television. Yet there are traditional rituals meticulously practised by these very individuals. One has only to observe the television-watching habits of Indians to know what appeals to them. Soap operas, which emphasise ritualistic behaviours, are widely watched by the general population which, at the same time, is equally at home with consuming chips and soft drinks or talking on the cellular phone.

Among all strata, irrespective of education, occupation or income, *karva chauth vrath* (fasting by wives for the welfare and longevity of the husbands, indicating a sexist bias) is practised, and the rituals of *annaprasana* (first weaning) and *mundan* (first head-shaving) continue to be in vogue for the young child. There is, thus, a dual track on which the Indian individual travels. The urbanised child, for instance, is quite different from the tribal child in social behaviour. Although the origin of behaviour is the same, it does not imply that we should fall into an easy trap of treating the individual in India as wholly westernised when he or she enjoys watching models on the catwalk on TV, when at the same time *nazar* or the evil eye is being removed from a child in the same household. Does the Indian individual growing in his environment obtain and process information, and express it differently from the western individual, or is it the influence of his/her relationship with the environment (human and geoecological)?

What does it mean when we hear these expressions when something goes wrong: *aisa hota hai* or *koi baat nahin* or *theek ho jayega* ('it happens', 'don't worry' and 'everything will be all right'), which are expressions of casual acceptance. Are these implications the workings of destiny or of hesitancy to put in effort to solve the problem? There seems to be fluidity of coping mechanisms by which the Indian adapts to fast-changing situations. For instance, the youth of today from the elite class is no less 'modern', if anything more 'modern', in customs, habits and mannerisms than his counterpart in the West.

In varying degrees, and under differing conditions, the Indian lives in elementary environments, like the Pangi tribe in northern Himachal Pradesh, or in transitional environments, like the migrants in Mumbai's Dharavi slums, while the middle class lives in high-rise apartments adjacent to the urban slums. What kind of perceptions, what kind of behaviours can be ascribed in any of these subcultures? Given the opportunity, the tribal who is assumed to show less cognitive behaviour in relation to urban-oriented norms, may in fact show more intelligent behaviour than the urbanite. It is well known from observation of slum dwellers and migrant encampments that there is a remarkable adaptive resilience to their stark facilities. We can very easily fall into the trap of labelling the poor, the tribal and the nomad in India as less intelligent and less creative, simply because of the norms the educated world tends to use. Unless we know the context it is difficult to assess such types of behaviour. Therefore, is there a hypothesis of deficit operating? Such intriguing questions will be looked into in this contextual volume. For these reasons of the qualities of the Indian psyche and ethos, the theoretical frames used in this textual reference will take into account such socio-religious ethnic habitat factors as are essential to the understanding of human development in India. The theoretical frames, however, will use the well-known structural concepts of development originating in the West as its bases in the face of no other adequate alternative, indigenous empirical theories. However, we must temper this statement by saying that there are a growing number of mini-theories in relation to the Indian psyche.

We must also state that in actual fact, we are still groping for norms in many spheres of development such as social, mental and personality development. To this day in India, there is very little data on standard reference norms. We have tried to use western norms, either directly or through adaptation, but they still do not completely convince us because of their origin in western societies. Differing perspectives of allied disciplines will also be interwoven in the holistic approach used in this volume. These are essential for a fuller understanding of the heterogeneity/homogeneity dimensions affecting the development and behaviour of the Indian.

This volume is an attempt to try and weave a contextual and a culture-based framework within the principles of behaviour and development in the child's progression from conception to adulthood. Where relevant, contrasts within subcultures, as conditioned by economic and social factors, will be presented.

Further, as this is a textual reference, it will also incorporate concepts that are classical and long-standing in the discipline, such as Piagetian, Lewinian and Freudian conceptualisations, as these concepts are based on observational data. At the same time, the contents of the book will not lose susceptibility towards traditional wisdom, prevalent in the Indian ethos and its philosophy. The writing of this volume is attempted in an informal style, illustrated with several examples of everyday life. Yet at the same time, the intention is to make the concepts more identifiable with the environment that is familiar to the reader. It should be evident to the reader by now that this preface is a précis of the themes in the chapters to follow, namely, given the long-standing concepts of the disciplines of psychology, sociology and anthropology, this volume moulds them to facilitate the interpretation of the Indian in his context. For much of the time that the author has been in the profession, there was an acute lack of referencing information that was empirical or well documented, that made sense to the reader in his or her own situation, and that was applicable to an understanding of the human psyche in India.

This volume is the first of a two-volume analysis of human development and behaviour in India and consists of nine chapters relevant to the concepts of behaviour and development. The second volume is more specifically relevant to students of development processes and their outcomes.

It is duly recognised that the basic theoretical concepts have been established through empiricism by western experts earlier than the Indian experts. Being latecomers, the discipline of sociology was the first to initiate field studies through ethnography while the discipline of psychology initiated its procedures from laboratory experiments. In the 21st century, there is a movement towards cohesion of these disciplines. It is recommended that the approach to the contexts given in this volume be viewed against the backdrop of an attempt of the author to bring about a holistic picture of human development set within a secular Indian context. The attempt is made on the availability and the accessibility of what Indian textual empirical data currently exists.

References

Anandalakshmy, S. and M. Bajaj, 1981, 'Childhood in the Weavers' Community in Varanasi: Socialisation for Adult Roles', in D. Sinha (ed.), *Socialisation of the Indian Child*. New Delhi: Concept.

Ostor, A., 1993, *Vessels of Time: An Essay on Temporal Change and Social Transformation*. New Delhi: OUP.

Acknowledgements

THE MEANDERING channels in the writing of this book have uncovered many challenging areas of knowledge. In this attempt, I gratefully acknowledge the help and support given to me by Shakuntala Dixit, Radhika Takru, Ronica Arora and Meghna Chowdhury. I also need to acknowledge the technical assistance of M.K. Shaji who has diligently typed the manuscript. I am most grateful to my mentors, U. Bronfenbrenner, H. Riccutti and H. Levin of Cornell University, New York State, for an indepth understanding of the fundamentals of the social science disciplines. I am thankful to my colleagues Nandita Choudhry, Deepti Mehrotra, A. Sharma and Renu Gulati for their helpful comments and suggestions. The silent support of my two children, Asheena and Arshad, has helped give me the energy and the volition to finalise this document. My son-in law Rolando Montecalvo has been my initial guiding spirit in the writing of this volume. For the innumerable assistance given to me in little ways by various generous people, I acknowledge my gratitude. Last, but not least, I am greatly indebted to Dr Kirit Parikh, Member, Planning Commission, who is not only an outstanding colleague, planner, strategist and economist in the human development process, but has also exhibited in his writing a deep insight into the problems of the disadvantaged. Dr Kirit Parikh is not only a national but also an international figure of worldwide fame.

Introduction

THIS MAY be an unusual introduction to a subject that ambitiously attempts to span a view across the scope of the psychosocial developmental process of humans. We start with a story, and this true story can be a more telling introduction. Here is its narration: A developmental specialist teaching a course on rural community extension took her students from the metropolis to have some practical experience in a nearby village. They got busy with the females of the cluster of households, collecting information and advising them on health and hygiene subjects. Outside a hut, an old man sat on a *charpoy* smoking his *hukka* and looking on with amusement. He finally called the teacher:

> *Masterni*, what do you know of our lives? You come in the morning in your jeep and go back to your city in your jeep. You do not know us. You do not live with us. What do you know of what happens in our daily lives? Do you share our joys and our sorrows; know what we feel and do?

A simple tale, but so telling; a lesson to those of us who write erudite theses on psychosocial aspects while knowing so little of the large masses of people who comprise the Indian subcontinent. We know about conceptualisations, but to what extent do they tally with the social ground realities to which they should apply?

Therefore, what I venture to write in the following pages could indicate what we ought to know about the vast majority who comprise the Indian society. These make up a motley of individuals with whom we move, jostling shoulders in the marketplace, in the railway stations and in shopping centres. If we are to know them, how do we relate what we know to their lifestyles? This volume proposes to present in detail selected aspects of such knowledge. These aspects are for sharing knowledge with those wishing to know more about how psychology, sociology and anthropology relate to the individuals in their society. Generally speaking, this first volume of a two-volume set is foundational knowledge. Chapter 1, 'The Hexagon of Human Development: The Indian Setting', deals with the rationality of thinking as applied to everyday life experiences without becoming mundane descriptive storytelling. It is meant to overview the picture of development, reflecting the philosophy of Indian society, and the inclusion of the social sciences in a framework that draws upon social, political and economic events (Misra and Tripathi, 1993).

The events related to the concept of holistic development of socio-political changes in the 21st century are mentioned herein (Cole, 1992: 5–31). They, in a sense, indirectly but compellingly affect the contextual parameters of the Indian. Although it has been asked whether there is a unique Indian way of thinking that puts the Indian into a specialised category apart from other societies (Ramanujan, 1990: 41–58), we hasten to add that basic thought processes are the same the world over. It is the cultural learning process that largely determines whether the individual is from India, from Indonesia, or from any other society (Cole et al., 1971). As globalisation and international politics dominate the relations between countries, modifications/aberrations between the North and the South affect developing countries, especially in the formulation of a national identity (Robertson, 1992).

Developing countries are usually at the receiving end of international decisions, with little power to participate in the process substantially. The consequences are that we in India are faced with economic issues like the flooding of markets with foreign goods. This perception of plenty, a recent and growing phenomenon, motivates consumer spending. Consumer spending is provoked by media advertisements and gimmicky incentives. Thus, family budgets usually take a spin. Surmounting this, however, is the increase in market economy by the Sensex indices. Where before, average Indians had to carefully consider priorities on spending, they now have easier access to money under instalment/housing/discount schemes. The domino effect therefore operates incisively. Children in most strata demand more possessions. Parents tend to capitulate to these demands so that, for instance, an upper-class teenager possesses unlimited pocket money, a car and designer clothes. The relatively poor children in the same milieu aspire for the same and therefore are frustrated, resulting in either greater motivation or lessened self-esteem.

It is another story with families in areas prone to natural disasters. Scraping a meal together every day is the beginning and end of the major and perhaps greatest priority. In this century of accelerated changing economic phases, the lesser or greater accessibility to products creates a greater inequality between the very rich and the very poor (Jodhka, 2001: 13). Therefore, in our understanding of these totally different ranges of small societal groups, we need to examine their respective proximal and distal interactive variables, which affect the various strata of the Indian psyche. For example, the lower-caste Shudras are in many instances faring better economically than the higher-caste Brahmins; and the daughter of an elitist family marries an up-and-coming Harijan (Singer, 1972). These juxtapositionings challenge conceptual frames of psychology, sociology and economics, and destabilise anthropological tenets. Even when we present, analyse and discuss conceptual frames, the underlying dynamics of social and technological change are intervening, and of unknown quantity and quality. As such, our statements are the products of here and now and in this complexity of fluctuations, variations and vicissitudes of social reality, social sciences need to be flexible in the interpretation of their conceptual frames. The extent of diversity and its effect on whether Indian society is homogeneous or not, whether it is more or less collectivistic in behaviour or how entrenched is being modern at one time and traditional at another requires further intensive evidence. This prompts the writing of this book to incorporate at every relevant step illustrations of the combined influences of these disparate disciplines. It also underscores the phenomenon of dynamism in overt behaviour forms cohabiting with traditionalism in the family structure (Bhatt, 1999). The resilience is apparent in a transitional society, which destabilises at one level before it stabilises at the next.

The first chapter attempts to set the generic stage of human development, homogeneous in essential features of physical growth, social and mental development. However, the individual is influenced by both his human and material environment and in this respect politics, economics and ecology are influential as they impinge on processes within the human. For instance, wars destabilise families, floods destroy the means for normal survival, and so on. The ethos of this volume is a strong belief in the holistic nature of development in an environment where changing times and spaces add to the development process, since development is coterminus with time.

Chapter 1 sets the stage for later chapters in bringing together a host of independent and intervening variables to demonstrate the kaleidoscopic nature of the Indian's development. The themes of indigeneity and homogeneity encapsuling heterogeneity are both puzzling and challenging in unravelling their dimensions, as they overlap in different combinations. This is precisely why the Indian, when given the opportunity, is versatile, for he has experienced the whole range of having nothing to having something, and to some extent having much. His generic nature is fast rooted in Hindu philosophy, and even if of another religion, is tempered to the socio-cultural norms of the dominant society—the Hindu society. Secularism and ethnicity, dominance and subservience in caste, all play their role. However, in an inexorable way, the heterogeneity is gradually amalgamating into a hierarchy of values of Indianness—of being a Hindu or Muslim, of being a tribal or urbanite, and so on. These attributes coexist without much dissonance and make up the unique character of the representative Indian.

Chapter 2, 'Human Development: Bases and Processes', attempts to deal with the meaning of human development. This term has been widely used to describe actual growth and development of the individual, both in a generic and phylogenetic form, as common to the human race, such as the foundations of psychological and sociological perspectives in viewing development from conception onwards. At the other end is the global view of human development using demographical indices of the quality of life in different societies, used by international organisations, as contained in their annual reports (World Bank, 2005). Here we are concerned with the socio-psychological developmental process so as to understand humans and their societies more closely, by examining principles, the axes of development and the various parameters surrounding the meaning of the development process.

Chapter 3, 'Origins of Knowledge on Human Development', attempts to detail, in as simple a manner as possible, the way humans think and act in relation to principles of logical thinking and ordering, and how they perceive themselves and others in the interactional process. This is by way of an introduction to systematic thinking, which is the basis of all disciplines attempting to arrive at facts. This chapter gives a generalised description of the basic principles of growth and development of the human being. Since the human is the highest form of the primate world, the chapter will also describe his* ability to think and act rationally. The emphasis here will be on the human being's capacity to develop not only through his own perception of himself but also through the perceptions of others about him (Mascolo and Bhatia, 2002: 55–91; Pratkanis, and Greenwald, 1985: 311–32). Hence, identity is described as an important conceptual frame, supported by linkages and interrelationships with his ecological environment. The individual's ability to arrive at logical deductions is based on the physiological mechanisms, especially the brain mechanism, which articulate the thinking processes. The role of neuroscience is stressed as being one of importance (Posner, 1998). The environment consists of both the human and the geoecological surroundings, which influence his development.

Chapter 4, 'Sources of Knowledge on Human Development', relates to the major bases of information accumulated since the inception of the systematic study of human development first documented in the West (Darwin, 1859). The disciplines of biology, sociology, psychology, anthropology and their correlates have contributed to the formulation of such information, as human development is a composite of all. What began as child study (Spock, 1945), and then child psychology (Jersild, 1949), was followed by the introduction of psychoanalysis of children (Freud, 1946), and then child development (Baldwin, 1980), and is now human development (Saraswathi, 1993) to give a few examples of the trend. It has enlarged its scope to the study of development throughout the individual's chronological stages (Dacey, 2004). A newly emerging area of empirical concern is the environment of the family as an ecological framework (Barker, 1968). As such, the scientific focus in India began with scattered and isolated pieces of knowledge, originating with philosophy, some educational treatises and more especially ·sociology (Dube, 1974: 145). In the field of psychology, such scientific information began with psychological experimentation and theoretical knowledge (Pandey, 2004), while sociology and anthropology concentrated on ethnographic studies. The origins of knowledge in these areas came from the West, with anthropology being the first, as colonial power influenced the study of 'primitive villages and their peoples' (Prakash, 1990: 383–408).

Newly evolving Indian universities scrupulously followed the western theories and methodologies, and applied them to the Indian situation, initially in laboratory experiments, while sociology explored the field of myths and mythology, social life and tribal customs (Jha, 1993: 165). However, with the growth of the discipline, discerning scholars, both from the West and in growing numbers from India, quickly became aware of the local and social realities of India and its socio-political independence status (Sinha, 1997: 129–70). Indian scholars sought to turn away from westernised influences. They began to explore indigenous sources and discovered that there were sparse indigenous data (Dube, 1992).

The place of ancient scriptures in articulating human behaviour, while pervasive throughout the ages, has found little documentation in empirical data. Notwithstanding this, the concepts as evolved from the scriptures have dominated human behaviour in the beliefs, especially of *karma* and *dharma* and their correlates in the 'philosophy of science' (Belwalkar and Ranade, 1927).

---

*The pronouns 'his', 'he', 'him', 'himself' and the noun 'man' are not intended to connote only the male gender but represent both genders of the human species.

Since the mid-1990s there has been an acceleration of academic interest in the 'localness' and social relevance of Indian data. Nandy, for instance, enquires into the biases of contemporary Indian psychology, as to whether the data is related to social realities at the ground level (2002: 393–502). To this day they relate to the unique Indian psyche in many subtle ways. There has been some attempt to understand Vedantic theoretical concepts, but they still remain hypotheses to be tested.

The chapter on sources of knowledge on human development attempts to present available information on documented knowledge on how the intermix of disciplines contributes to an understanding of human development. If the sources are available and if there are reliable methods to systematic psychological conceptualisations, then there should be information on how the study of the field of human development came about, which is contained in Chapter 5, 'The Methodological Study of Human Development'.

Chapter 5 will consider how human development has become an area of study, as well as the influence of historical events on beliefs and practices in the process of development. The effect of social change and its influences on these trends will be examined in the light of growing scientific knowledge and national efforts to improve the quality of life. Social historicity and socio-political knowledge give glimpses of sparse information of human development in the pre-colonial era (Basham, 1981) since there was little documentation except in philosophical discourses based on the scriptures (Bhattacharya, 1960: 1–12). We have a scanty generic idea of what was thought to be human development in the pre-colonial era. In the colonial era, there was much superimposition of anglicised ways, more readily adopted by the urban elites (*raja*s and *nawab*s) rather than the ruled masses. After Independence and with the impetus of democratic rule and a regularised attempt through five-year plans to benefit the neglected masses and to raise the production of the country, there was a simultaneous interest in higher education. This education was mainly through the various universities and national organisations. Anthropology, together with experimental psychology, spurred analytical investigations in the Indian context.

However, almost all theoretical conceptualisations and methodological strategies were either adopted wholesale or superficially adapted (Mohanty and Prakash, 1993: 104–21). It has only been in the last three decades or so that Indian experts have further redefined the context and the content as being indigenous in nature (Hussain, 1982). From simplistic nomenclature such as childcare, child study and child development, the field of human development came into its own in the latter part of the 20th century. Recognising that human development is a hybrid of several related disciplines, the contributions of the latter have added to the holistic tenor of the concepts of human development. Experts in the fields of socio-cultural psychology, sociology, social action and ethnographic anthropological strategies are being profiled to seek, analyse and propose models. There are tentative hypothetical concepts and some mini theories that inculcate Vedantic philosophy and its correlates to understand the 'Indianness' of the individual and his society (Atal, 1981: 89–97; Sinha, 1993). Arising out of these chapters, is scientific information on the steps employed in researching socio-psychological problems. This process is expected to give the reader a scientific basis as to how credible facts are arrived at.

The emergence of valid hypotheses should, in turn, be amenable to theory building in these social sciences, which affect human development in the Indian context. Chapter 6 'Research Concerns', introduces the reader to the methods of scientifically eliciting reliable and valid data to add to information in a systematic and structured way. This is further analysed in the different techniques used for eliciting data, and the ways in which they can be analysed and summarised for theory-building hypotheses. The role of design is pivotal and this will be further explained in terms of designs to elicit descriptive and inferential data through the use of sampling techniques. The use of probability statistics is meant to further enhance the reliability and validity of data. The explanation of the use of statistics will be to introduce the reader to the main themes of hypotheses, variables and types of summarisation, and whether the data are indeed true to the conceptual framework designed.

This chapter on research concerns deals with the systematic steps required to arrive at valid conclusions when examining social science problems to give the reader information on the relevant aspects in searching for facts. In this volume, we have dealt with abstract concepts, historical events and strategies that lead to an understanding of human development. However, who is this human being about whom we are studying various facets? While we talk about the human being/the individual in society, we also need to know what the psychological make-up of this individual is (Misra et al., 1990). How does he know he has an identity, how does he recognise that others have identities apart from himself? Therefore, Chapter 7 entitled 'Identity and Inter-personal Competence' attempts to describe the psychosocial dimensions of the self and others in the whole network of human relations. This chapter deals with the contextualised aura of the individual around whom these abstract concepts of thinking, studying and what is studied revolve. What is this aura? In terms of social reality, it comprises customs and values of the individual Indian and the habitat in which he lives, as linked to his group. The individual as a member of the group, however, needs an identity and an awareness of who he is and how he relates to his environment. The perception of self and the perception of others in an interactional social network, abiding by its rules and customs, are significant for becoming a competent individual (Mahajan, 1998).

Chapter 8, 'The Development of Critical Skills', details concepts and relevant factors influencing the individual and his coping skills to find a homeostasis between self and the environment. Among the myriads of such innate potentials that can be nurtured and developed are: motivational levels, language ability, intelligent performance and, especially in the Indian context, the ability to adapt to environmental vicissitudes. Humans are socialised to be motivated towards social goals. Under normal circumstances, the individual is expected to achieve academically, to communicate well, to process information and to adapt to changing circumstances, without much cognitive dissonance. Witness the resilient acceptance of devastation caused by famines or terrorist attacks. A belief in karma and its attendant strength dharma is the pillar of the Indian psyche. In the passage through life, these abilities, when developed, enable the individual to adapt to a variety of situations. Through the growth stages, the individual learns that *moksha* is the ultimate, and so tempers his behaviour and thought. Changing stimuli bring about changing cognitive adaptation, which challenges man's potential.

The less abled can only perform that much, the economically deprived have limited resources, but motivation and intelligence can make a king out of a beggar, and so the modern concepts of achievement orientation are gaining academic popularity. This is especially true in the current economic, global context of competition and power. However, the Indian uses his socio-spiritual background to temper such ego-oriented strivings, so that he is also sociocentric in his behaviour.

In Chapter 9, titled 'Societal Mores: Their Implications for Human Development', we speak of the situation in which the Indian lives, as to how it affects his development. There is growing concern among academicians that we are studying the trees and losing sight of the perimeters of the forest. The Indian situation sets the stage of influences throughout the lifespan. Over the years there has been a period of accumulation of habits, beliefs and values. This is more especially in the domain of socio-religious normative thinking and behaviour. Indians are rooted in their socio-religious norms, and however diverse the myriads of communities that exist, the generic character is more or less the same.

This chapter specifies a few major parameters of values and beliefs, and the Indian's adherence to moral and religious values, whether Hindu, Muslim, Christian or any other. The living arrangements range from small hamlets on rough terrain and thatched huts on the plains to huge high-rise urban conglomerates and the mansions of the rich. This pattern of geoecological living is not uncommon in other countries, for example, in South America. What makes it unique in India is that there is a coexistence of centrifugal and centripetal systems and their values, which makes a long-standing traditional country accept and attempt to adapt to democratic living in a global context (Cole, 1992: 5–31).

The conclusion, titled 'A Concluding View', deals with several foundational concepts. For instance, the development of critical skills is potentially innate in all human beings. The degree may differ and their development goes through a process of refinement and re-definement so as to enable the individual to cope with the events, problems and issues in his environment. We attempt in this chapter to suggest to the reader that while the area of human development is an amalgam of various disciplines, it is packaged into a group of conceptualisations, which should contribute to a holistic understanding of human development.

What are the philosophical and religious beliefs that pervade the process of development? In other words, how do we get to understand the Indian in his specific environment that affects his phylogenetic and cultural characteristics? For instance, how do deprivation and impoverishment, or surfeit and overabundance, act upon the Indian psyche in his ecology? While there are no definitive answers to these issues because of sparse empirical data, this volume will attempt to explore available and accessible avenues of discourse, discussing existent data on the Indian in his situational environment. As Saraswathi, Misra and Tripathi point out, 'the lack of data makes hypothesising at best tentative, presenting a challenge for further *in situ* and indigenous theory building' (Saraswathi, 2003).

The awareness of information and its sources, as to how the study of human development came about, is certainly fundamental. How will the reader use it, unless he has some conceptual understanding of the milieu in which the human, in this case, the Indian lives?

References

Atal, Y., 1981, 'The Call of Indigenisation', *International Social Science Journal*, 33: 89–97.

Baldwin, A.L., 1980, *Theories of Child Development*. New York: John Wiley.

Barker, R.G., 1968, *Ecological Psychology: Concepts and Methods for Studying the Environment of Human Behaviour*. Palo Alto, CA: Stanford University Press.

Basham, A.L., 1981, *Aspects of Ancient Indian Culture*. Delhi: Asia Publishing House.

Belwalkar, S.K. and R.D. Ranade, 1927, *The History of Indian Philosophy, Vol. 2: The Creative Period*. Pune: Bilvakunja.

Bhatt, P., 1999, *Ancient Indian Tradition and Mythology*. Delhi: Motilal.

Bhattacharya, K., 1960, 'Modern Psychology and Hindu Thought', *Philosophical Quarterly*, 33(1): 1–12.

Cole, M., 1992, 'Context, Modularity and the Cultural Construction of Development', in T. Winegar and J. Valsiner (eds), *Children's Development within Social Context: Vol. 2, Research and Methodology*. Hillsdale, NJ: Lawrence Erlbaum.

Cole, M., J. Gay, J.A. Glick and D.W. Sharp, 1971, *The Cultural Context of Learning and Thinking*. New York: Basic Books.

Dacey, J.S. and J.F. Travers. 2002. *Human Development Across the Life Span*. Boston: McGraw-Hill.

Darwin, C., 1859, *On the Origin of Species by Means of Natural Selection*. London: J. Murray Publications.

Dube, S.C., 1974, *Contemporary India and its Modernisation*. Delhi: Vikas.

———, 1992, *Understanding Change: Anthropological and Sociological Perspectives* (Studies in Sociology and Social Anthropology). Delhi: Vikas.

Freud, A., 1946, *The Ego and the Mechanisms of Defence*. New York: Universities Press.

Hussain, F. (ed.), 1982, *Indigenous Anthropology in Non-western Countries*. Durham: Carolina Academic Press.

Jersild, A., 1949, *Child Psychology* (3rd edn). New York: Prentice-Hall.

Jha, M., 1993, *Glimpses of Tribal Life* (Tribal Studies of India Series). New Delhi: Inter-India Publications.

Jodhka, S., 2001, 'Introduction', in S. Jodhka (ed.), *Communities and Identities: Contemporary Discourses on Culture and Politics in India*. New Delhi: Sage.

Mahajan, G., 1998, *Identities and Rights*. New Delhi: OUP.

Mascolo, M.F. and S. Bhatia, 2002. 'Culture, Self and Social Relations', *Psychology and Developing Studies*, 14(1): 55–91.

Misra, G. and K.N. Tripathi, 1993, 'The Concept and Context of Human Development', in T.S. Saraswathi and B. Kaur (eds), *Human Development and Family Studies in India*. New Delhi: Sage.

Misra, G., U. Jain and S. Bhargava, 1990, 'Applied Social Psychology in India: Challenges and Possibilities', in G. Misra (ed.), *Applied Social Psychology in India*. New Delhi: Sage.

Mohanty, A.K. and P. Prakash, 1993, 'Theoretical Despairs and Methodological Predicaments of Developmental Psychology in India: Some Reflections', in T.S. Saraswathi and B. Kaur (eds), *Human Development and Family Studies in India*. New Delhi: Sage.

Nandy, A., 2002. 'The Politics of Application and Social Relevance in Contemporary Psychology', in A.K. Dalal and G. Misra (eds), *New Directions in Indian Psychology, Vol. 1*. New Delhi: Sage.

Pandey, J., 2004, 'Psychology in India Enters the 21st century: Movement toward an Indigenous Discipline', in J. Pandey (ed.), *Psychology in India Revisited—Developments in the Discipline*, Vol. 3: Applied Social and Organisational Psychology. New Delhi: Sage.

Posner, M., 1998, 'Current Research in Cognitive Neuroscience', in I. Singh and R. Parasuraman (eds), *Human Cognition: Multidisciplinary Perspectives*. New Delhi: Sage.

Prakash, G., 1990, 'Writing Post-orientalist Histories of the Third World: Perspectives from Indian Historiography', *Comparative Studies in Society and History*, 32(2): 383–408.

Pratkanis, A.R. and A.G. Greenwald, 1985, 'How shall the Self be Conceived?' *Journal for the Theory of Social Behaviour*, 15: 311–21.

Ramanujan, A.K., 1990, 'Is There an Indian Way of Thinking? An Informal Essay', in M. Marriot (ed.), *India Through Hindu Categories*. New Delhi: Sage.

Robertson, R., 1992, *Globalisation: Social Theory and Global Culture*. London: Sage.

Saraswathi, T.S., 1993, 'Child Development Research and Policy Linkage: A Mirage or Reality?', in T.S. Saraswathi and B. Kaur (eds), *Human Development and Family Studies in India: An Agenda for Research and Policy*. Delhi: Sage.

———, (ed.), 2003, *Cross-cultural Perspectives in Human Development: Theory, Research and Applications*. New Delhi: Sage.

Singer, M., 1972, *When a Great Tradition Modernises*. New York: Praeger.

Sinha, D., 1993, 'Indigenisation of Psychology in India and its Relevance', in U. Kim and J.W. Berry (eds), *Indigenous Psychologies: Research and Experience in Cultural Context*. Newbury Park, CA: Sage.

———, 1997, 'Indigenising Psychology', in J.W. Berry, Y.P. Poortinga and J. Pandey (eds), *Handbook of Cross-cultural Psychology, Vol. 1*. Boston: Allyn & Bacon.

Spock, B., 1945, *The Common Sense Book of Baby and Child Care*. NY: Duell, Loan and Pearce.

World Bank, 2005, *World Development Report 2006: Equality and Development*. Washington, DC: World Bank.

The Hexagon of Human Development: The Indian Setting

Introduction

IF ONE were to attempt to understand the individual psyche from the perspective of only one discipline, it would be limited. If, on the other hand, one envisioned the individual as being in the centre of a hexagon with the disciplines radiating from the perimeters onto the centrifugal individual in the centre, then there would be a dynamic and simultaneous impact of criss-crossing disciplines and their variants: psychology, sociology, anthropology. These include their variants, such as social anthropology and socio-political factors (social psychology and cross-cultural psychology) and the derivatives of other disciplines. In their conceptualising them, they interact and interweave to give a holistic picture of human development. This interaction is depicted in Figure 1.1.

The Indian environment has a many-faceted scenario of various strands of development, namely, the psychosociological, the cultural–ecological and the eco-political bases (Kagitcibasi, 2002: 1–6). Each strand is related to the other in a complicated weave. In order to understand what human nature is and how the human mind thinks and acts, it is necessary to first understand the psychosociological make-up of the human being.

'No man is an island'; he cohabits and interacts with others, not only across the range of different types of people, but also knows of others across the oceans. Time is inexorable and it imposes its dimensions on patterns of living from one generation to another, from one geographical terrain of India to another. Individuals are different among classifications

FIGURE 1.1   The Interactive Disciplines Affecting Development

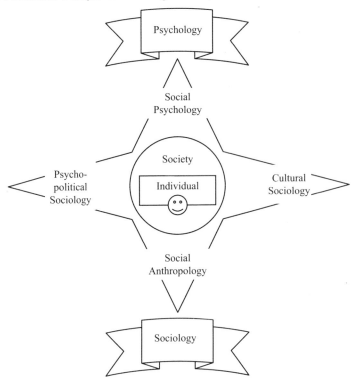

of people: demographically, ecologically and sociologically according to caste, class, ethnicity and religion. Dominating the scene is the economic factor. Therefore, we are concerned with the conceptual framework of how the Indian survives in his setting.

Spectacularly, the frames are as varied as the permutations and combinations of geo-socio-economic aspects. Underscoring these variations is the foundational structure of traditionality first perceived by early sociologists like Srinivas (1996) who comments that caste still operates as a system rather than a diffused reality. Concomitant with this is the waning of the purity–pollution differentiation identifying the lower castes from the higher castes. In spite of this diffusion, caste boundaries are sustained by the process of sanskritisation, democratisation, the policy of reservation of seats and jobs, and the patriarchal culture.

However, with the advance of liberalisation, caste may become a further diffused system. Caste seems to be acquiring an ethnic avatar, especially in urban areas, where caste boundaries overlap with ethnic boundaries. Srinivas also initiated a lively debate in his analysis of sanskritisation and westernisation (Srinivas, 1962: 42). Other luminaries, like Dube (1965: 421–23), Ishwaran (1966), Majumdar (1958), Marriot (1990) and Sirsikar (1965), in most of their writings, focus mainly on the analysis of caste in the community, and also caste boundaries which are forces to contend with, in the path towards socio-economic progress. A second factor in the current scenario is the different levels of adaptation to science and technology in its material form. However, there is, simultaneously, inadequate progress in the social sector areas such as sustainable growth for the neediest sections of society, specifically in health, education, sanitation, water, urban governance, child labour, especially for the marginalised groups, such as women, across social indices (Council for Social Development, 2006). The Indian, like many Far Eastern nationalities, is in juxtaposition between traditionality and being scientifically oriented towards developmental progress. Third, the carry-over of social historicity has much fracturisation. To this day, ritualistic behaviour is a significant aspect of behaviour, in the practice of socio-religious events at birth, marriage and death. It acquires sophisticated aspects of the West, among the upper elite and also, currently, the middle class. During a marriage ceremony, for instance, *havan* and *kanyadaan* are performed, after which there is the dance floor and the psychedelic disco lights. There is still the horse and the carriage but also the BMW rubbing shoulders with these antiquated modes of conveyance. The Brahmin in the city, drawn away from his traditional village context, becomes one among the many low and high castes eating together at the same restaurant, though neither would dare to do so in their own caste and community environs. Fourth, there has been a steady dissolution of the joint family in clustered living residences, of both the patrilocal and matrilocal type (Ross, 1961). Fifth, even though the nucleus is the biological family, there continues to be a collectivist spirit underscoring attitudes towards those of the extended family, clan and the community (Oyserman et al., 2002: 3–72). The unique resilient ability of the Indian to adapt to varying circumstances, however dire, is a psychological trait, especially in the deprived sections (who perhaps have no alternative). This adaptive resilience is born of a long-standing history of acceptance of individual differences. Major contributors towards the modernity pattern are the relentless stimuli of the electronic media, and the opportunities for education and for becoming achievement-oriented. For some, the impulse is to become a tycoon, and there are a fair number who do so, whether it is exporting rags or managing call centres, or, over the years, expanding market-oriented businesses. The adaptive resilience is a remarkable trait in the personality of the Indian (Barone et al., 1997: 107), who has lived through generations of forefathers existing under different feudal regimes, and maintaining in between the sense of identity of being an Indian during the colonial period. With the advent of independence and after over 60 years of experience as a democracy, these factors have now brought about a resurgence (Bhattacharya and Choudhry, 2000: 189). So that, while we trace the socio-economic history of development, we also know that the effects of the past bring with them social realities of a large majority living under conditions of poverty, being illiterate, becoming immune to unhygienic conditions and unable to create or use opportunities (Misra, 1983: 1–21). There are so many of the population jostling for first place. Where there is simultaneously a preoccupation with finding means for daily survival, the economically deprived, particularly, have inadequate incentives for improvement. Complicating the issue is the fact that the government itself has two sides. On the one hand, are the plans to better the conditions of the disadvantaged, but the trickle-down effect does not occur and the powerful minority of the beneficiaries siphon off the benefits intended for the neediest. On the other hand, the rich become richer, not knowing how to spend their secondary source of income, and with a small proportion of wage earners paying taxes.

Taxes are meagre and are spent over the large poorer population in the provision of minimum public facilities. Further, whatever efforts are made by the government in planning and programming, the inevitable evaluation carries the usual refrain: 'the implementation falls short of its target … the budget has not been spent on time … the infrastructure is poor', and so on. The result is that the efforts in the democratic set-up are siphoned off by the powerful and the wealthy. On the other hand, there is a discernible trend of the less privileged, spurred on by observing the rich with whom they have a 'cheek by jowl' contact, becoming frustrated and so falling into disreputable ways. The private economy is being spurred on by a bank finance loan phenomenon, so that more consumers are prompted to borrow and spend more, especially in the upper classes.

However, this backdrop has to be observed against the inexorable hands of time in relation to demographic concerns. Over a billion people have to be catered to and given minimal facilities for survival. The economically unproductive proportion of the young, the elderly and the housebound female are in a more fragile position, having to depend upon the smaller ratio of the productive young generation. Over two-thirds of the population live in villages, hamlets in difficult hill terrain, as nomads in the Thar desert and in urban slum conglomerates. According to a recent household survey, across 593 districts in 35 states and union territories, there are 179 million households with an average of six members each, with more places of worship than schools, colleges and hospitals combined (Saran, 2003). A closer look indicates that most of the places of worship are funded by donations of the rich. Two-thirds are rural and tribal households, with the probability that more than the average number live under one roof. The latter have learned to live with economic limitations in their lifestyles, yet their major strength is their sense of resilience to the vicissitudes of deprivation. We often hear such sayings in the idiomatic language—'aisa hota hai, chalta hai, koi baat nahi'—all taken to mean 'things will happen when they have to happen', a tenet enjoined in them from childhood over the generations of living an Indian philosophy of dharma and karma (Comarswamy, 2000). This is uniquely Hindu in its context of a philosophy that has been adapted by other socio-religious groups as an attitude to life.

We have deliberately stressed the above points so as to indicate that since 'no man is an island' the average Indian lives on a continent of other Indians sharing the same Indian ethos. This is so in spite of the fact that over the length and the breadth of India, the differing ethnic groups, spread over several states, over several religions, subcastes, hill and forest tribals, and nomads, do not know much about each other's lifestyles. The study on the Rajputs of Khalapur and the study by Seymour of a community in Bhubaneswar over a period of time illustrate that changes take place in styles of living, but few changes are observed in the core values of socio-religious norms (Minturn and Hitchcock, 1966; Minturn et al., 1978; Seymour, 1999). For generations, there have been mutual exchanges of goods and services among the castes which held the village community together through a unique *jajmani* system.

Although these transactions are not rigidly caste-bound in the world of today, especially in urban areas where geographical and occupational mobility is hastened, there is still a cohesion in these transactions in the Hindu cultural philosophy (Marriot, 1976: 109–42).

Deeply ingrained in the maturing Indian psyche is a sense of ethical conduct among family, kinship and community (Menon 2003: 431–49). However, each ethnic group practises its rituals somewhat differently from the other. This behaviour in part is propped up by the attitudes that each ethnic group can be discreetly differentiated through the differences in patterned behaviour. For instance, the Kashmiri knows more about Afghani food habits than the Tamilian who is more attuned to vegetarian food. Again, a Naga knows more about Tibetan lifestyles than he does about Gujarati. Yet they are all brushed with an 'Indianness' arising out of their inherent socio-religious philosophy (Mascolo and Bhatia, 2002: 55–91).

How does an individual, and in this context the Indian, get to know what he is? How does he progress from infancy to toddlerhood, from childhood to adulthood and finally to old age? Human development covers a lifespan. The major thesis of human development is the interaction of the individual with his environment, within time and space (Gould, 1977). In an extensive review of available material on human development, Kaur et al. have stated that there is a need for alternative paradigms to suit the Indian milieu and psyche (Kaur et al., 2001: 163–227). Efforts by scholars concentrate mainly on known variables like caste, class and ethnicity, mostly in isolation of each other, hardly in a factor-analytic manner (Misra and Srivastava, 2003: 210–43). Consequently, intervening variables are untouched. For instance, poor cognitive development might be observable in a low-caste child not because he is of a low caste, but because other factors, perhaps more potent, are left out of the analysis (Misra and Tripathi, 2004: 118–92). Part of the problem is that theoretical assumptions are left outside in the pale, when development is essentially a theoretical and abstract construct.

Development, physically and mentally, continues in a progressive, orderly fashion according to epigenetic rules (Thomas, 2001: 188) and according to the orthogenetic make-up of the individual (Werner, 1966). Development is both a process and a product transforming and transferring from one stage to another, monitored by time, which when operationalised means the age-cum-maturity package of the individual. Each stage is built upon the previous in a complex manner. Some traits are invariant (Piaget, 1950), while others are malleable (Skinner, 1953); still others are replaced by intragenetic, orthogenetic and sociometric factors, as in the case of puberty affecting adolescent behaviour, or changing social needs. The same phenomenon might also affect each individual differently because of their individual ontogenetic potentials; for instance, children have differing innate potentials to express emotions. Thus, similar phenomena could cause different emotive reactions in different individuals.

Development is based on systematic laws of progression and complexity and can be simultaneously influenced by multiple variables, known and unknown (Valsiner et al., 1997). There is also a hierarchical progressive complexity. For instance, an incident of a child losing a toy generally evokes some degree of emotional behaviour, but as an adult he learns to control his emotions and may show little overt emotion. Development is therefore a fusion of psychological and socio-cultural factors. Which one of these is more affective than the others can be more discoverable by ethnographic and narrative reporting from individuals, rather than from psychometric cross-sectional studies. When such studies are experimental they are geared to find behaviour specific to a particular time and place, without reference to the previous or predicted behaviour (Eckensberger, 2003: 70–101). Development is therefore both a continuum of universal characteristics such as the ability to speak and learn a language (however well or poorly), and specific characteristics such as the ability to compute complex mathematics (Aries, 1962).

The interactive responses between the developing individual and his environment are reciprocal, either proactive or reactive, at any one time. Since the environment is changeable, so is the human being influenced by environmental changes. As age increases, mechanistic development has less of an influence than the organistic. In other words, it is more chance-dependent than age-dependent. For example, an adult can behave like a child (immature), but a child hardly behaves like an adult. The latter's development is more predictable than the former's. The institutional framework of an individual's life development processes has its own developmental channels irrespective of the dynamics of human interaction. For instance, each caste ascribes significance to the caste occupation which is spontaneously and often non-verbally learned by the maturing individual in the community, such as among the potters, weavers and craftsmen (Anandalakshmy and Bajaj, 1981).

The nature of development is such that it is open to several avenues of interpretation, depending upon the focus of the discipline. For instance, sociology views the individual as one entity among others. Individual psychology views the internal workings of an individual mind. Ecology views the individual in his habitat, while anthropology views the individual as embedded in a culture of beliefs, attitudes, values and a physical setting. However, from a holistic viewpoint, the fusion of all these perspectives gives a fuller understanding of the development process (Pandey, 1998: 205–34). Therefore, the concepts of these disciplines impinge upon the individual's way of life in some way or the other. Time is unstoppable, it causes development, it causes deterioration, and it does so by change. Clearly, India is a society undergoing overt change, and in its transitional stage there is a period of instability before it settles down onto a plane of equilibrium, till time again causes change. Indians are travelling the path of modernisation, sophistication, globalisation and westernisation, long foretold by reputed sociologists (Ishwaran, 1970; Singh, 1977). Adaptation takes time, but new adaptations also cause other unintended consequences, or what is called 'the serendipity of change', in this case economic change, with social change trailing behind. This backdrop, briefly presenting the setting, is essential, before we go on to the tenets of development of the human being in a holistic manner. In the case of the Indian, holism is interpreted from two points of view: one from the interaction of the various disciplines, and the other from the interaction of the environmental influences in the framework of an analysis (general analysis) of socio-psychological events (Burman, 1994).

The Psychosocial Developmental Aspects of the Indian in his Situational Setting

It is possible to derive the basic facts of human development from the amalgam of concepts of various disciplines. These processes are inherent in the ontogeny of the human, irrespective of culture (Gottlieb, 1998: 792–802). In the understanding of the process, we return to the saying of sages from ancient India that 'the mind is related to the soul'. 'It is the function of the soul, the "atman", to control the living processes in the mind' (Orme-Johnson et al., 1997: 288).

The honing of the thinking processes increases the understanding of self and of others. In the process of this interactive understanding of self and others, we follow systematic, cohesive directions. This is because development takes place in unison, is effected and affected by each and every other part of the organism. The relationship between mind and body is well known, and it is the focus of ayurvedic precepts and yogic practices. 'Some of the most significant psychological insights of the Indian cultural development relate to spiritual self development and self realisation' (Paranjpe, 2003: 24).

While knowledge of scientific development has gradually increased, the boundaries of human development remain more or less the same, waiting to be discovered by man's ingenuity. Earlier theories of heredity and environment are changing their format to become more specific, and like the proverbial 'domino effect', the more that is known, the greater is the knowledge to be known. For a while, in the 18th century, knowledge was about socio-philosophical facets of human development, but when scientific information came to be known in the West, it first began to be documented in the early 17th century. It began to be documented in the West in psychology when a great deal of attention was paid to nature and environmental influences (Cole et al., 2004). But, as science and technology grew, so did man's knowledge of himself as a genetically formulated and regulated structure, with the potentiality to change himself. For instance, genetic engineering has narrowed down to the genome map and stem cell analysis, with emphasis on the sophisticated modification of ontogenetic forms (Langer et al., 2003).

On the other side of the spectrum, namely, environment, enquiry has fissioned out into specific areas like epidemiology of the human. This relates to ecology and disease effects, as also the effects of deforestation, polluting gases and effluents, which affect human stress levels and coping behaviour, and, therefore, well-being (Wissing and Van Zeden, 1997). This is frequently caused by stress in the economic and emotional orientation of the individual (Freeman, 1994: 107–30). These lead to more dissonance and less consonance. The individual in given circumstances has a degree of inbuilt mechanisms, which lead to self-efficacy, or otherwise, in dealing with the given situational parameters (Bandura, 1982: 122–47). We have also moved away from the formal psychometric forms of researching to include more specific idiographic and narrative styles of social reality, as evident in the works of Kumar, Chatterjee and Chaudhary on the process of socialisation, which emphasise the dominant role of contextual factors (Chatterjee, 1999; Chaudhary, 1999; Kumar, 1999). While generalisations are empirical guides, they are more acceptable for static variables like caste, class, ethnicity, and so on. The study of human behaviour fragments into several splinter descriptions in dynamic ways, and often deflects generalisations. Any one splinter is unlike the other. Besides, the more variables we tend to discover, the more these variables tend to throw up further intervening variables. For instance, to find valid causes for the behaviour of a disabled child living in a hill ecology, we need to understand influences like heredity, foetal vulnerability to inheritance, maternal nutrition, foetal stress, delivery practices, infant nutrition and morbidity. Further, there are other factors like tribal values, attitudes and practices, many of them based on myths and superstitions (Bhattacharya, 1995) and geoecological constraints. If this is so, then we are talking about the interactive processes in development. Thomas, for instance, in his overview of theories and theoretical concepts, states the need for 'a more complete understanding of family life', wherein he suggests, 'the combination of multiple view points of experts implies a fusion of ideas' (Thomas, 2001: 271–72).

While we look at the development processes philosophically, the ability to hypothesise, to theorise and to find evidences in real-life situations has to inevitably depend upon empirical data. This process, as a consequence of having been attempted and documented in western literature much earlier, influenced Indian information in the social sciences. Such handed-down information tended to be a transposition from the colonial field of interest. Many of these concepts are alien to the Indian psyche. For instance, we can only hypothesise that Indian mores prescribe filial duties and hierarchical statuses. These are the relative antithesis of values and attitudes in the West, where autonomy is prized, and observance of rights and obligations is more according to the formal laws of a civic society than according to personalised and informal relationships (Angel, 1994). The Indianised areas/domains of knowledge therefore are shortchanged for lack of availability of such corresponding empirical data in India. Indian expertise, and increasingly so in the 19th century, has stressed the existence of such lacunae (Sinha, 1965: 6–17). With continued dependence upon western-oriented conceptual/empirical data, research in the Indian context is sparse (Sinha and Mishra, 1993: 140–43). The initial empirical data were mainly on physical and nutritional indices (Reddy et al., 1992) and generic psychological attributes like social behaviour and cognition (Pandey, 2004a: 18).

From an assessment of the indices of economy, India is a developing nation of the Third World, but moving rapidly towards western patterns of living. This is not due to conscious educative decision-making processes, but a mental construction that the 'West is the best'. For the present, since economic status is, generally speaking, heavily skewed towards minus 2 standard deviations in many geoecological curves of the normal distribution, communities are still traditional and circumspect. This is evident in the socio-religious roots of Hindu ritualism and its significance in marking the stages of the life span (Saraswathi, 2003a: 127). For instance, stages of development in adulthood have long been included in Indian philosophy, marked by the important ceremony of *upanayana* or investiture implying the introduction to knowledge and initiation into manhood consisting of four *ashramas*, namely: (*a*) *brahmacharya* (a period of chastity); (*b*) *grihastha* (raising a family); (*c*) *vanaprastha* (spiritual maturity and renunciation of secular possessions and family life); and, lastly, (*d*) *sanyasa* (signifying detachment). In Hindu metaphysics, the second stage is indispensable. In this stage, dharma and *moksha* coexist with *arth* (wealth, goal of man during grihastha ashrama) and *kama* (enjoyment of the sensual pleasures), signifying the balance between the pursuit of the well-being of the mind and body in a coexistential form (Sinha and Tripathi, 2002: 245). Thus, we observe the mix of traditional socio-religious beliefs as an important base to the understanding of the scientific aspects of sociology and psychology. Within the parameters of Indian society, the Indian philosophical point of view is that development is holistic and continuous, where one stage leads systematically to the other and is necessary before the next. Since philosophical thought, and its metaphysical context, is not of a heuristic nature, it does not lend itself as yet to empiricism. Therefore, description of Indian thought comprises concepts that are socio-moral, philosophical and spiritual in content. Awareness of the inclusion of such concepts has been observed by concerned experts in their writings in the latter half of the 20th century (Berry et al., 2003: 1–17; Sinha and Kao, 2000: 9–22). The Indian experts, among others are: Dalal and Misra (2002: 19–49); Kak (2000: 83–116); Kakar (1981, 1982); Malhotra (2003: 3–13); Misra and Tripathi (1993); Nandy (1974, 2002: 393–404); Pandey (2004b: 396); Paranjpe (1984); Saraswathi (1993: 400); and Sinha (1988: 239–58; 1994: 20–23). Consequently, available Indian data are scattered, of small-scale samples and, in many respects, overlapping. In other studies, what is available is inconsistent and non-cohesive in providing a broad and connected picture of development in the Indian context. This trend reoccurs, unfortunately without much regard to theoretical constructs (Saraswathi, 2003b). Part of the problem is that India is multicultural, multiregional and multireligious, with a great deal of heterogeneity.

Unlike countries in the West, where homogeneity in community living patterns occurs, India has a mixed bag of ecological, economical, psychological and ethnocentric living. Even in a homogeneous area such as Tamil Nadu, for instance, there are several castes that to this day have their own separatist rituals and norms of interaction, though all are Tamilian Indians. Tamilians do not relate to other Indians, say, Punjabis, who speak a different language, eat different foods, have a different religion (mostly Sikhism) and have subcultural ways of living. We have therefore emphasised that culture is a dynamic, multifaceted picture of values, attitudes and beliefs, a mixture of homogeneity and heterogeneity. In contrast to the western ethos, Indians are by and large more family- and kinship-oriented, which originates from lineal ties of patrilineal norms (Khatri, 1970: 389). Gender-wise information, on the other hand, indicates a contradiction between religious beliefs towards the female in her form as a deity (the beliefs in *dharti mata*, *devis*) and customary practices towards the female in real-life situations. The abstract female is deified and the real-life female is discounted vis-à-vis the male (Katz, 1996). Further, ecological models demonstrate the ways in which they influence patterns of living during the development process in various *in situ* habitats and childcare in different ecologies (Lamb et al., 2002: 31–56). However, in the absence of empiricised theoretical frames dealing with the Indian psyche directly, several experts have utilised available theoretical concepts of naïve or intuitive thinking, of psychoanalysis and of social behaviour theories, in their contextual writings and empirical formulations (Pandey, 1984; Paranjpe, 1984). This is done to reinterpret them in the Indian context. This is especially true of social learning and imitation, as they relate to generic developmental traits found the world over. Together with other variables, they offer more relevant explanations of human behaviour in the Indian, modified by his cultural values and beliefs. They present a mix of sociological and psychological concepts in tandem. In dealing with the lifespan there is a connectivity from one stage to another, both from the physiological and the psychological standpoint as maturity is the basis of potential learning abilities.

Again, given the bonding of family members and interdependency, typical of the Indian psyche, there is a linkage between cultural norms notated by anthropology, and behavioural traits emphasised by socio-psychology. The latter has stretched across national boundaries to compare and contrast psychological dimensions across cultures. These extensions of basic social sciences give further insights into human development, especially in the context of changing social scenarios, where, with growing alternate choices, the individual has to take risks in weighing the pros and cons of decision-making processes, so as to gain a perspective on his identity (Giddens, 1998).

However, in this chapter we have also branched out into considerations of the environment of the socio-political system, which indirectly affects the quality of life of the Indian. India has carried with it a motley of events in social history from the early days. There was, first, the feudalism of warring chieftains, and subsequently a major Hindu dynasty, the Mauryas, the Mughal dynasty and a non-Indian alien culture superimposed by the British, the French and the Portuguese. Such a pseudo-culture confined to the upper elite further emphasised the chasm in an already divided country. So that even when we comment sanctimoniously about the quality of 'Indianness', somewhere there is an uneasiness as to whether there is in actuality greater heterogeneity rather than a homogeneity about our generic conclusions on development. After the colonial period, the colonists left behind a primary education system, a system of law and revenues, and the railway system (Khalakdina, 1998: 167) mainly to suit those in urbanised areas to serve British trade and commerce purposes and their bureaucratic administration.

These aspects of development were far removed from the lives of those living in scattered villages whose only contact was through the bureaucracy conveyed by the village *patwari* (a village officer in charge of collecting taxes and levies). These contacts were less for developmental purposes, and more for the collection of tithes. The latent and potential initiative and enthusiasm of the average Indian were hardly touched, leaving behind a trail of unquestioned subservience to a bureaucratic authority. India's culture has not changed in its core systems or in its philosophy (intellectual formulation of problems and their resolutions and analyses of Indian thought) (Mascolo and Bhatia, 2002: 55–91).

Generically Indian philosophy is no different from world philosophy, but differs in its spiritual interpretation (in art, religion, mythology and allied areas). It is unlike, for instance, the Christian philosophical ethos, its major difference being of the continuity of the *atman* over many lives and its absorption into creativity when it arrives at the stage of moksha (Bhattacharyya, 1989: 10–16). The interaction of Indian philosophy emanating from the Hindu religious ethos dominates the other ethnic religious groups. Most Indians, irrespective of their allegiances to differing religions, ethnicities, castes and classes, have a common ethos of non-violence, collectivism, interdependency, adherence to norms of lineage, hierarchy and ritualism. So much so that in many pockets, irrespective of these differences, beliefs in astrology and mythological superstitions still exist in the generic Indian psyche.

In the context of the 21st century, India is a proclaimed democracy notwithstanding its several constraints such as unfavourable socio-economic conditions, low income levels, pockets of poverty and inequality of wealth. They also include illiteracy, inegalitarian conditions, divisions by caste plurality, poor civic culture and primordial loyalties. This type of Indian democracy is still workable, barring a few hiccups. It is mainly because of the adherence to constitutional mechanisms put in place by the founding fathers of India's independence, and the avowed respect for the political system (in spite of nepotism and *jajman* prevailing), that the country, carrying the weight of its population burden, is moving ahead. Underlying this is the existence of an Indian philosophy that has a distinct world vision, which sets it apart, just as Taoism sets apart the Japanese. Both societies are in pursuit of productivity enjoined by spiritual philosophy (duty and its obligations), simultaneous with the pursuit of happiness through morality. The Asian systems of psychology inculcate a philosophy of the emancipation of self: *tattva-jnana* in Hinduism; the attainment of transcendence or nirvana in Buddhism; and an ideal personality reflecting a harmonious peaceful state between yin and yang in Taoism and Confucianism (Dorcas, 1997: 232; Sinha and Sinha, 1997: 28). Further, the roots of political stability in India are anchored in the roots of interdependence and *swaraj*, with constitutional directives holding the country together (Kohli, 2001: 298). In detailing the current problems and prospects, one of the major variables is the lack of ethical ethos (Mallikarjunayya, 2002: 459) embedded in civic and moral justice, which, in the Indian psyche, still remains a part of the social history of feudalism. It is suggested that the public ethos is going through a period of dissonance, obvious in contemporary India (Appadurai, 1990: 1–24). However, its interpretation is elusive as the society in this era is in a constant flux, and is being exacerbated by extra-national processes, especially the confrontation between traditionality and modernity observable in the present adolescent and adult generation (Saberwal, 1996: 199).

Against this background is the opening of the markets due to trade liberalisation policies, which have their own repercussions on the economy (Martinussen, 2001). These policies interact with the institutional infrastructures of implementation, and industrial development, initiated in the past half century, jostling with bureaucracy and the remnants of a feudal colonial framework.

Irrespective of the comments on the moral ethos, there is the fact that the Indian polity has held the country together through several vicissitudes. These are the events of Partition, famine and floods and the constraints of poverty on the larger masses of the country. It has, however, had its upswings: a green revolution followed by a white revolution, industrialisation in gradual and steady progress, and now globalisation in the 21st century. India has come a long way in its economic progress (UNDP, 2004). There is a drop in the infant and maternal mortality rates (IMR and MMR), a rise in life expectancy at birth, higher educational enrolment and job expansion, especially in technology. There is, however, a confrontation between quality and quantity. The task is enormous in terms of attempts to cover as many as possible of the burgeoning population and the developmental dissonance phenomenon. The interface between traditionality and modernity will continue as science and technology proceed faster than the average Indian is capable of absorbing them. The diaspora is opening up to the average Indian through media information and through increased understanding of the widening world, in search of an identity within the collective context (Robertson, 1992). Thus the human development process is affected by the churning changes around (Barrow, 2003). The average Indian living in a district town may be uneducated but he can certainly use a cell phone without understanding its mechanism. The mechanic who repairs it deftly does not necessarily need to be college educated. He may be just a 'high school student'. Thus, juxtapositioning is going on dynamically but slowly, and inexorably moving along the time dimension. We therefore need to stress the effects of globalisation on human patterns of living in India, where the illiterate vote, the rural folk watch the lifestyles of the rich and famous on the panchayat television set, and continue with rituals and customs as of the old.

Socio-political Changes Affecting Human Development

Generically speaking, in any socio-political arena, changes in one area of the social science has repercussions on the other. There is a simultaneous increase in men, methods and materials challenging developmental processes. The rise of new socio-political movements cannot be explained by modernistic development occurring during the 1980s. Incidentally this also eroded the 'Nehruvian agenda' (Jodhka, 2001: 15). Problems of lack of cultural homogeneity and the absence of institutional mechanisms for regulation of differences require strong states for ensuring order-based rational and scientific principles of interaction and management in South Asian societies (Das, 1994). India is generally considered a fairly stable society, yet there is the quest of communities for their identities within the secular framework (ibid.). The Chipko movement, the protests against the Bhopal tragedy and the Narmada Bachao Andolan, together with the Dalit movement and the North East Frontier Agency (NEFA) uprisings, indicate the concerns that these communities raise about their identities (Javeed, 2001).

However, there is also the potential of the breakdown of the old community village structure, the homogeneous tradition, and the voice of communities for rights and privileges in the framework of modernisation (Mahajan, 1998). This includes the Scheduled Castes and Tribes who seek developmental and environmental changes (Schlegel and Barry, 1991). These happenings/risings indicate the issue of India's emerging eco-political scenario. Although the Constitution has been stable over the past half century, most of the elected governments have not had an absolute majority and have had to contend with confrontations and hindrances from the opposition benches. This has slowed the progress of democratisation. Further, there is the inevitable interaction with the developed nations in forming a global spectrum of regulations, freeing or restricting imports and exports, as well as with the world financers, the World Bank and the International Monetary Fund (IMF). These are geared primarily towards the interest of the industrialised nations. It can be argued that they are the tax payers for India's economy in the form of loans. Their interest charges lead to debt-plagued economies of the developing world. Globalisation is literally opening the windows and doors of the economies of the world for trading, bargaining and for profiteering on a worldwide scale (Martinussen, 2001).

If we trace the history of India's debut in the various machineries of the financial world, there are several interesting factors which show the rise and fall of various components. Historical trends will put in place the changing facets of the trade, investment and profit picture of India from the 1980s to this day. These are important facets of the vortex of developmental trends. The trends impinge upon the tenets of equality and justice as facets of the democratic processes (Deutsch, 1975: 137–49). There is an increase of experience in the interchanges among nations in trade and commerce mainly due to the opening of world markets. However, a rider to this process is that its beneficial effects on the produce of the rural in the hinterlands is increasingly minimised (Appadurai, 1997).

What, therefore, is globalisation? The blueprint for globalisation was an economic and political theme proposed in the American transnational corporations (TNCs) and through multinational agencies. It was disseminated throughout the world by the World Bank, the IMF and later through the World Trade Organization (WTO). The EU and Japan took advantage of these channels of globalisation which meant 'free trade' (with no hidden and non-tariff barriers) and 'investment flows', but in practice there is a yawning asymmetry between industrial and developing countries. The latter have been mostly on a debt track record over the last two decades. Under the surveillance of the IMF, borrowing countries are obliged to 'consult' the IMF on economic policies. This has encouraged them to open up economies whereas industrial nations continue on their own tracks. Hence, the impact of subsidy reduction under WTO has been minimal. For instance, developed countries have been exporting agricultural products to Sub-Saharan and East European countries. Thus, the comparative advantage of the impact of globalisation has been tilted in favour of the industrialised countries.

There has been much debate on impact of opening up of world markets on the indigenous industries, especially small-scale and more especially the agricultural sector, which have to face sophisticated competition (Martinussen, 2001). Previously developing countries could, under the old General Agreement on Tariffs and Trade (GATT), protect indigenous industries. Now this right has been forfeited. This is a fundamental change. There is no protection for Japan, South Korea, Taiwan, India, Brazil and South Africa, which were able to emerge with large modern industrial bases. The Indian Patent Act of 1970 forbade any product patent on food, agriculture, chemicals and pharmaceuticals, granting only process patents. Alternate processes were found in India to manufacture a whole range of patented drugs emulating the West, and to sell them at lower prices (Chandra, 2001). As of 2005, however, there is a new law mooted to forbid the patenting of high-priced generic drugs in India, so as to equalise the competition. This reduced the threat to TNCs. This action also assisted the lowering of priced drugs in the West, thus ending the patenting between industrialised and developing countries. These are illustrations as to how trading takes place among industrial countries so as to balance the export costs of items for export. Another concession from developed countries was 'in foreign direct investment inflows'. The IMF and World Bank removed the restrictions on these inflows to developing countries, including India. Imports therefore displaced indigenous goods in high-value-added sectors from capital goods to luxury consumer goods, adding to the modernising trends fast catching up in India, especially in urban, living patterns (Appadurai, 1997).

As a consequence, the Indian market experienced a sudden influx of foreign goods. Not only were the latter competitive in price and standard of quality, but in the long run they displaced indigenous goods which were of poor quality. As the stock of inflows rose, developing reserves faced a costly holding rate or sharp currency fluctuations owing to the speculative movement of capital. Therefore, India, like other countries in the developing world, was forced to adopt such policies as would attract foreign investment even at the risk of national interest. Thus we see an increasing investment of turnkey projects, call centres and infrastructure to facilitate the industrial progress of the developed countries. These events have caused a sudden surge in job opportunities in Indian urban areas, especially for the young, educated urban Indian. This, in turn, has created an increasing sophistication in the lifestyles of the now well-to-do middle class and changed value systems causing a divide between the young and the old.

Macroeconomic policies and structural adjustment have become necessary to stabilise such developing economies. This led to a drastic cut in subsidies especially for capital formation and the social sector, which in respect of India were education, health, poverty alleviation programmes, food subsidies and rural development. Hence deficits continue, internal debts accumulate and an increasing part of the expenditure is absorbed by interest payments on domestic and foreign debts. Public firms in India are, therefore, greatly handicapped. Privatisation of state assets is being done at lowered prices than would ordinarily happen, since the scarce revenues are being diverted to meet maintenance expenditures. For these reasons, many of the publicly financed infrastructures like state education and health institutions are in poor shape (Misra and de Berumis, 2002). These events have their rebounding effects on the lower middle and the poorer classes, who either do not have or afford health insurance, unless they are government employees, and thus, who, for instance, have to resort to low-fee charging educational institutions for their children. Thus eco-political policies continue to affect the more vulnerable in the population.

The service sector growth has resulted in a steady increase in GDP (which need not necessarily be a suitable trend) as compared to more important sectors, such as the social sectors (Mitra, 2002). Consequently, producers will continue to receive a smaller proportion of profits. The Indian scenario is therefore different from that in developed countries, where there is a strong commitment towards privatisation and social security measures. In India, there is no regulation of minimum wages in the unorganised sector, and for most of them in the private sector there is no social security (Van Ginneken, 1998). For government employees, however, there is the security of provident fund, part of which is contributed from wages.

As such, with increasing capital inflow and therefore privatisation, the 'insurance capacity' for workers in such organisations is fragile where, ironically, capitalism is the working ethos (Breman, 1996: 279).

Given these constraints, however, the service sector has expanded in output and employment. The growth of India's economy in the year 2005–06 was 7.4 per cent (Government of India, 2006). Ordinarily, consumers do not realise that by and large they are paying as much for items of consumption from the free trade zones that are available in the open market, as in any of the comparable developing countries. This creates a curious juxtaposition, in that when consumers are faced with the alternative of buying cheaper home-made items vis-à-vis similar such items with 'foreign' labels, they tend, perhaps prompted by the prestige factor, to buy the latter. The increase in purchasing power of most strata of society, fewer investments and the attraction of better living have made for a larger 'purchasing' clientele of imported goods. No less supportive of this situation is the immense number of attractive loans and instalment plans that support the consumer spending tendency. What impact does this have, therefore, on the immediate ecology and styles of living of the family, the major agent of the psychosociological process in the family?

Without reference to the masses in the poorer rural areas of drought-prone, flood-prone, geoecologically-deprived areas, one might say, most families in the 21st century have better lifestyles in comparison to the previous decades. More parents are aware of healthy eating, knowledgeable about childhood vaccines and play centres for their young. Encouragingly, more children are completing a school education, with a greater emphasis (though inadequate) than before, on female education. The occurrence of the tsunami, for instance, has raised an awareness of the tragedies due to natural disasters (Robert, 2005: 48; Thomas, 2006). These are only a few instances of the effects of globalisation. The effect of upward spiralling economic trends and the promise of a higher GDP are bound to create newer 'visions of enterprise on newer aspirations'. In the 1990s, for instance, even though there was no declaration of GDP growth, no evidence of increase in poverty or fall in wages, there were no great signs of structural regression in the market, thus making it difficult for the country to step out of the 'lakshman rekha' (movement within a limited boundary) marked by the international finance capitalist structure (Acharya et al., 2004: 202–28).

Again, although employment in the organised sector has increased, the burgeoning population in effect does not show compatibility with a rise in wages/profits in the industrial sector (Rothermund, 1993) or employment rates (Sundaram, 2001b: 3039–49). India, possessing a labour-intensive pattern of economic growth, has created a lopsidedness in that it has reduced the expenditure on agricultural growth and facilitated the influx of foreign goods from the Far East (Sundaram, 2001a).

However, employment trends followed those of world markets. The rising price of oil has swelled the prices of other industrial outputs, and therefore a 'tightrope' balancing approach has been adopted by the Indian government (Madhab, 1999: 320–22). The uprisings by the naxalites along coastal Andhra (Upadhya, 1997) and the protest against the Narmada valley project (Baviskar, 1995) indicate that the oppressed are now aware of their rights and privileges and want to gain a place 'under the sun' (Rajan, 1998).

India's overall position in becoming a highly productive liberalised economy is still fraught with an accelerating population. This population is educated only half way around the professional mark. Its economy, like the proverbial tortoise and hare race, is dragged down by this human axis of an illiterate, non-professional mass of population. Its balancing between population and GDP is unlike China. China maintains its sovereignty and formulates its own policies, where the West has no strong input or leverage into its economy. Politically strong countries like China and India are able to resist the potential or actual threat from the powerful rich countries. India has resisted overly excessive investments into its economy, and therefore correspondingly large outflows occur from its coffers. Nevertheless, once set in motion, the Indian economy is struggling to maintain its financial reserves in the face of a fragile world policy of globalisation.

The Human Development Track

In view of the above picture of fragile juxtaposition there are some impressions on the state of development studies, across the broad range of theoretical assumptions of the development triad—modernisation, dependency and world system theory—which have not functioned as expected (Schurman and Leyes, 1996). In the face of their inability to explain the socio-economic and political changes in recent decades, globalisation has thrown development studies into a paradigmatic stalemate by offering new viewpoints of micro-social analysis. Development studies in the social sciences, far from being non-political, have an essentially political theme which has spawned two emerging paradigms: liberalisation and institutional approaches. There is a historical development in the world political economy that has diffused developmental studies. It is said that the rise of developmental studies is as much a political as a scholarly concern (Khare, 2006). The concept of modernisation was developed according to westernised thinking including the spread of capitalism in underdeveloped or developing nations. Modernisation is in actuality the synchrony of power relations, political projects and intellectual production (Gendzier, 1985).

The modernisation theory came under sustained attack in the 1960s for its concept and methods. The political climate in the Third World changed the theoretical underpinnings of modernisation concepts. Mass movements in the Third World overthrew the conceptualisations as oligarchic and exclusive. We are now witnessing the fragmentation of the principles of oligarchy, for example, the struggle between the North and the South, ostensibly the western thematic concerns, vis-à-vis the eastern. The systems maintenance bias of modernisation towards rich countries and local elites was exposed, despite world systems and dependency theories. Both underdevelopment and development were considered as two aspects of the same phenomenon, historically existent. This was a system of simultaneous functionality linked to conditioning situations (Rose, 2002).

The demise of the Soviet Bloc, and the increase of awareness of experiments in socialist governance, has brought about many upheavals in the world polity. The recognition of the growing importance of the oil rich countries and the rapid economic growth in Far East countries have caused different equations in the world polity. Therefore, world politics is assuming different balances. In this flux, India is emerging as the largest growing democracy and economy, with a more or less secular socio-polity. Globalisation, therefore, has, and will have, its own repercussions. The open market has a snowballing effect on the employment of cheap labour, many working in dehumanised conditions (Frobel et al., 1980). However, globalisation at the ground zero level fragments again into disparities, for instance, on gender and ethnic issues of differentiation. Here globalisation is in the melting pot of its sub-variables: liberalisation, poverty reduction, and providing a better quality of life and underlying the needs of the neediest. This is happening in the face of growing social changes due to the socio-economic development process (Robinson, 2002: 1047–71). For this reason, the *Human Development Report* (World Bank, 1998: 1) does not in essence give a descriptive picture of the relationships between the widening human choices and their framework, and the role of rich countries in promising human development to the poor. The human development concept at the global level has also failed to address the growing disparities which encourage power strangleholds in the guise of 'debt cancellation', increased loans at high rates and 'hanging donor contributions' (Sagar and Najam, 1999: 743–51).

When we talk of development with a human face we are aware that the rural areas are the most neglected, and in a sense the hinterlands contribute to the exploitative international labour market. This proportion is not only the greatest but also the most precious of our social capital as yet underdeveloped, which is now the concern of the 2004 elected government (Roy and Malek, 2002). The corporative approach to rural development has been most neg-lected so far due to the global giant that is overriding developing countries, which in essence is underwriting the industrial worth of developed nations. There are, however, some unique geoecological areas of human development and social capital in India, like Kerala, Punjab and Gujarat. Kerala is also an example of development of social capital in the sphere of women's education mainly due to the matrilocal and matrilineal social structure and the expansion of education in Cochin and Travancore right from the pre-independence era (Dreze and Sen, 1995). Thus we see that the polity and economic policies of globalisation have affected the Indian econ-omy and social structure in this changing era.

References

Acharya, S., R.H. Cassen and K. Mckay, 2004, 'The Economy—Past and Future', in R. Cassen, T. Dyson and L. Visaria (eds), *21st Century India: Population, Economy, Human Development and Environment*. Oxford: OUP.
Anandalakshmy, S. and M. Bajaj, 1981, 'Childhood in the Weavers' Community in Varanasi: Socialisation for Adult Roles', in D. Sinha (ed.), *Socialisation of the Indian Child*. New Delhi: Concept.
Angel, L., 1994, *Enlightment: East and West*. New York: State University of New York Press.
Appadurai, A., 1990, 'Disjuncture and Difference in the Global Cultural Economy', *Public Culture*, 2(2): 1–24.
———, 1997, *Modernity at Large: The Cultural Dimensions of Globalisation*. New Delhi: OUP.
Aries, P., 1962, *Centuries of Childhood*. New York: Random House.

Bandura, A., 1982, 'Self-efficacy: Towards a Unifying Theory of Behaviour Change', *Psychological Review*, 84: 122–47.

Barone, D.F.J., J.E. Maduax and C.R. Syneder, 1997, *Social Cognitive Psychology: History and Current Domains*. New York: Plenum Publishing Com.

Barrow, C., 2003, *Environmental Change and Human Development: The Place of Environmental Change in Human Evolution*, New York: OUP.

Baviskar, A., 1995, *In the Belly of the River: Tribal Conflicts Over Development in the Narmada Valley*. New Delhi: OUP.

Berry, J.W., R.C. Misra and R.C. Tripathi, 2003, 'Introduction', in J.W. Berry, R.C. Misra and R.C. Tripathi (eds), *Psychology in Human and Social Development*, pp. 1–17. New Delhi: Sage.

Bhattacharya, N.N., 1995, *Religious Culture of North Eastern India*. Delhi: Manohar.

Bhattacharya, P. and A.R. Choudhry (eds), 2000, *Globalisation and India: A Multidimensional Perspective*. New Delhi: Vedam Books.

Bhattacharyya, K., 1989, 'Indian Philosophy in the Context of World Philosophy', *Journal of Indian Council of Philosophical Research*, VI(2): 10–16.

Breman, J., 1996, *Footloose Labour: Working in India's Informal Economy, Vol. X*. U.K: Cambridge University Press.

Burman, E., 1994, *Deconstructing Developmental Psychology*. London: Routledge.

Chandra, A.K., 2001, 'India in the 1990s: The Impact of Globalisation', Paper presented at the Trilateral Academic Conference held at the Russian Academy of Sciences' Institute of Far Eastern Studies, Moscow, September.

Chatterjee, G., 1999, 'Nursery Rhymes and Socialisation', in T.S. Saraswati (ed.), *Culture, Socialisation and Human Development*. New Delhi: Sage.

Chaudhary, N., 1999, 'Language Socialisation: Patterns of Caregiver Speech in Young Children', in T.S. Saraswathi (ed.), *Culture, Socialisation and Human Development*. New Delhi: Sage.

Cole, C.G., E. Bearer and R. Lerner, 2004, *Nature and Nurture: The Complex Interaction of Genetic and Environmental Influences on Humans*. New York: Lawrence Erlbaum.

Comarswamy, A., 2000, 'Perception of the Vedas', in V. Das (ed.), *Oxford Indian Companion to Social Psychology and Social Anthropology*. New Delhi: OUP.

Council for Social Development (updated by A. Kundu), 2006, *India Social Development Report*. New Delhi: OUP.

Dalal, A.K and G. Misra, 2002, 'Social Psychology in India: Evolution and Emerging Trends', in A.K. Dalal and G. Misra (eds), *New Directions in Indian Psychology, Vol. 1*. New Delhi: Sage.

Das, V. (ed.), 1994, *Communities, Riots and Survivors in South Asia*. New Delhi: OUP.

Deutsch, M., 1975, 'Equity, Equality and Need: What Determines Which Value will be Used as the Basis of Distributive Justice?', *Journal of Social Issues*, 31: 137–49.

Dorcas, A., 1997, 'Chinese Qigong Research: An Overview', in H.S.R. Kao and D. Sinha (eds), *Asian Perspectives on Psychology*. New Delhi: Sage.

Dreze, J. and A. Sen, 1995, *India: Economic Development and Social Opportunity*. New Delhi: OUP.

Dube, S.C., 1965, 'Problems in Economic Development in India', in S.C. Dube (ed.), *Religion and Progress in Modern India*. New Delhi: Prentice-Hall.

Eckensberger, L.H., 2003, 'Wanted: A Contextualised Psychology. A Plea for a Cultural Psychology Based on Action Theory', in T.S. Saraswathi (ed.), *Cross-cultural Perspectives in Human Development: Theory, Research and Applications*. New Delhi: Sage.

Freeman, H., 1994, 'Stress, Mental Health and the Environment', in J. Rose (ed.), *Human Stress and the Environment*. London: Gordon and Breach.

Frobel, F., J. Heindrichs and O.I. Kreye, 1980, *The New International Division of Labor: Structural Unemployment in Industrialsed Countries and Industrialisation in Developing Countries*. UK: Cambridge University Press.

Gendzier, I.L., 1985, *Managing Political Change: Social Scientists and the Third World*. Boulder, CO: West View Press.

Giddens, A., 1998, *Modernity and Self-Identity*. Cambridge: Polity Press.

Gottlieb, G., 1998, 'Normally Occurring Environmental and Behavioural Influences on Gene Activity: From Central Dogma to Probabilistic Epigenesis', *Psychology Review*, 105: 792–802.

Gould, S.J., 1977, *Ontogeny and Phylogeny*. Cambridge, MA: Harvard University Press.

Government of India, 2006, *Economic Survey 2005–06* (quoted in *Indian Economy: An Overview*, www.ibef.org).

Ishwaran, K., 1966, *Tradition and Economy in Village India*. London: Routledge and Kegan Paul.

———, 1970, *Change and Continuity in India's Village*. New York: Columbia University Press.

Javeed, A., 2001, 'Caste Appeal Casteism? Oppressed Castes in Politics', in S. Jodhka (ed.), *Community and Identities: Contemporary Discourses on Culture and Politics in India*. New Delhi: Sage.

Jodhka, S., 2001, 'Introduction', in S. Jodhka (ed.), *Community and Identities: Contemporary Discourses on Culture and Politics in India*. New Delhi: Sage.

Kagitcibasi, C., 2002, 'Autonomy, Embeddedness and Adaptability in Immigration Contexts: A Commentary', *Human Development*, 20: 1–6.

Kak, S.C., 2000. 'On Understanding Ancient Indian Science in Science and Tradition', in A.K. Raina, B.N. Patnaik and M. Chadha (eds), *Science and Tradition*. Shimla: Indian Institute of Advanced Study.

Kakar, S., 1981, *The Inner World: A Psychoanalytic Study of Childhood and Society in India*. New Delhi: OUP.

———, 1982, *Shamans, Mystics and Doctors: A Psychological Enquiry into Indian and its Healing Traditions*. Bombay: OUP.

Katz, S.N., 1996, *Devi: Goddess of India*. Berkeley: University of California Press.

Kaur, B., S. Menon and R. Konantambigi, 2001, 'Child and Adolescent Development Research', in J. Pandey (ed.), *Psychology in India Revisited, Vol. 2*. New Delhi: Sage.

Khalakdina, M., 1998, 'Early Childhood Care and Development in India: A Perspective', in M. Swaminathan (ed.), *The First Five Years*. New Delhi: Sage.

Khare, R.S., 2006, *Caste, Hierarchy and Individualism: Indian Critiques of Louis Dumont's Contributions*, Oxford India Reading in Sociology & Social Anthropology. New Delhi: OUP.

Khatri, A.A., 1970, 'Personality and Mental Health of Indians (Hindus) in the Context of their Changing Family Organisation', in E.J. Anthony and C. Koupernik (eds), *The Child in His Family*. New York: John Wiley and Sons.

Kohli, A., 2001, *The Success of India's Democracy, Vol. XIV*. Princeton: Princeton University Press.

Kumar, K., 1999, 'Children and Adults: Reading an Autobiography', in T.S. Saraswathi (ed.), *Culture, Socialisation and Human Development*. New Delhi: Sage.

Lamb, M.E., D.M. Teti and M.H. Bornstein, 2002, *Development in Infancy: An Introduction*. New York: Lawrence Erlbaum.

Langer, G.L., S. Rivera, M. Schlesinger and A. Wakeley, 2003, 'Early Cognitive Development: Ontogeny and Phylogeny', in J. Valsiner and K.J. Connelly (eds), *Handbook of Developmental Psychology*. London: Sage.

Madhab, J., 1999, 'North East: Crisis of Identity, Security and Underdevelopment', *Economic and Political Weekly*, 6 February: 320–22.

Mahajan, G., 1998, *Identities and Rights: Aspects of Liberal Democracy in India*. New Delhi: OUP.

Majumdar, D.N., 1958, *Caste and Communication in an Indian Village*. Bombay: Asia Publishing House.

Malhotra, S., 2003, 'Social Cultural Diversity and Ethnicentricism in Child Mental Health', in J.G. Young, P. Ferrari, S. Malhotra, S. Tyano, S. Caffo and E. Macmillan, *Brain, Culture and Development*. New Delhi: Macmillan.

Mallikarjunayya, G., 2002, 'The Indian Society: Problems and Prospects', *Journal of Public Administration*, 48, July–September: 459.

Marriot, A.M., 1976, 'Hindu Transactions: Diversity without Dualism', in B.C. Kapferer (ed.), *Transaction and Meaning: Directions in the Anthropology of Exchange and Symbolic Behaviour*. Philadelphia: Institute for the Study of Human Issues.

Marriot, M.K., 1990, 'Changing Chariots of Cultural Transmission in Indian Civilisation', in V.F. Ray (ed.), *Intermediate Socieites*. Seattle: American Ethnological Society.

Martinussen, J., 2001, *Policies, Institutions and Industiral Development: Coping with Liberalisation and International Competition in India*. New Delhi: Sage

Mascolo, M.F. and S. Bhatia, 2002, 'Culture, Self and Social Relations', *Psychology and Developing Studies*, 14(1): 55–91.

Menon, U., 2003, 'Morality and Context: A Study of Hindu Understandings', in J. Valsiner and K.J. Connolly (eds), *Handbook of Developmental Psychology*. Thousand Oaks: Sage.

Minturn, L. and J. Hitchcock, 1966, 'The Rajputs of Khalapur, India', in B. Whiting (ed.), *Six Cultures: Studies in Child Rearing*. New York: Wiley.

Minturn, L., D. Boyd and S. Kapoor, 1978, 'Increased Maternal Power Status: Changes in Socialisation in a Study of Rajput Mothers of Khalapur, India', *Journal of Cross Cultural Psychology*, 9(4): 493–98.

Misra, D., 1983, 'Deprivation and Development: A Review of Indian Studies', *International Education Review*, January: 1–21.

Misra, G. and A.K. Srivastava, 2003, 'Childhood in India: An Overview of Psychological Research', in A. Agarwal and A.K. Saxena (eds), *Psychological Perspectives in Environmental and Developmental Issues*. New Delhi: Concept Publications.

Misra, G. and K.N. Tripathi, 1993, 'The Concept and Context of Human Development', in T.S. Saraswathi and B. Kaur (eds), *Human Development and Family Studies in India*. New Delhi: Sage.

Misra, G. and K.N. Tripathi, 2004, 'Psychological Dimensions of Poverty and Deprivation' in J. Pandey (ed.), *Psychology in India Revisited—Developments in the Discipline, Volume 3: Applied Social and Organisational Psychology*, pp. 118–92. New Delhi: Sage.

Misra, R.K. and G. de Berumis, 2002, *Privatisation of Public Enterprise*. Delhi: Manik Books/Vedams Books.

Mitra, A., 2002, 'The Halting Economy', in S. Patel, J. Bagchi and K. Raj (eds), *Thinking Social Science: Essays in Honour of Alice Thorner*. New Delhi: Sage.

Nandy, A., 1974, 'The Non-paradigmatic Crisis in Indian Psychology: Reflections on a Recipient Culture of Science', *Indian Journal of Pyschology*, 49: 1–20.

Nandy, A., 2002, 'The Politics of Application and Social Relevance in Contemporary Psychology', in A.K. Dalal and G. Misra (eds), *New Directions in Indian Psychology*. New Delhi: Sage.

Orme-Johnson, D.W., E. Zimmermann and M. Hawkins, 1997, 'Maharishi's Vedic Psychology: The Science of the Cosmic Psyche', in H.S.R. Kao and D. Sinha (eds), *Asian Perspectives on Psychology*. New Delhi: Sage.

Oyserman, D., H.M. Coon and M. Kemmelmeier, 2002, 'Rethinking Individualism and Collectivism: Evaluation of Theoretical Assumptions and Meta-analyses', *Psychological Bulletin*, 128: 3–72.

Pandey, G.C., 1984, *Foundations of Indian Culture: Spiritual Vision and Symbolic Form in Ancient India*. New Delhi: Books & Books.

Pandey, J., 1998, 'Environment in the Indian Context: Social Psychological Issues and Research', *Indian Psychological Abstracts and Reviews*, 5(2): 205–34.

———, 2004a, 'Introduction to Volume Three', in J. Pandey (ed.), *Psychology in India Revisited—Developments in the Discipline, Vol. 3: Applied Social and Organisational Psychology*. New Delhi: Sage.

———, (ed.), 2004b, *Psychology in India Revisited—Developments in the Discipline, Vol. 3: Applied Social and Organisational Psychology*. New Delhi: Sage.

Paranjpe, A.C., 1984, *Theoretical Psychology: The Meeting of East and West*. New York: Plenum Press.

———, 2003, 'Contemporary Psychology and the Mutual Understanding of India and Europe', in J.W. Berry, R.C. Mishra and R.C. Tripathi (eds), *Psychology in Human and Social Development*. New Delhi: Sage.

Piaget, J., 1950, *Psychology of Intelligence*. New York: Harcourt Brace.

Rajan, N., 1998, 'Multiculturalism, Group Rights and Identity Politics', *Economic and Political Weekly*, 4 July, 83: 4–10.

Reddy, V., M. Shekhar, P. Rao and S. Gillespie, 1992, *Nutrition in India*. Hyderabad: National Institute of Nutrition.

Robert, D., 2005, *Southeast Asia Tsunami: One of the World's Greatest Natural Disasters in Modern Times*. Chicago: Amer Products Corp.

Robertson, R., 1992, *Globalisation: Social Theory and Global Culture*. London: Sage.

Robinson, W., 2002, 'Remapping Development in Light of Globalisation: From a Territorial to a Social Cartography', *Third World Quarterly*, 23(6): 1047–71.

Rose, Euclid A., 2002, *Dependency and Socialisation in the Modern Caribbean: Superpower Intervention in Guyana, Jamaica and Grenada, 1970–1985*. Lexington, MA: Lexington Books.

Ross, A.G., 1961, *The Hindu Family in its Urban Setting*. Toronto: University of Toronto Press.

Rothermund, D., 1993, *An Economic History of India from Pre-colonial Times to 1991*. New York: Routledge.

Roy, M.K. and M.A. Malek, 2002, 'Human Development through Building Social Capital in Rural Areas: Some Experiences', *Journal of Rural Development and Administration*, 34(1–4): 37–59.

Saberwal, S., 1996, *Roots of Crisis: Interpreting Contemporary Indian Society*. New Delhi: Sage.

Sagar, A.D. and A. Najam, 1999, 'Shaping Human Development: Which Way Next?', *Third World Quarterly*, 20(50): 743–51.

Saran, R., 2003, 'How We Live: Census of India Household Survey', *India Today*, 28 July.

Saraswathi, T.S., 1993, 'Child Development Research and Policy Linkage: A Mirage or Reality?', in T.S. Saraswathi and B. Kaur (eds), *Human Development and Family Studies in India*, pp. 25–56. New Delhi: Sage.

———, 2003a, 'Being and Becoming—A Child, Youth, Adult and "Respectably" Aged', in J.W. Berry, R.C. Mishra and R.C. Tripathi (eds), *Psychology in Human and Social Development*. New Delhi: Sage.

———, (ed.), 2003b, *Cross-cultural Perspectives in Human Development: Theory, Research and Applications*. New Delhi: Sage.

Schlegel, A. and H. Barry, 1991, *Adolescence: An Anthropological Inquiry*. New York: Free Press.

Schurman, F.J. and C. Leyes, 1996, *The Rise and Fall of Development Theory*. Indianapolis, London, Nairobi: EAEP/Indiana University Press, James Curry.

Seymour, S., 1999, *Women, Family and Child Care in India*. Cambrige: Cambridge University Press.

Singh, Y., 1977, *Modernisation of Indian Tradition: A Systemic Study of Social Change*. Faridabad: Thomson Press.

Sinha, D., 1965, 'The Integration of Modern Psychology with Indian Thought', *Journal of Humanistic Psychology*, 5: 6–17.

———, 1988, 'Some Recent Changes in the Indian Family and their Implications for Socialisation', *International Journal of Intercultural Relations*, 18(2): 239–58.

———, 1994, 'The Joint Family in Tradition', *Seminar*, 424: 20–23.

Sinha, D. and H.S.R. Kao, 2000, 'The Journey to the East. An Introduction', in H.S.R. Kao and D. Sinha (eds), *Asian Perspectives on Psychology*. New Delhi: Sage.

Sinha, D. and M. Sinha, 1997, 'Orientations in Psychology: Asian and Western', in H.S.R. Kao and D. Sinha (eds), *Asian Perspectives on Psychology*. New Delhi: Sage.

Sinha, D. and R.C. Mishra, 1993, 'Some Methodological Issues Related to Research in Developmental Psychology in the Context of Policy and Intervention Programs', in T.S. Saraswathi and B. Kaur (eds), *Human Development and Family Studies in India: An Agenda for Research and Policy*. New Delhi: Sage.

Sinha, D. and R.C. Tripathi, 2002, 'Individualism in a Collectivist Culture: A Case of Co-existence of Opposites', in A.K. Dalal and G. Misra (eds), *New Directions in Indian Psychology*. New Delhi: Sage.

Sirsikar, V.M., 1965, *Political Behaviour in India*. Bombay: Manaktala.

Skinner, B.F., 1953, *Science in Human Behaviour*. New York: Macmillan.

Srinivas, M.N., 1962, 'A Note on Sanskritisation and Westernisation', in M.N. Srinivas (ed.), *Caste in Modern India and Other Essays*, p. 42. London: Asia Publishing House.

———, 1996, 'Introduction', in M.N. Srinivas (ed.), *Caste: Its 20th Century Avatar*. Delhi: Viking.

Sundaram, K., 2001a, 'Employment and Poverty in the 1990s: Further Results from the NSS 55th Round Employment–Unemployment Survey, 1999–2000', *Economic and Political Weekly* 35(2), 17 March: 931–40.

———, 2001b, 'Employment–Unemployment Situation in the Nineties: Some Results from NSS 55th Round Survey', *Economic and Political Weekly*, 35(32), 11 August: 3039–49.

Thomas, A., 2006, *Lessons of Disaster: Policy Change after Catastrophic Events*. Washington, DC: Georgetown University Press.

Thomas, R.M., 2001, *Recent Theories of Human Development*. New Delhi: Sage.

UNDP, 2004, *UN Role in Promoting Democracy: Between Ideals and Reality*. New York.

Upadhya, C., 1997, 'Social and Cultural Strategies of Class Formation in Coastal Andhra Pradesh', *Contributions to Indian Sociology* (NS) 31(2): 169–93, New Delhi: Sage.

Valsiner, J., A.U. Branco and C.M. Dantas, 1997, 'Co-construction of Human Development: Heterogeneity within Personal Belief Orientations', in J.E. Grusec and L. Kuczynski (eds), *Parenting and Children's Internalisation of Values*. New York: John Wiley & Sons.

Van Ginneken W. (ed.), 1998, *Social Security for all Indians*. New Delhi: OUP.

Werner, H., 1966, *Comparative Psychology of Mental Development*. New York: Science Editions.

Wissing, P. and C. Van Zeden, 1997, 'Psychological Well-being: A Fortogenic Conceptualisation and Empirical Clarification', Paper presented at the 3rd Annual Congress of the Psychological Society of South Africa, Durban.

World Bank, 1998, *World Development Report: Knowledge for Development*. New York: OUP.

2

Human Development: Bases and Processes

Basic Principles of Development

DEVELOPMENT PROCEEDS along certain regulated principles, which form the basis of development in its theoretical frame. These are:

(i) The individual is a dynamic organism with given innate tendencies. He follows epigenetic rules. Lerner (2002) has quoted Gottlieb as saying that a new definition of epigenesis is:

> Individual development is characterised by an increase of complexity of organisation—i.e., the emergence of new structural and functional properties and competencies at all levels of analyses (molecular, subcellular, cellular, organismic) as a consequence of horizontal and vertical coactions among its parts, including organism–environment actions.

Thus we see that development follows initially biophysical rules.

(ii) The individual behaves on an involuntary basis at first, and then voluntarily. He comes in contact with the environment through the stimuli in his surroundings, which influence covert and overt behaviour. There are phylogenetic and ontogenetic roots that predate the acquisition of symbolisation. Over a period of time, the latter are reinforced and developed into those traits appropriate for the individual to find a homeostatic level (Bernard, 1999; Cassirer, 1953).

(iii) The individual progressively exhibits complex behaviour dependent upon his innate tendencies (drive, motivation, cognition and intelligence) and their maturational correlates. By themselves, however, these innate tendencies may lie sterile, unless otherwise provoked or stimulated. These maturational correlates refer to interaction of the concepts of maturational regulatory mechanisms (Finlay and Darlington, 1995: 1578–84).

(iv) No matter what generalisations are made through research monologues or dialogues, an individual has unique qualities that differentiate him from others. These concepts relate to differential individual abilities, particularly achievement motivation and intelligence (Gottlieb, 1992).

(v) The individual learns to cope with his environment through a series of adjustments and adaptations. The latter concepts relate to theories of the socialisation process and the human being's competence in adapting to his environment (Cairns et al., 1990: 49–65).

(vi) The human being is psychologically moulded by the particular culture in which he lives, as distinct from people in other cultures (Cole, 2005: 25–54).

These themes are valid for any human society in generic terms. However, when we apply them to a specific geoecological group, such as the Indian society or the African society, we recognise that when these basics are applied, they assume different forms, related to the culture in which the specific society is rooted. In recent years, several erudite Indian scholars have appealed for emphasising the cultural content of human development in the Indian context with culture-specific connotations, emphasising the 'crisis of identity' (Dalal and Misra, 2002: 40; Dash and Kar, 1993: 77–89; Kumar, 1993: 67–72).

Among the many, two examples are: *(a)* the treatise on individualism and collectivism, a thoughtful application of McClelland's achievement–motivation concept to Indian society (Sinha and Tripathi, 2002: 242–55); and *(b)* language development in a multicultural society (Mohanty, 1991). Therefore, when translating these 'universal attributes' to the Indian situation for the purpose of collecting adequate empirical data, it becomes essential to discuss them in the *in situ* situation of social realities. Traditional social psychology is derived from the Dharmashastras[1], the Nitishastras[2], Smritis, Arthashastra and Puranas (Dalal and Misra, 2002: 36).

Their concepts, in a philosophical sense, are akin to that of socio-psychology, inasmuch as indigenous concepts have more in common with the aforesaid six themes of basic principles of human development. Social psychology is expected to explain life. Because Hinduism is the dominant religion, it is frequently described as denoting 'a way of life', the way of life of the dominant group in India. These are two facets of the same coin, namely, a way of life enjoined by religion and a way of life reflecting patterns of culturally attuned lifestyles.

---

[1]Dharmashastras are the ancient law books of Hindus which form the basis for the social and religious code of conduct for Hindus. These are post-Vedic works by different law givers that emerged during the rule of many Hindu dynasties. Manusmriti is an important work of this group of texts.

[2]Nitishastras are a class of ancient Hindu texts on politics and statecraft. The most important text of this group is the Arthashastra by Kautilya, a statesman of the court of Chandragupta Maurya.

Bearing this underlying condition of socio-religious ethos in mind, we turn to the concept of 'universals', which, we acknowledge, could have applicability in generic terms to the Indian context. The Indian culture being unique, abstract universals such as achievement and dependency may have an overall global interpretation; these need to be modulated in their cultural frames in each society. These were accepted conceptualisations since psychology and its themes were first documented by European psychologists on the basis of their own empirical evidences in the early 18th century (Sinha and Kao, 2000). Although the major emphasis in the development of psychology was decontextualised when it applies to India which is a unique culture (as indeed in other cultures), the contours become differentially defined (Misra and Gergen, 1993: 225–53).

Western conceptualisations are subtly different from Indian thought, which emphasises the socio-secularism approach of Hinduism within the cosmic energy. In the 1960s, with the emergence of cross-cultural psychological research, it became evident that the comparison between western and eastern societies was untenable. Human behaviour was/is considered adaptive to the context of the cultural system (Berry et al., 1983: 13–21). Therefore, concerns culminated in a movement towards an indigenous psychology. Simple illustrations will bear out these facts. In the early ad hoc adoption of Eurocentric terminology from the West, the dissonance became apparent when applying western norms of physiological growth related to nutrition intake. By and large, genetically, the western physique and frame is heavier and taller than that of the easterner, and even though the average Indian, for instance, does not consume the same amount and quality of nutrition, he still is healthy, despite being smaller and lighter. Therefore, western norms are rather misleading (Gopalan et al., 1998).

Again, with the great enthusiasm given to Piagetian schemas, and their appearance at strictly different ages, Indian evidence using the same protocols showed that they generally appeared later in the Indian and do not in any way deplete the potential cognitive development of the Indian child (Stryker, 1991: 19–41).

The fact of the matter is that most western tests, initially translated or cursorily adapted, were measuring the non-contextual bases of the Indian child's thought/behaviour processes in his culture. For instance, the Indian child's colour concept is different when labelled. The colour purple is called *jamuni* or the colour of a fruit. The colour blue is called *asmani* or the colour of the sky. As his world vision widens, the Indian can classify and categorise many other abstract colours with concretisation in terms of material objects. Further, how does one measure personal social abilities according to Gesselian norms, if the child is not familiar with such items as shoe laces and spoons, especially if he is used to *chappals* (slippers) and eating with his right hand? What we are saying is that the applicability of concepts requires correct operational definitions that are familiar in the given environment and not borrowed from another (Muralidharan, 1983). Therefore, the emphasis on culture- and context-specificity is underscored. It is said that the hermeneutics strategy is a method to find alternative conceptual ways to explain what are termed universals (equivocal definitions of the trait/characteristics/attributes), which is the antithesis of culture-specific indigenised traits/attributes/characteristics (Smith et al., 1995). The use of ethnography and observational methods is being encouraged towards culture specificity with greater impetus in relation to the 'positivist-empiricist metatheory and strategies of reductionism and operationalism' (Misra, 2003: 34). This has been enhanced by the increasing importance of ecological *in situ* observations (Berry et al., 2000). Thus, we see that there is something unique about the Indian pattern of thinking and acting, which is anchored in socio-cultural norms, and bonded by the social realities of regional, ethnic, caste and, in this case, religious parameters of the Indian psyche. The more psychologists and social psychologists delve into the ways of Indian thought, the greater is the trend towards finding differences between discovering 'ethics' (cultural universals) and 'emics' (culture-specific focus), in spite of the fact that there is still a search for pandemic, pluralistic attributes, which are comparable or contrastable (Berry, 1969). The search for 'emics' is a more constant one in the Indian sphere of psychological search, for the simple reason that the Indian psyche is a composite of dynamic permutations and a combination of culturally rooted variables. There is, for instance, the universal concept of socialisation of a child, where he is either dependent or independent, similar to the concept of being egocentric and being socio-centric. Independence during childhood is not as much stressed in the Indian situation as it is in the West, when compared to other priority traits of deference to elders or consideration of the others' needs. Why is this so? Let us go back to the roots of the basic forms of Indian thought as aptly stated by Pandey (1972: 86):

> The Indian mind has sought to govern social relations not by abstract reasoning but by intuition and compromise. It has sought to meet challenges by modifying rather than recycling older solutions. Instead of seeking freedom through power, it has sought freedom through self control. It is said ... the older and the newer forms have continued side by side and this continuity and heterogeneity within the ambit of the overall progress and unity.

Some of the salient features common to the traditional understanding and interpretation of Indian thoughts are contained in the following (Mishra, 2003: 50–52):

(i) The Indian mode of thinking is context-sensitive (Ramanujan, 1990). For instance, in metaphysical thinking, the Indian is a part of his space or country (*desh*), and his locale.

(ii) There is emphasis on harmony or coherence, rather than unity. Civilisation (*sabhyata*) is based on respecting the secularism of the various subcultures and diffusions of caste and class.

(iii) The person is one aspect of a socio-centric and organic conception of the individual's relationships in society. In this society social roles are foundational.

(iv) Existence is rhythmic in character. The antitheses determine the organisation of worldly processes. The universe is represented by an organic view, where units are interdependent (Capra, 1983). This concept is akin to quantum physics and the behaviour of subatomic particles.

(v) Attitudes towards time transcend historicity. Man is temporal and yet not temporal. His temporality is viewed on one plane, and his potentiality of being involved in time and space is viewed on another plane.

(vi) Indian thinking assumes cosmic plurality and cosmic inter-changeability. *Rta* is the dynamic immanent order of the cosmic manifestations. *Dharma* is followed as the imminent principle of order in nature, social and moral life. Life is organised and coordinated at every level through the operation of this principle.

(vii) Indian thought accepts that knowledge brings freedom from ignorance. The search for truth makes the human free.

(viii) Inward contemplation and self-analysis are emphasised. Intuition is perceived as the method for access to the ultimate self (*darsana*). Humans adapt themselves to nature without reconstruction.

(ix) A multiplicity of world views are recognised. The Rig Veda mentions that though God is one, he is called by many names. This leads to religious and intellectual tolerance.

(x) Humans are not only agents (*karta*) but ones who experience (*bhokta*) as well. There is an emphasis on sacrifice and not self/individual/egocentric aggrandisement.

(xi) The law of *karma* is the major principle governing everything. It is the cause and effect of the universe in its entirety and time dimension. It is also the major leading scriptural document on observations leading to mandates on what is moral and what is not, through the cosmic justice of rebirths. The contemporariness of karma is enjoined to this day in the way of thinking of the average Indian.

(xii) The four goals of life (*purusharthas*) are duty or dharma, enjoyment or *kama*, earning of wealth or *arth*, and liberation from the eternal cycle of birth, death and rebirth, or *moksha*.

(xiii) The unity of all life is the core of this tradition where the concept of individuality is subservient to the collective others. The ultimate source of reality is the *atman* in oneself and the cosmic temporal world is illusionary.

(xiv) From the above, it is deduced that the individual is situated in a cosmic web of relationships. Boundaries between others and self are not fixed, the individual is embedded in the group. Thus, we see that the philosophy of Indian thinking rests on being a part of the cosmic world of time, space and spiritualism. It notes that man is a part of his social world, that truth seeking or knowledge gives intellectual freedom, that secularism is emphasised, that duty is important as a basis of attainment of nirvana or self-harmony, that man is a temporal being going through successive reincarnations, that the world is illusionary and that due respect and value for traditions, for ancestors, for elders and the hierarchy should be ensured.

Therefore, we may infer that the development process in Indian thought is one in which traditional values are re-instilled (Kamlesh, 1981: 13–17). Many of them are ethical and perhaps aesthetic, and certainly connote a 'world vision' of the unity of all types who are allocated different roles working in unison. These are mainly roles of reciprocity and interdependence, in a socially organised world, even though changing modes are influenced by science and technology (Kedia and Bhagat, 1988: 559–73). Since concepts are expressed through language, the type of idioms, axioms, modes of address and grammatology in the Indian languages are quite distinct from the western (Ochs, 1986: 276–320). For instance, to describe the concept of *atman* as the soul robs it of the intensity of meaning in the connotational communication of the Indian psyche. There is a specific ontology of language in India, which is not the same epistemologically as a supposed English synonym (Marriot, 1990). Hence, there is an incompatibility of reproduction of the same meaning from one language to another. Such differential concepts are moral reasoning, achievement dependence, and such like (Sinha, 1980). According to the Upanishads, the atman, the vital essence of man, is the same as in the ant, same in gnat, the same in the elephant, the same in these three worlds, the same in the universe (Brhadaranyaka Upanishad: 1, 3, 22, quoted in Misra, 2003: 49). Thus we see, according to the underlying concept of the ancient scriptures, the world is analysed as described in these ancient sayings. They are considered akin to the understandings of social science documented in the last few centuries. Man has not suddenly acquired reasoning or cognitive powers, documented in the recent past, but has possessed them since inception, and they are yet to be understood and documented by the current science of social thought. With these concepts in mind, we need to analyse the underlying dynamics that direct/guide this thinking. At the same time, we need to keep in mind that these are not 'constancies'. There is always a state of mobility both of physiological and of mental development. This concept is termed 'dynamism', to indicate that the individual is constantly in a state of change, with stops and starts, in this flux of developmental mobility. Many experts call it progressive states of chronological development. While standards have been evolved for physical and mental development, when we deal with particular individuals there is always a wide range within which the individual evolves at his own pace.

Therefore, how does this dynamism operate? The importance of the concepts of innate physiological and biological development processes (nature) cannot be underestimated. So also, the various conditions under which the human adjusts and adapts in his constantly changing scenario of chronological stages, and situational scenario (nurture) cannot be over-emphasised (Berry, 1980). The individual uses the genetic endowment from both parents depending upon the interaction between dominant and recessive genes (Hasan, 2005). In this chapter, however, we do not expect to give an eclectic theory of human development precisely because the unfolding processes that go on constantly in the growing individual are somewhat unpredictable. We will deal only with the conceptual understanding of human development, its correlates and the linkages that organise it.

The reader will at once see that when we talk about human development we are forced to talk about an abstract generic person, for there is no such thing as an abstract human being in a developmental frame. We may, in common parlance, label a person as an extrovert or an introvert. In the use of such concepts we pick upon prominent attributes, but in reality development operationalises a composite bag of contributing concepts. For instance, we popularly describe a newborn thus: 'He looks like his father', 'He is the spitting image of his father/grandfather'; and 'He does not look like anybody in the family'. Even as lay people, we try to look for inherited genetic characteristics. But there is more to a personality than physical appearance. In other words, there are other inherent/acquired traits that make up particular and unique traits exhibited by a particular person during the developmental process, irrespective of whether or not he looks (physically) like his forefathers.

Definitions of Development: Thematic Conceptualisations

One of the more recent descriptions of development is the one expressed by R.M. Thomas as 'the way people change with the passing of time' (2001: 1). Although simplistic, Thomas argues that its amplification connotes both physical maturation and accumulation of experiences in an interactive process. The significant point made from a review of conceptualisations about human development is that the canvas is widespread, the variables are multiple and the foci are different. Some emphasise stage in chronological ages; others specify traits of individuals and groups. And still others emphasise the environment, and yet others go back to the origins of the biogenetic strains of phylogeny and ontogeny.

Ontogeny is a lifelong process (Misra and Tripathi, 1993: 95). Some areas are a priori considerations. Others are post facto considerations. By this we mean antecedent events (a priori) leading to consequent events (post facto)—such as a harmonious emotional environment builds up a sense of identity (Erikson, 1995: 18–164). We might group these factors into hypotheses/assumptions: how should development take place? The answer to this question is frequently based on comparisons of different theoretical concepts, such as the development stages according to Piagetian schema (Piaget, 1954: 156ff) and the development stages according to Erikson. Many of these are based on empiricism and argumentatively developed, like the IQ (Intelligence Quotient) tests such as Raven's Progressive Matrices (Khare, 1976: 33–37); Thorndike's Intelligence Test (Kakkar, 1976: 20–23); the Incomplete Man sub-test of the Gesell Developmental Scale (Pathak, 1977: 45–51); and other ecological models like Bronfenbrenner's ecological model (Bronfenbrenner, 1979). Others are on the basis of empiricisms like the learning theories and Piaget's schema of concepts (Piaget and Inhelder, 1969). Although the learning theories were based on quantitative studies, and the latter (Piaget's theory) was based on idiographic analysis, both of them have validity in their own conceptual frameworks.

Thus, theories and models of human development have appeared in a staggered fashion since the early 1990s. We give here a synopsis presented by R.M. Thomas (2001: 309) who has brought some order to the categorisation of the major theories. He has categorised the theories with respect to different time frames and according to their similarity. There are nine thematic theoretical types: (a) Spiriticism, (b) Mentalism, (c) Dynamism, (d) Functionalism, (e) Behaviourism, (f) Holism, (g) Constructionism, (h) Marxism and (i) Cognitivism (ibid.: 3–26).

Thomas describes this collation of theoretical concepts as, 'the inclusion of the concept of human thoughts'. His inclusion of the theories he has described are based on key empirical concepts evolving over the last two decades in the successive theories which attempted to explain human development in their own contextual frame (ibid.: 2). 'Spiriticism' is, according to Thomas, a naïve/cultural/folk psychology, composed mainly of people's beliefs and convictions without any underpinnings of empiricism. The system indicates the supernatural, and the relationships between that and human development. It is a form of the society's folk psychology that builds the belief system incorporating the soul, mainly propounded by creative and godlike individuals. Spiriticism is concerned with the development of values and ethics rather than the physical body and the intellect. The individual perceives the mortal world through moral precepts laid down by supernatural edicts, channelled through godmen. Violation of these precepts brings down the wrath of the supernatural. The physical part of the individual is the mind, and the non-physical, the soul. The latter continues to exist after the former ceases. In Christian belief, the good and the bad are characterised by the godhead and Satan, respectively (The Father, the Son and the Holy Ghost in Christianity). In Hinduism, the body disintegrates into four elements that are tangible, namely, earth, fire, water and air, and the mind also disappears. The most important aspect that differentiates Hinduism from the other religions is that the soul transmigrates in the former, while in the latter the soul is either banished to hell or lives in heaven or paradise. In Hinduism, the transmigration to another life or reincarnation depends upon the moral deeds or karma accumulated in the current life. Consequently, the primary aim of the finite life is an objective attachment to the material aspects and concentration on karma or good. These are based on the principle of cosmic justice (Reichenbach, 1990). Thus, there is a kind of inherent justice: people get in life what they deserve for their actions in the past. This is an exposition of the Hindu philosophy of life, which is an informal belief/ideology that is not subject to empiricism but is based on common sense inherent in logical psychology, where, for instance, children develop their skills on the basis of communication as a necessary vehicle for learning behavioural roles related to their responsibilities (Bernard, 1999). Thus, it is apparent that the supernatural aspect of Hinduism cannot be concretely tested by finite means, and so is the case with all religions. Hindus are operationally defined by karma, dharma, moksha and *punerjanam* (rebirth) (Ramamurthy, 2006). As these concepts exist in the mind, unlike the other types of psychological thinking in the other theories, mentioned by Thomas, spiriticism as a theory is informal and non-testable. However, it is important to underscore that the definitions of this theory are closely allied to the spiritual philosophy as attitudes, values and beliefs enunciated by the Dharmashastra, which is the spiritual text of Hinduism and is known as 'eternal and ageless' (*sanatana*): 'the essence is changeless, but the forms in which they express themselves are ever changing' (*Encyclopaedia of World Religions*, 1975: 118). It must not be assumed that all Hindus strictly think and behave according to religious mandates. Living in the real world, social realties overtake them and therefore most Indians adhere to a mix of spiriticism and other theories, expressed by other experts in the field of the social sciences.

The next movement towards the end of the 19th century was the traditional, philosophical mode of hypothesising through actual multiple events—a process termed 'mentalism'. The original proponent was Kant (Wood, 2004). Kant revolutionised the foundations of philosophical ethics, changing it to scientific philosophy with logical reasoning (Kant, 2002: 226). Tichener and Wundt conceived of the mind as differentiated into different physical processes such as willing, attending, sensing, thinking, communicating, and such like (Wundt, 1904). Their attempts were to explore the conscience through introspection. Tichener, however, conceived of the mind as a 'basic construct of images recorded in the mind based on perception' and elicited through intensive recall methods. Tichener used a parallel course of history to evince his themes. Examples used were the history of cultural products, of how language, myth and custom develop through differentiating experiences. Wundt went on to explain that human culture represents various stages in culture, mental evolution from primitive tribal to civilised, a type of recapitulation theorising. Tichener, on the other hand, asserted that the mind develops on an accumulation of sensations. He subscribed to the concept of positivism based on the methods of natural sciences. He applied the term 'Structuralism' to identify this theoretical thinking (Tichener, 1984).

While these two philosophers and educationists were continuing with their different modes of explaining human development, 'Dynamism' also grew at that time. Its main proponent was Freud (1920: 3–64). Freud started out by developing identities of covert function of the self through dreams and recollection of childhood experiences. Essentially, he assumed that human thoughts and actions are driven by a pair of contrasting internal forces, one of despair and the other of life/hope (Kenny et al., 1972–73). The life instinct is interpreted to mean a sensual pleasure-seeking energy. The despair/death instinct is a counterpart and these instinctual drives compete for homeostasis. Prominent neo-Freudians were Sullivan and Erikson, among others (Murray, 1938; Erikson, 1963; Horney, 1937; Sullivan, 1965: 281; Jung, 1928). The chief functionary in the psychoanalytical theory is the 'Id' residing solely in the unconscious as the major energy driving the personality and operating on the pleasure pain principle. The ego is the reality-based umpire. The superego is the kind of internalised parent, punishing and rewarding behaviour, while the ego deflects the Id's drives by adjustment mechanisms called 'ego defence mechanism'. We will discuss his theory in detail in Volume II. Suffice it to say that Freud's series of psychosexual stages between birth and adolescence relates to the zones of satisfaction such as anal, oral and genital and discusses conflict situations. However, his major focus was on the relationship between the caregiver and the childhood upbringing process, and, therefore, his interest was not on subscribing to how development took place normally but what could go wrong if it took place abnormally. What could be the cause and how could normalcy return?

From the middle of the 19th century, mentalists and Darwinists propounded a theory in Europe and a new theme emerged (Darwin, 1859). The aim of this new trend called 'functionalism' was to show how human beings adapted to their social and physical environment. It originated on the basis of Darwin's *On the Origin of Species* (1859), in which survival and its maintenance were regarded as the motivation behind behaviour. Such theorists at the turn of the century were James Dewey (1891), Angell (1904) and Baldwin (1897). The latter drew a parallel between the phylogenetic development of the human species and ontogenetic development of children in particular societies. The functionalists emphasised the superior capacity of humans to learn, to evolve physical and mental skills, and to control their environment.

During this period, 'behaviourism' as a theme was ushered in by J.B. Watson (1913: 159–77). In the early 20th century, Watson deflected from the concept of consciousness, to assert that thinking is behaviour and not a state of mind. The most significant theorist in this field was Skinner (1974) whose central tenet was that the habitual ways through which people learn are determined by the consequences of their actions in the past. Over the lifespan there is an accumulation of response techniques with rewarding consequences (reinforcers), which increase the strength of the action. Punishment weakens the recurrence of that behaviour, and in many instances eliminates from the repertoire of the learner the existence of past experiences. Thus, over a period of learning through these rewarding and non-rewarding behaviours, techniques used by adults in these constructs are called 'behaviour modification' techniques.

Around the middle of the 20th century, development theory from Europe assumed a profile of the Gestalt or the holistic view. which emphasised the development of the child as a unitary, integrated organism (Woldt and Toman, 2005: 5). Subscribers to this view included W. Kohler (1929). It was Kurt Lewin (1936) who exerted the most lasting influence on developmental theory emanating from all the Gestalt models. His concepts were composed of life space, where at any given time certain facts existed in a person's life space and a fact was defined as an objectively verifiable real-world observation. As the child grew, forces from the external world (weak or strong forces) modified his behaviour, increasing the life space of facts. In different regions of the life space, as the child grew, boundaries became increasingly rigid. This is akin to the concept of habit. As the life space expands further, facts when modified become too complex to maintain a sense of realism, and are encircled by boundaries, very much like a physics model. These regions become organised and interdependent, reorganising themselves dynamically as further life experiences replace the old ones.

The next sequential step of theoretical understanding was that of 'constructionism', the main proponents of which were Piaget (1965) and Vygotsky (1978). Vygotsky also included in his models Marxian concepts. Piaget was the major proponent of cognitive theory subsumed under constructionism. He built a series of schemas which were age-related, which, in his words, were 'a structure or organisation of actions as they are transferred, or generalised by repetition in similar circumstances' (Paranjpe, 2002; Piaget and Inhelder, 1969: 4). We will deal with Piaget's theory in greater detail in Volume II, as he is much used in the studies on the concept of cognitive development, by the enhancement of age and the physical structure of perceptual objects. These are again similar to several foregoing theories, such as 'functional invariance' (Lewin's concept of habit formation). Piagetian concepts like 'assimilation' and 'accommodation' are akin to the theories of the behaviourists and mentalists who emphasise accumulation of experiences in behaviour and their modification. The major differences are that Piaget bases his conceptualisation on neuro-maturation and the processes of logical thinking in construct formation. He also uses an age synthesis in unfolding the complexity of cognitive thinking, recognition of stimulus sensation and their construction/reconstruction during childhood. Vygotsky (1962), as one of the neo-Piagetians, suggested that cognitive development had its early origins in the perception of the physical world (composed of contingent, causal objects, spatial and temporal relations based on the field of perception). This is different from the logico-mathematical representation, which requires objective symbolic language. This conceptualisation went a step further to develop stages but linked them to concepts such that the individual was a result of action and not thought. Central to this model is the concept of 'lead activity', marked by three features. The first is that a lead activity occurs on the basis of a priority need to activate a process leading to goal attainment. The second feature is that somewhere along the line of the process, alternative strategies occur cognitively as intervening variables inhibiting goal attainment. The third feature is that the inhibition towards goal attainment depends upon the strength of these cognitively occurring alternative strategies that confront the individual. Translated into simple everyday action, this means that an individual, for instance, needs to obtain top grades in test performance. The lead activity is to study, revise, experiment and rehearse in order to perform well. Other alternative strategies include using tutorials, surfing the Internet, studying with peers in a group and so on. The individual knows that the major lead activity is the individual's comprehension which he must apply on his own volition. The other support strategies are easier to use, but may inhibit the goal attainment. Similarly, one lead activity may also signify that other activities are also necessary for the accomplishment of a goal and the individual may then use a sequential activity to accomplish the goal. To continue with the same stimuli example, when an individual finds that trying to comprehend information for the test also requires interpretation by a teacher to support his understanding, this then becomes the next lead activity. Cognitive learning took another direction when it included the social learning concept (social cognition and information processing models). The best known theory is Bandura's modelling theory (Bandura, 1969), which was formulated by observation and direct learning, or learning vicariously. This implies that the learning of action is based on the performance of others. The major functions are: perception of the model, coding the action of the model in memory, retaining the images in memory, carrying out the remembered actions and activating motivation to imitate the model. Information processing also involves similar pathways. In the classical version of information processing, the following occur: availability of sense organs; means of translating sensory stimuli into electrochemical codes; means of combining codes from different senses into a unified sensation; a short-term working memory function; a long-term memory that accumulates past experiences; and finally the muscle system that acts on the outer world. At birth, these systems are immature; but over a chronological age span they gain maturity, depending upon the neuromuscular system. This was evident in the work of Piaget, who proposed four causal processes affecting the development process: heredity, physical experience, social transmission and equilibration (Piaget, 1973).

In recent years there have been demonstrations of new techniques, influencing theoretical concepts with invention and widespread dissemination through electronic imaging. In the 1980s, artificial intelligence schemas and their related information-processing techniques were developed. The cognitive revolution took birth some 40 years ago (Miller, 1963). It began as an anti-mentalistic approach to the excesses of behaviourism. It retained the parameters of experimentation. Computer science provided the metaphor of information processing and, more recently, connectivity. Cognitive neuroscience has witnessed explosive growth in the neural mechanisms of human mental processes. A multidisciplinary approach, which is appearing on the scene in terms of understanding human development, is a combination of experimental psychology, computer science and neuroscience (Warm, 1998).

Indian philosophy, although discursive and analytical, also recognises both individuation and integration (Kagitcibasi, 1997: 1–50) and revolves around the major principle of dharma. Culture, in Hindi, is called *sanskriti*, which implies purification and transformation. While the potential interpretations are difficult to summarise, we could turn to the Dharmashastras focussing on the concept of dharma. This concept was first mentioned in the Rig Veda and elaborated in Gautam's Dharmashastra in 600 _` (Dalal and Misra, 2002: 22). Its interpretation implies the obligations and duties of man towards the world, that is, morality; responsibilities to other than self; the behavioural appropriateness between self and nature (the other inhabitants of the world, like animals, birds and growing plants); and the obligations to oneself (Bharati, 1985: 185–230). The intellectual reasoning and logic is from within oneself or the atman, which is maintained in constant communication with its spiritual essence. The other side of dharma, translated into social world realities, implies primarily the responsibilities of the adult to his/her progeny, implying, in turn, teaching or interpretation of the environment, both material and social, around the nurtured individual (Anandalakshmy, 2002: 33–41).

Thus, we see a transference of dharma, as understood by the adult, to the maturing child in terms of the social framework, the spiritual framework, the ecological framework and cultural framework. By being inducted into these frameworks, we mean the appropriate types of behaviour with respect to one's ecological habitat, respecting and nurturing one's ecology (Mascolo and Bhatia, 2002: 55–59). With respect to the sociological framework, we mean the appropriate interactions with family, kinship, community and others in society. By the spiritual world, we imply the understanding of one's identity in the cosmic sense in terms of morality, honesty, charity and other such virtues, which, when practised, bring the individual closer to obtaining nirvana or realisation of moksha, freedom from worldly egocentric motivations. In essence, therefore, dharma is inclusive of its operational definition of karma, which is actionised behaviour, reflecting dharma. Thus, there is, in terms of indepth analysis, an underlying concept, that when we talk about different academic theories about human development, we are in reality talking about the transitional self (or the 'I' which is known only in this world).

An Analysis of the Themes

Thus, we see that Thomas has systematically traced the development of theoretical thinking, indicating how the various schools of progressive thoughts on human development, over time, assumed different bases. The first theorising termed 'spiriticism' was built upon man's relation to the supernatural. In the early days of documented thoughts, such descriptions were merely exploratory and philosophical in nature and, to some extent, as in ancient India, dealt with myth and mythology. Out of these arose the philosophies of religion and thought relationships of governance between man and man, and man and nature, as viewed in the philosophies of Plato and Aristotle (Cooper and Hutchinson, 1997: 1808). These were reported in the 18th and 19th centuries. In India, much before the European Renaissance and the Industrial Revolution, unbeknownst to the western world and preserved by oral tradition in India, sages of ancient times such as Valmiki and Vyasa were the first to propound theories of man and his interrelationships in philosophical discourses (Swami Venkatesananda, 1999: 409). The former is said to have been the author of the Ramayana and the latter of the Mahabharata. Sant Gyaneshwar, Tulsidas, Kabir and Sai Baba have been some of the revered sages through whom Indians have been handed down a tradition of the mind, the conscious and the uniqueness of man's temporal existence in relationship with the supreme being. This relationship is in tandem with cosmic energy and nature as expressed in the Dharmashastras, through role allocation during the lifespan (Kane, 1941). These philosophies served to form the forerunners of the next set of categories which dealt with the mind and the soul in terms of man's development (mentalism). They dealt with the mind and matter (Baleson, 1909).

Mentalism delved deep into the human mind by the early European psychologists, who evoked the dynamics of the relationships of the mind to its inner stimuli and need-fulfilment, which then gave rise to further conceptualisations. These were the explorations of the mind and its inner workings (Vygotsky, 2006). There grew out of these mentalistic philosophies a further exploration of the workings of the mind. They gave rise to a third set of categories, namely, the modification of thought processes and modification of overt expression (behaviour modification process), first explained by Watson (1914), an experimentalist in behaviour study who stressed the linkage between thought processes and their overt expression. The objectivity of studying the mind through only its behaviour was a little tenuous, for it gave little recognition to the interplay with the environment (Smith et al., 2000).

This analysis gave rise to the next set of categories (constructionism) originating with the Darwinian concepts of survival, of coping mechanisms, and of differentiating between the mechanisms of the mind and body, which were general to the given species and called 'phylogenetic' processes. Those relating to the individual's innate differential processes, uniquely modified by his environment, were termed 'ontogenetic' processes (Thomas, 2001). Thus, this progression allowed an interplay between mentalism, behaviourism and constructionism, for the empiricism arising out of them provided a more holistic picture of the development processes over the human lifespan conditioned by time (maturational processes). These environmental influences, which have been gradually honed by man himself, have given rise to greater scepticism in science and technology. The pace of the latter seems to outrun the pace of man and his natural surroundings.

It is well known that increasingly science and technology are greatly influencing man's development. DNA processes, modern medicines and chemical alterations through mechanical devices, such as mental imaging, laser surgery, interventions into living organs with non-organic materials such as artificial limbs (prosthetics) are now increasingly common. The science of the genome offers explorations of gene manipulation. Serendipitously, they have extended the understanding of the development of human behaviour. As such, we might predict that the heterogeneity in human development across time may be more homogenised in the coming years given the fact that non-human development is more in the control of the human will and mind. Therefore, development in the future, at various stages in the lifespan, has the potential to be modified. For instance, babies are being born at improved levels of physical and related mental health in developing countries; differences in levels of intelligent behaviour are becoming more apparent in the recognition of gifted children and differently abled children, for whom there are special programmes, although mostly in the West (Eysenck, 1985: 1–34).

Again, primary school children in the 21st century are learning more than their parents did when the latter were school children. Children are now becoming 'parents of their parents', and are reversing the order of teaching and learning (Prout and Prout, 1997). The fact that globalisation has expanded space and increased the rate of geographical mobility implies that children have become more challenged, with increasing world vision. The more fruitful areas of investigation in development are not as much in areas of toilet training and weaning as in the previous decades, but more as to how to develop coping mechanisms against stress of various kinds—emotional stress, academic stress, personal stress, parenting stress and professional stress. There are now more sophisticated and perhaps more dangerous drugs for treatment of disorder in human behaviour when aberrant, and a greater growing antagonism between generations in the child's search for autonomy (Smetana, 2005).

In the progressive scenario of India's interaction with the global world, many westernised ideas are being adopted by the upper classes. By the very process of filtration their ways are being imitated by the lower classes, who do not have the means but have the aspirations. This leads to a double-barrelled coping with stress in their daily lives between the chasm of their dreams and their social realities. Besides the description of human development, it can be seen also as an emergence of behaviour that is simultaneously a process as well as a product. Development is a combination of biological growth processes that are linked to emotional maturity and mentally reinforced perceptions. In other words, as the child develops the use of finer muscles, from the gross neuromuscular motor abilities to intricate ones, he also learns to use them for more complex activities. For instance, an acrobat does not spontaneously exhibit acrobatic skills. These skills are obtained from long periods of exercise, training and practice through the growing years, where ontogenetic skills are developed (Gould, 1977).

It is apparent that there are elements of refinement of behaviour in the maturational process that intimately produces a product, such as the ability to use fine muscular coordination of eye and hand in a child, which enables him to paint or sew. There is also an element of progressive change, fused with this maturing process. In other words, maturation or refinement of the attribute increases with age, both physically and mentally, during the growing years where it is said that mental growth occurs, even though at a slower rate. Physical growth, however, is complete at the attainment of adolescence or thereabouts. For instance, in a study by Katiyar and his colleagues it was found that the peak height and weight gains were at 13 years 8 months and 14 years 4 months, respectively (Katiyar et al., 1985). This is the stage where physiologically, the human being attains the height of his graphic upward trend of physical development.

Axes of Development

Development has six axes. The first is maturing of characteristics that are phylogenetic, that is, characteristics inherent because of race. All human beings are alike in physiological characteristics (Gould, 1977). However, there are ontogenetic differences. An Eskimo is unlike an African: his language is far different, his skills and world perception are different. These are his ontogenetic characteristics, distinguishing him from others. The Eskimo orders his world of survival in relation to ice and cold while the African wears the least amount of clothing, and has to find ecologically-influenced adaptations to adjust to his surroundings. Both, therefore, develop skills to enable them to cope with their environments (Berry, 1974: 129–40).

The second axis emerges from the first. As development takes place the child becomes more and more independent and therefore becomes more involved in the world of culture. As has been said by Thorpe and Schmuller (1958: 3): 'a human being is enmeshed in a social order—and symbolic culture—which influences his every action' during this development period. Super and Harkness (1933: 221–31) in their discussion on the 'developmental niche' emphasise the role of the environment, both human and concrete, which shapes his behaviour (see also Pandey, 1998). In an informative study of three South Pacific cultures, Munroe and Munroe (1975: 1) traced the development process in selected conceptual domains of these traditional societies, using major conceptual frames like physical growth, motor skills, language, perception, cognition, dependence, aggression, sex roles and social motives. In their conclusion, these authors make a very strong case for the differentiation between the western and non-western child, while ethnographically finding differences among the three cultures in these domains except in early childhood dependency (ibid.: 181). The development of these domains in the western child in contrast was said to be due to 'developmental hypertrophy', stating that the western child's development is one of high stimulation in a regimen that is purpose-fully designed to maximise smartness, competitiveness, achievement and self-orientation (ibid.: 150).

The third axis states that whatever the interpretation of development, it must have a suitable fit within the culture to which the growing individual is being acculturated and which provides him with a meaning of his self (Kitayama and Markus, 1994: 17–37). The cultural nexus gives the individual a place in his societal environment from which he draws his norms of behaviour.

The fourth axis is that every individual is different from every other, physically and behaviourally, even though there may be only small nuances of difference. This has been empirically established by the study of identical twins (Bouchard et al., 1990: 223–28). These concepts of differences in development are explained by the theory of individual differences (Anastasia, 1965).

A fifth axis of development, and perhaps the most important, is that chronological age development is an unfolding process and is characterised by age-related incremental progressions, more apparent in the physical rather than the mental realm. The former is observable and the latter can only be inferred. It is in the latter area that the meaning of development gets diffused, as mental age does not always keep pace with the physical. Some exceed the norm of what is expected at certain ages, while others fall below. We have widely differing IQs, for example, the brilliant and the below average. At the same time, each individual proceeds on the basis of his needs. This is the sixth axis, which revolves around an individual's primary and secondary needs.

Primary needs are basic to the individual's survival, such as food and shelter. Secondary needs arise from needs stimulated by his surroundings such as the need for affiliation, for security and for achievement. Maslow has advanced a set of conceptualisations based on his theory of needs. Man has two sets of forces within him: one which moves towards defence and safety of the self and the other towards growth. Thus, one set clings to safety and defence, and the other regresses and clings to the past. The first is risk-taking, moving towards independence, freedom and separateness. The latter impels him towards wholeness of self, towards full functioning, and towards accepting his past and his unconscious self (Maslow, 1948: 402–16). The process of growth is a never-ending series of facing challenging situations, some large, some small, some achievable, some insurmountable. Where one has a choice of alternatives, one moves forward, or remains stagnant, or even regresses, and thereby meets with success or failure. Such processes include emotional situations of conflict, anxiety and final resolution. According to Maslow's theory of self-actualisation, needs are placed on a hierarchy from basic needs which expand to higher levels, similar to primary and secondary needs of behaviourism. In the dynamic context of competing needs, the satiation of one leads to the prominence of another (Maslow, 1943: 514–39). In other words, when two conflicting needs possess similar strengths of drive, they become resolved, by one gaining prominence and fulfilment over the other. For instance, this is a familiar situation with shoppers when they cannot decide on choice. There are some obsessive shoppers who agonise and spend hours on deciding which one of the two items to purchase while others make quick choices.

The Indian Philosophy on Human Development

It would be useful to note philosophical writings in Indian scriptures which try to find a meaning for personality development. In social metaphysics, explaining the essence of socially relevant models in India, social action (or doing or behaving) falls under one of four categories: dharma (related to religious practices), arth (related to wealth and material goods), kama (related to desires) and moksha (related to ultimate salvation). Social behaviour (which emanates from a person, by which he is identified) is either righteous (dharma) or non-righteous (*adharma*).

Therefore, action (behaviour) which is dharma can combine with arth without violation of the laws of Manu (an ancient sage who codified the modes of behaviour according to the scriptures and according to caste/hierarchical levels). For instance, a Brahmin on whom the rites of purity and pollution are strictly enjoined, is socially expected not to touch the skin of dead animals (polluting). However, in these modern days, it is accepted that he can work in a leather factory or sell leather goods.

An enterprising person can consistently practise *adharma* (profiteering, for instance, through adulteration of food) and be absolved through practice of ritualistic penitent behaviour (to appease the gods) through acts of dharma (such as giving charity out of the profits from the adharma profiteering.) Indians are, therefore, not lacking in achievement orientation, but work around it for the purpose of the desired karma (Mukerjee, 1976: 91–97).

Therefore, we need to question the assumption that traditional institutions are obstacles to industrialisation. The average Indian lives in two worlds. He learns to adjust and compensate, and can coexist with both dharma and adharma (Mukerjee, 1965: 15–58). Thus, reformulation and resilience are modes by which the Indian personality in society attempts to find levels of equilibrium, and like quicksilver can change from one mode of behaviour to its near opposite. We find, therefore, that caste is a 'nexus value' in the social structure in which man behaves, as he is appointed a particular position in the social structure, which integrates the social group. This positioning exists in spite of Aryanisation (Anglo-Saxonisation) and sanskritisation, where the individual continues to abide by socio-religious norms and beliefs. What is happening is dynamic changes around the individual's periphery are occurring constantly. For instance, it is not unusual for the daily worship (*puja*) performing Indian to wear a caste mark or a mark of the ritualism, and comfortably 'scam' account books.

To the Indian mind, the Creator is a supra-rational mind. His ultimate laws are probably unknowable, but there is an underlying cosmic law, *rta* that encompasses cosmic phenomenon testifying to the existence of the real absolute (*Brahman*)... *rta* necessitates synchronisation of life events ... and the prediction of events and the differentiation of these in terms of propitiation theology led to phenomenal knowledge of astronomy (of Jyotish Vedanga of Lagadha, siddhantas of Gargeya, Aryabhata, Varahamihir, Brahmgupta, etc), geometry of altar design (of Baudhayana's Sulbha Sutra, etc.) (Raina, 2000: 61).

According to A. Gupta (2006: 25–26), there are six philosophies of Hinduism inscribed in *Vedanta* which form the foundational principles of the spiritual life of the Indian. They emphasise that all is unity, and diversity is an illusion or *maya*. Thus, even though subreligions revere different forms of gods or goddesses as their household deity, all these represent, symbolically, one God, which explains the basic Indian-ness of the Indian psyche.

One of the interpretations of the acquisition of knowledge is based on the *Samkhya* philosophy. This philosophy presents the cosmic and individual principles of evolution. It describes how the mind, the senses, the intellect and cognition manifest themselves (Dwivedi, 1971: 171–85). The *yogadarsana* evolved from the Samkhya, a psychological framework of human behaviour (Singh et al., 1998: 21–35). The contention is that this thesis comprises the whole gamut of Indian psychological thinking supported by experiments on yogadarsanas as a doctrine of the mind. Western social scientists C.S. Hall and G. Lindzey, on the other hand, comment that the Pali text of *Abhidhamma* is wholly psychological in nature (Hall et al., 1998: 347–82). Buddhism is stated to link its philosophy to the five senses, a sixth sense possessing intentionality (Gunther, 1971). The mainstay of these shifts is the belief in *purushartha*, which provides meaning to existence, and validates its subsystems of the levels of adaptation to the environment.

For instance, if a person has attempted to attain a certain level of achievement but fails, he ascribes it to his karma and, therefore, adapts to a different level of equilibrium. This is often misinterpreted as 'rationalism' and 'apathy' by psychologists in their study of human behaviour in the Indian context (Mahadevan, 1980). In the familiar framework of social situations, Indians have a tendency to empathise with those in distress or in problematic situations. It is not uncommon to hear fellow men talk of their companions who have tried and not achieved, as being 'crossed by fate': *'bechara woh koshish toh kiya hai, magar kismet nahin hai'* (poor man, he has tried, but that is his fate). The practice of self-resilience is related to an affiliative trait of tolerance of 'bad fate'. In other words, frequently, westerners are amazed to find rich people passing by in their luxurious cars looking askance at beggars. Apparently, in the context of social–structural categorisation, caste/class differences are maintained.

The social maintenance systems have a thematic strain of social reality, namely, there must be poor and there must be rich. There must be well-fated and there must be ill-fated. There must be division of labour by virtue of the caste into which one is born as fated. Of course, one might move out of the occupational caste structure, for 'even cabbages can look at a king', (Carrol, 1865), but the effort enjoined upon the individual should be such that he should not adhere to the structural system. It is socio-religiously enjoined that one should be a vegetarian in a Brahmin household; but one may choose to be a non-vegetarian in a foreign country without castigation, where the Indian social structure has not followed him. We find this ideology has social relevance, for in order to fit into a societal structure one must abide by its norms or feel a sense of *social anomie*. This construct of social reality is much akin to Lewin's field theory of core and peripheral value systems. He postulates that deep embedded values are more difficult to eradicate than peripheral ones because of the different degrees of prevalence of energy, and the permanence of life space or what could be construed as the abiding inner self in Indian philosophy (Lewin, 1951).

Cosmic theory is a deeply embedded socio-religious value in the Indian subsystem. It is supported by the ayurvedic system of the self in relation to cosmic energy (for example, the art of reiki or transference of positive energy). It is also the bedrock of the relationship between the body and the mind, which is very much like the psychoneurological system in the explanation of a person's development. Conceptualisations of the developing personality offer snippets of behaviour within the given parameters of the theory/model/construct of most theories. We therefore state that, at any one time, development is the observed, frequently occurring behaviour of a person in relation to his own innate needs, and those related to the outside world. The human being, through the foundational stages (up to six years or so, as stated by most child development specialists), is seen to have embedded the roots of the essential traits that determine his later personality (Eysenck, 1952). We observe that almost all theories contribute towards an understanding of personality development of the individual, but do not compose themselves into any one single eclectic theory. Baldwin, for instance, in analysing the need for an integrated theory of development, comments that 'there do not seem to be areas of agreement among theories', and goes on to say that 'there is a need for a neural molecular nontheoretical language which should emphasise a theory of behaviour and action and a theory of behavioural change' (Baldwin, 1980).

Postulates of Development

As said before, development, implying a progression, can be directed either positively or negatively. However, not all change is development. It is a continuous process with every phase subscribing to a set of unique criteria. For example, infant development has its own set of characteristics (related mostly to motor and initial speech development).

Also, gerontology has its own characteristics such as loss of hearing, sight and lessened motor ability. The stages of development are logically related to chronological time. Therefore, time, out of all these factors relating to change, is the major criterion. Time dictates movement into certain directions. The concept of a stage is not progressive, not regressive, not static—it is a process of elaboration, a system of interface and a system of exchange in a contextual, dynamic composition, in which each component influences the other towards adaptation. For instance, the pre-operational stage precedes the concrete operational stage, which precedes the stage of abstract conceptualisation (Piaget, 1964).

The world to the individual is constructed through experiences of time at different levels (interfaces with nurturing peers and media), evolving and devolving through adaptive mechanisms, a self-reflexive movement of an introspective type. Development is that which exists, and is additive (Epstein, 1980: 81–132). There is no value judgement, no epistemology, no spiritual dissonance akin to the concept of the yogic thought of 'I am therefore I am'. That which I want to be is added onto 'I', but the 'I' can itself be modified. In the course of chronological progression, the 'I' has the potential to be modified and redefined (Fawley, 1999). Gergen considers the self concept as being socially constructed, existing in a cultural context. For instance, the cultural context for the Indian is composed of his gotra, his ethnic group, his socio-religious group and the regional group in which he is located (Gergen and Collins, 1971). Thus, human development is constantly influenced by the environment in which the individual lives (Gottlieb, 1999).

Because of the 'individualism' of development, the importance of qualitative analyses is growing in methodological recognition, so as to better understand development *in situ*. For this reason, current emphasis is on patterns that are ethnographically obtained, such as language development in elaborated speech formation (Bowerman, 1981: 93–185). Social scientists are attempting to highlight biological and physical attributes in development. The concept of epigenesis, relating to increased and new complex forms of organisation of how the human mind works, began in the 1900s, with the study of behavioural embryology (Gottlieb, 1998: 792–802). In actuality, this is based on evolutionary change resulting in behavioural change—from homogenesis to heterogenesis. Old concepts have been given new formats, where, for instance, heterogeneity has been refined to the concept of individual difference, where developing organisms of the same species can reach the same standpoint along different pathways (ibid.: 4). These have been empirically demonstrated: for example, manual skill and dexterity (Miller et al., 1990: 1207–12). This has brought to the forefront, in higher profile, the dynamic modelling of cognition in the form of connectionism (Van Gelder, 1995: 231).

The lowest form of organisation (molecular geneticism) to its higher form (complex intercellular integration) occurs throughout life (Weiss, 1959: 11–20), some generating and some degenerating, such as the loss of baby teeth in childhood and of permanent teeth in old age. Some of the major diseases that deplete intellectual development, besides brain damage and trauma, occur due to degenerative diseases in old age such as Alzheimer's and general senility (Parasuraman and Greenwood, 1998). Besides genes, individuals inherit not only a standard embryonic and foetal stimulative environment, but also places, parents and peers who modify the ontogenetic niche. This emphasises the stimulating effect of the outer embryonic sensations on the developing foetus. Such a process contributes to the experience in the early forms of interactive development (Moore, 1993).

Definition of the Developing Person

One of the first definitions of the developing person was in terms of the end product or the person's personality. This was expressed in 1950 by the Fact Finding Report of the Mid-century White House Conference on children and adults: 'A personality is the thinking, feeling, acting human being who, for the most part conceives himself as an individual separate from other individuals and objects. The human being does not have a personality—"he" is a personality' (Witmer and Kolinsky, 1950: 3). By this definition, we extrapolate that there is a synonymity between personality and a person, except that when we are talking about personality, we describe the person in a socio-psychological context. Thus, the individual personality is the identification of the self as an entity apart from others. But, the next question is, what is this identity? Unfortunately, even in attempting to theorise about what this identity is, we have fragmented information. It has been argued that a theoretical framework taps the underlying rather than the manifest. Those called genotypes are comparatively more meaningful, rather than the manifest phenotype (Argyris, 1970).

With regard to the social interpretation of identity in the individual, S.C. Dube pointed out in a keynote address, to another problem when he said 'the major weakness of social sciences, especially in a meaningful context, namely the Indian generic personality, as is well known … is … an excessive reliance on foreign models' (1976: 27–38). In this respect, we find that in the Indian context, out of sheer scarcity of data or relevant theories about personality, we depend heavily on the analysis of theorists from the West. Some theorists from social psychology and anthropology offer abstract constructs and models. From the viewpoint of their own disciplines, they study the structured concepts conceived by the logic of their theories, and have tried to best fit the identity of the person within that structure. For instance, sociology calls the entity a socialised person, who forms his self-constructs as influenced by the environment (socialisers). He perceives and is perceived as the outcome of the process of socialisation. In this connection, D.P. Mukerjee (1958) argued that many metaconcepts of social sciences derived from the West do not have relevance for the

Indian society. They are abstractions from a different culture and, he contended that, the assumption of Talcott Parsons on the definition of the 'actor/situation' does not hold good for the Indian situation as the Indian social system is inherently structured on a normative teleological basis (Mukerjee, 1958). At the same time, a holistic understanding of identity is essential, as the individual needs a niche to be more fully understood (Yardley and Honess, 1987). This niche is the package of associative identities, such as religious identity, ethnic identity and regional identity. The expression of ethnic identity and religious identity begins as early as three to four years of age, and promotes an emotional bias of irrationality of either being superior or inferior to individuals of other religions (Singh, 1979: 231–44). Again, religious identity is linked in a binding way to ethnic identity and political identity, given the generic nature of identity in a nation. Ethnically, Hindus, for instance, are scattered all over India and even in the diaspora; they continue their identification of caste and community, and national cum political identity. One has only to notice Indians abroad in malls and in places of leisure who talk more freely to other Indians who are strangers, rather than to the local people (Kumar, 1998). India, moving along the fast track of development, and, as a non-aligned country, developing nuclear power for peaceful purposes, is gaining a foothold in the global profile. Global happenings impinge upon the daily life of ordinary persons in terms of consumer index, oil prices and terrorist events. This calls for cautious interpretations in the face of international events, especially in the handling of multiculturism in a secular context (Rajan, 1998).

In attempting to find an average ground for developmental concepts, we find, instead, divergences. Take, for instance, the concept of self. Psychology depends heavily on the constructs of the individual as a 'self' (Baldwin, 1980). Anthropology tells us that the individual is acculturated to norms and behaves as a representative of such norms, such as being a conformist/non-conformist, towards parental and societal belief systems, or parental ethnotheories (Harkness and Super, 1996). Goodnow (1990) terms the process as parenting, giving it a general rubric. While it is acceptable that each discipline tries to maintain its own identity in terms of separate concepts, we are encouraged to see, in recent years, evidence of academic work in such areas as cross-cultural psychology (Berry et al., 2002).

The problem in finding a holistic concept of development is further compounded by the fact that each of the contributory theories has subtheories called molecular theories. For example, the subtheory of motivation in psychology, the subtheory of self in Erikson's schema (Erikson, 1950), the defence mechanisms in psychoanalytic theory, and so on. Thus, we have packages within each theory. Psychoanalytic theory tells us that the human being is egocentric rather than socio-centric and that trauma in the early years frequently leaves an indelible mark on behaviour in adolescence and adulthood. Learning theory, the major proponent of which was Hull (1943), emphasises the stimulus-conditioned response and reinforcement theories.

In Volume II, the theory of behaviour will be discussed in detail. Suffice it to say here, that at that point we will deal with experimental data, which allows for the interaction with modification through conditioning. It may be said that the conditioning principle may be considered the most fruitful paradigm of understanding learning at all levels of maturation. Other definitions of development grapple with the same problem: how far do we spread the parameters of the discipline/theories in trying to understand development.

We are really limited by the fact that none of these theories gives a meaningful, complete picture. In the 1950s, J. Whiting and I. Child, in their classic study on Child Training and Personality, (1953: 2–15) related their conceptions to theoretical formulations, by stating that 'personality is the extent to which a person's characteristics differ from one to another, the extent of uniformity within one person, the effect of different cultures on differences in personality among different societies'. This is, of course, a description related to their model of psychoanalytical concepts within cultural parameters (Kardiner, 1939: 110). The latter identify the effect of different cultures as primary institutions (the family producing the basic personality structure) and secondary institutions (peer group, neighbourhood, community, classroom, world information, and so on), influencing the development of a personality.

Most theories explain segments of behaviour or development through 'behaviourism' and limit themselves to conduct research to support the hypotheses of their disciplines. However, when we come to generalisations, we find that we are caught in stereotypes, such as, 'he is an aggressive personality', or 'she has a meek personality', and so on. But these are just clichés, from which we go on to typing persons to fit into categories on the basis of stimulus questions of methodologies. Here, we evoke only what we have set ourselves out to evoke. The psychoanalyst because of his theoretical background observes whether there is any science of fixation, either positive or negative in the individual studies. This is one of the major themes of the aforementioned classic study by Whiting and Child (1953). The behaviour theorist tries to find out whether the child has achievement motivation or not through the overt behaviour of the individual.

There is no linkage between one trait and another, nor are there linkages among theorists. As soon as psychologists take a sample and try to find out whether the group can be divided on the basis of authoritarianism or submissiveness, and do elaborate analysis of these bipolar dimensions by analyses of regression and covariance, all they are able to say is yes or no: authoritarianism exists or submissiveness exists, but a personality is more than that, and, what is more, is dynamic, and may be authoritarian before peers whom he can bully and be submissive before his parents who finance his education. Even when we try to find some typology like Sheldon's on the basis of body mass (1940), we are in fact bordering on the untenable. 'There is more to a human being's dynamic nature than just the basic fact of skeletal tissue which makes him out to belong to one category or another.' Thorpe, after much review of the available theories, states that:

> The process of personality formation and development, though they result in a distinct unity, are integrated. Although individual variation is the basis of psychological measurement, this uniqueness must be viewed as a total process of personality and should not cause us to lose sight of the patterns of experience which have produced it (Thorpe and Schmuller, 1958: 354–55).

But how do we know that there is a developing personality in a human being? What do we see or perceive? Is it a commonality or is it an individual characteristic or are there combinations of characteristics which make up what we see and typify? In the early days when philosophy seemed to be the only intellectual theory on the workings of the human mind, personality was viewed as a mask (Latin, *personae*) akin to the verb *personare*, 'to speak through', referring to the mask used by an actor on the stage. Greek and Roman drama employed the use of masks extensively in order that the audience identifies characters. In Shakespearean days, while the mask did not exist, Othello was obviously a villain and Romeo was a lovesick irrational. Some scholars still believe that personality is a façade. Psychoanalysts believe that the ego represents the individual and that social constraints and laws cover the ego with apparently several layers of veils.

Many experts believe that a developed human being can only be interpreted by behaviour and that theories of behaviour are really theories of personality (Klien and Krech, 1952: 5). But we know by now that all theories of behaviour rest on the fundamentals of the stimulus response bond, and are observable overts. How then do we come to know about the inner world of the person, which is also organised in a covert fashion, such as emotions and their suppression, anxiety, conflict and guilt. In order to find an adequacy of correlates to explain personality, some experts use the concept of 'correlation of events'. If the personality shows dominance, overbearingness and a tendency towards control, conflict models, such as Mowrer's model (Hall et al., 1998: 184), tell us that the person may have low self-esteem, low self-image, low self-confidence, and so on.

Psychoanalysts tell us the person has experienced some trauma which has become indelible or repressed and their outcomes in behaviour are really exhibits of such correlated covert happenings in the mind. Thus, we see that very few theorists of personality are able to present a holistic picture. They represent differing combinations of constructs of the individual's field space, depending upon the variables of parenting, ecology and environmental reinforcers or negators (Sharma and LeVine, 1988). Some psychologists try to overcome this limitation by saying that while it is not possible to cover all correlates adequately, there is a possibility of 'surplus value' (Thorpe and Schmuller, 1958: 15).

This surplus value is described as that potential which a theoretical model has for explaining additive personality dimensions, or further linkages. For instance, while the subtheory of motivation may explain how motivation takes place, it also has the potential to incorporate socialisation for motivation, much like a football coach would try to instill confidence in a football team playing a match. The subtheories of patterns of socialisation then incorporate socialisers, channels of socialisation, communication modes and language (both verbal and non-verbal). These then link up with positive and negative reinforcement in child rearing patterns, and their effect on the child's personality.

Let us take two examples from the Indian situation. One is language development, and the other is cognition. Language development as a theory has several principles (Chomsky, 1986). As language development will be discussed in detail in the chapter on Development of Critical Skills, we will continue to use its assumptions here in the context of bilingualism and or multilinguism characteristics of growing up in India, where children, as they grow up, are exposed to several languages and even within tribal areas to several dialects. The major principle of 'social speech interaction' occurs in the context of a learning situation, where the adult reinforces the child's phonemes and speech styles by encouraging imitation of adult speech patterns. The initiation into speech learning by the adult is the imitation of words and sentences which are short, terse and are according to the norms of the given community/society (Valsiner, 1989). We will narrate here statements in the mother's report about a segment of children's behaviour. This is to illustrate the content and the codes conveyed to the child.

Both are urban mothers. They were given a simple story to relate to their primary school children in their own manner after they understood the theme. The illiterate mother said:

Ek pitaji they. Us ka ek beta tha. Ladka ka nam Raju tha. Raju problem tha. Vo school nahin jata tha. Us ka pitaji bahut dhamkey deta tha ki tum school nahi jayega to biscot aur methai bund karega. Vo jub padai nahin kiya us ka pitaji nay us ko TV dekhne nahi diya.

(There was once a father. He had one son. His name was Raju. Raju was a problem. He did not go to school. His father used to scold him and say he would not get sweets and biscuits if he did not study. Then his father stopped him from watching TV.)

The literate mother was a little more elaborate:

Jasay apke pitaji hai ek bahut naughty boy ke pitaji the. Pita vo little boy ko bahut love karte the. Magar little boy baat nahin sunta tha. To ek din pitaji ne kaha, 'Hum apka TV dekhna, bahar jana, ice cream khana band karengey, jab tak apna homework nahin complete karengay and good marks nahin milengay and good boy nahin banengay aur bade ban kay doctor hona hai.'

(Just as you have a father, there was one naughty boy, who also had a father. The father loved the little boy very much. But the boy never used to listen to his father's instructions. So one day the father said: 'I will stop you from watching TV, going out and eating ice cream, till you finish your homework, and if you don't get good marks and behave like a good boy, and become a doctor when grown up.')

The above, in a simple manner, illustrates the differences. The illiterate mother used mainly Hindi. She also used deference norms and called the father by his deferential name. She did not use illustrative terminology, nor gave any motivational aspirations. Her utterances were limited to the here and now. Her sentences were terse and to the point, and did not move into adverbial or adjectival clauses. The educated mother, on the other hand, used many English words, but which required greater encoding and decoding like 'love', 'good marks', 'doctor', 'naughty boy', 'complete'. She also used words that were motivating, like becoming a doctor, if he were a good boy, and mentioned rewards. The two mothers lived in a world of social reality presented to them with words that easily identified the items in their environment. Thus relational social speech in idiomatic language is the means of communication for the child who learns to imitate and use language that is presented to him by the nurture. The illiterate mother restricts her codes to the immediacy of the environment since her vocabulary is limited and, therefore, the child gets used to expression in a restricted, rather than elaborate, manner (Kumar, 1999). In North America, English being the major language, it is used with idiomatic terminology which conveys depth of meaning to the child. Also, in that culture, cartoon models are used, such as Ninja, Pokemon, Hulk, and the like, to convey ideas of fantasy. Paranormal and interplanetary concepts, reinforced by the world of simulated toys and the almost psychoanalytic doll play techniques used by the child, depict heroism, villainy, hatred and love. In the Indian context the heroes and villains, and themes of morality and immorality, are from the Ramayana, the Mahabharata and the Panchatantra, as well as the mythology of *devi*s, *rakshasa*s, and so on.

In the Indian context, language in the form of multilingualism, and its relation to the acquisition of knowledge, affects the lifestyle of the child and therefore his personality (Chaudhary and Sriram, 2001; Roland, 1980: 73–87). We will discuss the domain of language in the chapter, 'The Development of Critical Skills' in detail. The acquisition of language as a skill links the individual's needs to the bonding of his society. It reinforces the bonds of affiliation (need-affiliation) and profiles his identity in his social group (Mohanty, 1991). The vehicle of cognition and transactions is language in its varied symbolic forms of art, literature and documentation. Cognitive development has an evolutionary as well as ontogenetic history: it predates the acquisition of symbols (Langer et al., 2003: 141–70).

The other area of cognition in the social reality of the Indian environment is ecological determinants of behaviour. Several authors have shown how ecology is an intervening variable, that it limits behaviour, that it interacts with behaviour and that behaviour adapts to ecological pressures (Berry, 1976a: 112). Using basic ecological influences as enunciated by J.W. Berry and his associates, we can extrapolate the following, relating to tribal areas, as an illustration of perceptual skills moderated by ecological factors.

In tribal areas, where the mode of sustenance is mainly hunting, the ecology impacts on perceptual cognitive skills as an intervening variable in moderating awareness of detail, in sharpening visual range, in enlarging the spatial periphery of perception, and so on (Berry, 1976b). These types of moderation are honed by cultural aids such as language cues, encoding of non-verbal messages, practising the art of shooting and crafting tools, so that there is alignment between hand–eye coordination skills and target. This functional adaptation is limited by the ecology (terrain, animal footprints, odours of animals, and so on). These skills are reinforced by the socialisation process, as functional adaptation is a need for survival. There is some data from the Indian situation which traces such skills (Misra and Agrawal, 2002). We may extrapolate from studies by Barry et al. (1959) who found that visual spatial skills vary systematically with a cluster of ecological and cultural determinants among hunting tribes (see also Goodnow, 1976). Similarly, we may hypothesise that the urban school child learns to use calculators and does not have to do mental arithmetic as did the children in the previous generation who counted laboriously on fingers or added digits and carried over to the next. In fact, we observe that even adults who have to do calculations tend to use the language of origin in the use of numbers, thus emphasising the underpinnings of acculturation or the process of socialisation towards cultural norms. In the next volume we shall discuss socialisation in detail, as it denotes the interaction between the child and his environment, mediated deliberately by adults in his environment. While there is no one such theory of ecologically circumscribed personality, there is sufficient evidence that ecology shapes access to the environment, and influences behaviour patterns (Berry, 1986: 59–74). For instance, among the hill people of Almora it is stated that songs sung by women pasturers are a way of communication with each other about the trials of life and household relations. Hill people of Himachal Pradesh have different perceptions of distance as related to townsfolk. If one asks for directions the usual response is 'just a little further', whether it is 10 yards or 10 km, it is further than the standing place of interaction. In the same way if one wishes to know where a specific place is on the hill top, it does not matter to the hill man whether it is 10 feet or 10 km the answer is 'it is up'; how far up, is not a priority for the informer.

Thus ecological influences form part of the package of what influences personality, as perception and its correlative cognition are a part of behaviour that is exhibited in problem-solving abilities (Berry, 1978). However, like the biogenetics theory mentioned earlier, of ontogenesis, phylogenesis and etiology, the human being uses adaptive mechanisms, either through outer stimuli (socialisers) or through his own innate tendencies. He tends to develop a sense of self which he tries to maintain in equilibrium with the demands of the outer world and his own innate needs.

We now are becoming a little more clear as to what development of a human being is likely not to be. It is not one characteristic or another, no matter which theory subscribes to it empirically. Each theory subscribes to a part of the explanation of the total parameters of what makes a personality. Neither is its description a monolithic theory. The understanding of development of a person is subscribed to by several theorists, who use hypotheses, several of them inadequately tested. It seems to be easier to describe one human being's personality at a time, rather than to club or categorise human beings as depicting clusters of characteristics/traits of personalities. There is no static description for any one person's personality, which is dynamic and can change from time to time and under differing conditions for the same person (Thorpe and Schmuller, 1958). Each theory has its own constructs and limits description to its own parameters; for example, the theory of cognition to adaptive behaviour, the theory of psychogenetics to the origins of intelligence, the theory of psychoanalysis to emotionality and its deviations, and so on. We also have a set of molecular theories that deal with smaller ranges of behaviour. Behaviour is both overt and covert in the explanation of as large a package as that of human attributes. We will examine the aspects of theories which attempt to explain those segments of behaviour that are more frequently used by theorists, than to hypothesise what personality could be, even though there is room for added or surplus value within each one of these theories. There is still room for conceptualisations, as yet unexamined or not explainable by the methodology or principles of such molecular theorists. For instance, in examining psychoanalytic theory and its constructs of how human beings feel, cope with and exhibit emotionality, there are still possibilities for explaining how situational pressures change or affect such emotionality. There are questions like: does a child become deviant because he has the innate potential to be a deviant or is he driven to deviancy by the pressures of his family, peer group or what? Why is it then that one child in the family can become a deviant and another not, although they live in the same environment? Such issues are still unanswered in the larger context of human development.

References

Anandalakshmy, S., 2002, 'The Physical and Social Environment of the Indian Child', in A. Mukhopadhyay (ed.), *Seen But Not Heard*. New Delhi: Voluntary Health Association of India.

Anastasia, A., 1965, *Individual Differences*. Hoboken, NJ: John Wiley.

Angell, J.R., 1904, *Psychology: An Introductory Study of the Structure and Function of Human Consciousness*. New York: Holt Publications.

Argyris, C., 1970, *Intervention Theory and Method: A Behavioral Science View*. Reading, MA: Addisson-Wesley.

Baldwin, J.M, 1897, *Social and Ethical Interpretations in Mental Development*. New York: McMillan Press.

Baldwin, A.L., 1980, *Theories of Child Development*. New York: John Wiley.

Baleson, W, 1909, *Mendel's Principles of Heredity*. Cambridge University Press.

Bandura, A., 1969, *Principles of Behaviour Modification*. New York: Holt, Rinhart and Winston Press.

Barry, H., I.L. Child and M. Bacon, 1959, 'Relations of Child Training to Subsistence Economy', *American Anthropologist*, 61: 51–63.

Bernard T., 1999, *Hindu Philosophy*. New Delhi: Motilal Banarasidass.

Berry, J.W., 1969, 'On Cross-Cultural Comparability', *International Journal of Psychology*, 4: 119–28.

———, 1974, 'Ecological and Cultural Factors in Spatial Perceptual Development', in J.W. Berry and P.R. Dasen (eds), *Culture and Cognition: Readings in Cross-cultural Psychology*. London: Methuen.

———, 1976a, 'Ecological and Cultural Factors in Spatial Perceptual Development', in J. Wolfenson (ed.), *Personality and Learning 2*. London: Hodder and Stoughton.

———, 1976b, *Human Ecology and Cognitive Style: Comparative Studies in Cultural and Psychological Adaptation*. New York: John Wiley.

———, 1978, *Human Ecology and Cognitive Style: Comparative Studies in Cultural and Psychological Adaptation*. New York: Sage/Halsted.

———, 1980, 'Social and Cultural Change', in H.C. Triandis and R. Brislin (eds), *Handbook of Cross Cultural Psychology, Vol. 5*. Boston: Allyn & Bacon.

———, 1986, 'The Comparative Study of Cognitive Ability', in S.H. Irvine, S. Newstead and P. Dann (eds), *Intelligence and Cognition: Contemporary Frames of Reference*. Dordrecht: Nijhoffe.

Berry, J.W., P.R. Dasen and H.K. Witkin, 1983, 'Developmental Theories in Cross Cultural Perspective', in L. Alder (ed.), *Cross Cultural Research at Issue*. New York: Academic Press.

Berry, J.W., J.A. Bennett and J.B. Denny, 2000, 'Ecology, Culture and Cognitive Processing', Paper presented at the 15th Congress of International Association for Cross-Cultural Psychology, Pulturk, Poland.

Berry, J.W., Y.H. Poortinga, M.H. Segall and P.R. Dasen, 2002, *Cross-cultural Psychology: Research and Applications*. New York: Cambridge University Press.

Bharati, A., 1985, 'The Self in Hindu Thought and Action', in A.J. Marsella, G. Devos and F.L.K. Hsu (eds), *Culture and Self: Asian and Western Perspectives*. London: Tavistock Publications.

Bowerman, M., 1981, 'Language Development', in H.C. Triandis and A. Heron (eds), *Handbook of Cross-cultural Psychology, Vol. 4: Developmental Psychology*. Boston: Allyn & Bacon.

Bronfenbrenner, U., 1979, *The Ecology of Human Development*. Cambridge, MA: Harvard University Press.

Bouchard, T., D.T. Lykken, M. McGue, N.L. Segal and A. Tellegan, 1990, 'Sources of Human Physiological Differences: The Minnesota Study of Twins Reared Apart', *Science*, 250: 223–28.

Cairns, R.B., Gariepy, J.-L. and Hood, K.E., 1990, 'Development, Microevolution and Social Behaviour', *Psychological Review*, 97: 49–65.

Capra, F., 1983, *The Tao of Physics*. Boulder, CO: Shambala.

Carrol, Lewis, 1865 (originally published), *Alice in Wonderland* (Web edition by eBook@Adelaide, 2004).

Cassirer, E., 1953, *Philosophy of Symbolic Forms, Vol. 1*. New Haven, CT: Yale University Press.

Chaudhary, N. and S. Sriram, 2001, 'Dialogues of the Self', *Culture and Psychology*, 7(3): 379–93.

Chomsky, N., 1986, *Knowledge of Language: Its Nature, Origin and Use*. New York: Praeger Publishers.

Cole, M., 2005, 'Culture and Cognitive Development: From Cross Cultural Research to Creating Systems of Cultural Mediation', *Culture and Psychology*, 1: 25–54.

Cooper, J.M. and D.S. Hutchinson (eds), 1997, *Plato's Complete Works*. Illinois: Hackett Publishing Company.

Dalal, A.K. and G. Misra, 2002, 'Social Psychology in India: Evolution and Emerging Trends', in A.K. Dalal and G. Misra (eds), *New Directions in Indian Psychology, Vol. 1*. New Delhi: Sage.

Darwin, C., 1859, *On the Origin of Species by Means of Natural Selection*. London: J. Murray Publications.

Dash, U.N. and B.C. Kar, 1993, *Nature of Knowledge in Developmental Psychology*, in T.S. Saraswathi and B. Kaur (eds), *Human Development in Family Studies in India*. New Delhi: Sage.

Dewey, J., 1891, *Psychology*, 3rd edn. New York: Harper Press.

Dube, S.C., 1976, 'Role of the Social Science', in S.C. Dube, *Social Sciences and Social Realities*. Shimla: Indian Institute of Advanced Study.

Dwivedi, B., 1971, 'Samkhya Framework of Mind, Senses and Intellect and its Relationships to Language and Thought', *Prajna*, 16: 171–85.

Encyclopaedia of World Religions, 1975, 'Hinduism'. London: Octopus Books Ltd.

Epstein, S., 1980, 'The Self Concept: A Review and the Proposal of an Integrated Theory of Personality', in E. Staub (ed.), *Personality: Basic Aspects and Current Research*. Englewood Cliffs, NJ: Prentice-Hall.

Erikson, E.H., 1950, *Childhood and Society*. New York: Norton Press.

———, 1963, *Childhood and Society*, 2nd edn, New York: W.W. Norton.

———, 1995, 'Identity and the Life Cycle' (Monograph), *Psychological Issues*, 1: 18–164.

Eysenck, H.J., 1952, 'The Organisation of Personality', in D. Krech & Klein S. George (eds), *Theoretical Models and Personality Theory*. Durham, North Carolina: Duke University Press.

———, 1985, 'The Theory of Intelligence and the Psycho-philosophy of Cognition', in R.J. Sternberg (ed.), *Advances in the Psychology of Human Intelligence, 3*. Hillsdale, NJ: Lawrence Erlbaum.

Fawley, D., 1999, *Yoga and Ayurveda, Self-healing and Self Realisation*. Wisconsin: Louis Press.

Finlay, B.L. and R.D. Darlington, 1995, 'Linked Regularities in the Development and Evolution of Mammalians Brains', *Science*, 268 (5217): 1578–84.

Freud, S., 1920, 'Beyond the Pleasure Principle', in J. Strachey (ed. and trans.), *The Standard Edition of the Complete Psychological Works of S. Freud, Vol. 8*, London: Hogarth Press.

Gergen, K.J. and W.A. Collins, 1971, *The Concept of Self*. New York: Holt, Rinehart & Winston.

Goodnow, J.J., 1976, 'Cultural Variations in Cognitive Skills', in J. Wolfson (ed.), *Personality and Learning 2*. London: Hodder and Stoughton.

Goodnow, J.J., 1990, *Development According to Parents: The Nature, Sources and Consequences of Parents' Ideas*. Hillsdale, NJ: Erlbaum.

Gopalan, C., N. Sharma and H.P.S. Sachdev, 1998, 'Relationship of Current Nutritional Status and Cognitive Functioning in 3–10 Year Olds Living in Slums' (Unpublished report). New Delhi: Nutrition Foundation of India.

Gottlieb, G., 1991, 'Experimental Canalisation of Behaviour and Development: Theory', *Developmental Psychology*, 27: 4–13.

———, 1992, *Individual Development and Evolution: The Genesis of Novel Behaviour*. New York: OUP.

———, 1998, 'Normally Occurring Environmental and Behavioural Gene Activity: From Central Dogma to Probabilistic Epigenesis', *Psychological Review*, 105: 792–802.

———, G., 1999, *Probabilistic Epigenesis and Evolution*. Worcester, MA: Clark University Press.

Gould, S.J., 1977, *Ontogeny and Phylogeny*. Cambridge, MA: Harvard University Press.

Gunther, H.V., 1971, *Buddhist Philosophy in Theory and Practice*. Boulder, CO: Shambhala.

Gupta, A., 2006, *Early Childhood Education, Postcolonial Theory, and Teaching Practices in India: Balancing Vygotsky and the Veda*. New York: Palgrave Macmillan.

Hall, C.S., G. Lindzey and J.B. Campbell, 1998, *Theories of Personality*, 4th edn. New York: John Wiley.

Harkness, S. and C.M. Super, 1996, *Parents' Cultural Belief Systems*. New York: Guilford Publications.

Hasan, H., 2005, *Mendel, the Law of Genetics*. New York: Rose Publishing Group.

Horney, K., 1937, *The Collected Works of K. Horney*. New York: Norton Publications.

Hull, C.L., 1943, *Principles of Behaviour: An Introduction to Behaviour Theory*. New York: Appleton Century Crofts Inc.

Jung, C.G., 1928, *Contributions to Analytical Psychology*. New York: Harcourt Brace and Co.

Kagitcibasi, C., 1997, 'Individualism and Collectivism', in J.W. Berry, M.H. Segall and C. Kagitcibasi (eds), *Handbook of Cross Cultural Psychology, Vol. 3: Social Psychology*, 2nd edn. Boston: Allyn & Bacon.

Kakkar, S.D., 1976, 'Linguistic Background and Intelligence', *Asian Journal of Psychology and Education*, 1(1): 20–25.

Kamlesh, 1981, 'A Study of the Effect of Personality on Value Patterns', *Indian Psychological Review*, 20: 13–17.

Kane, V., 1941, 'History of Dharmshastras', *Sasmskaras*, Vol. 2, Part 1, Chapter 6. Poona: Bhandarkar Oriental Research Institute.

Kant, I., (trans. by S. Wernder), 2002, *Critique of Practical Reason*. Indianapolis: Hacket Publishing Company.

Kardiner, A., 1939, *The Individual and His Society*. New York: Columbia University Press.

Katiyar, G.P., D. Sehgal, B.B. Khare, A.M. Tripathi, D.K. Agarwal and K.N. Agarwal, 1985, 'Physical Growth Characteristics of Upper Socio-economic Adolescent Boys of Varanasi', *Indian Paediatrics*, 12(12): 915–22.

Kedia, B. Landh and R.S. Bhagat, 1988, 'Cultural Constraints on Transfer of Technology Across Nations: Implications for Research in International and Comparative Management', *Academy of Management Review*, 13(4): 559–73.

Kenny, A.J.P., H.C. Longuet, J.R.L. Higgins and C.H. Waddington, 1972–73, *The Nature of Mind and the Development of Mind*. Edinburgh: Edinburgh University Press.

Khare, U., 1976, 'A Report on Exploration Study of Advanced Progressive Matrices: Growth of Reasoning Capacity and Some Correlates', *Indian Journal of Applied Psychology*, 13(1): 33–37.

Kitayama, S. and H.R. Markus, 1994, 'Culture and Self: How Cultures Influence the Way We View Ourselves', in D. Matsumoto (ed.), *People: Psychology from a Cultural Perspective*. Pacific Grove, CA: Brooks/Cole.

Klien, G.S. and D. Krech, 1952, 'The Problems of Personality and its Theory', in David Krech and George S. Klein (eds), *Theoretical Models and Personality Theory*. Durham, NC: Duke University Press.

Kohler, W., 1929, *Gestalt Psychology*. New York: Liveright Press.

Kumar, K., 1993, 'Study of Childhood and Family', in T.S. Saraswathi and B. Kaur (eds), *Human Development in Family Studies in India*. New Delhi: Sage.

———, 1999, 'Children and Adults: Reading and Autobiography', in T.S. Saraswathi (ed.), *Culture, Socialisation, Human Development: Theory, Research and Applications in India*. New Delhi: Sage.

Kumar, S., 1998, 'Identity, Ethnicity, and Political Development: Some Reflections', *International Studies*, 35(3): 365–71.

Langer, J., S. Rivera, M. Schlesinger and A. Wakeley, 2003, 'Early Cognitive Development: Ontogeny and Phylogeny', in J. Valsiner and K.J. Connolly (eds), *Handbook of Developmental Psychology*. London: Sage.

Lerner, R.M., 2002, *Concepts and Theories of Human Development*, 3rd edn. London: Psychology Press.

Lewin, K., 1936, *Principles of Topological Psychology*. New York: McGraw-Hill.

———, 1951, *Field Theory in Social Science*. New York: Harper & Row.

Mahadevan, T.M.P., 1980, *The Hymns of Samskara*. Delhi: Motilal Banarasidass.

Marriot, M., 1990, *India through Hindu Categories*. New Delhi: Sage.

Mascolo, M.F. and S. Bhatia, 2002, 'Culture, Self and Social Relations', *Psychology and Developing Studies*, 14(1): 55–59.

Maslow, A.H., 1943, 'Dynamics of Personality Organisation I & II', *Psychological Review*, 50: 514–39, 541–58.

———, 1948, 'Some Theoretical Consequence of Basic Need Gratification', *Journal of Personality*, 16: 402–16.

Miller, D.B., G. Higginbottham and C.E. Blaich, 1990, 'Alarm Call Responsivity of Mallard Ducklings: Multiple Pathways in Behavioural Development', *Animal Behavior*, 39: 1207–12.

Miller, P., 1963, *The New England Mind: Seventeenth Century*. Cambridge, MA: Harvard University Press.

Misra, G., 2003, 'Implications of Culture for Psychological Knowledge', in J.W. Berry, R.C. Mishra and R.C. Tripathi (eds), *Psychology in Human and Social Development*. New Delhi: Sage.

Misra, G. and K.J. Gergen, 1993, 'On the Place of Culture in Psychological Science', *International Journal of Psychology*, 23: 225–53.

Misra, G. and K.N. Tripathi, 1993, *Perspectives on Human Development*. New Delhi: Sage.

Misra, G. and R. Agrawal, 2002, 'A Factor Analytic Study of Achievement Goals and Means: An Indian View', in A.K. Dalal and G. Misra (eds), *New Directions in Indian Psychology, Vol. 1*. New Delhi: Sage.

Mohanty, A.K., 1991, 'Socio-psychological Aspects of Languages in Contact in Multilingual Societies', in G. Misra (ed.), *Applied Social Psychology in India*. New Delhi: Sage.

Moore, K.L., 1993, *Before We were Born*, 4th edn. Philadelphia: Saunders.

Mukerjee, D.P., 1958, *Diversities*. New Delhi: People's Publishing House.

Mukerjee R., 1965, *Historical Development and Present Problems in Social Sciences and Social Relations*. Shimla: Indian Institute of Advanced Study.

———, 1976, *Social Action: Historical Development and Present Problems in Social Sciences and Social Relations*. Shimla: Indian Institute of Advanced Study.

Munroe, L. and R.H. Munroe, 1975, *Cross Cultural Human Development*. California: Wadsworth Publishing Company.

Muralidharan, R., 1983, 'Developmental Norms of Indian Children Two and a Half to Five Years: Part III', *Personal Social Development*. New Delhi: National Council for Education Research and Training.

Murray, H.A, 1938, *Explorations in Personality*. New York: OUP.

Ochs, E., 1986, 'Introduction', in B.B. Schieffin and E. Ochs (eds), *Language Socialisation Across Cultures*. Cambridge: Cambridge University Press.

Pandey, G.C., 1972, *The Meaning and Process of Culture*. Agra: S.L. Agarwala and Co.

Pandey, J., 1998, 'Environment in the Indian Context: Social–Psychological Issues and Research', *Indian Psychological Abstracts and Reviews*, 5(2): 205–34.

Paranjpe, A.C., 2002, 'Indigenous Psychology in the Post-colonial Context', *Psychology and Developing Societies*, 14(1): 27–43.

Parasuraman, R. and P.M. Greenwood, 1998, 'Attention and Brain Function in Aging and Alzheimer's Disease', in I. Singh and R. Parasuraman (eds), *Human Cognition: A Multidisciplinary Approach*. New Delhi: Sage.

Pathak, M, 1977, 'Influence of Supplied Cues in Human Figure Drawings of Preschool Children', *Journal of Psychological Researches*, 21(1): 45–51.

Piaget, J., 1954, *The Construction of Reality in the Child*. New York: Basic Books.

———, 1964, *The Construction of Reality in the Child*. New York: Basic Books.

———, 1965 (1932), *The Moral Judgement of the Child* (trans. M. Gabin). London: Routledge and Kegan Paul.

———, 1973, *The Child and Reality*. New York: Viking.

Piaget, J. and B. Inhelder, 1969, *The Psychology of the Child*. New York: Basic Books.

Prout, A. and A. Prout, 1997, *New Paradigm for the Sociology of Childhood: Constructing and Reconstructing Childhood*. London: The Falmer Press.

Raina, A.K., 2000, 'Metaphysical Bases of Science', in A.K. Raina, B.N. Patnaik and M. Chadha (eds), *Science and Tradition*. Shimla: Indian Institute of Advanced Study.

Rajan, N., 1998, 'Multiculturalism, Group Rights and Identity Politics', *Economic and Political Weekly*, 83 (July): 4–10.

Ramamurthy, A., 2006, *Vedanta—Contemporary Researches in Hindu Philosophy and Religion*. Delhi: D.K. Print World Pvt. Ltd.

Ramanujan, A.K., 1990, 'Is there an Indian Way of Thinking? An Informal Essay', in M. Marriot (ed.), *India through Hindu Categories*. New Delhi: Sage.

Reichenbach, B.R., 1990, *The Law of Karma: A Philosophical Enquiry*. Honolulu: University of Hawaii Press.

Roland, A., 1980, 'Psychoanalytic Perspectives on Personality Development in India', *International Review of Psychoanalysis*, 7: 73–87.

Sharma, D. and R.A. LeVine, 1988, 'Childcare in India: A Comparative Developmental View of Infant Social Environments', in D. Sharma and K.W. Fischer (eds), *Socioemotional Development Across Cultures: New Directions for Child Development*, No. 81. San Francisco: Jossey-Bass.

Sheldon, W.H., 1940, *Varieties of Human Physique*. New York: Harper Press.

Singh, A.K., 1979, 'Development of Religious Identity and Prejudice in Indian Children', in A. Dsouza (ed.), *Children in India*. New Delhi: Concept.

Singh, I., R. Parasuraman and G. Mathews, 1998, 'Diversity in Cognitive Theory', in I. Singh and R. Parasuraman (eds), *Human Cognition: A Multidisciplinary Perspective*. New Delhi: Sage.

Sinha, J.B.P., 1980, *The Nurturant Task Leader*. New Delhi: Concept Publishing Co.

Sinha, D. and H.S.R. Kao, 2000, 'The Journey to the East: An Introduction', in H.S.R. Kao and D. Sinha (eds), *Asian Perspectives on Psychology*. New Delhi: Sage.

Sinha, D. and R.C. Tripathi, 2002, 'Individualism in a Collectivist Culture: A Case of Coexistence of Opposites', in A.K. Dalal and G. Misra (eds), *New Directions in Indian Psychology*, Vol. 1. New Delhi, Sage.

Skinner, G.F., 1974, *About Behaviourism*. New York: Knopf Press.

Smetana, J.G., 2005, 'Adolescent–Parent Conflict: Resistance and Subversion as Development Process', in Larry Nucci (ed.), *Conflict, Contradiction and Contrarian Elements in Moral Development and Education*, Part-II. New Jersey: Lawrence Erlbaum.

Smith, J.A., R. Harré and L.K. Langenhove (eds), 1995, *Rethinking Psychology*. Thousand Oaks, CA: Sage.

Smith, Leslie, Peter Tomlinson and Julie Dockrell, 2000, *Piaget, Vygotsky & Beyond*. London: Routledge.

Stryker, S., 1991, 'Exploring the Relevance of Social Cognition for the Relationship of Self and Society: Linking the Cognitive Perspective and Identity Theory', in J.A. Howard and P.L. Callero (eds), *The Self-Society Dynamics: Cognition, Emotion and Action*. Cambridge: Cambridge University Press.

Sullivan, H.S., 1965, *The Collected Works of Harry Stack Sullivan*. New York: Norton Publications.

Super, C.M. and S. Harkness, 1933, 'The Cultural Construction of Child Development: A Framework for the Socialisation of Affect', *Ethos*, II: 221–31.

Swami Venkatesananda, 1999, *World Book of Religions*. New York: State University of New York Press.

Tichener, Wilhelm, 1984, *Mensch und Gott in der Entfremdung oder die Krise der Subjektivität*. Munich: Alber.

Thomas, R.M., 2001, *Recent Theories of Human Development*. Thousand Oaks, CA: Sage.

Thorpe, L.P. and A.M. Schmuller, 1958, *Personality: An Interdisciplinary Approach*. New York: D. Van Nostrand Co.

Valsiner, J., 1989, *Human Development and Culture: The Social Nature of Personality and its Study*. Lexington, MA: Lexington Books.

Van Gelder, T., 1995, 'Modelling, Connectionism and Otherwise', in L.D. Niklason and M.B. Bode (eds), *Current Trends in Connectionism: Proceedings of the Swedish Conference on Connectionism*. Hillsdale, NJ: Erlbaum.

Vygotsky, L.S., 1962, *Thought and Language*. New York: Liley and M.T.

———, 1978, 'The Development of Higher Mental Processes', in M. Cole, V. John-Steiner, S. Scribner and E. Souberman (eds), *Mind and Society*. Cambridge, MA: Harvard University Press.

———, 2006, *Mind in Society*. Cambridge, MA: Harvard University Press.

Warm, J.S., 1998, 'Foreword', in I. Singh and R. Parasuram (eds), *Human Cognition*. New Delhi: Sage.

Watson J.B., 1913, 'Psychology as a Behaviourist Views it', *Psychological Review*, 20(2): 159–77.

———, 1914, *Behaviour: An Introduction to Comparative Psychology*. New York: Henry Holt and Co.

Weiss, P., 1959, 'Cellular Dynamics', *Reviews of Modern Physics*, 31: 11–20.

Whiting, J. and I. Child, 1953, *Child Training and Personality*. Yale: Harvard University Press.

Witmer, H.L. and R. Kolinsky (eds), 1950, *Personality in the Making*. New York: Harpers and Bros.

Woldt, A. and S. Toman (eds), 2005, *Gestalt Therapy: History, Theory and Practice*. London: Sage.

Wood, A.W., 2004, *Philosophy*. New York: Blackwell Publishers.

Wundt, W., 1904, *Principles of Physiological Psychology* (trans. by T.E. Bradford). Toronto, ON: Yorker University.

Yardley, K., and T. Honess (eds), 1987, *Self and Identity: Psycho-social Perspectives*. New York: Wiley.

3

Origins of Knowledge on Human Development

Informal Everyday Observations of Human Development and Behaviour

THE HUMAN being is the highest form of mammal with known thinking powers of a higher order. Much debate on the concept of the origins of man as evolving from primates is still speculative, although physical and physiological similarities have been extensively explored by anthropologists, showing similar genetic strains (Palimer, 2005). Man is a biological being with a structured entity. He follows a certain order of development in terms of sequence and appearance of physiological, physical and mental characteristics. When we observe a particular individual closely, there are certain traits and modalities of behaviour that differentiate him from other individuals. Even when comparisons are made between twins, whether identical or fraternal, there is still a question as to how similar and how different they are in subtle ways of behaviour (Wilson, 1976: 1–10). The common features of development are phylogenetic, moulded by the requirements of their specific race/ethnological features of the same racial stock, which are innate, genetically embedded patterns. The special features of any one individual develop into ontogenetic traits, that is, features unique to the individual as a separate entity, different from others of the same biological stock, such as the difference between one individual and another belonging to the Dravidian race. Information on human development comes mainly from analyses and documentation of studies in the West, which are the initial empirical grounds for our understanding of these basic genetic concepts. These are biophysical, phylogenetic and ontogenetic traits. The latter are those that are developed intellectually and emotionally to make up a distinct entity or a person's personality (Krech and Klein, 1932: 1).

For instance, individuals are born with the potential to be compassionate, to share and to give. Whether they develop these traits or suppress them depends upon innate dispositions, motivation and environmental influences. Over the growth span, even into adulthood and further, some individuals deliberately reduce expression of such tendencies while others intentionally emphasise them. For instance, some children exhibit hyperkinetic energy and are usually uncontrollable in early childhood. Over a period of time, through medications and guidance techniques, these children learn to control their innate energy. Most human beings, however, learn to modulate their childhood egocentric tendencies, and hence to amplify their socio-centric ones (Markus and Kitayama, 1991: 224–53).

The basics of human development rest on the following assumptions: The human being is born with unique innate tendencies. These tendencies, which early western experts equated with 'instincts' common to all animals, can now be manipulated in genetic engineering (McKonkey, 2004). However, further study has indicated that human beings do moderate these basic animal instincts by their own reasoning and power to control events and happenings, and hence these tendencies have come to be conceptualised psychologically as traits/characteristics/attributes (Atkinson, 1964: 77). Initially these tendencies are unmoderated, like the first cry of the newborn. Such tendencies occur when the child is hungry or wet, as expressions of discomfort (Sherman, 1928: 385–94). Research indicates that such unique traits exist from the foetal stage itself (Arduini et al., 1995: 83–99). However, a casual observation shows that infants continue to have differential patterns. For instance, as in the case of sleep patterns, some infants may sleep peacefully, others fitfully and still others need to be rocked or walked to sleep. Each human, therefore, has a specific pattern of demands and their satisfaction is related to their unique individualised tendencies.

The individual reacts to, and acts upon, his environment. Initially, these movements are through involuntary tendencies called reflexes, like the plantar and the grasp reflexes of the newborn (McGraw, 1943). Gradually, in a sequenced manner, the infant reacts to things/events that stimulate him mentally. As he grows older, he reacts in a willing or voluntary manner, at an orderly pace of increasingly complex patterns (Langer, 1986). For instance, a child has nightmares and wakes up in the dark, crying and in fear. He soon learns to associate the darkness with nightmares and so transfers his fear to the darkness of the night. This occurs through associating or linking experiences, which form a pattern. For instance, the child accumulates experiences (similar or different), thus identifying/sorting them into groups, such as objects/events/persons, through increasing perceptual discrimination (Baldwin, 1980: 137–285). The child continues to modify experiences, which grow in complexity, organisation, categorisation, memory storage and retrieval (Dehaene et al., 1998: 509). The learning of differences and similarities is through adaptation, assimilation and accommodation of stimuli (internal or external) (Piaget, 1930: 114–32). For instance, the child grows to learn, through maturational processes, that all men do not bear the label of 'father'. He distinguishes a figure called his father from others with events associated with this figure. He comes in contact with various such men, who look very much like his father, but who do not possess the minute differences of size, shape, voice, gestures, and so on, associated with the one figure labelled father. He identifies as father the figure associated with him in more intimate ways than other male figures. These stimuli influence his covert (internal) and overt (outwardly observable) behaviour, and the figure is labelled, and has specific qualities of interaction with him. This detailed explanation of continual and consistent associative experiences connotes the beginnings of interlinking concepts. This accumulation of experiences is dependent upon the growth of age-related maturational abilities. For instance, a newborn cannot discriminate between outer symbols of expected pain or pleasure, but a preschool child is mature enough to do so. For example, when the latter goes shopping with his mother, he anticipates being bought a toy or a chocolate (Baillargeon et al., 1995: 79–116). However, physiological development sets limits. As an infant, the child cannot learn to fit a jigsaw puzzle. He must first know how to use his fingers in a coordinated manner, and then with increasing chronological age, he moves from simple to complex jigsaw puzzles successfully. This is when he achieves dexterity of manipulation, the skill that is concurrent with coordinated physical and mental factors. This process is well analysed by early western psychologists, such as Bayley (1955: 805–18) for the infancy period, and Havighurst (1946) and Gesell (1946) who described developmental norms from the early years of childhood. Concurrently, developmental theorists like Freud (1935) and Piaget (1926) provided idiographic data, to give further explanations on the intra dynamics and cognitive abilities of young children, respectively.

The process of coordination is both on the physical and mental–emotional planes. Physical coordination is gradual in the early years, when the child learns self-mobility, and coordinates motor and perceptual developmental processes simultaneously. An infant, for instance, cries frequently when frustrated, but by the time adolescence and adulthood are reached, the individual has learned mastery and control over his levels of emotional expression (Harris, 2000: 281–92). Reinforcement through parental modes of behaviour (parents being his major models) modifies his socio-emotional expressions towards socially approved norms of behaviour (Miller and Dollard, 1941). These are gradually individualised to belong uniquely to his personality alone. For instance, in a school situation, he may be enraged at his teacher's behaviour towards him, but having been socialised to behave in an approved manner, he may jokingly deflect his aggression by turning to his school mates and saying, 'What can one expect of her, she is such a cranky old woman', thus rationalising the event (Super and Harkness, 1986: 545–69).

In the Indian culture (and perhaps in many other societies), the behaviour of crying when faced with an unmanageable trauma is not expected of grown men. However, crying in females at such events is not only acceptable, but also anticipated. It is well known that in some rural areas when women relatives meet each other after a long interval, they relate their experiences in a sing-song, crying manner. The human being learns through a process of action and reaction, combinations and permutations, to modulate his abilities and his motivations. He learns this according to his perception of adaptations required by him in his environment, both human and material (Markus and Smith, 1981: 233–62). They may be correct or incorrect perceptions, but they are his interpretations of his perceptions as to how he should cope with his environment. In times of scarcity of facilities such as water, individuals learn to adapt by storing up or using minimal water for essentials. The Indian learns to adapt to situational constraints of scarcity of facilities, even if due to negligence of the civic authorities, unlike the West, where, when civic amenities become suddenly scarce, there is chaos and civil suits are filed, as a right to facilities for which taxes are paid. A growing conceptual frame for understanding the individual's psychology is to understand the linkages between him and his human ecology, where families in scarce geoecological areas, because of lack of choices, are pressurised to adapt to their environs (Buttel, 1986: 337–56). Through these experiences, the individual's mind is attuned to adapt to the conventional systems of the culture by adopting individual modalities, and in the case of the Indian it is the adaptation to cultural norms evolving out of socio-philosophic connotations of the morality of life (Gupta, 2006: 20–23).

Correspondingly, the human being seeks pleasure and avoids pain. Situations that are painful, like physical punishment, are avoided. Those that are pleasurable are sought after. Over a period of socialisation, the young child learns that he will be punished by his father, but not his grandfather, who is usually more indulgent and less of a disciplinarian than the former. As a young child, the individual is satisfied with physical love through cuddling and hugging by his major caretaker. However, as he grows older, his affiliative needs widen to playmates, friends and, ultimately in adulthood, to include others of all ages, especially adults. Over his lifespan, the individual is identifiable by his socio-cultural systems: the family, the caste, the *gotra*, the clan and the ethnic group. The difference between him and others in the group is his unique construction of social reality as it relates to him (Misra et al., 1999: 191–218). In Indian society, there is a close physical-emotional proximity between the biological mother and the child, unique to many eastern and African societies (Ainsworth, 1973: 1–94). As an adult, however, he seeks adulation, approval and approbation for his skills from his fellow men. A child's pain is appeased when he is comforted by his mother/a familiar adult. In the Indian situation, the core of nurturance is connected to the biological female parent, the mother. However, unlike the West, through the period of childhood into adolescence, there is multiple care-giving by other female relatives, including older female siblings. Thus, these surrogate mothers interact, with varying experiences imbibed by the child, unlike those emanating from only a single caretaker, such as a biological mother. Kurtz's innovative ethnography meticulously enmeshes psychoanalytic thought and modern psychological theories to explain the phenomenon of multiple mothering in the Hindu context (Kurtz, 1994), even when contributed to by others than just the family members. Thus, the socio-cultural system prompts behavioural reactions (Haggis and Schech, 2002). This interaction develops into an ideology that pervades the personality and acts as a monitor on each progressive behavioural system (Geertz, 1973). Besides, the society and culture also influence the thinking, feelings and emotions of the individual in a different way. For instance, the child's anxiety for approval in primary years is appeased when his peers cheer him in sports. This pleasurable emotion is sought as it adds to his repertoire of positive experiences that build up the positivity and reduces the negativity of his societal image (Shweder and Haidt, 2000: 397–414). The individual seeks occasions to evoke these experiences from his family, kin group and peers. Such patterns, if overly frequent, become attention-seeking behaviour, which if inordinate turns pathological in nature (Feldman et al., 1979). More often than not, the range of attention-seeking behaviour is muted in adulthood as the child is socialised to develop control over his emotions and to modify this self-seeking or egocentric behaviour, as he grows to understand social norms in his culture (Shweder, 1993: 417–31). If the child strives and persists in realising goals, the traits he exhibits are more apparent as orientations towards high achievement and avoiding failure in his attempts to succeed (McClelland et al., 1953). In adults, this achievement-motivating behaviour is culturally distinctive in many non-western societies, as being more social rather than individual-oriented in contrast to the western societies (Mehta, 1971–76: 577–615). Another point of view that subscribes to the ability of the individual to initiate and respond to stimuli is the psycho-organic construct of epigenesis. Von Baer defined this process as formulated in his theory that vertebrate species progress from homogeneous cellular organisation towards a differentiated progression (Von Baer, 1928).

Rational Thinking and Human Development

The social sciences regularise informal observations into specific areas of scientific or logically ordered thinking. These orderings are based on the tenets of scientific thinking to analyse and infer verifiable data. When we ask the question: 'What is rationality?', we move into the realms of epistemology, philosophy and the essence of cognition (Inhelder and Piaget, 1964). Rationality is that aspect of thought processes and/or the acting out of behaviour that is morally proper or right or accepted among human beings as being correct and true. This at once distinguishes human beings from animals. This is not to say that animals do not behave rationally. Research has indicated that our understanding of learning behaviour derives much of its themes from experimental observation of behaviour in animals using the concepts of learning theory (Griffin, 1982: 241–50). Animals may behave in a way that we may not understand at times, but that does not mean they are irrational. What it could mean is that animals do not have the type of communication with which human beings are familiar, except in rare cases of human beings and their pets. This implies that we use standards as to what is right or what is wrong; and these differences may differ from one country to another as well as from one culture to another. When we attempt to interpret thought processes or observe acted-out thought processes in behaviour, we are in a sense seeking a frame of reference that is normative. These standards are usually based on the logic of inductive and deductive reasoning, which in Indian philosophy is rooted in the Indian text of *Sruti*s (different strands of the *sutra*, which has been explored in the Indian conception of rationality, both theoretical and practical) (Mohanty, 1992). To explain the concept further, we use syllogistic reasoning, which although known to most, bears repetition as it is foundational to logical thinking. For instance, when we say, 'All girls who go to school dress in school uniform, so as to be identified as belonging to school A. If I go to school A,

I also dress in the same uniform. Why? Because I wish to be identified as belonging to school A.' Two concepts are implied here: (*a*) logical reasoning, and (*b*) the identity of the self and others. A further explanation is that there is an inbuilt system of conceptual constructs, namely, 'I am like others who are like me. Others do or become X. Therefore I can also do or become X.'

We will first attempt to explain logical reasoning. Logical reasoning uses three premises in a syllogistic format (Baker, 1981: 28): major premise, minor premise and deductive/inductive premise. Logical reasoning using this syllogism moves from deducing facts from the generic to the specific and is called deductive reasoning. When it moves from the specific to the generic, it is called inductive reasoning. An example of deductive reasoning is as follows: (*a*) all human beings are mortal, (*b*) I am a human being and, therefore, (*c*) I am mortal. An example of inductive reasoning is: (*a*) I am a female and somebody's daughter, (*b*) all my friends are females, therefore, (*c*) all my friends are daughters of somebody.

Often, we do not rationalise in this way. We also feel and act irrationally or illogically. Familiar examples include getting ready to go to school or college; time is short, and we delay in getting ready on time, misplace our belongings and irrationally accuse others in the family of mishandling them. There is no logic to this but, because we wish to absolve ourselves from the blame, we put the blame on others. These types of precepts guide our daily lives. This is called rationalisation (Freud, 1938). Why is this so? Perhaps because as human beings we tend to use strategies (defence mechanisms or dynamisms) which lay the cause or the blame on somebody else, something else or some other event but not on ourselves (ibid.). The concept of defence mechanisms will be dealt with in detail in Volume II. Suffice it to say here that these are mechanisms whereby the self, or what is called the ego, attempts to justify irrational, illogical thought and/or action in a socially acceptable form. When we analyse these thought processes or their outcomes, namely, the sequential activities (since we often do not have access to thought processes of others), we ascribe this analysis to reasoned thinking from observed behaviour.

What credibility does the term 'reasoned thinking' have and what are its uses? We have said earlier that human beings ordinarily use an ordered thinking process as the basis to arrive at facts. What is ordered thinking and how does the human being use his mind to arrive at the ordering of a sequence of interlinking events/happenings? Over the centuries, there has been growing knowledge about the human being's ability to increase his reasoning capacity by exercising his brain functions. Man uses a system of suppositions based on a logical order of how human beings think and behave and use their overt symbols to discover truth in the objective environment (Sarukkai, 2000: 35–36). For instance, we use many assumptions about the relationship of man to the supernatural by identifying signs and symbols. When a *mannat* (vow) is made to a revered idol representing an incarnation of the Supreme Being, symbolised in the idol as Kali Mata and if a child is cured of a disease, the cure is attributed to godly intervention. If the child is not cured, then the cause is attributed to *karma*. In either case, as with all religions, there is no scientific empirical data. On the other hand, irrespective of time and place, ice will melt when exposed to heat. Anti-disease injections will help prevent the occurrence of disease, as in immunisation. These are basic physical-cum-chemical, experimentally arrived at as empirical data. However, human beings do not exist only on the basis of the outer world. There is a belief in the soul or *atman* and a belief in the supernatural, which is an inward conviction distinguishing human behaviour from animal behaviour.

We have explained earlier the meaning of logic, but how does logical ordering, like logical numbering and equations, take place? What, therefore, is logical ordering? It begins from simplistic explanations: If a man is hungry, he will want to eat to satisfy his hunger. The goal is to find ways and means to satisfy his hunger. The goal of satisfying hunger (which is an internal feeling) creates a need to consume food. This is accomplished by seeking and ingesting food, thus giving physiological and perhaps psychological satisfaction, reducing hunger and, therefore, decreasing the want for food, till the need arises again. If this hunger occurs from time to time, as it does, and the sequence is repeated, then we know for a fact that 'hunger creates a need for food'. And further that since this is a need for survival, it is a primary or priority need (Maslow, 1946: 22–48).

It is important here to emphasise that there is a relationship between the human and his needs, and his movement or action to satisfy these needs. To describe these events as concepts, the chapter on learning theories in Volume II will detail the foundational characteristics of needs classified on the basis of primary needs, secondary needs and derivatives of these needs (Murray, 1938), to show that such simple actions and reactions build up a foundation for theoretical reasoning or reasoning which is either deductive or inductive, both logical reasoning. Also, the levels of these needs, their satisfaction or deprivation influence the development of the personality. For instance, *sanyasis* deprive themselves of earthly goods and go on starvation for long periods of time. This is an activity that deprives the self of satisfaction of primary needs (primitive needs) and, therefore, said to raise the status of the human being's morality or saintly stature. Such behaviour is considered to draw one closer to attainment of *moksha*, which is a coveted form of human endeavour in Hindu philosophy. But the average human being is composed of physical tissues, which need earthly means of sustenance and nutrition to replenish or sustain them. Hence importance is given in religious philosophy to the relation of a healthy body to a healthy mind, through the tenets of Ayurvedic or natural herbal medication propounded by the Ayurveda in the Vedic scriptures. A. Gupta states that

> Indian philosophy is primarily Hindu philosophy and draws upon the Hindu texts…. There are six recognized systems or schools in Hindu philosophy and they are Nyaya, Vaisheshika, Sankhya, Yoga, Purvamimamsa, and Uttaramimamsa. The base for all the schools is the same and together they provide an interpretation of what is the ultimate reality (Gupta, 2006: 20).

In his discussion on methodological issues of assessing objectivity and reality in science, Sundar Sarukkai (2000: 31–32) states that:

(i) The logic of objectivity in science is diffused between the reality and imaginary perceptions of the same event.

(ii) The idea of objectivity indicates different characteristics in relation to different components of a theory.

(*iii*) What is loosely defined as objectivity may just be a weakly structured notion.

(*iv*) Objectivity in its strongest sense is the exact opposite of subjectivity, which may be found in 'modelling' and 'mathematisation'. This inverts the focus of objectivity from perceptual to the imaginary realm of symbols and characteristics.

(*v*) Objectivity in a contextual frame refers to the solidarity of a theme.

(*vi*) The differing nature of concepts distort the concept of objectivity.

(*vii*) Further, objectivity differs by the nature of the perceptions of an object made from different perspectives. For example, gravitation is well known as a causal agent and as a consequence of a previously held idealised principle of motion and inertia. These examples point to the complexity of the spread of objectivity as a scientific notion when it itself is a diffused concept.

(*viii*) Most theories have subjective elements in their discussions. Therefore, the co-existence of objectivity and subjectivity in assessing truth is untenable.

This is very much akin to our understanding that human beings are not perfect. There is always a deviation from the optimum nature of truth and its objectivity. Thus, we see that physical scientists question the very nature of objectivity, in its truest form, as being open to subjectivity, in some form or the other, mainly because of the subjectivity of human perception. This is admissible, since all laws that are statements of truth exist till such time as new laws replace them. Therefore, in the area of social sciences, the issue of subjectivity is all the more fundamental, as data obtained from humans beings can distort the nature of truth. Perhaps, it is for this reason that empirical data is always qualified by 'the concept of statistical probability'.

The logical psychological inferences we make, however, are based on years of experiments on human needs and their satisfaction (Maslow, 1954). Experiments with concrete objects (outside the human being), however, are more predictable than experiments with humans. For instance, Newton went through several experiments to arrive at a conclusion that unsupported weight falls to a base strong enough to hold it up (Cartwright, 1983). Such experiments occurred with physical and chemical concrete objects. These are observable with organic and inorganic materials, which can be manipulated. For this reason, the physical sciences are known as the exact sciences, for no matter how many experiments are conducted using the same processes, when a ball is thrown up it must come down. When sulphur is mixed with nitric acid in certain proportions, nitrogen sulphate is unvaryingly produced. A human being does not react so consistently. He reacts in different ways when a ball is thrown up. This is because the human being is experimenting with his individual human reactions (reasoning processes), which are not as observable as the concrete material of chemicals and energy.

The functions of the brain are internal and not observable. The outcomes of these functions can only be inferred from human behaviour, as to their related thinking processes. However, in understanding human behaviour, we try to be as exact as possible. We assume, for instance, that if the ball is a red ball of fire appearing out of nowhere, the dramatic intensity in most cases should cause a human being to perceive it. But if there are several such balls of fire, we do not know which among several human beings will perceive which ball. We can only conjecture that in all probability, the one that has the greatest size, intensity of colour and dramatic appearance will be the one perceived by most people in the vicinity.

The point we are making here is that, while physical objects are more controllable because they can be manipulated and modified, the mind of man is not so 'mouldable'. His internal self needs, aspirations, the influence of the external world, his perceptual ability, the situation in which he exists, and the consequent interactions are all interacting influences on his thinking, feeling and doing, in a dynamic way (Das and Thapa, 2000: 151–207). What is more, behaviour is liable to change from one time to another, and from one place to another. For this reason we can only assume that if a child is in distress, he will express crying behaviour. If this is done repeatedly, and done by many such children, we can generalise that children in distress will cry. But there are always the occasional ones who may not. If an adult has lost a beloved one, we presume he should look sad. On the other hand, there will be those who may be philosophical about their loss, and try to console themselves and therefore exhibit unexpected behaviour. We work on the basis of reactions that occur among a known group of similar human beings. If the same thing happens the same way, we can state, with some exactitude of logic, that human beings 'feel this way or that', that human beings will 'behave this way or that'. However, the given set of conditions must be known (contextual reference). There is more frequently than not the rider that some may not behave the way that is logically expected. This then becomes a matter of challenge in the pursuit of collecting further verifiable evidence called empirical data.

Ordered Basis of Human Behaviour

We have talked about the ordering of events in human behaviour. We need to expand it further. The ordered basis of human behaviour is attributed to the following:

(i) We observe that human beings, in certain sets of conditions which are repeated, tend to produce the same/similar reactions, such as students who imbibe the contents of teaching in a classroom. This is with a rider, as each student has a differential ability to learn. Again, taking away a prized toy from a child will tend, more often than not, to elicit a negative reaction from the child. These expectations are more likely to occur than not occur, and thus through the accumulation of such repeated expected behaviour, linkages are possible in understanding how human behaviour exhibits itself, when certain events occur, or do not occur. We set hypotheses/postulates on the basis of such assumptions. For instance, when a need is thwarted or not satisfied, we expect to see symptoms of frustrated behaviour. This set of observations is called an observable situation.

(ii) We can observe events in a sequential order, that could happen one after another, or together, to/in human beings. This sequence can either be observed (but it may not be convenient to wait for it to happen) or reported. When it is observed, it is called an experiment (a priori). When it is reported, it is called post facto or a fact known after the occurrence. For instance, experiences accumulated through repeated trials show that if a child is frustrated (for example, when refused a coveted toy), he is likely to become aggressive, throw temper tantrums, and he will not be pacified unless he gets it back, or is given something just as desirable or even better. Even here, we have to condition our statements by saying 'in most cases/at most times'. However, rarely does a child meekly concur to give up a prized toy without a negative reaction. We then hypothesise from these events that, frustration (first event) leads to aggression (the second event) in most children, which is a theoretical concept about such behaviour (Rosenzweig, 1944: 248–56). This is called a cause and effect situation.

(iii) There are other types of behaviour where more than one event can cause another event. For instance, there may arise a situation where a child wants a prized toy and at the same time knows from previous events that the adult will always give him what he wants. So when the toy is withheld his aggression is a combination of his desire for the toy and his frustration (barrier to motivation) that he has been refused when he was not before. Therefore, the frustration is compounded because of these two previous known events and not just one negative reaction. The withholder is also a part of the antecedent events that effect the reaction. This then is a situation where the observation is compounded by intervening unexpected antecedents related to the consequent behaviour.

When more than one event is related to a follow-on effect, these two are called correlatives. This type of situation occurs, when conceptually related events, such as frustration in being rejected by peers, together with a low self-esteem frequently leads to introverted or withdrawn behaviour. These two antecedent events occur prior to the withdrawn behaviour and, so to speak, simultaneously impel the withdrawn behaviour. These are correlative events or several such antecedents occurring simultaneously before the observed consequential behaviour. Thus, scientific enquiry about the development and behaviour of human beings is disciplined observation and a follow-on logical deduction/induction from such repeated situations. Disciplined observation has four distinctive qualities:

(i) It has to be observed with one or more of the senses. It has to be seen or touched or heard or smelt, involving sight, hearing, skin contact, tongue application or inhaling. The sense(s) have to be reliable, in that they are not impaired, otherwise the event observed may be 'not true', not because of the event being ambiguous but because of the impaired sense(s) assessing the event.

(ii) The sensor does not impose his own bias, even before the observed event, in that the observation is objective and is not touched with the emotionality or bias in the observer. For instance, a colour that is pure white is observed as creamy white by an observer who is partial to or likes creamy white and therefore imposes his bias of assessing white as creamy white. The observation should assess the true quality or attribute of the event and should not be tainted by the presupposed interpretation of the observer (Peak, 1953: 243–99).

(iii) The observation has to be isolated from the tendency to observe other events at the same time. For instance, if a teacher is concentrating on observing that no student is cheating during an exam, if distracted this interferes with the observation of children's behaviour. Her observation is also said to be contaminated by other factors. For instance, in observing which colour cube a child picks up, the observer must not be distracted by the size or the way the child picks up the cube, for the intent is to observe only the colour selected.

(iv) Most importantly, the observer must be able to isolate the event preceding the one to be observed, so as to distinguish it as causative or correlative to the follow-on event. For instance, a driver brakes suddenly (the antecedent event) over a road hump and swerves into a pothole (the consequent event). This may be due to several simultaneous variables, such as: he forgot to press the brake earlier; he was thinking of the quarrel he had with his wife before leaving; his child sitting next to him was complaining she was late for school; he suddenly had had a crick in the neck and was reacting to the pain, and such influencing variables. We do not know what other variables preceded the fact that he was not observant of the road hump.

When we re-examine the event, all we can say is that he was careless and did not observe the bump. All these preceding factors occur correlatively as antecedents. That is why it is safe and realistic to say that these are correlated with the subsequent event, namely, 'the bash into the pothole'. To illustrate further, a child is shy of making friends because he has low self-esteem, while other related factors might be that he is not talkative, or comes from a less well-to-do family, or he cannot show off with as much money as do other children in his class, and so on. Again, we cannot say which is a more prominent variable as compared to others. All may occur to some degree or the other at the same time.

Thus, the above processes may be simplified as follows. The events/ideas/happenings must be:

(i) **Unambiguous:** For example, if the intention is to study behaviour showing independence, it must not be interpreted as behaviour showing aggression.

(ii) **Exclusive:** The event should not fall into more than one category. For example, if a child's jealousy is being studied, it must not overlap with a category of anger exhibited by the child.

(iii) **Exhaustive:** The event/act should be exhaustively defined. For example, if a child's friendship patterns are being studied, all types of friendship patterns related to the situation studied must be included.

(iv) **Distinguished as correlative/causative:** The relationship between one event and another must be distinguishable as either correlative or causative. For instance, a child is satisfied because he is rewarded (causative), as opposed to a child who is satisfied because not only is he rewarded, but a high achievement need has also been satisfied. Therefore, operationally defined, the study of the event/act must take into consideration the total definition of the correlated/causative event/act to the segment of behaviour being studied. In real-life situations, however, human behaviour is hardly ever related to any one single cause. It is precisely because we do not know the other covert variables influencing the observed behaviour. There are several reasons as to what causes human behaviour and what is related to the behaviour being observed. A child achieves or does well in the examination, not only because he is intelligent but also because he is hard-working and wishes to please his parents. These are three interacting causes. Being mental processes, there is no known way of assessing the thought processes, unless elicited. The assessment, however, is done by the observer and can be biased unlike assessing physical scientific information. It is true, though, that as science advances, information processing is becoming a more reliable tool for assessment of behaviour (Rammsayer, 1998: 55–78).

This detailed explanation is essential, as it is the basis of reasoning in a scientific way about relationships between/among events in the human situation: cause and effect (where one event causes another event) and correlation and effect (where two events occur together). Such rigour is essential, if facts are to be accumulated to explain human behaviour and to develop reliable and valid concepts.

In psychological terms the causative/correlative events are termed stimuli and the effects are termed responses (Hull, 1945). We see this pattern happening frequently, for instance, among peers in schools. There are school breaks, where there is a tendency for friends to automatically get together at break time. This pattern becomes automatic or habitual, and is caused initially by an occurrence of repeated stimuli and the relevant conditioned responses. It is important here to introduce the concept of cognition. It is the acuity of reasoning, ordering, logically deducing or inducing from premises based on man's capacity to recognise the relationship between cause and its logical effects, i.e., the object or event existing within 'reality parameters' (Raina et al., 2000: x). The degree of accuracy (reliability) of observation is based on the individual's perceptual acuity and the extent of repeated knowledge regarding the perception. This acuity implies cognising concepts that are preformulated, that can be operationalised and that can be eventually evolved into several abstract forms. Let us illustrate. People have different levels of cognition based upon how well developed their perception is, how knowledge-built that perception is, and how this perception can be quickly discriminated/compared/contrasted and assimilated by mental processes about the object. A person from a rural area who does not know how a computer operates will possibly and probably attribute it to causes that are not accurate. Similarly, an urban child may not be able to read the relationship between weather conditions and crops and agriculture. Thus, cognition is not only related to human competence but also to the repertoire of experience in perceptual acuity (Gooding, 1989).

Academicians quite early realised and explained that cognition arises out of accurate perception and is 'cognitive labelling'. Spelke states that perceptual representation of innate reasoning and knowledge is the predominant factor in perceptual cognition and recognition (Spelke et al., 1992: 605–32). Cognitive development in its evolutionary frame has a phylogenetic base (the attributes of thinking logically and accurately given in the genetic make-up). It forms the basis for the acquisition of language and symbolisation, beginning in infancy (Langer et al., 1998: 107–24). In a later chapter on research concerns (Berko-Gleason and Bernstein, 1993), we will detail the specific regular processes involved in assessing truth and validity in searching for conceptual and behavioural events/acts in various domains of sociology and psychology. The above procedures could give a fuller explanation of the process of deriving logical conclusions (Butterworth and Bryant, 1990).

The Onion-layer Factor in Human Development

Currently, there are several conceptual frames attempting to explain human development (Thomas, 2001: 3–22). There are some concepts, not as yet full-blown theories, which lean towards a perspective and a generalised, structured approach (Baldwin, 1980). This views the human being from a mini perspective to a major perspective, much like enlarging the range of a telescope. The mini perspective views the developing human being in relation to his socio-physiological development, monitored by his own maturational levels. For instance, if he has lessened ability to be of normal intelligence, his maturational monitor will be slower than that compared to a normal individual (whether this lowered ability is due to malformation or malfunctioning of his neurological cells).

It is apparent that we are now dealing with the conceptual theories of social cognitive perception, of intrapersonal and interpersonal perception (Mishra, 2000: 94–150). This may also be viewed by Lewin's field theory (Lewin, 1935) in relation to valences and forces that affect the human being's perception. Thus through this process, core habits, attitudes and values are more deeply embedded, while the peripheral are not. Those patterns, which the self considers as essential to his identity, cannot be easily changed, but those which are new and not embedded in his personality can. For instance, it is easier to change dress styles (peripheral) than it is to become a non-vegetarian. The nature–nurture theory which centralises on heredity and environmental factors described in the next chapter are also central to thematic concerns of development (Newman et al., 1937). Further, human development theoretically does not exist in a vacuum, but its laws and theories offer a window to understanding the contribution of culture to human development (Thomas, 1997). This also indirectly refers to the traits with which one is born and brings to the world such as the traits of a passive child vis-à-vis a cranky child, and the nurturing quality of the caretaker, which can modify either of these major traits in children through the process of socialisation. Trauma, as in J. Bowlby's description, can deplete a child's ability to be normal when deprived of a nurturant who is security-giving (Bowlby, 1969). On the other hand, it is well known that early attachment and care is perhaps a priority need with young children as demonstrated by Harlow's study. His study shows that when deprived of security and food, the need for the former is stronger (Harlow and Harlow, 1962: 136; Hunt, 1944). Bowlby in his analysis of attachment and loss discusses case studies of how children separated from their loved ones suffer trauma, sometimes of psychoanalytic dimensions of autism (Bowlby, 1969: 428).

Also prevalent are meta-theories related to individualistic profiles of the human being, which have been propelled by resurgence of academic interest in subjectivity, self-reported experiences, and their relationship to cultural thought and action (Bruner, 1991). The individual skills which arise from such a milieu supersede the forces of the environment and show how man hones his skills to meet the challenges of his changing environment, such as predicting the weather or earthquakes. These theoretical concepts are in the redefining stages, but it must be remembered that they are, in reality, analyses of specific components of thought and behaviour. Unlike the physical science, therefore, these analyses are relatively incomplete in their explanations.

Thus, it is not possible to describe human behaviour or thought in its totality at any given time. Given an antecedent event (the cause), there may be varied consequent events (the effect). A thunderclap may cause varied responses from different people exposed to it. This response is not isolated, and is an accumulation of other past responses from which this response springs. If past responses are traumatic or fearful, the same overtones may persist in individuals thus exposed. Much of behaviour theories deal with the phenomena of stimuli and responses between the individual and his environment (Skinner, 1974). However, there are other theoretical concepts dealing with group behaviour in the individual's social ecologies.

If one were to follow just one individual's behaviour at most times, they may tell us about the pattern of behaviour for that one individual. This method is called the idiographic method of studying behaviour. Studying one individual does not tell the whole story. It is by studying group behaviour over a period of time that we are able to generalise about how human beings develop and behave generally. For instance, as an embryo, the first layer of effect is in the mother's womb, followed by the infant–mother symbiotic bonding and then the nurturant figure(s). The latter is a combination of many nurturant figures of grandparents, siblings, aunts and uncles, with whom the child is in proximity (the micro-level). When he goes to school, the child's interaction with teachers and playmates occurs (meso-level), so the patterns of stimuli and responses grow in number in widening circles of contact. Further, they dynamically influence each other, causing change from one chronological age to another. Further on, in the lifespan, the individual perceives and interacts with other people in the environment of marketplaces, at festivals, at family gatherings, weddings, and so on (exo-level). Still later, he meets other people in the larger environment and interacts with them (macro-level).

The child moves from the familiar to the unfamiliar, from one layer of effect to the other. It stands to reason, therefore, that the innermost layers are more difficult to understand or change as compared to those of the outer layers. These are the interactive concentric circles of his human ecology. The interaction from the micro to the macro tends to be less intense, depending upon the quality and quantity of interaction (Bronfenbrenner, 1989: 185–246).

In sum, therefore, as a child, the individual is more likely to use the experiences that he has absorbed in interacting with the innermost layers (the mini perspective), using his own unique innate abilities. These are developed during the years of infancy, the preschool and then the primary school stages, which are foundational in learning years. Through a gradual process of osmosis during the lifespan, he absorbs experiences gained from interactive/relational processes of the widening world. In the abstract, he only hears reported events with which he has no contact, such as war, floods and famines, or who is the prime minister, or what is in the newspaper, unlike the social realities of real-life experiences such as day-to-day life patterns (James and Prout, 1997: 280). The child is more likely, for instance, to react to shortage of money in the house for obtaining textbooks, than he is to the shortage of petroleum in the market. This is an instance of where the child's world vision is limited to proximal variables rather than distal variables corresponding to Bronfenbrenner's model of ecological systems wherein he describes the macro-level concentric circle encompassing the individual's world. But as he grows to adulthood, the individual is more exposed to the effects of petrol shortage (Bronfenbrenner, 1989).

The individual's behaviour is, therefore, an outcome of the interaction of his own innate potentials and the stimuli of his environment (Berry, 2003). Those people or events, with which the individual has close everyday proximity such as his major nurturant, the mother, are of more significance than those who are distant like relatives living in another state, relatives from his *sasural* (family of in-laws) or other individuals in the diaspora. If, for instance, the child is a Bhil tribal of Rajasthan, he may belong to a tribal parameter circumscribed by ritualistic habits and practices embedded in animistic religious rites. He is related to his tribe and community living in a particular geoecological area of Banswara, to its folklore and limited facilities.

He may probably not know what a mobile telephone is, whereas a middle-class boy going to a private school in a city probably carries with him a mobile phone (Doshi, 1971: 284). It must be stated, however, that even the Bhils are affected by the surrounding parameter of influx of industry, of social interventions and the return of transient migrants who sporadically work on construction sites in urban conglomerates (Sekhar, 1993: 277–94). They are betwixt and between and are at their level learning to adapt and synthesise their experiences, which belong to two worlds. A boy reared in a city, on the other hand, would be more exposed to sophisticated technology than a rural or a tribal individual. Opportunities to be exposed to the outer concentric circles, to interact within them and to be able to satisfactorily cope with them through a learning process are differently available to children living in different ecologies (Goodnow, 1976: 97–111). The family is the origin of the individual's first set of values, inter-generationally known, which moulds his attitudes and behaviour (Leslie and Komran, 1989). He thus develops the ability to cope and mediate with the environment. This is the first layer of interaction. Then his religion, his caste, his socio-economic class and his identity as an Indian give him widened knowledge of himself and his status. Thus, we see that, in effect, there is relativity operating between the child's micro-, meso-, exo- and macro-systems of environmental influences (Bronfenbrenner, 1982: 648). A paradigm given below illustrates the relationships among the variables impinging on the individual embedded in the varying micro and the extraneous systems.

In Figure 3.1, the criterion of increasing experiences is the domain of human contact in the environment. The growing individual has a constancy of interaction with his immediate relations in close proximity. As he develops, he moves out of that environment more frequently with increasing contacts and therefore increasing experiences laterally among peers. With further increases in age-related maturity and human interdependence, his increasing mobility exposes him to human and other related experiences (media, cultural activities, and so on). As he further matures into independence and self-responsibility for his lifestyle, he moves into occupational/professional circles. The reader will note a similarity to the various concentric

FIGURE 3.1   Influence on Development of Contacts in the Human Ecology

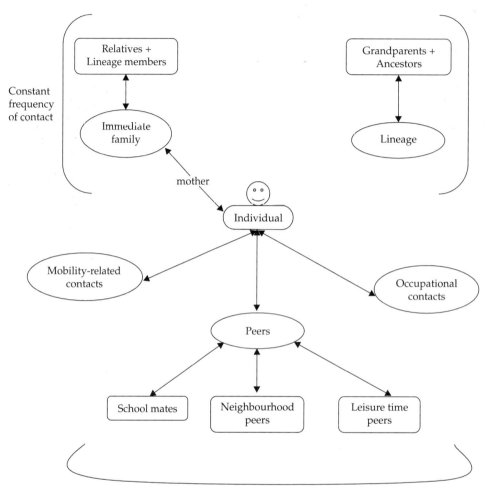

Increasing frequency of contact

ecological circles of Bronfenbrenner's model. While the criterion there is environmental ecology, the criterion here is specific to the rate, intensity and volume of other human contexts and therefore interpersonal experiences.

Thus, we see from the above paradigm that the basis of development works on two levels (the genetic mode and the environmental mode). The domains act and react consistently and continuously, with 'stops' and 'starts', during the tenure of the individual's lifespan, in a dynamic and multidimensional manner. Further, the process involves construction of the self-image. This process is enhanced by cultural forms of communication. The genetic mode is composed of the interaction of phylogenetic (the givens) and the ontogenetic (the building up of characteristics on the basis of the givens) characteristics. As a child, the individual is involved in his self to the exclusion of the needs of others. However, as he matures into primary school age and further, he learns to be sociocentric by conforming to societal norms and cultural beliefs. During the process of socialisation, he harmonises his own needs and moves in conformity with these norms and beliefs.

References

Ainsworth, M.D.S., 1973, 'The Development of Infant–Mother Attachments', in B. Caldvell and H. Ricciuti (eds), *Review of Child Development Research*, Vol. 3. Chicago: University of Chicago Press.

Arduini D., G. Rizzo and C. Romanini, 1995, 'Foetal Behavioural States and Behavioural Transitions in Normal and Compromised Foetuses', in J.P. Lecanuet, W.P. Fidfer, N.A. Krasnegor and W.P. Smotherman (eds), *Foetal Development, A Psychological Perspective*. Hillsdale, NJ: Erlbaum.

Atkinson, F.G., 1964, 'Conceptual Analysis of Motivation and Conflict', in F.G. Atkinson, *Introduction to Motivation*. New York: Van Nostrand.

Baillargeon, R., L. Kotovsky and A. Needham, 1995, 'The Acquisition of Physical Knowledge in Infancy', in D. Sperber, D. Premack and A.J. Premack (eds), *Casual Cognition: A Multidisciplinary Debate*. Oxford: Clarendon Press.

Baker, M.O., 1981, *Syllogisms—If–Then Statements*. Pacific Grove, CA: Midwest Publications.

Baldwin, A., 1980 'The Theory of Jean Piaget', in A. Baldwin, *Theories of Child Development*. New York: John Wiley.

Baldwin, A., 1980, *Theories of Child Development*, 2nd edn. New York: John Wiley.

Bayley, N., 1955, 'On The Growth of Intelligence', *American Psychologist*, 10: 805–18.

Berko-Gleason, J. and R.N. Bernstein, 1993, *Pyscholinguistic*. New York: Harcourt Brace.

Berry, J., 2003, 'Eco-cultural Perspective on Human Psychological Development', in T.S. Saraswathi (ed.), *Cross-cultural Perspectives in Human Development: Theory, Research and Applications*. New Delhi: Sage.

Block, F., 1987, *Revising State Theory: Essays in Politics and Postindustrialism*. Philadelphia: Temple University Press.

Bowlby, J., 1969, *Attachment and Loss*, Vol. 1. London: Hogarth Press.

Bronfenbrenner, U., 1982, 'Ecological Systems Theory', in C.B. Kopp and J.B. Kaslow (eds), *The Child Rearing*. Massachusetts: Addison-Wesley.

——, 1989, 'Ecological Systems Theory', *Annals of Child Development*, 6: 185–246.

Bruner, J.J., 1991, 'The Narrative Construction of Reality', *Critical Inquiry*, 18: 1–21.

Buttel, F.H., 1986, 'Sociology and the Environment: The Winding Road toward Human Ecology', *International Social Science Journal*, 109: 337–56.

Butterworth, G. and P. Bryant, 1990, *Causes of Development: Interdisciplinary Perspectives*. Hillsdale, NJ: Lawrence Erlbaum.

Cartwright, N., 1983, *How the Laws of Physics Lie*. Oxford: Clarendon Press.

Das, J.P. and K. Thapa, 2000, 'Intelligence and Cognitive Processes', in J. Pandey (ed.), *Psychology in India Revisited, Vol. I: Physiological Foundation and Human Development*. New Delhi: Sage.

Dehaene, S., G. Dehaene–Lambertz and L. Cohen, 1998, 'Abstract Representations of Numbers in the Animal and Human Brain', *Trends in Neuroscience*, 21(12): 355–361.

Doshi, S.L., 1971, *Bhils between Societal Self-awareness and Cultural Synthesis*. New Delhi: Sterling Publishers.

Feldman, S.A., E. Denhoff and J.I. Denhoff, 1979, 'The Attention Disorders and Related Syndromes: Outcome in Adolescence and Young Adult Life', in E. Denhoff and L. Stern (eds), *Minimal Brain Dysfunction: A Developmental Approach*. New York: Masson Publishers.

Freud, S., 1935, *A General Introduction to Psychoanalysis*. New York: Liveright Publishing Corporation.

——, 1938, *The Basic Writings of Sigmund Freud*. New York: Modern Library.

Geertz, C. 1973, 'Ideology as a Cultural System', in C. Geertz (ed.), *The Interpretation of Cultures*. New York: Basic Books.

Gesell, A., 1946, 'The Ontogenesis of Infant Behaviour', in L. Carmichael (ed.), *Manual of Child Psychology*. New York: John Wiley.

Gooding, D., 1989, 'Though in Action: Making Sense of Uncertainty in the Laboratory', in M. Shortland and A. Warwick (eds), *Teaching the History of Science*. Oxford: Basil Blackwell.

Goodnow, J.J., 1976, 'Cultural Variations in Cognitive Skills', in J. Wolfson (ed.), *Personality and Learning*. London: Hodder and Stoughton in association with Open University Press.

Griffin, D.R., 1982, 'Animal Communication as Evidence of Thinking', in T.W. Simon and R.J. Scholees (eds), *Language Mind and Brain*. London: Lawrence Erlbaum.

Gupta, A., 2006, *Early Childhood Education, Postcolonial Theory, and Teaching Practices in India: Balancing Vygotsky and the Veda*. New York: Palgrave Macmillan.

Haggis, J. and S. Schech, 2002, 'Introduction: Pathways to Culture and Development', in S. Schech (ed.), *Development: A Cultural Studies Reader*. Oxford: Blackwell.

Harlow, H.F. and M.K. Harlow, 1962, 'Social Deprivation in Monkeys', *Scientific American*, 207(5): 136–46.

Harris, P.L., 2000, 'Understanding Emotion', in M. Lewis and J.M. Haviland-Jones (eds), *Handbook of Emotions*, 2nd edn. New York: The Guilford Press.

Havighurst, R.J., 1946, 'Child Development in Relation to Community Social Structure', *Child Development*, 17: 85–99.

Hull, C.L., 1943, *Principles of Behaviour: An Introduction to Behaviour Theory*. New York: Appleton Century Crofts.

Hunt, J.M., 1944, *Personality and Behaviour Disorders*. New York: Ronald Press.

Inhelder, B. and J. Piaget, 1964, *Early Growth of Logic in the Child: Classification and Seriation*. New York: Harper and Row.

James, A. and A. Prout, 1997, *Constructing and Reconstructing: Contemporary Issues in the Sociological Study of Childhood*, 2nd edn. London: Falmer Press.

Krech, D. and G.S. Klein, 1932, 'Preface', in D. Krech and G.S. Klein (eds), *Theoretical Models and Personality Theory*. Durham, NC: Duke University Press.

Kurtz, S.N., 1994, *All the Mothers are One*. New York: Columbia University Press.

Langer, J., 1986, *The Origins of Logic: 1–2 years*. New York: Academic Press.

Langer, J., M. Schlesinger, G. Spinozzi and F. Natale, 1998, 'Developing Classification in Action: 1. Human Infants', *Human Evolution*, 13: 107–24.

Leslie, G.R. and S.K. Komran, 1989, *Family in Social Context*, 4th edn. London: OUP.

Lewin, K.A., 1935, *Dynamic Theory of Personality*. New York: McGraw-Hill.

Markus, H. and J. Smith, 1981, 'The Influence of Self Schmeta on the Perception of Others', in N. Cantor and J. Kihlstrom (eds), *Personality, Cognition and Interaction*. Hillsdale, NJ: Lawrence Erlbaum.

Markus, H. and S. Kitayama, 1991, 'Culture and the Self: Implications for Cognition, Emotion, and Motivation', *Psychological Review*, 98: 224–53.

Maslow, A.H., 1946, 'Theory of Human Motivation', in P.L. Harriman (ed.), *Twentieth Century Psychology*. New York: The Philosophy Library.

———, 1954, *Motivation and Personality*. New York: Harper and Bros.

McClelland, D.C., J.W. Atkinson, R.W. Clark and E.L. Lowell, 1953, *The Achievement Motive*. New York: Appleton Century Crofts.

McGraw, E., 1943, *The Neuro-muscular Maturation of The Human Infant*. New York: Columbia University Press.

McKonkey, E.H., 2004, *How the Genome Works*. New York: Jones and Bartlett.

Mehta, P., 1971–76, 'Political Process and Behaviour', in U. Pareek (ed.), *A Survey of Research in Psychology, Part II*. Bombay: Popular Prakashan.

Miller, N. and J. Dollard, 1941, *Social Learning and Imitation*. New York: Yale University Press.

Mishra, R.C., 2000, 'Perceptual Memory and Learning Processes', in J. Pandey (ed.), *Psychology in India Revisited, Volume 1: Psysiological Foundation and Human Cognition*. New Delhi: Sage.

Misra, G., A.K. Srivastava and S. Gupta, 1999, 'The Cultural Construction of Childhood in India: Some Observations', *Indian Psychological Abstracts and Reviews*, 6(2): 191–218.

Mohanty, J.N., 1992, *Rationality and Tradition in Indian Thought*. Oxford: Clarendon Press.

Murray, H.A., 1938, *Explorations in Personality*. New York: OUP.

Newman, H.F., F.N. Freeman and K.J. Jolzinger, 1937, *Twins, a Study of Heredity and Environment*. Chicago: Chicago University Press.

Palimer, D., 2005, *Seven Million Years: The Story of Human Evolution*. London: Weidenfeld and Nicolson.

Peak, H., 1953, 'Problems of Objective Observation,' in L. Festinger and D. Katz (eds), *Research Methods in the Behavioural Science*. New York: Holt, Rinehart and Winston.

Piaget, J., 1926, *Judgment and Reasoning in the Child*. New York: Harcourt Brace.

———, 1930, *The Child's Conception of Physical Causality*. New York: Harcourt Brace.

Raina, A.K., B.N. Patnaik and M. Chadha (eds), 2000, *Science and Tradition*. Shimla: Indian Institute of Advanced Study.

Rammsayer, Thomas, 1998, 'Mechanisms Underlying Temporal Information Processing', in I. Singh and R. Parasuraman (eds), *Human Cognition*. New Delhi: Sage.

Rosenzweig, S., 1944, 'Converging Approaches to Personality: Murray, Allport, Lewin', *Pyschological Review*, 51(4): 248–56.

Sarukkai, S., 2000, 'Symbols of Truth, Objectivity and Reality in Science', in A.K Raina, B.N. Patnaik and M. Chadha (eds), *Science and Tradition*. Shimla: Indian Institute of Advanced Study.

Sekhar, T.V., 1993, 'Male Emigration and Changes in the Family: Impact on Female Sex Roles', *Indian Journal of Social Work*, 57(2): 277–94.

Sherman, M., 1928, 'The Differentiation of Emotional Responses in Children', *Journal of Comparative Psychology*, 8: 385–94.

Shweder, R.A., 1993, 'The Cultural Psychology of Emotions', in M. Lewis, and J.M. Haviland (eds), *Handbook of Emotions*. New York: The Guilford Press.

Shweder, R.A. and J. Haidt, 2000, 'The Cultural Psychology of the Emotions: Ancient and New', in M. Lewis and J.M. Haviland-Jones (eds), *Handbook of Emotions*, 2nd edn. New York: The Guilford Press.

Skinner, B.F., 1974, *About Behaviourism*. New York: Knopf Press.

Spelke, E.S., K. Brienlinger, J. Macomber and K. Jacobson, 1992, 'Origins of Knowledge', *Psychological Review*, 99: 605–32.

Super, C. and S. Harkness, 1986, 'The Developmental Niche: A Conceptualisation on the Interface of Child and Culture', *International Journal of Behavioural Development*, 9: 545–69.

Thomas, M.R., 1997, *Human Development Theories: Windows on Culture*. New York: John Wiley.

Thomas, R.M., 2001, 'Theory Trends', in R.M. Thomas (ed.), *Recent Theories of Human Development*. Thousand Oaks, CA: Sage.

Von Baer, K.E., 1928, *Ueber entwickelungsgeschichte der Thiere*. Konisberg: Borntrager.

Wilson, R.J., 1976, 'Concordance in Physical Growth for Monozygotic and Dizygotic Twins', *Annals of Human Biology*, 3: 1–10.

4

Sources of Knowledge on Human Development

The Potpourri of Information

THIS CHAPTER is a collation of the available scattered information from various disciplines offering conceptualised explanations on human development. In the Indian context, social psychologists, for instance, expand concepts that are culture-sensitive and content-specific, while psychologists pursue cross-cultural and longitudinal empirical studies. Both directions are legitimate and essential. In fact, there need to be many more interdisciplinary foci. We see the beginnings of these directions, such as the Indian philosophical view of development, and concerted scientific attempts. Sociologists tend to dwell in their own framework, and cursorily focus on areas of family, kinship, caste and community relationships. These are usually in a descriptive way, of well-defined groups, in their institutional and relational structures. It has been only in recent years that Indian experts have attempted to bring about the 'Indianness' aura into their writings and to eschew the interpretations of domains according to westernised conceptualisation. Innovative-minded experts have moved into the realm of indigenising theoretical domains, and have included conceptual frames relating to Indian thought. However, the latter have been limited to logical reasoning, and have not been subjected to empirical data-gathering to build up theoretical frameworks. There are mini theories, such as bilingualism and multilingualism, attitudes and values and child rearing practices as examples of what was happening in the space of cross-cultural and Indian-specific settings. These were the bases for contrasting the Indian ethos with those of other cultures. After that plateau of inertia in sources, except anthropological data and some sociological descriptions of little communities, there were also explorations into the domains of education, of various kinds: agriculture, rural development, nuclear sciences, and so on. These widened the scope of information collection in the Indian context. It will probably take some time and concrete effort to find valid theories of development that are credible in the Indian context. It is essential to clarify that this chapter is not exhaustive in providing information in each discipline, as this is not the priority here. The priority is to give a general idea of information on disciplines gathered from the West and the emerging theorising by Indian scholars. However, there is a necessary interweaving of physiological and biogenetic concepts into the discussion, as these are universally accepted scientific concepts, irrespective of culture. It is when we proceed into the domain of sociology and psychology, and of other social sciences, that we are unable to provide a synthesis, a smooth process, because human development being a hybrid, with its tendency of borrowing, has a lopsided source base. It has a greater relationship with psychology and its derivatives, and somewhat less with sociology and much less with anthropology. Some theorists touch on structures, institutions and their relationships in sociology, and a very few on narrative idiographic descriptions of tribal lifestyles. While we stress a holistic perspective, it will still contain strands of these disciplines as, reasonably, (*a*) no discipline would like to lose its identity and (*b*) these conceptualisations will need to zoom in on the Indian psyche in the best possible fit.

Physiological Mechanisms Articulating Development

Basic to understanding human development is an understanding of the physiological system, which articulates the thinking and acting of the individual, as thinking is related to the functions of the physiological brain system (Thomas, 2001: 61). There are two types of genetic mechanisms operating in the physiological system, that orchestrate ideation and behaviour. These are the phylogenetic and ontogenetic traits inherent and potential at birth, respectively (McGraw, 1935).

The phylogenetic traits are shared by all humans alike and they refer to the generalised types of physical behaviour and the existence of organic systems, which enable the individual to walk, talk, move, operate his muscular system and exhibit behaviour generalised to the species. The species, in turn, evolve their own ontogenetic characteristics adapted to their given environments, shaping the individual (Elrod, 2002: 299–312). The ontogenetic traits are those which are evoked by the specific environment of the individual, when he has to develop coping skills (through practice and experience). These are essential skills for interacting with the environment in terms of productivity (Dewsbury, 1991: 198–205). These skills are usually occupational skills like carpentry, engineering, scientific experimentation, and so on. It is obvious that, therefore, these are learnt skills. Thus, ontogenetic skills are fundamental skills, which articulate the genetic (biophysical) abilities common to all humans. Given the basic materials or the ontogenetic abilities inherent from conception, a person's thinking or cognition arises mainly from the brain structure (Van Gelder, 1995: 217–35). For instance, the relationship of ontogeny to cognitive and symbolic processing of messages is channelled through the cortical synapses and neurons, and their operations (Kohler, 1925), but these are orchestrated by the environmental structures. The brain structure exists in the limbic system in the oldest part of the cerebral hemisphere and is called the rhinencephalon. This system includes differentiated but related parts: the hypothalamus, mamillary bodies and cingulate gyrus. The latter plays an important role in emotion, motivation, learning and memory (Mandal et al., 1995: 235–41).

Mendel's laws of hereditary transmission stated that each distinct characteristic was itself inherited and that they occurred in pairs (Mendel, 1866). Bateson called these 'unit characters', accepted in pre-formalistic embryology as a mosaic pattern of chromosomes in pairs (Bateson, 1913). Early Mendelism influenced psychology, especially in relation to individual differences. For instance, feeblemindedness was thought to be the result of a single defective gene that ran in families (Gould, 1996). Theoretically, genes are assumed to be the transmitters of hereditary characteristics. Johannsen differentiated between genotypes (characteristics inherited from the parents) and phenotypes (observed characteristics unique to the individual) (Johannsen, 1911: 129–59). It was Lundberg (1975) who studied the biological foundations of language, providing the developmental psychologists with psycho-biological evidence of the relationship where the nervous system organises itself according to the communication needs of the individual (Chugani, 1996: 187–95).

Greenough, Black and Wallace (Greenough et al., 1987: 539–59) expanded the theme to indicate that developmental opportunities present themselves to the growing individual as an 'experience-expectant'. This means that the organism, in the evolutionary sense, expects the events to occur within a specific context and time frame. When these occur with regularity, the organism's growth relies upon their continued occurrence making a circuit of enabling events. However, there is also the occurrence of 'experience-expedient' networks, which present a pattern through specific experiences throughout life. This process characterises normal learning and is supported by the recently discovered scientific basis of lifelong growth of neurons in the hippocampus (Gross, 2001: 67–72).

The knowledge of evolutionary history depends upon communication and/or cultural heritage. It is the cultural interface between man and his environment over the years (Keller, 2003: 102–27). It also requires specifying the development of ontogenetic skills as they arise from the genotype of the human being. In the examination of brain size, brain ontogeny, life history and cognition among primate species, including humans, were studied. Various sources indicated the growth of brain patterns varying across species. The findings revealed that primates are characterised by significant variation in patterns of brain growth and its development during the pre- and post-natal periods. Other life history variables were found to be correlated which indicate maternal metabolic adaptation with important implications during foetal growth of the child. These implications relate to maturational age, necessitating 'late maternal maturation' in the pre-natal period, enabling 'early maternal maturation' in the post-natal period. Such processes also indicate patterns of cognitive development due to maternal maturational indices. Thus, there is a strong relationship between foetal development and maternal genetic sources that influence later development in the child (Keller, 2003).

The genetic brain, which is the basis for individual behaviour, becomes the template on which subsequent relational experiences between the infant and its caretakers/environment are conducted. Infant 'hard wiring' is not immutable and from conception onwards into early adult life there is an interactive process among these relational experiences, which modify each other (Gunnar, 1998: 208–11). It is said, for instance, that the computer is a simulation of the thinking processes of the brain (Ambardar, 1983: 903–82). Simply put, the two orthogenetic processes, ontogenesis and phylogenesis, represent the inherent genetic traits, which are predispositions to developmental processes. Phylogenesis, which was previously called 'nature', and the process of ontogenesis, which was previously termed 'nurture', and its attendant nurturing are interdependent, lifelong processes (Fuller, 1960: 41–70).

How do we know that these progressions take place? With the rapid advances in science, it is increasingly evident that it is necessary to know what embryos are, and what their chromosomal make-up is like, as they are the foundational growth of the individual's development processes, so that we understand the basis of the progression of human development (Smotherman and Robinson, 1995: 15–32). The advances in genetic engineering where manipulation of chromosomes takes place, can alter the attributes of the physical embryo. In medically modifying the physical growing organism, not only are the physical attributes of the foetal development processes altered, but also the mental make-up, by genetic selectivity. Genetic markers lay special emphasis on DNA, indicating the direction of genetic selectivity (Zhao and Stodolsky, 2004). In a study on internal perceptions and certified gene therapy, clinical trials of gene therapy have caused concern in the general public about ethical standards. Covering many strata of society in several countries, including India, several aspects of genetic usage, including gene therapy and genetic engineering, were investigated in a survey. About three quarters supported personal use of gene therapy to save life, to increase its quality and 'to improve genes' as reported by Thai and Indian respondents (Macer et al., 1995: 791–803). For instance, genetic selectivity of sperm can give an embryo a specified physical make-up. But these experiments in genetic engineering and cloning, at this stage in scientific knowledge, are still under experimentation and are monitored by ethical principles (Berk, 2001: 88). In this century, with the discovery of the genome map (tracing the linkages between various chromosomes) the possibilities of genetic engineering (testing and mutation of cells) are accelerating (Miklos and Rubin, 1996: 521–29; Paabo, 2001: 1219–20). Stem-cell research is now an accepted area of study for the purpose of curative medicine (Panno, 2004: 178).

What, then, is this genetic formation, and what is its importance to the development process in the human? Scientific trends have increased the interest in the age-old controversy of nature versus nurture. Jensen's study on different groups of whites and African Americans gave a new twist to the concept that blacks have less of the generic genetic material for coping mechanisms in comparison to whites, in the testing of intelligence (Jensen, 1969: 1–123). Biologically, the inherited genetic make-up is a combination of genes from both parents. This implies the transference of the interactive genes and their inherent quality from one generation to another, which follow the epigenetic rules of biophysical development (Lumsden and Wilson, 1981). In earlier experiments of studies of behaviour in the West, emphasis was on the outcome of physical behaviour, the child's initial conceptual classifications, sensory/perceptual cognising, recognising, imprinting, mapping, grouping and categorising, which formed the basis of formal learning. This information accelerated research on behaviourism (Watson, 1913: 159–77).

Following on, the study of differential psychology made its impact in the understanding of individual differences. This was illustrated by studies on the behaviour of identical twins (Newman et al., 1937). The tendency was for identical twins to behave similarly and to use their intelligent functions similarly. Even though one twin may proceed maturationally at a faster pace than the other, there is a 'catch-up period' when the second twin nearly equalises his behaviour with the first (Gesell and Thompson, 1929: 1–124). Then came evidence of differentials in birth order, where the later-born offspring exhibited more creative functioning than the earlier born (Adler, 1928: 14–52; Sulloway, 1996). The later born is distinctly different from the earlier born, who being less privileged obtains his own niches by sheer persistent patterns of competition with the older sibling.

Information processing in the individual is obtained mainly through methods of tapping the movements of the brain through encephalographs. In these procedures the linkages in the processes as related to mental experiences are traced and any aberrations are noted to indicate malfunctioning. This body of knowledge does not give a consecutive, collative picture of the functioning of each domain with the other. For instance, some people may suffer from lapses of memory (amnesia) but could be intelligent in reasoning powers. For this reason, perhaps, standard intelligence tests tap separate domains in intellectual capacity (for example, non-verbal reasoning, creativity, problem solving, and so on). Information from tracing graphs through encephalographic methods is mainly obtained from studies on brain-damaged individuals. For instance, it was found that right hemisphere brain-damaged patients showed poor performance on non-verbal tests such as the Bender Gestalt test, which analyses general cognition (Sabhesan et al., 1991: 143–48). We can only infer that development as it originates from brain functions, indicates inheritance of traits as exhibited in twins, although ontogenetically they may not exhibit similar patterns of thinking and behaving.

The Processes of Neurosciences in Physical Development

The role of neurosciences in human development was high-profiled in 1967 by interest in Lindbergh's theses on the biological foundations of language. His theses provided psychobiological evidence of plasticity when the nervous system organises the self according to needs. This process extends into the second decade after birth implying that maturational changes have their own spurts, plateaus and deceleration during the lifespan. The question is how vulnerable the periods are, in between these differing periods. For instance, there are spurts of growth during the early childhood and adolescent periods. In between, during the primary school years the growth is relatively less. Dramatically, in old age there is a decelerated rate of growth with degenerative processes taking over (Demetriou et al., 1998).

The progressive developmental stages, such as revealed in the Piagetian schema of concept formation (Inhelder and Piaget, 1958), are evolved from the developmental opportunities, which are called 'experience-expectant', implying that the organism expects, in an evolutionary sense, certain events to occur within a context and a time frame on a probabilistic basis. A second source was the experimental works of Wallace (Greenough et al., 1987: 539–59). Here, the characteristics of normal learning are supported by the recently discovered life growth of neurons in the hippocampus, stimulated by experience (Gross, 2001: 67–73; Shors et al., 2001: 372–76). Experience, however, is development-dependent and implies reconstruction of original experiences, which are qualitative increments. For example, a two-year-old child distinguishes the major basic colours; later on he can differentiate among hues of a colour. There are factors that influence these experiences such as levels of health status, nutrition and activity level, which can lead to quantitative changes in brain tissue. Given the current uncertainty of well-grounded evidence, however, one can only hypothesise that there should be further evidence and therefore research to be able to offer explanations. The 'tissue' hypothesis explores whether it benefits neurological function to have a larger-sized brain, or whether the functional aspect of the brain, namely, its quality, is more significant. In relation to this, one area that has been studied extensively is language: functions of phonetics, syntax and semantics, represented primarily by the left hemisphere of the brain, especially in right-handedness (Dronkers et al., 2000: 65–71). Other language functions are less obvious in the left hemisphere. The upper surface of the left temporal lobe, however, is involved intimately in language processing. The tissue hypothesis predicts that the greater the symmetry in favour of the left hemisphere, the greater the likelihood that language representation remains the same, or perhaps leads to better functioning (Pieniadz et al., 1983: 371–91). The importance of neurosciences towards an understanding of the development processes is a recently growing phenomenon. These evolutionary circuits have a tendency to develop along a genetically planned way but require 'triggering' (environmental stimuli), so as to provoke events to occur (Mower et al., 1983: 178–80). Limitations cause short-changing of the process. For instance, the recently discovered tendency for lifelong growth of neurons in the hippocampus stimulated by experiences increases the chances of survival of neurons already created (Gross, 2001: 67–73). These concepts support the twin interaction of maturation and learning networks. There are certain factors that lead to the quantitative development in brain tissue according to measures for brain growth, such as overall thickness of cortex, number of synapses and dendritic spread.

Does this mean that more brain (brain size) is better in terms of intelligence, or should there be more tissue for adequate functioning (Lowitz and Scmidt, 2003: 52)? While research in this area is debatable, in one study it was found that tissue size correlated with spatial skills but not with verbal skills (Gur et al., 1999: 4065–72). But part of the problem is that measurement is gross, such as measurement of head size, which does not reveal the anatomical aspect.

In partial response to this issue, two domains studied with respect to brain functioning were hand preference and language skills. Magnetic stimulus and non-invasive cortical mapping techniques gave the first indication of the influence of large asymmetries in the development of hand skills (Rushworth and Walsh, 1999: 125–35). These experiments showed that the preferred hand shows more representation in the motor cortex (Peter, 2000: 191–222). It was also found that the corpus callosum links homologous regions in the two hemispheres and is responsible for most of the communication between them in relation to handedness, and to the brain in relation to cognitive/affective development (Driesen and Raz, 1995: 240–47). Thus, we see that there is little adequate research to indicate whether the quantitative or the qualitative aspect is more important in defining and refining behavioural traits (Elman et al., 1996).

The Development of Brain-related Behaviour

To understand how the physiological system of mental development and ideation takes place, we need to know the physiobiological characteristics, domains and their functions. The brain is composed of several trillion neurons and glia (from the Greek word meaning glue) (Kelso, 1995). The structures are detailed as follows.

The Limbic System and its Domains

The aforementioned structures lie in the limbic system, which lies in the oldest parts of the cerebral hemisphere called rhinencephalon (Adey, 1958: 621–44). The limbic system also includes the hypothalamus, the pons and the amygdala septal area, the hippocampus, mamillary bodies and cingulate gyrus. The limbic system designates the structure on the limbus or margin of the cortex (Bailey and von Bonin, 1951). The limbic lobe, as it is called, decides how the systems mentioned earlier work in collaboration with other brain systems. It provides the organism with a means of coping with the environment and with other members of the species. The basic parts of the system are concerned with primitive activities like food and sex, while other parts are related to sophisticated systems of feelings, emotions and higher cognitive functioning. The limbic system is the foundational system for survival of the species. For instance, the use of olfactory cues for protection from danger, like the smell of smoke related to fire occurs in the limbic system.

The olfactory connections connote the bases for emotional aspects of olfaction (Brodal, 1947: 179–222). The different parts in the limbic system have differential functions. The hippocampal formation is the source of information arriving from the emotional cortex. On the other hand, the amygdaloid nuclear complex has access to integrated sensory formation (Gloor, 1997). The hippocampal structure is also important for storage and recall of information. Feedback signals from the hippocampus to sensory association areas are important in consolidating memory (Buzsaki et al., 1990: 257–68). Memory is believed to reflect a cognitive map inherent in the hippocampal formation (Jarrard, 1993: 9–26). Verbal and contextual memory is hypothesised as developing from mechanisms already in place in this formation. It is also stated that there is a relationship between the septal nuclei (contentment) and the amygdala (anxiety) where the limbic system performs a balancing act (Davis, 1992). The orbital cortex, which is related to socially acceptable behaviour, is composed of neurons, which create either a sense of well-being or anxiety. This, in turn, is related through the nuclei to the brain stem, the hypothalamus and the anterior temporal lobe, where the latter also relates to the chemical balance of the endocrinological system (Kandel and Kupfermann, 1995: 595–612). From experiments with animals, it has been found that the limbic system plays an important role in motivation, emotion, learning and memory, which are the higher functions in the brain (Mandal, 2000: 60).

The limbic system with the hypothalamus has a major role, where the latter is in control of emotions (Adolphs et al., 1994: 669–72). The hippocampus is the area where affective and cognitive systems interact, wherein a cognitive mapping system is hypothesised. The cerebellum is the 'organiser' which sorts, interprets, organises and sends response messages, thus performing a balancing function.

The Cortex, Neurons and Messaging Functions

The cerebellum is connected to the spinal column, which is the nerve bundle of shafts carrying messages to and from the network of the smaller nerves (Herrick, 1891: 188–89). Neural systems develop almost immediately after conception, constructing the nervous system, which consists of neurons, supportive neural glia and neurotransmitters. A complex network of about 50 billion neurons and neurotransmitters make connections at any one of the 1,000 or so points for each neuron (Kol and Whishaw, 1990). Brain tissues are also composed of these trace pathways, although not much is known as to how these 'trace paths' occur. Messages are brought in by the peripheral system (outer sensors), which returns messages to the brain's stimuli nerves. The neurons of the nerves interpret the messages and send back the messages. The less complicated the neuron stimulus, the quicker the brain sends back the interpreted message, such as touching a hot surface and immediate removal of the body part in contact (Squire, 1987).

These neurons are sets of controls more like a computer panel. The cerebral cortex controls automatic movements. For instance, the brainstem channels emotional and cognitive messages, which are thus controlled by the cortex. The thalamus is the major reporting system for messages from the sensory transducers and appears to be important for the maturation of the post-natal cortex, as understood from laboratory experiments, extrapolated to humans (Rubenstein and Rakic, 1999: 521–23). The two halves of the brain have primary responsibilities, although they interact together through a bundle of fibres called corpus callosum, a neuron network which is found to be reinforced through learning by experiential responses (Hallonet et al., 1990: 19–31). Thus we see that the brain as the physical seat of ideation is not only complicated in terms of the various synapses and neurons performing different functions in the limbic system which is the master-board for the other parts of the brain, but is also dynamic in its complexity. Like a control panel, there are multifarious switches (outer sensations), which trigger interweaving and intertwining aspects originating from and to these different parts. For instance, emotional messages from the hippocampus are related to cognitive deductions, and also to the type of behaviour that is expressed or repressed.

The Process of Cell and Tissue Formation

Much of the development of the brain occurs during the embryonic and foetal periods (O'Rahilly and Muller, 1994). In understanding when development of the brain is related to its operational functions, studies indicate that much of the development processes/functions begin in the embryonic stage. Approximately, on the eighth day after conception, progressive development of cells causes a separation between the ectoderm (the beginnings of the nervous system) and the endoderm (the digestive system). The mesoderm (the beginnings of the skeletal, muscular and circulatory systems) appears a week later. Reflex action occurs in the foetus by the end of the first trimester. Exposures to a series of dangers, like rubella, have been studied during this growth spurt. A retardation of growth or spontaneous abortion due to the chemical interaction of the disease cells with the foetus is likely to occur during precarious foetal development. Poor diet, drugs like thalidomide, smoking and AIDS affect the normal growth of the foetal brain (Wilson, 1975). In the second trimester of pregnancy, reflex action is faster. Responses are firmly connected, while fissures are still forming on the cortex.

Rapid development during the second trimester requires extra protein and oxygen from the placenta, and the lack of these are often responsible for asphyxia as soon as the child is born, leading to dead cells in the brain, where regeneration is difficult and some form of mental retardation occurs. Hormone development and balance occur during this period of foetal development, leading to characteristically different ways of responding to stress out of the womb (Tronick and Giannino, 1987). Long emotional crises of the mother during the pregnancy stages lead to lowered levels of tolerance to anxiety-provoking stimuli in the infant, and continuing anxiety in later life (Bowlby, 1973).

Years of research have yielded some information on the relation of cognitive development to brain functions, which could be impaired due to head injuries (Gupta and Ghai, 1991: 55–61). Clinical recovery after head trauma has been found to be affected by neuropsychological deficits of processes such as ideation, fluency, verbal learning, and psychomotor and memory functions (Mukundan et al., 1987: 381–88). The most significant part is the cerebral cortex. This is a large mass of tissue of neurons and fibrons folded into many creases to fit into the skull.

Most neurons, through synapses and through chemical transmitters, send electric charges to the receptor neuron by signals not unlike radio transmitters (axons with multiple terminals). The short arms of neurons called dendrites form their connections with synapses and axons and convey impulses (Erulkar, 1994: 785–98). Studies have shown that electrode stimulation identifies areas of function, which are mainly used to guide brain surgery (Brazier, 1961).

Available Studies on Brain Functions

In understanding brain functions, a large part of our information is obtained from brain-damaged humans. Studies on brain-damaged humans offer support to the hypothesis that the left hemisphere mediates verbal functions while the right mediates non-verbal functions (Nagaraja and Rao, 1986: 71–76). For instance, the visual input is through the occipital lobe situated at the back of the brain. Experiments indicate light flashes in the visual field when electrically stimulated. A second area around this lobe provides the formation of visual pictures, which process incoming data, with a right cerebral dominance in right-brain damaged patients impairing visual functions (Dwivedi and Mukundan, 1993: 27–33).

The auditory area is in the fold of what is called the Sylvian sulcus on the temporal lobe, which produces high and low tones. Stimulation of the area processes words on the left side of the brain and sounds on the right side of the brain. Olfactory stimulation exists along the area called the fissure of Rolando, processing sensations of taste (Levinthal, 2003: 63). The conjunction of the parietal, occipital and temporal lobes processes visual, auditory and sensory patterns, either together or alone. Intentions or voluntary acts are stimulated in the forebrain, where commands from the motor cortex originate to produce specific muscular sensations which are selective.

As we have said before, in all these areas, responses sometimes occur separately, but more often simultaneously, in a complex fashion. Interactions among them occur through a bundle of corpus callosum nerve fibres. The two sides of the brain called the left and the right hemispheres are a whole system and operate in conjunction with each other. The resilience is such that when one side is damaged the other side compensates by taking on partial functions of the former, depending on how severe the damage is. We see this happening clearly in the area of vision. Thus, locations in the hemispheres are specific to each of the sensory functions: the perceptual, the auditory and the olfactory.

Psychologically Related Functions of the Brain Domains

Since development relating to behaviour is primarily the function of the brain, it is important to know which areas of the brain are related to learning and storage patterns. Much of this knowledge is available from medical research, especially in the area of diagnosis in brain damage. For instance, when the front portion of the left hemisphere is damaged, it tends to cause expressive aphasia. When the right side is damaged, it affects expressive speech related to hearing, vision and temperature. The regulatory systems operate to decode incoming messages. For instance, the electrical manipulation of the auditory system concentrates and magnifies sound waves, producing motion in the inner ear (Davis, 1939: 494–99). The input to each ear reaches both sides of the medial geniculate body, the thalamus and both sides of the cortex where processing of the sound waves is done. For operating the visual area, the cortex picks up the information through millions of rods and cones, which sort, consolidate and pass on information to the retina; the visual folds receive separate information. For instance, vision from the right field of the visionary region of both eyes goes to the left lateral hemisphere, and vice versa. The thalamus connects with the cortex and feeds back information through loops from the various areas of sight and sound. It is possible to operate any or all information at one and the same time. For instance, the cognitive and the affective areas are brought together by the hippocampus where memory is activated from a patterned learning experience. Laterality of the brain function is primarily related to neurological control of the language and muscle groups of one side of the brain. Mixed laterality is usually related to reading difficulties when proper connections are not made between the left lateral hemisphere, the thalamus and the hippocampus (Morgan and Hynd, 1998: 79–93).

How are these brain processing sets of information systems developed? In the embryonic stage, a hierarchical system of masses of specialised cells with their specific functions develop (Driesch, 1929). These cells are basic genetic cells, which divide and subdivide in the embryonic stage, retaining trace patterns of their genetic materials. When the egg is fertilised it begins with an embryonic cell enclosed in the genetic material called cytoplasm, an environment composed of various biochemical structural arrangements. While the genetic material is supplied by both parents, the cytoplasm is mainly maternal in origin. Through cleavages subdivisions occur, ending in a spherical collection of cells. When they are moved around and folded into masses, a process called gastrulation occurs, and one side of the sphere called the blastula moves inwards. Three layers of cells evolve: the outer is the ectoderm producing the skin. The middle layer called the mesoderm produces muscles and the third layer is the endoderm or the innermost layer of nerve and blood cells. On differentiation, they rapidly assume specialised forms and functions related to the specificity of the genetic material. Each individual has regional areas, which are called histogenetic, and the integration of the formative cells in each specific organ/limb changes in shape and size through a process called morphogenesis where each cell develops separately, but in integrative links with others (His, 1888: 287–98).

The Biophysiological Development of Cell and Tissue

The inner layer, the endoderm, develops rapidly, fissioning into the various organs. It is important to remember that the genes assume a predetermined arrangement with the phenotype, which changes to new levels of organisation and function. Differentials in genes produce variations in their structural arrangements, directing differential variability in the functions of the brain, like differential motor abilities.

While identical sets of genes from both parents compose a cell, each cell follows a different development process by the nature of chemical differences of the cytoplasm within each one. The process involves the transformation of simple organic compounds into complex proteins. For example, sugar and ammonia are converted into ornithine, into citrulline and then into argimine. They are propelled through these processes by enzymes, which are controlled by specific genes (Stein et al., 1975: 46–57). Much depends upon the initial compounds, which are essential for the proper transformation. If this process is inhibited in producing an end product, say, for instance, a muscle or a limb, by another chemical, then a deficiency is likely to occur. However protection is offered by two different metabolic pathways, which act as safety valves. These structurally arranged protective genes are only a small proportion of the total in an organism. Most of them are controlled by operator genes, which turn off and on the system of transformation, when there is an inhibitor. Other genes known as regulator genes monitor the transformation, so that at any one time the chemical environment stimulates the regulator, the inhibitor and the controller genes to act in consonance. Their action in turn changes the chemical environment in which they move, with many levels of dynamic interaction. These interactions contribute to the production of proteins for various muscles, nerve tissue and bone formation.

Genes exert their influence on behaviour through their effects at the molecular level of organisation (Morgan, 1988). Enzymes, hormones and neurons may be considered as the sequence of complete path markers between the genes and their behavioural characteristics (Fuller, 1957: 403–07). For instance, in the genetic system, the cytoplasm acts and reacts to produce an end product, while maintaining cell equilibrium in its specific chemical composition. The pathways involve many biochemical intermediaries, which contribute to the metabolic end state. The fruit fly, for instance, has been the subject of many experiments of these processes (Aluja and Norrbom, 1999: 984). It has been found that specific genes interact to mould the length, the width and the thickness of cells. These specific genes also maintain a balance among cells. For instance, in creating a wing in the fruit fly, a hormone is found to harmonise the process unless the deviation is too wide. However, when any gene is mutated, others interact to attempt a balance. This harmonising process is called a canalisation process. It offers compensating systems to complete the task of the end process. It may also be an explanation for the occurrence of dominant and recessive gene formations (Gottlieb, 1991: 4–13). In the formation of identical twins for example, when the embryo splits, two identical sets of human beings are formed, even though they began with half the cytoplasm material (Juel-Nielsen, 1965).

The process by which a region becomes a specific organ is also monitored by canalisation. Development of pre-term infants and of twins indicate the 'catch-up process' when canalisation sets the limits to the parameters (Gottlieb, 1976: 215–34). These changes occur during the development of the physiological time span, and range from conception till about 18 years, at the end range of puberty (Eichorn, 1970). Therefore, certain principles operate in the physical development of the human being, which also sets the limits of their brain and its mental capacities. The orthogenetic principle, for instance, illustrates that development begins globally and in an undifferentiated way, to become one that is differentiated, articulated and operative in a hierarchical systematic way. Piagetian theory rests on such an organismic explanation of the sequence of cognitive differentiation, specialisation and integration (Piaget and Inhelder, 1969). These sequences are based on the biological phased development of the human.

Here the human is dependent upon these biological processes of the sequence of differentiation, for instance, of colour, size, matter and distances, which are usually the first concrete operations at the preschool stage of development. This is achieved through a process of adaptability and assimilation to the environment and is known as the ontogenetic process, as distinct from the phylogenetic process, which is undifferentiated sensory operations in the human being at birth. The discipline of physical science and the aura of physiology in cognition indicate the interdependence of one upon the other in the study of diseases, for example, Alzheimer's disease and other forms of malformation of the physiological system affecting intelligent functioning (Parasuraman and Greenwood, 1998: 126–43). Thus, we have come a long way in identifying areas of the brain as related to functions frequently based on hypotheses. The main process through which behaviour-related brain processes are known are based on the study of embryos, foetuses and brain damage. The mysterious ways of the brain and its pivotal role in articulating human behaviour is still an enigma and perhaps can only be known sequentially through the newer methods of neuroscience, namely, genetic engineering and stem cell research for disease prevention and genome typing.

The Psychological Sources of Human Development and Related Behaviour

The two concepts 'human development' and 'human behaviour' require explanations. Development is a progression from simple to complicated forms, as mentioned earlier, where the child goes from one stage of physical growth to another. In the same way, his mental development follows a simple to a progressively more complicated form. Behaviour relates to the outward expression of the inward mechanisms of the physiological and mental processes as exhibited differently in different cultures. However, if we assume that phylogenesis is the first operant stage, we can readily understand how children at different ages behave similarly within an age group and differently among age groups. For instance, in the early stages a child sees something and puts it into his mouth without discrimination, reacting to his own biological world (Wolf, 1949: 198).

He later learns to discriminate between that which he can and that which he cannot eat from the outside world. His discrimination faculties become more acute through the accumulation of experiences and growing maturity (Werner, 1957). When he is one year old, for instance, the objects in his sensory field look like objects, which he could put into his mouth. Later, he is able to discriminate that it is only food placed before him that can be put into his mouth. Still later on, he learns that there are special types of foods, which he can accept or reject, where voluntary motivation comes into focus. His social perception, in the initial stages of development, relates mainly to his immediate situation: toys to play with and friends to play with (socio-centric behaviour).

It is only later, that he knows there are many people around him, and much later that there are not only Indians but also among Indians, some are Harijans, others Brahmins (the concept of social discrimination), that Brahmins can also live in Nepal (concept of expanded attributes of people other than Indians). Later still, this extension of perception of social structures extends to other peoples and other places (Piaget, 1976: 907). In Africa, there are those who believe in totems, in witchcraft, in the existence of the godhead in air, stones and trees (animism). These people have tribal bonds and no caste structure unlike people in India. In their writings, L.R. Munroe and H.R. Munroe used three cultures—the Ainu, the Trobrianders and the Gussi—to describe differences in cultural practices arising from different psychophysiological perceptions (Munroe and Munroe, 1975). Similarly, in the Indian situation, childcare practices are differentially influenced by their specific subcultures, such as the differences in childcare practices among hill tribes as compared to childcare practices in middle class metropolitan areas (Krishnan, 1998: 25–55). This is to say that human development assumes different patterns of behaviour in different cultures. In some, the origin is primitive, in others it is tribal and in yet others, it is sophisticated. The more simplistic the pattern of childcare, the greater the dependence on oral communication, modelling and imitation (Miller and Dollard, 1941). Therefore, we observe that strands of concepts both sociological and anthropological contribute to our understanding of how humans are reared (Munroe and Munroe, 1975: 7–25). As the individual in India advances chronologically, a unique feature of development in the Indian situation is the exposure to an ethnic group, to a caste group, to a kin group, and all their various fragmentations and fissions in subcategories.

For instance, in the development process, the individual learns that the caste divisions are man-made discriminations for a society to harmonise occupations with certain groups who do different occupational tasks (Beteille, 1991). Therefore, in sum, in man, development is progressive, sequential, simple to complex and general to discriminatory within a cultural niche.

Several conceptualisations in the child development were mooted from time to time by experts in the field. One, for instance, was that the child was a miniature adult (John Locke, cited by Gay, 1964). Another view, propounded by Rousseau, was that the child was born of nature, and natural surroundings were the best for teaching him his initial understanding of the world around him. This is very much akin to the Tagore school of thought in later years in India (Khalakdina, 1998: 166). Yet another view was the evolutionary hypothesis that development of the child was a recapitulation of the past history of man's development and the child enacted the stages in play of being huntsman, farmer and technician (Thompson, 1952: 10–11). John Dewey (1891) proposed yet another formulation—the pragmatic functionalism approach or learning by doing, which was revived in the Indian scenario by the concept of basic education propounded by Gandhi in the early 1940s (Biswas, 2000: 211). The older theories of the Calvinists, of the early Americans (the pilgrim fathers), who were of British origin, opposed the principle of 'spare the rod and spoil the child' as being anathema to their strictly principled Calvinistic religious upbringing. Gradually, however the protagonists of liberal and democratic educa-tion came into being. It says much for the vision of the Indian planners of independent India that we recognise these liberal, democratic and equal opportunity principles in proposing various forms of education for different age groups. Since much of the early years of children are spent in informal and formal education, these principles play an important part dovetailing with the traditional values of tolerance and emotional guidance given to children in India. In the early years of growing up in India, punishment was withheld as the child was perceived as immature, dependent, innocent of guile and god-given (Baig, 1979: 104).

However, human development by most experts is claimed to be related to the major theory of maturation and its correlates, and to learning by experience, practice and training, both in physical and mental abilities (McGraw, 1943). For instance, the child progresses in his mobility and manipulation of objects, from first using his fingers and palms for holding a ball with two hands, to holding a stick with one hand, to coordinating the eyes with the hand movement to grasp the stick. Then the progression moves to finer coordination of the eyes directly on the hole in a needle, using the thumb and first finger to thread the needle. This process is also related to the perceived outcome. The child has observed others using the thread and needle, and so constructs the perception in relation to his own skills, and attempts the same through the same types of eye and muscle coordination. Through trial and error, he accomplishes the same. Without the potential of the skill, the relevant behaviour cannot occur.

In the same way, the use of addition and subtraction of items in elementary arithmetic is the basis of multiplication and division. These processes have to first occur by cognising and doing, and then can be done by abstraction or mental calculations. Piaget carefully described these progressions in his analysis of the schema related to age maturation: from the pre-operational to the concrete operational and to the formal abstraction stages in preschool and primary school children (Inhelder and Piaget, 1958). Development can, therefore, be assessed by behaviour. This theme is contributed to by behaviour theorists, who focussed on experimental psychology as their main source of evidence (Skinner, 1974). These behavioural outcomes are more clearly observed in the initial stages of development, for example, in the operation of gross and fine motor coordination skills (Bayley, 1935: 26–61). Other relevant studies correlate the fact that such development, both mental and physical, occurs in a sequential order (Gesell and Ilg, 1943). By comparison with standardised measures, the development process of children is assessed by statistical techniques of quantification, means and standard deviations to arrive at a representative sample of behaviour (Kline, 2000: 240).

Approximation is made whether the required development/behaviour has taken place or not, whether or not mental development has occurred in keeping with the chronological age. For example, when a child of six cannot speak whole sentences (behaviour), we say that speech development relative to his age (chronological development) has not occurred.

In India, research in psychology began with the first department of psychology at Calcutta University in 1915. For lack of indigenous material, studies were adopted in design from the West such as concepts of form, perception, cognition and physical development in the early years of childhood. In recent decades there has been a growing interest in examining personality in a holistic manner from the viewpoint of cross disciplines, for example, psychology and physiology, psychology of gerontology (Bornstein and Lamb, 1999) and in the phenomenon of deprivation (Ganguli and Baroota, 1973: 21–48). But the replication continues. For instance, the pattern set in the West in studying perception has been replicated in the Indian context using Müller-Lyer illusion test (Chatterjee and Kundu, 1959: 58–63; Gupta and Prasad, 1967: 5–7; Mitra and Datta, 1939: 91–94). This emphasis, however, has moved over into perceptual cognitive tasks using socio-ecological factors such as perception of children in different ecologies (Sinha, 1976). Also used is replication of test measurements on Piagetian concepts of children from different socio-economic backgrounds (Bevli, 1977). Some psychological studies have moved into the area of assessing deprived children from various castes, using Raven's progressive matrices and other tests. Inevitably, these studies found that those of the higher castes who were not economically deprived did better than those of the lower castes who were deprived (Panda and Das, 1970: 267–73; Rath, 1974). However, Das and his colleagues put a rider to this conclusion when they noted that not all children who grow up in a disadvantaged environment suffer intellectually because of it. Some of them get to be as brilliant as those from the advantaged background (Das and Molloy, 1975: 213–20). Other factors found to influence individuals in comparative studies of varying socio-economic backgrounds were education, innate higher levels of intelligence and parental reinforcement in the case of the upper classes. However these static independent variables may not be as influential as the individual's own level of intelligence, competence and motivation to attempt to reach higher levels of competence. Kagitcibasi comments that in societies undergoing rapid socio-economic change, it is essential that the development itself and competence be understood from the cultural, contextual and functional perspectives (Kagitcibasi and Poortinga, 2000).

In the Indian context, there are inadequate indigenously developed measures. Many of them are adaptations of the available standardised measures developed earlier in the West, such as the Bayley Scale (Phatak, 1977) and the Mooney Problem List (Vasantha, 1978: 117–26). More recently, studies on academic achievement have provided indigenous analyses to the results (Misra and Agarwal, 1985: 250–66).

There have also been successful attempts to assess indigenous traits such as values (Sahu, 1981: 59–65) and similar attributes. In a refreshing move towards indigenous concepts and measures, more recently there have been other successful attempts to estimate deprivation (Misra and Tripathi, 2004: 118–215), specifically the PASS test for measuring intelligence (Naglieri and Das, 1990: 303–37) and the Temperament Measurement Schedule (Malhotra, 2002a: 220–27), among others (see Appendix I for some selected tests in use in the Indian context).

While development relates to the ability of the body and mind to interact in relation to each other, behaviour relates to the ability of the individual to demonstrate specific types of development. In other words, maturity of the physical capacities is related to the state of intelligent functioning of the mind, as maturity is the basis of physiological development beginning from conception in a progressive and sequential manner (Shirley, 1931: 507–28).

The understanding of human behaviour in India took a turn towards indigenisation in the late 1950s when there was a surge in expertise towards a comprehension that there was a dissonance between western-oriented psychological connotations and social realities in India (Adair et al., 1993: 149–69; Singh, 1980a: 93; Sinha and Kao, 1997: 9–22).

There is also a correlative movement towards context-sensitive conceptualisation and, therefore, a focus on social psychology, psychosocial acculturation, the eco-psychological parameters and ecological boundaries related to development.

Thus, conceptualisation of development in India and, for that matter, the Far East (China and Japan) is slowly expanding its theoretical dimensions towards specifics that apply to their own cultures (Befu, 1986: 13–27). However, there is no gainsaying that the phylogenetic principles remain the same the world over (Keller et al., 2002). Their interpretations differ with the best fit in their own contexts, such as inter-dependency (Malhotra, 2003: 6) in the Indian context.

The Socio-psychological Constructs of Human Development

How does the logic of ideas function? We have described earlier the deductive and inductive processes which lead to the formation of concepts. For understanding the process, we will emphasise the knowledge that has accrued over the years in the area of psychophysiological development on the basis of studies, mainly experimental, initiated in the West, and adapted/adopted/indigenised in India.

Psychophysiology tells us that the child begins to understand his world, initially through his senses, in the area of sensory development. He is said to recognise objects as differentially labelled categories. Later, it is reported by various psychologists and social biologists that they are given verbal expressions to identify them in their attributes of similarities/differences, such as: 'This is red and therefore cannot be black.' The concepts are repeated by the adult and imitated by the learning child, either through positive or negative reinforcement.

These are simplified processes and are based on alternate labelling through language development, but with increasing maturation they ripen to higher, more complex levels. Simple concepts begin with perception. These are said to relate to the initial perceptions begun in infancy, of shape, size, colour, volume, and so on, which increase in complexity as experiences accumulate. In describing the relevance of cortical evolution and development of visual perception, Purves, Williams and Lotto stress that perhaps the simplest visual attribute appears to be determined probabilistically (Purves et al., 2000). Empirical data on perception of light indicate that stimulus-induced activity of visual cortical neurons does not encode either the image or the stimulus but associations called precepts, which determine the relevant probabilities of possible stimuli. Given the basis of this conceptualisation, it is said that prolonged post-natal construction of visual circuitry and evolution of the visual schema is strengthened, dependent upon feedback from determined associations. What this implies is that the associative neural responses bring about a pattern of simultaneous brightness illusions. On the basis of experiments regarding figure-ground perception, the probabilities in initiating patterns of synaptic connections are determined by the experiences during the course of chronological evolution and by the active dependent feedback effect of developmental experiences (Rewal and Broota, 1990: 7–16). The biological impression, therefore, is that visually guided behaviour will be attended by the highest probability of successful stimuli. For instance, the infant in his perception of the world focuses on the brightest object. By probable association with other objects, he is able to observe through a process of developmental selectivity the relative attributes (of dissimilarity and similarity) of the perceived object. For instance, red is red but what is red? Red has depth, intensity and a certain brightness. Developmentally, through the post-natal period, there are indications that colours are grouped into a series of categories according to their attributes. Thus, the basis of 'labelling' is a combination of perception, cognition and recognition (Malhotra and Broota, 1986: 62–67). It is communicated through a structured auditory system called language. All societies of human and the mammal world utilise a sound system of communication, remembering that the brain functions through specialised areas in carrying messages. It follows that these areas process the messages and then send back the responses. We assume that conceptualisations related to sensations are primary. For instance, it is said that colours will attract the infant if they are within the perceptual range of the infant's vision, and if the vision is normal. For instance, in the physiological–psychological arena, P.K. Brown and G. Wald have discovered the existence of three kinds of cones in the retina, each with a cone pigment sensitive to a particular portion of the spectrum (Brown and Wald, 1964: 45–52).

Experiments done by varying the stimuli of colours show that the child stays with one colour longer than with others (primary sensations). It is also assumed that the stimulus of this is stronger. It is found that intense colours like red are colours with which the child's vision stays the longest, verifying the findings of E. Hering that the most contrasting colours in the visual pathway are the most dominating in sensory perception (Levinthal, 2003: 214).

We need to differentiate here among environment-specific situations. But there is no way in which the labelling of colours can be validated as being universally true. There is no scientific basis for calling any particular colour 'X' or 'Y'. It is simply the syntax of a language, socially constructed. In another culture, it may be called 'B'. The point is that the particular object has only cultural relevance. The object perceived may have depth and intensity, but its objectivity is labelled by environmental forces. The more elementary the culture, the closer is the labelling of colours to natural phenomenon. For instance, the colour 'orange' in English is related to a fruit; similarly, in Hindi, it is also related to a fruit, but the colour blue in English, in contrast, is called *aasmani* in Hindi, relating to the colour of the sky, and 'turquoise' in English is called *ferozi* (colour of a precious stone) in Hindi. Therefore, it is the social reality which constructs labels, which are commonly understood in that culture and therefore have abstract attributes (Sarukkai, 2000: 26–38). We may take this a little further in intercultural perceptions.

Besides the relevance of conceptualisation in its socio-historicity, the role of contextual factors is an important theme, such as the ecology of the individual (Bronfenbrenner, 1989: 185–246). An Indian may look askance at the Japanese eating raw fish, the Australians eating crocodile steaks and the French eating eels and frogs, without himself realising that some tribes in India consume roasted beetles. In time, some of the cultures may adopt the eating pattern of others as a part of their collective cuisine. However, it is difficult for a vegetarian to convert to non-vegetarianism, as from childhood, eating flesh is anathema to his religious convictions. What we are attempting to say here is that most of the patterns, like culturally-toned communication (idiomatic language) and emotional displays in interpersonal interaction, are patterns culturally learned from early childhood (Valsiner, 2002–03). One has only to observe a group of young children in an international school to be able to trace the culturally different behaviours towards similar situations. The point here is that perception is coloured by bias, but when there are other reference groups in contact, biases gradually disperse and disappear. For instance, the stereotype of the lower class in the social reality becomes blurred through constant interface and communication with other castes, with the eventual reality that all human beings live with what they have (Tripathi, 2001: 128).

To continue the example of colour, it becomes more complex with increasing perceptions of the individual. As he grows older, the individual transfers the concept of 'red' to other objects which are red: an apple, a ball, a cube, without seeing the outline or distinguishing one red from another. All are reds. The adults around, who try to impress the communicated label on the young child, utter sounds that the child imitates. It is 'red'. It is *laal* in Hindi and red in English (Piaget, 1954). So, now, he has attached a sound. Then the process of differentiation of red in different structures is heard, messaged to the brain through synapses and returned for coordination with its vocalisation of encoded symbolic auditory behaviour (Piaget, 1926a). It is said that language learning begins early in infancy (Chomsky, 1986). Further, the child learns that a ball does not have to be of similar structure to be red. The child also learns to differentiate colour from shape, volume and weight (Piaget, 1954). These symbolic utterances are labelled, coded and stored in memory for retrieval and presentation of similar stimuli. These are based on conceptualisations of Piaget's theory (Piaget, 1929). Thus, from the above illustration of the concept of colour (perception), causality of logical thinking and of intelligent behaviour has been developed by Piaget and other cognitive theorists (Piaget, 1974).

The Relationship of Environmental Ecology to Developmental Categories

It is in the area of cognition that ecology assumes importance. A nomad mother will induce in the child the sensation of the desert air, the wind and the dust; colours will also be highlighted in long sandy dunes of brown, and the occasional green and blue pools found in the desert. But, for the most, the world of sound for the nomad child is the rasping sound of camels, and the wind and dust howling during storms. This is quite different from the environment introduced to the urban-born child. Sensation and perception fight to have a place in his cognition, which is overwhelmed with stimuli and sound. These children, nevertheless, grow to attune perceptual ability in relation to their specific environments (Morton et al., 1996).

Logic also helps the child in the growing years, as he strings along events and objects, forming linkages (Mullick, 2000: 67). A ball is to play with, apple is to eat, and so on. So the beginnings of correlates are formed: if he eats an apple it will satisfy hunger, but if he eats paper, he will most likely throw up; and, therefore, by association, he later learns that hunger is appeased by eating food items, and that pain is caused if he eats the paper. He learns to move towards the former and avoid the latter for eating purposes. A child of four for instance experiences that the pressing of the button causes the brightness in the bulb. Later he learns that there is a wire connecting the switch to the bulb, which if activated brings energy, causing electricity to be transmitted to the bulb. Similarly, the infant thinks that milk is produced by the bottle or carton, or a container in which the milk is placed. Later, he learns that it originates in the market and, much later, that it is from a cow. Thus, the superimposition of more attributes, coded and decoded, enlarges or makes more complex the concept (Beg, 1991) as more and more characteristics are identified and labelled with the object. Throughout his contact with the environment, the child learns to replace old concepts with new ones. He moves from the familiar to the unfamiliar. When first perceiving a nurturant, it is mainly the initial caretaker, his mother or a substitute. Among large kin groups, for instance, every adult woman is a nurturer. Often the mother who works in the fields leaves her child in care of the grandmother or the older sister (Shaah, 1964: 48–50). If she is nursing the baby, it is only at these times he recognises her as the 'nourisher'. Thus, we see that the pattern of rearing of the child has to be moulded around the themes of the culture in which the child is socialised (Levine, 1977: 15–27).

In the Indian family, a child is taken care of informally by all members, especially females and older siblings (Arulraj and Raja Samuel, 1995). The biological mother is freely given advice on dos and don'ts and welcomes it as practical oral tradition. Thus, the ecology of the kin group forms a network of supportive and interactive family relations (Alavi, 1972: 1–27). This interaction of family members with the child is unlike the pattern in the West. Perhaps, it is the joint family ethic that prevails in India, which leads to such patterns of interaction. In the West, the child belongs to the nuclear family and any intrusion by others into this 'private space' is only with the acceptance of the biological family. These are not comparisons—they are only contrasts—as the basis is not the same but culturally differentiated.

In the West, terms like 'private space' and 'own space' are highly cherished by the individual, whereas in the East and particularly in the subcontinent, there is little privacy of space or barriers to interaction. In the West, it is preferred that children sleep in their own beds if not in their own rooms. In India and such like cultures, there is no such exclusion. In fact the mother–infant symbiosis is well known, where the child sleeps with the mother and is hip-carried by not only mothers, but other nurturants like the older female siblings. This proximity is sometimes misconstrued by western norms as precipitating in the child a sense of binding dependency. In the West, the child is literally allowed to carry his 'security blanket'; in the East and in African countries the swaddling, back-carrying and hip-carrying provide security to the infant (Ainsworth et al., 1978). Not only is space shared in the Indian household, but also thoughts among family members, and advice of family members is sought in times of personal problems. There is very little recourse to psychological counselling, unlike the West, except perhaps among the very rich/elite. In most Indian families, the spiritual philosophy of *dharma* and *karma* permeates many facets of life. Perhaps, in the context of information interaction as described earlier, there are linkages to certain socio-religious values that are inculcated early in life. These may be identified as follows:

   (i)   the joint family ethic (Gore, 1968);
  (ii)   the self as a unitary part of the family (Roland, 1988);
 (iii)   the spiritual contemplative philosophy enjoined by the Vedantas (Gupta, 2006: 25);
  (iv)   the learned, adaptive resilience to economic deprivation (Rath et al., 1979);
   (v)   the acceptance of differences in a secular society as in India (Raju, 1985);
  (vi)   the ethos of collectivism, rather than individualism (Sampson, 1988: 15–22);
 (vii)   the closeness of kinship and reverence for patriarchal hierarchy (Dube, 1974);
(viii)   the female nurturer as a nexus of love and security in childhood (Caldwell et al., 1963: 653–64).

Modern psychological theories have been derived from western thought, such as Hegel's 'rationalism'; Schopenhauer's philosophy of 'will-to-live'; and Nietzche's 'will-to-power' and 'assertion of individuality'. J.W. Atkinson commenting on William James' conceptualisation of psychology stated that James conceived of 'psychology as science of mental life both of its phenomena and its conditions' (Atkinson, 1964: 14). The western psychological theories as applied to modern psychiatry have only been recently introduced to the traditional systems of health and healing in India (Malhotra, 2002b: 2–3). But in the West, one is expected to manage one's problems and, in critical situations, to seek the advice of a professional who is assumed to be objective, namely, a therapist. The values of parents vis-à-vis the therapist are more significant in India (Pruett, 1991: 215–21). In the Indian family, such values and attitudes prevail and are expected to be imbibed throughout the developmental period when the child learns deference to elders, abiding by the locus of power and authority (Dahl, 1957: 210–19) and subscribing to kinship values. In recent years, the global concern for human rights, gender rights and child rights is being adopted in conventional forms by the governments, which are reflected in the Indian government (Himes and Saltarelli, 1996). Thus, the Indian is on a dual track of subservience to others and control of self-rights in group situations (Marriot, 1976: 109–42); his diversity of values is not a confrontation, but an alignment (Verma, 2004: 69–117).

With the growing academic interest in the part that the environment plays in the development process, scientific enquiry went from the cognitive stages of interest to the interactive processes. E.H. Erikson contributed to this interactive concept with his classic writings on the stages of development, from basic trust and mistrust in the early years to the attributes of gerontology (Erikson, 1969). The same schema is used to explain the most profiled behaviour which appears chronologically, such as autonomy versus shame, and so on, till the age of adolescence when the individual shows either a sense of identity or is confused about his identity (Erikson, 1964). Thus, the major theories of Werner (naïve theory) (Werner, 1948), Piaget's analysis of biogenesis (Piaget, 1981) and Freud's psychoanalysis (Freud, 1946) were supported by mini theories of motivation (Atkinson, 1964), of field forces (Lewin, 1951) and of socialisation through modelling (Miller and Dollard, 1941), with continual modifications of their concepts. For instance, discussions by R.M. Thomas examine concepts beyond Piaget's theory and beyond Vyogtsky's theory (Thomas, 2001: 105–34). It is essential that these conceptual theories are linked to basic genetic and environmental factors, namely, maturation and learning. These are articulated by the three constant variables of age, time and change. For instance, the occurrence of rapid social change in India has affected the relationship among and between classes, especially in urban areas (Caplan, 1987). Social change also affects the psychological domains of certain bipolar dimensions (Welzel et al., 2001). For instance, during the growing process the personality may vacillate between being either aggressive or non-aggressive for a period of time in trial and error attempts, but eventually settles down to being one or the other in the moulded form attained at adulthood (Chattell, 1985). We must also assume that these changes occur because of the effect of social and cultural variables. However, the personality during the adolescent and adulthood periods changes in some traits, but in some others there is stability. For example, adherence to religious norms is a continuous belief, whereas moral traits may change over time (Kakar and Chowdhry, 1970).

Whether the source is philosophy or any of the social sciences, it has been established that the primary contextual reference is the mother/nurturant or any similar substitute, who is the constant figure in the nurturance process. In the Indian context, the concept of the nurturant female is undifferentiated as there are many female figures who are perceived to have relative nurturant care-giving abilities (Kurtz, 1992). The meaning of nurturance in the Indian setting is different from that of the West, as it is generalised to significant 'others'. For instance, the baby in a family is handled by several female figures as a natural process (Khatri, 1970: 392–95). There are many labelling categories of female nurturants, which the child learns to elaborate. There is no one mummy or no one daddy, as in the West. The differentiation fissions out to many: men are either *chachas* (paternal uncles) or *mamas* (maternal uncles). If they are younger or older the labelling continues: *chota chacha* (younger paternal uncle), *bada chacha* (elder paternal uncle), *chota mamu* (younger maternal uncle) or *bada mamu* (elder maternal uncle), *dada* (paternal grandfather), *dadi* (paternal grandmother), *nana* (maternal grandfather) or *nani* (maternal grandmother), and so on. These are concepts, which are acquired from the learning environment as labelling concepts with varied interpretations as to the relational labels in language acquisition (Chomsky, 1986).

Relational concepts (correlatives) are formed earlier in informal associations than in causative relations. For instance, in rural areas, the lack of clouds is related to the consequent lack of rain, although there is little scientific reasoning and more of associative conceptualisations. The concept of famine is related to water, to rain and eventually to the monsoon clouds. That these factors loom large in the contextual reference of the Indian in his habitat, has given rise to studies on poverty and deprivation (Misra and Tripathi, 2004: 118–215). These are supported by political interest in intervention programmes of the governance (Acharya, 1989: 125–33). Therefore, there was much dovetailing in the early years of independence, of poverty, caste and community-change studies initiated by sociologists (Dube, 1976: 27–38; Singh, 1976: 51–61; Singh, 1980b) and psychologists (Misra and Gergen, 2002: 405–24; Tripathi, 2003: 235–59), and additively by ecologists in the Indian situation (Keller, 2003: 102–27). There have also been tentative attempts to dovetail multidisciplinary approaches (Singh and Parasuraman, 1998) and physical sciences (Young et al., 2003). The large regional differences in the Indian subcontinent with its myriad languages, and still more numerous and various dialects, the many variegated terrains of the grasslands, the tundra and the desert, has made ecology a growing conceptualisation of importance. It has also compelled scientists, especially psychologists, to move out of their own geo-ecological boundaries to examine contrasting concepts with other cultures (Kukla, 1988). Together with these types of field studies, there has been a continuance of experimental psychology (Pandey, 2000: 13–18). In both psychology and sociology, annotated bibliographies and publisher companions to psychology and sociology have been undertaken to expose the reader to available information (Berry et al., 1997 and 1999; Das, 2003; Gore, 2000a; Naidu and Nakhate, 1985; Sarawati and Dutta, 1987a). The existence of the gap between the poor and the rich, especially the rural poor in the less economically developed states of India (like Bihar and the north-east) has widened. This has occurred because of the introduction of liberalisation and free trade, and with India signing the WTO pact (Ahluwalia, 2002). Further, the divide between the North and the South in the global scenario has accelerated differences, more especially in the power struggles for territory and control. India is one of the less developed countries in the UNDP reports. As such, therefore, academic interest has moved into the world of the socio-political, such as domestic economy and trade (Britt, 1966). In the diaspora (the global village), amenities and facilities are taken for granted in the West, but in the developing economy of India, this availability is unpredictable.

Thus there have arisen a spate of studies on values and related attributes associated with early learning, furthering linkages with Indian philosophical concepts (Gupta, 2006). Take, for instance, water: it is both wanted (in times of famine) and rejected (in times of floods). Thus we see that, as the human being develops and learns complex concepts, their retention or rejection or even indifference depends upon the environmental cues that give meaning to the concepts so labelled. In essence, that which is less available like concrete and material goods, is more valued in the Indian context (Rath, 1982: 239–59). Thus, both academic and political interest surged to examine the politics of power and control in the institutional infrastructures so as to elicit data on the benefits of developmental programmes. Studies found that the more particular and the more powerful siphoned off the benefits. This occurrence led to evaluations of programmes implemented by the government. In many cases, there was a linkage between programme implementation and evaluation by academicians, who were associated with such evaluation, conducted mainly by the Planning Commission of the Government of India (Muthayya, 1972: 153–59; Shah and Junnarkar, 1976). A workshop on early childhood development (Report of the National Workshop on Early Childhood Development, 1996: 11–13) has indicated that we do not know what is going on in the human mind, until we elicit behaviour to identify and interpret. Many of the studies undertaken in the sociological and psychological field are stereotyped, with small segments of small samples making generalisations difficult (Khalakdina, 1974). Other critics of studies and methodologies have also examined the designs, methods and findings of these researches (Mohanty and Prakash, 1993: 104–35; Saraswathi, 1993a: 50–51). Much of psychological research findings are deduced and inferred from overt behaviour, and are therefore limited to stretching verifiability and reliability. Both processes are subject to probability. We use hypotheses from our observation to elicit empirical data. Small-scale scattered studies arising from the interest of scholars and their graduate students have been undertaken in variegated areas of developmental domains, for instance, aggression altruism, academic achievement and parental variables (Naidu and Nakhate, 1985; Saraswathi and Dutta, 1987a). There has been little planning on a large scale or in the continuity of variables studied (Kaur, 1987: 317–35). There is a prevailing acceptance that for every attempted description, there is an equally valid example illustrating exactly the opposite (much of the mores that are age-old come from folk tales repeated from one generation to another) (Ramanujam, 1994).

There is also a prevalent accommodation to and coexistence of seemingly contradictory perspectives (Marriot, 1976: 109–42). With this kind of contradiction inherent within its social and psychological landscape, it is certainly true that distant methods, simple frames and uniform categories will always remain inadequate to describe overall patterns of development in India. Nandy has said that he hopes that his review would help to encourage researchers to take the lead provided by well-intentioned research scholars in the pursuit of a culturally appropriate developmental psychology that has finally cleansed itself of the after-effects of colonialism (Nandy, 1983).

The sources of information are scattered, disengaged from each other, and the process has happened in fits and starts. In order to understand human development, it is also essential to use common sense to see how progression has taken place in the collation of information. First, during the successive reigns of the Mauryas and the Mughals there was greater emphasis on the study of arts, music, literature, philosophy and drama than on the study of physical sciences (Jaffar, 1972: 172; Kishori, 1992). Then came the colonial period of the English, the Dutch, the Portuguese and the French. All were intent on their first priority, namely, colonisation, and then, coincidentally, on specific systems of their culture, proselytising their religion and their forms of education. Since the British colonised the largest part of India as compared to the Portuguese and the French, the English system of education was emphasised as it was an essential part of the Raj's communication with the ruled. This system of education was far removed from the vast majority (Atal, 1976: 75). It was only after independence and the formulation of a Constitution that feudal India adopted a courageous democratisation process, underwritten by independent

India's Constitution. Through the democratic process of their visionary leaders, primary school education was made free and compulsory for all (*Constitution of India*, 1952). As there was no ready alternative, the British system of formal education was retained and in rural and tribal areas the vernacular was the medium, as again there was no alternative. The legacy of the British was the English language and English-monitored visages of an alien culture, which continued in the elite schools (Thompson, 1999). Because of the inbuilt traditional fortress of a Hindu ethos, values long dormant were out in the open and were researched for understanding the human in the Indian situation. In the field of academia the first thrust was by sociologists and anthropologists in the field situation. However, Mahatma Gandhi's basic education formula, similar to Dewey's concept of learning by doing was also introduced (Dewey, 1968).

It is reasonable to assume that given the opportunities to develop in several spheres academicians in their research policies would have dovetailed their research to understand developmental processes in India on longitudinal and cross-sectional groups of the population. There is a need for an interface between policy programmes and researches (Sinha and Mishra, 1993: 139–50). As behaviour occurs developmentally, and sequentially through the various chronological stages of growth (physical) and development, it would have been reasonable to assume that knowledge in social sciences would have proceeded along those lines. We have very little information on the growth and human developmental processes in the Indian situation in such a manner, except for the growth norms and human human nutritional indices as developed by the National Nutrition Monitoring Bureau. They have been isolated items at studying socio-personal development of young children (Muralidharan, 1983). At infrequent times, we have had annotated bibliographies (Saraswathi and Dutta, 1987a) of socio-psychological research in India. At best, emphasis was laid on nutrition, growth studies and some adaptations of physical growth measures from the West, to explain segments of developmental processes, such as Bayleys and Gesell's studies on physical mental and emotional growth (Bhandari and Ghosh, 1980: 289–302; Phatak, 1977). Sociology, on the other hand, continued its ethnographic field studies, studies on caste and class, and regional variations in normative and ethical behaviour. Realising that the influence of the caretaker and the interaction with the environment is significant, studies were informal and mainly related to infant care in the early stages of human development concerns. These further became studies on the play of children, the conceptual development of children and various ad hoc traits (Saraswathi and Dutta, 1987a).

It is also understood that in the field of psychology, there existed the continuous relationship between learning and behaviour. Therefore, experiments in the East were replicated in patterns of designs and measurements adapted or adopted from the West (Saraswathi and Kaur, 1993: 370). However, there were also strenuous efforts to study human development in its cultural context (Nsamenang, 1992). It was also realised that there was a continuous relationship between maturation and learning, both learning of the informal kind where the child learns from speech and behaviour of models in the family (Bandura and Walters, 1963) and through formal processes of deliberate teaching in the school systems (positive reinforcement).

Often, in the Indian context, there is a clash between what is taught at school and what occurs in the home. For, it must be realised that while education has begun to filter down to the masses, the curriculum has yet to be tailored to their eco-cognitive development. In other words, the familiarity of the concept can be understood in the abstract, but is yet to be contextualised in most school textbooks. For example, nursery rhymes like 'Jack and Jill', 'Mary had a little lamb', 'John Brown baby' are alien to the languages spoken in Indian homes. It was only two decades after the educational system came, in a faltering manner, to India, that it began to be de-contextualised from the alien scene to a localised context. As book production increased, so also did the revival of books related to mythology and classical tales such as the Panchatantra, which were used in the teaching situation. There was, on the part of the government, a similar revival of the ancient Hindu heritage through the opening of national museums and of institutions studying and publishing ancient Indian history. This was done to root the Indian psyche in its social historicity. As early as the 1990s, there was documentation on the Hindu psyche (Radhakrishnan, 1927). In the teachings of child development, in the early 1950s, there was a growing realisation that study should research the growth and developmental processes of the Indian child. Academicians also made a major thrust in this area. They still continued to borrow concepts from the West, hypothesising that the child moves from relative immaturity to maturity, and also that the child moved from relative dependence upon his environment to relative independence in the attainment of skills through practice and training (emphasising generic phylogenetic and orthogenetic learning processes) (Whiting and Child, 1953). However, the importance of environmentally oriented practice was hardly considered, and such writings were repetitive of westernised conceptualisations. We have used the word 'relative' cautiously as these traits of dependency/independency are viewed differently in the developing traditional societies as contrasted to the developed world where independence and achievement on a competitive basis are highly prized (Metha, 1971–76: 577–615).

However, academicians also realised that, with various institutional bases, such as departments of anthropology, psychology, sociology, political science, economics and several national institutes, the outcome from Indian institutions in terms of research information was localised. It was sociologists who moved out into field studies of caste, community and village, mainly because they were continuing the interest of the erstwhile rulers in these so-called 'attractive segments of society'. Psychology and its growing derivatives like social psychology, psycho-anthropology and psycho-economic analyses zoomed in on the Indian psyche. At the same time, there was an acknowledgement that adhering to colonial linkages with past systems of education short-changed the understanding of the Indian psyche.

Therefore, erudite scholars like Durganand Sinha, R.C. Mishra, T.S. Saraswathi, Ajit K. Dalal, A.C. Paranjpe and Janak Pandey (Pandey, 2001) and others scanned more deeply the various domains of psychology to unearth its deep-rooted indigenous interpretations as is the case of studies of values, achievement, language development, and such like areas (Pandey, 2004). Further, as scientists began to delve into the analysis of such traits/attributes/characteristics as they occurred in the Indian situation, they realised that the classical 'independent variables' existent in the Indian situation like caste, ethnicity, religion and regionality were important operating variables (see chapter on 'Research Concerns'). These variables in and of themselves were abstract and static, and only came into vibrant dynamism when attached to development and behavioural processes. For instance, it is well known through social case studies (Ishwaran, 1970) that in the subcategories of class, caste, religion, ethnicity and regionality, subtle differences occur between one group and another. For example, the Harijan has a low profile, the north Indians are as different from the south Indians as Punjabis are from the Bengalis, or a Keralite is from a Kashmiri. What we are saying is that the fissioning of these independent variables has brought out into the open the need for carefully circumscribed research designs, when contrasting the differing groups. The Hindu is different from the Muslim and from the Christian, in this secular society, in terms of their religious affiliations, just as the tribal from Madhya Pradesh is different from the tribal in the Coorg district. Likewise, examining the variation within the Hindu caste structure, we find that the value aspirations for occupations also vary among the Brahmins, the Kshatriyas, the Shudras and the Harijans, perhaps because of the circumscribed limitations of their caste status (Chatterjee, 1994). Therefore, it became a situation where 'if you do, you are unsuccessful', and where 'if you don't, you still continue to be unsuccessful'. In other words, is there a generic Indian psyche or is it as variegated as its fissioned independent variables? Social scientists, therefore, had to come to grips with the concepts of universals and specifics. Courageously, many of them studied across cultures to analyse these universals (Diaz-Guerrero, 1967).

The disciplines continued to propound their own areas in their cause of enquiry when expanding into other disciplines with their own parameters. For instance, psychology moves into cross-cultural psychology, social psychology, individual psychology, differential psychology and industrial psychology. Very few have moved across their individual parameters to link their researches using similar groups. Although several decades old, studies like those of Whiting and Child (1953) and Munroe and Munroe (1975), which used both anthropological and psychological dimensions in their study of behaviour, are few and far between. Indian academicians use religion, ethnicity, age and like variables, but within their own constructs (Naidu and Nakhate, 1985; Saraswathi and Dutta, 1987a). Generally speaking:

> Still there have not been national multi-sectoral studies that have established a wide database as well as an in-depth analytical framework in child related areas to obtain a profile of the child in India (Naidu and Nakhate, 1985).

Thus, we see that in reality the environment is not static, nor is it the same for any one individual in a pluralistic society. The relational ties with the human environment (family solidus peers solidus neighbourhood) and the interaction with the household, the playground (concrete objects) in the situation vary from one independent variable to another. Sociology from its inception has stressed the importance of social stratification and social institutions; it has further added another dimension, that of social change (Singh, 1980a). By this we mean that within this context, there are changes in the categories of the structure in terms of mobility and/or the aspirations towards upward mobility.

M.N. Srinivas's classic discourses on westernisation and sanskritisation are concepts well known and yet at the same time well disputed. For instance, he indicates that within the caste hierarchy, the lower castes adopt and practise the patterns of behaviour of the upper castes (Srinivas, 1955/56: 492–96). Thus, social change spurred on by economic changes is a continuous variable underlining many of the studies of varying groups (Marriot, 1990). Scales to measure the socio-economic status in order to assess the differences and change have been used (Kuppuswamy and Singh, 1967). Many of them, however, have only class variables; others include occupation, income and social prestige and these are factored into study designs. They do not take into account structural adaptation and caste resilience and, therefore, give static information, which is applicable only to a time and a place. In the 21st century, research concerns are moving towards understanding the Indian psyche mainly in the following areas:

(i) movement in economic status towards higher/prestigious occupations;
(ii) rural–urban mobility, which is impacting on conglomerate conditions in metropolitan areas and straining civic amenities;
(iii) the influx of other cultural values through the outsourcing from foreign countries;
(iv) the globalising patterns of trade, communication, tourism and the world of media, which are compacting the society towards modernisation.

Thus we see that social change is inevitable and as the decades progress, technology accelerates this change. For instance, from the pre-colonial, colonial, zamindari system and the untouchability phenomenon, India has moved towards the abolition of the zamindari system, the creation of a democratic Constitution, agrarian reforms and industrialisation. However, discrimination against the Harijan community continues to exist especially in the social sphere. Sociologists have used several theories of social change to explain these phenomena. The theories of social change in India are still influenced by the social theory from the West (Levy, 1952; Merton, 1967). However, they are only partially used in the analysis of phenomena derived in the Indian context. New and emerging phenomena which cannot be deflected from the Indian scenario of modernising effects are such areas as youth conflicts/stress, need for guidance, counselling and psychiatric treatment; domestic violence; and child labour. Also compounding the situation are increase in social disorganisation, the growing gap between generations and the effects of transnational mobility between and within generations. There are not yet reliable and valid indices of social change in the fast expanding world vision of movement from traditionality to transnationality to modernity and perhaps supermodernity in the Indian situation.

Existing theories of social change, such as evolutionary, functionality and neoevolutionary theories or, for that matter, sanskritisation and westernisation (Srinivas, 1966) and varying structural approaches in the last analysis, do not lend themselves to clear conceptualisations within the parameters of social change (Singh, 1980b). Clearly, a broader framework is essential and, therefore, in researching concepts described as 'little and great traditions' (Dube, 1965: 423). Thus, the plurality of the Indian situation needs to be further examined. For instance, it is not just belonging to upper or lower social class that functionalises 'change proneness' within these traditions, but also the motivational levels of given groups. We might ask what makes for the mobility (occupationally and geographically) of the Keralite, the Gujarati and the Punjabi in contrast to other ethnic groups? We might also ask what makes for the accumulation of wealth among the Marwaris in Uttar Pradesh, Delhi and West Bengal, or, for that matter, the intellectual and artistic nature of the Bengali. These may be stereotypes, but in reality their behaviour connotes a relationship to these attributes. It is often said that education is the handle to development. This might be a truism as it seems to be operating functionally (the function approach) in some ethnic groups, whereas in others it depends upon the natural progression of knowledge (the evolutionary approach), or the availability of reinforcing institutions like the occupational infrastructure, entrepreneurship facilities, government incentives, and so on (institutional approaches).

Thus we see that the utilisation of the indigenous variables like caste, ethnicity, family/kinship values and religious fervour must be taken into account when analysing social change (Singh, 1980b). In viewing social change, the parameters need to be widened to include the growing significance of human ecology (Berry, 2003 51–69; Kagiticibasi, 2003; Keller, 2003: 102–27). These also need to be examined for their continual reinforcement from perception to behaviour, especially those constructed by adults involved in the developmental process of their progeny (Baumrind, 1978: 239–76). Also important are the beliefs and customs which have endurance (like religious beliefs and rituals) (Desai, 1964; Kapadia, 1966). In the chapter on socialisation in Volume II, we will examine in detail such domains as modes and outcomes of socialisation. Suffice it to say now, that social change theories have yet to be adequately examined in relation to the dynamism of psychological development. Consequently, dovetailing theories of sociology and psychology. Further, although an initial start has been made by social psychologists to include the values of Hindu philosophy in the Indian psyche (Paranjpe, 1998) they need to be empiricised to add to scientific generality of data. For instance, we have mentioned the *samskaras* as stages of development, but they have yet to be further analysed in relation to normative behaviour (Kapur, 2003: 97). They need to be examined not as milestones as described in western psychology, but of mental states or attitudes during the lifespan. These cut across the lifespan and are: (a) achievement of appropriate balances between independence and dependence patterns; (b) relationship to changing social groups; (c) learning psychosocial–biological sex roles; and (d) learning to understand and control the physical world.

The related tasks/obligations/duties during the lifespan assumes different packages of role expectations, role performances and values of the hierarchical norms (Reichenbach, 1990).

The major theme in the Hindu philosophy is for the individual to perceive and abide by the norms of value, mainly for placing the collective good of the group before oneself. There is also emphasis on deference to age, hierarchy, authority and intergenerational norms.

These domains have yet to be fully explored by tracing the ethics of the joint family (Dube, 1997). This ethic, perhaps, still continues in muted forms in family relations and except for a few explorations in this phenomenon by some experts like T.S. Saraswati, A. Dalal and G. Misra and their colleagues, these themes have yet to be fully explored (Dalal and Misra, 2002a; Saraswathi, 1999). In recent years, discourses in the *Oxford Companion to Psychology* (Das et al., 2003) and the handbooks on sociology, psychology and anthropology have indicated a vast array of such documentation (Saraswathi and Dasen, 1997: xxv–xxxvii). These together with bibliographies and handbooks of researches, and studies in sociology, psychology and human development could perhaps offer a comprehensive critique of the documentation which exists as of today. Such empirical data could indicate what further domains require exploration in terms of lacunae in theoretical conceptualisations.

It is essential to view these concepts of change, traditionality, modernity, mobility and globalisation against the backdrop of the origins of socio-religious belief. India, being a secular society, not only has Hinduism as a dominant religion, but also its variations, namely, Buddhism, Jainism and Sikhism, together with the religions of Islam, Christianity and segments of Judaism and Zorastrianism. It is necessary, therefore, in discovering further information, that these influences of religion be taken into account (Robinson, 2004: 359). It is said that the temporal life is transient, and the fruits of this life are in the next, whether it is *nirvana* or *moksha*, whether it is *jannat* or heaven. We need further linkages of how these precepts, though covert, influence everyday life (Venugopal, 2004: 13). For instance, rituals in these religions are to mark events which remind the performer that they are important in daily life, such as the rituals to the household deity, observance of Ganesh Chaturthi in west India, Teej in north India, Lakshmi Puja during Diwali/Shivratri, *ashtottara* (offering prayers 108 times) and *kotyarchana* (offering prayers 19 million times) collectively organised in towns and cities. There is a morning invocation by most Hindu businessmen/shopkeepers. For instance, there is a Gujarati saying: 'A Vaishnavite spends his money on kitchen (food); and a Jain on stone (temple).' Account books are placed before the Goddess Kali who is worshipped in Bengal on the Bengali new year's day (Wolfson, 1976).

Learning is a very important tool in the progression of mature behaviour. Principles of the learning theories developed in the West, also apply to the Indian child. Strategies used may be different. The importance of such differential strategies is the same, namely, to help the child towards a goal-directed behaviour by enforcing or persuading through incentive or reward, and sometimes punishment. The practice of reward giving for good behaviour in early childhood is a common phenomenon. The importance of intervention programmes has been discussed in early childcare efforts (Swaminathan, 1979: 16–35). In these discussions, different strategies are used to interest, motivate and guide young children towards cues directed towards goals (Tolman, 1925: 36–41). Here, however, we need to mention that most of the programmes are based on casual and informal play-way methods in play school or in kindergarten. In the context of learning, there are experimental schools of high calibre dealing with cognitive models of the learning process, most of them are in urban, elite academic institutions. For the mass of the population, about 70 per cent of whom live in rural and tribal areas, and often in difficult terrains, learning is mostly by rote with most primary school children being expected to learn the three R's and recite numbers and alphabets (Swaminathan, 1998: 24).

In the past two decades, socio-political changes have had their effect on human development in India. As far back as 1966, K. Ishwaran indicated that there are pockets of resistance to social change in his sociological description of several small communities (Ishwaran, 1966). The burgeoning middle class, the reports of the drop in mortality rates and the increase in education have effected more purchasing power. Enlightenment through education has affected the living styles, especially those of the middle class (UNDP, 2002). The opening up of the markets has created an increased motivation to achieve, in most strata. This, in turn, has its effect on attitudes and values related to economic advancement (McClelland and Winter, 1969). In the process of analysis of change, the concepts of time and place assume importance in the Indian context, which is reflected in the current milieu of science and technology impacting upon the Indian psyche. We need to ask, for instance, how 'multinationalism' in the technological services influences the psyche of the middle class Indian. The western ethic is attuned to punctuality, efficiency and productivity. What is the process of osmosis transferred to the Indian personality who has to abide by these work ethics if he is to be successful in these transnational organisations?

We have yet to gain adequate information in these newer emerging areas of knowledge. Given India's myriad subcultures, even though commonalities prevail, such as (a) socio-religious observances, (b) the multicultural nature and (c) the multiplicity of various subcastes, the class differences still play a role in the vortex of change and in work ethics. There seems to be a struggle between rooted traditional values and the demands of modernisation. For instance, how does this adherence to the new milieu of change in work ethics at the office place relate to the resilience and adaptability attributes which the Indian has learned in his socialisation milieu? R.K. Mukherjee comments that the individual in his community is self-sufficient (R.K. Mukherjee, quoted in Singh, 1977: 184). However, over the last two decades, social change has eroded the concept of a self-contained community, except, perhaps, in the still remote and inaccessible areas, like the Pangis in the Himalayan ranges, who are snow-bound for most of the year, and, therefore, like Eskimos, are an interdependent community. Given the flux of change, this interdependence has widened from rural areas to the hinterlands of urban areas, and the urban areas to the international network, galvanising the Indian economy (Srinivasan and Tendulkar, 2003). The rising aspirations of the middle class and the juxtaposition of caste and political power disturbing the caste hierarchy also cause dynamic changes (Basu, 2003). However, even though the various subcultures are different from each other in some minute details, taken together they are held by common mutual bonds of nationality and commitment to a common historical heritage. No doubt, this phenomenon also occurs in other societies where individuals identify themselves with their own nationalities (Geertz, 1973: 221). We see clearly that leadership strategies give a charismatic picture of policies and goals, and the tendency of individuals is to identify with those goals and policies. We have had in India charismatic leaders who have left their mark in terms of their cultural heritage (Marsella et al., 1985).

The political scenario, therefore, has its impact on the individual national identity. We have a few explorations in analysing the Indian identity (Chakrabarty, 1995; Misra, 2003).

Priority Domains of the Development Process

The ordered bases of concept development in the scenario of social and technological change depend upon logic, established as a foundation, early in its documentation in the development of scientific thinking. It gives rise to the following interlinking concepts:

 (i) The first is the replacement of primary sensory concepts by more complex additive correlated concepts, so that the base of the given concept has many attributes. For example, the mother whose major role was homemaker and childcare nurturer is now no longer bound to one role. She now has multiple roles. In almost all strata, mothers work, either as domestic help or labourers in construction sites, or in offices or industries; the multiple roles of the female continue. It then becomes necessary to expand the concept of nurturing to include such frameworks as 'substitute care' and 'alternate care', where parents become part-time child caretakers, due to the phenomenon of extrafamilial care (Swaminathan, 1996).

 (ii) The process of formation of concepts can only be observed by elicited or observation of spontaneous behaviour and the ability of the observer to make an accurate deduction or inference. This is furthered by the accuracy of the interpretations/observation. R. Day discusses two complementary systems of thinking in the domain of economic theory: one deals with equilibrium and the other with properties of disequilibrium (Day, 2003: 256). Changes affecting the equilibrium of lifestyles and the observance of behaviour and its accurate recording have increased the number of variables affecting the individual. For instance, in the earlier days, interaction was with family, kin group and community. It is now expanded to include the electronic world, the economic market and the global diaspora. In this process, the Indian has also acquired the propensity to accumulate wealth for its own sake and in the process exclude its possession by others (Gadgil, 1955: 448–63).

 (iii) The interpreted behaviour should be repeatedly observed as it occurs. Hypotheses remain undeveloped if they are not exposed to the rigour of scientific research. For instance, there is the uncensored information available in print and visual media, to which individuals and communities are exposed. Most often information processed through these channels may not be entirely valid. What is important here is that news communication and media information should be verifiable through either multiple observations of the event or recorded and documented information.

 (iv) Repeated valid observations contribute to a logical theory. Theorising of human behaviour is more susceptible to inaccuracies than is material behaviour from the physical sciences. For this reason, valid, repeated observations are essential for constructing a theoretical frame, such as studying public behaviour in response to disasters. By this we mean that repeated and constant observation of news, advertisements, information over the Internet and interpersonal communication in public places are required to be carefully hypothesised to help understand the products in theorising on communication.

(v) Even so, a theory (collation of concepts) can be displaced or less favoured over a period of time, with the discovery of more credible newer concepts or additions/furtherance of the concept. For instance, while Erikson's psychodynamic concepts have stood the test of time, the theory of stimulus response has been modified to include the theories of conditioned response and reinforcement (Skinner, 1938). However, the view on development is neither wholly a schematic progression as in Erikson, nor a situational frame of the interaction between stimuli (inner or outer) and human behaviour. The view is currently that the human being acts upon his environment and in turn is acted upon (Leahey, 1987). These interactions occur within the dynamics of cultural–environmental frames (Altman and Rogoff, 1987: 7–40). Therefore, social scientists are moving in the direction of developing a framework for intergrated conceptualisation (Sinha, 1965: 6–17). This is not to say that there is general agreement among scientists from the various disciplines. They tend to still run around the race-track in parallel lines, with blinders. Psychologists who have viewed the indigenousness of Indian-documented data have indicated that the shift away from western conceptualisation has been clearly indicated in the research done in certain areas. Besides the relevance of conceptualisation in its socio-historicity, the role of contextual factors is an important theme. These factors are from the specific ecological context as influenced by the habitat (Bronfenbrenner, 1979). These variables vary within and among themselves, in depth and in degree, to the extent that they are reliable and valid indices.

How have such theories and their relevant concepts developed? In the next chapter, we will give a brief idea of the history of how the study of the child, which enlarged to human development, came into prominence. As in the West, reflections on development as to its origin, began with man's reflections in philosophy (Comte, 1988: 70). In the Indian situation, the rich heritage of Hindu philosophy and its interpretations by sages has laid the background for human development. The early history of science in India began with Vedas and Vedantas. 'The six Vedas deal with *kalpa*, performance of ritual with its basis of geometry, mathematics and calendrics; *siksa*, phonetics; *chandas*, metrical structures; *nirukta*, etymology; and *jyotisa*, astronomy and other cyclical phenomena' (Kak, 2000: 83–107). However, Indian philosophy did not have its reflection in the science of behaviour because it stopped at the spiritual and philosophical level, while the world of education in India continued on the knowledge obtained from the West. We are indebted to the West for information about the development of scientific disciplines, where they are being increasingly expanded due to newer forms of research in the technological era. However, to be based in social realities, research needs to reflect the Indian ethos to understand development in its milieu. The theories, their bases and their development, derived from the West, will be discussed in Volume II. The examples are derived partially form western frames, with an attempt to correlate them with the Indian frames of culture, ecology and the socialisation ethos. Just as changes in the sociological frame affect human development, so also geo-ecological frames affect the lives of people, especially in times of war, natural disasters and man-made deleterious phenomena, such as pollution and depletion of the ozone layer.

Contributions of Indian Philosophy to Information on Human Development

Vedic literature which includes the sum and substance of how a human being should live, can be dated to the 3rd or 4th centuries BC, or even earlier. In 1949, P.C. Sengupta attempted to chronologically date the Brahmanas, Sutras and other Vedic literature (quoted in Kak, 2000: 84). A comparison is made between self and self-identity by an illustration of a chariot being driven by the self and pulled by horses (different senses). Next to the driver sits the true observer, the eternal reality (ibid.: 84–85). It is interesting to note the parallelism between this interpretation of the mind which is the self and its identity to psychoanalytic theory with its fundamentals of the ego (the driver), the id (the horses) and the superego (the supreme observer). If we take the illustration a little further, it can be seen that several other theories match in some area or the other with the Vedic concepts of how man should behave. The concept of dharma, for instance, relates to morality and differs very little from Kolhberg's theory of morality (Kohlberg, 1969: 347–480). The *samskaras* (the fourfold stages called *ashrama*s in the life of a Hindu) are very much akin to the categories of the stages of man in Erikson's theory, except that the former details practices and the latter interprets behaviour in psychological terms. These ashramas are (*a*) *brahmacharya* (stage of learning and strict celibacy), (*b*) *grihastha* (stage of householder's life), (*c*) *vanaprastha* (stage of relative withdrawal to exclusive pursuit of moral and spiritual goals without leaving the family) and (*d*) *sanyas* (stage of complete withdrawal from affective-particularistic social obligations, and devotion to pursuit of spiritual values and its propagation in society) (Singh, 1977: 34; Bhattacharya, 1996: 305).

From the time of ancient India where spirituality was aligned to philosophy, it was perceived by academicians as a part of the processes of thought and behaviour. The theory of *guna* in Hindu cultural tradition gives a systematic foundation of the principles of charismatic recognition. This quality of charisma is in caste hierarchy and kinship hierarchy. The gunas or charismatic qualities are conceived on the principle of hierarchical levels. *Satva*, the quality of brightness and virtue, is considered the highest and the most desired level and is usually attributed to sages and Brahmins (Gould, 1987). Next in the hierarchical level is the *raja*s, the charismatic quality of passionate commitment to action attributed to Kshatriyas and kings; *tamas*, which represents innate endowment of dependency and ignorance attributed to the Shudras; while the Vaishyas (the traders) are positioned between the Kshatriyas and Shudras. The Vedic literature also talks about goal orientation. These are at different levels of increasing merit: relating to material goals of *kama* (pleasure) and *artha* (wealth); dharma, the goal of moral obligations; and moksha, the pursuit of salvation, which has a meta-social significance. These goal orientations seem to be similar in interpretations from western theoretical domains.

One of the major thrusts of Indian academicians is to 'outgrow the western approach' (Sinha, 1980) where a hermeneutic or alternative interpretation may be incorporated in analysing human thinking and behaviour, relevant to the conduct of the Indian society (Moore, 1989: 26–48). Such alternative interpretations can add to the richness of already existent knowledge (Powell et al., 1991). The richness of Indian philosophical thinking arises from rethinking about the place of the self, the *atman*. 'The atman is the vital essence of man, is the same in the ant, the same in the gnat, the same in the elephant, the same in the three worlds and the same in the whole universe' (Yati, 2000: I, 3, 22[c.]). The concept of karma underlined the Hindu attitude towards life and daily conduct (*purushartha*). The concepts of duty, rightness and virtue were embodied in the major overriding concept of dharma. However, man is not debarred from seeking material wealth (artha) or from seeking of pleasure (kama) and finally, the injunction of renunciation in order to devote oneself to religious or spiritual activities with the aim of gaining freedom from this finite world (moksha). If one looks at these concepts through the hermeneutic approach, the resemblance to the concepts of moral development (Misra, 1991: 179–94), the concept of justice (Misra and Mishra, 1989) and achievement motivation (Fyans et al., 1983: 1000–13) is seen in the spiritual injunctions of other scriptures like the Bible, the Torah, and the Guru Granth Sahib. Yoga was and still is a system of knowledge as well as a system of practical training for the well-being of the mental and physical states of man (Mukerji, 1981). Therefore, it goes far beyond theorising into idiographic empiricism (Pandey, 1972). Apparently, restitution and compromise were the two advocated actions of man towards man and nature, implying, besides others, the influence of ecology on man and vice versa. Ayurveda emphasises the three *dosha*s or causes of illness: *vaata* (related to the intake of excessive air or its production in the digestive tract), *pitta* (related to the liver functions) and *kapha* (related to the lung functions) (Kak, 2000: 83–107). These are the cues by which Ayurveda recognises that there are distinct personalities based on these on a consistent basis: namely, persons who suffer from liver complaints (pitta), persons who suffer from indigestion (vaata) and persons who suffer from coughs and colds (kapha). Gunas (satva, rajas, tamas) are constitutional psychological predispositions or 'temperament', also expressed in developmental psychology within their parameters (Kapur et al., 1997: 171–77). Also explicit are the ashramas connoting the early stages of the child's development. These are similar to the different chronological stages of development as expressed in western psychology.

Since the spirituality of the individual is a part of his identity, it has a strong influence on thinking and behavioural processes. Concepts like karma, dharma, *kalyug* and *rahukaal* (inauspicious time) are all familiar idiomatic expressions used in everyday communication. The Vedic and post-Vedic periods made references to social relationships, earlier than 1500 BC. These references revolved around dharma first mentioned in the Rig Veda elaborated in Gautam's Dharmashastra about 600 BC (Dalal and Misra, 2002b: 22). The psychophysical concept of dharma has stood steadfast during all the years of Hinduism, up to date. According to Kakar, dharma is an inherent force in human being which holds the individual and his society together. It is part of the broader cycle of Hindu theory of life cycle and changes (ashrama dharma). Dharma is considered both a process and mechanism of social integration to maintain harmonious relations within a society (Kakar, 1979). Compromise and coexistence are at the heart of the concept of dharma. Further, the Ramayana and the Mahabharata are intensive and extensive theses on the tri-cycle relations among man and man; man and nature; and the reciprocity of nature towards man. The theme of ecological homogeneity which is stressed in these principles is that all are existentially expected to share the same energy available in the cosmos. From these concepts we can observe the implications of the scientific logic of nature and nurture, and the influence of the environment on man's behaviour, as expounded by social psychology, ecology and anthropology. Within the parameters of the concepts of dharma and karma, we also see a similarity to the psycho-analytical concepts. These concepts are the 'ego' akin to the self, 'superego' akin to the teaching of the godheads and 'libido' akin to kama. The psychological concepts of rationality and rational thinking are also reflected in dharma as it deals with righteous social conduct. Indian thought is, therefore, context-sensitive, as illustrated in the Mahabharata, the Ramayana and folk tales (Shweder, 1990: 1–42). Their major emphasis is living together in harmony, not different from the concepts of *ahimsa* and secularism of today. The *grama* (village) is focussed on unity, which is explicitly for community well-being (Murti, 1955).

The Vedas expound six philosophies, based on contemplated approaches to life, and contained (according to A. Gupta) a theory about the universe. Gupta argues that Hindu philosophy is ingrained in the Hindu mind and might explain that in spite of the multiple representation of gods and goddesses, Hindus believe that there is one Supreme Being and that these different forms represent different attributes of the godheads (*avatars*). Gupta also states that there is non-duality in the meaning of life. She maintains that Indian philosophy is not just a philosophy as interpreted in the western context, but is a synthesis of various streams like religion, psychology, education, ethics, political thinking, social thought, and so forth (Gupta, 2006: 26).

In the social organisation of a community in which these concepts were practised, the governance by the *panchayat* also existed from the days of the Hindu dynasties. In its modified form, the panchayat continues to be the core of rural development/community participation. These role performances were recognised in the scriptures by the expectation and performance of one's duties, similar to social psychology of role perception and role performance in varying ecologies, given the cultural pluralism in the Indian context. These communities vary from Aryans to Dravidians; from the people of the north-east who are more like the Tibetans than the average Indian, to the Keralites whose lifestyles in terms of human ecology are very much like that of the Sri Lankans; and yet all are Indians, and subscribe to the composite Indianness (Schweder et al., 2006). The worldview is conceived as composed of antithesis: good/bad, and so on. The negative and positive attributes of the object represent an interconnected view of all things related to all other in the last analysis, as similar to quantum physics (Capra, 1983). Temporality of 'being' is related to time and space (Misra, 1971: 363–73). History and social reality were conceived as part of an explanation of man's behaviour, as it continued from one generation to another, assuming dynamic forms at every generational period. In Indian thought much emphasis is placed on the use of intuition as the major analytic form of one's behaviour according to social standards (Pandey, 1984). The belief exists that human beings are also experiencers: (*bhokta*), besides being doers (*kartas*) (Paranjpe, 1984). Paranjpe gave a vedantic model of *jiva* (living self). As in Bronfenbrenner's ecosystems, the inner self here consists of five concentric layers. These are food or the physiological support of living (*annamaya kosa*), the need for air (*pranamaya kosa*), the need for activity of the mind (*manomaya kosa*), the ability to formulate cognitive concepts (*vijnanamaya kosa*) and the ability to be happy and content and attain an equilibrium in harmony with those around (*anandmaya kosa*) (Paranjpe, 1988: 185–213). We see from the interlinkages of concepts that the most essential aspects of the co-harmony of the mind and body are related. The displacement in any one of the *kosa*s leads to an imbalance in equilibrium of the cosmic energy that humans share with others. This is not too dissimilar from the western conceptualisations of the relationship between the mind and body in order to create a harmonious equilibrium.

The interferences with the state of equilibrium are due to the continuous and dynamic interaction of the three gunas: tamas or inertia; rajas or energy; satva or reason. If according to karma all actions have consequences, then the dominance of any one of those actions causes instability, which then causes the self to reorganise towards stability. In the interim, experiences of confusion, indecisiveness and conflict occur. Human beings are always striving to find a balance. When the jiva is dominated by inertia (tamas), there is a lack of progress or advancement and the human is not motivated to use his full potential. When the jiva is dominated by rajas or energy, there is a tendency to accumulate more to oneself at the expense of others. When the jiva is dominated by satva, the self pursues affairs of the mind to the detriment of the needs of his physical well-being. The moral discourse of Manu, Gautam and Yagyavalka of the Vedic period and Kautilya of the post-Vedic period are not dissimilar from the philosophies of the Greek philosophers in the West (Dalal and Misra, 2002b: 21)

Social Psychological Implications for the Indian Psyche

Social psychology is a branch of study that is closely related to the psychophysical interpretation of man and his environment in nature. Social psychology, therefore, in the academic context, straddles the bridge between pure psychology and pure sociology. Thus, social psychology like cultural sociology, social anthropology and social demography delves into more complex and intricate analyses of man's behaviour in relation to his environment (in a generic sense) and vice versa. This is unlike the single target of looking at social structures and social relationships in pure sociology. Cross-discipline areas of domain in psychology occurred in the late 1970s. It has gathered momentum since. Psychology has fissioned out into social pyschology, psychoanthropology, individual psychology, group psychology and is now moving further still into areas of economics, by examining leadership roles and management, productivity and efficiency, and similar economic variables which influence behaviour. However, from the foregoing analysis of sources of information in Vedic literature, we find the strong underscoring of philosophical thought (Mukherji, 2000). Such areas of cross-discipline concerns are, for instance, social realities (Sinha, 1982: 148–60), economic deprivation (Tripathi and Misra, 1975: 54–61) and interactive behaviour in little traditions (Marriot, 1976: 109–42).

It was only in the 1950s that a spurt occurred moving away from mundane laboratory animal experiments to the outer world of psychosociology in the area of social cognition (Ramakrishna, 1984: 1–8). Thematic research was in areas like interpersonal perception, attitudes, achievement and various areas of relationships to cognition extrapolated to human beings. Surveys of available research began in 1971. Among the researches, social and cultural processes, followed by attitudes/opinions and prejudices were seemingly most popular (Rath, 1972: 362–413; Sharma and Anandalakshmy, 1981: 10–16). Studies on equity, social justice and achievement motivation have used culturally toned indigenous constructs to arrive at findings that indicate the social milieu as a stronger influence than individualism. This is in contrast to the individualised achievement orientation of the West (Misra and Agarwal, 1985).

The Multidisciplinary Nature of Development: The Holistic Parameters

Our knowledge of human development increases in proportion to the research findings. For instance, anthropology gives us the idiographic method to study children on an individual basis, and the ethnographic method to study small groups in their habitats. Psychology gives us the psychometric methods by which groups are studied and their averages taken as an index of the group norm. Sociology gives us concepts on the structure, and influences of societies and their groups on the socialisation process. Physiology tells us about the relationship between physical health, cognitive processes and mental normalcy and, especially in the context of India, the role of nutrition in the growing years as it affects mental health (Cravioto et al., 1966: 319–72). Economics gives us concepts on deprivation. Politics gives information on how societies are managed, what are social and normative patterns of societal behaviour, laws and their implementation, and the effects of the political instability/stability on human development (UNDP, 2004).

Not all these disciplines have the same profile of research information in the Indian situation. Perhaps, the most profiled is psychology, both from the experimental and the ethnographic perspectives. The most relevant to development is the discipline of psychology, more especially developmental psychology, which is often treated synonymously with child development (Saraswathi and Dutta, 1987b). Developmental psychology has also become synonymous with human development, and is broadly operationalised in various side fields, such as the use of constructs in individual psychology, social anthropology, cross-cultural psychology, group psychology, and such like. It offers concepts about the construct of themes, the formation of ideas, the effects of nature and nurture, learning processes, memory and related process of conditioned and non-conditioned expressed behaviour. J. Pandey, who has edited three volumes on *Psychology in India Revisited*, has collated a valuable collection of studies in areas of importance to Indian psychology. These contain among others: studies on perception, language, intelligence, deprivation, and so on, which are useful sources for understanding Indian development and behaviour (Pandey, 2004).

The reader has been made aware that the thinking and acting processes originate from the physiological system. The brain is involved in the development of chromosomes and the functioning of hormones. Abnormalities lead to differentiation in patterns of behaviour. Such information has been provided for instance by Young et al., (2003), A.K. Raina et al., (2000) and several others, who have attempted to correlate different fields of interest to try and provide a forum for the understanding of human development in the Indian context. Suffice it to say, having in the foregone paragraphs given much stress to the physiological basis, we have proceeded to look at the contributions from the social sciences which assist us in understanding development. We will look briefly at the major relevant disciplines of psychology, sociology and anthropology, in terms of their major ideas included in this volume.

The Significance of Psychology in the Developmental Process

Psychology is the basis of concepts on development. From the time of conception, the child's brain evolves till it is mature, leading to our understanding of stimulus response theory as a generic theory to subtheories of conditioning theory, Gestalt theory, learning theories, theory of differences, and to their subcategories of motivation, achievement, intelligence, reward and punishment. We also observe a fine line of hierarchical structures linking the postulates of one theory to another.

Let us take the concept of maturity. Maturity is linearly related to chronological age as seen, for instance, in Piaget's thesis relating progressive cognitive development to chronological stages. A child of two should be able to coordinate eye and hand in completion of tasks appropriate to the age. What then is appropriate age? Studies done on completion task tests, show how groups of children of age two, when tested or observed, are able to throw and catch a ball with the eye and hand in synchronisation. They do so in a coordinated fashion in such a way that the eye perceives the flight of the ball, judges distances and impels the hand to move forward at the right or wrong time to catch or drop the ball (perception theory) (Mishra, 2000). But we do know that practice makes perfect, so that on repeated trials, the learning theorists tell us, the child should be successful more times than not in catching the ball. From a study of groups of children, we have a framework of what is called developmental tasks at each stage of development, concepts developed by several psychologists (Havighurst, 1953). Besides measuring physical tasks by age (Malhotra, 2002c: 70), psychologists have adapted/ adopted or used locally constructed measures to assess such constructs, like the Indian adaptations of Weschler Intelligence Scale for Children (WISC) and Malin's Intelligence Scale for Indian Children (MISIC) (Saraswathi and Dutta, 1987a). Research has provided empirical data on language development (Mohanty, 2000: 208–56) and intelligence (Das and Thapa, 2000: 151–207) and other such traits. These give us empirical data on behaviour, performance behaviour and, with the use of statistics, averages and deviations, from which normally expected behaviour is deduced. These concepts are tools for assessing general and specific performance/abilities.

However, differential psychology tells us that although averages may be expected, there are exceptions to the rule. More recently, for a holistic picture, the phenomenon of the physical quality of life is being examined in relation to individual differences in the following domains: social, psychological, emotional, and sub-domains like independence, social relationships and environmental influences (Holtzman, 1992: 3–18). There are gifted children who normally perform above the average, and there are children in need of special care who normally perform below the average, and exhibit various forms of mental disability. These disabilities have been assessed in the Indian situation mainly by clinical psychologists using measurements adapted from the West.

S. Malhotra has given a list of a series of such tests in her analysis of child psychiatry (Malhotra, 2002c: 66–67). Theological derivatives in the Indian context, such as values of morality and cooperation, are mainly from the socio-psychological nexus of traditionally communicated thinking and its correlative behaviour. They are derived from the scriptures, whether it is Hinduism and its derivatives, or Islam and its derivate Sufism (Kao and Yang, 1991). It is important here to state that there is a unique form of Indianism that prevails irrespective of core religious preachings (Madan, 1992: 394–409). Each religious group respects and enters into the spirit of the celebrations of other religions; the sages from religions who have attained a superior place in their context are venerated by members of other religions, like Khwaja Moin-ud-din Chisti, Sai Baba of Shirdi, and so on.

Only recently have experts in the discipline been emphasising the need for indigenisation of the subject, so as to make it relevant to the social realties of the Indian psyche (Dalal, 1996: 1–41). Therefore, while the common characteristics of the human phylogenetic traits are shared by all humans, the way a society or culture moulds thinking and behaviour is different from others.

These specifics in the Indian context have some empiricism to afford a rational beginning on development, credible and valid for Indian society (Kakar, 1982; Marriot, 1990; Misra, 1988: 16–21; Mistry and Saraswathi, 2003: 267–91; Paranjpe et al., 1988; Sinha, 1997: 129–69).

One of the first specialisations in psychology that contributed to an understanding of human development is the psychology of the child. Child psychology uses concepts of general psychology (Saraswathi, 2003a: 125–37), differential psychology, socio-psychology, behavioural psychology and other strands of general psychology. While we will deal in detail with the various significant theorists in Volume II, we must mention here a few of the outstanding theorists of the West who in studying early childhood have contributed much to our understanding of the basics of psychological development. They are E.H. Erikson (1950), S. Freud (1935), F. Heider (1958), C.L. Hull (1945), I.P. Pavlov (1927), J. Piaget (1929), B.F. Skinner (1950) and L.S. Vygotsky (1962). Hull, in dealing with the major criteria of development, also mentions that the system of delayed gratification is an important concept in learning. This behaviour of waiting is a very important phase in the learning process. It means that the growing individual learns to condition his first reaction to delaying his own gratification so that he is in line with socially approved behaviour. In this way he learns coping mechanisms leading to competence in adjusting to the human environment, by adjusting his own responses. These types of conditioned responses are evident in the typical Indian child, during his interactions with his family members. We make mention here of Inhelder and Piaget (1958) for their contribution to cognitive theory. They have, in the course of their theorising on the stages of development from the sensory motor to the abstract conceptualisation stage, emphasised that the concept of experiences in the human species is common to all. However, there are differences in particular learned experiences which make one individual different from another. The self is categorised as familial (Roland, 1987). They, thus, underscore the 'nature and nurture' contributions to development, as being parts of the whole process. However, in looking critically at these concepts, it has been observed that heredity cannot be satisfactorily separated from the environment. In fact, it usually overlaps with developmental psychology, as each explains the same phenomenon, but from different perspectives (Furth, 1973: 61–67). While child psychology has a limited age coverage, developmental psychology covers the whole lifespan, or the eight stages of man as Shakespeare puts it, and according to the Dharmashastras, the stages of life (samskaras) (Kane, 1941).

Differential psychology is perhaps the most widely used for distinguishing individual behaviour from normative group behaviour through tests and measurements. These are useful tools in clinical psychology and in academic guidance and counselling (Malhotra and Kohli, 1995). It is valuable in understanding how a child differs from other children, when his background and environment are the same or similar, but where performances are different. In this context, differential psychology is high-profiled. It is an important branch of developmental psychology, for it helps identify the individual child's attributes as distinct from others in his socio-economic class, religion and ethnicity.

The branch of educational psychology concentrates on how a child learns, what helps a child learn better, or find out motivational levels, levels of aspirations, vocational choices, and such like, which are used extensively in the educational field (Jonassen and Grabowski, 1993). This branch integrates concepts of difference and not deficits. Its area of psychometrics has its focus on the teaching–learning situation, exploring major parameters, such as positive/negative reinforcement, conditioned stimulus response, the role of reward (for example, recognition for passing class levels successfully) and the role of punishment (negative reinforcement, such as withdrawal of approval). These factors are contingent on self-image/esteem, and resolution of conflict, anxiety and guilt, which are critical psychological aspects, especially during the school years (Eysenck, 1947).

A further branch of psychology, which comes under the ambit of developmental psychology, is clinical psychology. This studies the individual's non-normative (non-normal or deviant) behaviour. It also relates to children with special needs (mental disability, psychosomatic disorders, deviancy from norms, psychiatric disorders, and curative and/or preventive measures). It also takes into consideration the role of the informed adult/counsellor/psychiatrist in interaction with children with special needs (Malhotra, 1995). Its principles and content form the basis for helping children who are socially and mentally non-normative. In the Indian situation, since the emphasis is on the normal child, there is limited and scattered published information on non-normal behaviour and its correlates. We have observed that there are various groups and their subgroups of disciplines contributing to human development as an amalgamation. In particular, this assumes importance given the unique features of the large population. Its various classifications, fissions and fusions such as ethnicity, caste and subcastes underlie the processes by which the human being is reared and from which habits, attitudes and lasting values are inculcated from early childhood (Tandon, 1981).

The Fundamental Importance of Sociology in the Development Process

Comte is considered to be the father of sociology. He brought together several types of concepts under the umbrella of sociology to mean the study of man in his society (Starton, 1936).

The conceptualisations adopted in the early documentation by Indian scholars followed the constructs dictated by the West in Merton's theoretical sociology (Merton, 1867b: 171), in Levy's structure of society (Levy, 1953) and the early classical theorising of Dumont and his colleagues (Dumont, 1970). These western sociologists proposed the rules of methodology, which are basic to understanding social phenomena.

Thus, by far, most of the knowledge that is contextual about the development of the individual in India is gained from the field of sociology. As such, its texture and fabric interweave in all walks of life and in the major differentiating variables of caste, class, ethnicity and regionality. Sociology is perhaps the first discipline of social sciences which undertook to study the Indian *in situ*. Such western experts as Weber, Durkheim, Cohen and Cooley, mentioned in Merton's classic writing (Merton, 1867b), dealt with the conceptualisations they were familiar with in the West, and analysed generalisations and universals. In the early 19th century, a breakthrough was made by outstanding scholars like Marriot (1955), Mencher (1970: 197–216), Mazumdar (1958), Hitchkock and Minturn (1956), Srinivas (1966), Singh (1973), Gore and Dube, to mention a few. These scholars explored the sociological background of the Indian on a scale larger than that available in small case studies of little communities to indicate the tangential effect of conceptualisations drawn from the West. Using their observations in field situations, they attempted to derive indigenous constructs valid in the Indian situation, which brought into relief the meaning of social reality in the Indian context (Moghadam, 1987: 912–20). Even so, the piecemeal information gathered cursorily from time to time lacked a common thread of constructs which if strung together could have made a logistic whole of continuity, since these were small scattered studies of 'little communities'. As Beteille commented in his treatise on a sociological perspective, there should be stress on hypothesis derivation on the present and future, rather than an overzealous preoccupation with the past (Beteille, 1991). It would be well to consider the suggestion by Beteille that there is need for more field work in contiguous areas of ecologies, so as to present a comprehensive linking picture of the sociological aspects, contributing to valid theories of development in the Indian context. As yet we have not dealt with the whole spectrum of the issues and problems facing the arena of childhood. For example, establishing an interface between research in child development and its policy implications has to be fully explored (Saraswathi, 1993b: 29–31). Prout and James (1990) in the western context have suggested a new paradigm for the sociology of childhood (Prout and James, 1990: 7–35). Early stalwarts in the area of studying childhood in India are S. Kakar (1968), D. Sinha (1986), G. Misra (2003), T.S. Saraswathi and others who have scanned the field of social psychology, cultural psychology and psychoanalysis to attempt to bring in a perspective on human development. M.S. Gore (2000b) in his review of sociology and anthropology has given a compendium of newer sociological writings, such as those of E. Asirvatham (1960: 123–30), P.D. Kulkarni (1964: 193–200), S.N. Agarwala (1965: 118–25), A. Bose et al. (1970) and M.S. Gore (2003). From a sociological perspective, Hinduism is a secular philosophical religion that is open to interpretations for human developmental aspects. This percolates down to the Hindu individual in his acceptance of friends being Muslim, Christian, Sikh or Jain, and in observing no distinctions in secular spaces such as the classroom, the office and public meetings. Because of their disadvantaged position in society, and the political will to protect their opportunities, the government has reservations for lower/deprived classes (Upadhyay, 1992) which then heightens the self-image of the underprivileged child, enabling him, for example, to be able to afford education in the same classroom situation as an upper-class child. Adherence to the principles of caste is a high-profiled sociological variable, insidiously affecting societal behaviour based on discriminatory beliefs such as purity and pollution (Gupta, 2000). The original intent was to allocate categories of tasks to different groups so as to harmonise the organisation of a community. Gradually this division became wedges of discriminatory relations. Gandhiji began a movement so that the untouchables, the Harijans, at the bottom of the rung of the social structure would not be shunned in societal structures and institutions (Gandhi, 1927).

Demographic variables which differentiate statuses on the basis of age, sex and similar variables, when utilised, do not present the total picture of differences. However, these need to be examined *in situ* for variations that may occur. Sociological studies, discussions and treatises emphasised the norms for patriarchy, family, kinship relations and societal relationships through the dimensions of role expectations and role performances by age and by sex. However, in the changing socio-technological era and the impact of global trade and mobility, these structures are fast rearranging themselves in different permutations and combinations. Modernisation has, therefore, affected the form of social institutions/structures from somewhat static forms to increasingly dynamic forms in the 21st century (Panda and Das, 1970: 267–73). Therefore, information on sociology describes conceptualisations of the past with those evolving over time and space (Deshpande, 2003). Sociology, coupled inextricably with psychology, like the proverbial Siamese twin syndrome, is of utmost importance to the understanding of the facets of family, kinship and societal structure in the Indian context (Srinivas, 1966). The intertwining of these two disciplines has been recognised by psychologists, who have introduced a relatively new field in their explorations of human development. Such expert writings are by academicians like T.S. Saraswathi (1999), Durganand Sinha (1997), G. Mishra (2003), A.C. Paranjpe (1988), S. Kakar (2002), A.K. Dalal, R.C. Tripathi (2001) and Janak Pandey (Saraswathi, 2003b), who have advocated a wider socio-psychological perspective on human development in the Indian context.

If one views the subsystems operating on the individual during the developing period from childhood to adulthood, one of the major systems is human ecology (Bronfenbrenner, 1993: 3–44). Human ecology, according to Bronfenbrenner's perspective, is the hierarchical dynamism of interaction from the micro-system (the family), to the meso-system (kinship, neighbourhood, peers), to the exo-system (the institutions of civic amenities like banks, stations and marketplaces, where the individual interacts with others in this system), and finally to the wider world of the macro-system (with which the individual rarely comes in contact, perhaps only through media and literature, such as other nations, ecologies and foreign institutions). Such a model is parallel to Lewinian field theory, which assumes a field theory of stronger versus weaker forces that impinge upon the individual (Lewin, 1935). In the centre of Lewin's perceptual field of forces is the core and in concentric circles one arrives at the periphery. Therefore, both Bronfenbrenner and Lewin emphasise proximal and distal influential variables such that the distal have less interactive power than the proximal. These analogies serve to look at different pathways advocated by different experts which converge on the fact that the individual is the centre of psychological, sociological and psychosociological models. To give an example, in the interaction of a father and a son about the son's future choice of occupation, there is dynamic interaction between the two in their forces of communication. This is an example of the micro-system. This situation can be enlarged to those in the exo-system, where executives meet to make decisions. Such conceptualisation leads onto another branch of behaviour called organisational behaviour, which is much used in the professional world (Kanungo, 2004).

As such those individuals who have internalised the values of the systems, perform according to expectations, and are therefore judged as 'good' children/adults/citizens. There have been varied attempts during the past two decades to include these models in the cultural framework of social psychologists, as documented by, among others, Berry et al. (2003), Dalal and Misra (2002a), Kao and Sinha (1997) and Saraswathi (2003b). There have been valuable contributions in the areas of perception, intelligence and language by R.C. Mishra (2002: 94–150), J.P. Das and K. Thapa (2000: 151–207), and A.K. Mohanty (2000: 208–55). These authors have collated discussions and empirical data as available in the latter quarter of the 20th century.

These conceptualisations have been viewed against prevailing social norms in order to understand their paradigmatic relationships (Maslow, 1943: 370–96). In Maslow's theorising, he moves from the dynamics of primary to secondary needs and their fulfilment through the human environmental systems. In the Indian situation, studies on needs have been viewed from a few domains like need-achievement, need-affiliation, need-dependency, and so on (Kakar, 2002: 132–40; Dalal and Misra, 2002b: 19–49; Paranjpe and Bhat, 1997: 127–43; Sinha, 1997: 218–35). These psychosocial needs have yet to be examined through adequate empirical studies. It stands to reason that since the primary needs are for basic need gratification, such as the need for food, for clothing and for shelter, these are significant to the Indian who lives in scarce subsistence ecologies, and where famine and floods threaten to destabilise his ecology which provides him with sustenance (Berry, 1979: 177–206).

Anthropological Contributions to Sources of Information

A little history of anthropology could serve to understand the setting of anthropological trends in sourcing information on human development. Anthropology as a discipline emerged in the late 19th century and became established in the 20th century. Two major landmarks associated with its inception are: Darwin's theory of evolution of species that all human beings have evolved from the same stock (Darwin, 1859), which gave rise to the study of the structure of society that was labelled as anthropology. The second landmark was the view on the colonised by the coloniser. A large number of anthropologists were employed by the colonisers in India to understand the 'native mind' so as to help them rule more effectively. The surveys and ethnographic studies in the colonial period led to the separation of sociology from anthropology (Hussain, 1982).

Anthropology was considered esoteric and abstract theorising, and was, therefore, limited to the study of underdeveloped communities considered as primitive, uncivilised groups such as the colonised in several geo-ecological areas. These people were considered as curious interesting species to be studied as a part of anthropology, or, at best, as social anthropology including theories in the psychoanalytic frame (Hartnack, 1987: 233–53). British anthropologists who brought anthropology as a discipline to India confined their study to universities. They advocated that their concepts and methods used to study western societies could not be applied to the study of 'natives'.

In the study of anthropology, the primacy of the species was very evident in the viewpoint of Darwin (1859). However, in their anthropological studies, B. Malinowski (1948), A.R. Radcliffe-Brown (1929) and M. Mead (1964) widened the scope to include structures, institutions and methodological concepts (Merton, 1948). In the 1960s, anthropology developed three major schools: symbolic anthropology, cultural ecology and structuralism (Lévi-Strauss, 1963), and these promptly got reflected in the teachings of anthropology in India.

However in the already existent disciplines of psychology and sociology, cultural anthropology and cultural sociology were becoming more profiled. The initial steps taken in India were introduced by the early sociologists such as Marriot (1976: 109–42), Mukherjee (1977: 38–59), Singh (1988: 159–233) and Srinivas (1993: 933–38) who began to break away form the colonial trend of viewing India as only composed of castes.

Anthropology also included the study of the family, the kin group and the community, within its parameters of study. The holistic approach to studying tribal communities and small caste or ethnic groups also reflected development patterns. Qualitative behaviour through ethnographic or idiographic methods became the material of anthropology. They reflected traditions such as myths, folklore, superstitions and social/cultural group behaviour in little 'traditions'/communities. Incidentally, sociologists who studied little communities provided *in situ* observation of traditional village communities for anthropology (Keyes and Daniel, 1983). These analyses offered deep insights into the contingent variables affecting behaviour, in intensive interaction of observers living in the groups studied. These formed the material for building up hypotheses, as in the study *Mothers of Six Cultures* by Minturn and Lambert (1964). Such studies facilitated the understandingof the relationship between culture and society (Dasen and Mishra, 2000: 428–34).

Following Darwin's theory of the survival of the fittest, anthropologists in the West fanned out to study behaviour in elementary groups so as to provide insights into concepts of behaviour arising from the Darwinian principle. Such anthropologists travelled to deep Africa, South Pacific islands and internal terrains of South East Asia to study tribes, and, therefore, came into Indian interiors. One reason for the separation of sociology from anthropology was that, conceptualisations in the latter were non-western in connotation, since there was an ethnocentric ecocharacteristic to the patterns of living of the inhabitants. Social anthropology focussed on descriptive living patterns, while sociology concentrated on structures, institutions and systems. In the growing awareness of the influence of science and technology, the concept of 'survival of the fittest' was replaced by 'functionalism'. Additive areas like 'cultural relativism', 'acculturation' and 'cultural assimilation' were also studied, and became extensions of anthropology.

Anthropologists in India began looking for new methodologies using these approaches, which provided data for hypothesis-building. Ontogenetic skills, skills for survival, beliefs and values were profiled for providing such data. Thus, anthropology consciously and unconsciously did serve the functionality of the society, through a series of relative studies. Mead (1964) and Benedict (1938: 161–67) were among the first to view living patterns as being differential in content, but universal in intent. It was accepted that human beings, being of a higher order, used intelligent behaviour to nurture their young and so ordered their lives along geo-ecological influences of their habitats (Bruner and Cole, 1976: 165–80; Goodnow, 1976: 97–111).

It is a well-known truism that all societies rear their young to maturity. In India, this anthropological concept found fertile ground for studies on child-rearing, traditions and practices of small communities like Bhils (Nath, 1960), Akas (Sinha, 1962), Yanadis (Raghaviah, 1962), Grasias (Dave, 1960), Lodhas (Ray, 1965), Shikligars (Sher Singh Sher, 1966), Mala Ulladan (Nandi et al., 1971), Murias (Elwin, 1947), Padam Minyong (Roy, 1960) and Oraons (Das and Raha, 1963). Indian folktales, myths and mythologies were also used to explain group behaviour. Starting in the colonial period, departments of anthropology, both at the university level and in the government, came into being to study tribal life in India, especially childcare (Naik, 1971). While activists like the NGOs believe that the tribes should be rehabilitated in their own ecologies, the government felt that they should be integrated into the general population. Over the years, therefore, studies on change have become a popular area of enquiry into how tribes change their lifestyles, like S.L. Doshi's study of the Bhils in relation to their synthesis into the mainstream of society (Doshi, 1971). There ensued studies on naturally migrating groups of tribals (Ray, 1972: 1–24). Conceptualisations that arose from such studies revealed that these migrants considered themselves 'as transients' and they experienced a nostalgia about their original habitats. The result was that productive men left their families for temporary work in urban areas, with their roots in the original place of habitat. The attraction of studying culture in both psychology and social psychology motivated the experts to move into the area of study of small group behaviour. This gave an impetus to cultural anthropology.

It is obvious, therefore, that these three disciplines were moving towards looking at culture, namely, the same phenomenon, but from the standpoint of their own parameters. Thus, for instance, cultural anthropology served a useful basis for understanding context-specific societies which had their own modes of functionality as structural systems (Pandey, 1972). Like elsewhere, India has its own progressive levels of quality of life in its movement towards a scientific way of life. It uses the tools of technology to sustain and improve its patterns. In India, there exist various subcultures that are sufficient unto themselves, as they use the functionality of their environment to sustain their patterns (Anandalakshmy and Bajaj, 1981). Ecology, therefore, is an important concept, which has yet to be fully reflected in conceptual terms in anthropology and sociology. Such little traditions as the nomadic tribes of the Thar desert and the hill tribes like the Paharis of the upper mountains of the Himalayas form fruitful areas of study for providing conceptual frames (Beremann, 1963: 289–304).

Thus, cultural anthropology, with which human development is concerned, developed alongside with symbolic anthropology and structuralism (Ortner, 1984: 126–66). In his discussion on the future of anthropology, V.K. Srivastava (1999: 545–52) looks critically at the utility of anthropology, as anthropologists feel that the future of anthropology is incumbent upon its immediate market value. The author states that the future of anthropology can be enhanced by giving primacy to an interpretive understanding of societies and cultures, useful to policies and programmes for development (Giddens, 1996). To date, anthropology in India exists in a multicultural milieu, which demands newer forms of inventiveness and subtlety (Clifford, 1986: 1–26). The implication is that, in this era of postmodernity and globalisation, the task of anthropologists should also be prediction-oriented (in the form of hypotheses) for future channels to the understanding of the human in his milieu. Such far-seeing anthropologists, also advocate a holistic approach to the various subdivisions of anthropology, and its dynamic parameters—archaeological, physical, cultural and psychosocial—so as not to fragment the concepts of development in its interpretation. It is also essential to bridge the gap between anthropology and the physical sciences (Radcliffe-Brown, 1948). As such this means that anthropology should look at the facets of psychological dimensions of psychosociology, of cultural relativity and of culture assimilation and adaptation, in addressing its anthropological issues. In fact, anthropologists should enhance their exploration of linkages between anthropology and the traditional Indian medical systems. This is a fruitful source of information, for instance, on the concept of illness in traditional Indian society (Joshi and Mahajan, 1990).

This is not to say that there has been no cognisance of this lacuna. Several anthropological studies have examined communities in terms of social change. For instance, there have been several studies of social change in 'little communities' by Minturn and Hitchcock (1956), Pandey (1984) and Seymour (1975). Cultural anthropology was conceived as a dynamic process, shaping and being shaped through human action. Its understanding could be achieved through viewing it in its historical perspective. It could be viewd as the 'social history of a society', as the derivation of rituals and mores, for instance, socio-religious norms practised in the Hindu culture (Misra, 1988). The cultural aspect of anthropology concepts could then contribute to a society's identity. The old colonial patterns of investigation of 'we' and 'they' distinction is no longer tenable (Das, 1995). This has given place to an understanding of a society in transition within its own indigeneity (Pandian, 1985).

Anthropology also deals with the upbringing of the child in his social setting. The characteristics of the child, his family and socio-cultural and physical setting are often studied ethnographically (Super and Harkness, 1986). These characteristics are also coupled with in-depth qualitative analysis (Bowlby, 1969; Bronfenbrenner, 1989: 185–246; Piaget, 1926b; Whiting, 1963). India has a substantial population that is tribal and/or ethnic who are diverse in their characteristics and frequently cannot be subsumed under the definition of being average Indians. Additional anthropological findings therefore contribute to a fuller understanding of psychometric data, which are generally statistical numbers, identifying the samples in populations (Anandalakshmy and Sharma, 1981: 101–16). For instance, in studying prejudice, there is no way of knowing which among the biased individuals is more prejudiced than the others, unless one examines each score in the study. But, what does the concept of greater or lesser bias mean? It is only limited to the group studied. Its generality is in question. On the other hand, ethnographic data gives information about the societal structures, systems and interactions, as they exist at the time of data collection. It gives results, such as mothers are not very communicative in speech elaboration with their children (Chaudhary, 1966). Besides, idiographic narratives and records of anthropology have a great potential, especially if they form a larger multi-centric effort for developing hypotheses (Murdock et al., 1963). We owe much to anthropology for offering insights into such aspects as values, attitudes, beliefs and interpersonal relations, among the myriad diverse cultures. These provide substance to the concepts of 'multiculturality' and 'plurality' of the Indian society, which require from anthropology a realism when explaining modernising societies of today (Moore, 1996: 1–18). Studies on the various attributes of children (annotated bibliographies on areas like personality development, emotional development, social development, physical development), though sparse, give a fair indication of the problems facing the average Indian child in his milieu. These findings, however limited, provide a basis for policies and programmes, such as a national policy for compulsory primary school education (The Primary School Education Policy, 1986) and prevention of child labour (The Child Labour Act, 1986). A major theme, 'the rights of the child', has been propounded since the 1980s, emphasising the implementation of laws to protect the basic rights of the child in India (Khalakdina, 1998: 173–74). The referendum on the rights of the child is globally acknowledged. It is now well known that nearly 400 million people are below the poverty line (Ravallion, 1998: 35) and children constitute a sizeable proportion of this population. If products of consumption are insufficient, since human beings utilise available knowledge and skills to generate such products, it implies that skills, whether potential or observed, are below capacity to be able to utilise the fruits of science and technology. A large mass of the population is illiterate, lives under limited facilities and is underserviced (Department of Health and Family Planning, 1969: 272). The advance, therefore, in human productivity is less than that of the pace of science and technology. This phenomenon has yet to be looked at in large scale proportions as many illiterate and poorer sections of society lag behind in their technical and scientific skills, creating an imbalance between production and consumption. The consequence of this is that the more efficient and more productive upper classes accumulate more wealth to themselves, thus widening the gap and creating an open field of frustration, aggression and social disorganisation for the poorer.

Thus, when we view the sources derived from sociology, psychology, anthropology and their derivatives on human development and behaviour of the Indian, we need to ask several questions. How do we identify critical areas of development that form developmental goals? What are the critical skills needed for the successful realisation of these goals? What developmental strategies/socialisation techniques can help harmonise traditional values with scientific progress? Given the large number of underprivileged/disadvantaged Indians, more especially the vulnerable among them, women and children, how do we fuse patriarchal norms of hierarchical lines with the 'egalitarian' concept of modernisation (Safilios-Rothschild, 1982)? Most of these social groups live in remote villages and inaccessible tribal areas and, therefore, there is a need for studying them through anthropological methods, besides methods from other disciplines.

If the meaning of research and knowledge is to provide human beings with information that has utility, how much of it is eventually utilised by policy makers and planners? In what ways are these valuable sources of information, when utilised, evaluated for their successful implementation and realisation of goals? For instance, the gigantic Integrated Child Development Services (ICDS) programme, which has been stable since 1975, has dug roots deeply into project areas in urban, rural and tribal areas, covering a large number of preschool children, and, in some cases, girls, pregnant women and lactating mothers. It has been evaluated from time to time and has been fairly successful, though covering only a minute proportion of the target group. Much empirical data has emanated from this programme, especially on physical growth, nutrition and cognitive development. However, its future progress, like that of any other governmental programme, remains to be seen.

In the 21st century, economic power and wealth are being wielded by the powerful to renew the colonial forms in a new garb in shifting geopolitics. The impact of global technology and differential patterns of consumption are increasing. Most relevant of all are population theories hinging on to economically dynamic variables (Day, 2003). They affect the lives of the poor, as one in three children in India comes from poor families. We must then turn our attention to environmental conditions. We are aware that although a distal factor, poverty is an overriding variable in making observations or predictions about child behaviour in India, as the majority of children have no opportunities for the operation of their full-blown capacities, both economic skills and psychological abilities (Alam, 1992: 68–69). They are not taken as the basis for appropriate methodologies in programming. To give an instance, several studies discuss the success of teaching methods that stimulate cognitive development, according to Piaget's schemata. They have yet to be adequately implemented by the planners and programmers.

Economic insecurity (poverty) seems to have a debilitating effect on learning skills according to Gesellian norms. In a study by R. Muralidharan, it was found that urban children were faster in motor development than rural and migrant children (Muralidharan, 1974). With meagre adult reinforcement, the rural/migrant child is left to construct his world of reality from his immediate environment (Gergen et al., 1999: 496–503). When rural men migrate, women and children are left to take care of the occupations in the hinterland, leading to such fallouts as non-schooling children, dropouts, lessened maternal care and more sibling role models. These children also have fewer opportunities for absorbing scientific knowledge. On the other hand, mothers who are migrant workers at construction sites, also lose out on mothering, and hence the young are left to older siblings. But the fact is that in urban areas, there are more accessible facilities like health centres, nourishing food, and, what is now a growing phenomenon, a number of non-governmental organisations catering to the needs of the urban poor (Tripathi, 2003). These facilities are not available to the same extent in rural far-flung areas because of lack of infrastructure and personnel. Given these few examples, we at once underscore the factor of economic poverty as a constant, although distal, when studying developmental behaviour in Indian children, except in the well-to-do where the syndrome of availability, opportunity and utilisation of facilities are at once apparent. Thus, a growing area that requires further sourcing of information is the relationship among economic deprivation, social deprivation and psychological deprivation as a holistic package of effect on the human potential. Such holistic approaches are hardly apparent in current information on development of the Indian (Misra, 1983: 1–21).

Socio-demography gives information on the statistics prevalent in India of structures, age groups, ratio of males to females, and certain indices of the physical quality of life such as education and health statuses (WHO QOL Group, 1996: 354–56). From the human developmental point of view, although the importance of the concept of human development is acknowledged in recent WHO reports, sociologists, psychologists and anthropologists should take their cues from such data to further amplify the concept of human development through empirical data (qualitative or quantitative) in their disciplines. For instance, studies should be undertaken on a comparative disciplinary basis for assessing female nutritional standards in varying geo-ecological areas. It is well known that goitre and thyroidism are the fallouts of the lack of iodine (available in iodised salts), which is not available in rock salt used in the hills. This leads to a greater incidence of the disease. What we are stressing is that not only should there be other viewpoints on development like neurosciences, but also the parameters of epedemiology and, chronic geo-ecologically-borne diseases to give a fuller comprehension of the attributes of such demographic groups. A case in point about sex ratio is a study conducted in Karimpur by S.S. Wadley (1993: 1367–76), which gives recent evidence on female mortality and on what comprises human development.

A Perspective on Development in India

From the above detailed analysis of existent sources, however sparse, with plateaus and gaps in information, we may conclude as follows:

(i)   In the study of the Indian society and its cultural variations, several disciplines impinge upon it not only on domains of psychosociological development, but also offer dissimilar interpretations for the same domain, such as aggression and dependency.

(ii) The fact that each discipline itself gets fissured into various additive frames also confuses their contributions. For instance, psychology talks of cultural psychology and anthropology talks of cultural anthropology. If both are viewing the same phenomena (for example, culture), they must naturally devolve upon the same domain. Therefore, what aspect of culture does psychology interpret and what aspect does anthropology? We do not have clear-cut perspectives on these.

(iii) Within each discipline itself, there are theoretical boundaries. For instance, if we use the theory of reinforcement as handed down to us by Skinner and his associates, then we are limited to the explanation of development/behaviour to only that theoretical frame. We might speculate as to the relevance of other frames, but these do not have tried and tested hypotheses relevant to the one theory that is picked upon to explain results.

To exemplify this further, suppose we attempt to study friendship patterns, we might use psychological concepts like emotional bonding/age group preferences/age-related tasks/similar interests, and so on. When we talk about it in sociological concepts, we use neighbourhood patterns/similar social class variables, community norms and conformity. When we study this pattern using economic concepts, we talk about the variables of socio-economic classification (occupation, income/education and deprivation).

(iv) When utilising concepts from other disciplines, we sometimes find we are talking about the same concept, but described with different constructs. For example, when sociology explains the concept 'mother child dyad', we observe that psychology explains the concept as 'mother-child bonding'. When sociology uses the concept 'social anomie', psychology explains it with concepts of 'social isolation' and 'identity crises'.

(v) Irrespective of the discipline, development has its originating source in all, some with lesser intensity than others. The interesting point is that, being sciences of the human mind there is always a rider. Take, for instance, economics: it predicts behaviour with the assumption 'other things being equal', Which in reality are not. Psychology gives us results that in 95 per cent or 99 per cent of the cases, behaviour has been studied to be X or Y. Even statistics, the bedrock of numbers, rests upon the theory of probability. Anthropology gives qualitative descriptions valid for that group or the individual, which cannot be generalised and therefore remain as illustrations/untested hypotheses. Sociology gives the contextual reference, which in the Indian situation is imperative to understand if we wish to gain a holistic picture of the environmentally influencing factors on the individual, for example, the socio-ecological habitat of a particular 'little tradition'.

These conditional statements imply that the total variation in behaviour/development cannot be accounted for, for 'the mind is like a sword, it can cut everything else but itself.'

(vi) It is difficult to reliably identify all the conditions modifying the individual's development/behaviour, for we still do not know how changeable they are, at what instant and in what dimensions. We can predict earthquakes in the physical world, but there is no foolproof method for predicting earthquakes occurring in the human mind.

(vii) The foundations of behaviour continue to be basic: 'stimulus–response', as observed through the senses. We may look for antecedent events (cause/correlative) and consequent events (resultant/outcomes) to the specific behaviour, but unless it is a stimulus–response situation, whether experimental or spontaneous, whether elicited or naturally occurring, the studied segment of behaviour such as aggressive behaviour cannot be completely and factually explainable. Our conceptual frame is the human being in his environment, sharing common features with the basics of human nature all over the world, but differing in specific forms of behaviour articulated in this instance in the Indian environment.

(viii) In understanding the sources of development in the Indian context it is essential to realise that India has a long social history, the effects of which continue to influence behaviour, especially social behaviour such as differential behaviour among castes, ethnic groups, religious and regional groups as they trace their lineage to generational sources.

(ix) In understanding the Indian psyche, it is essential to understand the source of philosophy influencing thought and behaviour. The religious injunctions of the scriptures pervade daily life, and the beliefs of karma, dharma and their relative injunctions are strong beliefs which, while not amenable to scientific enquiry, are nevertheless held steadfastly.

Personal adaptation rests on the physiological and biological bases of human nature. Adaptation occurs on the basis of proximal and distal effects. Proximal effect occurs, for instance, when the individual is in immediate contact with stimulus, and distal is when the stimulus is further removed. Distal stimuli hardly affects the lifestyle of an individual in his everyday routine, like the war in Iraq for non-Iraqis, but is of consequence if that same individual is in Baghdad.

(x) Being a pluralistic society, it is essential to have a paradigm that encompasses understanding in socio-psychological terms of the plurality and the multidimensionality in the social sciences (Harris and Robert, 1996).

As yet, the dovetailing of different sources of information in a holistic manner for explaining behaviour and development has not yet been realised. Behaviour theorists explain behaviour in terms of stimuli and response. The emotive context is left out. On the other hand, psychodynamics depends heavily on the emotive system, and theories of societal structure and behaviour depend upon an understanding of the internal processes experienced by the developing individual, as he goes through the stages of his lifespan. The difficulty is in the 'mixture' of concepts from these various platforms to get an eclectic viewpoint. The fact remains, however, that the mountain (human) is the same, whichever angle the different disciplines view it from (Martinussen, 2001).

References

Acharya, S., 1989, 'Poverty, Unemployment Relationship in Rural India', *Journal of Social Work*, 49: 125–33.

Adair, J. G., B.N. Puhan and N. Vohra, 1993, 'Indigenization of Psychology, Empirical Assessment of Progress in Indian Research', *International Journal of Psychology*, 28: 149–69.

Adey, W.R., 1958, 'Organisation of the Rhinencephalon', in H.H. Jasper, L.D. Proctor, R.S. Knighton, W.C. Noshay and R.T. Costello (eds), *Reticular Formation of the Brain*. Boston: Little Brown.

Adler, A., 1928, 'Characteristics of the First, Second, and Third Child', *Children*, 3: 14–52.

Adolphs, R., D. Tranel, H. Damasio and A. Damasio, 1994, 'Impaired Recognition of Emotion in Facial Expressions Following Bilateral Damage to Human Amygdala', *Nature*, 372: 669–72.

Agarwala, S.N., 1965, 'Impact of Population Growth on Society', *Indian Journal of Social Work*, 26(1): 118–25.

Ahluwalia, M.S., 2002, 'The Indian Economy 1950–2001', *Business Today*, 20 January.

Ainsworth, M.D., M. Blehar, E. Waters and S. Wall, 1978, *Patterns of Attachment: A Psychological Study of the Strange Situation*. Hillsdale, NJ: Erlbaum.

Alam, Q.G., 1992, 'SES, Ethnic and Cultural Differences in Achievement Motivation', *Perpsectives in Psychological Researches*, 15: 68–69.

Alavi, H., 1972, 'Kinship in West Punjab villages', *Contributions to Indian Sociology*, 6(1): 1–27.

Altman, I. and B. Rogoff, 1987, 'World Views in Psychology: Trait, Interactional, Organismic and Transactional Perspectives', in D. Stokols and I. Altman (eds), *Handbook of Environmental Psychology, Vol. 1*, New York: Wiley.

Aluja, M. and A.L. Norrbom (eds), 1999, *Fruit Flies (Tephritidae): Phylogeny and Evolution of Behaviour*. London: CRC Press.

Ambardar, A., 1983, 'Individual Differences: Effects in Human Computer Interaction', *Technical Report*, US Army Contract MD, pp. 903–82.

Anandalakshmy, S. and A. Sharma, 1981, 'Prejudice in Making: Understanding the Role of Socialization', in D. Sinha (ed.), *Socialization of the Indian Child*. New Delhi: Concept.

Anandalakshmy, S. and M. Bajaj, 1981, 'Childhood in the Weavers' Community in Varanasi: Socialisation for Adult Roles', in D. Sinha (ed.), *Socialisation of the Indian Child*. New Delhi: Concept.

Arulraj, M.R. and S. Raja Samuel, 1995, *Balancing Multiple Roles: Child Care Strategies of Women Working in Organised Sector in Tamil Nadu* (Research Report). Madras: M.S. Swaminathan Research Foundation.

Asirvatham, E., 1960, 'Social Changes in India', *Indian Journal of Social Work*, 21(2): 123–30.

Atal, Yogesh, 1976, 'Indian Social Science in the Changing Environs', in S.C. Dube (ed.), *Social Sciences and Social Realities, Role of the Social Sciences in Contemporary India*. Shimla: Indian Institute of Advanced Study.

Atkinson, J.W., 1964, *An Introduction to Motivation*. New Jersey: De Van Nostrand and Co.

Baig, T.A., 1979, *Our Children*. New Delhi: The Statesman Press.

Bailey, P. and G. von Bonin, 1951, *The Isocortex of Man*. Urbana: University of Illinois Press.

Bandura, A. and R.H. Walters, 1963, *Social Learning Personality Development*. New York: Holt, Reinhart and Winston.

Basu, S., 2003, 'Caste and Class: Differential Response to the Rajbansi Caste Movement', in S. Basu (ed.), *Dynamics of a Caste Movement: The Rajbansis of North Bengal, 1910–1947*. New Delhi: Manohar Press.

Bateson, W., 1913, *Mendel's Principles of Heredity*. Cambridge: Cambridge University Press.

Baumrind, D., 1978, 'Parental Disciplinary Patterns and Social Competence in Children', *Youth and Society*, 9: 239–76.

Bayley, N., 1935, 'The Development of Motor Abilities during the First Three Years: A Developmental Study of Sixty-one Infants Tested Repeatedly', *Monographs of Society for Research in Child Development*, 1: 26–61.

Befu, H., 1986, 'The Social and Cultural Background of Child Development in Japan and the USA', in H. Stevenson, H. Azuma and K. Hakuta (eds), *Child Development and Education in Japan*, pp. 13–27. New York: Freeman.

Beg, M.A., 1991, *Psycholinguistics and Language Acquisition*. New Delhi: Bahri Publications.

Benedict, Ruth, 1938, 'Continuities and Discontinuities in Cultural Conditioning', *Psychiatry* 1: 161–67.

Beremann, D., 1963, 'People and Cultures of the Himalayas', *Asian Survey* 3(6): 289–304.

Berk, L.E., 2001, 'Meaning of Human Chromosomes and Cloning', *Child Development*, 3rd edn. New Delhi: Prentice-Hall.

Berry, J.W., 1979, 'A Cultural Ecology of Social Behaviour', in L. Berkowitz (ed.), *Advances in Experimental Social Psychology*, Vol. 12. New York: Academic Press.

———, 2003, *Ecocultural Perspective on Human Psychological Development*, in T.S. Saraswathi (ed.), *Cross-cultural Perspectives in Human Development: Theory, Research and Applications*, pp. 52–69. New Delhi: Sage.

Berry, J.W., Y.H. Poortinga and J. Pandey (eds), 1997, *Handbook of Cross Cultural Psychology, Vol. 1: Theory and Method*. Boston: Allyn & Bacon.

Berry, J.W., P.R. Dasen and T. S. Saraswathi (eds), 1999, *Handbook of Cross Cultural Psychology, Vol. 2: Basic Processes and Human Development*. Boston: Allyn & Bacon.

Berry, J.W., R.C. Mishra and R.C. Tripathi, 2003, *Psychology in Human and Social Development: Lessons from Diverse Cultures—A Festchrift for Durganand Sinha*. New Delhi: Sage.

Beteille, A., 1991, *Society and Politics in India: Essays in a Comparative Perspective*. London: The Athlone Press.

Bhandari, A. and B.N. Ghosh, 1980, 'A Longitudinal Study of the Fine Motor-Adaptive, Personal-Social and Language Speech Developments of Children from Birth to One Year of Age in an Urban Community', *Indian Journal of Medical Research*, 71: 289–302.

Bevli, U.K., 1977, 'Concept of Speed: A Developmental-cum-training Study', Ph.D. Dissertation, IIT, Delhi.

Bhattacharya, N.N., 1996, 'Rites of Passage', in N.N. Bhattacharya (ed.), *Ancient Indian Rituals and their Social Contexts*, Vol. xxiii (2nd revised and enlarged edition). Delhi: Manohar.

Biswas, A.K., 2000, 'History of Science Movement in India', in A.K. Raina, B.N. Patnaik and M. Chadha (eds), *Science and Tradition*. Shimla: Indian Institute of Advanced Studies.

Bornstein, Marc H. and M.E. Lamb (eds), 1999, *Development Psychology: An Advanced Textbook*, 4th edn. Mahwah, NJ: Lawrence Erlbaum.

Bose, A., P.B. Desai and S.P. Jain (eds), 1970, *Studies in Demography*. London: George Allen and Unwin Ltd.

Bowlby, J., 1969, *Attachment and Loss, Vol. 1*. New York: Basic Books.

———, 1973, *Attachment and Loss, Vol 2: Separation*. New York: Basic Books.

Brazier, M.A.B., 1961, *A History of the Electrical Activity of the Brain*. San Francisco, New York: Macmillan.

Britt, S.H., 1966, *Consumer Behaviour and the Behavioural Sciences*. Canada: John Wiley.

Brodal, A., 1947, 'The Hippocampus and the Sense of Smell', *Brain*, 70: 1–179.

Bronfenbrenner, U., 1979, *The Ecology of Human Development*. Cambridge, MA: Harvard University Press.

———, 1989, 'Ecological Systems Theory', in R. Vasta (ed.), *Annals of Child Development*. Greenwich, CT: JAT.

———, 1993, 'The Ecology of Cognitive Development: Research Models and Fugitive Findings', in R. Wozniak and K.W. Fischer (eds), *Development in Context*. Hillsdale, NJ: Erlbaum.

Brown, P.K. and G. Wald, 1964, 'Visual Pigments in Single Rods and Cones of the Human Retina', *Science*, 144: 45–52.

Bruner, J.S. and M. Cole, 1976, 'Cultural Differences and Inferences about Psychological Processes', in J. Wolfson (ed.), *Personality and Learning 2* (A Reader Prepared by the Personality and Learning Course Team at the Open University, Hodder and Stoughton, in association with The Open University Press, UK).

Buzsaki, G., L.S. Chen and F.H. Gage, 1990, 'Spatial Organisation of Physiological Activity in the Hippocampus Regions: Relevance to Memory Formation', *Brain Research*, 83: 257–68.

Caldwell, B.M., L. Hershwer, E.L. Lipton, J.B. Richmond, G.A. Stern, E. Eddy, R. Dracghman and A. Rothman, 1963, 'Mother–Infant Interaction in Monometric and Polymetric Families', *American Journal of Orthopsychiatry*, 33: 653–64.

Caplan, Lionel, 1987, *Class and Culture in Urban India: Fundamentalism in a Christian Community*. Oxford: Clarendon Press.

Capra F., 1983, *The Tao of Physics*. Boulder, CO: Shambala.

Chakrabarty, D., 1995, 'Modernity and Ethnicity in India: A History for the Present', *Economic and Political Weekly*, 30: 3773–80.

Chattell, R.B., 1985, *Structured Personality-learning Theory: A Wholistic Multi-variate Research Approach*. New York: Praeger.

Chatterjee, P., 1994, *The Nation and its Fragments*. New Delhi: OUP.

Chatterjee, R.G. and R. Kundu, 1959, 'Estimation of Visual Extent under Variable Conditions', *Indian Journal of Psychology*, 34: 58–63.

Chaudhary, N.C., 1966, *The Continent of Circe*. Bombay: Jaico.

Chomsky, N., 1986, *Knowledge of Language: Its Nature, Origin and Use*. New York: Praeger.

Chugani, H.T., 1996, 'Neuroimaging Developmental Non-linearity and Developmental Pathologies', in T.W. Thatcher, G.R. Lyon, J. Rumsey and N. Krasnegor (eds), *Developmental Neuroimaging*. San Diego: Academic.

Clifford, J., 1986, 'Introduction: Partial Truths', in Clifford James and G. Marcus, *Writing Culture: The Poetics and Politics of Ethnography*. New Delhi: OUP.

Comte, A., 1988, *Introduction to Positive Philosophy*. Indianapolis, IN: Hackett Pub. Co. Inc.

Constitution of India, 1952.

Cravioto J., E.R. DeLicardie and H.G. Birch, 1966, 'Nutrition, Growth and Neurointegrative Development: An Experimental and Ecological Study', *Pediatrics*, 38 (Supplement 2, Part 2): 319–72.

Dahl, R.A., 1957, 'The Concept of Power', *Behavioural Science*, 2: 210–19.

Dalal, A.K., 1996, 'A Science in Search of its Identity: 20th Century Psychology in India', in *Psychological Abstracts and Reviews*, 4(1): 1–41.

Dalal, A.K. and G. Misra (eds), 2002a, *New Directions in Indian Psychology, Vol. 1*. New Delhi: Sage.

———, 2002b, 'Social Psychology in India: Evolution and Emerging Trends', in A.K. Dalal and G. Misra (eds), *New Directions in Indian Psychology, Vol. 1*. New Delhi: Sage.

Darwin, C., 1859, *On the Origin of Species by Means of Natural Selection*, London: John Murray.

Das, A.L. and M.K. Raha, 1963, *The Oraons of the Sunderbans*, Bulletin of Cultural Research Institute, Tribal Welfare Department, Government of West Bengal, Calcutta.

Das, J.P. and K. Thapa, 2000, 'Intelligence and Cognitive Processes', in J. Pandey (ed.), *Psychology in India Revisited—Developments in the Discipline, Vol. 1: Psychological Foundation and Human Cognition*. New Delhi: Sage.

Das, J.P. and G.N. Molloy, 1975, 'Variates of Simultaneous and Successive Processing in Children', *Journal of Educational Psychology*, 67: 213–20.

Das, V., 1995, *Critical Events: an Anthropological Perspective on Contemporary India*. New Delhi: OUP.

———, 2003, *The Oxford India Companion to Sociology and Social Anthropology*, 2 vols. Delhi: OUP.

Das, V., A. Beteille and T.N. Madan (eds), 2003, *Sociology and Social Anthropology: Oxford India Companion to Sociology and Social Anthropology*. New Delhi: OUP.

Dasen, P.R and R.C. Mishra, 2000, 'Cross-cultural Views on Human Development in the Third Millennium', *International Journal of Behavioural Development*, 24(4): 428–34.

Dave, P.C., 1960, *The Grasias, also called Dugri Grasias: A Scheduled Tribe in Bombay and Rajasthan States*. New Delhi: Bharatiya Adimjati Sevak Sangh.

Davis, M., 1992, 'The Role of Amygdala in Fear and Anxiety', *Annual Review of Neuroscience*, 15: 353–75.

Davis, P.A., 1939, 'Effects of Acoustics Stimuli on the Waking Human Brain', *Journal of Neurophysiology*, 2: 494–99.

Day, R., 2003, *The Divergent Dynamics of Economic Growth: Studies in Adaptive Economising, Technological Change, and Economic Development*. Cambridge, UK: Cambridge University Press.

Demetriou, A., W. Doise and C.F.M. Vanlieshout, 1998, *Life Span Developmental Psychology*. New York: Wiley.

Desai, I.P., 1964, *Some Aspects of Family in Mahuva*. Bombay: Asia Publishing House.

Deshpande, S., 2003, *Contemporary India: A Sociological View*. New Delhi: Penguin Books.

Dewey, J., 1891, *Psychology*, 3rd edn. New York: Harper.

———, 1968, *Experience and Education*. New York: Collier.

Dewsbury, D.A., 1991, 'Psychobiology', *American Psychologist*, 46(3): 198–205.

Diaz-Guerrero, R., 1967, 'Social-cultural Premises, Attitudes and Cross-cultural Research', *International Journal of Psychology*, 2(2): 78–87.

Doshi, S.L., 1971, *Bhils: Between Societal Self-Awareness and Cultural Synthesis*. Delhi: Sterling.

Driesch, H., 1929 (1908), *The Science and Philosophy of the Organism*. London: Black.

Driesen, N. and N. Raz, 1995, 'The Influence of Sex, Age, and Handedness on Corpus Callosum Morphology: A Meta-analysis', *Psychobiology*, 23(3): 240–47.

Dronkers, N.F., B.B. Redfern and R.T. Knight, 2000, 'The Neural Architecture of Language Disorders', in M.S. Gazzaniga (ed.), *The New Cognitive Neurosciences*, 2nd edn. Cambridge MA: MIT Press.

Dube, L., 1974, *Sociology of Kinship: An Analytic Survey of Literature*. Bombay: Popular Prakashan.

———, 1997, *Women and Kinship: Comparative Perspectives on Gender in South and South-East Asia*. New Delhi: Vistaar Publications.

Dube, S.C., 1965, 'The Study of Complex Cultures', in T.K.N. Unnithan, Indra Dev and Y. Singh (eds), *Towards a Sociology of Culture in India*. New Delhi: Prentice-Hall.

———, 1976, 'Role of Social Science', in S.C. Dube (ed.), *Social Science and Social Realities: Role of the Social Sciences in Contemporary India* (Transactions of the Indian Institute of Advanced Study). Shimla: Indian Institute of Advanced Study.

Dumont, L., 1970, *Homo Hierarchicus: The Caste System and its Implications*. London: Paladin.

Dwivedi, P. and C.R. Mukundan, 1993, 'Lateralisation of Visual Attention and Distrastability', *NIMHANS Journal*, 11: 27–33.

Eichorn, D.H., 1970, 'Physiological Development', in P.H. Mussen (ed.), *Carmichael's Manual of Child Psychology, Vol. 2*, 3rd edn. New York: John Wiley.

Elman, J.L., E.A. Bates, M.H. Johnson, A. Karmiloff Smith, D. Parisi and K. Plunkett, 1996, *Rethinking Innateness: A Connectionist Perspective on Development*. Cambridge, MA: MIT Press.

Elrod, S.S., 2002, *Schaum's Outline of Genetics*. New York: McGraw-Hill.

Elwin, V., 1947, *The Murias and their Ghotuls*. London: OUP.

Erikson, E.H., 1950, *Childhood and Society*. New York: Norton.

———, 1964, *Identity, Youth and Crisis*. New York: Norton.

———, 1969, 'Human Strength and the Cycle of Generations', in *Insight and Responsibility*. New York: Norton.

Erulkar, D.E., 1994, 'Form and Function of Nervous Systems', in *Encyclopaedia Britannica*, Vol. 24, Chicago: 785–98.

Eysenck, H.J., 1947, *Dimensions of Personality*. London: Kegan Paul.

Freud, S., 1935 (1916), *A General Introduction to Psychoanalysis*. New York: Liveright.

———, 1946, *The Ego and the Mechanisms of Defense*. New York: International University Press.

Fuller, J.L., 1957, 'Comparative Studies in Behavioural Genetics', *Aca Genetica Statistic Medica*, 7: 403–7.

———, 1960, 'Behaviour Genetics', *Annual Review of Psychology*, 11: 41–70.

Furth, H.G., 1973, 'Catholic University of America: Piaget, IQ and the Nature-Nurture Controversy', *Human Development*, 16(1): 61–67.

Fyans, Jr. L.J., F. Salili, M.L. Maehr and K.A. Desai, 1983, 'Cross-cultural Exploration into the Meaning of Achievement', *Journal of Personality and Social Psychology*, 44: 1000–1013.

Gadgil, D.R., 1955, 'Indian Economic Organisation', in S. Kuznets, W.E. Moore and J.J. Spengler (eds), *Economic Growth: Brazil, India, Japan*. Durham, NC: Duke University Press.

Gandhi, M.K., 1927, *The Story of My Experiments with Truth*. Ahmedabad: Ahmedabad Navjivan Trust.

Ganguli, H.C. and K.D. Baroota, 1973, 'The Cultural Factor in Organisation of Perception', *Indian Journal of Experimental Psychology*, 48: 21–48.

Gay, P. (ed.), 1964, *Classics in Education, No. 20: John Locke on Education*. New York: Teachers College, Columbia University.

Geertz, C., 1973, 'Ideology as a Cultural System', in C. Geertz (ed). *The Interpretation of Cultures*. New York: Basic Books.

Gergen, K.J., A. Gulerce, A. Lock and G. Misra, 1999, 'Psychological Science in Cultural Context', *American Psychologist*, 51: 496–503.

Gesell, A. and F.L. Ilg, 1943, *Infant and Child in the Culture of Today*. New York: Harper.

Gesell, A. and H. Thompson, 1929, 'Learning and Growth in Identical Infant Twins', *Genetic Psychology: Monographs*, 6(1): 1–124.

Giddens, A., 1996, *The Future of Anthropology in the Defense of Sociology: Essay on Interpretations and Rejoinder*. Cambridge: Polity Press.

Gloor, P., 1997, *The Temporal Lobe and Limbic System*. New York: OUP.

Goodnow, J., 1976, 'Cultural Variations in Cognitive Skills', in J. Wolfson (ed.), *Personality and Learning 2* (A Reader Prepared by the Personality and Learning Course Team at The Open University). London: Hodder and Stoughton/The Open University Press.

Gore, M.S. 1968, *Urbanisation and Family Change*. Bombay: Popular Prakashan.

———, 2000a, *Sociology and Anthropology*. Delhi: Manak.

———, (ed.), 2000b, *Third Survey of Research in Sociology and Social Anthropology*, 2 vols. Delhi: Manak.

———, 2003, *Social Development: Challenges Faced in an Unequal and Plural Society*. Jaipur: Rawat Publications.

Gottlieb, G., 1976, 'Conceptions of Prenatal Development: Behavioural Embryology', *Psychological Review*, 83: 215–34.

———, 1991, 'Experiential Canalisation of Behavioural Development: Theory', *Developmental Psychology*, 27: 4–13.

Gould, D., 1987, *The Lord as Guru: Hindi Saints in North Indian Tradition*. New York: OUP.

Gould, S.J., 1996, *The Mismeasure of Man* (revised edn). New York: Norton.

Greenough, W.T., J.E. Black and C.S. Wallace, 1987, 'Experience and Brain Development', *Child Development*, 58: 539–59.

Gross, C.G., 2001, 'Neurogenesis in The Adult Brain: Death of a Dogma', *Nature Reviews Neuroscience*, 1(1): 67–73.

Gunnar, M.R., 1998, 'Quality of Early Care and Buffering of Neuro Endocrine Stress Reactions: Potential Effects on the Developing Human Brain', *Preventive Medicine*, 27(2): 208–211.

Gupta, A., 2006, *Early Childhood Education, Post Colonial Theory, and Teaching Practices in India: Balancing Vygotsky and the Veda*. New York: Palgrave Macmillan.

Gupta, A. and D. Ghai, 1991, 'Memory in Head Injured Patients', *Journal of Personality and Clinical Studies*, 7: 55–61.

Gupta, D., 2000, *Interrogating Caste: Understanding Hierarchy and Difference in Indian Society*. New Delhi: Penguin Books.

Gupta, G.C. and B. Prasad, 1967, 'A Study of the Effect of Increasing Intensity of Shock on the Estimation of Visual and Auditory Temporal Duration', *Indian Journal of Experimental Psychology*, 1: 5–7.

Gur, R.C., B.I. Turetsky, M. Matsui, M. Yen, W. Bilker, P. Hughett and R.E. Gur, 1999, 'Sex Differences in Brain: Grey and White Matter in Healthy Young Adults: Correlations with Cognitive Performance', *Journal of Neuroscience*, 19(10): 4065–72.

Hallonet, M.E.R, M.A. Teillet, N.M. le Douarin, 1990, 'A New Approach to the Development of the Cerebellum Provided by the Quail Chick Marker System', *Development*, 108: 19–31.

Harris, P. and T. Robert, 1996, *Management of Cultural Differences: Global Leadership Strategies for the 21st Century*. Houston: Gulf Publishing Company.

Hartnack, C., 1987, 'British Psychoanalysis in Colonial India', in M.G. Ash and W.R. Woodward (eds), *Psychology in 20th Century Thought and Society*. Cambridge, UK: Cambridge University Press.

Havighurst R.J., 1953, *Human Development and Education*. New York: John Wiley.

Heider, F., 1958, *The Psychology of Interpersonal Relations*. New York: John Wiley.

Herrick, C.L., 1891, 'The Evolution of the Cerebellum', *Science*, 18: 188–89.

Himes, J.R. and Saltarelli, 1996, *Implementing the Convention on Rights of the Child: Resource Mobilisation in Low Income Countries*. Florence: Innocent Studies, UNICEF.

His, W., 1888, 'On the Principles of Animal Morphology', *Proceedings of the Royal Society of Edinburgh*, 15: 287–98.

Hitchkock, J. and L. Minturn, 1956, 'The Rajputs of Khalapur, India', in B. Whiting and I.L. Child (eds), *Six Cultures: Studies in Child Rearing*. New York: John Wiley.

Holtzman, W.H., 1992, 'Community Renewal, Family Preservation and Child Development through the School', in W.H. Holtzman (ed.), *School of the Future*. Austin, TX: American Psychological Association and Hogg Foundation for Mental Health.

Hull, C.L., 1945, *Principles of Behaviour: An Introduction to Behaviour Theory*. New York: Appleton-Century.

Hussain, F. (ed.), 1982, *Indigenous Anthropology in Non-Western Countries*. Durham, NC: Carolina Academic Press.

Inhelder, B. and J. Piaget, 1958, *The Growth of Logical Thinking from Childhood to Adolescence: An Essay on the Construction of Formal Operational Structures*. New York: Basic Books.

Ishwaran, K., 1966, *Tradition and Economy in Village India*. London: Routledge and Kegan Paul.

———, (ed.), 1970, *Change and Continuity in India's Villages*. New York and London: Columbia University Press.

Jaffar, S.M., 1972, *Some Cultural Aspects of Muslim Rule in India*. Delhi: Idrah-i-Adabiyat.

Jarrard, L.E., 1993, 'On the Role of Hippocampus in Learning and Memory in the Rat', *Behaviour Neural Biology*, 60: 9–26.

Jensen, A.R., 1969, 'How Much Can We Boost IQ and Scholastic Achievement', *Harvard Educational Review*, 19: 1–123.

Johannsen, W., 1911, 'The Genotype Conception of Heredity', *American Naturalist*, 45: 129–59.

Jonassen, D.H. and B.L. Grabowski, 1993, *Handbook of Individual Differences, Learning and Instruction*. Hillsdale, NJ: Lawrence Erlbaum.

Joshi, P.C. and A. Mahajan, 1990, *Studies in Medical Anthropology*. New Delhi: Reliance Publishing House.

Juel-Nielsen, N., 1965, 'Individual and Environment: A Psychiatric-Psychological Investigation of Monozygotic Twins Reared Apart', *Acta Psychiatrica et Neurologica Scandinavica*, Monograph Supplement 183.

Kagitcibasi, C., 2003, 'Human Development Across Cultures: A Contextual-Functional Analysis and Implications for Interventions', in T.S. Saraswathi, *Cross-Cultural Perspectives in Human Development, Theory, Research and Applications*. New Delhi: Sage.

Kagitcibasi, C. and Y.H. Poortinga, 2000, 'Cross-cultural Psychology: Isues and Overarching Themes', *Journal of Cross-cultural Psychology*, 31(1): 127–47.

Kak, Subhas C., 2000, 'On Understanding Ancient Indian Science', in A.K. Raina, B.N. Patnaik and M. Chadha (eds), *Science and Tradition*. Shimla: Indian Institute of Advanced Studies.

Kakar, S., 1968, 'The Human Life Cycle: The Traditional Hindu View and the Psychology of Erik Erikson', *Philosophy East West*, 18(3): 127–36.

———, 1979, *Identity and Adulthood*. Oxford: OUP.

———, 1982, *Shamans, Mystics and Doctors: A Psychological Enquiry into India and its Healing Properties*. Bombay: OUP.

———, 2002, 'The Theme of Authority in Social Relations in India', in A.K. Dalal and G. Misra (eds), *New Directions in Indian Psychology*. New Delhi: Sage.

Kakar, S. and K. Chowdhry, 1970, *Conflict and Choice: Indian Youth in a Changing Society*. Bombay: Somaiya.

Kandel, E. and I. Kupfermann, 1995, 'Emotional States', in E.R. Kandel, J.H. Schwartz and T.M. Jessell (eds), *Essentials of Neuroscience and Behaviour*. Norwalk, CT: Appleton and Lange.

Kane, V.P., 1941, *History of Dharmashastras*, *Vol. II*, Part I. Poona: Bhandarkar Oriental Research Institute.

Kanungo, N. Rabindra and Sasi Misra, 2004, 'Motivation, Leadership, and Human Performance', in J. Pandey (ed.), *Psychology in India Revisited—Developments in the Discipline, Vol. 3: Applied Social and Organisational Psychology*. New Delhi: Sage.

Kao, H.S.R. and D. Sinha (eds), 1997, *Asian Perspectives on Psychology*. New Delhi: Sage.

Kao, H.S.R. and C.F. Yang (eds), 1991, *Chinese and the Chinese Mind*, 3 vols. Taipei: Yuen Lin Publishing House.

Kapadia, K.M., 1966, *Marriage and Family in India*. Bombay: OUP.

Kapur, M., 2003, 'Child Care in Ancient India', in J.G. Young, P. Ferrari, S. Malhotra, S. Tyano and E. Caffo (eds), *Brain, Culture and Development: Tradition and Innovation in Child and Adolescent Mental Health*. New Delhi: Macmillan.

Kapur, M., H. Uma, M.V. Reddy, I.P. Barnabas and D. Singhal, 1997, 'Study of Infant Temperament: An Indian Perspective', *Indian Journal of Clinical Psychology*, 24(2): 171–77.

Kaur, B., 1987, 'An Agenda for Future Theory Building Research and Action', in T.S. Saraswathi and Ranjana Dutta (eds), *Developmental Psychology in India, 1975–1986, An Annotated Bibiliography*. New Delhi: Sage.

Keller, H., 1997, 'Evolutionary Approaches', in J.W. Berry, Y.H. Poortinga and J. Pandey (eds), *Handbook of Cross-Cultural Psychology*, Vol. I. Boston: Allyn Bacon.

———, 2003, 'Ontogeny as the Interface between Biology and Culture: Evolutionary Considerations', in T.S. Saraswathi (ed.), *Cross-Cultural Perspectives in Human Development: Theory, Research, Applications*. New Delhi: Sage.

Keller, H., Y.H. Poortinga and A. Scholmerich (eds), 2002, *Between Biology and Culture: Perspectives on Ontogenetic Development*. Cambridge: Cambridge University Press.

Kelso, J., 1995, *Dynamic Patterns: The Self-organisation of Brain and Behaviour*. Cambridge, MA: MIT Press.

Keyes, C.F. and E.V. Daniel, 1983, *Karma: An Anthropological Enquiry*. Berkeley, CA: University of California Press.

Khalakdina, M., 1974, 'A Critique of Research in Child Development', *Manuscript of UNICEF*, SCARO, New Delhi.

———, 1998, 'In Sight—Day Care for Construction Workers' Children', in M. Swaminathan (ed.), *The First Five Years*, pp. 44–59. New Delhi: Sage.

Khatri, A.A., 1970, 'Personality and Mental Health of Indians (Hindus) in the Context of their Changing Family Organization', in E. James Anthony and Cyrille Koupernik (eds), *The Child in his Family: The International Yearbook for Child Psychiatry and Allied Disciplines*, Vol. 1. New York: Wiley-Interscience.

Kishori, S. Lal, 1992, *Legacy of Muslim Rule in India*. Delhi: South Asia Books.

Kline, P., 2000, *New Psychometrics, Science Psychology and Measurement*. UK: Routledge.

Kohlberg, L., 1969, 'Stage and Sequence: The Cognitive Developmental Approach to Socialisation', in D.A. Goslin (ed.), *Handbook of Socialisation Theory and Research*. Chicago: Rand-McNally.

Kohler, W., 1925, *The Mentality of Apes*. New York: Harcourt Brace.

Kol, B. and I.Q. Whishaw, 1990, *Fundamentals of Human Neuropsychology*, 3rd edn. New York: Freeman.

Krishnan, L., 1998, 'Child Rearing: The Indian Perspective', in A.K. Srivastava (ed.), *Child Development: The Indian Perspective*, pp. 25–55. New Delhi: NCERT.

Kukla, A., 1988, 'Cross-cultural Psychology in a Post-empiricist Era', in M. Bond (ed.), *The Cross-cultural Challenge to Social Psychology*. Thousand Oaks, CA: Sage.

Kulkarni, P.D., 1964, 'Social Research and Social Planning', *Indian Journal of Social Work*, 25(3): 193–200.

Kuppuswamy, B. and Y. Singh, 1967, 'Socio-economic Status Stratification in Western Uttar Pradesh', *Sociological Bulletin*, 16(1): 62–68.

Kurtz, S. N., 1992, *All the Mothers are One: Hindu India and the Cultural Reshaping of Psychoanalysis*. New York: Columbia University Press.

Leahey, T.H., 1987, *A History of Psychology*. Englewood Cliffs, NJ: Prentice-Hall.

Levine, R.A., 1977, 'Child Rearing as Cultural Adaptation', in P. Herber Leiderman, Steven R. Tulkin and Anne Rosenfeld (eds), *Culture and Infancy Variation in the Human Experience*. New York: Academic Press.

Levinthal, C.F., 2003, *Introduction to Physiological Psychology*, 3rd edn. New Delhi: Prentice-Hall.

Lévi-Strauss, C., 1963, *Structural Anthropology*. New York: Basic Books.

Levy, M.J., Jr., 1952, *The Structure of Society*. Princeton: Princeton University Press.

———, 1953, *The Structure of Society*. Princeton: Princeton University Press.

Lewin, K., 1935, *A Dynamic Theory of Personality*. New York: McGraw-Hill.

———, 1951, *Field Theory in Social Science*. New York: Harper & Row.

Lowitz, S. and L. Scmidt, 2003, 'Developmental Psychology and the Neuroscience', in J. Valsiner and K. Connolly (eds), *Handbook Of Development Psychology*. London: Sage.

Lumsden, C. and E. Wilson, 1981, *Genes: Mind and Culture: The Co-evolutionary Process*. Cambridge, MA: Harvard University Press.

Lundberg, U., 1975, 'A Multidimensional Analysis of Involvement in Furute Events', Report from the Department of Psychology, University of Stockholm.

Macer, D.R., S. Akiyma, A.T. Alora, Y. Asada, J. Azariah, H. Azariah, M.V. Boost, P. Chatwachirawong, Y. Kato and V. Kaushik, 1995, 'International Perceptions and Approval of Gene Therapy', *Human Gene Therapy*, 6: 791–803.

Madan, T.N., 1992, 'Secularism in its Place', in T.N. Madan (ed.), *Religion in India*. New Delhi: OUP.

Malhotra, R. and K.D. Broota, 1986, 'Perception of Field Size as a Function of Brief Exposure Duration', *Journal of Psychological Research*, 30: 62–67.

Malhotra, S., 1995, 'Study of Psychosocial Correlates of Developmental Psychopathology in School Children', Report submitted to the Indian Council for Medical Research, New Delhi.

———, 2002a, *Temperament Measurement Schedule in Child Psychiatry in India*, pp. 220–27. Delhi: Macmillan.

———, 2002b, 'Child Psychiatry: Origins and Development', in S. Malhotra (ed.), *Child Psychiatry in India*, pp. 2–3. Delhi: Macmillan.

———, 2002c, *Child Psychiatry in India*, p. 70. Delhi: Macmillan.

———, 2003, 'Socio-cultural Diversity and Ethnocentrism in Child Mental Health', in J.G. Young, P. Ferrari, S. Malhotra, S. Tyano and E. Caffo (eds), *Brain Culture and Development*. New Delhi: Macmillan.

Malhotra, S., and A. Kohli, 1995, *Study of Psychosocial Determinants of Developmental Psychopathology in School Children*, ICMR Project Report.

Malinowski, B., 1948, 'Magic, Science and Religion', in J. Needham (ed.), *Science, Religion and Reality*. New York: Macmillan.

Mandal, M.K., 2000, 'Physiological Foundations of Behaviour', in Janak Pandey (ed.), *Psychology in India Revisited*. New Delhi: Sage.

Mandal, M.K., H. Asthana and R. Pandey, 1995, 'Asymmetry in Emotional Face: Its Role in Intensity of Expression', *Journal of Psychology*, 129: 235–41.

———, (ed.), 1990, *India through Hindu Categories*, New Delhi: Sage.

Marriot, M., 1955, 'Little Community in an Indigenous Civilisation', in M. Marriot (ed.), *Village India: Studies in the Little Community*. Chicago: Chicago University Press.

———, 1976, 'Hindu Transaction: Diversity without Dualism', in B. Kapferer (ed.), *Transactions and Meaning*. Philadelphia: Philadelphia Institute for the Study of Human Issues.

Marsella, A.J., G. de Vos and F.L.K. Hsu (eds), 1985, *Culture and Self: Asian and Western Perspectives*. London: Tavistock.

Martinussen, J., 2001, *Policies, Institutions and Industrial Development: Coping with Liberalisation and Industrial Development in India*. New Delhi: Sage.

Maslow, A.H., 1943, 'A Theory of Human Motivation', *Psychological Review*, 50: 370–96.

Mazumdar, N.D., 1958, *Caste and Communication in an India Village*. Bombay: Asia Publishing House.

McClelland, D.C. and D.G. Winter, 1969, *Motivating Economic Achievement*. New York: The Free Press.

McGraw, M., 1935, *Growth: A Study of Johnny and Jimmy*. New York: Appleton Century Crofts.

———, 1943, *Neuromuscular Maturation of the Human Infant*. New York: Columbia University Press.

Mead, M., 1964, *Continuities in Cultural Evolution*. New Haven: Yale University Press.

Mencher, P.A., 1970, 'Tamil Village: Changing Socio-economic Strucutre in Madras State', in K. Ishwaran (ed.), *Change and Continuity in India's Villages*. New York: Columbia University.

Mendel, G., 1866, *Versuche über Pflanzen-Hybriden* (Experiments on Plant Hybridization), Verh. Naturforsch. Ver. Brünn (Proceedings of the Natural History Society), 4: 3–47 (in English in 1901, *Journal of the Royal Horticulture Society*, 26: 1–32).

Merton, R.K., 1948, *Social Theory and Social Structure*. Glencoe, IL: The Free Press.

———, 1967a, *Social Theory and Social Structure*. The New York/London: The Free Press.

———, 1967b, *On Theoretical Sociology, Five Essays, Old and New*. New York: The Free Press.

Metha, P., 1971–76, 'Political Process and Behaviour', in U. Pareek (ed.), *A Survey of Research in Psychology, Part 2*. Bombay: Popular Prakashan.

Miklos, G.L. and G.M. Rubin, 1996, 'The Role of the Genome Project in Determining Gene Function: Insights from Model Organisms', *Cell*, 86: 521–29.

Miller, N.E. and J. Dollard, 1941, *Social Learning and Imitation*. New Haven: Yale University Press.

Minturn, L. and J.T. Hitchcock, 1956, 'The Rajputs of Khalapur, India', in B. Whiting and I.L. Child (eds), *Six Cultures: Studies in Child Rearing*. New York: John Wiley.

Minturn, L. and W.W. Lambert, 1964, *Mothers of Six Cultures: Antecedents of Child-Rearing*. New York: John Wiley.

Mishra, R.C., 2000, 'Perceptual, Learning and Memory Processes', in J. Pandey (ed.), *Psychology in India Revisited— Developments in the Discipline, Vol. 1: Psychological Foundation and Human Cognition*. New Delhi: Sage.

Misra, G., 1983, 'Deprivation and Development: A Review of Indian Studies', *Indian Education Review*, January: 1–21.

———, 1988, 'Relevance of Indian Thought to Contemporary Psychology', in F.M. Sahu (ed.), *Psychology in Indian Context*. Agra: National Psychological Corporation.

———, 1991, 'Socio-cultural Influences on Moral Behaviour', *The Indian Journal of Social Work*, 52(2): 179–94.

———, 2002, 'Perceptual Learning and Memory Processes', in J. Pandey (ed.), *Psychology in India Revisited—Developments in the Discipline, Vol. 1: Physiological Foundation and Human Cognition*. New Delhi: Sage.

———, 2003, 'Implications of Culture for Psychological Knowledge', in J.W. Berry, R.C. Mishra and R.C. Tripathi (eds), *Psychology in Human and Social Development: Lessons from Diverse Cultures—A Festschrift for Durganand Sinha*. New Delhi: Sage.

Misra, G. and R. Agarwal, 1985, 'Meaning of Achievement: Implications for Cross-cultural Theory of Achievement Motivation', in I.R. Lagunes and Ype H. Poortinga (eds), *From a Different Perspective: Studies of Behaviour Across Cultures*. Lisse: Swets and Zeitlinger.

Misra, G. and K.J. Gergen, 2002, 'On the Place of Culture in Psychologiacl Science', in Ajit K. Dalal and Girishwar Misra (eds), *New Directions in Indian Psychology—Vol. 1: Social Psychology*. New Delhi: Sage.

Misra G. and A.C. Mishra, 1989, 'Contextual Effects of Distributive Justice Judgements of Children' (unpublished study). Bhopal: Department of Psychology, Barkatullah University.

Misra, G. and K.N. Tripathi, 2004, 'Psychological Dimensions of Poverty and Deprivation', in J. Pandey (ed.), *Psychology in India Revisited—Developments in the Discipline, Vol. 3: Applied Social and Organisational Psychology*. New Delhi: Sage.

Misra, V.N., 1971, 'Relevance of the Indian Concept of Civilisation in the Modern Context', *Journal at Ganganatha Jha Kendriya Sanskrit Vidyapeeth*, 27: 363–73.

Mistry, J. and T.S. Saraswathi, 2003, 'The Cultural Context of Child Development', in R.M. Lerner, M.A. Easterbrooks and J. Mistry (eds), *Handbook of Psychology, Vol. 6: Developmental Psychology*. New York: John Wiley.

Mitra, S.C. and A. Datta, 1939, 'The Influence of Colour on the Estimation of Area', *Indian Journal of Psychology*, 14: 91–94.

Moghadam, F.M., 1987, 'Psychology in the Three Worlds: As Reflected by the Crisis in Social Psychology and the Move Toward Indigenous Third-World Psychology', *American Psychologist*, 42: 912–20.

Mohanty, A.K., 2000, 'Language Behaviour and Processes', in J. Pandey (ed.), *Psychology in India Revisited—Developments in the Discipline, Vol. I: Physiological Foundation and Human Cognition*. New Delhi/Thousand Oaks/London: Sage.

Mohanty, A.K. and P. Prakash, 1993, 'Theoretical Despairs and Methodological Predicaments of Developmental Psychology in India: Some Reflections', in T.S. Saraswati and Baljit Kaur (eds), *Human Development and Family Studies in India: An Agenda for Research and Policy*. New Delhi. Sage.

Moore, H.L., 1996, 'The Changing Nature of Anthropological Knowledge: An Introduction', in H.L. Moore, *The Future of Anthropological Knowledge*. London/New York: Routledge.

Moore, S.F., 1989, 'The Production of Cultural Pluralism as a Process', *Public Culture*, 1(2): 26–48.

Morgan, A.E. and G.W. Hynd, 1998, 'Dyslexia, Neurolinguistic Ability and Anatomical Variation of the Planum Temporale', *Neuropsychological Reviews*, 8(2): 79–93.

Morgan T.H., 1988, *The Theory of the Gene (Genes, Cells and Organisms)*. New York: Garland.

Morton, D., E. Friedman and C. Carterette, 1996, *Cognitive Ecology, Handbood of Perception and Cognition*. California: Academic Press.

Mower, G., W. Christen and C. Caplan, 1983, 'Very Brief Visual Experience Eliminates Plasticity in the Visual Cortex', *Science*, 221: 178–80.

Mukerji, P.N., 1981, *Yoga Philosophy of Patanjali*. Calcutta: University of Calcutta Press.

Mukherjee, P.N., 1977, 'Social Movement and Social Change: Towards a Conceptual Clarification and Theoretical Framework', *Sociological Bulletin*, 26(1): 38–59.

Mukherji, N., 2000, 'Traditions and Concept of Knowledge', in A.K. Raina, B.N. Patnaik and M. Chadha (eds), *Science and Tradition*. Shimla: Indian Institute of Advanced Study.

Mukundan, C.R., G.N. Reddy, A.S. Hegde and J. Shankar, 1987, 'Long-term Effects of Head Trauma on the Middle Latency Components of Evoked Potential Responses', *Pharmacopsychoecologia*, 3: 9–16.

Mullick, M., 2000, 'Rationality and the Limits of Reason', in A.K. Raina, B.N. Patnaik and M. Chadha (eds), *Science and Tradition*. Shimla: Indian Institute of Advanced Studies.

Munroe, R.L. and R.H. Munroe, 1975, 'Life Stages in Three Cultures', in R.L. Munroe and R.H. Munroe (eds), *Cross-cultural Human Development*, pp. 7–25. Monterey, CA: Brooks/Cole Publishing Co.

Muralidharan R., 1974, *Motor Development of Indian Children: Developmental Norms of Indian Children 2½ to 5 Years.* New Delhi: National Council for Educational Research and Training.

———, 1983, *Developmental Norms of Indian Children 2½ to 5 years, Part III: Personal–Social Development.* New Delhi: National Council for Educational Research and Training.

Murdock, G.P. and Associates, 1963, 'Ethnographic Atlas', *Ethnology,* 2: 109–33.

Murti, T.V.S., 1955, *The Central Philosophy of Buddhism.* London: Allen and Unwin.

Muthayya, B.C., 1972, *Child Welfare: Existing Conditions and Parental Attitudes.* Hyderabad: National Institute of Community Development.

Nagaraja, D. and P.M. Rao, 1986, 'Comparative Neuropsychological Evaluation of Dominant and Non-dominant Hemispheric Lesions in Occlusive Cerebrovascular Disease', *Indian Journal of Clinical Psychology* 13: 71–76.

Naglieri, J.A. and J.P. Das, 1990, 'Planning, Attention, Simultaneous and Successive Cogntive Processes as a Model for Intelligence', *Journal of Psycho Educational Assessment,* 8: 303–37.

Naidu U.S and V.S. Nakhate (eds), 1985, *Child Development Studies in India.* Bombay: Tata Institute of Social Sciences.

Naik, T.B., 1971, *An Evaluation of the Studies Conducted by the Tribal Research Institutes of India.* New Delhi: The Planning Commission.

Nandi, S., C.R. Rajalakshmi and I. Vergheese, 1971, *Life and Culture of the Mala Ulladan.* Calcutta: Anthropological Survey of India, Government of India.

Nandy, A., 1983, *The Intimate Enemy: The Loss and Recovery of Self under Colonialism.* New Delhi: OUP.

Nath, Y.V.S., 1960, 'Bhils of Ratanmal—Analysis of the Social Structure of a Western Indian Community' (unpublished Ph.D. Thesis), Baroda, M.S. University.

Newman, H.H., F.N. Freeman and K.J. Holisinger, 1937, *Twins: A Study of Heredity and Environment.* Chicago: Chicago University Press.

Nsamenang, A.B., 1992, *Human Development in Cultural Context. A Third World Perspective.* Newbury Park, CA: Sage.

O'Rahilly and F. Muller, 1994, *The Embryonic Human Brain.* New York: Wiley.

Ortner, S., 1984, 'Theory in Anthropology Since the Sixties', *The Comparative Study of Society and History,* 26(1): 126–66.

Paabo, S., 2001, 'The Human Genome and Our View of Ourselves', *Science,* 291: 1219–20.

Panda, K.C. and J.P. Das, 1970, 'Acquisition and Reversal in Four Subcultural Groups Generated by Caste and Class', *Canadian Journal of Behavioural Science,* 2: 267–73.

Pandey, G.C., 1972, *The Meaning and Process of Culture.* Agra: S.L. Agarwala and Company.

———, 1984, *Foundations of Indian Culture: Spiritual Vision and Symbolic Forms in Ancient India.* New Delhi: Books and Books.

Pandey, J. (ed.), 2000, *Psychology in India Revisited—Developments in the Discipline, Vol. 1: Physiological Foundation and Human Cognition.* New Delhi: Sage.

———, 2001, *Psychology in India Revisited—Developments in the Discipline, Vol. 2: Personality and Health Psychology.* New Delhi: Sage.

———, 2004, *Psychology in India Revisited—Developments in the Discipline, Vol. 3: Applied Social and Organisational Psychology.* New Delhi: Sage.

Pandian, J., 1985, *Anthropology and the Western Tradition: Towards an Authentic Anthropology.* Illinois: Waveland Press.

Panno, J., 2004, *Stem Cell Research: Medical Applications and Ethical Controversy.* New York: Facts on File Incorporated.

Paranjpe, A.C., 1984, *Theoretical Psychology: The Meeting of East and West.* New York: Plenum Press.

———, 1988, 'A Personality Theory According to Vedanta', in A.C. Paranjape, D.Y.F. Ho and R.W. Ribber (eds), *Asian Contributions to Psychology.* New York: Praeger.

———, 1998, *Self and Identity in Modern Psychology and Indian Thought.* New York: Plenum Press.

Paranjpe, A.C., and G.S. Bhat, 1997, 'Emotion: A Perspective from the Indian Traditon', in H.S.R. Kao and D. Sinha (eds), *Asian Perspectives on Psychology.* New Delhi: Sage.

Paranjpe A.C., D.Y.F. Ho and R.W. Rieber (eds), 1988, *Asian Contributions to Psychology.* New York: Praeger.

Parasuraman, R. and P.M. Greenwood, 1998, 'Attention and Brain Function in Aging and Alzheimer's Disease', in I. Singh and R. Parasuraman (eds), *Human Cognition: A Multidisciplinary Perspective,* pp. 126–43. New Delhi: Sage.

Pavlov, I.P., 1927, *Conditioned Reflexes: An Investigation of the Physiological Activation of the Cerebral Cortex* (translation). London: Oxford University Press.

Peter, M., 2000, 'Contributions of Imaging Techniques to Our Understanding of Handedness', in M.K. Mandal, M.B. Bulman-Fleming and G. Tiwari (eds), *Side Bias: A Neuroschological Perspective.* Dordrecht: Kluwer Academic Publishers.

Phatak, P., 1977, *Pictoral Monograph of Motor and Mental Development of Indian Babies from 1–30 Months*, Baroda (Self-published).

Piaget, J., 1926a, *Judgement and Reasoning in the Child*. New York: Harcourt Brace.

———, 1926b, *Language and Thought in the Child*. London: Routledge and Kegan Paul.

———, 1929, *The Child's Conception of the World*. London: Routledge & Kegan Paul.

———, 1954, *The Construction of Reality in the Child*. New York: Basic Books.

———, 1966, 'Need and Significance of Cross-cultural Studies in Genetic Psychology', *Journal of International Psychology*, 1: 3–13.

———, 1974, *Culture and Cognition: Readings in Cross Cultural Psychology*. London: Methuen.

———, 1976, 'Need and Significance of Cross Cultural Studies in Genetic Psychology', *American Anthropologist*, 78: 907.

———, 1981, *Intelligence and Affectivity: Their Relationship during Child Development*. Palo Alto, CA: Annual Reviews.

Piaget, J. and B. Inhelder, 1969, *The Psychology of the Child*. New York: Basic Books.

Pieniadz, J.M., M.A. Naeser, E. Koff and H.I. Levine, 1983, 'CT Scan Cerebral Hemispheric Asymmetric Measurements in Stroke Cases with Global Aphasia: Atypical Asymmetries Associated with Improved Recoveries', *Cortex*, 19: 371–91.

Powell, R., G. Bhatt, B. Grady, R. Tonks and J. Carpendale, 1991, 'United We Stand? Our Disciplinary Commitment as Psychologists', Paper presented at the annual convention of the Canadian Psychological Association, Calgary.

Prout, A. and A. James, 1990, 'A New Paradigm for the Sociology of Childhood? Provenance, Promise, and Problems', in A. James and A. Prout (eds), *Constructing and Reconstructing Childhood*. London: Palmer Press.

Pruett, K.D., 1991, 'Family Development and the Roles of Mothers and Fathers in Child Rearing', in M. Lewis (ed.), *Child and Adolescent Psychiatry: A Comprehensive Textbook*. Baltimore: Williams and Wilkins.

Purves, D., S.M. Williams and R.B. Lotto, 2000, 'The Relevance of Visual Perception to Cortical Evolution and Development', in G.R. Bock and G. Cardew (eds), 'Evolutionary Development Biology of the Cerebral Cortex', Novartis Foundation Symposium, 228. New York: John Wiley.

Radcliffe-Brown, A.R., 1929, *The Sociological Theory of Totemism*. Reprinted from the Proceedings of the Fourth Pacific Science Congress, Java.

———, 1948, *A Natural Science of Society*. New York: The Free Press.

Radhakrishnan, S., 1927, *The Hindu View of Life*. London: George Allen and Unwin.

Raghaviah, V., 1962, *The Yanadis*. New Delhi: Bharatiya Adimjati Sevak Sangh.

Raina, A.K., B.N. Patnaik and Monima Chadha (eds), 2000, *Science and Tradition*. Shimla: Indian Institute of Advanced Study.

Raju, P.T., 1985, *Structural Depths of Indian Thought*. Albany: State University of New York Press.

Ramakrishna, T., 1984, 'Interaction of Biological and Experimental Variables in Development: An Ethological Perspective', in B.S. Rao and P.S. Shetty (eds), *Studies in Animal Behaviour*. Bangalore: St. John's Medical College.

Ramanujam, A.K., 1994, *Folk Tales from India*. New Delhi: Penguin.

Rath, R., 1972, 'Social Psychology', in S.K. Mitra (ed.), *A Survey Research in Psychology*. Bombay: Popular Prakashan.

———, 1974, 'Teaching-Learning Problems of Disadvantaged Tribal Children', Presidential Address, 12th Annual Conference of IAAP, Utkal University, Bhubaneswar.

———, 1982, 'Problems of Integration of the Disadvantaged to the Mainstream', in D. Sinha, R.C. Tripathi and G. Misra (eds), *Deprivation: Its Social Roots and Psychological Consequences*. New Delhi: Concept.

Rath, R., A.S. Dash and U.N. Dash, 1979, *Cognitive Abilities and School Achievement of the Socially Disadvantaged Children in Primary Schools*. Bombay: Allied.

Ravallion, M., 1998, 'Poverty Lines in Theory and Practice', LSMS Working Paper No. 133. Washington, DC: World Bank Publications.

Ray, N., 1972, 'Introductory address', in K.S. Singh (ed.), *Tribal Situation in India Today*. Shimla: Indian Institute of Advanced Study.

Ray, P.C., 1965, *The Lodhas and Their Spirit Possessed Men*. Calcutta: Anthropological Survey, Indian Museum.

Reichenbach, B.R., 1990, *The Law of Karma: A Philosophical Enquiry*. Honolulu: University of Hawaii Press.

Report of Department of Health and Department of Family Planning, 1968–69, New Delhi: Ministry of Health & Family Planning and Works, Housing and Urban Development.

Report of the National Workshop on Early Childhood Development, 1996. New Delhi: National Institute of Public Corporation and Child Development, Government of India.

Rewal, V. and K.D. Broota, 1990, 'A Chronometric Study of Differential Reinforcement in Figure-ground Perception: A Further Study', *Journal of Indian Academy of Applied Psychology*, 16: 7–16.

Robinson, R. (ed.), 2004, *Themes in Indian Sociology, Vol. 3: Sociology of Religion in India.* New Delhi: Sage.

Roland, A., 1987, 'The Familial Self, the Individualised Self and the Transcedent Self: Psychoanalytic Reflections on India and America', *Psychoanalytic Review*, 74: 237–50.

———, 1988, *In Search of Self in India and Japan, Towards a Cross-Cultural Psychology.* Delhi: Ajanta Publications.

Roy, S., 1960, *Aspects of the Padam Minyong Culture.* New York: John Wiley.

Rubenstein, J.L.R. and P. Rakic, 1999, 'Genetic Control of Cortical Development', *Cerebral Cortex*, 9(6): 521–23.

Rushworth, M. and V. Walsh, 1999, 'A Primer of Magnetic Stimulation as a Tool for Neuropsychology', *Neuropsychologia*, 37: 125–35.

Sabhesan, S., R. Arumugham and M. Natarajan, 1991, 'Cognitive Deficits after Head Injury', *Indian Journal of Psychology*, 33: 143–48.

Safilios-Rothschild, C., 1982, 'Female Power: Autonomy and Demographic Change in the Third World', in R. Anker, M. Buvinic and Youssef (eds), *Women's Roles and Population Trends in the Third World.* London: ILO.

Sahu, S., 1981, 'Verbal Competence of Socially Disadvantaged Children', *Journal of Social and Economic Studies*, 9(1): 59–65.

Sampson, E.E., 1988, 'The Debate on Individualism: Indigeoeus Psychologies of the Individual and their Role in Personal and Societal Functioning', *American Psychologist*, 43: 15–22.

Saraswathi, T.S., 1993a, 'Child Development Research and Policy Linage: A Mirage or Reality', in T.S. Saraswathi and Baljit Kaur (eds), *Human Development and Family Studies in India: An Agenda for Research and Policy.* New Delhi: Sage.

———, 1993b, 'General Introduction—Child Development Research and Policy Linkage: A Mirage or Reality?', in T.S. Saraswathi and B. Kaur (eds), *Human Development and Family Studies in India: An Agenda for Research and Policy.* New Delhi: Sage.

———, (ed.), 1999, *Culture, Socialization and Human Development.* New Delhi: Sage.

———, 2003a, 'Being and Becoming—A Child, Youth, Adult, and "Respectably" Aged in India', in J.W. Berry, R.C. Mishra and R.C. Tripathi (eds), *Psychology in Human and Social Development: Lessons from Diverse Cultures—A Festschrift for Durganand Sinha.* New Delhi: Sage.

———, (ed.), 2003b, *Cross-cultural Perspectives in Human Development: Theory, Research and Applications.* New Delhi: Sage.

Saraswathi, T. S. and B. Kaur (eds), 1993, *Human Development and Family Studies in India: An Agenda for Research and Policy.* New Delhi: Sage.

Saraswathi, T.S. and P.R. Dasen, 1997, 'Introduction to Volume 2', in J.W. Berry, P.R. Dasen and T.S. Saraswathi (eds), *Handbook of Cross-cultural Psychology, Vol. 2*, 2nd edn. Boston: Allyn & Bacon.

———, 1987a, *Developmental Psychology in India, 1975–1986: An Annotated Bibiliography.* New Delhi: Sage.

Saraswathi, T.S. and R. Dutta, 1987b, 'Some Assessment Measures', in T.S. Saraswathi and R. Dutta (eds), *Developmental Psychology in India 1975–86*, pp. 299–318. New Delhi: Sage.

Sarukkai, S., 2000, 'Symbols of Truth, Objectivity and Reality in Science', in A.K. Raina, B.N. Patnaik and M. Chadha (eds), *Science and Tradition.* Shimla: Indian Institute of Advanced Studies.

Schweder, R.A., H. Markus, and D. Sharma, 2006, 'Socialistation and Cultrural Pluralism', Conference on Culture and Children. Cambridge, MA: Harvard Graduate School of Education.

Seymour, S., 1975, 'Child-Rearing in India: A Case Study in Change and Modernisation', in Thomas R. Williams (ed.), *Socialisation and Communication in Primary Groups.* The Hague: Mouton Publishers.

Shaah, P.G., 1964, *Tribal Life in Gujarat: An Analytical Study of the Cultural Changes with Specific Reference to the Dhanha Tribe.* Bombay: Gujarat Research Society.

Shah, P.M. and A.R. Junnarkar, 1976, 'At-risk Factors and the Health of Young Children in India', KASA Model Integrated Mother–Child Health Nutrition Project (Mimeo). Bombay: Institute of Child Health, Grant Medical College.

Sharma, A and S. Anandalakshmy, 1981, 'Prejudice in the Making: Understanding the Role of Socialisation', in D. Sinha (ed.), *Socialisation of the Indian Child*. New Delhi: Concept.

Sher Singh Sher, 1966, *The Sikligars of Punjab: A Gypsy Tribe*. Delhi: Sterling Publishers Ltd.

Shirley, M., 1931, 'The Sequential Method for the Study of Maturing Behaviour Patterns', *Psychological Review,* 38: 507–28.

Shors, T.J., G. Miesegaes, A. Beylin, M. Zhao, T. Rydel and E. Gould, 2001, 'Neurogenesis in the Adult is Involved in the Formation of Trace Memories', *Nature,* 410: 372–76.

Shweder, R.A., 1990, 'Cultural Psychology—What is It?', in J.W. Stigler, R.A. Shweder and G. Hertz (eds), *Cultural Psychology: Essays on Comparative Development*. Cambridge: Cambridge University Press.

Singh, A.K., 1988, 'Intergroup Relations and Social Tensions', in J. Pandey (ed.), *Psychology in India: The State-of-the-art*, Vol. 2, pp. 159–223. New Delhi: Sage.

Singh, I. and R. Parasuraman, (eds), 1998, *Human Cognition: A Multidisciplinary Perspective*. New Delhi: Sage.

Singh, Y., 1973, *Modernisation of Modern India*. New Delhi: Thomson Press.

———, 1976, 'Role of Social Sciences in India: A Sociology of Knowledge', in S.C. Dube (ed.), *Social Science and Social Realities, Role of the Social Sciences in Contemporary India* (Transactions of the Indian Institute of Advanced Study). Shimla: Indian Institute of Advanced Study.

———, 1977, 'Orthogenetic Changes in Cultural Traditions and Modernisation', in Y. Singh (ed.), *Modernisation of Indian Tradition (A Systemic Study of Social Change)*. Faridabad: Thomson Press.

———, 1980a, *Social Stratification and Change in India*. New Delhi: Manohar.

———, 1980b, 'Concepts and Theories of Social Change', in Y. Singh (ed.), *Social Stratification and Change in India*. New Delhi: Manohar.

Sinha, D. 1965, 'The Integration of Modern Psychology with Indian Thought', *Journal of Humanistic Psychology*, 5(1): 6–17.

———, 1976, 'Some Social Disadvantages and Development of Certain Skills', Paper presented at the IPA International Symposium on Cognition, Delhi University, March.

———, 1980, 'Towards Outgrowing the Alien Framework: A Review of Some Recent Trends in Psychological Researchers in India', Paper presented at the XXII International Congress of Psychology, Leipzig, 5–12, July.

———, (ed.), 1986, *Psychology in a Third World Country: The Indian Experience*. New Delhi: Sage.

———, 1997, 'Indigenising Psychology', in J.W. Berry, Y.H. Poortinga and J. Pandey (eds), *Handbook of Cross-cultural Psychology, Vol. 1: Theory and Method,* 2nd edn. Boston: Allyn & Bacon.

Sinha, D. and H.S.R. Kao, 1997, 'The Journey to the East: An Introduction', in H.S.R. Kao and D. Sinha (eds), *Asian Perspectives in Psychology*. New Delhi: Sage.

Sinha, D. and R.C. Mishra, 1993, 'Some Methodological Issues Related to Research; in Developmental Psychology in the Context of Policy and Intervention Programs', in T.S. Saraswathi and Baljit Kaur (eds), *Human Development and Family Studies in India: An Agenda for Research and Policy*. New Delhi/Newbury Park/London: Sage.

Sinha, J.B.P., 1982, 'The Hindu (Indian) Identity', *Dynamic Psychiatry*, 15 (74–75): 148–60.

———, 1997, 'Indian Perspectives on Leadership and Power in Organisations', in H.S.R. Kao and D. Sinha (eds), *Asian Perspectives on Psychology*. New Delhi: Sage.

Sinha, R., 1962, *The Akas: The People of NEFA*. Shillong: Research Department, Adviser's Secretariat.

Skinner, B.F., 1938, *Behaviour of Organisms*. New York: Appleton Century Crofts.

———, 1950, 'Are Theories of Learning Necessary?', *Psychological Review*, 57: 193–216.

———, 1974, *About Behaviourism*. New York: Knopf.

Smotherman, W.P. and S.R. Robinson, 1995, 'Tracing Developmental Trajectories into the Pre-natal Period', in J.P. Lecanuet, W.P. Fifer, Krasnegor and W.P. Smotherman (eds), *Foetal Developmental: A Psychobiological Perspective*. Hillsdale NJ: Erlbaum.

Squire, L.R., 1987, *Memory and the Brain*, New York: Oxford University Press.

Srinivas, M.N., 1955/56, 'A Note on Sanskritisation and Westernisation', *The Far Eastern Quarterly*, 15: 492–96.

———, 1966, *Social Change in Modern India*. Berkeley: California University Press.

———, 1993, 'Changing Values in India Today', *Economic and Political Weekly*, 28(19): 933–38.

Srinivasan, T. and S.D. Tendulkar, 2003, *Reintegrating India into the World Economy*. New York: Institute of International Economics.

Srivastava, V.K., 1999, 'The Future of Anthropology', *Economic and Political Weekly*, 34(9): 545–52.

Starton, George, 1936, *The Study of the History of Science*. Cambridge: Harvard University Press.

Stein, G.S., J.S. Stein and L.J. Kleinsmith, 1975, 'Chromosomal Proteins and Gene Regulation', *Scientific American*, 232: 46–57.

Sulloway F.J., 1996, *Born To Rebel: Birth Order, Family Dynamics and Creative Lives*. New York: Pantheon.

Super, C.M. and S. Harkness, 1986, 'The Developmental Niche: A Conceptualisation at the Interface of Child and Culture', *International Journal of Behavioural Development*, 9: 545–69.

Swaminathan, M. 1979, 'Children of the Urban Poor: Problems and Opportunities', in A. De Souza (ed.), *Children in India*. New Delhi: Manohar.

———, 1996, *The First Five Years*. New Delhi: Sage.

———, 1998, 'Introduction', in M. Swaminathan (ed.), *The First Five Years*. New Delhi: Sage.

Tandon, T., 1981, 'Process of Transmission of Values in the Indian Child', in D. Sinha (ed.), *Socialisation of the Indian Child*. New Delhi: Concept.

Thomas, R.M., 2001, *Recent Theories of Human Development*. New Delhi: Sage.

Thompson, E., 1999, *History of British Rule in India*. Delhi: Vedams Books Ltd.

Thompson, G., 1952, *Child Psychology*. New York: Houghton Mifflin and Co.

Tolman, E.C., 1925, 'Behaviourism and Purpose', *Journal of Philosophy*, 22: 36–41.

Tripathi, L.B. and G. Misra, 1975, 'Cognitive Activities as a Function of Prolonged Deprivation', *Psychological Studies*, 21: 54–61.

Tripathi, R.C., 2001, 'Aligning Development to Values in India', in A. Dalal and G. Misra (eds), *New Directions in Indian Psychology, Vol. 1*. New Delhi: Sage.

———, 2003, 'Culture as a Factor in Community Interventions', in J.W. Berry, R.C. Mishra and R.C. Tripathi (eds), *Psychology in Human and Social Development: Lessons from Diverse Cultures—A Festschrift for Durganand Sinha*. New Delhi: Sage.

Tronick, E.Z. and A.F. Giannino, 1987, 'The Transmission of Maternal Disturbance to the Infant', in E.Z. Tronick and T. Field (eds), *Maternal Depression and Infant Disturbance*. San Francisco: Jossey-Bass.

UNDP Human Development Report, 2002, New York: UN.

UNDP Human Development Report 2004: Cultural Liberty in Today's Diverse World, 2004, New York: Oxford University Press.

Upadhyay, H.C., 1992, *Reservations for Scheduled Castes and Scheduled Tribes*. Columbia: South Asia Books.

Van Gelder, T., 1995, 'Modelling Connectionist and Otherwise', in L.D. Nikalson and M.B. Bode (eds), *Current Trends in Connectionism: Proceedings of the Swedish Conference on Connectionism*. Hillsdale, NJ: Erlbaum.

Valsiner, J., 2002–03, *Culture and the Development of Children's Action: A Theory of Human Development*, 2nd edn. New York: John Wiley.

Vasantha, A., 1978, 'Study of Science Talent and its Correlates', *Journal of Psychological Researches*, 22(2): 117–26.

Venugopal, C.N., 2004, 'Foreword', in Rowena Robinson (ed.), *Sociology of Religion in India*. New Delhi: Sage.

Verma, J., 2004, 'Social Values', in J. Pandey (ed.), *Psychology in India Revisited, Vol. 3: Applied Social and Organisational Psychology*. New Delhi: Sage.

Vygotsky, L.S., 1962, *Thought and Language*. Cambridge, MA: MIT Press.

Wadley, S.S., 1993, 'Family Composition Strategies in Rural North India', *Social Science and* Medicine, 37(11): 1367–76.

Watson, J.B., 1913, 'Psychology as a Behaviourist Views It', *Psychological Review*, 20(2): 159–77.

Welzel, C., R. Ingle Lart and Hans-Dietes Klingemann, 2001, *Human Development as a General Theory of Social Change: A Multi-level and Cross Cultural Perspective*. Berlin: Wissenschaftszentrum [Fur sozialforschung Gmbtt (WZB)].

Werner, H., 1948, *Comparative Psychology of Mental Development* (revised edn). Chicago: Follet.

———, 1957, 'The Concept of Development from a Comparative and Organismic Point of View', in D.B. Harris (ed.), *The Concept of Development*. Minnesota: University of Minnesota Press.

Whiting, B.B., 1963, *Six Cultures: Studies of Child-Rearing*. New York: John Wiley.

Whiting, J.W.M. and I.L. Child, 1953, *Child Training and Personality*. New Haven: Yale University Press.

WHO QOL Group, 1996, 'What is Quality of Life?', World Health Forum, 17.

Wilson, E.O., 1975, *Sociobiology: The New Synthesis*. Cambridge, MA: Hardward University Press.

Wolf, W., 1949, *The Personality of a Preschool Child*. New York: Grune and Stratton.

Wolfson, J., 1976, 'Cultural Influences on Cognition and Attainment', 'Introduction', in *Personality and Learning 2* (A Reader Prepared by the Personality and Learning Course Team at The Open University). London: Hodder and Stoughton/The Open University Press.

Yati, N.C., 2000, *The Brhadaranyaka Upanishads* (with Original Text in Roman Transliteration, English Translation; Contributor, Nancy Yielding). New Delhi: DK Print World Ltd.

Young, J.G., P. Ferrari, S. Malhotra, S. Tyano and E. Caffo (eds), 2003, *Brain, Culture and Development: Tradition and Innovation in Child and Adolescent Mental Health*. Delhi: Macmillan.

Zhao, S. and M. Stodolsky, 2004, *Bacterial Artificial Chromosome, Vol. 2: Functional Studies* (*Methods in Molecular Biology*) Clifton: Humana Press.

5

The Methodological Study
of Human Development

Early Western Documentation on Human Development

W E HAVE stated in the first chapter that before the Industrial Revolution in Europe and the availability of printed material most knowledge on human development was orally communicated. Again, much of what we know is from the early documentation of western writers. For instance, social thinkers like Aristotle and Plato ignored the so-called uncivilised countries of the East altogether (Aristotle, 1885; Dewey, 1910; Locke, 1924; Rousseau quoted in Qvortrup, 2003). They divided humanity into two—the civilised and the uncivilised. During the colonisation period in India, newly emerging trends in sociology studied the structure of society in its divisiveness, such as different ethnic groups, castes and class structures (Dange, 1949). These studies also indicated how these structures emerged in a given village community (Dumont, 1966). Thus, the village communities of India became a focus of sociological studies. In Europe, it was Comte who first postulated the theological root of modern social science, the development of *la morale*, a science of the highest order, a 'natural philosophy' and the anti-metaphysical stance of his own positivistic view of knowledge (Comte, 1973). The philosophy explained at that time was distinctly Eurocentric indicating no cognition of the developing world (Scheler, 1970) and became, no doubt, the forum for philosophical discussion. This ethic was initiated by the Anglo-Saxon rule into the colonised territories through means of the forerunner of the pragmatic ethos of the Protestant ethic (Hegel, 1969). This ethic was one of the major approaches used in the education of the colonised. A. Ross and W. McDougall were among the first to introduce social psychology as an academic field through their writings (McDougall, 1908; Ross, 1908).

Historically, on the physiological side, the first scientific account of man's development can be traced to Darwin's treatise on the 'evolution of man', and the first mention of the child in his biographical sketch of an infant (Darwin, 1859). Darwin's discussions dealt with genetic endowment and environmental experiences. He differentiated humans from animals, although they have a genetically similar physiological make-up. He emphasised man's ingenuity and creativity in manipulating his environment and his ability to communicate through language (Atkinson, 1964: 8–9). The infant is pictured as a biological organism, extracted from familial and material genetic environments, as indicated in Chapter 2 in the explanation of the concepts of ontogenesis and phylogenesis. Arising from these concepts, the theory of 'cultural recapitulation' was posited. It explained patterns and stages of development of the species as ontogeny modifying phylogeny (Deacon, 2000).

These concepts developed in the western world, which had the facility of communicating such thinking about the origins of man, led to much debate. The child was considered a 'savage', leading to the study of primitive tribes as 'savages', in order to understand the development process.

In a set of equivalences, elaborated by J.B. Lamarck (1944) and L. Moss (2003: 267–76), experiences were considered to be the basis of development (knowledge) rather than innate dispositions. These experiences were said to be reproduced in childhood and dreams, and were hypothesised as being akin to the child, the prehistoric man and the savage. They followed a unilateral developmental process in an ordered hierarchical manner from uncivilised to civilised. The basis of comparison was the undeveloped primitive as against the developed westerner, mainly the colonisers: the British, the French, the Spanish, the Portuguese (Brass, 1966). These nationalities, through their sea-faring abilities, colonised other nations and brought their own bases of thinking to establish the differences between themselves and the conquered. The argument of the evolutionists was that savages eat anything edible, that their behaviour was elementary, so are children's behaviours and, therefore, should be treated as elementary in nature. Unfortunately, several experts indicate that even in this century the imitation of western models is still carried through as a colonial effect, albeit in muted form (Nandy, 1983; Sinha, 1986).

Through a process of trial and error, that which was unpalatable was discarded. Through a pattern of natural selectivity, the savage was denoted as being on the lowest rung of hierarchy of civilisation. It is in the process of experimentation that we see the first signs of a pristine scientific process, where physical needs were matched by environmental resources. Savagery was believed to exist in the early history of the colonised. In the early history of hunters and tribal warfare there were no written records, except etchings in caves and the ruins of early life of the Stone Age dug up by anthropologists in the West. However, these ancestors were not identified as being uncivilised savages by the westerners. Their recorded information was available from excavations, from etchings and household items, and the irrigation systems utilised by them. These were the first signs of civilisations that lived and died but left behind evidence of an elementary pattern of living and social life. However, excavations of the Inca and the Indus Valley indicate that these civilisations were highly developed (the use of metal, wood work, stone) and had urban centres which preceded the colonisers' initial perceptions that India was a country of primitives. However, there is little recorded or narrative data.

Although excavations in south India indicate civilisations in the Stone Age, the first major civilisation flourished around 2500 _` in the Indus valley, much of which now lies in present-day Pakistan. This civilisation continued for another 1,000 years, and was known as the 'Harappan Culture' (Plunkett et al., 2001). In its earliest forms, the pattern of living was depicted as group clusters, with apportioned division of labour, especially land- and sea-bound occupations. For instance, there was trade between India and other countries by sea (Possehl, 2002b).

At this point, we should emphasise that the western world had opened up trade and commerce through sea mobility, colonising many parts of the Far East and Africa, including India where the inhabitants were treated as being in need of indoctrination.

This indoctrination was not only in terms of religion but also in subtle forms of bureaucracy, which kept the inhabitants under the surveillance of their colonisers, especially through the mechanism of paying tithes, which often could not be afforded and left the small and marginal farmers in continual debt (Banerjee and Iyer, 2006). The latter's behaviour was compared to the un-nurtured child. In fact, the colonisers perceived the inhabitants as being less able than themselves. This historical trend has persisted in some muted form decades after independence (Nandy, 1983). Feudalism was the first form of governance and the payment of tithes gradually streamlined the social group into categories of nobility and serfdom. In India, the earliest form of organised governance was one of feudalism and overlords, the *rajas* and the *nawabs* who were the landed gentry and perpetuated their status by virtue of the *zamindari* system. (Singh, 1970). Thus, there were three parallel lines of power, which descended upon the poor masses living in unserviced villages. The first was the immediate government— the *panchayat*, the *patwari* and the *zamindar*. The second was the caste structure, overseen by the Brahminic priest. The third was the colonial power, which held the zamindari system under tight control (Das, 1977). Under this burden, the average villager lived isolated from any form of progress. The strictures on relations between man and the godheads were mainly written by sages or courtiers commandeered by the nobility (King, 1999).

The scanty information that was recorded by hand contained little or no information about the course of human development, except the origins of *atman*, the revolutions of the atman through reincarnations, the teachings through the laws of Manu, the *shastras* (Sathe, 1967: 595–600) and the belief in yoga (Chandler, 1987: 5–26). The only contact, therefore, that the forgotten villages had with knowledge was through the sustained teachings of Hindu philosophy, interpreted by the Brahmins. Knowledge was also imparted through *gurukuls*, *madhukaris* and discourses at temples.

Historical Trends in the Study of Human Development

Pre-colonial Period

We can assume here that the kind of discourses the believers in the Hindu religion were exposed to were classical orthodox themes. Since the masses were illiterate, except in their idiomatic language, their behaviour was virtually under Brahminic power. Thus far, we have indicated the very sketchy information of knowledge and how it was gained during the Vedic period (Basham, 1934: 10–43), and during the Mauryan and Gupta periods of rule (Koshambi, 1964). The primary sources of orthogenetic information and secondary or heterogenetic sources of knowledge on development were little known except through hypothetical 'guesstimations'. For instance, there are gaps in the understanding of the prehistoric Indus (Harappan) valley civilisation and the traditional Vedic cultures in India (Possehl, 2002a). The trail of civilisation seems to have emerged from the Middle East, from Mesopotamia (Possehl, 2002b: 322–40). How these components of civilisation carried from one era to another is probably based on the discourses of religious advisers to the nobility. Because of the power they wielded, the Brahmins, by assigning to themselves the purity rites and the power to absolve pollution (especially amongst the lower castes) through purifying sacrificial *pujas*, ascribed to themselves the highest profile among the caste groups (Raghavan, 1959).

Education in those days was the prerogative of the higher castes, and by virtue of their status they and their *chelas* (assistants) taught children of nobility (Gore and Soares, 1960). There were popular edicts by Ashoka (275 _`), Chandragupta and Vikramaditya (300 ^a). One of Ashoka's edicts enjoins: 'Dharma is a collection of moral precepts, loyalty and obedience towards elders and generosity' (Antonova et al., 1979). Kalidasa, Tulsidasa and Tukaram reinforced such morals in their oral teachings, mostly communicated in their family circles by siblings, caretakers of children and grandparents (Mandelbaum, 1972). The emphasis was on role modelling (Vidyarthi, 1969). They dealt mainly with morality and relevant behaviour, encoded in Indian socio religious philosophy (Gupta, 2006: 37–54).

Beyond this, dependence on information was for piecing together historical events such as wars and rebellions, which however did not focus on human development in terms of physical/ psychological progression, except for the samskaras which marked the rites of passage during childhood and in adulthood. They indicated crucial development phases, and although there is no empirical evidence, they were practised for the purpose of modifying 'constitutional vulnerabilities' and controlling the course of 'psychosocial development' or the stages of development through the lifespan (Grihasutras, 700–300 _`) (Khalakdina, 1979: 14).

Clearly, there was no evidence of knowledge on human development, except for non-empirical information from religion and philosophies of sages. What seems to emanate, on a general basis, are the following themes that have a continuity in some modified form or the other to this day, namely, familialism (Anandalakshmy, 1998: 274–77); kinship, loyalty and networking (Dube, 1997); acquiescence to age in the patriarchal hierarchy (Appadurai, 1988: 36–49); differentiation in the treatment and upbringing between the sexes; the principle of hierarchy, holism, continuity and transcendence (Singh, 1977a: viii) and the compact between the individual and his caste group (Singh, 1980: 21). These attitudes, beliefs and customs emanated from oral teachings at religious congregations at the times of festivals, *yatras*, *bhajan mandals* (gathering of devotees to sing devotional songs), and where swamis held discourses quoting from and interpreting the scriptures. There was no way of validating the teachings of sages and establishing their similarity related to the scriptoral teachings as these were based on individual interpretations by the priesthood and sages. In a sense, the net of ignorance over the masses kept them bound to these precepts and practices, in the manner in which unquestioned authority is heeded to in traditional patriarchal families.

This informal information on the ways of life also contained prohibitions and prescriptions at times of ritualistic events, such as birth, death and marriage. The priesthood also monitored the daily behaviour of the people by enjoining upon them how they should behave during times of certain religious events such as Shivaratri for all, karvachauth, pregnancy and lactation rituals for women (Valsiner, 2000). Many of these injunctions exist to this day and are based on the themes of auspicious and inauspicious days for certain types of behaviour.

Group living was considered essential as a source of identity and security. The existence of the group has its origin in what was called tribal behaviour. Elementary forms of organisation and interactions kept them distinct from others, like the landed *jagirdars* and noblemen at the various courts of rajas and nawabs. To preserve their identity, their rituals and ritualistic behaviour, the masses residing in the hinterlands inculcated distinct forms, patterns of rights and responsibilities, assuming the nascent form of caste division of labour and a hierarchy coincidental with the hierarchy of feudalism (Ghurye, 1986).

Interaction among groups took the form of exchange of goods and services and patterns of filial communications through a *jajmani* system (Wiser, 1959). India at that time was mainly agricultural in its economic domain. In the absence of technology, dependence upon the monsoons was critical for a good harvest. This dependence on agriculture was precarious and often led to famines where the smaller farmers were at the mercy of the patwaris (Baden-Powel, 1982). The major occupation, namely agriculture, revolved around family, *gotra* and kin group, insulated in the village community (Baden-Powel, quoted in Singh, 1977b) and thus heightened knowledge only about these networks. Milton Singer has stated that:

(i) India is primarily indigenous, fashioned on pre-existing folk and regional cultures, its great traditions continuous with little traditions.

(ii) In 'little traditions' of diverse ethnic groups/castes/tribes, cultural continuity was a product and cause of a common cultural consciousness, as the Indian ethos.

(iii) This continuous cultural consciousness has existed with the help of certain processes and factors mediated by sacred books and sacred objects.

(iv) The Brahmins were the main agents of cultural transmission.

(v) The phenomenon of cultural continuity is so deeply rooted that it forms a resistance to the impact of modernisation (Singer, 1955–56).

These patterns depicted, at the same time, cohesiveness within the groups, while simultaneously segregating them by differential obligations and duties in the community network. Thus, roles and role prescriptions, duties and obligations were orally communicated injunctions. In order to keep the phenomenon of segregation-cum-interaction in place, sets of normative behaviour were prescribed by elders (as in the gotra system). The individuals' relationships to the hierarchy of the gods followed a pattern of obedience to Brahmins, who interpreted the sayings of gods, so as to keep the group structures in place (Carstairs and Kapur, 1976). There were sets of beliefs interpreting science through traditional ways, helping to infer scientific phenomena through natural phenomena (like the structure of the Jantar Mantar in Delhi which used geometrically constructed pillars as the sundial to infer time). Energy in its many forms of 'water, fire, stone, air' gave rise to the worship of these forms (animistic) as life-giving, as there were no other scientific explanations available, especially since they were shrouded in mysticism. Recorded in stone and on leaves (images carved in temples and the palmyrus used in *janampatrika*s [horoscopes] preserved by ancient sages), these were the beginnings of communication patterns, passed down from generation to generation orally. The system of writing and reading had not yet found its place in the communication system among the general populace, except for the discourses of the charismatic leaders of their times (K.M. Panikkar, cited in Singh, 1977b).

In India in the Vedic period, there was hardly any distinction between philosophy and religion. The relations between dharma, *kala* (art), *shrama* (labour) and *guna* (quality) were considered bio-mental abilities (Kakar, 1979). In the West, information was recorded in knowledge of the Neanderthal man, giving rise to the theory of evolution and instinctive behaviour (early man was the Neanderthal man, *Homo neanderthalensis*). The first Neanderthal skills were discovered in 1856 by workers quarrying for limestone in the Neander Valley near Düsseldorf, Germany (Bischoff et al., 2003).

Man's needs in the early years were identified as primary and secondary needs. The primary needs were needs for protection against hazardous forces, lack or overabundance of water, lack or overabundance of fire or lack or overabundance of earth (Dubois, 1906) The vicissitudes of these sources of energy (floods and famine) gave rise to a sense of unpredictability and, therefore, insecurity in relation to natural elements. The natural elements were appeased as animistic forms of energy. These appeasements in the form of ritualistic customs were ostensibly to draw down the benignity of the godheads or to avoid their wrath. These gods were mostly female in figures like Durga or Kali Mata (Gross, 1989: 217–30). Rituals became translated into a system of oral folklore, superstition and dependence on nature.

Man sought protection from the unpredictability of nature through venerating these supernatural forms (Wilkins, 2004: 520). The practice of these rituals, their meanings and their relationships towards the supernatural are recorded through retrieved anthropological data and knowledge gained from excavations (Plunkett et al., 2001).

Thus the early written history of human behaviour could be attributed to hypothetical constructs, concerning elementary social organisation and the rules and role tasks for the survival of the community, usually the village community (Karve, 1961). Their status depended upon defending territory and possessions through modes of instinctual survival, a response mainly reactive to unknown forces, a kind of a naïve theory propounded by Werner (Werner, 1984: 630). Emphasis was mainly on language learning by symbols, used in the early days for communication, usually through the cognition of symbols and signs (Ault, 1983). For instance, the nomad, in the face of lack of alternatives for survival, grew to read the signs of dust storms, the seaside fisherman to know about tides and waves, and the farmer to know about the lack or otherwise of the formation of rain clouds. These experiences were based on trial and error methods, much like that of an infant learning through repeated reactions to gain mastery over his immediate environment.

Life then became a process of routine reaction to overt natural stimuli and reactive behaviour monitored by elders and chieftains of the tribe (Satyanarayanan, 1990). Civilisations rose and fell, depending upon their stability in the face of war and strife, where villages often changed hands depending upon whose victory it was. Some inkling of their lifestyles is available from the monuments left behind at places like Ellora, Ajanta and Konark, to give a few examples. However, community life continued within its self-sustaining parameters unvarying and unchanged, as its security depended upon the village as a continuous community (Marriot, 1955a).

The British Colonial Period

In the early 18th century, when human beings became the focus of scientific study, the emphasis initially was on physical development in physiology and biology. The linkages with social sciences came much later, beginning with education and child welfare policies in the Indian context (Government of India, 1961). Knowledge of the developing processes in the individual had its origins in this context. The individual was viewed as a member of a family and kin group network. Thus, while philosophy and sociology were the two linkages to discourses in the abstract on the human in his social setting, the systematic enquiry into human developmental processes began in the socio-educational field. Naturally, philosophy as propounded in the epics of the Mahabharata and the Ramayana dwelt on man's relation to the godheads and nature and man's relation to man. Development of the human in his human setting and habitat appeared on the scene in writings of the western scholars like Mandelbaum (1971), Marriot (1990) and Dumont (1965: 85–99). They dealt mainly with social structure, social issues and societal interactions. Man in India was not seen as an individual in sociological writings, but as a member of a group in which he coexisted with others (Parsons, 1951). Understanding of the human mind was still based on spiritual discourses of Manu, Gautam, Yagyavalkya and Kautilya (Dalal and Misra, 2002). It was only during the period of colonisation that Indians came in contact with the type of education propounded by the British, mainly through various reformist movements introduced by them during their rule.

The most famous of them was the Macaulay report (Antonova et al., 1979). It dealt mainly with primary school education, where education was confined to the rich and the noble through tutorials. Education was anglicised. Interest in early childhood education was borrowed from Frobel and Montessori, and gave rise to a system of primary school education that was rote-learning and was contextually British-oriented. Segmentally, in the few universities that sprang up in the major cities, departments of sociology and then psychology and anthropology were set up.

The study of anthropology came into focus due to the need for knowledge of tribal areas in order to better govern them. Without much interaction each of these sciences was focussed on its own areas, and were isolated from each other. In independent India, the first structured time-bound strategies came with education and community development of the human, while greater emphasis was laid on agricultural and industrial development encompassing community participation as its focus (Krishna, 2001: 158).

The study of the human as an entity came into focus when the child's mental and emotional development was viewed through the earlier writings of psychologists on the education of children. This profiling was further emphasised by the plight of children during and in the aftermath of the world wars. There was little knowledge of how the scattered ethnic groups living in India brought up their children, leave alone educate them. In the West, however, the welfare of the child in terms of physical and mental care was emphasised. Gradually, as the post-WWII situation assumed some normalcy in the West, the child's several aspects of growth and development were studied in institutions of higher learning in Britain and Europe. Because of the colonial ties, some attention was paid to the education of the urban child in larger cities. In the institutions of higher learning in India, course curricula were copied from the British system.

Because of the impetus of the interest of British anthropologists, several Indian scholars undertook the study of 'little traditions' in the descriptions of tribal life. Marx and Locke in the West dominated the area of sociology (Locke, 1960; Wheen, 2000), while in India it was Karve, Srinivas, Dube and their colleagues (Dube, 1988; Karve, 1961; Srinivas, 1962). Psychology was a late entrant, and dealt initially with general psychology. It was in the early part of the 20th century when branches of psychology were established that child psychology came into existence. Child psychology, mainly textual, was confined to British conceptualisations dealing with physiological links to the development of the mind and the growth stages of the human (Havighurst, 1953). It dealt generally with developmental stages, and consequent behaviour during childhood.

There was not much emphasis on the later stages of the lifespan in India. In fact, cognisance and study of gerontology emerged from an understanding of the plight of the elderly in old folks' homes (Dave and John, 2003: 109–16). These areas of study first occurred in the West, especially as an outcome of the phenomenon of modernisation.

These studies gave an impetus to documentation (Chakraborti, 2004), which had a trickle-down effect in the colonies, especially India. Interest in reviewing information on the child at the first stage of human development mainly began through philosophical writings. Plato, 400 years before Christian era, generalised child development and training (Cooper and Hutchinson, 1997: 1808). It was only in the 17th century that philosophers like Locke, for instance, laid special stress on natural impulses and habit-training of the child (Locke, 1960), while Rousseau, a century later, emphasised the back-to-nature principles (social and motor activities) (Rousseau, 1762). Taking a strand from this, Montessori (1964) emphasised practical activities as the major form of learning. John Dewey later on discussed his theory of pragmatic functionalism, that is education through activities (Thompson, 1952: 6–7). These forms of education had a trickledown effect in the urban areas of India. In 1947, during the partition of India, the country was disrupted in terms of any development due to the upheaval of millions in north India. It was only in the 1950s that some forms of immediate development took shape through the declaration of the Constitution of India. Attention was first paid to tribal and rural welfare as they were severely neglected under the colonial regime (Luthra, 1979: 89–103). With the advent of a planned economy, envisioned in the first Five Year Plan, statistics emerged about the plight of the tribals and the rural people which challenged the intelligentsia to put forward plans for universal primary education. At the same time, the largest programme which covered the entire country, namely the Community Development Programme, advocated awareness-building (conscientisation) of the masses and an elemental structure for self-reliance. This was meant to empower people to participate in the development of their socio-economic lives.

The influence of planned economic change was of great importance in stimulating focus on the science of human development. As a matter of fact, the trends towards the conceptualisation of research and teaching of human development, initially arose from other than child concerns. Young children and mothers were clubbed together as 'the vulnerable groups', mainly because of demographic concerns about the high rate of infant and maternal mortality (Kaur, 1978).

In its first ever recognition of rural people, the idea of community development was first mooted in the flush of independence. Community development encompassed agricultural development and, therefore, economic development as its fulcrum. From it emerged sub-areas like women's development through women's participation in *mahila mandals* and representation in village panchayats.

Also, because of the major concerns regarding the health of the 'vulnerable' (women and young children), major emphasis was placed on maternal and child health. However, these required tremendous planning, outlays and trained personnel. These tasks had to be worked at from scratch. Too much was being done too soon in the eagerness of the government to raise the quality of life of the rural/tribal poor, and in the initial stages was in a sense disorganised, with results less than expected. From the concern for women and children sprang the notion of *balwadis* (nursery care for the preschoolers) and a limited form of primary school education. Higher education was mainly confined to the cities. Over the last 50 years, these developmental systems have become full-fledged areas of governmental and non-governmental action with much policy making (Government of India, 2000).

India has subscribed to the UN Convention on Education for All, primarily by emphasising the priority initiated in the Constitution for Universal Primary education (UNESCO, 2000). The Integrated Child Development Services (ICDS), initiated in 1975 with 33 pilot project areas in rural, urban and tribal India, has over the years proved to be a programme with staying qualities, and now more than 30 years hence, is a gigantic programme benefiting preschool children in health, education and nutritional inputs. As of 2000, it is said to be the world's largest and unique child care programme, reaching out to 5.6 million expectant and nursing mothers and 26.5 million children in the age group of 0–6 years, through nearly 10 lakh (0.1 million) frontline workers in 4,348 projects being implemented in 4,079 community development blocks (Punhani, 2000).

The population has grown uninhibitedly in spite of several measures to curb this growth. The realisation came about in the late 1970s that awareness and education were the major prongs for curbing population growth, especially among the deprived sections. S. Khandekar has given a vivid description of the disadvantaged children of Greater Bombay (Khandekar, 1976). Coupled with other small-scale studies, the case for the economically poor, termed 'the fragile section', the 'deprived' or 'the disadvantaged', took preponderance. Since economic deprivation was characteristic of the lower classes, their opportunities for education and jobs through the reservation policy of the government was enacted in the late 20th century (Upadhyay, 1992). Even to this day, educational and social development has lagged behind other economic indicators (Saraswathi, 1999: 31). Children are still at risk especially on account of the growing problems associated with modernisation (Garbarino, 1995: 235–78). B.C. Muthayya in his report of the disadvantaged rural child (1977: 560) and Saraswathi and her colleagues (1993) observed that there is a need for a radical change in the research directions in human development towards policy-oriented research. Such research would give greater clarity on the living conditions of the poorer segments of the population, most of whom live in rural and tribal areas.

India is deemed to be a subcontinent, where the lacunae for social and psychological development facilities are still large. The country is now in the Tenth Plan period (Government of India, 2001). Some encouraging signs of economic development have occurred. Massive efforts like the ICDS, and programmes of both government and non-government agencies for health (especially maternal and child) and education, have gradually had effect, although still inadequate (World Bank, 1997). It is particularly the economic development spurt, which has spurred improvement among the lower economic groups who make up 75 per cent of the population (Myles, 1995), rather than any planning processes for societal community concern or community participation. Over the years, research has shown a marked improvement in the attention paid to preschool children, in for their health, nutrition and cognitive development (Swaminathan, 1998: 23–24). The ICDS has been regularly monitored so as to give a feedback to the nodular ministry, the Ministry of Human Resources Development, so as to realign inputs to outputs (Sood, 1992).

Concern for the disabled is slowly catching the attention of both government and non-governmental organisations, even though resources for them are still scarce. As such the attempts are minimal. They only touch the fringe of the needs of such groups. With the advent of independence and constitution emphasising freedom, equality and justice, highly sophisticated in nature (in many respects incomprehensible to the illiterate masses), a gigantic task of development was undertaken. Since the system of governance was already the familiar British bureaucratic system, there continued to be top-heavy preparation, planning and project formulation. Much of these highly sophisticated labels were incomprehensible to the masses who, however, adapted to the new functions of the state as they dispelled the labels of the colonial era. For the first time, the deprived, the disadvantaged, the rural and the tribal were brought into the orbit of development. Primary education, balwadi programmes, rural development programmes were instituted and interfaced with the highly traditional society (Dube, 1988).

However, this did not displace the work of non-governmental agencies, for they were supported by grants-in-aid by the government ministries, namely Health, Human Resources Development, Rural Development and Law and Justice, and such like. Non-governmental enterprises have moved from the charity-giving ideology to economic growth of remote communities so that the economic standards could be raised through self-initiatives (Lalitha, 1987). There was a curiously ironic phenomenon developing: the government had all the finance but little infrastructure since its target was large populations, while the few scattered non-governmental organisations (NGOs) concentrating on smaller coverages accomplished their tasks more effectively with fewer facilities. Some of these NGOs existed even before the independence era: for instance, the Brahmo Samaj began in 1824, the Ramakrishna Mission in 1897, the reformist movement of Raja Ram Mohan Roy in 1859, and the Harijan Sevak Samaj in 1932. Since then, many agencies have sprung up in various parts of the country (Khalakdina, 1998: 163–94). These non-governmental agencies were committed to raising the standards of living of the poor. Thus, we see that in India from the early 1940s, the emphasis was on the provision of facilities for the vulnerable groups. However, there was little organisation, administration and technical acumen to achieve them.

Whatever knowledge existed was ad hoc through simultaneous training of personnel and implementation of projects. Parental perceptions in these project areas was to perceive such interventions as charitable organisations not dissimilar from the *daan* (charity) given by the rich (Khalakdina, 1973). There was hardly any interaction between programmes and parents and, therefore, little parent education, so that a schism occurred between the infrastructure group and the parent group.

The early stages of programming of the ICDS, the largest in India today for young children, began in 1975, as a pilot project. Since then the programme has incorporated women and young girls, successfully in its developmental aegis (Government of India, 1996a: 11–13). The emphasis on encouraging ontogenetic skills was lacking. For instance, little children were supposed to read and write at early stages even if they were not neurally mature. The reasoning was that it was a required skill based on phylogeny. Individual differences and talents went unnoticed in the regime. However, with the growing recognition of the importance of ontogeny, strategies began to change, and the concept of the slow learner, the gifted and the educable began assuming focus.

In their probing to understand the development of the individual chronologically, the disciplines of psychology and sociology began focussing not just on experimental psychology and theoretical sociology, respectively, but on field studies, case studies and existing life situations of the growing individual. Some of these concerns were based on Lewin's field theory (Lewin, 1938), and Miller and Dollard's classic analyses of how children unconsciously model their learning on the basis of an admired adult in the family (Miller and Dollard, 1941: 440, 485). Therefore, borrowing from the West, Indian experts undertook the study of normal behaviour which gave rise to the concept of averages: averages in intelligence, developmental norms, psychometrically obtained, such as Weschler, Bellevue, Gesell and Raven's progressive matrices (Saraswathi and Dutta, 1987), all based on norms of western children. The study of the non-normal gave rise to the idiographic study of irrational behaviour (Freud, 1935; 1946).

From the psychological point of view, beginning in the West, there has been a movement towards viewing development in a holistic interdisciplinary manner, paying more attention to the cultural traits of a society, doing in-depth studies of individuals in their *in situ* situations. Further, research and critiques of long-standing theories were concerned by newer theories such as the social learning theory and the Lewinian theory of field forces (Lewin, 1938; Miller and Dollard, 1941).

In India, there was a growing emphasis on the validity of applying cultural and ecological concepts for reliable information on development in the Indian context. Modifications of some theories such as the strictly Freudian by the neo-Freudians, the theories of Gestalt by more dynamic models looked at a whole perspective of human development as interlinked in action and reaction (Koffka, 1935). Vygotsky, a neo-Piagetian, theorised that any particular mental function must have both environmental as well as psychological frames. In other words, Vygotsky added that Piagetian theory dealt specifically with a focus on the individual's cognition, without adequate reference to the environmental influences (Vygotsky, 1981: 145–72). This was further stressed by the enlargement of this concept by Bronfenbrenner in his model proposing different systems of interaction, from the micro-, meso-, exo-, to finally the macro-systems of human ecological interaction. Bronfenbrenner gave a cognitive mapping of a model indicating the human interaction of man with his environment (Bronfenbrenner, 1977). The introduction of the concept of human ecology is a more acceptable form of explanation of human behaviour than just the individualised explanations of stimulus–response, operant conditioning and similar segments of human behaviour (Bennett, 1983). This is especially acceptable in the Indian context, given the variegated categories of caste, ethnicity, regionalism, religion and other factors, which are sociological in nature.

Therefore, the interaction of psychology and sociology in a socio-psychological context is much favoured in theorising human development. Some of the outstanding experts who make out an argument for this coalition are: A.C. Paranjpe (1998), D. Sinha (1986), P.R. Dasen (1990), R.C. Tripathi (2002: 307–25), S.C. Kak (2000), and T.S. Saraswathi (2003).

These suggested modifications do not in a sense shake the foundations of the basic concepts of development. They are varying perspectives on development using specific themes such as the schemas of Erikson and Piaget (Erikson, 1943; Inhelder and Piaget, 1958, 1964). They continue to be salient but in a contextual frame.

However, progressively, new theories are moving towards a more eclectic conceptualisation of the meaning and nature of human development. These emphasise the intricate intertwining between the biophysical genetic nature of the human being and the moderating influences of the environment. This is especially significant as the human environment in the Indian context is more intense compared to the West and its concomitant values and loyalties are more heterogeneous than in the West (Ramanujan, 1972).

Notwithstanding these information sources, it is important to remember that in India very little was done in researching/documenting the individual's development beyond the adolescent years. The young adult, the middle-aged and the elderly were inadequately analysed in the orbit of human development.

From the Indian perspective, Indian thought on development was embedded in theosophical thought. This emanated from the injunctions of the belief in *karma* and *dharma* (O'Flaherty, 1980).

This appeared in its earliest forms of writings about the behaviour of man in relation to his environment. Philosophical writings have existed from the early 17th century, where the themes included some emphasis on the role of the nurturer in the family, namely the mother, as the nexus of caring. This theme was especially profiled in the family (Baig, 1979; Khatri, 1965), which was supported by the kin group, the caste and the community networks (Habib, 1963). It was reflected in Indian mores, which articulated the values of the individual in the family. For instance, in the Hindu joint family, the status of the Hindu male and the Hindu female was strictly demarcated (Khatri, 1970; Madan, 1962: 3).

More recently, there has been an upsurge of information on the contribution of Indian philosophy to the thinking processes of science, and in its rediscovery of Indian conceptualisations contributing to scientific thought (Raina et al., 2000: ix). These have been re-examined by discussions on yogic origins of scientific living (Devananda, 1988), understanding ancient science and the traditional concepts of knowledge, which were partially neglected under the colonial agenda. These discourses have stated that the Indian mind developed a profound system of mathematics, astronomy, physics and biology as emanating from yoga, and that ancient scholastic tradition is quite in conformity with the latest scientific information obtained in the science of the West (Raina et al., 2000). Very clearly, there is a strong movement to consolidate this generic process in the bid for underscoring that Indian psychology in the 21st century is making a movement towards becoming an indigenous discipline, incorporating scientific Indian thought (Pandey, 2004, 342–66). It is well known that the birth of child, especially the male, was heralded with much joy. The Grihasutras point out to the stages of development marked by events such as the first feeding, the first weaning, tonsuring and so on, indicating the recognition of varying and chronologically increasing years of maturity. In some elementary tribes, rites of passage were events heralding the boy into manhood (Verma, 1996).

The characteristics of kinship, caste and community were also recognised as being important in the early political history of rajas and nawabs. This was important in the situation where there was constant warring, and change of rulers, between dynasties: for instance, from the Mauryas to the Mughals, and among them the various chieftains. There was a differential notion of who was the ruler at one time and who was not in the mind of the masses, thus creating a dissonance. Some of the moral injunctions of the rulers to the ruled were hailed as ethical mandates (Antonova et al., 1979). At about the same time, cognisant of the strife in society, sages like Kalidasa, Tulsidas and Tukaram, through their writings, reinforced morals, hierarchical deference, patriarchal norms and loyalty towards kinship, *jati* and community. This was highlighted by later-day experts in the field of sociology (Mandelbaum, 1968).

In the period prior to independence, some beginnings were made in paying special attention to children under the guidance of selected gurus. These were, however, mainly of children of the higher castes, who attened special religious gurukuls (Gore, 1966). During the late Mughal period madrasas were introduced as centres of learning, mainly for teaching the Quran. Females were debarred from entering these various religious centres, initiating early the concept of 'discount' of the female. Their main task was to be trained as future *bahus* (daughters-in-law) for the *sasural* (in-laws' house). The major emphasis in learning was imitation of the same-sex parent, as the model (Vidyarthi, 1972).

When children were about six or seven, around the primary school age, they were taught the locus of control (*paterfamilias*) in the mainly patriarchal family. The bond between the mother and child was strong, especially between mother and son. Childhood was considered a period of dependency for both sexes. There was greater laxity in the upbringing of the male and overprotection of the female child. The infant in the early years was closely attached to the mother in physical proximity, much more than in western cultures. This also emphasised the dyad relationship between mother and child (Malhotra, 2003: 3–13). In available writings on the Indian family (Anandalakshmy, 1998: 274–75; Dube, 1965; Khatri, 1970; Kumar, 1993; Srinivas, 1962) both sociologists and psychologists have viewed development as the effect of the reinforcement by families (in their verbal and non-verbal communication) of traditional values, respect and obedience to elders, stratification of caste/gender roles and statuses, and hierarchical structures. (UNICEF, 1973). Thus, informal education continued in a parallel manner in relation to the few efforts made by the colonisers, mainly the British in the north and east, the French on the south-east coast and the Dutch and Portuguese along the southern and western coasts, respectively.

They brought with them their colonial processes used in the West in education and in social behaviour, imitated by a miniscule proportion of the rich Indian feudal lords. With the establishment of the East India Company in 1815, the British were firmly entrenched in India. They started out in establishing educational institutions and psychology was given a boost with the establishment of the first psychology department in Calcutta University by N.N. Sengupta (in Dalal and Misra, 2002: 36). These institutions of higher learning did not affect the lives of the masses, but only served to 'intellectualise' the elite. For purposes of administration and more importantly tax collection, it was essential that the principalities collected tithes through their patwaris, to be paid regularly into the coffers of the British (Baden-Powell, 1892). The society became a world of '*sahibs*, *babus* and *naukars*'. Villages which formed almost 95 per cent of the population were forgotten, and the major cities became areas of commerce and industry for trade with the West. Jute in Bengal, coal in Bihar and Orissa, gold in the south, metal in Central Provinces and tea in the hillside provinces became the leaching ground for the British Raj (Gopal, 1965). Nawabs and rajas who could favour the British overlords became their minions and their spies for quelling rebellious insurgents.

However, because these cities were also populated by the sahibs, some modicum of learning the English way came into existence and it was imitated by the princely class. Some of the earliest schools like Doon in UP, Lawrence in Himachal Pradesh and Tamil Nadu, and convents run by European nuns came into existence for the gentry and the British families, mainly at hill stations. Two parallel forms of interaction from the West occurred. First was the charismatic relationship of the foreigner with the elite Indian. This linkage did not displace the Indian's firm bonding with his traditional cultural heritage (Mandelbaum, 1972).

The second was the interaction of the Britishers who imposed their own caste system of *jajman*: the ruler and their henchmen, the babus and patwaris, and the ambigous masses, each category being beholden to the level above. (Wiser, 1959). In many such situations, the ruled sought refuge further in the nexus above them, so as to find a safe haven of security. In times of stress and distress, the family appealed to its caste group, the caste group to its community and so the lines of loyalty were established. In the last analysis, a colonial future-oriented system of the British Raj was imposed upon a past-oriented traditional system (Kluckhohn and Strodbeck, 1961). For the majority of rural and tribal areas there was no form of schooling experience for the upgrading of their elementary skills in the occupations followed by the caste groups. Thus, the beginning of acceptance and tolerance of a sophisticated mode of living (the rulers and their henchmen) found its rooting in the psyche of the Indian who moved from one form of feudalism to another with indifferent acceptance. During this period of acceptance of that which could not be changed, it is important to remember that the average Indian took refuge in the security of the wisdom of the teachings of the Ramayana, the Mahabharata, and the gurus. This attitude helped cement their linkage with their godheads through the conduit of Brahmins, who were the priestly interpreters of the scriptures. This was a reaction formation to the insecurity of the threatening foreign overlords. In many situations because of the superstitious adherence to rituals, 'the twice-born', the Brahmins, had control over them (Carstairs, 1957). Perhaps this ability of the Indian to coexist with many forms of superior headships has given him, over the ages, the resilience to perform the role tasks suitable to the occasion, namely subservience to authority, and, alternatively, authority over the subjugated, with the freedom to control the subjugated. In more recent research on self-abnegation, a research study done in Mexico raises the question as to whether abnegation as (perceived) in the Mexican society can be generalised to (most) similar traditional societies such as India. We do know that in the Indian society, the practice of being courteous may also be inferred as being reciprocal in interactional relations, 'khatirdari'. As such, one may ask whether abnegation long drawn from a tradition of being subservient to several different rulers could be a cultural mode for an inherently developing country, or it is an expression of stoicness or resentment (Diaz-Guerrero, 2003: 65–85). For instance, a worker in the government service says 'ji sir' to his boss and when he returns home vents his frustration by punishing his victim(s), usually the wife and children. Since forms of behaviour were orally communicated in the traditionally Indian system, the Indian's ability to change role performance to suit the occasion also gave him the ability to retain his own conventional forms of social behaviour. Even though acknowledging the foreign ways of life, the average Indian has not changed his core values, that is respect towards godheads, the priesthood and the family; and obedience to them, followed by observance of hierarchical rites of conventional behaviour. Perhaps, this adherence to core values are the rooted behaviour tendencies which, in spite of the onslaught of science and technology, continue in Indian homes to this day.

Be that as it may, the major information that existed in the pre-colonial days were orally communicated to be put into action. These were the teachings of Manu, the scriptures of the Mahabharata and the Ramayana. However, it is doubtful as to whether the correct interpretation was expounded by the Brahmins who wielded power over the illiterate masses. These masses could only imbibe what they heard. It is only when the upper classes came into their own through the British system of education, that they and their compatriot scholars, sufficiently knowledgeable to translate the Vedic literature, could document them more intelligibly for the educated.

Even so, to this day there is the necessity of the pundits who are the only ones to perform the sacred rites, who themselves resort to individualised interpretations. Some of the pundits are so sophisticated today that they even intertwine English in their interpretations. As such the realistic interpretations were in the form of dos and don'ts, hardly in the form of understanding the reasoning behind the scriptures, especially when communicated to the masses in the still illiterate rural and tribal areas and among the urban poor. What was understood, however, was the following:

- Rites and rituals should be practised at the right time for the appropriate person.
- Pujas and *mantras* must be performed to bring down the benignity of the godheads and to avoid their wrath.
- Pilgrimages and visits to shrines were an essential part of religious activities in order to gain *moksha*.
- Dharma should be widely practised. The rites of pollution and purification should be observed.
- The observance of custom and convention among the age groups, between the sexes and in family/kin group should be maintained for creating a viable and harmonious community.

These injunctions automatically put the Brahmins on the highest rung of the hierarchy of respect and reverence, and the untouchables at the bottom, till the actions of Mahatma Gandhi and the coming of independence removed untouchability in law, but not necessarily in daily interactions among the castes. However, with the growing prosperity of the general populace, there is a movement of the lower castes to demand their rights (Mahajan, 1998) and attempt to incorporate nodes of sanskritisation and westernisation simultaneously into their practices, beliefs and attitudes (Das, 1994).

Thus we have a backlog of unknown territory regarding the exposition of the teachings of Hindu scriptures to the populace at large. What is apparent, however, is that in the post-British period, the Indian psyche seems to have recovered its self-esteem, previously submerged in the British Raj (Nandy, 1983). There continues to be general public apathy towards seeking valid information. This is understandable since the masses were/are concerned more with their daily needs for survival rather than seeking information for their edification. Except for the public address system in the early years, there was not much evidence of an orchestrated system of public communication. Over the past 30 years, however, communication has accelerated to such an extent that not only are there numerous channels of television, but there are advertisements, rail and road systems of communication, banks, post offices and more importantly the cell phone. The major contact between the masses and erudite information was mainly from interpretations by agents of intervention. These information sources were from the block headquarters personnel, the developmental agencies and the communication between the rural and urban people. These made it possible for the illiterate adult to know something about the happenings in governance. For the most part, in the earlier days, the primary education, which was mandatory, hardly covered one-third of the target group. It has now expanded to over 60 per cent on a general basis with many more females than before attending primary school (in spite of dropout rates). Thus, there has been a steady filtration of information and education into the family circle with the advent of independence.

It was only in the British era, when English was taught in the elite schools, that the elite Indian scholar became interested in the social-anthropological aspects of Indian living. The independence era brought in governmental and non-governmental implementation of knowledge. At about the beginning of the 20th century, a number of voluntary organisations came into existence. Initially begun on the mould of the charity-giving missionaries, several voluntary organisations spread themselves out into the fields of early childcare, care of the abandoned, widowed and sexually harassed women, delinquents and those in need of special care. A host of them operated in many regions of the country, with varying degrees of success. Some of them persisting from the colonial period are the Balkan ji Bari (1924), the Guild of Services (1923), the Children's Aid Society (1927), the Council for Women (1925) and the All India Women's Conference (1926). To this day, these stalwart organisations together with other organisations like the Indian Council for Child Welfare (1952) continue to interact with the poorer masses, especially in remote areas. However, even though they were well-intentioned, given the vast majority to be serviced, the result of the work of these non-governmental agencies is infinitesimal. It was in the independence era that the constitution gave a new face to efforts to raise the status of the masses, however gigantic the tasks seemed. These masses were poor and illiterate and had not a clue about what democracy implied.

In the field of academics, there was a spurt of interest in the study of small communities, (Marriot, 1955b) laboratory experiments (Mondal, 2000: 58–93) and field ethnography studies. These were mainly by departments of anthropology of the few well-known universities that existed in Mumbai, Delhi, Chennai, Kolkata and Allahabad. Gradually, however, with the growing encompassing of larger target groups in higher education, there was a spurt in not only pure psychology, pure sociology and pure anthropology, but also their derivatives. These derivatives are social psychology, cross-cultural psychology, social anthropology, and the like. The concept of insularity within the disciplines was thus broken.

Having begun in the colonial era, the work of well-known educational philosophers continued to grow: Tagore (for universal values and aesthetics especially of nature), Annie Besant (for spiritual and mystical areas of knowledge), Vivekananda (for religion and social service), Raja Ram Mohan Roy (for ethics and value of education), Jyotiba and Savitri Bai (for pioneering education for Dalit women), J. Krishnamurti (for family and education) and Jijubhai (for educational methodology). These pioneers put their mark on the need for simpler forms of education and development. Mahatma Gandhi consolidated this theme in propounding basic education in India. Philosophical education was the basis of infrastructure development (primary schooling), community development and adult education. These were a few efforts of democratic India to improve the living conditions and the health and education of families.

However the anglicised pattern of education continued in its original form, for want of a viable alternative. This continued without a cultural basis, initially, for even the efforts of the few educated Indians to try and change the structure and format proved feeble in the face of the gigantic structure set forth by Macaulay (Evans, 2002). This happened in spite of the proponents of basic and national systems of education. We observe four parallel patterns emerging from the spread of education in India. These are as follows: (*a*) a highly educated, but minuscule, proportion of those educated in higher institutions of learning, who could further educate themselves in research and teaching within the same circle; (*b*) a growing young population being educated in formal school learning; (*c*) a large proportion of illiterate adults; and, finally, (*d*) a lack of communication, transmission, translation, and trans-interpretation of educational principles between those who knew and those who did not.

It is true, though, there was a linkage, however poor, between those who knew and those who did not by a group of paraprofessionals, namely health workers, multipurpose workers, child workers, and others. They carried messages from the educated elite in the areas of social, psychological and anthropological information to programmes/project levels. However, as indicated by several discerning scholars, the interface between information givers, researchers and policy/programmes was and continues to be fairly unsystematic (Sinha, 1993: 57–63).

This malaise has occurred because of three phenomena: the ready availability of the British system of education, western borrowed information in the social sciences and the lack of sources of such information in the Indian educational system.

Therefore, erudite empirical data on generic empirical facts like learning and reinforcement theory, formation of attitudes and values, childcare (weaning, toilet-training, independence and achievement) were followed in the western mode. These were popular areas of enquiry by Indian scholars in education for early childhood. The scholars who taught were themselves frequently products of the British system. Therefore, there was a lacuna in the Indian ethos of who the Indian was.

Information Sharing between Government and People

As we have said before, the Indian government has taken up the highly ambitious programme of development in a pluralistic, illiterate and traditional population. This population is as heterogeneous as a kaleidoscope. Few perhaps have benefited from a knowledge of what human development is (given the potpourri of the various disciplines). If one were to ask the question, what is the purpose of this knowledge on human development, there can be no two answers. The answer is to understand and to better the lifestyles of the various heterogeneous groups of the population spectrum. However positive we might want to be, while all strata are improving their lifestyles, given the spurt in economic growth, some are improving more than others. These 'some' are the extremely rich, economically better-off and powerful in contrast to those who are poor and helpless. India is, therefore, faced with an ever-increasing challenge, though with a few hiccups it is managing to balance democratic ideals with its actions. Still there is a yawning gap between those who have and those who do not.

The challenge facing developmental specialists, whether they are sociologists, psychologists, anthropologists or economists, is that they cannot ignore the fact that development is holistic. If this challenge is further analysed, there are several sub-challenges. First, Indians freed from the shackles of colonisation used their potentials and their priorities. Second, in that era, scientific thinking on the workings of the mind took into account the influences of the environment such as ecology. Third, the challenge accelerated the concentration on the study of human development and psychosociological aspects of societies (Dube, 1965: 423). For this spurt in the latter, we owe our knowledge to insightful socio-anthropological studies which examined small group behaviour of inhabitants in their own environs (Benedict, 1934; Malinowskwi, 1959; Mead, 1983). Fourth, ethnographic detailing showed how behaviour was articulated by the forces in the natural habitat (Vayda, 1969). Fifth, the upper classes were educated and were articulate to document their thoughts in print (Dalton, 1970). By force, therefore, studies related to the developmental processes in the urban areas were the focus of the disciplines of psychology and sociology. The Indian elite needed to make an effort to prove how useful their contributions were towards 'upliftment' of the downtrodden. Several were jailed in the cause of Indian freedom and were still imbued with the spirit of national ardour.

Economic concepts like poverty and deprivation emphasised the lack of learning facilities for the underprivileged rural poor, and were popular themes for analyses and action by these upper class scholars. In this academic pursuit, analyses, discourses and even research indicated that the upper classes, who came from better educational levels, were better-off. These analyses overlooked the intervening variables of cognitive ability, opportunity, aspiration and persistence.

With the advent of many institutions of higher education and research, several organisations came into being: National Institute of Public Cooperation and Child Development (NIPCD) for women and children; National Institute of Health Education (NIHE) for health services; National Council for Educational Research and Training (NCERT) for education, especially preschool and primary school education; the Institute of Public Administration (IPA) for governance and the Indian Institute of Advanced Studies (IIAS) which dwelt on the social sciences. These are a few examples of the plethora of institutions set up by the Planning Commission. Several national institutions were created to plan and implement programmes. They, however, remained within their parameters, and did not look at the problems from a total perspective of benefit to the whole human being (Pareek, 2002).

Reference norms in India were devised on tests of intelligence, aptitude, values and conditioned behaviour which originated from the West. School textbooks still prescribed items of consumption like 'red apples', 'tables' 'cots' and nursery rhymes, all constituted to do exactly the opposite of learning for the masses of rural/tribal children, who knew only oral communication through their dialects. When the country established official languages, then national organisations, like the NCERT and its state branches, and the National Book Trust began translations of the literature into the state languages. Given the problem of tri-lingualism in many states, where English, Hindi and the vernacular had to be learned, it followed naturally that expertise was limited in the less known state languages. To give an illustration, the rural/ tribal children are more familiar with their items of ecology than those of the urban areas (*peedas* versus chairs, slippers versus shoes). Thus tests invariably showed, as expected, that rural tribal children performed less successfully. Likewise, tests of aspirations/vocational choices were tangential concepts for children whose family occupations were unvaried and elementary. Psychometrists eventually found that the stylised fashion of using unconditioned tests from the West like Weschler's tests of intelligence (Weschler, 1992) had its reliability vitiated by cultural and subcultural factors, mainly arising from the environment. In the United States in the early 1970s, much debate was generated around the deficit versus the difference hypothesis regarding intelligence. It arose out of Jensen's study whether intelligence was more a racial factor than a nurtured one (Jensen, 1969). While the racial factor has a genetic basis, most academicians comment that nurturance has much to do with the expression of intellligence (Eysenck, 1971).

It was only in the 20th century that the focus on some tests moved from adoptions to adaptations. In the early years of higher education, departments of psychology incorporated these in their testing situations without much adaptation. Those adapted were mainly of intelligence, psychiatry and vocational aspirations.

The net result of these adaptations, using western reference norms, invariably indicated that Indian children performed less well and, therefore, were less intelligent/capable or had lesser mental abilities. Then psychometrists in India began to translate, 'adapt' such tests, and still continued on the same pathway. In recent years, however, attempts are being made to devise indigenous norms. Unfortunately, the comparisons are still between the 'less' and the 'more' within the country, for example, economic deprivation, lower and higher castes, rural and urban children (Naidu and Nakhate, 1985: 5–10; Saraswathi and Dutta, 1987: 127–232). Therefore, a variety of adaptations of the western tests like the Gesellian norms, Havighurst's (1953) developmental tasks and Binet's intelligence tests (Binet and Simon, 1905), which were supposedly related to the Indian scene, became popular. Since in the 1930s, the study of the human began with early infancy, and the episodes of childcare such as weaning, toilet-training and discipline, studies in India reflected the same preoccupations. Whereas in the departments of psychology, emphasis was given to experimental and general psychological tenets, sociology, on the other hand, had made strides in social structure, social analysis and social interactional studies (Dube, 1965). The area of child studies remained, during the 1940s and 1950s, under courses teaching home craft, homemaking and, later, home science. The sphere widened gradually as sociologists turned to studying child-rearing in different societies, (Minturn and Hitchcock, 1956), some of them using psychological terminology; and psychology itself moved from the laboratory to study the child in the network of the family, peers and the social environment. Academically, variables for measuring socio-economic class improved their operational definitions, including quantifying rural income which before were either guesstimates, or took into account important items like possession of cattle, and estimating their costs. As yet, standardised scales of socio-economic status have yet to be satisfactorily devised. In trying to transform the populace towards adopting and adapting to modern progressive ways of thinking and acting, sociology was in a quandary, as to how to innovate methodology in socio-psychological dimensions, consonant with the prevailing traditionality dimension of the populace (Yang, 2003). The government's effort has been to revise the curricula in order to meet the target of compulsory education for all. It has to be realised that the targets fall short, given the constraints that rural/tribal masses experience in continuing a primary school education, completing it and procuring satisfactory jobs.

The concern of the rural/tribal Indian was, 'How does this education help us in making a living?' Several evaluations have shown that while about two-thirds of the population of school-going children are supposedly enrolled in school, the proportion actually going to school is much less (Singh, 2003). Early childcare programmes of preschoolers were only a scratch on the surface. Moreover, the female child is at a great discount, aggravated by the situation that in most states, especially in the north, maternal and child mortality is still alarmingly high, with the population growth going unabated. The psychology of differences was then examined, and eventually studies which discussed the interface between psychology and culture (Cole, 1996). The results of these studies showed that hypotheses were mainly tested on assumptions of deficits rather than differences (Cole, 1992: 5–31). For instance, a child from a lower socio-economic group, given opportunities for training, can exhibit the same or similar skills as a child from an economically higher group and is therefore not deficit (Basvanna and Rani, 1984: 121–28).

The fact remains that many schools are poorly equipped and are one-room schools in rural areas (Sharma, 1998). Despite this lack of quantity and quality of education, institutions of higher learning continue to conduct degree courses in all areas of social sciences and, in some colleges, in the areas of child development.

Trends in the Study of Human Development

The study of human development per se is an area of scientific enquiry, which originated with 'childcare' in the early 1920s. It assumed scientific labels congruent with available knowledge in research on the parameters of childhood, maturation learning and physical development in the early 20th century. It was labelled child development in India. In the West, the area of study went further, recognising that environment was increasing in importance in studying the child. Therefore, the domain was labelled 'human ecology' giving a wider contextual base and a recognition that the changing environment of science and technology made it necessary that it be reflected in the educational and research programmes in the West. In India, it still continued to be child development, and was mainly taught in home science colleges while other colleges taught the traditional psychology/sociology/anthropology courses.

In the latter part of the 20th century, cognisant of the lacunae in describing the development of the human in his total lifespan, many home economics colleges in the West changed their nomenclature: child development was labelled human development, home economics colleges were relabelled colleges of human ecology, and such like. In trying to find a niche for this amalgamated discipline which still borrows concepts and empirical data from other disciplines, there is no true identity for human development, for it is the human who has developed his environment, and yet the study of his own development is still incomplete.

Human development as an area of study became more complex with the increase in factors (independent variables) affecting it. Sociology began spurting out information on social patterns of behaviour affecting child upbringing. For instance in child-rearing patterns, even in urban populations, religious norms like the ceremonies relating to age (feeding of the first solids, head shaving, and recognition of the stages of man according to the Vedas) existed side by side with modernised ideas on development (Singer, 1972). Further, superstitions were still carved in these patterns (evil eye, auspicious times, horoscope readings and so on). Such sociological patterns, which could not be divested from their psychological connotations (perception of values, the formation of beliefs and attitudes leading to behaviour), influenced the domain of socio-psychology, and therefore affected child development in its socio-psychological research. Some of the earliest universities to give precedence to research in sociology, anthropology and psychology, the bases of the study of human development, were the universities of Kolkata, Delhi, Mumbai, Chennai and Allahabad.

Historically, psychology departments were established since 1915, well before child/human development in many universities. However faculty was limited and topics were usually included as a part of philosophy. In India, there were only three postgraduate departments at the time of independence. The discipline of psychology rapidly expanded to 57 departments and more than 400 doctoral students and 96 doctoral graduates per year by the early 1980s (Dalal, 1990: 87–136). The Indian Council for Social Science Research commissioned three reviews for the discipline of psychology (Adair et al., 1995: 392–407). The first survey of psychological research was published in 1971 edited by S.K. Mitra and the second by U. Pareek in covering researches conducted up to 1980 (Pareek, 1981) and the third review was by Pandey (1988). Much of the studies were in experimental psychology, tribes in anthropology and village communities in sociology (Srinivas, 1966: 153). Studies on child development were scarce since the vicissitudes of the populace, the majority of them moving from one kind of sub-servience (the chieftains and the rajas) to another (the British Raj), meant that the core of childcare practices and value systems continued to be the same.

Given the fact that each tribe was warring with another, adjusting and readjusting, controlling their tribesmen by authority, there was an ambivalence about the state of care of the populace and therefore development. Added to this insecurity were the ravages of nature and the demands for tithes; the average Indian (more especially in the villages) gradually assumed an attitude of self-abnegation. In a study in Mexico, the findings have been discussed in relation to the individual being 'amiable, courteous, accommodating' (Diaz-Guerrero, 2003), but of being in their own control in their own communities. One might extrapolate such findings in relation to the Indian culture, where the Indian psyche shows similar personality traits, such as deference (Tripathi, 2002: 307–25) towards age, sex and hierarchy in the societal milieu. This phenomenon of socio-religious traditions is that the majority of Indians live under poverty conditions in rural and tribal areas. These are the landless, the subsistence farmers, the daily wage earners and those who depend upon fragile ecological conditions. It is said, further, that the prolonged deprivation increases the adaptability to deprivation, in the face of no other alternatives (Sinha and Tripathi, 2003: 192–210). Again, one might speculate that there is a carry-over effect from the feudal and colonial eras of subservience towards authority (Kakar, 2001: 132–40) and locus of power. These factors taken together might account for the fact that the Indian sees himself more as a part of a collective identity. Therefore, it is not unreasonable to assume that all these traits form a dynamic network with which the average Indian attempts to negotiate in constructing his social environment. Perhaps it is this ambivalence, this hesitation at risk-taking for fear of negative consequences, that is viewed as the timid dependent nature of the average Indian of today. This contrasts with the aggressive western model which forges ahead in being proactive in coping with the environment. Perhaps to this day the strong ties between family members of the extended network has its roots in this non-divisive approach to the family in its community (ethnic group). For this reason also, perhaps, the close relationship between man and his ecology from ancient times is reflected in these strong ties of visiting family members and keeping in contact. For instance, the worker in the city still has strong ties with his family or relatives in his 'village'; these give a contextual reference to his identity with his childhood ecology of working in the fields, pasturing cows and drawing water from the village well. What we are hypothesising is that many of the psychosocial attributes seen in the Indian of today have a strong relationship with the orally communicated values of forefathers, and the culture and ecology from which they have emerged. The ethos of the family as a valued institution, in spite of changes, exists today as an identity marker for the individual.

On the national front, the beginning of census taking revealed some stark realities. The high mortality and birth rates which were revealed forced experts to look at the fact that the child population was increasing, but at the same time dying out at early ages. Research and related programmes, therefore, focussed on maternal care and childcare in order to keep the born child surviving. Hence, there was a high profile given to health and nutritional studies and care of the mother and child (through establishing institutes of health and nutrition, communicable disease and so on). But then the question arose: to keep the child surviving at what quality of life?

Therefore, besides increased healthcare, the area of preschool development also came into focus in the national programmes through the first ever instituted balwadis of the community development programme. Since the ground work was new, there was not much research to indicate the need for preschool education. The priority for implementing primary school education was uppermost in educational plans and programmes. Subsequently, professionals realised that without preschool intervention programmes for stimulation and development, primary school would be at a discount, especially with the growing knowledge that the early years were the foundation for habits, values, health and nutritional statuses. It was in 1977 that the long-term effects of preschool education were evaluated in USA by a consortium of experts. Long-lasting effects were reported in four areas: school competence, increased abilities, attitudes and values and a positive effect on the family (Lazar and Darlington, 1982). Such studies indicated the relevance for preschool education, especially for developing countries like India.

Enquiry into the behaviour and development of the infant through the childhood stages was based on the Piagetian principles of cognition and cognitive behaviour, and also on Vygotsky, but mainly from the western point of view. They had the salutary effect on the Indian situation of encouraging child development studies to focus on cognition in early childhood dealing mainly with concept formation (Piaget, 1929). This in turn impelled research to turn to environmental and cultural milieux affecting cognitive behaviour. These raised isssues as to how a rural child, who might not be having a red ball in his perceptual environment, would recognise the colour of red, and similar cognitive concepts. Several well-known NGOs came into existence to tackle such problems at the environmental level (Kosabad, Tilonia Bharat Sevak Sangh, Paras and other philanthropic organisations). There was also the question of how to bridge the gap between professionals educated in higher educational institutions and the paraprofessionals who themselves were from the community in which they worked, like *balsevika*s, *mukhya sevika*s and balwadi workers. It was expected that the professionals would train the paraprofessionals in the community development programmes through pre- and in-service training. The major institutions at this point catering to these services are NIPCCD (National Institute of Public Cooperation and Child Development), NIRD (National Institute of Rural Development), NIPA (National Institute of Planning Administration), NIHAE (National Institute of Health Administration and Education), NIN (National Institute of Nutrition) and NCERT (National Council of Educational Research and Training). Other auxiliary institutions originated from time to time mainly at the state levels.

Demography (numbers of people, age/sex and caste-related factors), geography (habitat and the physical environment), anthropology (tribal behaviour, role of mythology, religious behaviour and village communities), economics (number of children deprived and living at substandard levels) and sociology (sociometric behaviour, social organisation/disorganisation) affected the domain of child development. These gave rise to a spate of studies on the effects of economic deprivation on intellectual and cognitive development (Agarwal and Tripathi, 1984: 451–53) and modes of behaviour. Granted that basically the theories are similar as they deal with generic human nature at the grass-roots level the divergence as influenced by family and culture has not been fully explored in the Indian context. Only recently attempts are being made to be culture-specific in the context of the modern-day India (Featherstone, 1990).

Current Status: The Study of Human Development as it Exists Today

We may sum up the above fluctuating historical events of the study of human development in India as follows:

(i) The assumptions regarding biological and physical development are as credible today as when they were first recognised in the West, as the bases have not changed. The variables studied—anthropometric measures, nutrition levels, physiological mat-

uration by age—continue to be stable and consistent concepts.

(ii) The assumptions regarding psychological development have varied as various theories were propounded and studies made in their frameworks from time to time. Darwin emphasised ontogenetic and phylogenetic traits, and assumed that the human being was a primitive when born. Continuing on this premise, psychology treated a child as a clean slate to be moulded (conditioning concepts), who could learn progressively, according to age and maturational levels (learning concepts). The child could be rewarded or punished (reinforcement theories), his/her personality could assume certain characteristics (personality theories), he/she could be highly competent/incompetent (intelligence theories), and so on.

(iii) At the same time, with the fissioning of psychology into various approaches towards study of development, such as instinct/intuition, Gestalt perception, conditioning, reinforcement, intelligence, learning, cognition, and so on, the child was analysed differentially depending upon the framework of each approach.

(iv) Research and communication having increased, the realisation grew that psychology could not stand by itself. The incorporation of concepts from other disciplines were necessary.

(v) In the Indian situation, all these disciplines are derivatives of concepts from the West. They have been borrowed and are being adapted. Although many experts have criticised the dominance of western thinking there seemed to be no way initially to break away from the model of 'copy and imitate'. Indigenous concepts have been slow to develop (Agarwal, 1975; Nandy, 1974). While the cultural and context-specific factors are assuming importance, the cultural factor itself is fissioned into several subcultures, and the context factor is itself changing as societies move from traditionalism towards modernised styles or mixed styles of living. What may be true of a Pangi child from the Himalyas may not be true for a child in Manipur, although both live in the same geoecological framework.

(vi) The concept of intervening variables is growing stronger, given the fact that modernisation touches all walks of the individual's life but in varying degrees, and depending upon the subculture/specific context. In the Indian society, the conceptualisation and the study of the child is deemed to be more reliable when explained on the basis of specific factors of his/her human and material environment.

The study of human development reflects changing social structures and systems, increasingly sophisticated technology and economic vicissitudes. Additionally, global situations of war and strife, and political domination and submission of nations exacerbate the situation. It is obvious that influences of change are more directly felt by changing social and economic vicissitudes than by the far removed political and global events. By and large political changes in power structures have changed political profiles of nations. For instance, Russia has lost its communistic stronghold, while China has muted its communist ideology. The ushering of free trade and economic acceleration in some of the eastern countries has created lifestyles that compare with the sophistication of the West. Most of them however have a curious mix of sophisticated western patterns with traditional beliefs and practices. In India this has been largely contributed to by the rising middle class caught between trying to be authentically Indian and yet modern. This has been commented upon in an examination of human development processes through the lens of a mix of social development and psychoanalytic theorising based mainly on Kakar's theses (Sharma and Gielen, 2004). For instance, many large nouveau-riche business houses are owned by families with traditional lifestyles like the Marwaris and the *bania*s. At the same time they have fabulous cars, servants, marble flooring and chandeliers, town and country homes, use sophisticated gadgetry and imitate modern trends of partying and drinking, without any signs of dissonance, moving rapidly and easily from the traditional to the modern and back again, according to the situation. One might almost term it a stage of transition for the society, and during this period of trial and error, a state of instability occurs till it settles down to one of relative stability. The current Indian cultural ethos is a mix of inconsistencies (Derme, 2004: 88–114).

Planned changes came into being with constitutional directives in 1950. In their nascent stage, as far as the child was concerned, they related mainly to netting large populations of primary school children into a so-called compulsory education frame, and systematically providing healthcare in maternity and child welfare centres. These were mainly institutional concerns. The family was not considered a part of the child training process, except to provide physical and emotional care. Considering the huge population, the geographical inaccessibility and the unfamiliarity with allopathic medicines, rural families were initially cautious in their use of modern medicine. Through the years the process of evaluating the programmes by the Planning Commission gave rise to the realisation that infrastructures were weak, personnel were poorly trained, facilities hardly available, and so the programmes were more often than not tangential to supplying facilities to the neediest group targeted by Government of India (UNICEF, 1973: 19–36). Much governmental interdepartmental soul-searching went on, till ultimately the child and the female were categorised as 'vulnerable and disadvantaged'. A series of projects for the young child were implemented and discarded, throughout the initial five-year plans. In the fifth plan, a pilot project for the young child called Integrated Child Development Scheme (ICDS) was set up, which over the following plan periods became a permanent feature. The evolution of the ICDS shows success in the areas of health status, nutritional status and psychological development. In the main the ICDS reports show that some improvement has taken place nutritionally and educationally (Sood, 1992). For women, there are projects by the different ministries, especially the Health Ministry, for improving the health status of the mother. The Ministry of Education has projects for improving the literacy levels of out-of-school females and the Ministry of Labour for occupational opportunities expanding and small-scale entrepreneurship. The Nodular Ministry of Human Resources Development through its Department of Women and Child Development caters to the specific needs of the vulnerable group and the Department of Social Welfare has instituted programmes for the alleviation of poverty and for women and children in distress (orphans, destitute, abandoned and so on). These are practical programmes implemented on the basis of existing knowledge of human development, the sources of which are multifarious: education through NCERT, nutrition through NIN, child and women development through NIPCCD and community development through NIRD, to mention a few. It is however the universities that conduct research on human development, although in separate fields. Anthropology fissions out into cultural, physical and ecological anthropology; sociology into psychological, anthropological, behavioural and organisational sociology; while psychology proliferates into developmental, sociological, anthropological, child–adolescent and experimental psychology. In other words these disciplines grow vertically rather than horizontally and do not give a holistic picture on human development. This phenomenon has been aptly stressed by T.S. Saraswathi in her plea for an interface between researchers, and between researchers and policy makers.

It is reasonable to assume that the state of knowledge imparted through educational institutions reflect these vicissitudes. Therefore, as has been said before, the understanding has moved from one of childcare and mothercraft and the theoretical study of societies, especially societies embedded in anthropology, social structure and stratification, into specialised areas of human development. Human development offers, a generic field of understanding, and therefore can be understood in a generic framework. However there are many fissions, such as the various areas of specialised psychology and sociology, and the various areas of human behaviour: applied, organisational, labour management and so on. Additional conceptualisations have been applied to the field of human development, such as welfare, community development, family ecology and more especially women and child rights (Flavia et al., 2004).

If we trace the current status, the beginnings of the study of human development began in post-WWII Europe when in the aftermath of the wars, hundreds of children became destitute and orphans. From concerns about their welfare, studies concentrated on children in distress, such as Bowlby's classical theory on attachment and loss (1969). In India, beginning in the British regime, the nobility (rajas and nawabs of principalities) were euphemistically considered as 'native advisors' to the overlords, the British (Ishwaran, 1966). Thus, in the Indian subcontinent, the Far East, the countries of Africa, and in the tropical/mountainous areas of South America, concerns about instituting programmes for the uplift of the 'natives' were not in the purview of the western colonisers. European-flavoured educational institutions were replicated, and 'Spockism' was, for a while, popularised, together with a borrowed system of education. As the institutions proliferated there was a reflection that childcare was too limited a study of human development. In India this pattern of copying the West continued in educational institutions. Therefore, the structures and curricula became similar. Unfortunately, the Indian was exposed to literature emanating from the West, and every change in the syllabi of countries like Britain and the US was reflected in changes in educational institutions where English was the medium of instruction, for it was considered prestigious. As yet, it had not percolated to the Hindi medium, leave alone the regional languages. When child development became human development in the West and changed from human development to human ecology, the Indian institutions reflected the same tendencies. This was because the West was the pioneer and leader in scientific and technological information. In its early stages, there was a tendency to follow classical traditions in experimental psychology, experimenting mainly on components of psychology such as perception of form and space. Only recently with increasing emphasis on motivational and personality variables has there been a growing tendency to link the development process with a different facet of the Indian personality (Sinha, 1979). In the 1970s and the 1980s, there was a perceptible movement towards indigenisation, where experts began to concentrate on the contextual dimensions of the Indian society (Atal, 1981: 89–97).

This was especially because of the immense diversity of cultural contexts. However, educational infrastructures were not the only sources of knowledge. The governmental ministries planned their own developmental programmes in the sectors of health, agriculture, community development and welfare, thus instituting field-level programmes especially aimed at disadvantaged groups. Simultaneously, many non-governmental programmes of various types mushroomed all over the country, several assisted by grants from international and national agencies. These were interventions in the lives of the people, again the deprived sections of the population.

There are three types of broad-spectrum services for human development, one is national, the second is state and the third is inter-sectoral at the field level. It is fair to say that from the first plan onwards the only area of human development of major concern was that of the infant, the mother and the primary school child. The former two were in the infrastructure of the Health Ministry, and the latter was the concern of the Education Ministry, both at national and state levels. Starting with an emphasis on primary education, as enjoined by the Constitution of India, and literacy programmes for adults, education has expanded to institutions of higher learning at vocational colleges and colleges of the universities. In recent years, the Indira Gandhi National Open University (IGNOU) correspondence courses and in-service training (pre- and on-the-job) as offered by NIHE, NIN, NIRD and similar such institutions are targeting the youth. The vocational institutions are geared towards competence in various channels—media, fashion, entrepreneurship and other specialised avenues. There are other prestigious institutions which run short-term training courses for staff development of those already in professions. There are some government run programmes for infant and preschool care like the state-run crèches, balwadi programmes and the still continuing programme of the ICDS. These programmes however cover a miniscule number of the population. In a way the ICDS was the first holistic programming initiated on a large scale. It is now recognised as the largest government-initiated and implemented programme for children in the developing world. This is not to say that this programme is adequate but that this mammoth developmental programme has existed for over 30 years, and is being maintained, overseen and monitored by the Ministry of Human Resources and its auxiliary departments.

A major contribution has been made steadily by NGOs who cater to the deprived in various contexts: some for entire families, others specifically for women and children. In recent years, economic activities are being emphasised for the eradication of poverty, especially with the enunciation of the minimum needs programme in 2004. In the current scenario there have been four successful trends:

(i) In the interlinkages with world events, a number of global policies have been ratified by the Indian government also: Basic Education for All (1990), Convention on the Rights of the Child (1992) and World Summit Conference on Children (1992).

(ii) A dialogue between the state and the voluntary sector is gaining ground in collaborative interface (Querashi, 1995).

(iii) Outside the parameters of government efforts, media and social marketing have begun to emphasise aspects of mental and physical health statuses (Unnikrishnan and Bajpai, 1996).

(iv) Documented information has identified areas of greater social concern like abuse and exploitation of children and women. These identified areas have furthered professional concerns in research and ameliorative efforts both at governmental and non-governmental levels (Khalakdina, 1998; Querashi, 1995).

Beginning as a course of study mainly in the few urban colleges of home science that existed in the 1940s and 1950s in Chennai, Delhi, Kolkata, Mumbai, Baroda and Hyderabad, child development spread into the state agricultural universities. Initially it was a course for the elite in colleges and was labelled childcare, then it was renamed child development and later had the appendage 'family relationships' added to it. This area of study was modelled unvaryingly on the western pattern, with western-oriented textbooks in their trappings of an alien culture. This programme was modelled along the lines of home science in the agricultural universities in the USA. It also came to be termed a science course in some universities. Other universities introduced the course in the humanities departments. Still later it became part of the course work in sociology and psychology, sponsored by the University Grants Commission (UGC). The UGC was solely responsible for financing and monitoring the academic content, the structure and administration/staffing patterns of colleges seeking affiliation to universities for conducting such course. Thus a hybrid of courses encompassing child development came into being. Starting mainly as undergraduate courses they expanded to postgraduate programmes mainly in colleges of home science and allied national institutions. Human development courses were also offered by institutes of technology and national institutes like NCERT and others.

The number of professionals and paraprofessionals in human development is inadequate. There are 'pure' psychologists and sociologists who, by virtue of the training they have gained at university levels, man the various departments, mainly in teaching and research, and so create more 'pure' psychologists, sociologists, and so on, rather than holistic human development specialists. The administration of child intervention programmes is run mainly by bureaucrats. Technocrats are few and far between for the various intervention programmes.

Human development, as we have seen, includes various related fields: differential psychology, sociology, sociopsychology, anthropology, social anthropology, social economics, organisational psychology, clinical psychology, psychometrics, educational psychology and cultural anthropology, besides others. We find that there are several levels of specialisation, the most popular being education in high schools, followed by institutions for training nursery school teachers, clinical psychologists, school psychologists, researchers and extension workers in agricultural and home science colleges. In recent years there have been paraprofessionals trained for the various levels of ICDS: trainers, supervisors, mukhya sevikas, *gram sevikas* and balsevikas (Khalakdina, 1969: 32–33). A smaller number are employed in government and non-government organisations at various levels, but rarely at senior levels in the government sectors. In the larger cities and towns there is an increasing number who take short-term courses in early childhood education to begin childcare centres: many of them commercial enterprises with poor quality services geared mainly towards providing supervisory services. For the higher trained professionals, there are as yet no steady career paths other than teaching research and extension. Some with added specialisations are branching off into television media and communication which are popular career avenues.

By far, the greatest change to the education sector of human development is the increasing technology in self-learning tools. The advances in science and technology have also far-reaching effects. Various experiments are under way such as: modifying brain waves to help the disabled and the mentally challenged by medication; genetic engineering experiments with brain functions; and accelerating curative measures for treating brain damage. Clinical psychologists, neurosurgeons, therapists and similar highly trained professionals in brain and mental processes use sophisticated medication for cures and recoveries. While human cloning is being clandestinely carried out, the far-reaching implications of creating a highly technical brain and mind are futuristic possibilities (Brown, 2006).

Media is a very popular means of introducing mental principles in a three-dimensional format. Television, magazines and cinema have a great stranglehold on people's minds and imaginations. Studies have indicated that many hours are spent watching TV. There are several shows which have a positive effect—discovery and geography channels, children's channels, talks, seminars and conferences, which have programmes whereby viewers are informed and educated. However, there is the downside of the ill effects of watching horror, war and crime movies, especially for children who have impressionable minds. Even though there is a strong censorship, there are covert means of distribution of pornography and harmful drug-related information, inciting or stimulating delinquent behaviour.

On the other hand, newspapers and scientific and technological journals offer much information on developments in the world that add to the information on the various aspects of human development. From the above brief picture it is apparent that:

(i) As of today, there is no strong commitment of investment in the young child and his future development as a human being. Several streams of interest wind their own way in a curiously non-creative fashion. Among professionals, for instance, there is little interaction among disciplines such as paediatrics, and guidance and counselling of parents. A paediatrician will refer young parents to marriage counsellors or parental classes, as the business of paediatrics is strictly the health and perhaps the nutrition of the child. In the West this is even more specialised; there are demarcated areas of the gynaecologist, the paediatrician, the nutritionist (and even a lactologist), the parental counsellor, the daycare centre, the psychiatrist and the media (nuclear families consult books avidly for learning how to care for their young, or gain some knowledge from impersonal media information on how to bring up children).

(ii) In India, we find that the more institutionalised the profession, the less is the contact of growing adult with the family of origin. In urban upper classes it is fashionable (perhaps because it is affordable) to consult a paediatrician on a regular basis and to send children to similar fashionable nursery schools. With the urban poor it is mainly a one-time affair with the hospital. The more informed may attend a few prenatal classes and fewer postnatal ones, but for the vast majority of the poor, except for the occasional visit by the midwife, there is also little interaction except in times of emergency and little information about pre- and post-natal development of the child's psychological make-up. What then is the impact of educators and researchers on child development (as one integrated discipline or as separate sectors), on improving the lives of this very critical majority?

Curiously, professionals (educators/practitioners/researchers), imbued with scientific and western-oriented concepts, experience much difficulty in interpreting such westernised information for the majority. There are several problems in simplifying and interpreting such sophisticated information for the end users, the very large numbers of the uneducated, tradition-bound parents of young children, who are not really able to understand, leave alone implement, such concepts in their daily lives. Take, for instance, the concept of rehydration. The educated urban mother at once recognises the concept (replenishment of essential salts in a water conduit).

But what does one say to a rural uneducated adult, except perhaps that a child loses water during diarrhoea and should have more water? To some mothers, who see a simplistic relation between input and output, all forms of food are to be avoided or reduced to stop the flow of output (a simple cause and effect relation). To an educated urban mother, the injunction that 'you should stimulate your child by talking to him/her so that he/she develops a language base quickly and accurately', is comprehensible; but to tell a rural mother, 'you must keep talking to your child so that his language develops faster' might only bring the tolerant response, 'he will learn when he is able to, and understand' (a simplistic understanding of maturational levels). Professionals might argue that they use demonstration methods/result methods and the whole range of extension methods to induce this learning. While this is demonstrable in wheat growing (agriculture is a more exact science), and perhaps in continued dehydration of a diarrhoea-stricken child (medical science), how does one demonstrate the effectiveness of home stimulation and other psychological/sociological conceptualisations to such mothers?

This is not to say that the professionals are handicapped. There are several teaching manuals and training programmes, but the problem still remains at the grass-roots levels. To circumvent this there is usually a requirement that paraprofessionals have some educational bases so that they themselves understand the concepts.

Let us take a detailed example of imitation and modelling in a preschool education centre for children of uneducated mothers. There is a wide chasm between school and home environments to begin with. The preschool teacher says 'wash your hands before/after eating' (principle of hygiene). This is done at school. The child goes home; there is no water even for simple ablutionary purposes, so the practice is non-valued in the home situation.

We might as well ask: What is the child's perception of the two types of reinforcing environments in his everyday life? How does it affect his cognition, his development? Such instances can be multiplied. The school environment is verbal and positively reinforcing; the home environment is not necessarily so. Again realising this predicament, professionals find several strategies: educate mothers/female siblings who are caretakers, or better still employ a paraprofessional from the environment itself who understands the culture and more importantly can speak the dialect. The permutations and combinations are ongoing, but what is meant in this discussion is precisely its thesis. How much do we know or can know of the cultural frames in which we translate our knowledge realistically? Therefore, the emphasis is on contextual references in the subcultures with which we deal, whose fine nuances should be in the repertoire of our scientific knowledge (Markus and Kitayama, 1991: 224–53).

This is not to say, though, that such problems are not being tackled by the Indian professional cadre. There are, in many institutions, feedback and interaction between teaching research and extension. The quality of such interaction, however, is unknown. Till such time as these issues are addressed, such problems of interface between the community and body of knowledge will continue. In this respect we see some alternatives working. There are several valued NGOs where professionals live in the community habitat and interact on a day-to-day basis. They have shown successful results in motivating communities to implement improved practices.

NGOs have projects conducted on a voluntary basis, which are only illustrative. They cannot be replicated, although even the government recognises the worth of their interventions, and has taken steps to form partnerships (Lata, 2000). They are usually developmental in their ethos and each one is unique, such as mobile crèches conducting services for construction workers, SEWA for the development of entrepreneurship among women, and such like. It is difficult to duplicate the strategies of such organisations by the government infrastructure and so an alternative is for them to be nodular NGOs assisting/training other NGOs.

We have come a long way in this chapter in tracing the scientific conceptualisations of the study of the human being. However, it is more concentrated on the child up to adolescence than over the lifespan. Although our limitation is that we have to depend heavily upon western-oriented conceptualisations, Indian studies being mainly reinterpretations of western concepts and frameworks, we still have to make an effort to teach and communicate with the users the information drawn from research based in our own milieux. We have to straddle two worlds: the world of technological communication and global interaction, and the world of a tradition-based society still holding on to its socio-religious values and mores.

Increasingly human endeavour cannot afford to make mistakes with the threats of environmental degradation, political instability, fatal epidemic diseases, and so on. A quick look at the vital statistics of the country shows many positive signs which indicate that the directions in which planning and programming move should be commensurate with the needs. More are being born and more are living. The IMR is 94.9 (per 1,000). The MMR is 408 (per 100,000 live births). The percentage of underweight children among children under 3 years of age is 47 (National Family Health Survey-II, 1998 cited in Government of India, 2002). Thus, while some indices are improving steadily, they are being offset by the alarming growth in population from 683.4 million in 1981 to 1,027 million in 2001. Provision of services has not increased in proportion to the rapid growth in population. Hence, there are a larger number of those under the poverty line, estimated to be around 260 million, who have inadequate services and lack the opportunity to gain access to them. For example, in remote areas, villagers have to walk for miles to get to a health center or to procure emergency health services, which is not the picture in the urban elite groups (Azad India Foundation: http://azadindia.org/social-issues/poverty-in-india.html).

A parallel phenomenon is the rapid increase in technological knowhow. Social and personal capacity is unable to cope with the output of the technological era. Those who are last will have to run faster to keep pace as the growing hiatus between the rich and poor among countries and within our own country leave the less advantaged in a more precarious situation than ever. India's economic quality of life is measured by GNP, but how is its quality of life in the social sense measured? The modern state is now expected to clothe its economic policies with a human face. How relevant is humanity in the face of warring politics and changing policies? We have watched the aftermath of terrorism (both from the Middle East and in neo-Nazi variegated forms of internal rebellions), of tribal ethnic warfare both in African nations and in Serbia in Europe. In India, there are several problems created by uneven educational systems which are available and are being differentially utilised. From time to time, there are stirrings among different groups, but as yet nothing volatile enough to cause countrywide insurgencies. We cannot ignore the inroads created by scientific discoveries which upset the demographic picture. These inroads affect, for instance, the fertility rates where sex determination is practised, and female foetuses are aborted. The relative neglect of the health and nutrition of the female child also leads to this process of the reduction of the female populations in proportion to males.

Huge shifts in our rural populations are creating an unstable life for young children born and living under slum conditions. How do the living conditions of such children affect their levels of frustration and perhaps consequent aggression? Frustration is built up by lack of access to amenities available to others. While the ontogenetic basis of child development has been accepted in understanding human development, what do increased scientific discoveries do to the phylogenetic traits of the child, when the sperm is intrauterinely implanted, especially by surrogate donors? Children of today are much smarter and healthier than the children of previous generations. Their environment has changed. Child development is not fixed, unilinear or timeless (Burnam, 1996: 59), but is individually oriented and dependent upon epigenetic regulations. Therefore in the changing environment of the universe we cannot get lost in a forest for want of specific trees. In a fast-moving target range of technology, the modalities of being precise and accurate are becoming more important, especially in the study of man, and man in his formative stages or childhood. In the Indian context, it must be admitted that there has not been much stress on human development as an area of study in the holistic sense. Segmented areas in the various social sciences exist, but they form scattered pictures, and leave the reader with the deduction that by and large industrial development has outstripped human development, with the poor and rural populations gaining less than their share.

Research in human development is sparse in the Indian context and therefore suffers from an incomplete picture of human development through the lifespan, especially during adulthood and old age. Many theories are illustrated with examples from the West, and thus short-change the Indian context or, for that matter, the eastern ethos, which creates a hiatus between the East and the West in terms of interface. This is especially true when it is realised that the world is being telescoped at an accelerated rate.

Census data of the year 2000 indicates some improvement in health and education indicators. However the composite index of quality of life still shows a high rate of infant and maternal mortality. Thus in spite of the heartening figures in Kerala and Maharashtra, the fact is that the progress is minimised by the burgeoning population which stands over one billion in the 21st century. The major thrust has been in the technological sphere where industry and communication have grown by leaps and bounds.

The average Indian is now better informed about the benefits of health, good nutrition and a clean environment. But the cities are still amassing great slums as the infrastructural system cannot keep up with the population growth. Services to early childcare for the urban child are inadequate. Three out of every 10 children live in cities (Saran, 2003). Urban slum children suffer from multiple forms of deprivation of a familial social nature. About 30 per cent work in street jobs and do not attend schools. The National Slum Development Programme, which began in 1966, still makes a major thrust on housing but hedges on the need for a child-friendly environment for 6 million urban children in the major cities. It is important to note that the ICDS is a reflection of the holistic concept in child development, and operationally integrates all services for the young child, the girl child and mothers of young children, but beyond that there is an abyss (Government of India, 1996b). The child's world vision has widened in comparison, and the children of today are less apathetic as compared to those of the previous generation, as they are constantly battered with more stimuli which they have to contend with.

The picture of human development in the world today is one that occupies ethical and scientific thought, given increased mobility and the shrinkage of distances, accelerated by fast-paced communications. We have come a long way in the diaspora, from the Neanderthal man to the probable cloning of the human through DNA reproduction. According to the UNDP's Human Development Index 2005, which is based on economic, social and demographic indices, India stands 128th in rank. Also, the UNDP's measure of Gender-related Development Index (GDI) ranks India as 138th out of 177 countries. The GDI captures inequalities in achievement between women and men. The rate of development in India in the economic sphere has been accelerating as indexed by the GDP. However, sociologically and demographically, it is lagging behind several other countries.

We have to admit that in the overall picture we cannot afford to harp on our traditional origins and be sanctimonious about it. We have to find a bridge between the old and the new, 'traditionality' and 'modernising scientific technology' (Khutiala, 2003). As such, how do we make sense of all the empirical data we have: that the brain is related to culture, that cognition is ecologically influenced, that human beings can be cloned, that individuals can live comfortably betwixt and between two cultures being modern in one situation and traditional in another. Displaced children in war-ravaged areas, destitute children and families in disorganisation are all challenges requiring a different order in the establishment of relations within families and in communities. Yet, if the average Indian is traditional at home and modern in a disco, well then that is what he is: a hybrid of many parts, but he may also be a brother to a tribal. This coexistence is perhaps the Indian's greatest quality of adaptive resilience. Therefore when we look at the data, the empiricism and the documentation of how the human being develops, we must realise that the kaleidoscope is changing all the time. We have the average shopkeeper who can pull out his cellphone while a 'sadhu' is waiting for his Tuesday alms with his bowl. They do not eschew each other but, given the roots of social history, live in a jointed fashion with their traditional core values. We have repeated these values again and again, and can only say that the average Indian like the average Japanese has learnt to 'coalesce' the traditional and the modern, and to exhibit them in different sets of situations.

Therefore, we need to study behaviour and development at the generic level and yet be able to interpret these generics in the specific system and structure that is Indian (Deshpande, 1979: 1–28). The application of methods and theory, according to many specialists, should be ultimately context-specific (Dash and Kar, 1993: 84–85). We have seen the one-way, parallel-line approach of various disciplines to understand human development, and except for a few courageous, far-seeing academicians (Pandey, 2004) the rest continue to look at the Indian segmentally, though now, when more than ever, it is essential to view development holistically. The bases of information are the theoretical assumptions that man has come into this world with generic skills that are phylogenetic in character, and then develops further skills suited to his acculturation to a specific society's requirements such as a carpenter or a genetic engineer (ontogenetic), as well as simultaneously suited to his cognitive development (dependent upon his innate abilities) and skills acquired in his environment (outer stimuli). In this world of high-speed technology, compared to the earlier years, it is the development of ontogenetic skills stimulated by environmental experience such as those from media and technology which are becoming dominant; for example, learning to read and write on a slate has given way to computerised learning which challenges motivational levels. We also have to contend with differences in the exposure of the elite child and the street child, the urban child and the rural child. What social differences do these environments create? Such discontinuities are widening in our culture. Even in urban areas we see young men working in their father's traditional occupation, where the father has not even passed high school, and does his *hisaab kitaab* according to generationally communicated ways of management, and the son, though he has completed a university degree, has to work in his father's shop. Does frustration build up? Is there apathy? Do the motivational levels heightened by a college education and degree get subdued or do they create anxiety levels suppressed by traditional norms in such situations? The study of human development in India is challenged by such changing frames of reference for the Indian of today.

References

Adair, J.G, J. Pandey, H. Aktar, B.N. Pohan and N. Vohra, 1995, 'Indigenisation and Development of the Discipline', *Journal of Cross-cultural Psychology*, 26(4): 392–407.

Agarwal, A. and K.K. Tripathi, 1984, 'Influence of Prolonged Deprivation, Age and Culture on the Development of Future Orientation', *European Journal of Social Psychology*, 14: 451–53.

Agarwal, K.G., 1975, *'Psychology or Adaptology'*, *Social Scientist*, 3(10): 69–73.

Anandalakshmy, S., 1998, 'The Cultural Context', in M. Swaminathan (ed.), *The First Five Years: A Critical Perspective on Early Childhood Care and Education in India*. New Delhi: Sage.

Antonova, K.C., Bongard-Levin and G. Kotovsky, 1979, *A History of India*. Moscow: Progress Publishers.

Appadurai, A., 1988, 'Putting Hierarchy in its Place', *Cultural Anthropology*, 3(1): 36–49.

Aristotle, 1885, *Politics* (trans. by B. Jowett). Oxford, New York: Clarendon Press.

Atal, Y., 1981, 'The Call for Indigenisation', *International Social Science Journal*, 33: 89–97.

Atkinson, J., 1964, 'The Implications of Darwin's Theory of Evolution', in *An Introduction to Motivation*. Princeton, NJ: Van Nostrand.

Ault, R.L., 1983, *Children's Cognitive Development: Piaget's Theory and the Progress Approach*, 2nd edn. New York: OUP.

Baden-Powel, B.H., 1892, *Landsystems of British India* (3 vols). London: OUP.

Baig, T., 1979, *Our Children*. New Delhi: Ministry of Information and Broadcasting.

Banerjee, A. and L. Iyer, 2006, *History, Institutions, and Economic Performance: The Legacy of Colonial Land Tenure*. Cambridge, MA: Department of Economics, Massachusetts Institute of Technology.

Basham, A.L., 1934, *The Wonder that was India*. New York: Groove Press Inc.

Basvanna, M. and M.U. Rani, 1984, 'Differential Impact of Social and Economic Factors on Intellective and Scholastic Abilities', *Journal of Psychological Researches*, 28: 121–28.

Benedict, R., 1934, *Patterns of Culture*. New York: Houghton Mifflin.

Bennett, J.W., 1983, *Human Ecology as Human Behaviour: Essays in Environmental and Development Anthropology*. Mahwah, NJ: Erlbaum.

Binet, A. and T. Simon, 1905, 'Méthodes nouvelles pour le diagnostic du niveau intellectuel des anormaux' (New Methods for Diagnosing the Intellectual Level of Abnormals), *L'Année Psychologique*, 11: 191–244.

Bischoff, J.L., D.D. Aramburu Shamp, A. Arsuaga and J.L. Carbonell (eds), 2003, 'Neanderthals', *Journal of Archaeological Science*, 30: 275–80.

Brass, P.R., 1966, *New Cambridge History of India*. London: Penguin Books.

Bronfenbrenner, U., 1977, 'Toward an Experimental Ecology of Human Development', *American Psychologist*, 32: 513–31.

Bowlby, J., 1969, *Attachment and Loss, Vol. I: Attachment*. London: Hogarth.

Brown, T.A., 2006, *Genomes 3*. New York: Garland Science Publishing.

Burnam, E., 1996, *Deconstructing Developmental Psychology*. London: Routledge.

Carstairs, G.M., 1957, *The Twice Born: A Study of the Community of High Caste Hindu*. London: Hogarth.

Carstairs, M. and R.L. Kapur, 1976, *The Great Universe of Kota*. London: Hogarth Press.

Chakraborti, R.D., 2004, *The Greying of India: Population Ageing in the Context of India*. New Delhi: Sage.

Chandler, K., 1987, 'Modern Science and Vedic Science: An Introduction', *Modern Science and Vedic Science*, 1(1–4): 5–26.

Cole, M., 1992, 'Context, Modularity and the Cultural Construction of Development', in L.T. Winegar and J. Valsiner (eds), *Children's Development Within Social Context: Research and Methodology, Vol. 2*. Hillsdale, NJ: Lawrence Erlbaum.

———, 1996, *Cultural Psychology: A Once and Future Discipline*. Cambridge, MA: Harvard University Press.

Comte, A., 1973, *System of Positive Polity, Vol. 1*. New York: Lenox Hill Pub. and Dist. Co.

Cooper, J.M. and D.S. Hutchinson, (eds), 1997, *Plato: Complete Works*. Indianapolis, IN and Cambridge, UK: Hackett Publishing Company.

Dalal, A., 1990, 'India', in G. Shouksmith and E.A. Shouksmith, *Psychology in Asia and the Pacific*. Bangkok: UNESCO.

Dalal, A.K. and G. Misra, 2002, 'Social Psychology in India: Evolution and Emerging Trends', in A.K. Dalal and G. Misra (eds), *New Directions in Indian Psychology, Vol. 1*. New Delhi: Sage.

Dalton, D.G., 1970, 'M.N. Roy and Radical Humans: The Ideology of an Indian Intellectual Elite', in E.R. Leach and S.N. Mukherjee, *Elites in South Asia*. Cambridge: Cambridge University Press.

Dange, S.A., 1949, *India from Primitive Communism to Slavery*. Bombay: Peoples' Publishing House.

Darwin, C., 1859, *On the Origin of Species by Means of Natural Selection*. London: John Murray.

Das, V., 1977, *Structure and Cognition: Aspects of Hindu Caste and Ritual*. New Delhi: OUP.

——— (ed.), 1994, *Communities, Riots and Survivors in South Asia*. New Delhi: OUP.

Dasen, P.R., 1990, 'Theoretical Frameworks in Cross-cultural Developmental Psychology: An Attempt at Integration', in G. Misra, *Applied Social Psychology in India*. New Delhi: Sage.

Dash, U.N. and B.C. Kar, 1993, 'Nature of Knowledge and Developmental Psychology', in T.S. Saraswathi and B. Kaur (eds), *Human Development and Family Studies in India—An Agenda for Research and Policy*. New Delhi: Sage.

Dave, P. and G. John, 2003, 'A Look into the Lives of Older Persons', *Indian Journal of Gerontology*, 17(1&2): 109–16.

Deacon, T., 2000, 'How Flexible is the Neuro-developmental Clock?', in S.T. Parker, J. Langer and M.L. McKinney (eds), *Biology, Brains, and Behaviour: The Evolution of Human Development*. Santa Fe, NM: School of American Research Press.

Derme, S., 2004, 'Culture, Family Structure and Psyche in Hindu India', in D. Sharma and O.P. Gielen, *Childhood Family and Socio-cultural Change in India, Representing the Inner World*. New Delhi: OUP.

Deshpande, M., 1979, 'History: Change and Permanence: A Classical Indian Perspective', in G. Krishna (ed.), *Contributions to South Asian Studies*. New Delhi: OUP.

Devananda, V.S., 1988, *Yoga: The Complete Illustrated Book*. New York: Rivers Press.

Dewey, J., 1910, *Influence of Darwin on Philosophy and Other Essays in Contemporary Thought*. New York: H. Holt and Co.

Diaz-Guerrero, Rogelio, 2003, 'Is Abnegation a Basic Experimental Trait in Traditional Societies? The Case of Mexico', in J.W. Berry, R.C. Mishra and R.C. Tripathi (eds), *Psychology in Human and Social Development*. New Delhi: Sage.

Dube, L., 1997, *Women and Kinship: Comparative Perspectives on Gender in South and South-east Asia*. New Delhi: Vistaar Publications.

Dube, S.C., 1965, 'The Study of Complex Cultures', in T.K.N. Unnithan, I. Deva and Y. Singh (eds), *Toward a Sociology of Culture in India*. New Delhi: Prentice-Hall.

———, 1988, *Modernisation and Development*. London: Zed Books.

Dubois, J.A., 1906, *Hindu Manners, Customs and Ceremonies* (trans. H.R. Beauchamp), 3rd edn. Oxford: Clarendon Press.

Dumont, L., 1965, 'The Functional Equivalents of the Individual in Caste Society', *Contributions to Indian Sociology*, 8: 85–99.

———, 1966, 'The "Village Community" from Munro to Maine', *Contributions to Indian Sociology*, 9: 67–89.

Erikson, E., 1943, 'Observations of Yurok: Childhood and World Image', *The International Journal of Psychoanalysis in American Archeology and Ethnology*, 35(10): 257–301.

Evans, S., 2002, 'Macaulay's Minute Revisited: Colonial Language Policy in Nineteenth-century India', *Journal of Multilingual and Multicultural Development*, 23(4): 260–81.

Eysenck, H., 1971, *The IQ Argument, Race, Intelligence and Education*. New York: Library Press.

Featherstone, M., 1990, *Global Culture: Nationalism, Globalisation and Modernity*. New Delhi: Sage.

Flavia, A., S. Chandra and M. Basu, 2004, *Women and Law in India. An Omnibus Comprising Law and Gender Inequality, Enslaved Daughters, Hindu Women and Marriage Law*. New Delhi: OUP.

Freud, A., 1946, *The Ego and Mechanisms of Defense*, New York: International Universities Press.

Freud, S., 1935, *A General Introduction to Psychoanalysis*. New York: Liveright (Originally published in 1916).

Garbarino, J., 1995, 'Growing up in a Socially Toxic Environment: Life for Children and Families in the 1990s', in

G.B. Melton (ed.), *Nebraska Symposium on Motivation, Vol. 42: The Individual, the Family and the Social Good: Personal Fulfilment in Times of Change*. Lincoln, NE: University of Nebraska Press.

Ghurye, G. S., 1986, *Caste and Race in India*. Columbia, MO: South Asia Books.

Gopal, S., 1965, *British Policy in India*. Cambridge: Cambridge University Press.

Gore, M.S., 1966, *Urbanisation and Family Change*. Bombay: Popular Prakashan.

Gore, M.S. and I.E. Soares, 1960, *Historical Background of Social Welfare in India*. New Delhi: Popular Prakashan.

Government of India, 1961, *Constitution of India*. New Delhi: Publications Division, Ministry of Information and Broadcasting.

———, 1974, *Report of the Evaluation of Family and Child Welfare Projects*. New Delhi: Department of Social Welfare, Ministry of Education and Social Welfare.

———, 1994, *The ICDS and Other Child Care Programmes in India*. New Delhi: Ministry of Human Resource Development, Dept. of Women and Child Development.

———, 1996a, *Integrated Child Development Services (ICDS)*, New Delhi: Ministry of Human Resource Development, Dept. of Women and Child Development (Mimeo).

———, 1996b, 'National Workshop on Early Childhood Development', pp. 11–13. Delhi: Ministry of Human Resource Development, with World Bank and UNICEF.

———, 2000. *Mid-term Appraisal of Ninth Five Year Plan, 1997–2002*. New Delhi: Planning Commission.

———, 2001, *Approach Paper to the Tenth Five Year Plan, 2002–07*. New Delhi.

———, 2002. *National Health Policy*. New Delhi.

———, Five Year Plan 2000–2007, New Delhi: Planning Commission.

Gross, Rita M., 1989, 'Hindu Female Deities as a Resource for the Contemporary Rediscovery of the Goddess', in C. Olson (ed.), *The Book of the Goddess: Past and Present*. New York: Crossroad.

Gupta, A., 2006, *Balancing Vygotsky and the Veda*. New York: Macmillan.

Habib, I., 1963, The Agrarian System in Mughal India, Bombay: Asia Publishing House.

Havighurst, R.J., 1953, *Human Development and Education*. New York: Longmans, Green.

Hegel, G.W.F., 1969, *Hegel's Science of Logic*, (trans. by A.V. Miller). London: Allen and Unwin.

Inhelder, B. and J. Piaget, 1958, *The Growth of Logical Thinking from Childhood to Adolescence*. New York: Basic Books.

———, 1964, *Early Growth of Logic in the Child : Classification and Seriation*. New York: Routledge and Kegan Paul.

Ishwaran, K., 1966, *Tradition and Economy in Village India*. London: Routledge and Kegan Paul.

Jensen, A.R., 1969, 'How Much Can We Boost IQ and Scholastic Achievement', *Harvard Educational Review*, 39(1): 1–123.

Kak, S.C., 2000, 'On Understanding Ancient Indian Science', in A.K. Raina, B.N. Patnaik and M. Chadha (eds), *Science and Tradition*. Shimla: Indian Institute of Advanced Study.

Kakar, S., 1979, *Identity and Adulthood*. New Delhi: OUP.

———, 2001, 'The Themes of Authority in Social Relations in India', in A.K. Dalal and G. Misra, *New Directions in Indian Psychology, Vol. 1: Social Psychology*. New Delhi: Sage.

Karve, Irawati, 1961, *Hindu Society: An Interpretation*. Poona: Deccan College.

Kaur, S., 1978, *Wastage of Children*. New Delhi: Sterling Publications.

Khalakdina, M., 1969, 'Training in Development Work', *Social Action*, 19(1): 32–33.

———, 1973, 'The Preschool Child in India', in *The Study of the Young Child: India Case Study* (Mimeo). New Delhi: UNICEF South Central Asia Regional Office.

———, 1979, *Early Childcare in India*. London: Gordon and Breach.

———, 1998, 'Early Childhood Care and Education in India: A Perspective', M. Swaminathan (ed.), *The First Five Years*. New Delhi: Sage.

Khandekar, S., 1976, *The Disadvantaged Preschooler in Greater Bombay*. Bombay: TISS.

Khatri, A.A., 1965, *Changing Family, and Personality of Hindus—A Few Broad Hypotheses*. Vidya, J. Gujarat Univ. 8.

———, 1970, 'Personality and Mental Health of Indians (Hindus) in the Context of their Changing Family Organization', in E.J. Anthony and C. Koupernik (eds), *The Child in his Family, Vol. 1*. New York: John Wiley.

Khutiala, S.K., 2003, *From Tradition to Modernity*. New Delhi: Abhinav Publications.

King, R., 1999, *Orientalism and Religion: Post-colonial Theory, Indian and 'the Mast'*. London: Routledge.

Kluckhohn, F.R. and F.L. Strodbeck, 1961, *Variations in Value Orientations*. Evanston, IL: Row Peterson.

Koffka, K., 1935, *Principles of Gestalt Psychology*. New York: Harcourt Brace.

Koshambi, D.D., 1964, *The Culture and Civilisation of Ancient India*. London: Routledge and Keegan Paul.

Krishna, S., 2001. 'Gender, Tribe and Community Control of Natural Resources in North-east India', *Indian Journal of Gender Studies*, 8(2): 307–21.

Kumar, K., 1993, 'Study of Childhood and Family', in T.S. Saraswathi and B. Kaur (eds), *Human Development and Family Studies in India: An Agenda for Research and Policy*. New Delhi: Sage.

Lalitha, N.V., 1987, *Voluntary Work in India*. New Delhi: NIPCCD.

Lamarck, J.B., 1944, 'Biologie ou Considérations sur la nature, les facultés, les développements et l'origine des corps vivants', in *La Revue Scientifique*, 82 année.

Lata, D., 2000, 'Early Child Care and Education', *Assessment Study of Programmes Supported by SCF (UK) in India* (Mimeo). New Delhi: Save the Children Fund.

Lazar, Irving and R. Darlington, 1982, 'Lasting Effects of Early Education: A Report from the Consortium for Longitudinal Studies', *Monographs of the Society for Research in Child Development*, Vol. 47(2–3). Chicago: University of Chicago Press.

Lewin, K., 1938, *The Conceptual Representation and Measurement of Psychological Forces*. Durham, NC: Duke University Press.

Locke, J., 1924, *Of Civic Government: Two Treatises*. London: J.M. Dent and Sons Ltd.

———, 1960 , *An Essay Concerning Human Understanding* (*Great Books in Philosophy*). Amherst, NY: Prometheus Books.

Luthra, P.N., 1979, 'The Child in India: Policy Provisions and Practices', in S.D. Gokhale and S.N. Sohoni (eds), *Child in India*. Bombay: Somaiya Publications.

Madan, T.N., 1962, 'The Joint Family: A Terminological Clarification', *International Journal of Comparative Sociology*, III: 1–16.

Mahajan, G., 1998, *Identities and Rights: Aspects of Liberal Democracy in India*. New Delhi: OUP.

Malhotra, S., 2003, 'Socio-cultural Diversity and Ethnocentrism in Child Mental Health', in J.G. Young, P. Ferrari, S. Malhotra, S. Tyano and E. Caffo (eds), *Brain Culture and Development*. New York: Macmillan.

Malinowskwi, B., 1959, *Crime and Custom in Savage Society*. London: Routledge & Kegan Paul.

Mandelbaum, D.G., 1968, 'Family, Jati, Village', in M. Singer and B.S. Cohn (eds), *Structure and Change in Indian Society*. Chicago: Aldine Publishing Company.

———, 1972, *Society in India: Continuity and Change*. Bombay: Popular Prakashan.

Mandelbaum, M., 1971, *History, Man and Reason*, Baltimore: Johns Hopkins University Press.

Markus, H. and S. Kitayama, 1991, 'Culture and the Self: Implications for Cognition, Emotions, and Motivation', *Psychological Review*, 98: 224–53.

Marriott, M. (ed.), 1955a, *Village India: Studies in the Little Community*. Chicago: Chicago University Press.

———, 1955b, 'Little Community in an Indigenous Civilisation', in McKim Marriot (ed.), *Village India: Studies in the Little Community*. Chicago: Chicago University Press.

———, (ed.), 1990, *India through Hindu Categories*. New Delhi: Sage.

McDougall, W., 1908, *An Introduction to Social Psychology*. Boston: Luce.

Mead, M., 1983 (1928) *Coming of Age in Samoa: A Psychological Study of Primitive Youth for Western Civilisation*. New York: Morrow Publishers.

Miller, N.E. and J. Dollard, 1941, *Social Learning and Imitation*. New Haven: Yale University Press.

Minturn, L. and J.T. Hitchcock, 1956, 'The Rajputs of Khalapur, India', in B. Whiting and I.L. Child (eds), *Six Cultures: Studies in Child Rearing*. New York: John Wiley.

Mondal, M.K., 2000, 'Physiological Foundations of Behaviour', in J. Pandey (ed.), *Psychology in India Revisited: Developments in the Discipline, Vol. 1: Physiological Foundation and Human Cognition*. New Delhi: Sage.

Montessori, M., 1964, *The Montessori Method*. New York: Schocken Books.

Moss, L., 2003, *What Genes Can't Do*. Cambridge: MIT Press.

Muthayya, B.C., 1977, 'The Disadvantaged Rural Child', *Community Development and Panchyati Raj*, 9(2): 560.

Myles, G., 1995, *Public Economics*. New York: Cambridge University Press.

Naidu, U.S. and V.S. Nakhate, 1985, 'Child Development Studies in India', *TISS Series*, 56: 5–10.

Nandy, A., 1974, 'The Non-paradigmatic Crises of Indian Psychology: Reflections on a Recipient Culture of Science', *Journal of Psychology*, 49: 1–20.

———, 1983, *The Intimate Enemy: Loss and Recovery of Self under Colonialism*. New Delhi: OUP.

O'Flaherty, W.D., 1980, *Karma and Rebirth in Classical Indian Traditions*. Berkeley, CA: University of California Press.

Pandey, J. (ed.), 1988, *Psychology in India: The State-of-the-art*, 3 vols. New Delhi: Sage.

———, 2004, *Psychology in India Revisited, Vol. 3: Applied Social and Organisational Psychology.* New Delhi: Sage.

Paranjpe, A.C., 1998, *Self and Identity in Modern Psychology and Indian Thought.* New York and London: Plenum Press.

Pareek, U. (ed.), 1981, *A Survey of Research in Psychology, 1971–76* (Part II), Bombay: Popular Prakashan.

Pareek, K., 2002, 'India Development Report', in *Human Development Report.* New York: UNDP.

Parsons, T., 1951, *The Social System.* New York: Free Press of Glencoe.

Piaget, J., 1929, *The Child's Conception of the World.* London: Routledge and Kegan Paul.

Plunkett, R., T. Cannon, P. Davis, P. Greenway and P. Harding, 2001, *Lonely Planet: South India.* Melbourne/London/Oakland/Paris: Lonely Planet Publications.

Possehl, L.G., 2002a, *The Indus Civilisation: A Contemporary Perspective.* Walnut Creek, CA: Altamira Press.

———, 2002b, 'Indus–Mesopotamian Trade: The Record in the Indus', *Iranica Antiqua,* 37: 322–40.

Punhani, R., 2000, *Children in India: An Insight.* Delhi: Rouge Communications.

Querashi, S.Y., 1995, 'Strengthening Interdepartmental and Government–NGO linkages for Integrated Women and Child Development', Paper presented at the National Consultative Meeting on Networking with NGOs. New Delhi: NIPCCD.

Qvortrup, M., 2003, *The Political Philosophy of Jean-Jacques Rousseau: The Impossibility of Reason.* Manchester: Manchester University Press.

Raghavan, V., 1959, 'Methods of Popular Religious Instructions in South India', in M. Singer (ed.), *Traditional India: Structure and Change.* Philadelphia: American Folklore Society.

Raina, A.K., B.N. Patnaik and M. Chadha, 2000, 'Preface' in A.K. Raina, B.N. Patnaik and M. Chadha (eds), *Science and Tradition.* Shimla: Indian Institute of Advanced Study.

Ramanujan, B.K., 1972, 'The Indian Family in Transition', in A. D'Souza, *The Indian Family: The Change and the Challenges of the 70s.* New Delhi: Indian Social Institute.

Ross, A., 1908, *Social Psychology: An Outline and Sourcebook.* New York: Macmillan.

Rousseau, J.J., 1762, *The Social Contract.* Harmondsworth: Penguin Books.

Saran, R., 2003, 'How We Live: Census India Household Survey', *India Today,* 28 July.

Saraswathi, T.S. (ed.), 2003, *Cross-cultural Perspectives in Human Development: Theory, Research and Applications.* New Delhi: Sage.

Saraswathi, T.S., 1993, 'Child Development Research and Policy Linkage: A Mirage or Reality?', in T.S. Saraswathi and Baljit Kaur (eds), *Human Development and Family Studies in India: An Agenda for Research and Policy.* New Delhi: Sage.

———, 1999, 'Introduction', in T.S. Saraswathi (ed.), *Culture, Socialisation and Human Development.* New Delhi: Sage.

Saraswathi, T.S. and A. Dutta, 1987, *Developmental Psychology in India 1975–1986: An Annotated Bibliography.* New Delhi: Sage.

Sathe, M.D., 1967, 'Dharmasastra', in M. Joshi (ed.) *Bharatiya Samskrtikosa (Indian Encyclopedia of Culture), Vol. 4.* Pune: Bharatiya Samskritikosh Mandal.

Satyanarayanan, M., 1990, *Tribal Development in India: A Trend Report of Tribal Studies of Indian States.* Delhi: South Asia Books.

Scheler, M., 1970, 'On the Positivistic Philosophy of the History of Knowledge and its Law of Three Stages', in J.E. Curtis and J.W. Petras (eds), *The Sociology of Knowledge.* New York: Praeger.

Sharma, D. and O.P. Gielen., 2004, *Childhood Family and Socio-cultural Change in India, Representing the Inner World.* New Delhi: OUP.

Sharma, N., 1998, *Paradigms for Evaluating Primary Education: A Study of Class V Children in Government Schools in New Delhi.* New Delhi: New Discovery.

Singer, M., 1955–56, 'The Cultural Pattern of Indian Civilisation: A Preliminary Report of a Methodological Field Study', *Far Eastern Quarterly,* 15(1): 23–24.

———, 1972, *When a Great Tradition Modernizes.* New York: Praeger.

Singh, S., 2003, *Lonely Planet India.* Oakland, CA: Lonely Planet Publications.

Singh, Y., 1970, 'Chanukhera: Cultural Changes in Eastern Uttar Pradesh', in K. Ishwaran, *Change and Continuity in India's Villages.* New York: Columbia University Press.

———, 1977a, 'Preface', in Y. Singh, *Modernisation of Indian Tradition.* Faridabad: Thomson Press.

———, 1977b, 'Village Community', in Y. Singh, *Modernisation of Indian Tradition.* Faridabad: Thomson Press.

———, 1980, *Social Stratification and Change in India.* New Delhi: Manohar.

Sinha, D., 1979, 'Cognitve and Psychomotor Skills in India : A Review of Research', *Journal of Cross-cultural Psychology,*

10(3): 324–55.

———, 1986, *Psychology in a Third World: The Indian Experience*. New Delhi: Sage.

———, 1993, 'Research–Policy Interface: An Uneasy Partnership', in T.S. Saraswathi and B. Kaur (eds), *Human Development and Family Studies in India, An Agenda for Research and Policy*. New Delhi: Sage.

Sinha, D. and R.C. Tripathi, 2003, 'Individualism in a Collectivist Culture: A Case of Coexistence of Opposites', in T.S. Saraswathi (ed.), *Cross-cultural Perspectives in Human Development: Theory, Research and Applications*. New Delhi: Sage.

Sood, N., 1992, *Preschool Education in ICDS, An Appraisal*. New Delhi: National Institute of Public Cooperation and Child Development.

Srinivas, M.N., 1962, *Caste in Modern India*. Bombay: Asia Publishing House.

———, 1966, *Social Change in Modern India*. California: Berkeley University Press.

Swaminathan, M., 1998, 'Introduction'. in M. Swaminathan (ed.) *The First Five Years*. New Delhi: Sage.

Thompson, G.G., 1952, *Child Psychology*. New York: Houghton Mifflin Company.

Tripathi, R.C., 2002, 'Aligning Development to Values in India', in A.K. Dalal and G. Misra (eds), *New Directions in Indian Psychology, Vol. 1: Social Psychology*. New Delhi: Sage.

UNESCO, 2000, 'World Declaration on Education for All: Meeting Basic Learning Needs', *Education for All: Meeting our Collective Commitments*, Dakar, Senegal.

UNICEF, 1973, *UNICEF Study on the Young Child I: Indian Case Study*. UNICEF (SCARO).

Unnikrishnan, N and S. Bajpai, 1996, *Impact of Television Advertising on Children*. New Delhi: Sage.

Upadhyay, S.C., 1992, *Reservations for Schedule Castes and Schedule Tribes*. Delhi: South Asia Books.

Valsiner, J., 2000, 'Cultural Organisation of Pregnancy and Infancy', in J. Valsiner, *Culture and Human Development*. London: Sage.

Vayda, P., 1969, *Environment and Cultural Behaviour*. New York: Natural History Press.

Verma, M.M., 1996, *Tribal Development in India: Programmes and Perspectives*. Moscow: Verign Inc.

Vidyarthi, L.P, 1969, *Conflict, Tension and Cultural Trend in India*. Calcutta: Punthi Pustak.

———, 1972, *Tribal Ethnography in India: A Survey of Research in Sociology and Social Anthropology*. New Delhi: Indian Council of Social Science Research.

Vygotsky, L.S., 1981, 'The Genesis of Higher Mental Functions', in J.V. Wertsch (ed.), *The Concept of Activity in Soviet Psychology*. Armonk, NY: M.E. Sharpe.

Werner, H., 1984, *Symbol Formation: An Organismic Development Approach to the Development of Language*. Hillsdale, NJ: Lawrence Erlbaum.

Weschler, D., 1992, *Intelligence Scale for Children*, 3rd edn. Sidcup: The Psychology Corporation/Harcourt Brace Jovanovich.

Wheen, F., 2000, *Karl Marx: A Life*. New York: W.W. Norton & Co.

Wilkins, W.J., 2004, *Hindu Mythology*. New Delhi: DK Print World Pvt. Ltd.

Wiser, W.H., 1959, *The Hindu Jajmani System*. Lucknow: Lucknow Publishing House.

World Bank, 1997, *India: Achievements and Challenges in Reducing Poverty*. Washington, DC: World Bank.

Yang, K.S., 2003, 'Methodological and Theoretical Issues on Psychological Traditionality and Modernity Issues in an Asian Society: In Response to Kwang-kuo Hwang and Beyond', *Asian Journal of Social Psychology*, 6(3): 263–85.

6

Research Concerns

Introduction

THE PURPOSE of writing this textual content on research is to emphasise that it is essential that research studies should be critiqued before acceptance (Muthayya, 1972). There are scores of unpublished theses lying on library shelves in postgraduate institutions, which leave much to be desired regarding validity both in terms of the theoretical framework and methodology. This chapter gives in broad strokes the possible lacunae in research studies. An academician needs to know which of the scores of studies, even those published, have valid and reliable parameters. A student of social sciences, and more especially of human development, which is a hybrid of many disciplines, should have knowledge of valid and reliable research.

We shall be concerned with logical induction/deduction, which is the prima facie requirement of analytical thinking in research. It is therefore necessary to relook at contextual frames and methodological strategies. We emphasise the word 'relook,' which is to search again in depth. The first step is to differentiate between 'development' and 'behaviour', and to find conceptual distinctions. As Baldwin states, 'behaviour is the occurrence of an acting out of the individual which is observable' (Baldwin, 1967: 3–34). For instance, if we state that Mohan is a hyperactive child, we mean that he is not within the normal range of behaviour commonly exhibited by children of his age. This is the observation of an event, 'a behaviour'. Development, on the other hand, is a chronologically changing behaviour pattern. This is generic in nature and represents phylogenetic characteristics, such as the progressive stages of physical growth. Development also indicates the ontogenetic development that is acquired as unique characteristics by a particular individual, such as developing musical skills. Let us take the example of Mohan again: he is not the same at age 10 as he was at age four. To explain further,

Mohan has gone from one stage of development to another. Thus, behaviour is one event and development a series of progressive events.

Therefore, we see two clear paths for assessing or estimating the existence of a unit of behaviour outcome (product), or a patterned development trait continuously exhibited by the individual (process). The researcher should be able to examine an event at one time and in one place as it occurs (immediacy), say, for instance, the occurrence of aggression after a frustrating experience (the classic frustration aggression hypothesis) (Rosenzweig, 1976). The other is to observe either acceleration or deceleration of a trait over time, in this case 'aggression'. Research enables one to find a repetitive pattern by examining a group of children on a long-term basis (longitudinal studies), to note change if any, or observe behaviour of different groups of children over time.

Thus, when we observe a pattern exhibited by a group of nursery school children recognising size, space and colour of objects, we attribute this cognitive behaviour to a generic development process in children at progressive ages during the preschool years. It is then possible to examine results as to their accuracy such as the occurrence of Piagetian schema of the pre-operational stage in preschool children (Piaget, 1954: 56). Thus, in fact, we use basic observation techniques. What are these basic observation techniques? Going back to Chapter 1, we had emphasised that in observing behaviour at one time or many times over a timespan, the observation must have the following characteristics:

(i)   The observation must be unbiased. Either the same behaviour is observed repeatedly by the observer to see if it has the same pattern, or it is observed by several independent observers who attempt to match their observation to achieve one reliable observation.
(ii) The observation must be clearly and not ambiguously reported. It cannot be conditional; it must be clearly unequivocal.
(iii) It must be clearly observable, otherwise it might lead to different interpretations. The observation must be isolated, otherwise other types of behaviour might interfere or contaminate the observation.

These conditions relate to both reports of the observer (when behaviour is elicited) and report of the observed (when behaviour is a response to stimuli). The first type belongs to what we call direct observation and experimentation, and the second is indirect observation or the report/record of the observed. The former is by far the more controlled and therefore more clearly interpretable. This method has been utilised by experimental psychologists, more often than not in a laboratory-like situation, to isolate the phenomenon to be observed. The second type or indirect observation is information elicited from the individuals themselves, like a report or a self-analysis by answering verbal questions or through written information. The latter is often used to assess personality or test a trait's existence or a feeling or attitude or a value or even what vocation the person aspires for. Information, which has been evolved through documented research, is obtained by vigorously following a disciplined method for eliciting behaviour or tracing the existence of a development process through a well-planned design (Creswell, 2002).

Methodologically, there is a sustained movement to use either 'number data' or 'narrated data', or both. The first is termed quantitative data, and the second, qualitative. As has been said before, number tests called psychometric tests have been adopted or at best adapted from the West. They have been infrequently translated into Hindi and other major Indian languages. Frequently, large samples use standards devised by large-scale normative studies such as the reference norms of height, weight and other anthropometric measures devised by the National Institute of Nutrition, Hyderabad, for measuring these indices in sample studies. There is also a movement to delve deep into idiographic data so as to evolve post facto hypotheses relevant to building up an indigenous theoretical model as that proposed by Paranjpe on the basis of Vedic concepts (Paranjpe, 1988: 185–213). Erikson presented a perspective on the life cycle and identity of the individual which has special relevance to the Indian psyche in its socio-psychoanalytical frame (Erikson, 1979: 13–34). As yet, these are meta-theories which require an immense amount of systematically collected data to refresh the scenario on the Indian psyche in its different settings. Forward-looking sociopsychologists, cultural psychologists and eco-cultural experts are moving in the direction of sustaining an indigenous basis for empirical data (Pandey, 2002). As commented by Saraswathi, the process of understanding the Indian psyche implies the need for arriving at a more complete, process-oriented, socio-culturally focussed theory of human development, systematically backed by human development (Saraswathi, 2003: 16).

Since we have taken the stance that human development is a holistic phenomenon, even if specific relevant factors are selected their value is in the strong association they evince in relation to the concept studied. It is euphemistically said that if one probes sufficiently, 'eventually, everything is related to everything else', but that is not the intention of researching into linkages between and among psychosocial concepts. The intention is to find the 'strength of association' between and among logically justifiable concepts. For instance, comparing urban and rural groups and finding differences where the urban people have better incomes/education/status may be biased towards the urban orientation. If not objectively studied, the results may be due to value judgements. Therefore, any research study should follow principles of rigour to be of acceptable standards. These strategies should indicate efficiency, economy and sufficiency. They should not be construed by any value judgement such as deficiency or sufficiency. They should be strictly viewed as bases of analysis.

The Path of Human Development Research

In the current milieu, child development, and now its changed form, human development, came to be born as a reluctant child, made up of various bits and pieces of theories and their empirical data from allied disciplines. These bits and pieces were hardly put together coherently, as each discipline was bent on furthering its own profile without little recognition of the influencing factors from other disciplines. For instance, psychology might dwell on the attachment bond between the mother and child as a psycho-emotional context in its research parameters, but often does not include the incidence or the influence of other mothering styles by surrogates, who are socially acceptable as mother substitutes (Burnam, 1996). In the same manner, sociology might talk about the child being 'everybody's child', and about multiple mothering, but may not delve into the phenomenon of the 'mother–child psychological bond of attachment'. Precisely because of this disjunction, none can by itself give us a total picture in spite of available cross-sectional studies or multicentric approaches in analyses. Even when there are attempts to do so, a multiplicity of multifarious, independent variables are used. Also, the statistical analysis partitions out the effect into many minute categories so that the result gets diluted. Such parametric studies can justify their stance by pointing out that these variables were controlled when subject to sophisticated statistics of variance/regression, and so on. But in the statistical process, the qualitative aspects get submerged. So the reader is left holding a study which says something like: when mother's protectionism is correlated to father's authoritarianism and the social status of the family, then X occurs. So, unless we take an aggregate of several independent variables theoretically, in the real situation it is not possible to identify each and every subject by these various combinations. It is only possible to stay with averages, means, standard deviations and percentiles to indicate the position of individuals along the dimensions of these variables. For instance, we can select a particular individual like Mohan, find his score in the results and state that Mohan exhibits X characteristics because he comes from a Y educational background and a Z structure of the family. It is evident that it is difficult to accept Mohan's behaviour on the basis of only these categories. There are several intervening and unknown variables operating.

The bottom line is that we arrive at a confusing complexity of variables responsible for the child's behaviour. For instance, a child behaves in this way because he belongs to a particular caste/class, is from a modernised family/traditional family (socio-economic variables), has domineering parents, is neglected (psychological variables), is naturally hyperactive or apathetic (biological variables), is independent, aggressive (personality variables), and so on *ad infinitum*, till we do not know what the child is uniquely like. At this point we stress our stance, namely: while the child should be looked at holistically, merely conglomerating a host of variables likely to affect the dependent variable of development/behaviour does disservice to the concept of holistic development. For instance, we make assumptions in these studies that caste being selected as an independent variable, a Harijan child would perform less well on achievement than a Brahmin child (Rath et al., 1979). It would perhaps have been more relevant to take cognitive intelligence and/or non-verbal language/occupation, and labour skills, with which the Harijan child is more familiar, than comparing him with the Brahmin child who is more academically inclined and has the reinforcing environment to study and achieve.

More recently, research has indicated that testing of skills and related intellectual behaviour is compromised by an environment that lacks stimulation, rather than any genetic or innate ability to perform or behave intelligently (Pandey, 2004: 15–16). J. Pandey states that the target-reoriented programmes have focussed on creating a sense of participation and responsibility in the deprived sections of the society. They now emphasise economic deprivation and do not consider other forms of deprivation such as social and physical deprivation.

Perhaps physical deprivation in the form of poor health and nutritional status and social deprivation in the form of disadvantage or discrimination may also be correlative factors. They are, however, not fully utilised in the researching on 'holistic deprivation'. Other factors like opportunity and native intelligence could be more at work affecting achievement behaviour in the economically deprived.

This is where the idiographic and narrative studies like Piaget's and Erikson's came into popularity as they concentrated on individuals and small groups, which were more cohesive than most. In more recent years, the case study approach is offering more insights into human behaviour than large sample studies, as the latter depend upon the normal curve scores, which in many instances is not normal in the real life situation (Guilford, 1936). To give an illustration of the misinterpretation of causes of a certain event/behaviour/happening, studies in the USA which interpreted intelligence to be a racially differentiating factor have been hotly debated upon, in relation to the study design said to be spurious.

If a child has an IQ of 110 (psychology), is from a tribal group (anthropology), is living in poverty (economics), in a large kin-group system (sociology) and happens to be a boy/girl (gender psychology), we deduce that the results are related to all these factors. The quandary is: which of these factors are more potent and which are not? We might attempt to find the potency of each independent variable using sophisticated parametric analyses, but then again the most we might be able to do is to portion out the resultant quotient (analysis of covariance), or indicate which is more potent when others are held constant (analysis of regression) and so on. We are then left holding numerical terms, and lose the qualitative aspects of the individual. We further deduce that the resultant behaviour (if the probability is high) is due to the variation in the independent variable/s as tested by analyses of variance or covariance or regression and so on (Giles, 2002: 3). Therefore, there is a movement now to construct tailor-made tests and stimuli to suit the context, like the methods of interview, questionnaires, observational records and similar methods, suited to geoecologically homogeneous groups. For instance, in testing the occurrence of the Piagetian stages, we have in mind the standard labels of colours, but if a respondent calls the colour purple *jamuni* and another, *baigani* or *ragi*, how do we transfer the perception of these different labels from the concrete to abstract, which is eventually the functional stage of formal learning? We have studies which relate to children from Bhubaneshwar, Orissa or Kolkata slums in Bengal which limit themselves to the populations from which the sample is studied. We refrain from generalising from the results for other populations and social/psychological groups, since the background assumptions of their lifestyles are culturally different. The tendency, however, especially in the face of scarcity of studies, is to quote the results of small samples (often biased) as being acceptable for other groups also, leading to misconceptions. Take, for example, the very popular area of 'stereotypes'. Just because a person is from south India, we cannot generalise that he is bound to like idli and sambhar—he may in fact dislike it; or say that Gujaratis are money-minded as their main occupation is business. We even have epithets like: he is a Marwari (meaning he is a miser, or that a person is not refined because he happens to be illiterate). This process is eventually narrowing down the variables studied to those which are more potent for the particular trait/event which should be the focus of the intended study, and to avoid stereotypes, unless it is the intention of the study to investigate why and how people use stereotypes for ethnic groups.

Currently, anthropology and sociology are being dovetailed in the study of large groups, so that a more clear picture of development is articulated by relevant environmental effects. The reasoning is that since the family is a by-product of the prevailing social system, and the social system differs across communities living in differing ecologies, with differing traditional values and habits, the child who is the product of the family behaves in a predictable way. However, more recently, because of the emphasis on the individuality of the person, idiographic methodology has become a popular methodology (Hairjete, 1997). Having given this general overview of data obtained through major techniques, namely quantitative and qualitative strategies, we now move to the systematic structure and analysis of deriving valid and reliable data.

The Meaning of Research

In the previous chapters we have referred to research studies and their findings in support of conceptualisations in discussions and in analyses through the use of logical reasoning. The basis of research information is factual, existent and predictable human thinking and behaviour in the social sciences. The various disciplines contributing to human development use their own conceptual framework. As a check against this dissolution into hybridism, scholars have debated on the type and quality of researched information. They have also said that there is a need for an integrative paradigm to understand the individual (Benttler and Marmat, 2003). They have argued for a paradigm which suitably observes and validly documents empirical data. There is now an accelerated search for relevant and culturally and socio-psychologically acceptable indigenous data (Dalal and Misra, 2002), and the understanding of their basics in psychology (Underwood, 1957). In this chapter, we concentrate on detailing the procedures for researching, as it is essential to know how to sift the wheat from the chaff, so to speak, so that the informed reader (from this information or otherwise) will know what is acceptable and tenable researched information. The major parameters guiding research are:

  (i)   the accuracy of defining the concept in all its possible ways;
 (ii)   a strict adherence to research principles;
(iii)   a justifiable enquiry;
 (iv)   the outcome of the enquiry contributes to theory and/or is applicable, or both; and
  (v)   remaining within the confines of available theoretical frames and yet searching for new extensions to other frames of reference, such as the motivational frame which can be linked to the frame of need achievement.

Thus, indigenous explanations for the conceptualisations should be explored. We have emphasised that generic conceptualisations from the West are useful platforms to divert research in the Indian context into relevant contextual domains of the Indian psyche. Having said this, however, we also need to understand the ways in which we have so far derived our information. One good way to know is to browse through the series of annotated bibliographies such as the one by U.S. Naidu and V.S. Nakhate (1985) and the bibliography in sociological/anthropological surveys, such as by V. Das et al. (2004) which collates and systematises scattered small sample research over a period of time in the disciplines. Critical reviews by stalwarts like Sinha, Mishra, Pandey and others have stressed, as Nandy puts it, that there is a lack of paradigmatic integration of such data (Nandy, 2002), that data is derived from two kinds of sources, namely longitudinal and cross-sectional, of which the former is hardly existent except for a few studies, while the latter is ad hoc and scattered over several variables, so that it throws up more intervening variables rather than the ones studied, leading to confusion as to what is an independent variable in relation to other variables in the design (Anandalakshmy, 1974). Further, there is data derived from parametric and non-parametric analyses. The former gives standards and norms from scores, like nutritional standards, while the latter are frequency data and only indicate major tendencies of the groups studied.

The data gives rise to deductive information, which then could form the basis of hypotheses leading to theorising suitable to the Indian context. For instance, research (even though in small-scale studies) indicates that there is a tendency for the Indian to be interdependent. This is a phenomenon which has been viewed differently by the western world as being a dependent trait. Research (however small) has indicated that the Indian is interdependent in his interrelationships with others (Sinha and Tripathi, 2002). If such findings are regularly and systematically obtained, they could give rise to hypotheses that the Indian child learns to be interdependent, rather than solely independent or solely dependent. Such explorations are important and imminent in theorising in the Indian context (Dasen, 2003: 128–65). Frequently emphasised concepts, for example, are achievement, authority, collectivism, leadership and justice, and the stress is on theoretical underpinnings of studies on the intervening variables of cultural tenets in behaviour, attitudes and values (Sinha and Mishra, 1993: 139–50). We must remember that given the wide field of discovery, for every verifiable study, there can be another that can negate the first. These various phenomena related to the subject of enquiry can be multiplied *ad infinitum*. Further, the interaction of such variables as time, temporality and deviations must be recognised when examining the interdependence of variables. Time occurs as a constant factor irrespective of other variables. For instance, the term 'chronological age' is time-bound and age increases with time. However, the occurrence of developmental milestones depends upon the physiological (maturational) and orthogenetic potentials of the individual.

How do we know that these arguments are in fact true? We need to understand how premises are developed, and how logical deductions are made through fact-finding and systematic enquiries. How do we view information logically to arrive at factual solutions to problems or queries? This process is not casual or informal, but proceeds on a scientific and systematic basis. In the context of human development, it is the evolutionary and de-evolutionary processes during the lifespan that require upgrading of scientific knowledge (Thomas, 2001). For instance, cognitive development as an embedded aspect of human development had a low profile until the 1940s and expanded with the growth of Piagetian theory in the 1950s. In the 20th century there was an accelerated development of other converging issues, such as the rights of various groups (children, women, the Harijans), the effects of deforestation and industrialisation (like the consequences of 'Narmada Bachao Andolan'), the greenhouse effects, and so on. These, then, become socio-ecological factors affecting the individual's identity and relevant behaviour (Moore, 1978). These are correlative facts, one impinging upon the other. Change, and the continuity of change, albeit in fits and starts, is the overriding factor of influence, as change directs regression or progression, in a slow or accelerated fashion. Change is the major permanent variable in assessing facets of human nature and behaviour. Therefore, we need to understand the meaning of research or re-searching in order to elicit what is called empirical data or data obtained through scientifically attempted methodologies, based on fact-finding processes. We should also recognise that since change is a major factor such research studies are bounded by the parameters of time. For instance, the results of research conducted in the 1950s on sanskritisation and modernisation assume different forms in the current-day context. Currently, the rights of the Scheduled Castes and Scheduled Tribes are recognised as legitimate and programmes of alleviation are being implemented to allow opportunities for them.

The Building of Indigenous Theory

In the larger context, since the field of human development has borrowed constructs and concepts from the social sciences, we need to build up an aggregate of relevant human development conceptualisation and its indices, which could substantiate theoretical assumptions in the Indian context. Saraswathi (Saraswathi and Dutta, 1987) in her insightful analysis has succinctly summed up the lacunae in processing satisfactory data, which are reliable and valid, and contextual in nature. These are:

(i) lack of clarity in the conceptual framework;
(ii) research designs, which are mainly descriptive and refer mainly to distal variables;
(iii) ambiguous criteria for sample selection;
(iv) the use of mainly borrowed tools from the West or the use of self-constructed tools without adequate attention to reliability and validity;
(v) the insufficient knowledge of existent previous data to form linkages with new researches; and
(vi) the use of inappropriate statistical tools and measures.

Traditional research in the social sciences, for lack of indigenous theorising, has accepted neo-western intellectual agendas, in the new phase of globalisation. Western social science agendas have caught the imagination of the upper middle class of the metropolitan universities, spurred on by donor support (Bhambri, 1998: 17–19). Often, scholars are not free to choose the area/topic of interest, and unfortunately, as reported, Indian scholars show a unique dependence on western scholars for ideas and techniques of investigation (Sinha, 1975: 10). Further, research is subject to meeting the needs of sponsors and, therefore, gets shortchanged in terms of fuller analyses, losing out on cultural sensitivity. A.K. Mohanty (1988a: 117–36) and other eminent scholars have advanced the plea that the indigenisation of data should be the foremost consideration if Indian themes on human development are to make some empirical headway.

Essential to accumulating credible and verifiable information is a disciplined procedure and a systematic methodology. The term 'empirical' is used here to connote scientific facts made evident in the micro- and macro-contexts of human development. It is no easy task to describe information that is qualitatively and quantitatively true, existent and factual. Searching scientifically for empirical data has, first of all, to be clearly preconceived in its conceptual or theoretical format. It must exhibit linkages between one set of known data and another set. These should be preformulated and are subjected to validity tests. In other words, even though such information is known to exist casually, it must be exhibited causally or correlatively in order to be accepted as tenable and scientific.

For instance, in a study of anxiety in a family, there may be members with high anxiety and others with less. Even before we ask the questions as to why casual observation indicates this difference, we need to know two processes. One is: What is the theoretical basis of anxiety? And the second is: What is the best scientific strategy to use in order to elicit anxiety behaviour? In the Indian context, there are scores of studies that do not have a theoretical framework. A critique of available studies has indicated that besides the shortfalls in research design, a matter of more concern is that they proceed to examine small areas of behaviour without much relevance as to whether these areas have been previously researched or not (Khalakdina, 1976). Myres (1992: 375) in his monumental work *The Twelve who Survive* also emphasises these lacunae. There is also a tendency to produce data without much adherence to a theoretical framework (Kaur, 1993). Frequently, studies are similar in purpose and content and, therefore, do not add much factual information to the theories of human development. In the ultimate analysis, empirical information, which in research terminology is called datum/data, should subscribe/add to the theoretical framework or at the minimum level develop hypotheses for further research. For instance, Kurt Lewin's field theory gives a physical paradigm of energy, forces and valences (Lewin, 1936). He emphasises that it is more difficult to modify core values than peripheral. Therefore, if we wish to study core or peripheral values, we need to specify how we are adding to research facts already available in the Indian situation, such as food habits which are core and are generally known to be difficult to change. It must be said at once here that there are no specific divisions among the variables, which are either inherent attributes in the human or existent in the external environment. Relationships intertwine in a dynamic fashion between the human and his environment. It is not a static situation. As more information and scientific knowledge are collected through scientific enquiry, there is correspondingly a change in the prevalent assumptions. For instance, on the basis of psychodynamic theory, it is known that social imitation takes place by children with respect to parental models (Freud, 1946).

This theoretical construct is then used to study further relevant patterns such as: Do sons imitate their fathers and daughters their mothers? Are there similarities in organised normal families as compared to disorganised non-normal families? Are imitative models from the family changing to newer models as influenced by the electronic media?

Further, it is essential to collect data relevant to the gaps in available knowledge, so as to have continuity of conceptualisation. For instance, in ancient days the moon was a faraway romantic sphere in the celestial space, but now we know it is made up of rocks and sands and is accessible. The latter has happened because of appropriate science and technology which was non-existent in ancient times. Before the computer age, there was the age of the wireless. Currently, school children can teach their parents sophisticated software programmes. A greater volume of information creates a more calculated field of risk taking and decision making. It also encourages creativity and innovativeness and further problem-solving abilities.

Centres of Research on Human Development

The major institutions, which conduct a degree course in the area called 'human development', are the colleges of home science/home economics and some institutes of technology. Fragmented courses are taught in arts colleges, mainly women's colleges, and are called child development, family living, and so on. The major theory-building social sciences are psychology, sociology and anthropology, with the first one contributing the most as it pertains to human physical growth and mental development, mainly in experimental laboratory studies, first initiated by extrapolating animal behaviour (Mandal, 2000). There is no focussed approach to the totality of conceptualisations on human development in institutions of higher learning. One has to look at the human being through various perspectives, and its relationship to policies in the Indian context (Kaur, 1993: 320; Sinha, 1993: 57–63). There are institutes of advanced study such as the Institute of Rural Development, Hyderabad, the Institute of Advanced Study in Simla and specialised courses in aspects of human development at the National Council for Educational Research and Training (NCERT), National Institute of Public Administration (NIPA), National Institute of Mental Health and Neurological Sciences (NIMHANS), Tata Institute for Social Sciences, and national councils like the Indian Council for Social Science Research (ICCSR) and National Institute for Public Cooperation and Child Development (NIPCCD), for example, which collate information on various aspects of development, with NIPCCD also being the nodular national organisation for the Integrated Child Development Services (ICDS).

One area of concern is the measurement in areas of human development such as intelligence, achievement motive and various domains such as justice, altruism, moral development and school performance. These enquiries are still sporadic and scattered. Besides, the tests available in India suffer from lacunae in several instances and their appropriateness has been decried by several experts (Saraswathi and Dutta, 1986; Sinha and Misra, 1982: 195–215).

Research in child and human development in India has a long way to go. We have depended for too long on western measurement techniques that have questionable credibility in the Indian society (Sinha, 1965: 6–17; Sinha and Kao, 2000). We have, until recently, hardly looked at the Indian scriptural ideology, philosophy and socio-psychological conceptualisation of man and his environment. Like other Asian countries, for instance Japan, China and the Philippines, India has also a long and rich cultural heritage of religious and philosophical ideology. India has hardly interacted with eastern thought till recently (Sinha and Kao, 2000: 9). Also, till recently, we have rarely studied our conceptualisations so as to place them into theoretical frameworks and designs and derive empirical data. For instance, we have many short shrift discourses/descriptions on the preference for a male child, but for what reasons?

As soon as we ask this question, we are given sociological explanations such as lineage, economic necessity, and so on. The Hindu and the Muslim ways of life have also injunctions about the stages of development, such as the *samskaras* in Hindu philosophy (Saraswathi and Kaur, 1993: 340). These philosophical phenomena have been overlooked in norms developed for infant growth (Gesell, 1928) and for developmental tasks (Havighurst, 1946: 85–90). Most of the studies are on infant growth patterns (Phatak, 1977), nutritional status (Radhakrishna, 1992) and developmental norms (Bevli, 1983). Most other studies are of small samples, geographically scattered, with varying operational definitions of the same variables (Saraswathi and Dutta, 1987).

Sinha and Mishra (1993: 139–50) in their comments on the status of policy and research state that there is still a need for a body of common conceptualisation among the various experts in their cocooned disciplines to give a holistic picture to the study of human development. This is particularly so when we view the existent fact that at the ground level there are many permutations and combinations of concepts when applied to the varying communities that make up India. The picture for each discipline is that each still remains in its ivory towers. It can be further demonstrated that the movement towards holistic development is hampered by the types of research currently conducted in institutions of higher education. Thus, without a framework which is sociologically, psychologically and culturally feasible, developmental ontogenetic characteristics in unique environments can be little understood, and we still continue to talk about the importance of toilet training and weaning in child rearing practices, and urging children to be aggressively independent since these are what are recommended as being the right research area in western literature.

Information collected from real life situations, or data, is collected in a quantified form. Such data is of two kinds. The first is collected over a long period of time, from a developmental point of view, sequentially and consistently, such as studying a group of infants through the infancy period, to observe their cognitive development processes. This type of research is longitudinal, differing from cross-sectional research which is collection of data at one time among groups—for instance, studying a consequent behaviour termed aggression as dependent upon the antecedent of amount of frustration (Elkind, 1980: 10–18). In summary, therefore, the progression in research in human development should be to emphasise four processes which stimulate enquiry. First, the process of enquiry has to be accurate, relevant and valid to the context (Mohanty, 1988b). Second, results should arrive at logical explanations based upon currently available data using recent technical acumen. In other words, there are certain principles which should guide an enquiry as to what is the existent status of enquiry, and to what extent it is status quo or changing. Third, the research should have relevance to theory building and/or applications in the Indian context. Thus, research should be systematic and scientific. Fourth, it should be based on a disciplined preplanned design. This preplanned design indicates not only a search but that the search should be looked at through a scientific telescope at the selected phenomena/events/situations with a specific purpose or objective (not biased). In other words, it should be true (valid) conceptualisations and give the same results if acquired in the same ways at different times (reliable methodologies). The data should reflect relevancy. This perspective has been emphasised by Sinha as there has been a great deal of borrowing from the West. We have used conceptualisations that are hardly ours. For instance, the child-centred approach used in the West may be totally inappropriate for the traditional Indian society, for which research should be indigenised (Paranjpe, 1998).

The Logical Basis of Research

Research is not 'guesstimation'. It is not loosely identifying a thing with one's subjective label. We often hear in conversation, judgments passed on people: 'he is such a bore', 'she is such a mouse', 'that child is very boisterous', or 'that child is very withdrawn'. If we were to ask a group of randomly selected people as to what was meant by the words bore/mouse/boisterous/withdrawn, we would get various biased interpretations. Therefore, the procedure has to be scientifically processed. But, what does 'scientifically processed' mean? It means examining problems or issues to derive valid and reliable information, implying that this can be only undertaken by those with expert knowledge on the subject. For instance, in social psychological research, we would expect the enquirer making the scientific inquiry to be a student of psychology/sociology/social psychology/human development. It would be difficult for a mathematician, however knowledgeable in his profession, to deal with social science enquiries. For instance, in researching into personality types of certain groups for introverted behaviour (withdrawn behaviour) or for indexing aggression, expertise in these areas is essential. How do we describe this aspect of withdrawn behaviour or aggressive behaviour, so that the definition is agreed upon? Let us assume that the definition of 'withdrawn' refers to a person who is unable or does not wish to interact socially, who has low self-esteem, who shows hesitancy in expressing his thoughts, is quiet most of the time and does not speak freely or does not take the initiative to do so. These imply that it is not any one indicator which identifies this trait, but several facets of 'withdrawnness' which operationalise the trait.

Having said that, however, there are various aspects of any behaviour, which can be used as indicators. Searching for the most appropriate in a disciplined manner implies three issues:

(i) How efficient and effective is/are these indicator/s (valid and reliable indices)?
(ii) Taken together, do they make up behaviour, which can be observed or elicited or reported (complete operationalisation or definition)?
(iii) Can this type of behaviour(s) be identified in a group (by the use of appropriate sampling techniques)? Or can this type of behaviour be elicited from an individual case study (idiographic methods)?

We may see that the points above refer to:

(i) relevancy of indicators;
(ii) congruence of indicators;
(iii) appropriateness of methodology suitable to the indicators; and
(iv) probability of eliciting the indices of such indicators.

Therefore, what do we mean by indicators?

The Meaning of Indicators/Variables

A variable is an indicator of an event/concept or happening. The very term variable implies that these traits/characteristics/events/situations are themselves varying among the members of the group studied. For example, the concept of leadership can vary from one leader to another.

In the area of social science research, it is essential to know what is the most appropriate index or operational definition of the variable. However, unless the researcher is fairly knowledgeable about the contents of the relevant discipline, in this instance all types of leadership, in available research and empirical findings, he might fall into the trap of operationalising the concept inaccurately. There are two types of variables in a research. The first is the independent variable and the second is the dependent variable. The very terms dependent and independent are indicators themselves. The independent variable can vary without being affected by the dependent variable. The dependent variable, however, can vary consequently, concurrently, concomitantly or correlatively with the independent variable. Its significance is influenced by the independent variable. For example, research indicates that there are three types of leaderships, namely, authoritarian, democratic and *laissez faire* (Lippitt et al., 1939: 271–99). Therefore, the operational definitions of these three types should be unambiguous, exhaustive and related to the theory of leadership.

Thus, a variable varies from one person to another, in different situations, from one methodology to another, and with similar types of variations in leadership. In fact, the same individual may behave differently (vary) in one situation at one time and react to the same situation differently at another time (within variation). Let us amplify these differences within a variable. Persons have different psychological make-up. One student, for example, may be calm, another excitable when given a test (same situation). The calm person may show more calmness when confronted with a test than when confronted by a dentist (different situations). To continue the example, the calm person may be shy to talk about his feelings in public, whereas he may be free to talk about them when writing them down on paper (different methodology). The same calm person when he/she grows older may be more vocal than another (varying times). The catchword here is variance, or changeability. Variations are the crux of the methodologies employed to study differences or similarities from person to person within the group and from group to group. If the intent, for instance, is to find differences in individuals from one culture to another and from one test to another used on the same group, then it is important to direct the study towards finding the differences between the two cultures as two separate groups or as two heterogeneous groups. Here, the significant term is heterogeneity (differences or variations). In order to posit that these are two heterogeneous groups, say, on the attribute of dependency, it is essential that the variable under study has an underlying force or strength to elicit group variance on the attribute of dependency. The strength of the group variance implies that there exist theoretical assumptions that indicate that these differences might exist. The research is to confirm whether they do exist or do not exist in reality. For example, in their study Munroe and Munroe described differences on the same variables (dependency, language and so on) in three differing cultures (Robert and Munroe, 1975). Again, based on existing literature or proven data, we proceed to find these differences (if any) through understanding the concept of variance. We assume that the group variance is more than the variance within the group. Again, it is important that an individual belongs only to one group and not the other, otherwise results would be contaminated. This variation between the two groups or among more than two groups is tested through statistical analysis against the variation within each group. It stands to reason that if the variance within the groups is larger than the differences/variations between the groups, finding out whether in reality these two groups are heterogeneous on the variable dependency is therefore not tenable (Jahoda et al., 1951). That is, the groups are more homogeneous than heterogeneous. It is vital that the planning of a research study be based on assumptions or hypotheses, which in turn are based on theoretical concepts.

Variables and their Types

There are two types of variables: the independent variable or the control or classificatory variable, and the dependent variable or the variable which is caused by or related to the independent variable. To continue the illustration, the guidance techniques can vary independently of the child's aggressive tendencies, but in this hypothesis children's aggressiveness depends upon variation in parents' techniques/situations. Thus, in any hypothesis, there are independent and dependent variables. We may take a host of independent variables and relate them to a host of dependent variables, either interactively or singly. However, as we have stressed before, defining a variable may be interpreted differently even among experts.

The variable, whether dependent or independent, must have the following characteristics:

(i) it must represent one attribute, symptom or construct and be unambiguously defined;
(ii) each item of enquiry or question must relate to one construct and not any other;
(iii) taken together, all stimulus questions or items of the variable should define the whole range of the selected variable, that is it should be exhaustive; and
(iv) the item or question must be related to conceptual constructs.

Each variable, whether dependent or independent, must have an operational definition. This is essential as the operational definitions are stimuli by which behaviour can be elicited. For instance, to find out whether behaviour is aggressive or not, there are several probe questions (stimulus questions), such as if the child is frustrated when not given a prized toy, what is his concept of behaviour like? Does he cry? Does he hit out at other children, does he want to grab the toy, and so on (according to behaviour theory), or does he show signs of inner conflicts such as rationalisation, projection, introjection or sublimation (psychoanalytical theory)? One may even observe the child's behaviour throughout a day to find out how many incidents of aggression occur (anthropological, narrative/verbatim descriptions).

Not all studies are framed with hypotheses. Some are descriptive, some are idiographic, some are case studies and some are surveys. It is either an a priori design or a post facto design that has the ability to hypothesise. Often a study is an initial enquiry into a particular sample, such as sex behaviour in adolescent females in rural areas. This is an area which is difficult to study, and therefore has very little research. So an initial enquiry may be termed as further 'exploratory study', so that hypotheses to be tested may be framed for quantitative assessment for future larger sample studies. Thus, we have different types of research designs.

A Systematic Process of Selection of Variables

The selection of relevant effective and efficient variables depends upon the purpose and posited design of the study. These variables are queried to find answers to the problems/issues posed. The design of the study then sets out to scientifically enquire who/when/where/how: who, meaning the identification of the respondents/subjects/sample; when, meaning the time at which the study is done; where, meaning the location; and, most important, how, meaning the design which includes the methodology.

The meaning of research may be summed up by saying, 'Research is a scientific enquiry based upon valid assumptions.' It is a systematic process of understanding events as they exist, naturally occurring or a priori, or after they have occurred or post facto manner. For example, observing the behaviour of people as their side loses a cricket match is post facto, in other words, a reaction to an event. Research is the systematic process of understanding events, as they are modified/manipulated/qualified.

The variables are to be valid and relevant. Validity implies that the concept truly exists like cognitive perception in children. It should be relevant to the study and not disconnected. Continuing with the same example, cognitive perception should be relevant to the respondent's age and ability to perceive cognitively.

Assumptions or Hypotheses

In wanting to know, for instance, whether one group of children in preschool shows more dependency than another, one must assume or hypothesise that when actually researched in the real situation, these differences will be relevant or not relevant.

Criteria for the Construction of a Good Hypothesis

(i) Hypotheses are statements about relations (similarities or differences) between/among variables.

(ii) Hypotheses carry clear implications for testing the stated relations.

(iii) Hypotheses are statements which contain two or more variables that are measurable or potentially measurable and should assume how the variables are logically related.

(iv) There is clarity and unambiguity in the format of the hypotheses.

(v) Hypotheses should be working instruments contributing to theory.

Let us amplify the term hypothesis further. There are three types of hypotheses between two variables X and Y. One hypothesis is termed the null hypothesis, that is, it is a statement of no differences, that are acceptable statistically between X and Y. The second is that there are differences (X is not like Y or bidirectional), and the third is that one is greater than the other (X is greater than Y or unidirectional). Each and every hypothesis should be logical, until tested and proved. The directional hypotheses are just as logical as the null hypothesis. They are mainly statements of the same relationship that lends itself to statistical analyses. The most popular format is to state the difference in either direction, not implying that anyone is more or less significant than the other. When the differences are acceptable, according to statistical principles it means that 'there is a great probability that these differences are in fact true' (valid) (Stevens, 1961).

To illustrate further about hypotheses, we say that the enquiry is posited on the basis of 'if' and 'then'. If children in a preschool group A are compared with children in group B for dependency, then we are assuming two concepts. One is that this hypothetical situation can be proven to be true or not true on the basis of relating the 'variance' of group A with the 'variance' of group B (namely the degree/amount/type of dependency). Second, the hypothetical situation can be formulated in any one of the three forms mentioned above.

The first hypothesis is called a hypothesis of 'no differences'. It does not automatically mean that they are similar, for a hypothesis can only prove or disprove what is stated. The second and the third hypotheses are called directional for they state one is greater than the other or vice versa. The last states definitely that one group is greater than the other. Hypothesising, as stressed repeatedly, should not be frivolous statements, for one can compare anything with anything in terms of a hypothesis and find differences. For instance, one can index the height of females to their intelligence quotients. But this serves no logical/scientific/relevant purpose in the social sciences. What we are saying is that, conceptually, there must be an assumed linkage. For instance, if a child is frustrated, he will either be aggressive or regressive. It is rarely that he is unemotional. The discipline of science directs one to base these assumptions/suppositions/hypotheses on theoretical facts. For instance, there is much ambivalence in the theory of intelligence. Some protagonists argue that intelligence is mainly through inherited genomes; while others argue that intelligence can be improved through stimulated nurturance. This is precisely the argument used by Jensen in studies of Anglo-Saxon Americans and African Americans in the early 1970s (Jensen, 1969), while on the other hand, those whose psychosocial philosophy is based on sociology/anthropology/ecology argue that environment or the stimuli around the human being are more potent than the inherited traits. In the Indian situation, while we have inadequate comparison on intelligence, there are data to indicate that institutionalisation depresses intelligent performance (Khatri, 1965). Research conducted to this effect amongst disadvantaged children has indicated that opportunity and motivation are the two major attributes that stimulate intelligent behaviour (Bharati and Ramamurthi, 1977: 192–95). However, unless the stimuli are free from cultural bias, measuring intelligence may be spurious. The reason why we have laid stress on current knowledge of theoretical frames is that we are strictly bound to proceed on the basis of sound premises.

To go back to the first illustration, observation of the two preschool groups on the dependency trait shows statistically that adults in the latter group do much of the activities for their children and do not encourage curiosity and so reinforce dependent behaviour vis-à-vis group A, where children are allowed to explore, innovate and follow their own lines of curiosity of knowledge. Therefore, we posit the hypotheses as follows:

(i) There are differences in dependency behaviour between groups A and B as related to parental stimulation.

(ii) Group A of the better educated class shows less dependent behaviour than group B of less educated class, or, to put it more succinctly, social class is related to dependency behaviour in children.

(iii) The reader will notice that these various ways imply the same premises, namely that educated parents are more likely to stimulate independent behaviour in their children.

There are various ways in which we can further elaborate these hypotheses. Therefore, a hypothesis is a logical conjecture between two or more variables. They are declarative forms, which relate, either generally or specifically, one variable to another variable. Therefore, we see that in assessing the significance of relationships between/among variables using quantitative data, necessarily the statement of the hypotheses is to be tested.

Criteria for Valid Hypotheses

We present some criteria for assessing the validity of a hypothesis. These are not exhaustive. The following are what we consider as central:

- (i) There is a statement of relationship between and among variables.
- (ii) There are clear implications for testing the stated relationships.
- (iii) The variables are measurable and the statement assumes how they are related.
- (iv) They are working instruments or operational definitions of a concept or construct.
- (v) They should evolve from a theoretical or conceptual frame and/or be extrapolated from findings of other studies, indicating further research.
- (vi) They should have within their construct/s the expectation of predictability that a similar or continuing concept will add to the knowledge and/or its applicability in real life situations.

The proving of the relationship or disproving of the relationship, according to statistical formulae, is not the whole story. The findings must be relinked to theoretical concepts. For instance, finding that children with psychosomatic disorders show more aggressive behaviour relates to the Freudian framework of defence mechanisms (Symonds, 1946). In these hypotheses, such studies look at two distinct variations: the variation in psychosomatic disorders and the variation in exhibited defence mechanisms. The study of these variations can be observed *in situ* on an experimental basis or by observing behaviour in real life situation (a priori hypothesising) or by reported incidence of psychosomatic disorder/aggressive behaviour (post facto hypothesis). Hypotheses can be positive in any of the three forms mentioned above: null, unidirectional and bidirectional.

Designs and their Types

A research design is a systematically thought out plan with several logical sequential steps. These are:

- (i) Preparation of a plan so as to select the most appropriate design for eliciting relevant, valid and reliable data in relation to the problem.

(ii) Informed choices should be made about whether a plan is to do an experiment, or collect verbatim data through interviews or reported information or questionnaires; their comparative value for the purpose of the study should be analysed.

(iii) The plan design should relate to the problem and develop its statement/s.

(iv) The problem should be based on empirical research already existing and/or available data, information, consequences, lacunae, need assessment and situational analysis.

(v) The design should specify the objective/s, variables and their operational definitions. This process presents a credible basis for justification of conducting the study, insofar as it will add to/substantiate/develop new directions towards theoretical concepts.

(vi) The purpose of building up a research design is also to identify indicators by which the data can be elicited. The design has to derive a valid and reliable sample according to the principles of sampling (Coolican, 1995). The study poses hypotheses on the basis of assumptions it makes regarding the cause or correlative factors associated with the problem.

(vii) The hypothesis is further stated in a workable form, that is, there are variables on the basis of which the sample will be exposed for elicitation of data. The plan or design needs to assess inputs/requirements and the strategies/technical programme of a calendar of events.

(viii) The hypothesis has working operational definitions of the variables. They are categorised as classificatory or independent variables, meaning that they can vary independently of others, whereas the dependent variable is hypothetically linked to the variation of the independent variable. For instance, in the study on aggression, the parents can vary their techniques (independent variable) without dependence upon the assumed dependent variables. Thus, if the design links the dependent variable of aggression to the parental techniques, then it depends upon the variation in parents' techniques. Other independent variables can be class, caste, religion and ethnicity. Here, one is either a Muslim or a Hindu, a low caste or a high caste. In other words, there are no variation between these castes or these religions. Findings are deduced through the use of 'descriptive' statistics and for the purposes of proving or disproving the hypothesis/es, 'inferential' statistics are used (Blommers and Lindquist, 1960).

(ix) In real life situations, costing also has a time frame; for instance, polls or surveys are large extensive studies of shorter durations, such as finding out preferences for voting patterns. But to conduct a longitudinal study requires a long period of time to observe developmental trends, such as growth patterns of children. The latter often requires expertise and intense investment and is more conducive to theory building.

(x) After the conduct of the research and the procurement of acceptable data, the outcomes should be discussed in relation to theoretical frames or the purpose for further research in the area, giving the significance of such results in a discussive manner.

(xi) The design should specify the facilities available. Also, grants/assistance and constraints may offer less facilities and, therefore, constrict the operational phase of the research project.

(xii) The conduct of a research study also involves the finances available in the budget and their utilisation over a certain span of time, estimating expenditure on personnel and other budgetary requirements.

(xiii) The procured data, their analyses, their significance and implications should be documented for publication and reference purposes for further research.

The Major Parameters of Research

Given the above example of a design, the major parameters are as follows: Research must be scientific both in its conceptualisation and in the carrying out of action-based programmes on the conceptualisation. For instance, if one wishes to study friendship patterns, one must have a sufficiently well-grounded knowledge of the socio-psychological patterns of friendship for understanding how friendship patterns emerge, stabilise and continue (psychosociological information). This should be obtained by reviewing previous research so that the researcher is cued in to the study of affiliative variables. For instance, one might study friendship patterns in rural schools and the evidence may prompt other researchers to study differences in friendship patterns by ecological *area*, by ethnicity, by caste or class, and so on. They have to be studied at a specified time ('when'), say when the children *are* at primary school stage; in a certain *place*, say the central schools of Ahmedabad ('where'); and using an appropriate method ('how') (Badke, 2004).

The study has to be systematic. In other words, there has to be a preplanned design as mentioned above. It means that the steps in the process have to be systematically planned one after another in a logically linked manner. The preplanning is based upon the purpose, and should explore possibilities of further knowledge based on the existent knowledge. For example, in studying moral behaviour of primary school children, one might experiment with allowing opportunities to cheat during an examination (Hartshone and May, 1928). If cheating is found to occur in the absence of the invigilator, then one can conduct further such studies, such as the development of conscience in primary school children, reactions to rewards and punishment by primary school children, sharing and cooperation in primary school children, and so on. Again, if one uses the same sample one can correlate honesty with rewarding/punishing behaviour. If one uses another sample, then comparisons may be made between the two. In other words, the same sample can be studied in relation to different dependent, variables, either cross-sectionally or longitudinally, either on an a priori design or a post facto design.

These are a few examples to indicate various possibilities of researching on the basis of known researched events, situations, phenomena or samples. This means that if we wish to study the effect of the moon on the behaviour of the human, it would be a far-fetched and a seemingly impossible task, except in highly sophisticated, secrecy-bound national or international organisations with extremely high funding, not within the purview of social science parameters in research studies at the academic level.

We know in general terms about human development, and all over the world experts are conducting studies on various aspects of human development, of which we hear, or we read about in scientific books/journals/periodicals. So we attempt to study with a purpose in mind of finding factual information for the purpose of adding to already known information. For instance, we have information of the schematic formation of conceptualisation, but little is known of how the cognitive schema are influenced by different ecologies in which humans live. Concepts of time and space are differently recognised within concrete city walls vis-à-vis remote hill terrains. Some scientific enquiries have been conducted on ethnicity, but not sufficient for us to say categorically that ethnicity creates divisiveness among groups within the same ecology. On the other hand, much is known about the cohesiveness of tribal behaviour of nomadic tribes; for example, their networking and bonding irrespective of time and space are highly developed. We do know that child-upbringing practices change over time and space (Bronfenbrenner, 1958). As in other cultures, in India also sociopolitical and cultural history have left their indelible mark on the psyche and therefore the need for alternative paradigms assumes importance in the Indian psyche. Hence, there is a dire need for alternative paradigms which have a suitable fit for the Indian psyche. It is reasonable to assume that a particular enquiry has the purpose of enlarging the already existing knowledge of human ecology.

Methodologies of Data Collection

Dependent upon the type of research designs, namely a priori and post facto, the method of data collection should be the most appropriate, the most relevant, efficient and effective. There are several methods of data collection. The a priori method is simultaneous and immediate with the event while the post facto method reports and documents after the event has occurred. Examples of a priori are the observation of children's play and an example of post facto is questioning subjects about their vocational aspirations.

In a priori designs the method is usually observations. These are controlled, non-biased observations where the variables are isolated or field observations where they are studied as they occur normally and naturally in real life situations (Shaw and Hammond, 2004). Observation becomes a scientific technique to the extent it (a) serves a formulated research purpose, (b) is planned systematically, (c) is recorded systematically and (d) is subject to checks and controls on validity and reliability. The four broad questions in observation methods are:

- What should be observed?
- How observation should be recorded?
- What procedures should be used to assure the accuracy of observation and what relationship should exist between the observed behaviour and the person acting out the behaviour?
- How can such a relationship be validly established in the research strategy/method?

A subsystem of observation is the strategy of participant/non-participant observation. In non-participant observation, the experimenter is present with the sample study, but only records the behaviour. In participant observation, the experimenter/observer interacts with the person/s in the sample. Observation as a methodology, both participant and non-participant, has a strong advantage of reliability. The stimulus and its reaction can be isolated from other contaminating variables. The behaviour can be viewed in circumstances where it is not possible for the respondents to vocalise or express themselves under laboratory conditions. In the former, there is full control by the experimenter, unlike post facto research designs, where the researcher has to depend upon the responses for reliability which may not always be so. In fact response can be spurious or 'halo', but physical observation is not, for the observed record is what is seen/heard.

Laboratory experiments are carefully controlled, whereas observations in the natural situations are not as controllable and can be contaminated by other intervening variables. For example, in field studies, when observing a particular phenomenon, the observer can be distracted and therefore the observation is not reliable. Further, there may be other factors like interruptions and movements which cause gaps in the observation. However, the applicability of this type of research to theory is more pristine than the laboratory experiment. The field observation technique is used largely to contribute to theory. In field observation techniques, where other than the intended behaviour occurs because of intervention by other variables, it is essential that there is more than one observer recording the same behaviour so that a tally may be made for reliability and the avoidance of subjective bias (inter-rater reliability). It is necessary to use probability statistics, to account for error that might occur due to contamination by other extraneous variables.

The methods used for post facto are many, like questionnaires, interviews, reporting, projecting, surveying and the case study method. The latter can take many forms. It refers to examining only one group qualitatively and following the particular behaviour/s to be studied over a period of time as it occurs in the group, such as friendship patterns. Thus, it is a specific group small enough to follow and observe as and when the friendship actions occur. A case study approach is directed towards small groups, where a variable is examined in depth as occurring/reported. Another form of the case study method is idiographic, where a single event/incident is observed and reported over a period of time such as anthropological studies of small group behaviour. Several such individual case studies are put together to draw generalisations from the total number of cases such as studies of single mothers and their child rearing methods. The case study method is often used for the purpose of identifying whether a hypothesis is in fact true for further exploration with a larger group on a sampling basis.

Therefore, it is an exploratory field for formulation of hypotheses. In an urban slum, for example, if there are cases reported of stealing by non-schooling youngsters in the community, then through a case study of each youngster, one can collate material to make the predictive hypothesis that lack of schooling in urban slums is related to disorganised behaviour. Using a case study approach automatically implies qualitative data and is mostly descriptive since social statistics is not amenable to a single or a few cases. These qualitative verbatim records are often useful for illustrating behaviour of small groups and the idiographic method is growing more popular, such as Piaget's study of causality in children (Piaget, 1928) and Freudian case studies (Freud, 1928). Data are elicited from the material for analysis, but it has to be collected from a group of people who form either the population or the sample of the population. This group is termed as the respondent group because it responds to stimuli which are expected to elicit or bring out the responses from the group/sample.

Survey Methods

Survey methods are usually used for quick estimation such as in polls (Weinberg et al., 1999). Surveys are usually conducted when the topic is fairly new, and a quick assessment is needed and is readily obtained, such as opinion polls and pre-analysis of voting patterns. The crux of the surveys is to plan and execute a design for the inclusion of a wide representation of the groups (samples) to be studied. The basis of prediction is made on percentages, ratios and fractions of a normal curve, and is especially useful in pilot and feasibility studies, so as to obtain a right estimate of the aspects the researcher intends to pursue in a more rigorous analysis. Further, surveys are useful when an area of study is relatively unexplored, for instance sex behaviour among adolescents, and the researcher wishes to formulate a feasible theoretical framework for an intensive study. Surveys are based on quota area and census or demographic population characteristics, such as a survey of food habits or preferences often used by the media as sales advertisement attractions. In general, survey data are not put to tests of significance. The populations and their samples are meant to indicate general tendencies and, therefore, descriptive statistics serve the purpose.

Questionnaire Methods

It is the questions/probes/information-seeking methods that form the stimuli. The stimuli can be in the form of questions in what is termed as questionnaire schedule. The data can be narratives, which are called verbatim or spontaneously spoken responses. They can be paper-pencil tests and, in the case of projective techniques, there can be responses to pictures/provocative stimuli/issues. We will explain each one by examples. But before doing so, it is essential to say that all the stimuli/questions/probes taken together must operationalise the total dimension of the variable(s) under study. For example, if one wishes to elicit information on vocational aspirations, all stimulus questions taken together must cover the whole range of possible occupations. This range might be presented in the questionnaire schedule, either open-ended or structured. Open-ended means the respondent is free to choose any occupation that he or she aspires towards, without being prompted to select from a given range. Structured, on the other hand, implies that the respondent answers only from the various professions given as choice, or can rank-order them or can give them equal weightage. Usually the second structured type is called multiple-choice selection. The format of eliciting data through a questionnaire depends upon the variable to be studied. For instance, if the researcher says 'What would you like to be when you have to choose an occupation', this is called free choice response. If the interviewer wishes to emphasise only blue-collared workers or paraprofessionals or professionals, then his question would be, 'Which of these X occupations would be your first choice?' It is important that the researcher knows what to do with the data he collects; in other words, he must already have conceived of a framework for analysis of the data.

The questions should not be equivocal, ambiguous, repetitive and overlapping. They should not be biased, and should not evoke a 'halo response', or confuse the respondent. The questionnaire should not be lengthy; if necessary it should be broken up in parts so that it might not lead to spurious or invalid responses.

The questions are put into a format called questionnaire schedules with pre-planned structures for placing the responses in a tabular format for analysis. This means that asking for ranked choices on an occupation schedule implies that the responses are amenable to non-parametric statistics (Siegal, 1956: 279–84). If the respondent gives a weight to each one of these choices, then scores are obtained for parametric analysis. It is important to remember that the questionnaire method can be asked of each respondent and marked one at a time. However, when there are large samples, the group method of administration is more economical in terms of time and efficiency, as the group is subject to testing at one time in one place. Again it may not be possible to conduct either individual or group responding situations. Therefore, it may be more convenient to mail the questionnaires. However, the latter technique suffers from the probability of less than the total respondents returning their completed questionnaires. It is usual to expect 10 per cent loss in mailed questionnaires and the researcher has to be disciplined in selection of the sample so that the probability of the returned questionnaires is high. Therefore, it is essential that the sample finds it easy to fill in the questionnaire and has the incentive to return the mailed questionnaire. These mailed questionnaires are most often used in survey research, marketing research and exploratory research studies.

Thus, we observe that the data from surveys and questionnaires can be treated with reference to the objective of the study. For instance, in survey polls, the researcher might be interested in the percentages responding to a particular question, like 'Who would you choose as president?' It may go further to rank-ordering of those preferred as the president. Questionnaires, on the other hand, do more than just asking particular questions for descriptive purposes. Questionnaires/responses may be subjected to further analyses of sub-hypotheses, such as gender-related responses and age-related responses.

Interview Method

In the interview method the interviewer has no option but to be face to face with the respondent in asking a question and getting an immediate response. The interview technique requires that the interviewer has requisite skills to make the respondent feel at ease to respond freely, uses the right tone, is non-threatening and reinforces the interviewee positively. These strategies are necessary so as to get non-halo, non-biased, spontaneous responses. It is a skilled ability, which requires much practice. The interview follows the same content as do the questionnaire schedules in terms of the criteria mentioned above. To repeat, these criteria are non-ambiguity, no equivalence, relevancy, accuracy and, taken together, these interview questions should operationalise the dependent variable. The interview technique is by and large a fairly reliable method. There are different types of interviews, classified depending upon the purpose or the method like non-directive which again is equivalent to the unstructured questionnaire method where the respondent is free to express himself or herself in any way he/she likes and the responses are then scrutinised by a panel and categorised on the basis of preset criteria; for example, if the question is 'Which feeling is uppermost when you are about to take a test?' responses will be varied. They may be the following: 'I am scared', 'I feel physically sick', 'I am excited', 'I feel like running away', 'I haven't studied so I don't know what I shall write', 'I have studied hard but I know I am going to fail', and so on. These are varied responses and need to be categorised on certain criteria like negative, positive and indifferent responses. Another type is directed interviews like true or false or multiple choices, where categories are predetermined and the responses fall into any one of the the the sets. Usually standard tests are of this type where correct responses indicate 'high' on the criteria and incorrect scoring a 'low'. The third type is client-centred. This type is usually used in psychotherapy, or psychological testing, where not only questions are used, but also probes to elicit data more completely. A variation of this type is the use of projective techniques in psychoanalysis where the respondent gives his own interpretation to an amorphous picture, to an incomplete sentence story or expresses defence mechanisms like introjection, projection, rationalisation, sublimation and so on. These techniques are used only by skilled psychologists who interpret the responses in relation to the problems presented. Verbatim responses and case history method of client's undergoing therapy or who are to be assessed for personality variables like introversion, extroversion, self-esteem and so on are also subjects of such techniques.

The fourth type is the in-depth interview where the dimensions are intensively probed in order to elicit responses which are more explanatory of the behaviour studied. For example, in trying to ascertain whether there is sibling rivalry in a family, the interviewer asks a number of indirect probing questions like, 'When your sister is praised for some task, do you feel you could do just as well or better?', and similar questions to find out the depth of the attribute, in this instance sibling rivalry. Thus, several questions then unfold the depth of the attribute, trait or event. Such in-depth interviews are frequently used in recruitment techniques through group discussions, buzz sessions and quizzes where an idea is floated and the reaction of the interviewees is sought in an open-ended manner. Thus, the administrator is able to judge the quality of the participants, their participation rates and the quality of participation in these sessions (indicating initiative, resourcefulness, innovativeness, decision-making and risk-taking abilities). It enables the interviewer to (*a*) direct the questions in such a way that they do not intimidate the respondent; (*b*) be casual and informal and, therefore, elicit responses which are not stressful and are more likely to be true.

For the interviewer, to be aware about establishing rapport before presenting the questions, it is necessary for the interviewer to prepare the set of alternate questions and expect probable responses. The interviewer (*a*) should have the ability to modify the question (retaining the same content), if it has to be further explained; (*b*) should have the opportunity to express the question in a way that it is comprehensible in a non-ambiguous and unequivocal manner; and (*c*) by judging the reaction of a particular respondent, should keep changing from one question to another, depending upon how comfortable the respondent feels.

Thus, what we are saying is that the interview technique can be a reliable method, because it offers all the necessary opportunities for accurate expression by the respondent. Necessarily, therefore, the data procured is as good as the quality of the technique/researcher.

Paper-pencil Test

This method is fast becoming popular as it is often based on standardised tests. Standardised tests are those which are present in a question and answer format. They are prepared on the basis of an analysis of pre-sample responses (pilot study). Many such tests emanate from the West and they are mainly used to assess an individual in a homogeneous group as to his rank order in that group on an attribute. Standardised tests are those, where questions are related to eliciting responses to the dependent variable/s. They may be adapted from standardised tests of the West like the Vineland Social Maturity Scale, the Apperception Test, Infant Developmental Scales, and a host of others. Some like vocational tests are adopted without much modification. Still others may not be standardised but are contrived, validated and made reliable through correlation analysis. The responses are pre-tested on a pilot sample, revised and used for the actual sample to be tested, much like validating a situation by rehearsals. Some IQ tests like Binet and Wechsler Bellevue are used, as adopted from the West, as they are said to test general intelligence assumed to be homogeneous in any group of humans. Some tests are devised to be 'culture-free'. Others, especially those devised by university students, are usually exercises for a thesis and are a one-time affair. Research institutes or institutes that have research units, like the Tata Institute of Social Sciences and the National Council for Educational Research and Training, have attempted to develop standardised tests for their use on a larger scale in a repeated manner. Standardisation using western tests which have been attempted are Gessell's norms used as standards by Bhandari and Ghosh (1980). On the other hand, Indian norms have been used in studies of anthropometeric growth utilizing Indian Council of Medical Research (ICMR) norms as in Shinde et al. (1980: 45–53). To give an example, cognitive development in Eysenck's Personality Inventory was adapted to the Indian context (Chattopadhyay et al., 1982: 104–8). Piagetian tasks have been used without adaptation in several studies, especially those related to conceptual levels and the Piagetian schema. Among the several experts who have commented on the current status of research, Saraswathi's (1974: 231–36) analysis has indicated many issues.

Anandalakshmy, in a critical review of major research studies relating to the young child in the late 1970s in India, emphasised that many of the studies did not use a theoretical base when utilising standardised tests, or used them inappropriately. A major suggestion was the need to focus on socially relevant problems (Anandalakshmy, 1979: 295–309). In standardising tests, the responses are scored and arranged on a normal curve distribution with calculations of the mean, standard deviations and percentiles. If a respondent scores correctly 25 out of 100 questions, he is then said to be at the 25th percentile or minus 2 standard deviations below the statistical average, and, therefore, is said to be a low scorer on the basis of a normal curve distribution. This adheres to the principle that in a random sample there are just as many scorings above the mean as below, which occurs in a normal distribution. Thus, standardized tests are used on similar samples, and provide reference norms for the variable/s studied.

In procuring data for the purpose of understanding fully or inferring from the data what the meaning of a statistic is, one should be aware that quantitative data only tells how many are significantly different from the average score in the standardised test. The limitations of the standardised tests are that they can only give quantities or numbers, and do not tell us much about the individual's qualities which these scores represent. Often it is said that a person who has a score can be converted into a percentile, but a percentile cannot describe the qualities of a person. For this reason, research studies in the social sciences are now going into a newer format of giving narrative descriptions to highlight the characteristic in the quantitative group. These are called verbatim illustrations and are usually procured from taped interviews, which give descriptive data supplementing quantitative data.

Sociometry

In his sociometric analysis, Moreno (1977) has broken grounds in the field of sociometric theories, concepts and techniques. Initially, these related to close groups in institutional settings, but have gradually widened to studying small groups under laboratory conditions, and in anthropological studies (Alphale, 1976: 167). For instance, sociometric techniques are used to assess associative ties among communities and to use them for programmatic purposes in identifying leadership and followership. This technique is essentially related to group interaction, and is based on the concept of affiliation. In this strategy there is one symbolic representation of interpersonal structures with notational schemes, describing features of the social structures. Sociometry is based on concepts of interpersonal affiliation, need affiliation, preferential selection and identification of friendship and group patterns.

The information relates to persons who select, who do not select, who mutually select each other, who are selected by few and who are selected by none, as being those with whom the person wishes to affiliate in varying situations of group membership. Labels are given to such persons identified in the group: one selected by all (leader), one not selected at all (isolate) and the in-betweens in the range, namely, non-reciprocal selection. Often, the choice of selection is also based on rank order, namely, who is selected as first, second and third choice. This preferential labelling/identification is embedded in the theory of social organisation. Like-minded individuals tend to herd in a group (the herd instinct). Still, within the herd, some are most frequently selected (leaders) while others are not at all selected, indicating the strength of the ties/bonds of the members of the group.

The need for affiliation (need affiliation) is a secondary need as stated by Murray (1938). Its converse is also true, that unlike the herd instinct there is also a tendency to voluntarily stand outside the group. In the network of interpersonal interaction the event for which the choice is made has its own conceptual frame. Persons can be selected based on the objective. For instance, if a person is to be selected to go into a dangerous jungle, then it could be one who is most indispensable or one who has the qualities of leadership to guide others into the jungle. This is dependent upon selective perception. Dispensable persons are not valued in the group, while leaders are.

Studies that use sociometry as a technique deal with organised behaviour by selecting a leader, a key person or a representative, for a special skill. Also, the person may be selected to be in a special situation like partners in a game, friends to go out with and so on. The data are often presented in matrix tables, but more frequently in a sociogram (diagrams of positions of members in the group) (Proctor, 1960). Sociometry is a simple tool used in natural situations in the area of preferential choice. One consequence of using these data is that there is a probability of bias occurring in the responses other than the stimulus question. For instance, if one were to ask who would you like to sit next to for your studies, the preference may be to select a person who is good in studies or selecting a friend for the sake of being close to him/her. Therefore, the researcher must be clear as to whether he is interested in obtaining personal biases or identifying qualities such as leadership, excellence in a certain skill or friendship patterns in the group.

The Critical Incident Technique

The critical incident technique is used as a short assessment identification of data that presents the major issues/problems/characteristics in a given situation. For instance, it is a method of defining the group concept of what makes a particular member of an organisation more effective than the other. In the use of a critical incident technique, it is essential to choose a criterion in which the identification of the dependent data is made. For instance, in a case study approach, where delinquents are observed for antisocial behaviour, the observer looks for behaviour which highlights destruction, cheating, lying or robbery, to illustrate the significant/critical characteristic sought. The observation of this incident occurring over time is recorded for its frequency to indicate whether it is a significant or a non-significant attribute (physical violence, cheating, stealing among a group of delinquents). It can also be used in the interview method; for instance, when a researcher wishes to elicit incidents of trauma, the respondent is asked to speak freely about particular incidents in the past, which have threatened/frightened or terrified him. If it is necessary to observe this behaviour, it is essential to observe and record incidents of unusual activities. Such activities may be collected over a period of time to underscore traits such as social disorganisation/mob behaviour/riotous behaviour and so on. Thus, the meaning of the critical incident technique is that it critically operationalises the occurrence of behaviour or event or trait which is highly significant in the repertoire of the person's range of behaviour. As in sociometry, the expertise of the researcher is essential for indicating non-bias in the observation and reporting.

Content Analysis

The analysis of the properties of verbal material is commonly referred to as content analysis. It may be considered as a method of studying the collective material to indicate patterns that emerge. For instance, in attempting to find out forms of communication, intensive analysis is made of the protocols collected, so as to indicate type, quality, direction and intensity of the communication in a particular sphere. The form of information may be written, like literature, leaflets, articles, journals, or verbal, like radio programmes, speeches, folk songs and so on, to collate the frequency of patterns.

The analysis may be qualitative or quantitative in nature. Content analysis, when used in the qualitative format, is usually descriptive, namely, 'a report may say from an examination of the activities of the terrorists over the past year, these activities are more frequently in area X than in Y.' It can also be other than reported information. In spoken information, it can be notating the number of times a person uses a particular phrase or concept, and then ordering them in intensity/extensity or reporting the data as such. Quantitative analysis reports the number of times a certain criterion/phase/concept/construct is used vis-à-vis others from narrative records/verbatim data/reports. These are usually in the form of categories: for instance, how many times the crowd booed the speaker on the podium or applauded the speaker and so on. It is also possible for the researcher to form a precis of the records or speeches to indicate trends. Frequently, illustrations of the sample are expanded to give a further in-depth picture of the quantitative data. Qualitative descriptions are given from the quantitative analysis. For instance, if a study indicates that many mothers significantly use verbal scolding, rather than rewarding behaviour, one might give examples of each in order to elucidate the more frequently occurring type under verbal scolding/verbal praise categories. Thus, we find that the technique of content analysis used in many studies that have idiographic data gives more meaning pertaining to individuals over the period of data collection, or description of case profiles as in the area of guidance and counselling.

Semantic Differential

Semantics refers to a specific language used and its various interpretations. For example, one person's language may indicate literal constructs. Another might use analogies, metaphors and similes to mean the same concept. Therefore, the concept of semantic differentials is based on differentials: unipolarity/bipolarity, and also idiomatic phraseology (Selitiz et al., 1969). This means that constructs like attitudes, ranging, for example, from 'agreeable' to 'disagreeable' (bipolar) and 'most agreeable' to 'least agreeable' (unipolar), can be assessments of degrees of difference in quality of expression regarding the same objects/situations. For example, lightning in the sky may be viewed differently. Respondents may find it either most agreeable or least agreeable (unipolar) or agreeable or disagreeable (bipolar). In either case, they are two ends of the same dimension describing the quality of the particular lightning. The technique of semantic differential is extremely useful for experimenting with people from different socio-economic classes, educational levels, occupational levels and even cross-culturally. The qualitative description such as exemplary, very good, outstanding, fair may be used in describing a play or a drama. It is a question of semantics or language-specific descriptions. They indicate the intensity of perception of people in relation to an event, an object, a person, a phenomenon, and scaling it from high to low. Also, the concept may mean different things to different people at different times. In other words, differences in the use of language as to their meaning indicate cultural nuances. Often, the word 'fine' is used. If asked to define the word fine when the person says, 'I am fine', it might indicate many things: good health, feeling bright, getting along well or achieving. If these are qualifying adjectives arranged along a score sheet, they will range from 'more' to 'less' in intensity. This type of measurement may be used in assessing attitudes, values and existence of traits as differentially perceived from person to person, from culture to culture, and expressed in verbal forms of given languages. For instance, what is appreciated in one culture may be not so in another, such as the forms of greetings, which differ from culture to culture, and even within a culture. In India, greetings can take the form of 'Ram Ram', 'Namaste' or 'Jai Shri Krishna'. Its major use is in psycholinguistics where labels are given differentially from person to person or culture to culture about the same concept.

Projective Techniques

These are tests based on the theory of psychoanalysis, and are devised to tap unconscious thinking processes mainly used in abnormal psychology or to test cases of abnormal personality and behaviour disorders (Kapur and Mukundan, 2002). The tests generally used are Thematic Apperception Test (TAT) and Children's Apperception Test (CAT), where ambiguous pictures are presented to the respondent to elicit the respondent's covert perception in an overt form. The questions usually used are ambiguous, 'What is the person thinking, feeling or doing?', or 'What do you think is happening in this picture?' The theory is that the respondent projects his own distortions and aberrations through these pictures. These are qualitative and give data which pertain only to individual cases and presented in a unique manner as related to the particular dynamic personality. There are other contrived projective tests such as the Rosenzweig picture frustration technique. These tests are designed to elicit the unconscious, innermost, repressed feelings of the respondent, who is non-threatened when he gives his interpretations of pictures, sentences and so on. The analysis, when examined for its psychodynamic structure, will indicate to an experienced psychiatrist or psychoanalyst the particular behaviour disorder or mental aberration, such as neurosis, psychosis and, in more severe cases, schizophrenia and manic depression. Such techniques elicit covert behaviour through over-stimuli (Edwards, 1956).

Statistical Procedures Used in Research

It is important to underscore the differences between the physical and the social sciences. They differ in:

(i)   The degree of exactitude, which is more prevalent in the physical sciences than in the social sciences. For example, measuring racial prejudice is a subjective, biased concept, interacting with several unknown intervening variables. In the physical sciences, all known variables are accounted for and are measurable with precision.

(ii)   The control over the events in the physical sciences is less limited than in the social.

(iii)   The degree of objectivity is more difficult to control in the social than in the physical sciences.

(iv)   Generalisations about a population from which the sample is drawn are stated as being either definitive (populations existing currently) or infinitive (populations ever continuous) in the physical sciences. Since people are dynamically changing over time and space, it is less possible to measure infinite populations.

Statistics is that science of numbers which identifies events as they occur (natural phenomena), and as they can be summarised for inferences (experiments). They are identified through mathematical formulae. In social sciences, the central focus is the human being in relation to his environment. The system has an economic aspect (affectivity and efficiency), the social aspect (compatibility with social concepts), psychological aspect (the individual's needs, attitudes, habits, values and behaviour). Human beings act and interact within these three systems, which exercise their own individual postulates pertaining to their sciences. In reality these systems are influenced by each other even as they influence human development and behaviour.

In statistical language, the information is the data and the interactions are those which cause variation in the data derived about humans. The research study may be one of events, for example, the number of times people participate in national voting during their adult lifespan. The research may be one of human traits, for example, studying patterns of aggression in young children. The study may be of phenomena, for example, the occurrence of famine and its relation to nutritional levels.

Statistics is, therefore, the scientific method of quantifying data from a sample of such observations/incidents in order to accept/reject suppositions/hypotheses about these observations (Levin, 1977). The information is called data. This information has also to be reliable, that is, it should be obtained in such a manner that there is no bias from the researcher or the researched event. The data thus collected is described in terms of numbers (totals, ranges, percentages, average means, modes and so on). It is a scientific method for summarisation of data, which is a convenient method for analysis of several hundreds of people in large samples. The results of these tests are then related to the normal curve. This normal curve gives reference tables. These tables are statistically prepared reference tables of random samples of normal ranges of statistical tests, which give formulated equations, such as the computation of numbers for placing in an equation format (T test/F test/regression/variance equations). These statistical systems are more advantageously used in analysing score data which assumes that scores have ratios, proportions, fractions quantifying the data, starting from a zero score. This is essential, for it assumes that if measured along a continuous line of scores, every interval between two scores is equal to every other interval in the scoring system.

It is to be remembered that statistics can only summarise data already existing. It is a tool and does not produce data. It does not add to or subtract from the validity or reliability of the measures. All aspects of the research design are interlocked in a systematic way and follow systematic rules. These rules pertain to the representativeness of the sample, appropriateness of the measure and use of relevant tools of statistics. These three are inextricably interlinked and faulting in any one affects the others. This is likely to result in production of spurious data. Although this statistical tool is in itself a valid measurement device, the data can become non-tenable due to errors in the above three systems, namely erroneous sampling, inappropriate measures and faulty variables.

Sample Designs and Sampling Techniques

We have mentioned the term samples/groups in several of the previous sections. We will now expand on this concept, remembering that this aspect of the design is as important as any other, for the selection of a wrong sample for obtaining the right responses will make the total effort of the research process invalid.

By now it is obvious to the reader that the steps in the sequence of setting up a research design is so interrelated that one invalid assumption/operational definition, incorrect analysis or illogical deduction makes the research invalid for the purpose for which it was planned. For the same reason, a correctly identified sample, selected in the most effective way, using a valid type of sample, is also accountable for the validity of the research study.

What is a sample? Popularly it means a piece of the whole. It assesses the qualities of the sample, extrapolating them to the whole from which the sample was taken. In other words, the sample reflects the identical properties of the population from which it is drawn. For instance, in interaction with people, to assess a characteristic, it is untenable and unnecessary to interact with every person in order to assess the characteristic of the whole group, which may number over hundreds. It would take a number of years and become obsolete by the time we finish assessing the whole. Using the premise of logical deduction that a randomly selected part is like the whole, we use sampling methods to select a sample from the total which is representative of the population. It is the same as picking up one gram of a chemical to represent the population of the chemical. There are strict criteria in sample selection based upon theories of sampling (William, 1974). It is essential to identify the population. Take the situation of census data. This involves the whole country, but only a percentage is taken. The larger the population, the smaller may be the percentage or portion of the sample. It is necessary to hypothesise that the characteristics we have proposed are existent in the population. The population should be accessible. One should be able to reach members of the population easily. Most importantly, the sample should be representative of the population. Representativeness includes three criteria:

(i)   The distribution of the characteristic/s in the population should be equally available in the sample; that is, if one were to select a sample from a population, the probability of picking one unity/entity/person is just as probable as picking up any other. In other words, there should be no bias in the selection of the units/persons making up the sample. This is called random sampling and is perhaps the most reliable method of sampling as there is no bias in the selection process.

(ii) The purpose of sampling is to generalise deductions/inferences about the population from the sample. In other words, what is true of the sample is true of the population to a lesser or larger degree (level of probability). The implication is usually that since one cannot study the total population from the sample results, it may be estimated that the results are true of the population in 95 to 99 per cent of the cases in the population.

(iii) Selecting a sample enables the researcher to use inferential statistics (depending upon whether the measures obtained are scores or frequencies). As has been said before, scores enable the researcher to compute score inferences like the statistical difference between two groups (t test) or more groups (f test or mutivariant analysis). The advantage of using score data enables the researcher to assess the outcome data in terms of a representative normal distribution of the scoring system: in other words, these are averages, standard deviations, normal distribution scores and their percentiles. It is essential to emphasise that a researcher can use sampling technique/s in any combination, as required by the research problem. For instance, the researcher might wish to study the incidence of HIV in a particular population. Then, it becomes necessary to identify cases for the sample. This is purposive sampling. He might be able to procure within the time limits about 50 cases. There is therefore no point in doing a sample study and instead it might be more fruitful to do a case study, where the sample is purposively selected. On the other hand, if he finds that there are about 2,000 cases of HIV/AIDS, identified from different age groups, from different economic and occupational classes, then he might choose one control variable for identifying the sample, such as age/class/ethnic group. In this case it would be necessary for him to take a proportionate sample of different age groups as the classificatory variable and then portion them out into class and ethnic groups.

Types of Samples

It is essential to point out that sampling types in a research design can be combined in any sequence. For instance, for census data one takes a random sample and from that random sample one can take proportionate subsamples, such as region or area samples. Thus, there is a combination of three samples: random/proportionate/area sampling. Again, the classification can be on the basis of quota sampling or the representatives of the criterion, in this case HIV/AIDS, so that the quota selected represents the quota of people who are assumed to have HIV/AIDS in a population. For instance, if there are statistics stating that in the demographic data of a country, 2 per cent suffer from malnutrition then the quota taken should be from that 2 per cent, which naturally in any country runs into large numbers, and so the actual samples may be 0.002 per cent of the population.

To summarise, there are various types of samples. The most significant and reliable is random sampling, followed by proportionate/quota sampling as they represent numbers, and numbers are more reliable indices to subject them to statistic inferential analyses. The population characteristics are known as parameters and, therefore, are absolute figures. It implies that the parameters are normally distributed. Normal distribution in simple terms implies that if one were to draw a bell, then the middle of the bell is the mean and the left half is equal to the right half, and each can be measured into three areas. Therefore, the total area is divided into six parts, where one half is equal to the other. Each one of the six is called a standard deviation, and because they lie to the left and right of the mean, those to the left of the mean are termed minus 1, minus 2, and minus 3 standard deviations, and those to the right of the mean are called plus 1, plus 2 and plus 3 standard deviations. The right-hand standard deviations imply that the scores are higher than the mean and those to the left are less than the mean in terms of deviations from the mean, which represents the average. Random samples are usually used with large populations like studies of census and surveys (Moser and Kalton, 1971).

In purposive samples, the sample units are selected by using a criterion for identifying the units/persons in the population. When the researcher is intent upon studying a particular group like school children or only adolescents, then the population consists of only school children or only adolescents. Immediately, this brings up the question as to where these children live or where they can be found. Therefore, the selection purposively identifies the persons/units by this criterion: for example, upper and lower castes in twelfth grade students in a particular area such as Delhi.

In area samples, a sample is taken from a particular region, or several regions are compared (multicentric). If the aim is to study particular characteristics, such as caste or various ranges of occupation, then, on the basis of consulting national data, the researcher can take quota samples of different castes. Thus, it is seen here that quota sampling is similar to proportionate sampling, ratio or percentage sampling, because these statistics imply a relationship among them.

Another essential point to remember in use of sampling techniques is that only scores from such samples can be subject to inferential statistics. These represent a normal distribution, since the measures are numerical and, therefore, continuous. However, in the actual plotting of scores, they may not, or usually do not, represent an absolute normal curve. The latter are referred to only as standard population quotients. The sample quotient may deviate from the population quotient or be skewed in either direction when compared to a normal curve distribution. For instance, in the statement of hypothesis in relation to the population, the resultant quotient is representative of the population parameters. If the results of the sample show deviations from the standard reference, they are reflective of the sample variations. This, therefore, relates to the results whether there are differences between or among groups of the sample, namely heterogeneity or homogeneity of the sample (Blommers and Lindquist, 1960: 528). When it is heterogeneous, it implies that the sample has differences between/among its classificatory groups. To illustrate, if the resultant value of the statistical test is equal to or greater than the value in the reference table of the normal curve, then there are differences greater than probability. If it is homogeneous, the resultant test value indicates that there are no significant differences when the value is compared to the expected tabled value of the population. To illustrate, a significant value of the resultant test between two castes in prejudice means that one caste is different from the other in their attitudes/values/ behaviour towards the other caste/castes. If the test value is less than the reference value, it implies that there are no significant differences, and that the group is homogeneous in their attitudes/values on the scores on prejudice. If in a test on value of orientations of two cultures the samples are appropriately drawn and there are no significant differences, the inference is that one is like the other.

Analyses of Data

Data are usually presented in two forms: quantitative and qualitative. Quantitative data are analysed and reported in the form of inferential analysis, based on assumptions of normal distribution of responses. Qualitative data are given in the form of description without the assumptions of normal distribution. The type of statistics used in quantitative analysis is termed parametric and the type used in analysis of qualitative data is termed non-parametric.

Descriptive Data

It is usually routine that the first attempt to summarize data numerically is on a descriptive basis in the presentation of analysis. These are called descriptive analysis. They make no attempt to test for significance. They only present the data in numbers or percentages of the samples selected. Descriptive data tends to be qualitative in nature (Kapala and Suzuki, 1999). If the sample has been selected on controlled variables, the description first indicates the total number (N) and a breakdown into classificatory variables. For example, if the controlled variable is sex, then the total number of the sample is presented, then it is divided into subcategories, such as males and females, and may be further divided into age groups and, if required, into other sub-categories. These are presented in a tabular form in a cellular arrangement, as given in Annexure 6.1.

Inferential Data

As stated in Annexure 6.1, each respondent is examined simultaneously for all three variables. At this point, it is necessary to suggest whether measures are continuous or discrete. The description of the sample is uniform (Blommers and Lindquist, 1960). When it is measured for a particular dependent variable, the tables are reformulated. For instance, if in a study of conservatism between rural and urban girls, we might also examine the same dependent variable among older rural girls and younger rural girls, older urban girls and younger urban girls. Therefore, this data can be classified and reclassified into various other categories. The hypothesis may be that rural girls of older age group are more conservative than the other three groups. This is in consonance with the socialisation techniques where conservatism is practised more in rural groups than in urban groups (because of the factor of modernisation).

Non-parametric Data

It is necessary to distinguish from the above analysis of tests between inferential statistics and descriptive statistics. Inferential statistics are based on tests of significance as they apply to standards derived from the population, whereas descriptive statistics refer to presentation of data as it exists without any reference to the population from which it is drawn. Inferential statistics usually use parametric measures while descriptive statistics use non-parametric measures. Both imply the parameters of the population, except that parametric measures are related to generalisation to the population whereas non-parametric are not.

It will be recalled that scores relate to continuous measures, while frequencies are used usually in non-parametric data. However, there are other types of data which do not logically lend themselves to scores. They are merely tallies and answer the question of 'how many' and, therefore, the numerical figures represent the number of people. They represent, as in the example given above, the frequencies of occurrence. These are called rank-ordered discrete variations, which do not have standardised scores or standardised procedures. As such, they are called non-parametric data and are analysed in terms of variations of the chi-square tests and other modes using the median instead of the mean (Hoel, 1971). Such tests used are also Mann Whitney test, Marshall test, Smirnov and Multi-cell Contingency Coefficient (Festinger, 1959).

Qualitative analysis and therefore non-parametric data are usually used in ethnographic studies, which are collected mainly through observational and in-depth interview techniques (Crabtree and Miller, 1999). These types of data give the flavour of styles, of patterns, of living situations of small groups, especially in relation to such areas like cultural, sociological and ecological variables. These types of data are obtained by first-hand observation or verbatim reports ob-tained from intensive information from small groups, usually cohesive communities. The data are recorded and analysed for content and categorised as such. Some research designs are such that these observations and verbatim records are obtained at different intervals of time. They indicate either developmental changes or static situations. Charting developmental milestones is one such type. Another is to document changes in lifestyles (Minturn and Hitchcock, 1966; Minturn et al., 1978: 493–98; Seymour, 1999). The reported categorised information is described for its contextual meaning. This data usually forms the basis for developing hypotheses to be tested on larger populations. A need for such qualitative data, especially for the Indian population, arises out of the fact that empirical data is sparse for theorising and there is need for qualitative foundational data to result in post-hypothesis from the available trends. For instance, in the ethnographic study by Munroe and Munroe, where descriptions were given of variables like physical development, language development and so on, they could indicate hypotheses, such as community A is more aggressive than community B, because of the differences in occupational pursuit in that A relies on hunting and B on non-hunting activities for food procurement (ecological variable).

Often experimental designs in the strict sense are based on before or after measures, such as the classical study of Rosenzweig (Rosenzweig, 1976: 885–91). These are experimental in nature (Kantowitz, 1978). Quantitative data can be reinterpreted by descriptive data. These types of data can also be interpreted in a narrative reported form (Mix et al., 2002). We hasten to add, however, that without the handle of averages of the sample reported, innermost feelings cannot be captured unless we have descriptive data (Chaudhary, 1999). Again this is not to be compared with data obtained from psycho-therapeutic counselling, when clients are asked to state their innermost thoughts and feelings. The averages are central tendencies, and form a fulcrum around which variations of the group are described. Such data collection techniques are usually used in anthropology, such as the 'Six Culture Study' (Whiting and Child, 1953) and 'Two Worlds of Childhood' (Bronfenbrenner, 1970). If one were to get an insight into how extra-familial care for preschool children works, such studies as reported in *The First Five Years* are an excellent example (Swaminathan, 1996). In a sense, such narratives and descriptions are akin to giving the reader in-depth insights into the topic researched. It also gives the academician the choice of selecting the best styles with which they are familiar and make the scenes they depict familiar to the social realities of life as it is lived, for instance the differences in living patterns in geo-ecological tracts (Khalakdina, 1979). Inferences are derived from the descriptive data without the need to be constricted by numbers and their averages in the reporting of data. This is not to say that quantitative research and analysis are not as essential, but that these two types of data complement each other and are essential for a fuller picture of behaviour and development (Searle, 1999).

Strategies for Designing Research Studies

Before beginning a research design, it is essential to define what is being examined. If it is a concept, it must be operationalised and drawn from a theory. For example, if the study is independence-training in young children, then it relates to the theories of motivation, the level at which the child feels inherently that he would like to do things on his own, and to the theory of reinforcement, which is the positive encouragement he receives from his environment, both human and natural. We might even relate it to an accepted theory like Erikson's theory of the development of autonomy or, in clinical situations, to psychiatric disorders/trauma.

Next, it is important to examine the types of research (a priori or post facto) and select the one most suitable to validate the research questions/problems posed. Typically the design consists of the following parameters:

- stating the problem (emphasising the purpose);
- offering justification for the conduct of the study;
- examining previous research studies/theories on which the design can be logically based (review of research);
- logically selecting the appropriate sample (sample design);
- delineation of the economic and effective way of eliciting data (with or without the use of hypotheses);
- identifying the independent and the dependent variables (the data to be collected);
- selecting a method that is the most appropriate and that will elicit new data economically and efficiently;
- selecting the type of analysis which offers a cohesive summary.

On the basis of a careful re-examination of the steps the study is then conducted according to the protocols of eliciting data from the selected sample, coding the data and then subjecting them to analysis or summarisation. When stating the purpose of the study, we assume some basic facts. As in the concept of affiliative pattern given earlier, we know that there is a tendency for like-status children to form friendship patterns because of the homogeneity of their psychosocial environment. Typically, therefore, there are several connections in the stages of a research design. Research design is the focus of the processes involved. It is a blueprint for examining linkages among various aspects of the study.

Annexure 6.1

Sample of an A Priori Research

We present the steps of a hypothetical research study:

(i) **Title:** A study of differences in dependency levels in preschool- versus non-preschool-going children in a community X.

(ii) **Problem statement:** In the area of child behaviour, the expression of dependency and the reinforcement of dependency is an important mode of child upbringing practices. From the years of early infancy, the child's behaviour, such as dependency behaviour, is best recorded by observation of qualitative actions. Qualitative behaviour is probably a more reliable form of analysis for observation of dependency exhibited by children.

It is often said that dependency behaviour which is positively reinforced in early childhood, might continue into a pattern in later years. In childhood years, parental discipline usually takes the form of either punishment or reward or both.

In reaction, children learn to behave in conformity to the social norms, such as listening to parental commands and instructions, showing obedience and respect, and therefore show a greater form of conformity to parental norms.

As such, this kind of conformity is said to suppress extrovert, outgoing type of behaviour and reduces the level of independent behaviour in the average Indian child. However, attending a preschool might indicate a lesser level of dependent behaviour as preschool teacher techniques are expected to reinforce independent behaviour. It is said that while dependency behaviour is more obvious in traditional families, it is less so in educated upper income families, who send their children early to preschools, thus encouraging independent behaviour. It is also said that the early years of childhood are foundational in the formation in lasting habitual behaviour. Therefore, it is important to find levels of dependency in the behaviour of preschool children, so that one might confirm or reject such popular notions.

(iii) **Justification of problem:** In the field of development, socialisation is an important sphere that reinforces personality traits. It is said that in today's global world it is essential for children to learn how to achieve and become successful in life. In the West, the need for achievement is very high and is often accompanied by marked levels of confident risk taking and independent decision making. As the child grows into an adult, he is weaned away from dependency upon parents and older generations and guided to depend upon his own logical deductions. By comparison an average Indian child continues to refer to the older members in his society for decision making, especially in critical periods of alternative choice making. If dependency is reinforced from early childhood onwards it follows logically that it becomes a pervasive trait into adulthood.

However several mothers send their children to preschools in the same milieu and same homogeneous group, which according to some research seems to reinforce independence in the child. Therefore, studying differences between preschool-going and non-preschool-going children in the same group will offer an understanding about this mode of behaviour.

(iv) **Hypotheses:** (a) There are differences in dependency behaviour between preschool- and non-preschool-going children in a community X. (b) There are differences in the upbringing practices between mothers of non-preschool-going children and preschool-going children.

(v) **Operational definitions:** The meaning of socialisation is the upbringing process, guidance and reinforcement by the adult towards the young child. Dependency behaviour is that behaviour observed in children when they do not do things on their own, ask for help, refuse to explore or create, and follow commands and instructions in behaviour. Mothers are those who are the main caretakers in the home situation. Teachers are those who have had training and are expected to implement the training in reinforcing exploration, curiosity and creativity, and let children experiment on their own.

(vi) **The sample:** The sample is from a homogeneous group of children of the same age, including purposively from non-preschool- and preschool-going children. Sub-samples may also be taken on the basis of the education of the mother and sex of the child. The sample will consist of equal number of boys and girls in the age range 3–6 years, from educated and non-educated mothers of both sets of children.

(vii) **Technique:** This includes observation protocols at periodic times in the various situations such as eating, playing alone, or with others in situations where the child interacts with the mother in the home situation and with the teacher in the school-going sample . Research questions may also include questions about (a) whether the mothers have imbibed new ideas about upbringing from observation of their children in the classrooms, (b) whether teachers reinforce or do not reinforce independent/dependent behaviour.

(viii) **Analysis:** This pertains to the application of non-parametric statistics showing the frequency of child dependency behaviour in various mother–child interactions in varying sub-groups.

(ix) **Results:** Data are analysed in relation to theories of dependency, conservatism versus liberalism in child rearing techniques and in some ways the benefits of exposure to preschool learning situations.

(x) **Interpretation:** If there are more dependent orientations in either of the sub-samples, the analysis will show this difference and will indicate whether this dependent behaviour is more frequent in non-preschool-going children vis-à-vis preschool-going children or vice versa. If the tests are significant, then the results are interpreted on the basis of theoretical concepts of dependency, socialisation and child rearing techniques. If there are none, it indicates that there are no significant differences between the preschool-going and non-preschool-going children in dependency behaviour. While an inference might be made that teacher/classroom effects are predominant on preschool-going children, another hypothesis may be posited that preschool teachers influence dependent/independent behaviour. And a third hypothesis may be posited on the basis of sex where perhaps preschool boys show less dependent behaviour than girls.

Some Aspects of Measurement of Quantitative and Qualitative Data

We give here some selected examples of measurement of quantitative and qualitative data. They are also based upon the reliability and validity of the tests/tools measuring the variables and the appropriateness of the statistics selected for summarising description and the inferences drawn.

Standard tests have an inbuilt measure on the basis of which they refer to a population; the numbers assigned to objects, events, phenomenon and people are numericals. These numericals belong to four categories or measurement types. In ordinary mathematics, 10 is greater than 1 but when measuring social phenomena, there is no way of knowing whether 10 is 9 times the difference between 1 and 2, for invariably unless it is the physical/biological sciences, there is no such evidence of zero attribute in social events and social phenomena. For instance, in terms of finiteness a human being is either dead or alive; he cannot be somewhat dead or somewhat alive. There is an irreversible dichotomy. Thus, human beings belong to any one of the two categories exclusively.

Measurement is the mathematical logic of assigning quantity. However a quantity has meaning when related to other quantities. For instance, people of different races have different physiognomies and can be distinguished by their facial structures as being Caucasian, Negroid or Mongolian. These types can be fissioned out but they display only qualities of the generic term 'race'. This is called a nominal measure.

To continue with the example, if one were to look at the fissioned racial groups there would be certain overlapping similarities: most people from Far East (for example Chinese and Japanese) have slanting eyes; most Africans have curly hair; most Caucasians are fair-haired and fair-skinned, but there are shades among all. These shades cannot be quantified as there is much overlapping among stereotypes, and therefore can be only qualitative or nominal data.

The next type of measure relates to the issue of how much of one is a percentage of another. In other words, what is the interval distance between one and another? If the length of a runway is one mile then the pilot knows for how much of the distance he can work up speed and at what distance he should take off from; there is an equivalence between these two which can be measured by interval frequencies.

With reference to an absolute starting point, the most weighted form of measure is the ratio scale, which assumes an absolute zero as in physical sciences where each person is exactly proportionate to any other on their scoring in a normal curve distribution. We have said before that the advantage of this ratio/absolute scale is most used in the realm of physical sciences and is assumed to be so in social sciences.

Generally in the social sciences the ordinal or the interval scale is used where the population parameters are not known. Ratio scales, based on parametric scores, are used for the purpose of finding deviations of samples derived from their actual or abstract population. Measures should have validity and reliability before they are put to test. Validity is of four types: first, face validity or that which is informally perceived to be accurate, such as, boys are more aggressive than girls. Second is the content validity related to known concepts such as aggression when measured as physical/verbal violence. Third is the concurrent validity, which implies that other studies have used the same operational definition as in the study proposed. Fourth is the correlative validity that refers to studies using guidance techniques and those using counseling techniques (which are similar in conceptualisation). Reliability refers to (a) inter-rater reliability, where several observers observing or assessing the same situation give somewhat similar ratings, (b) test–retest reliability, where the same test is given to the same group but at different times, which give similar or dissimilar ratings. Similarity indicates reliability of the test.

These two attributes of validity and reliability lay the foundation for scores/ranks being adjudged as more than probable (more related to the facts) depending upon the results of their tests (t test, f test and correlations) being greater than probability with degrees of freedom compared to standard reference values. If the resultant value is more than the standard value, it gives levels of significance which, in the social sciences, is accepted at 1 and 5 per cent levels (Siegal, 1956: 279–84).

Preparation of Project Proposal

The steps in preparing a project are systematic and attempted in a disciplined manner. They are:

- Conception of project proposal based on the need to study a problem, its justification, its applicability, its theoretical and pragmatic constructs.
- Its researchability, operationalisation, and goal orientation.
- Statement of the problem and review of empirical data/evidence leading up to the existence of a problem.
- Formating schedules, objectives and their operational definitions, measurable indicators/ parameters, feasibility approaches/piloting inputs/requirements/strategies/technical programme/ methodologies.
- Costing and its logical framework duration/time frame/calendar of events.
- Expected outcomes/results/interpretations/factual applicability.
- Facilities available/budget.
- Personnel requirements/numbers qualifications.
- Reporting schedules/final reporting and the research summaries.

The above are protocols used when doing large-scale research that covers a large sample and is in the form of a research project. For example, the evaluation of the supplementary nutrition programme project 'Poshak' was done by Cooperation, Assistance and Relief Everywhere (CARE). It covered a large field over several years. Being a large-scale study it required large input materials and methods. The ongoing evaluation of the ICDS project (started in 1975) on a nationwide basis is another large-scale example. For the most part however studies are of small samples of small duration and give very conservative results pertaining to small populations. The preconception of how data are analysed has to be already prepared in the design. Every stage is linked to every other stage backwards and forwards. The analysis is the real crux of whether or not the researcher has collected the data he should have or whether there is so much data that it cannot be structurally handled by the analytical frame. What is the analytical frame? The analytical frame relates to coding of data, the grouping of data in tables, results of the test (if used) and/or the results in terms of descriptive data (percentages and ranks ratio). The analysis also refers to hypotheses, if any. If there are no hypotheses, it refers to sample characteristics. For instance, if one is studying adolescent behaviour in relation to attitude towards parents, then there are several independent variables that can be selected:

- adolescents of different ages;
- adolescents who are either school/non-school-going;
- adolescents from different castes/classes/religions/ethnic backgrounds/regions/types of families; and
- adolescents from organised/disorganised families, and so on.

The type of data also depends upon purpose or objective. If the researcher is studying adolescents from tribal, urban or rural areas this selection is called purposive since it is directed towards one type of variable, namely region. This is a classificatory variable. Within these three groups other variables can be used for further selection, like sex, caste and so on.

There are two principles of analyses for applying tests of significance. One, there can't be too many classificatory or selection variables, because when set in a tabular form there is a likelihood of zero frequencies or scores in any one or more of the cells of the table. For instance, if one selects two variables like region and sex, there are N(N – 1) divided by two possibilities of comparison of scores in cells (matrix table), where N represents the total. Two, comparing sub-totals (groups), for instance, a group that is by classification Brahmin/non-Brahmin, educated/illiterate, joint/nuclear family, professional/non-professional, implies too many variables for comparison at one time and therefore the likelihood of having too few scores in some cells for statistical comparability, and therefore the sub-sections are less than an acceptable number, like 15 or 20, for parametric statistics. In such sub-categories, there is a likelihood that the test results may be spurious/false as the numbers are inadequate for distribution purposes.

Thus, the number of cells depends upon the number of variables selected and if they are interactive the number of cells becomes exponential and difficult to subject to tests of significance. To circumvent the interaction of too many variables at one time, parametric tests and variance tests are used. To manage discrete or frequency data, multiple cell contingency tests are used. Thus, in a tabular form, each variable must be subdivided into other variables so as to present data that is more holistic. For example, in studying the effect of region, sex and caste if there is significance in the test it says more about the individuals per se than just in terms of any one group at any one time. For instance, one could infer that Mohan who comes from an urban area belongs to a higher caste and has higher SES (socio-economic status), than Suresh who is from a tribal area. In such analyses the test due to the main effects of the separate variable can also be compared for interaction among variables (Wolf, 1960; Blommers and Lindquist, 1960).

Probability Considerations in Research Designs

It is important to note that the concept of probability exists in research, for one cannot be 100 per cent sure that human nature is 100 per cent predictable. Data may exist as either verbatim records (descriptive words) or numericals (number of respondents). It is the latter that is related to the science of numbers or mathematics. The purpose of using analysis of quantity is mainly to summarise data; instead of saying that 1 plus 2 plus 10 subjects equal the quantity of 13, we number them as n1, n2, and so on. In this fashion we can aggregate and disaggregate the respondents according to the variables. In a research study, for instance, using caste and religion as independent variables, the same person, for example, n1, belongs to both caste and religion and therefore his or her quantitative sum or score on each variable can be divided into those which connote caste a or b or c, and at the same time denote which religion he belongs to: x, y or z. This facility to use aggregated sums of responses is through sets of summary employing statistics. These summarisations afford the researcher the ability to apply such summarised data (scores or frequencies) to tests of significance.

Where the parameters are scores, the principle of number mandates that there is a zero from which the scores begin, that is the scores can be converted to ratios/fractions/proportions, and this is a continuous variable, such as degrees of aggression. A t test (of significance between two variables/groups), an f test (a test of variants among more than two variables/groups), Pearson product-moment correlation (a test of correlativity between/among groups' scores), covariance, linear regression and multiple regression are all examples of parametric tests. These are tests derived from representative samples of the populations and refer to the parameters of the populations themselves. These tests are of immense value because they give answers for probable facts. The facts are that not all respondent subjects in any one group will behave similarly and that there will always be a certain proportion that is out of the range of similarity. Thus, all tests give a probability figure. Probability here implies that the test results are true for most of the sample, but not for all. The acceptable standard is that one or five cases out of a hundred may not behave similarly. This implies that if there were 100 cases per sample, the results will be true for 99 per cent or 95 per cent of the cases. Thus, the usual acceptable probability levels are 1 per cent and 5 per cent, respectively. These are given in a standard tabular format for comparisons with test results. This standard reference table of random numbers is for testing whether the test result is equal to or greater than the standard reference given with the probability of its occurrence.

For instance, a test using caste and religion is subject to a t test (a test of difference between two variables). The resultant of the t test may be greater than the reference value and is therefore said to be significant or that the probability is greater than normal that these differences exist in the population from which the sample is drawn. Significance means that the differences/similarities are in fact accepted as being highly probable results. Probability level is therefore the crux of statistical analyses. The handle that is used here is that the smaller the sample, the more conservative should be the acceptance of probability level. For example, in a sample of 100 respondents, 1 per cent is acceptable. Translated, it means that out of a 100, one respondent is unlike the rest. Logically, therefore, the greater the number of respondents, the larger is the probability level of acceptance. Correspondingly, a sample of respondents of 100,000 could acceptably use a 10 per cent level (Blommers and Lindquist, 1960).

As explained above, the normal curve deals with the probability of occurrence of the dependent variable in the sample subjected to testing. Logically, the more complex the statistical analysis, the greater is the variation accounted for and, therefore, by inference, the 'error variance' within groups is less than among groups.

There are also intervening variables which may not be tested. For example, if one wished to study children's reactions to approaching exams, one might study the relationship of test anxiety to performance. A discerning expert would argue that test performance does not depend only upon preconditions of levels of anxiety, but also upon study patterns and interest. These are called intervening variables and can be accounted for in the analysis.

When there is discontinuity as in categories of variables such as caste or religion or ethnicity there can be no continuum of responses. These are therefore called discrete or ordinal data, that is, there is no basis of comparability or exchange or similarity between one group and another in terms of exact quantities. Here, it is usual to use non-parametric or rank-ordered data. All that these tests do is to indicate that one respondent is greater or lesser than the other/s. These can be again ordered in terms of frequencies.

Frequencies indicate the number of respondents within each category. For instance, in an attitude survey a question can be asked: Will the democratic party get elected in the next election? Answers may fall into following categories.

Category 1:   certainly
Category 2:   maybe
Category 3:   most unlikely
Category 4:   not at all

In these four categories rank-ordered agreement can therefore be accounted for from 1 to 4; 1 indicates full agreement and 4 indicates no agreement with the statement made. Frequencies can also be yes, fairly, somewhat fairly and not at all, agree mostly, agree somewhat and do not agree. The reader can observe that these are rank-ordered frequencies or discrete data. On the principles of parameters it is also observable that there are no parameters as in parametric statistics. The argument in presenting non-parametric data rests on the assumption that each respondent is greater or lesser than the other in ordering but not in quantification. The tests here are known as various form of chi-square, coefficient of correlation, rank-ordered, Spearman–Brown rho and various forms of multiple coefficients of correlation. To get an in-depth perception the case study method of qualitative description is complementary.

Types of Research Designs

In post facto research, the independent variable/s have already occurred. The researcher relates a dependent variable to the independent variable, which is studied in retrospect for its relation/effect on the dependent variable. The most important factor in this type of research is control because post facto design examines existing variables as they occur in situ. There can be no deliberate control by the investigator of the dependent variables. First, they have to be taken as having occurred. Second, they cannot be manipulated or modified; because the event has already occurred and there can be no change in their status. Third, they cannot be randomly selected.

The types of researches which are subsumed under this format are (*a*) descriptive studies such as living situations of urban slums; and (*b*) survey studies such as polls, market surveys and census data. Thus, post facto is the reporting of data after its occurrence. For instance if one is doing a study on parenting, it is typical to interview parents on certain criteria as to how they bring up their children in various areas of behaviour and in inculcating habits, attitudes and values. These may also be elicited by inventories/ questionnaires or standardised psychological or psychometric tests.

A priori designs are those which propose that an event or events will occur if preceded by a stimulus or event immediately prior to its occurrence. It is somewhat like predicting that if it is cloudy it will most probably rain. In this type of design there is an automatic tie-up with quantitative data to try and prove empirically (by analysis of quantitative data) that these events (independent/dependent) impinge upon each other. The data that arises from such enquires is called inferential data: we infer that if X occurs then Y follows. However, unlike post facto design, there is the possibility of actual control and manipulation of variables.

The strategy used is a manipulative one. In the early years of psychology they were mainly laboratory trials very much like the trials in a chemistry or physics laboratory. In such situations the environment is controlled except for the variable/s to be experimented upon. For example if heat is applied to ice it melts and the rate of melting is deduced or inferred. In animal experiments which preceded many components of learning behaviour, experiments were tried by reinforcing rat behaviour or conditioning rat behaviour. Pavlov's experiment with the dog has led to much diversion into human behaviour, reinforcement and conditioning (Pavlov 1927). These were followed by controlled experiments on children. Therefore, in an experimental design, the variables that are independent are observed in situ (as they occur) by isolating the experimental dependent variables from all other extraneous variables.

The greatest strength of laboratory experiments is that they attempt to discover relations under 'pure' and uncontaminated conditions. The prediction of results from hypotheses in human experiments were prompted by experiments in animals as humans could not be exposed to conditions that animals could. However, it is necessary to remember that because of the very factor of being controlled it is a simulated situation, whereas in real life the operation of extraneous variables occurs and to that extent contaminates the dependent event. The other type of experiment is the field experiment which tries to mitigate the artificiality of the experimental situation by selection of a real life situation where the dependent variables are observed as they occur. However, there is no guarantee that because of the spontaneous nature of the interaction of the known variables, the contaminating effect of extraneous variables cannot occur on the dependent variable. For instance in the observation of isolating aggressive behaviour in a free play situation in a nursery, there may be many other variables acting and reacting upon this behaviour. This is when the behaviour is observed by the experimenter and isolated as being aggressive. This is frequently overcome by having protocols for observing time-scheduled behaviour to indicate the frequency of acts (physical aggression, verbal aggression and so on). This is as near a balance as possible between controlled laboratory experiments and field experiments. The field experiment, however, has four unique virtues (Adams and Preiss, 1960):

- There is a one-to-one contact between observer and observed.
- The observer has the opportunity to interact and obtain explanations or elucidations of the observed behaviour.
- It is possible to have more than one observing the same behaviour so that subjective bias is minimized.
- The field situation is a situation of social reality which lends itself to validity and reliability of the data so collected.

The variables in a field experiment usually have a stronger effect than those of laboratory experiments. They are appropriate for studying complex social influences, processes and changes in life-like settings. They are well suited both to the testing of the relevent theory and to the solution of practical problems. A variation of field research is action research where a variable is deliberately introduced into a selected sample in the field situation where it is acted upon to bring about change. The variable is usually an intervention. These variables are clearly indicated in national programmes such as supplementary feeding which is an action introduced to bring about better nourished children. Another example is the immunisation programme implemented to prevent childhood diseases. The very term action implies introduction of an intervention variable and is usually conducted in a 'before and after' manner. In other words, children are measured for nutrition and health statuses before the intervention and after the intervention with the predictive hypothesis that if intervened, there is a beneficial effect. Such field programmes are carried out by national projects on development of women and children in deprived sections of society.

Tabulation of a Sample Study

A tabulation implies the setting of data in a tabulated form which further implies a logical distribution of the data. The cellular arrangement means that the categories are displayed thus (total number = 200):

Differences among Hindus and Muslims on Z Variable

Age Group	Sex	Religion	
		Hindus	Muslims
Above 25 years	M	25	25
	F	25	25
Below 25 years	M	25	25
	F	25	25

The cellular arrangement is given above

N = 200 (total sample), A = Hindus, B = Muslims and each of the eight cells contain equal distribution of respondents who are of one sex or the other, are in the older or younger age groups, and are either Hindu or Muslim.

The sums of X have the notational figure of ΣX and the variance of each score collated is Σx. It is the difference between the sums of scores squared and the square of scores that will indicate the amount of difference in an equation format, i.e., the variation is $(\Sigma X)^2 - \Sigma(x)^2$.*

When finding the difference between two groups, the test is usually called t test, and methods to find variances simultaneously among many groups are multivariate analyses, such as f test, analysis of regression, covariance and the like. To illustrate, in using a multivariate analysis for the scores which are square for each one of the variables and the resulting f test which examines these three variances simultaneously will give variance due to (a) age, (b) sex and (c) religion at the same time.

These are called the main variances. The computed interactional variance among age, sex and religion indicates the differences between the four groups categorised by a combination of age, sex and religion. If the error in this computation is larger than that of the variance due to these groupings then the variance in the groupings is not significant. In statistical terminology this means that the 'within groups' variation is more than the 'among groups' variation. In other words there is more heterogeneity within cells than among groups. And this indicates that the test shows no significant differences among them.

---

*Consult statistical tables for notational significance of variances: Blommers, Paul and E.F. Lindquist, 1960, *Statistical Methods in Psychology and Education*. Calcutta, New Delhi, Kharagpur: Oxford Book Company.

References

Adams, R.N. and J.J. Preiss (eds), 1960, *Human Organization Research*. Homewood, IL: Dorsey Press.

Alphale, C., 1976, *Growing Up in an Urban Complex: A Study of Upbringing of Children in Maharastrian Hindu Families in Pune*. Delhi: National Publishing House.

Anandalakshmy, S., 1974, 'How Independent is the Independent Variable?', in J.L.M. Dawson and W.J. Lonner (eds), *Readings in Cross-cultural Psychology*. Hong Kong: University of Hong Kong Press.

——, 1979, 'Recent Research on the Young Child', *The Indian Journal of Social Work*, 11(3): 295–309.

Badke, W.B., 2004, *Research Strategies: Finding Your Way through the Information Fog*. New York: iUniverse, Inc.

Baldwin, A.L., 1967, *Theories of Child Development*, 2nd edn. New York: John Wiley.

Benttler, L.E. and J.J. Marmat, 2003, *Integrative Assessment of Adult Personality*. New York: Guilford Press.

Bevli, U.K., 1983, *Developmental Norms of Indian Children 2½ to 5 Years, Part IV: Language Development*. New Delhi: National Council of Educational Research and Training.

Bhambri, C.P., 1998, 'The Globalisation and Social Science', *Economic and Political Weekly*, 33(12): 17–19.

Bhandari, A. and B.N. Ghosh, 1980, 'A Longitudinal Study of the Fine Motor Adaptive, Personal, Social and Language Speech Developments of Children from Birth to One Year of Age in an Urban Community', *International Journal of Medical Research*, 71: 287–302.

Bharati, V. and P.V. Ramamurthi, 1977, 'The Influence of Certain Stimulus Variants on the Experience of Muller–Iyer Illusion: A Cross-sectional Study of Children 6–11 Years of Age', *Journal of Psychological Researches*, 21(3): 192–95.

Blommers, P. and E.F. Lindquist, 1960, *Elementary Statistical Methods in Psychology and Education*. Calcutta: Oxford Book Company.

Bronfenbrenner, U., 1958, 'Socialisation and Social Class through Time and Space', in E.I. Hartley, T.M. Newcomb and E.E. Maccoby (eds), *Readings in Social Psychology*, 3rd edn. New York: Henry Holt and Co.

——, 1970, *Two Worlds of Childhood*. New York: Russell Sage Foundation.

Burnam, E., 1996, *Deconstructing Developmental Psychology*. New York: Routledge.

Chattopadhyay, P.K., S. Das Gupta and A.K. Bhattacharya, 1982, 'Estimation of Time in Children: Effects of Stimulus Length, Task and Personality, *Child Psychology Quarterly*, 15(3): 104–08.

Chaudhary, N., 1999, 'Language Socialisation: Patterns of Caregiver Speech to Young Children', in T.S. Saraswathi (ed.), *Culture, Socialistation and Human Development*. New Delhi: Sage.

Coolican, H., 1995, *Introduction to Research Methods: Statistics in Psychology*. Oxford: OUP.

Crabtree, B.F. and W.L. Miller, 1999, *Doing Qualitative Research*. Thousand Oaks, CA: Sage.

Creswell, J.W., 2002, *Qualitative, Quantitative and Mixed Methods Approaches*. Thousand Oaks, CA: Sage.

Dalal, A.K. and G. Misra, 2002, 'Social Psychology in India: Evolution and Emerging Trends', in A.K. Dalal and G. Misra (eds), *New Directions in Indian Psychology, Vol. 1*. New Delhi: Sage.

Das, V., A. Beteille and N. Madan (eds), 2004, *Oxford Indian Companion to Sociology and Social Anthropology*. New Delhi: OUP.

Dasen, P.R., 2003, 'Theoretical Frameworks in Cross-cultural Developmental Psychology: An Attempt at Integration', in T.S. Saraswathi (ed.), *Cross-cultural Perspectives in Human Development: Theory, Research and Applications*. New Delhi: Sage.

Edwards, A.L., 1956, *Techniques of Attitude Scale Construction*. New York: Appleton Century Crofts Inc.

Elkind, D., 1980, 'Developmental and Experimental Approaches to Child Study', in I.B. Weiner and D. Elkind (eds), *Readings in Child Development*. Huntington, NJ: R.E. Krieger Publishers.

Erikson, E.H., 1979, 'Report to Vikram: Further Perspectives on Life Cycle', in S. Kakar (ed.), *Identity and Adulthood*. New Delhi: OUP.

Festinger, L., 1959, 'A Theory of Cognitive Dissonance', in L. Festinger and J.M. Carlsmith, *Cognitive Consequences of Forced Compliance*. Stanford, CA: Stanford University Press.

Freud, A., 1928, *Introduction to the Technique of Child Analysis* (English edition). London: Hogarth.

——, 1946, *The Ego and Mechanisms of Defense*. New York: International Universities Press.

Gesell, A., 1928, *Infancy and Human Growth*. New York: Macmillian.

Giles, D., 2002, *Advanced Research Methods in Psychology*. New York: Routledge.

Guilford, J.P., 1936, *Psychometric Percentiles of a Normal Curve which Often is not Normal Guilford Methods*. New York: McGraw-Hill.

Hairjete, R., 1997, 'An Outline for the Main Methods in Social Psychology, Part II', in N. Hayes (ed.), *Doing Qualitative Analyses in Psychology*. Hore: Psychology Press.

Hartshone, H. and M.A. May, 1928, *Studies in the Nature of Character, Vol. 1: Studies in Deceit*. New York: Macmillan.

Havighurst, R.J., 1946, 'Child Development in Relation to Community Social Structure', *Child Development*, 17(1–2): 85–90.

Hoel, Paul G., 1971, *Elementary Statistics*, 3rd edn. New York: John Wiley.

Jahoda, M., M. Deutsch and S.W. Cook, 1951, *Research Methods in Social Relations, Vols I & II*. New York: The Dryden Press.

Jensen, A.R., 1969, 'How Much Can We Boost IQ and Scholastic Achievement', *Harvard Educational Review*, 39: 1–123.

Kantowitz, B.L. Roedinger, 1978, *Experimental Psychology: Understanding Psychological Research*. Chicago: McNally College Publishing Co.

Kapala, M. and I. Suzuki, 1999, *Using Qualitative Methods in Psychology*. London: Sage.

Kapur, M. and H. Mukundan, 2002, *Child Care in Ancient India from the Perspectives of Developmental Psychology and Paediatrics*. Delhi: Sri Satguru Publications, India Book Centre.

Kaur, B., 1993, 'An Agenda for Future Theory Building, Research and Action', in T.S. Saraswathi and B. Kaur (eds), *Human Development and Family Studies in India: An Agenda for Research and Policy* pp. 317–35. New Delhi: Sage.

Khalakdina, M., 1976, *Critique on Available Empirical Research Data on the Young Child in India*. New Delhi: UNICEF, SCARO (South Central Asia Regional Office).

———, 1979, *Early Child Care in India*. London: Gordon and Breach.

Khatri, A.A., 1965, 'Differences in Goals, Ideals, Interests, Intelligence, Scholastic Performance, etc. for Orphanage-reared and Family-reared Children', *Indian Journal of Applied Psychology*, 2(1): 28–38.

Levin, H., 1977, *Elementary Statistics in Social Research*. San Francisco: Harper and Row Inc.

Lewin, K., 1936, *Principles of Topological Psychology*. New York: McGraw-Hill.

Lippitt, T., K. Lewin and R.K. White, 1939, 'Patterns of Aggressive Behaviour in Experimentally Created "Social Climates"', *Journal of Social Psychology*, 10: 271–99.

Mandal, M.K., 2000, 'Psychological Foundations of Behaviour', J. Pandey (ed.), *Psychology in India Revisited: Developments in the Discipline; Vol. 1: Psychological Foundation and Human Cognition*. New Delhi: Sage.

Minturn, L. and J.T. Hitchcock, 1966, *The Rajputs of Khalapur, India*. New York: John Wiley.

Minturn, L., D. Boyd and S. Kapur, 1978, 'Increased Maternal Power Status: Changes in Socialsiation in a Research Study of Rajput Mothers of Khalapur,' *Indian Journal of Cross-cultural Psychology*, 9(4): 493–98.

Mix, K.S., J. Huttenlocher and S.C. Levine, 2002, *Quantitative Development in Infancy and Early Childhood*. New York: OUP.

Mohanty, A.K. 1988a, 'Psychology in India: Still at the Crossroads?', *Psychology in Developing Society*, 2: 117–36.

———, 1988b, 'Beyond the Horizon of Indian Psychology: The Yankee Doodler', in F.M. Sahu (ed.), *Psychology in the Indian Context*. Agra: National Psychological Corporation.

Moore, B., Jr., 1978, *Justice: The Social Basis of Obedience and Revolt*, London: Macmillan.

Moreno, J.W., 1977, *Who Shall Survive? Foundations of Sociometry: Group Therapy*. Boston: Beacon House.

Moser, C.A. and Kalton, G., 1971, *Survey Methods in Social Investigation*. London: Heinemann Educational Books Ltd.

Murray, H.A., 1938, *Explorations in Personality*. New York: OUP.

Muthayya, B.C., 1972, *Child Welfare: Existing Conditions and Parental Attitudes*. Hyderabad: National Institute of Community Development.

Myres, R., 1992, *The Twelve Who Survive: Strengthening Programs of Early Childhood Development in the Third World*. London, New York: Routledge, in cooperation with UNESCO.

Naidu, U.S. and V.S. Nakhate, 1985, *Child Development Studies in India*, Bombay: Tata Institute of Social Sciences.

Nandy, A., 2002, 'The Politics of Application and Relevance in Contemporary Psychology', in A.K. Dalal and G. Misra (eds), *New Directions in Indian Psychology, Vol. 1: Social Psychology*. New Delhi: Sage.

Pandey, J. (ed.), 2002, *Psychology in India Revisited—Developments in the Discipline, Vol. 2: Personality and Health Psychology*. New Delhi: Sage.

———, 2004, 'Introduction', in J. Pandey (ed.), *Psychology in India Revisited—Development in the Discipline, Vol. 3: Applied Social and Organisational Psychology*. New Delhi: Sage.

Paranjpe, A.C., 1988, 'A Personality Theory According to Vedanta', in A.C. Paranjpe, D.Y.F. Ho and R.W. Ribber (eds), *Asian Contributions to Psychology*. New York: Praeger.

———, 1998, *Self and Identity in Modern Psychology and Indian Thought*. New York: Plenum.

Pavlov, I.P., 1927, *Conditional Reflexes* (trans. G.V. Anrep). London: Oxford University Press.

Phatak, P., 1977, *A Pictorial Monograph of Motor and Mental Development of Indian Babies from 1 to 30 Months*. Baroda: MS University.

Piaget, J., 1928, *Judgement and Reasoning in the Child*. New York: Harcourt Brace.

———, 1954, *The Construction in the Child*, New York: Basic Books.

Proctor, H., 1960, 'A Sociometric Method for Distinguishing Social Structures', in Richard N. Adams and Jack J. Priess (eds), *Human Organization Research: Field Relations and Techniques*. Homewood, IL: Dorsey Press Inc.

Radhakrishna, R., 1992, 'Trends in Nutrition: Emerging Challenges'; 'Nutrition: Need for Effective Intervention', *The Economic Times*, 10–11 February.

Rath, R., A.S. Dash and U.N. Dash, 1979, *Cognitive Abilities and School Achievement of the Socially Disadvantaged Children in Primary Schools*. Bombay: Allied Publishers.

Robert, R.L. and R.H. Munroe, 1975, *Cross-cultural Human Development*. Monterey, CA: Brooks/Cole Publishing Company.

Rosenzweig, S., 1945, 'The Picture Association Method and its Application in a Study of Reactions to Frustration', *Journal of Personality*, 14: 3–23.

———, 1976, 'Aggressive Behaviour and the Rosensweig Picture Frustration (P–F) Study', *Journal of Clinical Psychology*, 32(4): 885–91.

Saraswathi, T.S., 1974, 'A Short Term Longitudinal Study of the Development of Colour and Form Concept in Preschool Children', *Journal of Psychology*, 49(3): 231–36.

———, 2003, 'Foreword', in T.S. Saraswathi (ed.), *Cross-cultural Perspectives in Human Development: Theory, Research and Applications*. New Delhi: Sage.

Saraswathi, T.S. and B. Kaur, (eds.), 1993, *Human Development and Family Studies in India: An Agenda for Research and Policy*. New Delhi: Sage.

Saraswathi, T.S. and R. Dutta, 1986, 'Cross-cultural Studies in Developmental Psychology in India: Problems and Prospects', Proceedings of the English Conference of the International Association of the Cross-cultural Psychology, Istanbul, Turkey.

———, 1987, 'Introduction', in T.S. Saraswati and R. Dutta (eds), *Development Studies, Annotated Bibliography in Development Psyshology 1975–1986*. New Delhi: Sage.

Searle, A., 1999, *Introducing Research Data in Psychology*. New York: Routledge.

Selitiz, C., L.S. Wrightsman and S.W. Cook (eds), 1969, *Research Methods in Social Relations* (Revised one volume edition). London: Methune & Co.

Seymour, S., 1999, *Women, Family and Child Care in India*. Cambridge: Cambridge University Press.

Shaw, C.T. and S. Hammond, (eds), 2004, *Blackwell M. Research in Psychology*. London: Sage.

Shinde, R., P. Parekh and K. Jaul, 1980, 'A Study of Some Selected Anthropometric Parameters in Upper Class Pre-school Children of Jabulpore', *Indian Journal of Paediatrics* 17(1): 45–53.

Siegal, S., 1956, *Nonparametric Statistics*. New York: McGraw-Hill.

Sinha, D., 1965, 'The Integration of Modern Psychology with Indian Thought', *Journal of Humanistic Psychology*, 5(1): 6–17.

———, 1975, 'Cognitive and Psychomotor Skills', *Indian Journal of Cross-cultural Psychology*, 10(3): 324–55.

———, 1993, 'Research—Policy Interface, an Uneasy Partnership', in T.S. Saraswathi and B. Kaur (eds), *Human Development and Family Studies in India: An Agenda for Research and Policy*. New Delhi: Sage.

Sinha, D. and H.S.R. Kao, 2000, 'The Journey to the East—An Introduction', in H.S.R. Kao and D. Sinha (eds), *Asian Perspectives on Psychology*. New Delhi: Sage.

Sinha, D. and R.C. Mishra, 1993, 'Some Methodological Issues Related to Research in Developmental Psychology in the Context of Policy and Intervention Programmes', in T.S. Saraswathi and B. Kaur (eds.), *Human Development and Family Studies in India: An Agenda for Research and Policy*. New Delhi: Sage.

Sinha, D. and G. Misra, 1982, 'Deprivation and its Motivational and Personality Correlates', in D. Sinha, R.C. Tripathi and G. Misra (eds), *Deprivation: Its Social and Personality Correlates*. New Delhi: Concept.

Sinha, D. and R.C. Tripathi, 2002, 'Individualism in a Collectivist Culture: A Case of Co-existence of Opposites', in A.K. Dalal and G. Misra (eds), *New Directions in Indian Psychology, Vol. 1: Social Psychology*. New Delhi: Sage.

Stevens, S.S. (ed.), 1961, *Handbook of Experimental Psychology*. New York: John Wiley.

Swaminathan, M., 1996, *The First Five Years: A Critical Perspective on Early Childhood Care and Education in India*. New Delhi: Sage.

Symonds, P.M., 1946, *The Dynamics of Human Adjustment*. New York: Appleton Century Crofts.

Thomas, R.M., 2001, *Recent Theories of Human Development*. London: Sage.

Underwood, B.J., 1957, *Psychological Research*. New York: Appleton Century Crofts.

Weinberg, H.F., J.A. Weisberg, B.A. Kronsnicla and D. Bowen, 1999, *An Introduction to Survey Research, Polling and Data Analyses*. New Delhi: Sage.

Whiting, J.W.M. and I.L. Child, 1953, *Child Training and Personality*. New Haven: Yale University Press.

William, G. Cochran, 1974, *Sampling Techniques*, 2nd edn. New Delhi: Wiley Eastern Private Ltd.

Wolff, K.H., 1960, 'The Collection and Organization of Field Materials: A Research Report', in R.N. Adams and J.J. Preiss (eds), *Human Organization Research*. Homewood, IL: Dorsey Press.

7

Identity and Interpersonal Competence

Identity in the Social Structure

THE UNDERSTANDING of human development perceived as occurring outside the self is one way by which we attempt to understand how we, each one of us individually and separately, have developed and are developing in a holistic manner. It has been aptly said, 'The mind is like a knife; it can cut everything else but itself' (Russell, 1945). Russell implies that we can analyse everything else objectively, except ourselves. If one persists, one can understand others in a reliable manner, but to analyse oneself is somewhat unreliable—precisely because we cannot at most times do so in a rational manner. Whenever we fall below our own expectations, it is frequent that we tend to excuse ourselves, or find some other reason outside ourselves, through the dynamisms of defence mechanisms (Hentschel et al., 2004).

However, connotations of the self are different in the West vis-à-vis the East. These connotations arise from differences in the cultural ethos comprising religious values, goals and goal attainment, both individually oriented and collectively oriented (Maslow, 1970). Psychology, as originating in the West, is based on objective and scientific discovery of facts through analysis of the individual psyche as embedded in a particular culture (Roland, 1996).

However, the perception of identity is not in isolation of the inner self alone (Kakar, 1991), but also in relation to one's encompassing ecology, which has subtle but telling influences on the perception of selfhood (Littlewood, 1999). Since psychology in a documented format in the East is a latecomer, it is interspersed with eastern philosophical thought, and more given to varied interpretations, as Confucianism and Taoism in China, Zen Buddhism in Japan and Hinduism in India (Sinha and Kao, 1997: 26). Over the ages, the Indian scenario has been interspersed with the dynamics of religion, politics and their various stratifications.

This has given rise to many strands of pluralism in the Indian society (Kaviraj, 1995). Let us take an analogy from what we are familiar with. Take the case of nouns and pronouns in English grammar. Pronouns such as 'it', 'they', 'she', 'he', 'them' and 'we', in the Indian context, are conditioned by prefixes or suffixes like *aap* (denoting higher status in the hierarchy) and *tum* (denoting lower status). In fact, it is not uncommon for youth in North India to address each other as *yaar*, which means 'friend' (indicating equal status). The word *ji* (sir) in Hindi is a common suffix indicating deference to the person in a hierarchical status. The identities of individuals have various additive connotations, such as place of origin, surnames indicating ethnic origin, and even to some extent the caste status. For instance, it is mainly from their surnames that it is possible to identify the state from which individuals originate, as for instance, the surname Singh belongs to individuals mainly from north India; names ending in 'an' are usually from south India like Janardhanan, Bhaskaran and Swaminathan. We can also, if we analyse the names more intently in terms of genealogical trees of lineage, 'guesstimate' their caste identity. For instance, Aggarwals are usually from the Vaishya caste in the north. Why are these indicators essential in identifying an individual? They are essential because they identify a person as not only being an individual entity, but also belonging to a particular social network (Markus, 1977: 63–78). These are of course generalities, and are termed 'classificatory categories', but here the matter of the individual is more incisive. He cannot be coded as a statistic. He is a vital human being, perceiving himself in sequential stages as being firstly, 'I', then finds relationships with others, like 'papa, mama, *didi* (elder sister)'. He expands this string of relationships: he has a name, a surname, an address, a date of birth and so on. These are formal indicators. However, they do not indicate the particular entity's personality and his specific relationships to his environment, both human as well as concrete. For instance, it is not unusual when travelling with others to exchange information about oneself like 'I am ___, I come from ___', and as the conversation proceeds, inevitably, there are exchanges about one's place of residence, occupation and so on. Thus, human beings strive to find a place that uniquely connotates themselves as separate entities (Lewis, 1991: 111–34).

As soon as we use the connotation of 'I' or 'self', we are in a sense trying to understand the unique individual both from an external and, more importantly, an internal perspective. The Vedantic philosophy is all encompassing in describing the self, in relation to enunciated religious principles, regarding the self, others and the external world (Hume, 1931). What are these external and internal perspectives? For this we need to describe and determine how we recognise ourselves for what we are, and be able to comprehend the perspective of the 'other selves'. Without digressing too much into the spiritual realms of *'atman, pehla janam,* and *agley janam'* (Soul, previous and future incarnations), *'rishteydari'* (relationship), or the conscious self and its evolution into self-realisation (or knowledge of the inner self), we will stay here with the psychological concepts of intraperception, interperception and extraperception. These deal with recognising individuals and their situational parameters. The 'who am I' is dealt within the self-analysis of feelings, attitudes, habits, motives, interests, likes and dislikes. Each individual is born with genetic traits, physical features and growth potentials, which, as we have said before, differ from one to another. The process of perception is possible through a second asset of adaptation to environmental challenges (Keller, 2003). With growing maturity, the individual increasingly learns to use strategies that build up his identity in the perceptions of others (Hofstede, 1991: 49–78). For instance, as an adult he will learn to be quiet, even to congratulate his opponent, when he is seething with anger. He tries to put on a 'social face'. Physical anthropologists attempt to trace civilisations through each era. There are compelling hypotheses that we are descendents of the ape, and, over time, have evolved from one genetic species to another improved species through selectivity and adaptability to the environment (Darwin, 1859). During the course of evolution, these traits accrue as mediated by the environment, so that the individual adapts to the environmental parameters (Durham, 1991). The ability to think rationally, to control and master the environment, increases dexterous manipulation of energy and molecules. The momentum has accelerated from one generation to another. Although little has been done to contrast the 'knowledge' of the parental generation with the child generation, it is obvious that children are more knowledgeable than the parental generation, especially when the parents were children. For instance, children supersede their parents in their skills at computation techniques. However, the perceptual abilities follow the same general principles of biophysiology. It is the individual differences in the inherent traits that humans bring along with them genetically, and their potential to modify them, that make up the difference. We cannot, however, rule out the influence of parental models affecting identity (especially same-sex identification) (Chakraborty and Basu, 1994: 1–8). Several studies have indicated that there is a strong tendency for the ontogenetic traits of females to be guided in such a way that they are expected to behave with 'femininity'. Several studies, both in India and with comparison to other cultures outside India, have indicated that irrespective of the family structure, sociologically Indian fathers are strongly patriarchal in their attitudes towards the upbringing of the female offspring (Patel and Power, 1996: 310).

All human beings perceive through their senses. It is through sense perception that we come to recognise the outer world. However, there is an inner perception of the self, the inner knowledge or wisdom or '*buddhi*', that there is a person within the person of the self. In the Indian culture, it is important to begin with the knowledge of the self or the atman. Then, it is said we are better able to know others. The Rig Veda, for instance, speaks of '*rta*' or cosmic order with the assumption that there are various equivalences between the outer and inner world. The lower or dual and the higher or unified orders were classified at the latter level where there is a unity, what in psychology is called homeostasis, or what some theorists call equilibrium. For instance, in Katha Upanishad and the Bhagavad Gita, the person is compared to a chariot pulled in different directions by the horses or the senses. The mind is the driver who controls the direction (Kak, 2000: 85). We find a similarity in Freud's analysis of the id, the ego and the superego, together with the libidinal energy and catharsis, where the driver is equivalent to the superego (Freud, 1935).

The true observer sits near the driver who represents the true self or universal unity. It is said that no coherent behaviour is possible without this self. The levels at which the individual self is described is in ascending order: the body (*annamaya kosa*), then follows the energy sheath (*pranamaya kosa*), the mental sheath (*manomaya kosa*), followed by the intellect sheath (*vijnanamaya kosa*), and finally the emotion sheath (*anandamaya kosa*). Above all these is the self or the atman. Kak, in his exposition of the meaning, indicates that this is relevant to the field of socio-psychology in examining the self.

He states that the major levels are the body, the energy and thoughts at the highest level, in ascending order (Kak, 2000: 86). Energy states may be changed either at the physical or at the mental levels. When agitated it is characterised by *rajas*, when dull it is characterised by *tamas*; the equilibrium is called *sattva*. *Prana* is the medium of exchange between the psychological and physiological systems. The three levels stated by Kak compose the mind (ibid.). The mind is the emergent entity but it is the self that articulates the mind.

It stands to reason that in the newly growing human being this development is nascent, but is not unearthed by the self, which itself grows in relation to the maturity of the individual and his knowledge of himself and the world around him. The mind is composed of the lower level, which is *manas*, collecting sense impressions. The sense of perception is *ahamkara*, or 'I-ness'. Buddhi is the intellect that reorganises these sensory impressions. These three, that is manas, ahamkara and buddhi, are the internal instruments of the mind. Memories are stored in the *chitta*, which organises and reorganises impressions as they occur with relevant emotions. This complex, according to the Vedas, forms the innermost nexus of the consciousness or the self, atman. In western psychology, the self is equated with the ego and the soul, which in themselves are heuristic and spiritual, and are only inferred. If one were to seriously examine the philosophical cum cognitive construction of concepts in the Vedic scriptures and compare them with those in modern science, there is a remarkable similarity (Alexander and Bower, 1989: 325–71). The concept 'being' (existence) is similar to the concept of '*jiva*' (life) and the concept of the self is similar to that of atman in Hindu philosophy (Paranjpe, 1975). Till his attainment of the knowledge of the self, the individual is still in a state of exploring himself and his *kosa*s (the body, the energy, the mental, intellect and emotion) in the understanding of the self in terms of strengths and weaknesses (Kak, 2000: 86).

According to the empirical psychological perspective, knowledge of the outer world is by the senses. In psychology, the term ego is akin to the conscious described in the spiritual context of the inner self (Allport, 1943). The ego originally began with the conceptualisation of Freud, 'the father of the theory of psychoanalysis', to connote that part of the mind in control of the self and in touch with social reality and its norms. The superego and the inner self of uncontrollability or the libido are assumed to be representative of the good and the evil, respectively, reflected in biblical sayings. Other neo-Freudians (Horney, 1939) interpret the ego or the self as composed of three parts: the parent ego (the superego) or the authoritarian part of the person that acts like a monitor; the child ego or that part which is genetically inherited with its passions and desires expressed in a spontaneous manner akin to the libido; and the adult ego (the self ego) akin to a computer, which collects facts and processes them and assesses probabilities and makes predictions, the nexus of reasoning rationally. The 'I' or the ego is composed of a set of consistent patterns of thinking, feeling and doing (Summerton, 1979: 8). It stands to reason that experiences are built up from early childhood into a foundation set, which monitors the rest of the thinking process (Arasteh, 1980).

Understanding of the self is obtainable by reports from narratives of children who emphasise the 'I' approach in terms of wanting space and privacy to be with themselves and to understand themselves (Chaudhry and Kaura, 2004). For this reason, adult guidance and encouragement in this direction are said to be of great importance during the formative years, where child rearing or parenting practices occur (Darling and Steinberg, 1993: 487–96).

This self uses its own accultured (trained and assimilated) bases in viewing the world of the others. For an understanding of the other, or other entities, a contextual reference is essential (to recognise the self) (Hirsch, 1982). According to Indian thinking, human nature (Hiriyanna, 1952) is an amalgam of philosophy, psychology and sociology, where concepts are described in a holistic manner. It is essential for the self to extend the boundaries of the senses because it implies reciprocal relationships and interactions which cannot take place in isolation of each other. The self needs to interact in relation to other entities or bodies, as exemplified by the kosas. Cosmic energy holds the individual and others together so long as they are finite (of this world). An individual belongs to a *desh* (country), *kala* (period of history), *dharma* (work, occupation) and *guna* (bio-mental attributes). Transgression is said to be the root cause of unrest of the self (Sinha and Sinha, 2000: 32).

The Hindu view of social life through the ages is explicit in the epics Ramayana and Mahabharata; and like the Bible and the Quran, these make explicit the types of relations that should exist between the self and the other, between nature and society (in its broad generic sense).

Interdependence emphasises the interrelatedness of the various strands of society. As a social being there is no identity outside this network of relationships. In gradual complexity the growing child comes to know his position in relation to the outer world, gaining a view as to his status in his family, kin group, community and eventually a 'worldview'. The latter concept is important, as interactional worldviews 'have been the dominant approaches in comparative psychology' (Altman and Rogoff, 1987: 7–40). These perceptions shape the ego identity, which is socially constructed dependent upon the individual's experiences and his social positioning. Thus, the social self is the individual's interpretation of his position in his social world which gives him his identity as perceived by others in his sphere. He is a son/father/grandfather (hierarchical); he belongs to a caste (his interactive world of professions and their related values); he is a person of a country (subscribes to the policies, laws and systems of the structures of the country: for example school, work institution, religious group and so on). He becomes aware of the appropriate tasks to be performed for meeting his expected roles (Bailey, 1957). For instance, a primary school child, when he enters a classroom, lowers his profile of also being a player on the playground, and assumes the mindset of a student intent on studies. In a day, he learns to switch roles and to confine himself to high-profiling the expected tasks in each situation. As an adult in an office, he takes on the role of a professional at the job tasks required of him (a strategy) to meet his goals. The latter consist of immediate goals (to be effective and efficient at his work) and long term (to meet the needs of his family, himself and his obligatory duties to kinship and community (dharma)). He learns prescriptions and prohibitions of social behaviour, which is controlled through his ego (Harter, 1988: 43–70).

Models of social behaviour in the Hindu dharma are prescribed in the shastras and the Puranas (Kane, 1941). In the other religions, such behaviour is also inscribed in the *hidayaat*s in the Quran, the injunctions of the Guru Granth Sahib and the tenets of the Bible.

The Indian mind comprises dichotomies, resolved by a higher level of abstraction. According to Indian philosophy, the psychosocial aspects of thinking range from spiritual to lower levels of spontaneous life processes (Hiriyanna, 1932). The Samkhya yoga model of consciousness (subject to distortions by three *kelesha*s or defilements of the mind: *aga* or passion, *dvesa* or hatred, and *moha* or delusion) prescribed by the Gita proposes the pursuit of *loka sangraha* (where everyone acts according to his destined station in life for the social good). For this purpose, four *purushartha*s are given: *dharma* (duty), *artha* (material pursuit), *kama* (passion) and *moksha* (enlightenment). Artha and kama are to be obtained within the societal network as also dharma. At times artha and kama may be in conflict with dharma and may be resolved by moving towards moksha by paying off *rena*s (debts) (Roy and Srivastava, 1986).

Again, an individual has to pass through various stages in life. For instance, if an individual does not perform the tasks at the stage of *grihastha*, he cannot move to the next level of detachment. It is also argued that the individual has to feel attachment before experiencing detachment. Control of the keleshas is to be developed at each stage if he is to pass successfully from one stage to another. The determination of consciousness is a precondition to coming to terms with one's state in life. Perhaps for this reason, the Indian psyche has much more of a sense of tolerance and acceptance of destiny, unlike the western psyche. The latter is interpreted in terms of behaviour modification concepts (Bandura, 1969).

Indian philosophy has embedded models of social behaviour well enunciated by the Mahabharata's three dominant characters: Krishna (a political strategist), Yuddhishtir (a righteous king) and Arjun (a warrior, who was most responsible for winning the war against the Kauravas). Arjun was counselled by Krishna to perform his *kshatriya* dharma (warrior duty) by doing away with the evildoers. The same is true of the depiction of the godhead Rama in the Ramayana, standing for optimal justice and divine power (Bharati, 1983).

Perceptual Knowledge of Self and Others

Feuerbach, over a hundred years ago, discovered that philosophy, pivoted around the 'I', with little reference to the 'you' (Laing et al., 1976: 14). Psychoanalysis also downplayed the 'you'. Perception of an object or thing or person, however, came to be viewed as a compound of many perceptions of many people in a given situation. Such situations are a compound of action and reaction, cyclically, jointly or disjointedly. In the West, Martin Buber, Scheler and Husserl used both the 'I' and 'you' as a composite interactive process. The major contribution to an understanding of the self from the West includes the classic theories of Fritz Heider (1958). Language was seen to be the means of the expression of such perceptions in the interactive situation. These are meta-perspectives of differential views of each other, and it is language (verbal or non-verbal) which gives meaning to expression of the self. Interpersonal perception is threefold: the perceiver perceives the other; the other perceives the perceiver; and further, each one assesses what the other perceives of himself. It becomes a three-way process in communication, based on the degree of intensity of perception. Interpretations are multifaceted meta-identities according to Laing et al. (1976). Self-identity, on the other hand, is a knowledge of oneself in relation to the structures of the psychological and the socio-physical world around the individual.

In the psychological sphere, the most used sense is sight. In this generalisation, however, there are several aids, even to the extent of creating virtual imagery, and the perception that the self is not only perceiving, but is actually reflected in the frame of reference that is perceived (Harris, 1995). Initially, in infancy and early childhood, the object physically perceived, animate or inanimate, has form, size, shape and colour, but is labelled only by other humans around the child. The child also learns to label through the process of social learning and imitation. He also learns to coordinate several senses in vision. For example, an infant sees a figure appear. It is his mother. He recognises her as familiar, from past pleasurable sensations with this figure. He stretches out his arms, makes gurgling sounds. He hears her voice, which further reinforces him that she is in fact his caretaker. She holds him and has a familiar smell. This reinforces his attachment to this caretaker, and like happenings in a kaleidoscope he puts all these frames of reference together to conclude that she is his major caretaker, and is labelled 'mom' or 'ma'. We have only to watch a baby among cooing women to see the perturbation on his face, and the smile of relief when he recognises his mother among them. Memories revive and frames get transposed in a complex and organised manner.

In most Indian families, even though the phenomenon of 'jointedness' is being dissipated by changing social circumstances, the ethic still prevails (Bassa, 1978: 333–43). The joint family is viewed within these parameters as a friendly, indulgent, mutual insurance society or a welfare state, and in intermittent forms and at various levels is observable to this day.

In complicated technological situations, an adult person can undergo scientific tests and be transposed in mental imagery from one world to another. This is possible by eliciting energy, through light waves, through digital processes and through chip configuration in photography and computers. Such processes make it a far more complex task to pick up the right cues to picturise the correct picture. For instance, to quote Thomas (2001: 25), magnetic resonance imaging (MRI) does not use X-rays, but instead depends upon the behaviour of protons (nuclei) of hydrogen atoms that are exposed to powerful magnetic and radio waves. When so exposed, the protons emit radio signals that are detected and then transformed by a computer into images on a screen.

Therefore, as an analogy, we might assume that the perception of a thing, when transposed through the neurological system, is filtered and interpreted through self-imagery. These perceptions are retained in memory as stored processes and eventually are recreated on recall through cumulative neurological responses.

For instance, we have often heard the expression 'déjà vu'. Here the senses perceive a situation, there is an immediate response process set in motion, retraced through past similar cues, which recreate the same situation as stored in memory. It feeds back into the interpretative neurons which then picturise similitude, and the perceiver feels or says, 'I have been in this situation before', when in actuality he may not have been (Gergen, 1971). 'The self-concept is socially constructed and exists in a cultural context', more in terms of group, caste and gender identities. The Indian society, being traditional in nature, emphasises values and norms pertaining to gender roles which are clearly culture-related.

The perception of the self is always with reference to a contextual frame, mainly the cultural frame, in which the self is constantly reconstructing his perception of the self in relation to the situational context (Markus and Kitayama, 1994: 22–37). 'I am what I am, and what I have made of myself/has been made by me.' What is this 'I'? Again, we will bypass the metaphysical world, and stay with the physical socio-emotional reality of the human being. The human being comes into the world with physical tissue composed of chromosomes that comprise the pheno- and genotypologies (McKinney and Namara, 1991), which are hereditary material, possessing potential capacities, which over the chronological lifespan either blossom or are attenuated. For instance, if a child has a certain intelligence level but is severely deprived of iodine in the early years, he develops cretinism, which stunts growth, physically and mentally. Deficiencies, whether nutritional such as protein, or emotional like lack of maternal care or isolation from other human beings, are physio-psychological factors affecting normal development. Under normal care and upbringing, perception is unimpeded, hearing can be increased to whatever crescendo required, the taste buds can be exposed to new foods and therefore normal development is maximised (Menon, 2003: 431–49). This then is the self perceived in a physiological sense.

In the West, European philosophy also contended with the concept of the 'self' or 'I'. Aristotle's theory of Neomachean ethics 2,000 years ago, which lay dormant, was revitalized by Kant's several expositions on logical thought and reasoning (Aristotle, 1998; Kant, 1929).

Also, 'the other' is as primary as the self, for in the epistemological sense, ideogrammatically, the 'I' is relative to 'the other' and the 'I' cannot exist without reference to 'the other'. For this reason, the human being is paramountly a social being and cannot exist for long in isolation.

George Mead (1934) related the concept of 'self' or 'I' as mediated by the 'generalised other' and suggested the effect of the 'looking glass' in examining the concept of 'I' (quoted in Laing, et al., 1976). Talcott Parsons (1955) in his theory of social action discussed the alter ego. There is a further dimension to this interface between 'I' and 'you'. These are the meta-perspectives 'you, him/her, them, me, I'. Each may not perceive the other the same way, and in a group situation there may be a series of multi-perspectives. 'I anticipate, expect and suppose them to see me in the ways I hypothesise' (Laing, 1961). However, through constant inter-action with some, like the nearest relatives, with whom an individual lives day in and day out, there may be a closer perception of how the other thinks and feels. This occurs often between immediate biological relatives, and more frequently with spouses, thus creating a sense of empathy. The individual constantly acts in the light of supposed attitudes, opinions, beliefs and actions that are expected of him. The individual thus perceives them as meta-identities, which are temporary when acted out by the individual. For instance, in the company of the peer group, there are expected perceptions of the individual by the peer group, which may not tally with his perceptions of himself as an identity, or with his interpretation of their perceptions (intra- and interpersonal perceptions).

Self-identity in the Indian philosophy is the atman, and meta-identities, as to what the individual thinks others perceive him to be, are called *samajik gahayita*. These types of perceptions change dynamically as changes occur during interaction of the identity of self and the meta-identity of others (Greenwald and Pratkanis, 1984: 129–77). For instance, a schoolboy in the playground perceives his friends and proceeds towards them in a positive manner expecting positive interaction. They turn away due to a previous misunderstood interaction. He is unaware and perceives them to be irrational and makes overtures. Their perception changes and they perceive him as a coward. He perceives them then as irrational bullies and so a vicious circle ensues leading to a greater distorted perception of the reality of the situation in relation to his self (Festinger, 1957). One can act against the perceived perception of others, just as a child stubbornly does the opposite of his mother's expectations even though he perceives the reality of her instructions. Here, the 'I' distorts the interpretation but not the perceived imagery. When we participate in a discussion, for instance, and we comment, 'I agree with you,' we mean the thought of the other is exactly how we or I also perceive the idea or object or event discussed (Heider, 1958). In most cases, there is an attempt to arrive at an equilibrium, agreeing to agree or agreeing to disagree. The latter is akin to saying, 'I respect the space of others or the views of others as applying to themselves but not necessarily to me.' Match and mismatch of perceptions can take place in dynamic interaction and in any combination of simplicity or complexity. The latter often ends in a statement 'I don't understand them/her/him'.

In all these processes the concept of communication is important. Language helps a person to say things as they are (in a factual manner), even though harsh and upsetting to the other. Therefore, we tend to use words which disguise the harshness but still convey the messages. We often refer to the latter as tactful or diplomatic communication, and consider it an asset in interpersonal relations. There is also a growing knowledge of the relationship between ecology, habitat and perception. These influence the variations in perceptual ability (Barker, 1968). If the ecology is desert land and the individual lives a nomadic life, his perception revolves around sand, space, water and survival. These are high-profiled in his perception as contrasted with urban conglomerates where the perception is bombarded with high technology and information systems. Ecology modifies habitat, which in turn modifies the patterns and quality of life and therefore its perception (Archer et al., 1984: 118–40).

There are also individual differences between the parent and the child, which modulate the emotional content of their interactive processes (Lynch, 1990). This occurs spontaneously from early childhood in the dyad relationship between mother and child, which is especially intense in the Indian situation. This process of reinforcement is based on the intentionality of the needs of each other, which motivates them (Mesquita et al., 1997: 255–97). We live in a world of perceptions of others that guide and influence us, for example, identity-labelling by others so that we perceive ourselves by what we are labelled in formal terms. This is essential in a social milieu where structured interactions take place as in a family, unlike that which takes place in unfamiliar public places as in a movie theatre or a railway station. We can justify our identity by documentation (ration card, place of residence, passport and other such factual material). But these are all varieties of labels about ourselves, some of which the individual hears about himself, some which is reported about him and some of which he infers from cues in situations where people are gathered around (Triandis, 1989: 506–20). Self-perception is constantly being modified by the perceiver himself. In some theories of development it is given a philosophical interpretation, like perceiving a vital consciousness of the inner self towards finding a balance, a homeostasis between the individual and the environment. At times, there are no differences between self-perception and the real 'I' as when the psychiatrist affords the patient an insight into his real self (good or bad). At other times the individual puts up a social façade, deliberately putting up a front that he wishes others to perceive. It is common to see in school gangs individuals trying to gain approval by being a loyal member of the peer group. At other times the self seeks emotional stability, like when one hears of a family tragedy and is trying to control himself from exhibiting distraught behaviour (Lynch, 1990). At other times, the emotive content is excessive as in a rage where an individual can either express the rage or depress the expression. These are quick fluctuations stimulated by quick changing self-perceptions of how the individual should act and react in specific situations. Sometimes, one acts impulsively without thinking rationally and this is perceived by others as acting 'without any sense'. It is therefore not only the impulses which the self feeds itself on in terms of thinking only, but also thinking and behaving, or behaving only (Kagitcibasi, 1996: 180–86).

Let us illustrate: A young adult just out of college and in a new job perceives he must make an impression. He grooms himself as if he were going to a party, practises how he should speak before the mirror, and counsels himself as to how to deport himself in the presence of his boss and colleagues. He literally perceives himself as a reflection in the looking glass (thinking only). Let us assume he arrives at work on the first day, well in time. He walks in feeling self-conscious hoping that others would notice him, greet him and help him out (behaving only). His colleagues just stare at him. One makes a remark, 'another new *bakra* (lamb) come to the slaughterhouse', and they all turn away doing their own things. Our young man perceives their perceptions as expressed in their behaviour. He feels deflated, crushed and making himself as inconspicuous as possible slithers onto his seat (thinking and behaving). On the other hand if our young man was practical, dressed ordinarily, walked in casually and smiled and said 'hi' to every one he met, even if he got surly glances back, he has perceived something extra. He would have counselled himself: 'So what if they don't accept me on the first day. They are also embarrassed . . . I should take it coolly and in a few days I can make friends with at least some of them, and then I will feel comfortable' (thinking and behaving). He has perceived beyond their expressed perceptions (verbal or non-verbal). He has perceived some concepts and thoughts about their inner selves. For instance the appointment of the young man is a threat to Mohan (a colleague) who was angling for the job and did not get it. Mohan's loyal friends are determined to express their solidarity with Mohan, and hence, even though our young man is innocuous, they literally gang up against him. But if his perception is right about their inner perception, that they really have nothing against him and he is likeable and sociable, then some will melt towards him and soon will accept him, even if minimally. Our young man has not only perceived their perception expressed in behaviour, but also is cued into their inner thinking. The 'concept of inner thinking' and related research in recent years have indicated two trends: an increasing academic interest in analysing the self, though not necessarily in psychoanalytic terms, but more in relation to self-perception, and the second is that intensive analyses indicate that the self is culturally toned in diverse cultures in different ways (Bharati, 1985: 185–230). For instance, a study between Americans and Indians indicated that the Indian's perception of self is more in relation to his familial and social identity and is more pronounced in females, whereas the American is more autonomy-oriented (Dhawan et al., 1995). Therefore, ideas, concepts and thoughts originating from oneself and interpreted from the thoughts expressed and the behaviour seen in others is perception (Markus and Kitayama, 1991: 224–25). When one says, 'he is a very perceptive person', one implies that the individual uses a high level of grasping or sizing up the situation, using an innate cue grasp. Again, perceptions of others, which make up our interpretation of the others, are gathered mainly through interpersonal perceptions. Sometimes, this is modified by a feeling of what we call good or bad rapport with the other or others. Often we avoid a person because his expressed thought or behaviour is displeasing to us. In these situations, there is often a spontaneous reaction to label the person a 'bore' or 'overly talkative' or some such negative label. A form of defence mechanism (or justification of one's action as caused by outside the self or 'I') utilised by the 'I' is an attempt to use meta-identities (the self temporarily adopts an alternative identity). This is common when the individual wills himself to add on extra qualities to himself to meet a situation such as a timid person trying to be brave against a bully or an ordinary-looking girl trying to behave as if she is attractive. These however are temporary and eventually the individual goes back to the real self. Negative or positive vibes are another indication of movement away or towards others.

There is a saying 'no man is an island'. Humans are gregarious, social people, and like primates live in groups. This tendency is sometimes called the 'herd instinct'. Take for instance, a gathering of young girls dressing up for a bridal party. There is much giggling, praising and encouraging of each other. Rani is not as good-looking as Sita so she dresses quietly without much chitchat, feeling inadequate. She perceives from the lack of contact with her and the great amount with Sita that she is not much liked; she is not one of the gang. This is an important aspect of an adolescent's lifestyle, namely to belong to the peer group. Rani is there because she is the bride's cousin. She hesitatingly goes up to Sita and says hopefully, 'Do I look OK?' She probably looks dowdy but Sita is a compassionate girl and says, 'Can I help you with your make up?' Now Rani perceives that Sita is saying, 'You look dowdy but I will help you look less dowdy.' Although the interpersonal perception is that she is getting help to look better, actually Sita is thinking she is a bore. Rani knows this, she perceives more than what is said because she intuitively recognises the expression and the effort made by Sita and the false gaiety in Sita's voice. Through all the chatter she overhears: 'She is like a clam and won't talk.' The same girl turns to her and says, 'Hi Rani, how nice you look.' But Rani knows she is not one of them, not a part of the gang (the collection of peers grouping together). This is an instance where perceptions are mutually tangential, but because of the social norms they are converted into another frame of reference, as did Sita towards Rani and Rani's reinterpretation of the reality of the episode. Thus we can infer that what we see as behaviour especially in social situations may be a put-on façade. For instance, a husband and wife have quarrelled at home before going to a party but at the party they call each other by endearing terms as if they were newly married. The more experiences one accumulates, the greater the knowledge and ability to introspect and analyse. However, it is like the old adage: 'Doctor, know thyself'. Unless the self is free from anxieties, guilt and biases, it is difficult using fair processes in analyses of events happening to oneself and to other individuals. Thus, in interactive patterns, human beings are modified in behaviour by their perceptions of their peers, their parents and the social environment in which they live (Allport, 1920: 159–82). Their personalities are shaped by the adjustments that continue to influence their selves. This is especially true of the effect of those who matter most to the self. To the child it is more frequently the parents and siblings. As the child grows, peers and teachers also assume importance. Often there are divided loyalties in the school and college years. One often hears the youngster rebelling and saying, 'but my friends don't do this, or my teacher says so'. It is common, for instance, to try to be like one of the peer group by wearing similar clothes, chewing the same kind of gum and exhibiting similar mannerisms. These types of behaviour can also lead youngsters to suffer from anxiety, guilt, anger and resentment.

Overcoming the negative vibes and balancing the positive is a combination of balancing and counterbalancing the effects of interactive perceptual variations affecting the self. We need to stress here that most families subscribe to the patriarchal norm and hierarchical authority. In the Indian situation, the father plays a secondary role in actual household and childcare practices. This is especially true in the traditional family set-up. More often than not he is viewed as an authoritarian figure, and although 'distant', in the child-caring context, is perceived as a dominant figure guiding family norms. However, when it comes to the operation of individual's initiative in that set-up, there is much baulking as the individual begins to experience independence and vacillates between it and the allegiance to the patriarchal norms. With the changing structure of the family, with both parents working and with the increasing competitive environment, the relationship between parents and their adolescent children is undergoing changes due to differential parenting patterns (Sartor and Youniss, 2002: 221–34). The maturing individual is in a constant state of flux especially in adolescence and young adulthood, when there is a struggle between a search for identity and avoidance of self-diffusion (Erikson, 1959).

Emotionality plays a great role in the maintenance of this balance. Interacting with others whom one knows as acquaintances is not as intense as when one interacts with one's close friends, creating closer emotional ties. What are the interactions with 'other selves', both close and far? How does one recognise the potential or analyse the strengths and limits of other selves? Who are these other selves? These are also selves with formal labels or identities. But here the similarity ends. Each is circumscribed by labels of past/current situations. The ability to recognise potentials, limitations and strengths of 'other selves' depends upon a great deal of unbiased introspection. To introspect implies using logical deduction and induction techniques in the process of analysis. It is often said: 'First know thyself that thou should know others.' This kind of introspective behaviour is one of the strongholds of Samkhya Yoga in that meditation not only exposes the self to the self, but also comes to terms with the balance between the self, the others and the supernatural. Meditators have reported many sublime experiences of higher states of consciousness, and in commenting on them, Maharishi Mahesh Yogi has explained that there is more to life than the ordinary three states of waking, dreaming and sleep (Orme-Johnson et al., 1997: 83). Unless the analytical perceptual powers are used on one self, the ability to analyse others is usually blurred. Human beings in stress often turn to others for unbiased analyses. In the traditional network of the *kutumb* (extended family), the *biradari* (relations) and *parivar* (immediate family), these others were essentially elders. In the sophisticated world in which urban Indians live today, in nuclear families, with both parents working, and children in schools, there is lesser opportunity to use informal networks of the family and the kin group. Guidance and professional counselling channels are being used more frequently by the upper classes. In the West, it is the fashion to consult psychotherapists. Public schools in India are now beginning to use counsellors to help children in high schools, especially in the academic spheres. Families tend to use family networks for counselling, arbitration and settlements where family disorganisation exists. In the metropolitan areas, where there is more public awareness of disorganisation (both social as well as family), non-governmental help groups offer assistance in extreme cases of spouse and child abuse, rape and sexual harassment.

India is in a state of flux, and there is a spurt towards gaining professional education, whether paraprofessional or otherwise. Professionally educated young men and women, whether they are software engineers or doctors or lawyers, are now immersed in acquiring additional skills in the areas of management and interpersonal skills, to enhance their upward mobility. In fact most state-of-the-art and sophisticated organisations have both a human resources development (HRD) cell and a staff development cell, to hone the skills of their management cadres. In this respect, a study by Gupta and Panda (2003: 1–29) reported that from a sample of qualified technocrats in a highly technological joint venture, they found a high degree of the existence of simultaneous individualistic and collectivistic tendencies called 'social connectiveness' in the sample (Earley and Gibson, 1998: 265–305). This phenomenon may be interpreted as a manifestation of a hybrid self as a self composed of many different sets of behaviour which then can be cohered into one entity (individual). For instance, a fairly good example is one individual playing multiple roles with the ability to move from one to another without cognitive dissonance. The results of the study also showed that the dominant value orientation-shaping behaviour patterns was the individualistic tendency. Given the implications of identity crisis as discussed by Erikson (1951: 234–37), there is also a tendency to disassociate the self from the other. The conflict between the self and the other in terms of self-achievement indicates that with the trend towards globalisation and sophisticated interactivity between the East and the West, the young generation has the tendency to adopt westernised strategies of management in their lifestyle (De Vos, 1968: 348–70).

Interpersonal Competence

Competence is a synonym for ability. It implies the degree of self-satisfaction with the ability to perform and accomplish tasks. Competence, as described by Foote and Cotrell (1955), exists in some degree or the other in all human beings. Competence in the performance of tasks differs widely depending upon the ability, comprehension and motivation of the individual and also the evaluation of others. Before we expand upon the concept of competence we need to assess what is social action, as competence is assessed only in behaviour and that too behaviour which is observable in action in the context of social reality. Parsons presents an action schema which, based on his theory of social action, classifies types of systems (1949). The theory of action means any theory, the empirical reference of which is to a concrete system, composed of the units referred to as 'unit acts'. A unit act has the following minimum characteristics:

- an end;
- a situation analysable in turn into a means and condition;
- at least one selected standard in which the end is related to the situation, wherein there is an actor(s)'s subjective point of view.

Unlike the theory of behaviour, it does not exclude the subjective aspect. The theory, through a process of interactions, is based on the empirical world of reality, not the creation of the human mind, and not reducible to order in the epistemological sense. There may be many representations which are directly and functionally related to the social action of the actors in the system (ibid.: 77). Interpreted in layman terms, this theory proceeds systematically to focus on the unit of action acted out by individual/s, in relation to subjective norms, and then converted to social reality. Competence is that exhibited behaviour, relative to a given time, given place and a given set of people. In these circumstances the individual understands that specific individuals exhibit an understanding of the situation as realistic strategies and find workable means to reach a common goal (Wilson and Ryland, 1949). It is obvious that when we add the qualifying concept of the interpersonal we are implying an individual in relation to others. Having illustrated the role of perception and the concepts of role expectation, performance and satisfaction, we see that unless and until there is a consensus that in fact the individual has performed according to expectations, he is said to be non-competent. Therefore, competency is both individual satisfaction as well as satisfaction of the others in the situation. When there is lack of competence, the individual personality through consecutive destabilising events begins, especially in early adolescence, to experience a lack of congruence between the self, ideal images and social orientation. Therefore, this dissonance affects his self-esteem (Smart and Smart, 1970: 107–15). Thus we see that there is an inverse relationship between social competence and social failure.

Competence has been studied in situ by a set of ethnographic analyses, as to what factors correlate with the adjustment of children in family occupational strategies where families as a collective of members are all engaged in the family occupation. Children are taught skills or they learn them by the process of observing and imitating. Using ethnographic methods, several interesting findings emerge. In studies by Anandalakshmy and Bajaj, children of illiterate potters and weavers (whether rural, urban or semi-urban) learnt their family's occupational tasks through observation and informal teaching. The tasks show that boys view occupation as a goal, while girls look upon the tasks as a process of socialisation (Anandalakshmy, 1978; Anandalakshmy and Bajaj, 1981). Competence has four aspects:

- perception of a task (mental or physical);
- mental and physical traits for its accomplishment;
- visualisation of the end product and strategies for its successful completion;
- heightened cue grasp of the totality of the perceived situation, called intuition in layman terms.

Pre-visualisation as to how a task should be accomplished better prepares a person for competence (namely precognition of the steps), which is less difficult than being exposed to the situation where there are many unknown factors and the individual is caught 'unawares'. This precognition also includes perception of clarity of role in relation to standards of behaviour (verbalised or non-verbalised). Therefore, non-clarity of role and its various aspects of the tasks to be performed in the eyes of others more or less leads to confusion and loss of confidence and self-esteem (Smart and Smart, 1970: 107–15). We see this behaviour in school children whose parents have high expectations of their performance on stage and who suffer loss of self-esteem when they do not perform according to expectations. In a study on parental expectations, it was found that a person who was frequently and consistently underacting in the role expected of him either due to a lack of knowledge, lack of empathy or lack of responsibility eventually moved in a downward spiral. This spiral was composed of conflict, guilt, high anxiety, and in a sense could lead to psychoneurosis. Understanding the needs of the others leads to monitoring and modifying one's own needs. When the perceptions of the individual and the others are incompatible or dissonant, then, cognitively, the individual can realign his perceptions and related action to harmonise the situation and to create a positive atmosphere. On the other hand, he can persist in being deliberately in dissonance with the situation and therefore aggravates the incompatibility. This attribute or trait for empathic cue perception is pivotal in role behaviour (Hassan, 1989). For instance, a leader is one who can competently gauge needs and aspirations of others in his group to find common strategies and goals through participation with others. But when the leader persists in emphasising his own egocentric ideas, incompatibility and dissonance ensue, destabilising the congruence of goals in the team. This takes us once again back to the concept of spirit of teamwork, for it implies further that a perceptive interpersonal 'perceiver' will know how and when to modulate his needs and strategies to be in unison with those of others within a cultural context (Sinha, 1997: 218–35).

Thus, there are two sides to the coin: competence as viewed by the inner self, and competence as viewed by others. Hence the importance of interpersonal perception in assessing competence not only in terms of one's ontogenetic ability but also 'in the eyes of others'. Ontogenetic abilities imply the competence achieved through self-development such as the competence in skiing, in acrobatics, the operation of computer techniques and so on. The perception of others as regards the perceived competence of an individual is often tangential to the perception of the individual about his abilities. We see this commonly exhibited when children interact with each other. One child may, for instance, dare another to jump over a wall, to tease a dog or steal fruit from the neighbour's tree. The perception of the boy who is thus challenged evolves into a process of self-evaluation where he weighs the pros and cons of his ability. If he has less confidence in his ability, he may back away. If he has a realistic perception of his ability, he may attempt the dare. At the same time, if he is apprehensive but still wishes to attempt the dare, he may take a risk.

In such situations of dual or heterogeneous interaction, there are occasions where stimuli evoke the abilities to be tested. It might also just happen, for instance, a child who studies hard for his exam but fails may perceive thus: (a) he did his best; (b) he was going to fail anyway; (c) he was undervalued. Most children in school have to gauge how they accomplish their school tasks and go through a process, therefore, of self-evaluation of internal competence which might be a mismatch with the perception of the teacher, the parent, the peer group and the relatives. Thus we arrive at the concept of interpersonal competence.

Interpersonal competence is based on genetically imbedded potentialities contributing to self-esteem. Components in the interpersonal competence stated by Foote and Cotrell (1955) are mental health, intelligence implying cue grasp, empathy or the degree to which one identifies with the other, autonomy or the degree to which the individual is free to associate with the others with no hindrances, judgement or knowing which areas are high profiled and creativity or the will to use new innovative thinking in the interactional process (Kagitcibasi, 2002: 1–6).

The individual living in a human environment composed of various strands of inter-action, which are culturally tinged, either develops an ability to relate successfully to these various strands in a harmonious way or is in conflict with them. What are these various strands of interaction? These various strands are relationships in the group of which the individual is a member. Sociologically speaking, these groups are those in which the individual grows from childhood through adulthood into old age. But these are not static groups; they themselves are constantly changing and dynamically arrange and rearrange themselves as the individual goes through his own lifespan. The child moves from a one-to-one relation with his nurturant or mother surrogate, and then to several in the family network, whether it is nuclear or joint. The situations in the social context of rituals, feasts, marriages, critical events like birth and death are normatively those where the kin group is the 'proximal' source of interaction. The child constructs his environment in relation to his sense of homeostasis with this proximal group (Markus and Cross, 1990: 576–608). Schools, offices and public places like markets are sources of 'distal' interaction. The individual carries layers of experiences which he cognitively selects in the interaction with different groups. For instance, when playing football he uses one set of experiences such as the rules of the game and when he moves to his family situation, he uses a different set of experiences, namely interacting with family members, again differently. As a father, with his child, he uses a subset of experiences in caring for the child, with his parents he acts with respect and accommodates their views, and so on. The individual attempts simultaneously to harmonise his interaction between one group and another (Nobert, 1991). For instance, as a primary school child, he would like to play with his friends during off school hours but then he is required to finish his homework, or to do some household chores. The more deprived the ecology, the greater the demand on the growing child to participate and contribute to family work. In this process of fitting the 'self' to the situation, the individual tends to review or reassess himself in relation to his needs and the facilities in the environment which could meet his needs (Epstein, 1988: 61–69). Nonetheless, he has to juxtapose his time to accomplish the tasks expected of him in each differing role. Frequently some role tasks suffer and disharmony occurs. In biological terms we call this lack of homeostasis, but in the world of human relationships this is called conflict, a conflict of interests when it comes to perceiving a particular behaviour from the others' point of view. There is an imbalance. The energy force in a human being directs him to find a sense of well-being or success in dealing with human relationships (Hurrelmann, 1995). As the individual proceeds to become a young executive or a worker in a factory or even a shop assistant, in management terms he is required to achieve a consumer-friendly or client-friendly relationship. This is all the more important when his profession depends on a one-to-one relationship, whether he is a salesman, a doctor or a lawyer. Most corporate organisations have a professional HRD cell where the main task is to develop the interpersonal abilities of their staff for the success of their outputs. A successful salesman is required to have certain characteristics. To paraphrase Shakespeare: 'Some are born with them, some acquire them and some have them thrust upon them' (Markels, 1964), meaning that few have the inborn tendency of being successful in human relationships. The disposition has to be cultivated in order to acquire the characteristics for dealing successfully with others (Drury, 1989). As the child grows into an adult, he has to learn successfully how to cope with family and work demands. He is increasingly involved in the chronological needs of the cycle of marriage, births and even deaths. Thus, we see that embedded deep within these characteristics are three concepts: the concept of acuity of perception, the concept of practice or repetition and the concept of being disposed towards understanding of others or the sense of empathy as distinct from the sense of sympathy. Overriding all these is the growing realisation that to be able to do all these successfully there is a requirement of accurate role perception and self-competence (Paranjpe, 1975; Roland, 1987). In formal situations of operating towards competence, which means being successful in attainment of a task whether it is in combination with others like being a member of a team in a debating competition or whether it is an individual task, the expectation of the self and that of others may be dissonant or congruent. There are, in this context, several aspects: (*a*) The perception of the self's competence in a particular situation/task/event; (*b*) the perception of others in the situation where the individual is attempting to be competent; (*c*) the dynamic criss-crossing of the perception of each other in quick succession in that situation. For example, in a cricket match where the bat is being flexed by the batsman for the incoming bowler's delivery, the perception of the batsman is a quick view of his own capacity to be competent before even attempting to hit the ball. He also perceives the intention of the bowler even before the ball is thrown. At that time, each, namely the bowler and the batsman, sizes up the other's competence to achieve.

The Perception of Self-competence in a Particular Situation/Task/Event

Interpersonal perception is the way an individual intercepts the perception of the other to encode the other's perception. He (the individual) pre-empts the anticipated barriers by expecting their occurrence, and cognitively assesses his chances of success in dealing with the situation/task/event to overcoming these barriers. For instance, when there are more than two individuals competing in the same situation/task/event, and the outcome is successful for one and not the other, it indicates that the person who has a higher cue grasp prepares himself beforehand mentally. He usually maps out different alternatives, using a maximum sense of cue perception and a preparation of the self-resources. The actual interpersonally perceived situation is dynamically interpreted, much like players in games of sport. The more acutely the individual observes the situation/task/event, and encodes the required behaviour, the greater is the probability of accomplishing his goal. Again, the larger the number of interactions, the greater the probability of increasing his misconception.

The accomplishment of a task in interpersonal relations is successfully correlated to the strength of the motivation to achieve. The ability to be competent cannot exist without a prerequisite of this motivation to achieve (Mehta and Mehta, 1974: 320–36). The ability to accomplish, to be competent, to achieve successfully is also related to self-esteem. Self-esteem/self-confidence is an important factor for being an optimal individual (Husain, 1974: 100–108). At the same time, individuals in collectivistic societies such as India are expected to use their skills to promote collective well-being. Perhaps in eastern societies which encourage group or collective behaviour, forms of aggression or egocentric behaviour are discouraged, as they lead to misperceptions of positive relations in family and other group situations (Ho, 1986: 1–37).

From the time the child is able to comprehend the identities of those around him in his family environment, he is gradually inducted into what sociologists call 'role perception', 'role performance' and 'role expectation' in the different situations he experiences as he grows chronologically. One can link this to a football team. Every player knows what his position is, what he is expected to do, and if he perceives this expectation accurately, he is likely to perform to the best of his ability in the roles expected of him. Perceptual ability depends upon several innate tendencies. It is the alertness of the individual to stimuli around him. To a large extent this is dependent upon the genetic make-up of the individual and his opportunities (Mishra, 2000: 94–150). For instance, it is common to observe that some people do not have much of a perception of their surroundings. They tend to be focussed only on one object. There is little ability to visually perceive many objects in the field and to size up the relation of one to another. A highly cued cognitive perceptual ability is an attribute one would find in leaders, administrators, organisers and those in charge of large-scale enterprises. They intuitively have the ability to perceive people in relation to each other and to the objective of the group, while others are unable to make these linkages and therefore perform poorly. The concept of performance in competence is the key to acuity of perception and the level of related and functional skills.

We see in our everyday life that people may have a high level of education but in performance in interpersonal situations, they have a poor cue grasp and perception of other's abilities. We therefore need to specify what types of competencies originate from inner dispositions when we say a person is a born leader or when competence is painstakingly acquired through learning processes. One type of competence is skill at expected physical tasks which can be observed. It also implies the use of cognitive processes (Cole and Bruner, 1971: 867–76). For instance, a mathematician who is skilled will provide exceptional mathematical ability. But it is difficult to assess whether this is an innate capacity or a learned capacity. All that is obvious is a skilled physical performance. A second type is the skill of interpersonal relations wherein the accomplished individual is, so to speak, 'an accomplished diplomat'. The concept of diplomacy implies a high cue perception of the situation in which the individual interacts verbally or non-verbally to convey an ideal impression. The third is an ability to use language and gestures couched in terms that are intended to raise the ego of the other and deflate the limitations of the other. The fourth is the competence to be able, through experience or rehearsals, to predict the outcome. In other words, a socially competent individual is able to do an empirical exercise in predicting the outcome of an interaction.

The origin of competence is a phylogenetic ability, which can be ontogenetically processed, namely, the potential through opportunity is used by the individual. It is through the process of socialisation, that competence in skill and performance in interpersonal relationships occur in early childhood where the foundations are laid (Anandalakshmy, 1975). The individual encodes, codes and decodes the experiences to fit into his repertoire of knowledge. For instance, an individual wakes up in fear at a flash of lightning; it is followed by thunder, which is also frightening. With several such similar occurrences the individual becomes competent in learning to curb his fear, as each episode does not have a consequent disaster. It could act the other way if an incident of lightning and thunder is followed by someone near and dear struck by lightning. No matter how many following episodes are harmless, the fright still remains. The depth of the trauma is always perceived as the constant fear of an object to be avoided. In an ecology which is arid and deprived of much human contact, as in nomadic groups, the individual deals with few people and lives in a vast desert with a few oases. He is likely to be more competent in his knowledge about his nomadic community, than in the ways of the city life. Take for instance the urban slums in the large cities of India. Children grow up learning to make do with little. People are living cheek by jowl, and because there is little space, interaction grows in a binomial manner. There are many possibilities for miscommunications, and the struggle for basic necessities like water often ends in social disorganisation till things are patched up and the cycle begins again. In such a situation, competence for dealing with deprived conditions is a paramount attribute (Sinha, 1976: 167–200).

Perceptual ability in the psychosocial sense depends upon important attributes governing physical acuity (Csikszentmihalyi, 1993). The first is the range of objects in the field of perception, the second is the individual's selectivity of a single perceived object and the third is the deductions made from the perception dependent upon the objective (Taylor, 1948: 3–12). The range of visual perception is necessary for the individual to make deductions dependent upon the objective. If an individual is listening to a discussion of which he is the audience, he is trying to make meaning of what is said, he observes the verbal and body language, while simultaneously listening to the content of what is said. He decodes the meaning of what is said by the speaker, and selectively deduces for himself the meaning and import of what is said through oral/facial expressions. This attribute of bias for or against is important in perception, for either bias in favour of or bias against can distort the factual meaning of what is said. One excellent example is rumour and gossip, as what is expressed is taken out of context of the original happening. Since the incident is in relation to the individual's own interest/feelings, he may be biased in his auditory perception in picking up what appeals to him and discarding that which does not. He may have a feeling of bias against the speaker/s and therefore most of what is said by the speakers is deduced in a negative manner. Another attribute of perception is the individual's own knowledge of the contextual reference. If he is a chemistry student, and is listening to information on the unconscious in psychology, he may find it difficult to interpret the information. In such a case his perception is tangential, and the ability of the individual to comprehend accurately and deal with it is minimised. Notwithstanding the perceptive attributes, the utilisation of these attributes in the appropriate context and time by the appropriate person or persons is what makes the perceiver competent. Therefore competence is that skill where given a depth of perceptual ability, an individual deals with his human environment to the best possible advantage, mainly to him, and those who concern him. The reader may be able to perceive that this acuity of perception and successful ability to deal with situations, simple or complex, arises out of the development of leadership skills. Among the skills which leaders are usually expected to possess, is the skill/competence (*a*) to understand the problem, (*b*) to find appropriate solutions to the problems in an organisational milieu and (*c*) to comprehend that this is not a lone task but arises in collaboration with others (Merei 1958: 522–31). A non-authoritarian personality is tolerant of ambiguity, is flexible and will attempt to incorporate the views of others, while an authoritarian personality is dominating and inflexible, discards others' points of view, is egocentric and rigid in his perception. Such a personality tends to ignore the spirit of teamwork (Adorno et al., 1950).

The term 'teamwork' is a simplistic explanation of the individual's inner interaction of the id, the ego and superego. The ego is self-motivated, where the individuals use the strategy that is most complementary to themselves. There are various degrees of egocentric behaviour such as 'exhibitionism' or showing off in a group situation. In the case of such an individual, he himself details his skills and prowess, boasts of his achievements and so on. These attempts subconsciously either belittle the listeners who feel that they are inferior to the individual or think poorly of him because they can see through his veneer of arrogance. Thus while some may admire him others may resent him, but most would be indifferent. This does not indicate competence in dealing with others, and misperceptions may occur. It only alienates others and may, in fact, lead to disharmony and non-productivity (Brusson, 1985). Therefore, competence also means a realisation of the capabilities of others, acknowledging them and utilising them towards a common goal. Competence implies an accurate perception of the roles of others and their contribution, and therefore the combined effort of those in the particular situation involved in the successful output (Broughton, 1967).

The individual either develops a competence to relate successfully to these various strands in a harmonious way or is in conflict with them, as said before. What are these various strands of interaction? Sociologically speaking, these are interactions with the various groups (families/ colleagues/relations/leisure-time friends) within one's own habitat and those across various states and now, in the context of globalisation, with different countrymen. The individual interacts to a large or small extent with other individuals in these groups. Each group has a separate context and non-verbalised, habituated patterns interaction, and formal or informal rules of such interaction. In a family one can informally tease, quarrel and make up with family members. In a formal group one cannot act in such a fashion without disapproval, and in some cases ostracism may occur. These actions however are not static like pegs in a pegboard, but are constantly changing and dynamically arranging and rearranging themselves at various times and places in various contexts. For instance, the brother can bully his little sister while having dinner in a home situation but when he is present at her marriage performing ceremonies in the *pandal* (dias used for marriage/formal function) he is expected to behave formally with her. As a young child, the individual begins to move from one relational network to another, gathering experiences of how to act and react within each group. The child in India is frequently exposed to events that are familial in nature like religious, cultural and family events. At births, deaths, marriages, festivals and national holidays, families tend to meet each other in a familial social context. It is somewhat mandatory that one visits or is visited by relatives and friends during Diwali and Dussehra, which are based on religious events. The child then moves further into the concentric circle of the peer group, which is added on to the family and kin group. In this context he has to switch on and off the characteristics of different roles, to deal competently both with informal and formal environments. These bring out his competence to deal with both successfully without contradiction in his perception. If the individual does not develop the competence, failure occurs in such experiences. Again, it is to be noted that in the Indian context, children live in various ecologies, some which are highly populated and call upon several types of interpersonal dealings. Each culture, each subculture within a culture, differs however slightly from the other in the perception of interactive behaviour. These perceptions are based on norms such as religious beliefs, patterns of ethics, morality and justice. Theoretical concepts are built up as hypotheses of behaviour, to describe the interactions of a given social group or a society (Graue and Walsh, 1998).

In some communities, as in isolated tribal areas in sparse ecologies, there is little interaction, except with the family and the village community. Thus, the more deprived the ecology, the more intensive is the individual's perception with smaller groups of human beings. By deduction he is not required to display interpersonal success with larger and various groups as is the urban child. For the urban child lives in an ecology with various kinds of people and situations, and therefore these increase his repertoire of differential interpersonal perceptions. In remote ecologies individuals live in routine and unchanging environments, as exists with the Paharis of Himachal or the tribals in Yelamanchilli forests of Andhra Pradesh. On the one hand, there is the socio-biological homeostasis with the tribal, and on the other hand is the technological dynamism of the urban setting.

In the interactive process, a tendency exists to align thinking and action with the egalitarian concept of justice distributed according to merits, very much like the codes and laws of a perfectly working legal system. Krishnan in an analytical discussion expands on the meaning of justice from the social point of view (Krishnan, 2000). She presents the traditional Hindu view of justice, and underscores the fact that religious beliefs about justice are pervasive among Indians, even those who are not Hindus, since they share the same cultural norms. Social justice from the indigenous point of view is most revealing. There is no one treatise in Indian scriptures, which deals exclusively with justice, but there are gleanings from several such as the Ramayana, the Mahabharata, the dharmashastras Manusmriti and Arthashastra. *Vyavahara* (behaviour in the social context) is distinct from *achara* (prescribed moral conduct) and *nyaya* (justice or fairness) (Dutt, 1979). Justice or fairness has been interpreted by sages throughout the centuries but with no underpinnings of empirical data as science knows it, which in the Indian context is also scarce. In a study, comparisons on the allocation of rules or preferences between equality and merit (equity and need) were studied. Need was highly profiled in the Indian subjects, and equity in the Americans (Berman et al., 1985). In another study by Misra, females showed more maturity in allocation of reward and punishment for moral behaviour than males (Misra, 1991). Justice is said to be an expression of *neeti* (policy or moral ethical codes). These are the sayings of authoritative interpreters of the scriptures and have been enjoined in discourses, *bhajans*, *kirtans* and *satsangs* and are therefore oral traditions. Such occurrences in the work-a-day world, especially of urban and technologically minded families, are becoming scarce. These traditional concepts still exist. On the other hand, modernising families are becoming more attuned to the egocentric rather than the socio-centric orientation that governs interpersonal competence. Some find a medium between the two, which again typifies the Indian psyche, which can be flexible according to the needs of the situation. In interpersonal relationships, there is a great need for ego satisfaction in order to experience a sense of accomplishment whether it is convincing a dissenting person, or cajoling a person to do what the individual would like him to do. In the case of non-achievement or non-success when dealing with human beings, there is often an impact on self-esteem, and in cases where there is conflict the person is unable to solve the problem or bring about a resolution, and loses confidence and esteem in himself, which colours perception (Kitayama, 2003). However, it is important to identify the cultural domains of childhood as foundational to our understanding of the parameters of growing up and the context of perception (Roland et al., 1976). These domains are:

(i) space and interaction within the household and outside the household: family interactional processes;

(ii) orientation past/present/future: these different orientations intensify generational disjointedness and the status quo of the known in relation to the unknown;

(iii) continuity and discontinuity;

(iv) family and work ethic;

(v) changing family composition;

(vi) transient and migrating families;

(vii) mobility shifts.

These parameters are in close dynamic interactions, sometimes being highlighted by one set of combination and at other times by others. In a nuclear family, for instance, there are fewer interactions per space and per time than in a joint family household. This leads to a situation of imbalance between the individual's perception of need and the strategies used to fulfil his needs. What is it that directs an individual to fulfil a need? Learning theory states that the individual responds to stimuli and that the process itself is a change either in thought or action or both. Because of his gregarious nature, the human being motivates himself to respond to the stimulus of another individual. What is it that impels him? It is the energy force in a human being which directs him to find a sense of well-being and success, to extricate from the situation those responses which satisfy him. The individual as an entity in the family is simultaneously and interactively influenced by three axes: (*a*) his sociopsychological state of development; (*b*) the development of social history embedded in sociological customs and conventions with which he is familiar; (*c*) the existence of an identifiable cultural context.

The extension of the self delves deeper into the context of social history, and his place as an individual in it, in an interconnected manner. As an adult, he can trace his lineage, and, perhaps, his genealogical tree. If one were to ask an elderly person living in north India about his antecedents, he will most likely tell you that his grandfather or great-grandfather came from what is today Pakistan, that they came with nothing, and that they worked the hard way to become what they are. This is his past orientation. In this way, the interconnectiveness of his perception is framed with the present and future orientations. His movement towards homeostasis with his environment is based on the strengths and limitations of his perception, and the positive or negative effects from the environment. These perceptions from the viewpoint of society relate to his developmental goals, which are transmitted through cultural channels of communication.

Let us give some examples. A child of five or six, for instance, perceives very little about his connection with the wide world around him. His chronological age permits him, with his small quota of experiences, to be able to operate within a restricted environment of experiences. He perceives limited geographical spaces—house, roads, market, school—and little of other countries or peoples or their habits. The state of his development limits his capacities. The state of social history refers to the past heritage, which he possesses: his origins, his lineage, the relatives and friends around him circumscribe his world. An adult is more able to describe his world than a child. As an adult, he may have read, or travelled, known others and had experiences with them in interaction, to the extent that he recognises how different their customs and habits are in contrast to his world. He has an increasing world perception as he grows older. The vegetarian Indian says to a Chinese: 'how can you eat rotten eggs' (a delicacy). The Chinese can say to the Indian: 'how can you eat curdled milk' (yoghurt), and so on. The Australian eats kangaroo's steak. The Japanese eat raw fish, the Ethiopians eat raw meat, and in some remote Indian tribes beetles are commonly eaten. Thus is the individual who is well informed who perceives others as different and does not judge them in relation to himself as higher or lower human beings. Further when an individual accumulates experiences of living in several countries over a period of time, he meets with people who are different culturally. If, for instance, an Indian has to work in France, he attends French classes. If an Indian lives for a while in an African country, he at least knows by minimal communication what to say for 'How are you?', 'Can I go to the market?', 'What is the price of this?', and so on. He extends his perception to other cultures and therefore by contrast perceives his culture more definitively. He says 'in my country we do this in a different way', or he learns to appreciate vegetarian food while living in a country of 'non-vegetarian' food habits. He holds on closely to his identity and therefore stabilises himself as being an Indian, as different from others.

What we are attempting to illustrate is that in the process of growing up into an adult, the person through various perceptions assembles concepts of differences and similarities among peoples/situations. We find that the acuity of interpersonal perception grows by such repeated experiences, which then qualifies the individual to deal adeptly with people of varying types. In the context of social interaction, it must be underscored that given the different types of personalities, each one emphasises particularly dominant traits (Lindzey, 1998: 1–20). Some exhibit authoritarianism, others submissiveness; some may be extroverts, others introverts; some may be obsessive speakers, others may be silent listeners. As the saying goes 'it takes all kinds to make a world' and an individual who is perceptive in an empathetic way, is more likely to find harmony and equilibrium than one who is unfeeling and non-empathetic. At the same time, it is essential to remember that empathy can very easily turn to irrationality. One can empathise with another person's trauma but if he loses objectivity then he is not dealing with the situation competently.

The reader will perceive by now that interpersonal competence is closely related to developmental goals of groupism. If the Indian society prefers to bring up children to share, to cooperate, to give and to be compassionate (a conglomerate of concepts which operationalise interdependency), then Indians are reared to show these traits. If the Indian is brought up on the socio-religious values of 'ahimsa' (non-violence), tolerance, acceptance of differences, and advocating 'samjhota' (compromise), and to learn from childhood not to be quarrelsome, not to be physically rough, and to forgive, then these actions are more along the path of non-aggressiveness. Non-aggressiveness is said to be similar to submissiveness and lack of definitiveness of the personality. In reality it connotes the finesse with which the Indian can play many different roles in any sequence. He is deferential to his boss and says 'yes sir' to him during office hours. He is authoritarian with his children, and rebukes them severely for making a noise when he is at home. He can chastise his wife for not cooking a good dinner. He can be obsequious to his father from whom he wants to borrow money, and he can be a rough comrade with his drinking friends. He can switch from one role to another in quick succession and there may be varied interpretations of roles by others' differential perceptions (Ramanujam, 1994). There are several illustrations in daily life; for instance, when an accident occurs people gather around and everyone who gets involved in the explanation of how the accident happened will give different interpretations according to their differential perceptions.

The ability to overcome obstacles, to find direction to life's processes, is linked with goals, engendered in socialisation. Knowledge of the self is an epistemological concept, dealing with the philosophical and psychoanalytical connotation of the 'Who am I?' question. As such, it is a spiritual understanding, and is, therefore, in the Indian context close to the understanding of the atman, and its correlates. Thus, as an individual the Indian is able to compartmentalise himself into various categories without compromising his identity (Marriot, 1976) as he is able to identify himself on the spiritual, the psychological, the social and, most importantly, the philosophical planes without discord. This is not to say that the Indian is able to do so neatly. Often, there is conflict and inability to resolve the conflict. It is reasonable to assume that with the pressures in the modern world, the Indian psyche has to cope with many more divergences than the individual from the West. Perhaps, the major difference is that the Indian tries to equalise his perception to harmonise his needs and feelings with that of the human world around him, whereas with the westerner, the coping mechanisms have to deal more probably with many more competing 'others'.

References

Adorno, T.W., B. Frenkel, E. Runswik, D.J. Levinson and P.N. Sanford, 1950, *The Authoritarian Personality.* New York: Harper.

Alexander, C.N. and R.W. Bower, 1989, 'Seven States of Consciousness: Unfolding the Full Potential of the Cosmic Psyche through Maharishi's Vedic Psycholopgy', *Modern Science and Vedic Science*, 2(4): 325–71.

Allport, G.W., 1920, 'The Influence of the Group upon Association and Thought', *Journal of Experimental Psychology*, 3: 159–82.

———, 1943, 'The Ego in Contemporary Psychology', *Psychological Review*, 50: 451–78.

Altman, I. and B. Rogoff, 1987, 'World Views in Psychology: Trait, Interactional, Organismic and Transactional Perspectives', in D. Stokols and I. Altman (eds), *Handbook of Environmental Psychology, Vol. 1.* New York: John Wiley.

Anandalakshmy, S. and M. Bajaj, 1981, 'Childhood in the Weavers' Community in Varanasi: Socialisation for Adult Roles', in D. Sinha (ed.), *Socialisation of the Indian Child.* New Delhi: Concept.

Anandalakshmy, S., 1975, 'Socialisation for Competence', in J.W. Berry and W.J. Loner (eds), *Applied Cross-cultural Psychology.* Amsterdam: Swertz and Zeitlinger.

———, 1978, 'Socialisation for Competence', Paper presented at the International Symposium on Agressive Behaviour at AIIMS, New Delhi.

Arasteh, A.R., 1980, *Growth to Selfhood: The Sufi Contribution.* London: Routledge and Kegan Paul.

Archer, S.E., C.D. Kelly and S.A. Bisch, 1984, 'Social Indicators', in S.E. Archer (eds), *Implementing Change in Communities: A Collaborative Process.* St. Louis: C.V. Mosby Company.

Aristotle, 1998, *Neomachean Ethics*. New York: Courier Dover Publications.

Bailey, F.G., 1957, *Caste and the Economic Frontier*. Manchester. Manchester University Press.

Bandura, A., 1969, *Principles of Behaviour Modification*. New York: Holt Rinehart and Winston.

Barker, R.G., 1968, *Ecological Psychology*. Stanford: Stanford University Press.

Bassa, D.M., 1978, 'From the Traditional to the Modern: Some Observations on the Changes in Indian Child Rearing and Parental Attitudes, with Special Reference to Identity Formation (The Toddler Period)', in E.J. Anthony and C. Koupernik (eds), *The Child in His Family, Children and their Parents in a Changing World*, Vol. 5. New York: Wiley Interscience.

Berman, J.J., V. Murphy-Berman and P. Singh, 1985, 'Cross-cultural Similarities and Differences in Perception of Fairness', *Journal of Cross-cultural Psychology*, 16: 55–67.

Bharati, A., 1983, 'India South Asian Perspectives on Aggression', in A.P. Goldstein and M.H. Segall (eds), *Aggression in Global Perspective*. New York: Pergamon Press.

———, 1985, 'The Self in Hindu Thought and Action', in A.J. Marsella, G. Devos and F.L.K. Hsu (eds), *Culture and Self: Asian and Western Perspective*. New York: Tavistock Publications.

Broughton, J.M., 1967, 'Piaget's Concept of the Self', in P. Young-Eisendrath and J.A. Hall (eds), *The Book of the Self, Person Pretext and Process*. New York: University Press.

Brusson, N., 1985, *The Irrational Organisation*. Chichester: John Wiley.

Chakraborty, U. and J. Basu, 1994, 'Relationship of Parental Gender Role Stereotype with Children's Gender Role Identity', *Samiksa*, 48(1&2): 1–8.

Chaudhry, N. and I. Kaura, 2004, 'Approaching Privacy and Selfhood through Narratives', *Psychological Studies*, 46(3): 132–40.

Cole, M. and S. Bruner, 1971, 'Cultural Inferences about Psychological Processes', *American Psychologist*, 26: 867–76.

Csikszentmihalyi, M., 1993, *The Evolving Self*. New York: Harper Collins.

Darling, N. and L. Steinberg, 1993, 'Parenting Styles as Context: An Integrative Model', *Psychology Bulletin*, 113(3): 487–96.

Darwin, C., 1859, *On the Origin of Species by Means of Natural Selection in the Preservation of Favoured Races in the Struggle for Life*. London: John Murray.

De Vos, G.A., 1968, 'Achievement and Innovation in Culture and Personality', in E. Norbeck, D. Price-William and W.H. McCord (eds), *The Study of Personality: Interdisciplinary Appraisal*. New York: Rinehart and Winston.

Dhawan, N., I.J. Roseman, R.K. Naidu, K. Thapa and S. Ilsa Rettek, 1995, 'Self Concepts across Two Cultures', *Journal of Cross-cultural Psychology*, November, 26(6): 606–26.

Drury, N., 1989, *The Elements of Human Potential*. Shaftesbury: Element Books.

Durham, W.H., 1991, *Co-Evolution: Genes, Culture and Human Diversity*. Stanford: Stanford University Press.

Dutt, M.N., 1979, *The Dharmashastras: Hindu Religious Codes, Vols 1 and 4*. New Delhi: Cosmo Publications.

Earley, C.P. and C.B. Gibson, 1998, 'Taking Stock in Our Progress on Individualism/Collectivism: 100 Years of Solidarity and Community', *Journal of Management*, 24(3): 265–305.

Epstein, M., 1988, 'The Deconstruction of the Self, Ego and Egolessness in Buddhist Insight Mediation', *Journal of Transpersonal Psychology*, 20: 61–69.

Erikson, E., 1951, *Childhood and Society*. London: Imago Publishing Co.

Erikson, E.H., 1959, *Identity and the Life Cycle*. New York: International University Press.

Festinger, L., 1957, *A Theory of Cognitive Dissonance*. Stanford: Stanford University Press.

Foote, N.N. and L.S. Cotrell Jr, 1955, *Identity and Interpersonal Competence*. Chicago: University of Chicago Press.

Freud, S., 1935, *General Introduction to Psychoanalysis*. New York: Liveright.

Gergen, K.J., 1971, *The Concept of Self*. New York: Holt Reinhart and Wolsen.

Graue, M.E. and D.J. Walsh, 1998, *Studying Children in Context: Theories, Methods and Ethics*. Thousand Oaks, CA: Sage.

Greenwald, A.G. and A.R. Pratkanis, 1984, 'The Self', in R.S. Wyer Jr and T.K. Srull (eds), *Handbook of Social Cognition*, Vol. 3. Hillsdale, NJ: Lawrence Erlbaum.

Gupta, R.K. and A. Panda, 2003, 'Individualized Familial Self: The Evolving Self of Qualified Technocrats in India', *Psychology and Developing Societies*, 15: 1–29.

Harris, H., (ed.), 1995, *Identity*. Oxford: OUP.

Harter, S., 1988, 'The Construction and Conservation of the Self: James and Cooley Revisited', in D.K. Lepsley and F.C. Power (eds), *Self, Ego, and Identity: Integrative Approaches*. New York: Springer-Verlag.

Hassan, A., 1989, *Dynamics of Leadership Effectiveness in Indian Work Organisations*. New Delhi: Commonwealth Publishers.

Heider, F., 1958, *The Psychology of Interpersonal Relationships*. New York: John Wiley.

Hentschel, U., G. Smith, J.G. Draguns and W. Ehlers, 2004, *Defence Mechanisms: Theoretical, Research and Clinical Perspectives (Advances in Psychology)*. Amsterdam: Elsevier.

Hiriyanna, M., 1932, *The Essentials of Indian Philosophy*. London: George Allen and Unwin.

———, 1952, *Popular Essays in Indian Philosophy*. Mysore: Kavyalaya.

Hirsch, E., 1982, *The Concept of Identity*. Oxford: OUP.

Ho, D.Y.F., 1986, 'Chinese Patterns of Socialisation: A Critical Review', in M.H. Bond (ed.), *The Psychology of Chinese People*. Hong Kong: OUP.

Hofstede, G., 1991, 'I, We and They', in G. Hofstede, *Cultures and Organisations*. London: Harper McGraw Hill International.

Horney, K., 1939, *New Ways in Psychoanalysis*. New York: Norton.

Hume, R.E., 1931, *The Thirteen Principles: Upanishads*, 2nd edn. Oxford: OUP.

Hurrelmann, K., 1995, *Einfuhrung in die sizialisationstheorie: Uber den Zusammenhang von Sozialstruktur und Personlichkeit*, 5th edn. Vienna, Basel: Beltz Verlag.

Husain, B., 1974, 'Achievement Motivation and Self-esteem: A Cross Cultural Study', *Indian Journal of Psychology*, 9(2): 100–08.

Kagitcibasi, C., 1996, 'The Autonomous–Relational Self', *European Psychologist*, 1: 180–86.

———, 2002, 'Autonomy, Embeddedness and Adaptability in Immigration Contexts: A Commentary', *Human Development*, 20: 1–6.

Kak, S.C., 2000, 'On Understanding Ancient Indian Science', in A.K. Raina, B.N. Patnaik and M. Chadha (eds), *Science and Tradition*. Shimla: Indian Institute of Advanced Studies.

Kakar, S., 1991, *The Analyst and Mystic: Psychoanalytic Reflections on Religion and Mysticism*. New Delhi: Penguin.

Kane, V.P., 1941, *History of Dharmashastras, Samskaras, Vol. II*, Part I. Poona: Bhandarkar Oriental Research Institute.

Kant, I., 1929, *Critique of Pure Reason* (trans. by N. Kemp Smith). New York: St. Mertin's Press.

Kaviraj, S., 1995, 'Religion, Politics and Modernity', in U. Baxi (ed.), *Crisis and Change in Contemporary India*. New Delhi: Sage.

Keller, H., 2003, 'Persönlichkeit und Kultur', in A. Thomas (ed.), *Kulturvergleichende Psychologie* (2. Aufl., S. 181–205). Göttingen: Hogrefe.

Kitayama, 2003, 'Culture, Self and Social Relationships', Keynote address at 'Cultures in Interaction', Regional Conference of the International Association for Cross-cultural Psychology, Budapest, 15 July.

Krishnan, L., 2000, 'Distributive Justice in the Indian Perspective', in H.S.R. Kao and D. Sinha (eds), *Asian Perspectives on Psychology*. New Delhi: Sage.

Laing, R.D., 1961, *The Self and Others*. London: Tavistock.

Laing, R.D., H. Phillipson and A.R. Lee, 1976, 'Interpersonal Perception', in J. Wolfstein (ed.), *Personality and Learning*. London: The Open University Press.

Lewis, M., 1991, 'Self-knowledge and Social Influence', in M. Lewis and S. Feinman (eds), *Social Influences and Socialisation in Infancy*. New York: Plenum.

Lindzey, G., 1998, 'The Nature of Personality Theory', in C.H Hall, J.B. Campbell and G. Lindzey (eds), *Theories of Personality*, 4th edn. New York: John Wiley.

Littlewood, R., 1999, 'Ecological Understandings and Cultural Context', *Philosophy, Psychiatry and Psychology*, 6(2): 133–34.

Lynch, O.M. (ed.), 1990, *Divine Passions: The Social Construction of Emotion in India*. Berkeley: University of California.

Markels, J., 1964, 'Shakespeare's Confluence of Tragedy and Comedy: *Twelfth Night* and *King Lear*', *Shakespeare Quarterly*, 15: 78.

Markus, H.R., 1977, 'Self-schemata and Processing Information about the Self', *Journal of Personality and Social Psychology*, 35: 63–78.

Markus, H.R. and S.E. Cross, 1990, 'The Interpersonal Self', in L.A. Pervin (ed.), *Handbook of Personaltity Theory and Research*. New York: Guilford Press.

Markus, H.R. and S. Kitayama, 1991, 'Culture and the Self: Implications for Cognition, Emotion and Motivation', *Psychological Review*, 98: 224–25.

Markus, H.R. and S. Kitayama, 1994, 'Culture and Self: How Cultures Influence the Way We View Ourselves', in D. Matsumoto (ed.), *People: Psychology from a Cultural Perspective*. Pacific Grove, CA: Brooks/Cole.

Marriot, K., 1976, 'Hindu Transactions: Diversity without Dualism', in B. Kapferer (ed.), *Transactions and Meanings: Directions in Anthropology of Exchange and Symbolic Behaviour*. Philadelphia: ISHI Publishers.

Maslow, A.H., 1970, *Religions, Values and Peak Experiences*. New York: Viking Press.

McKinney, M.L. and K.J. Namara, 1991, *Heterochrony: The Evolution of Ontogeny*. New York: Plenum.

Mead, G.H., 1934, *Mind, Self and Society*. Chicago: University of Chicago Press.

Mehta, P. and N. Mehta, 1974, 'Achievement Motive Research in India', *Indian Psychology*, 49(4): 320–36.

Menon, U., 2003, 'Morality and Context: A Study of Hindu Understandings', in J. Valsiner and K.J. Connolly (eds), *Handbook of Developmental Psychology*. Thousand Oaks, London: Sage.

Merei, F., 1958, 'Group Leadership and Institutionalisation', in E.E. Maccoby, T.M. Newcomb and E.I. Hartley (eds), *Readings in Social Psychology*, 3rd edn. New York: Henry Holt & Co.

Mesquita, B., N.H. Frijda and K.R. Scherer, 1997, 'Culture and Emotion', in J.W. Berry, P.R. Dasen and T.S. Saraswathi (eds), *Handbook of Cross-cultural Psychology*, Vol. 2, 2nd edn. Boston: Allyn & Bacon.

Mishra, R.C., 2000, 'Perceptual Learning and Memory Processes', in J. Pandey (ed.), *Psychology in India Revisited: Developments in the Discipline, Vol. 1: Physiological Foundation and Human Cognition*. New Delhi: Sage.

Misra, G., 1991, 'Socio-cultural Influences on Moral Behaviour', *Indian Journal of Social Work*, 52(2): 178–94.

Nobert, E., 1991, *The Society of Individuals*. London: Basil Blackwell, OUP.

Orme-Johnson, D.W., E. Zimmerman and M. Hawkins, 1997, 'Maharishi's Vedic Philosophy: The Science of the Cosmic Psyche' in H.S.R. Kao and D. Sinha (eds), *Asian Perspectives on Psychology*. New Delhi: Sage.

Paranjpe, A.C., 1975, *In Search of Identity*. New York: Wiley Interscience.

———, 1988, 'A Personality Theory According to Vedanta', in A.C. Paranjpe, D.Y.F. Ho and R.W. Rieber (eds), *Asian Contributions to Psychology*. New York: Praeger.

Parsons, T., 1949, *The Structure of Social Action*. Glencoe, IL: Free Press.

———, 1955, *Family, Socialisation and Interaction Process*. Glencoe, IL.: Free Press.

Patel, N. and T.G. Power, 1996, 'Socialisation Values and Practices of Indian Immigrant Parents: Correlates of Modernity and Acculturation', *Child Development*, 67: 302–13.

Ramanujam, A.K., 1994, *Folk Tales from India*. New Delhi: Penguin.

Roland, A., 1987, 'The Familial Self: The Individualised Self and the Transcendent Self: Psychoanalytic Reflections on India and America', *Psychoanalytic Review*, 74: 2377–508.

———, 1996, *Cultural Pluralism and Psychoanalysis: The Asian and North American Experience*. New York: Routledge.

Roland, W., J.R. Henderson and C.E. Bergam, 1976, *The Cultural Context of Childhood*. Columbus, OH: Merrill Publishing.

Roy, R. and R.K. Srivastava 1986, *Dialogues On Development*. New Delhi: Sage.

Russell, B., 1945, *The Problems of Philosophy*. London: OUP.

Sartor, C.E. and J. Youniss, 2002, 'The Relationship between Positive Parental Involvement and Identity Achievement during Adolescence', *Adolescence*, 37: 221–34.

Shakespeare, W., 2002, *Twelfth Night*. New York: Barron's Educational Series.

Sinha, D., 1976, 'A Study of Psychological Dimensions of Poverty: A Challenge and a Necessity', *Journal of Social and Economic Studies*, 4(1): 167–200.

Sinha, D. and H.S.R. Kao, 1997, 'The Journey to the East: An Introduction', in H.S.R. Kao and D. Sinha (eds), *Asian Perspectives on Psychology*. New Delhi: Sage.

Sinha, D. and M. Sinha, 2000, 'Orientations to Psychology, Asian and Western', in H.S.R. Kao and D. Sinha (eds), *Asian Perspectives on Psychology*. New Delhi: Sage.

Sinha, J.B.P., 1997, 'Indian Perspectives on Leadership and Power in Organisations', in H.S.R. Kao and D. Sinha (eds), *Asian Perspectives on Psychology*. New Delhi: Sage.

Smart, M.S. and R.C. Smart, 1970, 'Self-esteem and Social–Personal Orientation of Indian 12 and 18 Year Olds', *Psychological Reports*, 27(1): 107–15.

Summerton, 1979, *Of Transactional Analysis*. Delhi: Manohar.

Taylor, W.S., 1948, 'Basic Personality in Orthodox Hindu Culture Patterns', *Journal of Abnormal and Social Psychology*, 43: 3–12.

Thomas, R.M., 2001, 'Theory Trends', in R.M. Thomas, *Recent Theories of Human Development*. New Delhi: Sage.

Triandis, H.C., 1989, 'The Self and Social Behaviour in Differing Cultural Contexts', Psychological Review, 96: 506–20.

Wilson, G. and G. Ryland, 1949, *Social Group Work Practice*. Boston: Houghton Mifflin Co.

8

The Development of Critical Skills

Goal-related Skills

THE GOALS towards which the human being develops are mainly achieved through the process of socialisation. This process does not occur casually or unconsciously. Most adults' socialisation efforts are goal-directed, such as developing coping mechanisms to conform to social norms. Some of the major ones, relevant to the Indian psyche are: the reinforcement in the socialisation process to be non-aggressive; to attain a culturally accepted degree of interdependency; to be in line with role expectations and role performances of one's gender (gender differentials); and to be oriented towards the collective good of one's societal values (collectivism). But for these types of goal-directed behaviour to be reinforced by socialisers, certain crucial skills need to be developed in the young. At the same time there needs to be an inner or inherent potential for these skills in the individual. Enhancement of such skills, however, rests on two foundational bases: the maturational base and the will or the motivation to attain such skills, dependent upon the innate potentials (Rosenfels, 1978). Maturation also forms the foundation of the ability to learn and coupled with the will or the motivation to want to learn, development of these skills continues through the lifespan (ibid.). The process of learning takes place throughout the lifespan, initiated in infancy and attritioning in old age: very much like the stages of life recited by Jacques in Shakespeare's *As You Like It* (Dolan, 2000). They are encultured, and the group for whom they are reinforced derives such reinforcement through the environment which is conducive to such development (Anderson, 1995).

The development of critical skills is reinforced by the efforts of the adult socialisers of the young, and, as the individual grows, by the environment (Agarwal et al., 1987: 137–49).

They can be reinforced or otherwise by the conscious effort of a stimulating environment (human or ecological), to attain such skills along certain socially approved channels. For instance, we frequently hear: 'The parents did all they could to bring up the child the right way, but the child has turned out to be a black sheep of the family.' This implies lack of motivation on the part of the individual who is being guided or tended. What, therefore, are these critical skills? While it may be admittedly argued that there are a myriad of such skills, this chapter will limit itself to four major skills which are essential for the individual to develop towards selected goals in the individual's life and to develop coping mechanisms to attain them. Perhaps the most important skills are based on primary/secondary needs, which impel or motivate the individual to gain the means to survive. These are the primary and secondary needs described by Maslow and detailed by Murray (Maslow, 1970). If motivational levels are low or unstimulated, the basic foundation for attainment of developmental goals is adversely affected. The first and foremost skill that has the potential to be optimised is motivation and its levels. Once the individual is self-directed to achieve, other skills are more easily enhanced. A second major force or drive is the ability to optimise communication, which takes the individual along an accumulation of developmental experiences through exchange and interchange of ideas through language skills.

By and large, communication through language is the major force which when developed in the human is the highest form of interaction (Baig, 1991). As described later in this chapter, communication is essential for all forms of development: moral, spiritual, scientific and artistic. In the days of cave living, symbols on stone were the first initiated means of communication; today communication has advanced through microchip technology and cryptic codes. Thus, the development of language and the skill to use it is fundamental to the realisation of the goals of development. By itself language is not as effective as when it is impelled by man to find solutions to problems. Additively, unless there is interest and motivation to do so in all spheres of his life, the development of this skill will be less than optimum. Language is the expression of the individual's cognitive abilities and is necessary for the growth of the individual in society (Thompson, 1952).

However, neither motivation nor language abilities would be effective if man did not possess the acumen to utilise the potentials of understanding the ideas communicated. The ability to understand is based on levels of intelligence. For instance, a child who is severely mentally challenged may not follow the meaning of the language used and therefore is not amenable to guidance. In other words, an understanding of intelligence, its origin, its many functions, and its relation to environment and development are also essential for cognitive competence (Ganguly, 1988: 23–32).

Finally, we have added another skill, which in a developing country such as India is also critical for the attainment of goals. This skill is the skill for adaptive resilience, for we have pointed out how quickly the Indian has to adapt to traditionality in one situation, then change to modernity in another, and this back and forth goes on in quick succession. Given the fluctuations in availability of resources where a country has at least one-third of its population under the so-called poverty line, and where it is known that deprivation has its own dire consequences, the Indian through his unique development processes matures in coping with his meagre environment.

He does so by developing a resilience to contradictions and confrontations (Bardhan, 1970). He learns through experience that he has to make do with what he has, and to wrest the best out of his environment. He also learns to tolerate differences in caste, creed and ethnicity, and because of his deep-seated faith in fate or *karma* to accept what comes as destined.

Critical traits, which form the fulcrum of behaviour are those which are important in directing behaviour (Allport, 1966: 1–10). The traits selected here are:

- motivation to achieve;
- intelligence levels and their functioning;
- language development and its relationship to communication;
- adjustment or resilience.

Maturation for Optimisation of Skills for Development

The term maturation was popularised mainly by Gessell to connote the organic germination of brain cells to give the brain the necessary competence required at every chronological stage (Gesell, 1929: 307–19). Maturation is any change with age in the conditions of learning (formal or informal) which depend upon organic growth factors, rather than prior practice or experience (Megeoch, 1942). In other words, age-related behaviour occurs spontaneously under normal conditions of growth, like an infant who does not talk, but suddenly bursts into intelligible speech and then speaks rapidly, catching up with others of the same age. We have so far briefly highlighted the importance of key concepts of heredity, nurture and maturation. These are essential for a human being at any given age to develop optimally those skills for which he is expected to perform. For instance, an infant crawls, stands and then walks in sequence. Some children may skip a stage, but the important point to remember is that, according to the principles of maturation, progression is of essence (Johnson, 1991) Physical maturation is optimal to development, both physical and mental, from birth or even before, till adolescence when it gradually peters off. However there are two periods of rapid physical growth: one during infancy, which plateaus during the primary school years, and then sharply rises during adolescence (Frisch and Revell, 1970: 397–98). By the same token cells and tissues atrophy during old age, and the human being tends to shrink in size and in appearance. It is at the peak of adolescence that most development in terms of pubertal changes takes place. Development of primary language skills is mastered in terms of short and simple sentences during early preschool years, which occurs in most cultures (Schroeder and Gordon, 2002: 12). Such developmental milestones occur primarily in sequence but not necessarily optimally at any one time. Sometimes delays take place due to malnutrition and maladies in early years, which impede normal physical growth, such as lack of essential minerals and protein (Verma et al., 1976: 499–506). What is maturation geared towards? We have talked about the inherited genetic material in the individual, when we discussed physiological mechanisms mentioned previously (Gesell, 1946). Even before a human being begins to learn according to the societal norms, there is an organisational framework in place for reception, assimilation, coding and decoding of stimuli by internalising their meaning (Conel, 1939).

Nature and nurture have no separate identities or isolated functions (Thorpe and Schmuller, 1958: 40). They both contribute in different degrees to maturation which is two-pronged. It is observable in the extension of physical characteristics like height and weight, and similar anthropometric measures, but more importantly in the maturational processes occurring in the psychological domain. With increasing age during infancy and childhood there is a corresponding increase in the organisation of the central nervous system. Microscopic studies of the brain of deceased infants of different ages have indicated the changes which take place in the central nervous system over time (Conel, 1939). The maturation of neural tissues sets limits to a child's expected chronological behaviour. For instance, any amount of stimulation will not cause an infant to talk in sentences. In a normal environment, a child of two to three years talks in short sentences, yet if the same child is brought up by chimpanzees he would only learn their guttural and whimpering sounds. Language is the basis of communication and unless there are stimulating models, the child will not be able to express himself in the utterances of his society. These utterances occur in a systematically ordered manner as a language understood by its own cultural group. By the same token, a highly stimulating environment, especially that of the home, as studies in the Indian situation (Muralidharan, 1970) have shown, does give the child a higher level of language skills than expected. What we are saying is that the normal environment sets expected limits, but understimulation or overstimulation sets corresponding limits, which takes us to the question of intelligence. Intelligence levels are set by the genetic ability which is a combination of cue grasp of perceptive awareness and quickness in induction or deduction of a situation in terms of its premises. However, the basic level of intelligence does not rise or fall. What rises or falls is the experience accumulated and utilised through intelligent behaviour. Major disabilities from birth are mostly not repairable as the neurons connecting the brain functions, the synapses, are dysfunctional (Belfer, 2003: 131–40).

The place of genetics which was enshrouded in ambivalence in the 19th and early 20th centuries is now becoming clearer in the growing scientific knowledge of the place of innate or inherent traits. It begins with what is given to the human being in the genomes he inherits and in the innate potentials he possesses as an individual entity. The term heredity is popularly employed to describe the innate material of the individual at the time of conception. G.E. Conklin defined heredity as the continuity from generation to generation of certain elements of 'germinal organisation'. Heritage is the sum of all those qualities which are determined or caused by this 'germinal organisation' (Conklin, 1922: 134). Maturation, as defined in all textbooks in psychology, is an unfolding of what is inherent. It also implies the capacity of the human (or for that matter many of the primates and animal species) to imbibe what is perceived, and to retain, store and to recapitulate the learning when evoked by similar stimuli. In the initial stages of scientific thinking on human development two concepts assumed importance: nature and nurture, or heredity and environment. It will be recalled that phylogenetic development refers to the abilities that all human beings possess like walking, talking, and so on. Ontogeny, on the other hand, is what the individual species develops on his own like the ability of acrobats in the circus ring or the ability to produce literary achievements. These are developed through the individual's lifespan (called ontogenetic development) (Dewsbury, 1991: 198–205). On the other hand, it was thought that the cognitive sources of thinking were nascent and it required the environment through its stimulative processes to elicit cognitive thinking (Pylyshyn, 1991: 49–92). The early theorists vacillated between nativist and traditionalist sources of thinking in human development. Later on, however, these became encapsulated into one thinking, so that at any given time in the product of thinking behaviour, the two may operate in different degrees but, like Siamese twins, one cannot do without the other, as the material with which one comes into the world determines the way he develops (a psychology of science and a science of psychology). The brain and its related parts closely mediate thinking and behaviour. Chomsky (1965a), Lenneberg (1967), Johnson (1993), Filipek (1999: 113–28) and Young et al. (2003: 288) were some of the first to provide information on how language was related to biological dispositions.

Till the late 19th century, there was not much technical correspondence between the two trends of psychological conceptualisations, namely, nativist and traditionalist views. The breakthrough came with the evidence that foetal development, though biological in its origin, was also affected by the environment, namely, the maternal effects during the pregnancy period such as reaction to auditory stimuli, maternal drugs, and so on. Thus, this evidence gave effect to the interaction of nature and nurture even during the 'germination period'. Maturation or the staged development of the physical and biological self was found to be related to endowed genetic mechanisms that triggered off these stages like walking, talking and the development of skills (Havighurst, 1972), which were said to be milestones of development.

Gestalt theorists in viewing the development process referred to the interaction of several mechanisms and downplayed the effect of biological development as triggered off by the thinking processes in the brain. Piaget however deliberately used biological and physical development to explain the maturational processes through his development schemas which moved from the concrete to the abstract in explaining development (Piaget, 1947).

In Chapter 4 we have indicated that the left hemisphere of the brain is the dominant sphere for a single-language experience, which is quickly assimilated in the early years, between 2–5 years. This is empirically found to exist in the Indian culture (Kapur, 2001). In the area of brain development, perhaps because of the contributions of neurologists to the area of knowledge, much more is known about the function or malfunction of the brain in cognitive development. For instance, experiments in perception have shown that in the visual cortex where alternations could be made by critical changes in visual experiences, the ability or lack of vision is compensated by other sensory abilities (Posner and Raichle, 1994).

Studies in bilingualism are of two kinds: (a) cognitive processes and (b) consequences of bilingualism. Over time, bilingual individuals constitute a rationale of rules of their own to bridge the interaction between the two languages. There are inferences 'in switching', from the mental to the expressed as individuals usually think in their mother tongue but talk in another language. They infer this from one language to another (Mohanty, 1994). There are however pieces of information that can be only understood in one language such as science. But when attempting to understand music, arts and literature, the nuances in the mother tongue are apt to be more accurate than when translated (through coding and decoding) into the second language (Annamalai, 1986). Apparently, bilingual children are better able to decipher the meaning behind sentences which are ambiguous to monolinguists. This indicates that bilinguists have better abilities in metalinguistic abilities and cognitive flexibility in understanding the import of a communication (Mohanty, 1994).

Motivation

Motivation is revealed in the theoretical concepts of D. McClelland who is its major proponent (McCllelland, 1984). He begins with the technological argument that all human beings and mammals have purposeful activities directed towards a goal, whether they are well performed or not (McDougall, 1945). This concept is also borne out of naïve psychology (Thomas, 1997). Miller et al. (1960) have observed that behaviour is goal directed. Goal directedness is closely related to motivational energy, which is directed towards analysis of ambiguity. There are many ways of perceiving the two linked concepts: Goal implies a certain end product and directiveness implies a selected strategy (Woodfield, 1976).

   The theory of motivation postulated here is by McClelland (Atkinson, 1964a: 240). Its formulations are similar to the theory of Tolman and Lewin who based their analysis of motivation and individual differences on the need to achieve. It also has some of the general implications of Stimulus–Response (S–R) behavioural theory (Lewin, 1935; Tolman, 1936). The theory explains the determinism of direction, magnitude and persistence, which is innate in human behaviour. These occur mostly when the individual is aware that the consequence of his action will be evaluated. This theory might also be called the theory of achievement-oriented performance. McClelland explored risk taking factors in the orientation towards achievement, the effects of which are a sense of satisfaction, a higher level of confidence and self-esteem. It was said that low performance in task-attempts leads to a lowered sense of achievement, which can cause the individual to be either more motivated, or be apprehensive and therefore have lowered self-esteem (McClelland, 1958). Failure is related to anxiety of future performance (Moulton et al., 1958). It can also lead to the emotion of frustration especially when repeated attempts fail. Therefore we find that embedded in the theory of achievement motivation are subconcepts like frustration, guilt, conflict, regression or aggression, high or low self-esteem, and higher or lower motivation to achieve further. Over a period of time typical behaviour of success or failure reflects on personality traits such as indecisiveness, lessened initiative and fear of failure, on the negative side. While on the positive side it leads to progressive self-confidence, self-esteem and interpersonal competence. Thus, motivation is psychodynamic in concept and includes three domains: (*a*) personality tendencies, (*b*) immediate environment and (*c*) repeated cumulative experience of success or failure.

In a study of achievement and its relationship to success and failure, a sample of Caucasian and non-Caucasian respondents was studied. They were matched on sex and parental education, but not on religious and cultural backgrounds. The study revealed that Anglo-Saxons were more likely to assume responsibility for their success especially under conditions of high ego involvement (Miller, 1976: 901–06). Murphy and Murphy (1968) assumed that the prevailing dominant ethos dictated that individuals are responsible for their deeds and outcomes, whether negative or positive. The Caucasians denied responsibility for failure and stated they worked harder for success (ego protection). The Asians did not have a similar need for ego protection, as they were more ready to assume responsibility for their failure, and used little ego defence mechanisms to protect themselves. If we examine this tendency expressed by the Asians we find it is related to karma where the individual is responsible for his deeds, successful or otherwise. Studies across cultures on motivation indicate that the interpretation of motivation is differentially operationalised in cultural embeddedness (Kornadt et al., 1980).

There are studies in the Indian context that demonstrate the various facets of motivation in relation to achievement. We give below a set of studies on motivation and achievements. One such study showed a negative correlation between achievement and anxiety levels among students, those with low anxiety levels scoring better than those with high anxiety levels (Singh and Kumar, 1977: 56–60), especially in relation to task complexity Under-achievement and overachievement have received much attention in order to assess why especially underachievement is so persistent. In a study of overachievers and underachievers in Kolkata using seven reasoning numerical ability scales and other indices, overachievers were found to be less neurotic and anxious, did better in social service and in outdoor interests, scoring high on study habits, attitude to school, religion and cultural background as compared to underachievers. A further study concentrated on personality factors. Using an elaborate set of tools, results of this study showed that overachievers of both sexes had superior abilities because of their motivation towards achievement and an aspiration for higher levels of performance. Males showed a greater interest in aesthetic activities, while the overachieving females showed more interest in social activities. Both types of achievers were found to be influenced by economic, social and demographic characteristics (Menon, 1973, Ph.D. Thesis, quoted in Naidu and Nakhate, 1985). Overachieving girls tended to score higher also in adjustment of their background. Although scoring higher was evident in girls than in boys, there were no differences in social adjustment (Patel and Joshi, 1977: 178–84) and children of higher socio-economic status (SES) performed better (Vijayalakshmi, 1980). Continuing on the theme of underachievers and overachievers, environmental factors like socio-economic status in fact was differently related to both, in that high achievement was related to better background (Kohli, 1976, quoted in Naidu and Nakhate, 1985).

Geographical habitat such as urban or rural seems to make a difference. When the rural–urban question arose, it was observed that rural overachievers were generally more individualistic, reflective and internally restrained. Parental values were found to reinforce achievement. And underachievers seem to suffer from greater emotional immaturity (Agarwal, 1977: 105–10). On reinforcement, it was only the high achievers who showed a subsequent better performance, indicating that low achievers have a low cognitive ability in interpretation of their self-confidence (Sidana and Sahuja, 1978: 83–86). One study found that girls have a stronger feeling for internalising responsibility, attributing responsibility to themselves in success rather than failure situations (Panda and Panda, 1978: 88–100). In the same study male and female introverts and extroverts tested on several indices like Junior Personality Inventory by Mohan et al. Raven's Standard Progressive Matrices, Letter Completion and Serial Completion tests revealed no differences between extroverts and introverts on their performance in these tests. The authors who used these tests however suggested that high levels of aspiration for achievement or fear of failure could lead to greater anxiety and consequent work decrease in introverts (Mohan and Bhanot, 1976: 23–29). In another study, parental education and income had a significant influence on the educational aspirations of their children, with urban children showing higher levels of aspiration (Bisht, 1972). In the use of a personality inventory administered to high and low achievers in school systems, extroversion and introversion were of little significance in relation to achievement. However emotional stability was related to high achievement (Pandey, 1981: 1–4). Overachievers tended to be less neurotic and anxious than underachievers (Bhaduri, 1971 in Naidu and Nakhate, 1985: 120). Levels of aspiration among academic achievers showed that high achievers expressed higher aspirations when anxiety scores were low, and low achievers expressed higher aspiration when anxiety scores were high. It seems that achievement is related to anxiety levels which affected realistic aspirations (Tiwari et al., 1980: 46–51). How do other students perceive achievers? In one study using sociometric analysis, tests of intelligence and achievement scores showed that those with higher levels of intelligence and high scholastic ability were found to be more acceptable than those with less in either achievement or intelligence (Badami and Tripathi, 1973: 69–74).

We must underscore in this context that the results of such studies quoted depend mainly upon the type of measures used. For instance, in studies on classroom performance, the Anxiety Scale by Chattel and Sheller and the Persistent Test by Bhattacharya attempted to assess anxiety and persistence in various combinations. However, there were no statistically significant differences and it was concluded that anxiety and persistence do not significantly affect performance on a given programme (Gangopadhyay, 1973: 21–31).

Therefore, how is achievement related to these influencing variables? Studies in deprivation show that by and large children from poor areas are low achievers, influenced as they are by an insufficient and inadequately stimulating home background (Paranis, 1978). Are there differences between the sexes? Apparently there are. There is some indication that the motivation for achievement is birth order–differentiated; from a few available published studies, it was found that the firstborn in nuclear families and the last born in large or joint families are more anxiety-prone (Bharathi and Venkataramaiah, 1976: 11–17).

Along the same lines, verbal blame was significantly more effective than verbal praise in both sexes, especially for introverts vis-à-vis extroverts (Broota et al., 1985: 1–5). Also, reinforcement on academic achievement was found to lead to superior performance (Prasad, 1977 in Naidu and Nakhate, 1985). It has often been said that socio-personal attitudes can affect performance. In a set of schoolchildren, attributes found to discriminate between high and low achievers were self-effort versus fatalism, acceptance by others, independence versus conformity and being past-present-future-oriented. Further, social personality factors related to academic achievement such as scholastic performance, attitude to self, and positive reinforcement by parent, teachers and peers were found to be highly related indicators of academic performance. Does emotionality play a part in low achievement? In a study of low academic achievement, emotionality and low academic achievement in boys were significantly related. The females were more emotional than the males. There existed a negative correlation between low academic achievement and emotionality in girls (Seth, 1978). Females apparently are influenced by their academic achievement history, immediate performance and the magnitude of reinforcement they receive. Although reinforcement worked similarly for both high and low achievers, it was more effective with the subject's immediate performance when it was successful and low achievers were less able to discriminate between right and wrong responses indicating an inherent difficulty in intellectual abilty (Sidana and Saluja, 1978: 83–86).

Motivation being inherent, its dynamic energy force is not observable except in demonstrated behaviour. The predisposing factors are several strands of reinforcement much like the tenets of S–R theory where rewards and punishment affect the drive that motivates the individual. These snippets of studies on small samples give variegated results. It is, therefore, difficult to weave them into broad strokes. They demonstrate samples of available data, some results contradicting the others. The major concept that seems to emerge is that high achievers have high motivation levels and are reinforced by their background to be so. Sex differences were too contradictory to make any generic statement. We still have to find data in the Indian scene which are from large samples assessed on measures devised in the Indian context. It is true that even if the samples may be large, it is not tenable to say that they relate to the average Indian as there is greater heterogeneity than homogeneity in the Indian population from one region to another, from one ethnic group to another, from one religion to another, and so on. Nevertheless, larger populations need to be studied to give comprehensive results of a multicentric strategy applicable to the Indian psyche. We can hypothesise some generalisations. All human beings have the drive to meet their needs as indicated by Maslow in his theory of needs (Maslow, 1987). In the average Indian family there are two parallel lines of reinforcement related to needs. The first is positive or negative reinforcement to be dependent or independent. In early infancy and even up to preschool years the average Indian child is protected and negatively reinforced in attempting to do things on his own volition till such time as the nurturer feels that the child can explore his environment independently. Parallelly during this period of mobility, exploration and curiosity, the continual overseeing by the nurturant creates a trusting environment. We do know that Erikson's model emphasises the significance of trust in the early period of development which coincides with the dependency trait. This is not to say that the child is not being encouraged to be self-reliant. In most subcultures in India, with the appearance of the successive children, the older children are encouraged to be nurturant mother substitutes and therefore are given independent responsibilities. In fact considering the social realities of the substrata of the poor, disadvantaged tribal, rural and urban groups, the care-taking responsibilities are many (Khalakdina, 1979: 31). True, in the upper, elite groups where families can afford maids (*ayahs*), these tasks are delegated to them. In fact, though no studies are available to substantiate this phenomenon, the ayah culture has its own parameters wherein most instances they are the major nurturants, disciplinarians and perhaps models to be imitated, especially in elite, nouveau-riche families.

Motivation to achieve is used more often than not in the performance of tasks which are, for instance, comparatively equated. This occurs mostly in test and competitive situations. Test anxiety is usually revealed by tasks where various levels of anxiety are exhibited, related to personality variables which we term situational variants. Those whose personality shows high test anxiety exhibit poor performance (Atkinson, 1953: 381–90).

Again, if the incentive to perform is not need-based there is indifferent performance. When performance is evaluated against norms and the individual is almost certain of success the probability of success is high. However, where there is acceptance of failure the probability of success is low. Therefore the incentive value of success may be considered an 'immediate determinant' strength of motivation (McClelland, 1961).

Thus when we relate these concepts to the issue of aggression versus non-aggression we find that motivation to achieve is interdependent with competitiveness and doing better than the others, especially when the achievement is formally tested as in school exams. However, the motivation is not directly energised towards the bad karma of the other, but towards an abstract fatalistic situation. In general, Indian parents do not reinforce aggression when they state 'the child should have done better in his exam'. They specifically do not contrast and compare with others, the direction is unilateral and is often accompanied by the phrase 'do better next time'.

The general principle of motivation is that there is a generalised drive which is carried from one situation to another where two situational influences are competing: (a) the strength/weakness of acceptance and (b) incentive value of success for a particular activity. These concepts relate to Festinger's study on aspirations (Festinger, 1942: 235–50) and Lewin's theory of energy force fields (Lewin, 1935).

Each subculture has its own set of cultural activities where performance is applauded. For instance, in Jaisalmer, it is the camel race; among the sophisticated it is the horse race; in informal peer group activities in rural areas it is 'gilli-danda' (game of sticks and stones) and among almost all classes it is cricket. However elementary, it is the team spirit which is encouraged when there is difficulty in task accomplishment. This is obvious in team games in several subcultures in India. McClelland has also introduced the concept of situational determinant or the risk factor in high achievers, which in fact strengthens the achievement level (McClelland, 1961). But too unrealistic a risk tends to reduce motivational levels. We have seen this in little children who often back away from tasks which are chronologically over their age maturity.

On the other hand, we know that practice and training, as in the case of circus children, reduces the risk factor so that there is a greater motivation to achieve, especially in high achievers. Further, education is also a determinant. Those with higher education have lower levels of frustration in their motivation to achieve (Veroff et al., 1960). Thus the average Indian in situations of competition, incentive-giving and praise-giving or reward is more likely to attempt tasks even if he has to strive, but frequently not with the intention to outdo the other.

Therefore, aggression is deflected towards the situation and not to the human beings involved in the situation. The most clear examples are in school achievement where the child performs in relation to his last performance record. He is oriented to achieve by his parents/adults, which is reflected in the system of evaluated performance. The system of rewards initiated by the school structure is also meant to be a socially approved incentive for the child to judge himself by his previous ratings. Children are more rewarded for cooperation and altruism than for competition and physical aggression (Hamblin et al., 1971: 41–53). However, it is accepted that the classical study of frustration/aggression is as valid for Indians as for others and extreme frustration can lead to extreme physical aggression , as in communal riots in irrational 'mob frenzy' situations (Bettelhiem, 1958: 301). We must also emphasise that there is a build-up of frustration between those who do not have and those who do have in the social milieu, but which is rationalised by projection onto fate, which is used as a coping mechanism (Rosenzwieg, 1944). This is true in most of our deprived ecologies. Sometimes the expectancy of failure reinforces the tendency to avoid situations of failure, and therefore even trying, which is viewed as lack of motivation in the eastern psyche. It is perhaps for this reason that where children or adults are fearful of failure in competition they do not participate. Another situational determinant is conflict. The theory is that all individuals have both the motivation to achieve success and the motivation to avoid failure. This is the concept of approach-avoidance conflict (Vernoy and Huffman, 1991: 432). The assumption here is that conflict exists between the positive anxiety to achieve and negative anxiety about failure. When the motive to avoid is stronger than the motive to achieve, there is a conflict between the two, pulling in opposite directions. This is what happens when a person says 'I am in a dilemma' which is often resolved by taking the line of least resistance, namely, the tendency to avoid even attempting the task, which is the psychodynamic equivalent of 'escapism'. Another situational determinant that operates in this conflict avoidance approach is that a host of personal and socio-interpersonal influences relate directly to the goal of 'groupism' rather than 'individualism'. These are parental expectations, peer group judgements about ability and one's own perceptions about the pros and cons of a situation. The individual's inhibitions to avoid failure through the use of projective mechanisms such as projection, rationalisation, reaction-formation deflection, sublimation and conversion are commonly used.

In analysing the terms 'motivated', 'motivating' and 'motive', we have to take into account the doer, the doing and the deed, respectively. The doer has to have a need and an interest in attempting to either achieve mentally, like doing a crossword puzzle, or physically, like building a bridge. However, wanting to do something remains attritioned and therefore is inhibited by a barrier termed ambiguity (Kuhl and Heckhausen, 1985: 137). This barrier or intervening variable when disassembled comprises a number of interacting subvariables: insufficient and inaccurate knowledge, anxiety about one' ability, uncertain self-esteem, conflict with other compelling directions and with satisfaction, self versus social needs and frustration, all enveloped in a package called 'ambiguity barriers'.

In the Indian context, we can illustrate this by the frequently occurring example of adolescent aspirations. An adolescent, for instance, may wish to become a Bollywood star. Thus he has a need and an interest and he has an ambiguous idea of the end product. This ambiguity is compounded by barriers such as inaccurate ideas about planning and strategy, anxiety as to whether or not he really has the attributes, uncertainty about ability to meet the challenges, a conflict with parental aspirations and frustrated thinking as to how to overcome these obstacles. Clearly he has the motivation but it is unclear to him as to how to go about meeting his goal. We can find similar examples in other types of interpersonal issues such as marriage, family disorganisation, monetary difficulties, and so on. In the context of developmental goals, the motivation, ambiguities and barriers may clearly exist. For instance, in trying to create a sense of interdependence and togetherness, motivation can come in conflict with 'self-motive and other motive'. In relation to non-aggression where the ego is challenged and ego satisfaction is deflected, the motivation to want to be aggressive is dynamically curbed by moral and social values. In the developmental goal towards groupism, motivations that are socially approved and reinforced are done so by emphasising family/kin group and community bonds. In the developmental goal of moving towards engendered statuses, the motivation is bidirectional—both from the nurturer, who has a social image for the progeny, and the progeny himself/herself to abide by socially accepted role behaviour.

Motivation, simply put, is an inner energy directing individual behaviour to attain/possess/achieve a higher level of experience. This motivating energy may be to accumulate more experiences (extensity or quantity), such as seeing as many sights when on a vacation, or to increase the depth of an experience (intensity or quality). One of the earliest attempts to define this inner energy was made by W. James who compared it to instinct or acuity of acting in such a way as to produce certain ends without foresight of the end, and without previous education in the performance (James, 1890). These tendencies called instincts were described as 'tendencies to reflexive actions' initiated by sensory stimulus and called forth by sensory stimuli. The nervous system was conceived as a pre-organised bundle of reactions by James. Instinctive behaviour was considered to be blind and impulsive in character. To ask why an animal should act in a particular impulsive (instinctive) way is as meaningless as to ask a desperately hungry man who is eating food why he should want to eat. According to James, thus, an instinct is a movement to fulfil a primary desire impulsively without sufficient forethought or warning, as to what the eventuality would be, except to impulsively fulfil a primary need. Instincts relate to primary wants of the organism without which the organism cannot live, such as food, shelter, mating and protection. As cumulative studies were done, and the theory of conditioning and secondary reinforcement came into the purview of researchers, these concepts of instincts were modified (Pavlov, 1928). These modified constructs were related to needs, the chief being primary needs and secondary needs. These are: (*a*) the organic need: the need for relieving tensions of hunger, thirst, pain, fatigue, and so on, the neglect of which leads to frustration and physical disorders; (*b*) the self or ego need: the need for responsiveness, social recognition and autonomy and mastery over events and objects; and (c) the security giving or mutuality needs: for affection, belonging and safety (Thorpe, 1950). L. Goldstein added other features to these needs: human behaviour cannot be explained only on the conscious plane, but also on the basis of the non-conscious experiences (bodily processes and inner experiences such as moods and attitudes that have been previously accumulated). These make up a complex of inner forces that arouse the motivational force towards a specific direction (Goldstein, 1940: 150).

What is the basis of the development of such traits as motivation? In this context we emphasise that the inner forces within the human being are to close a perceived gap between desire and fulfilment of the desire. Man exists not as a vegetable but as a progressive, productive creature. The motivation to survive is the strongest of human forces. Existent in all humans is will or volition, the will to do or not do is a decision-making process in man's make-up. As studies of volition or will expanded, there also grew a realisation that instinct and will were insufficient to explain this phenomenon. For there was more to the directional behaviour of man than just instinct or will.

It was the classic thesis of J.W. Atkinson (1964b) which threw further light upon the concept of the inner drive, propelled by the concept of need which opened up avenues of constructs, the main being motivation. Motivation is assumed to be a process, an inherent energy in all known mammalian beings. In the earlier days of psychological development these energies were conceptualised, indicated earlier, as instinctual behaviour. Instinctual behaviour is a spontaneous reaction to an energising stimulus such as danger. This is obvious in a child's behaviour when he reaches out to touch a fire and is burnt. The reaction is reflexive, and this pattern is not repeated because of the associative pain. If a reaction brings pleasure, such as the sucking response of an infant, it is apt to be repeated and thus a reinforced pattern of behaviour is set in, identified by Piaget as being a circular response reaction (Piaget, 1954). This pattern, as G.C. Thompson (1952: 129–30) reiterates, is the child striving to attain a status of equilibrium by behaviour, indicating a seeking or motivated learning pattern.

According to Atkinson, the study of motivation has to do with analysis of the various factors which incite and direct an individual's actions. However, over time developmental psychologists began to use the term motivation in human beings as motivation was seen to connote more than just a spontaneous or reflexive response. One of the earliest discussions of the concept of need in early infancy was Bowlby's theory of attachment and loss in childhood (Bowlby, 1958: 350–73). He discussed this in the psychoanalytical approach, emphasising the view-points of D. Rapport and J.M. Gill (1959: 153–62). This point of view assumes the existence of the following: (a) the dynamic domain, connoting the psychological forces in a phenomenon; (b) the economic variable, indicating propositions of the energy involved in the phenomenon; (c) the structural aspect, indicating the psychological configurations; and (d) the genetic factor, indicating the psychological origin and development of the phenomenon.

The meaning of motivation is well explained by Atkinson who is one of the earliest proponents of the parameters of motivation. The theoretical aspects of motivation are as follows:

(i) Motive is defined generally as something (need or desire) that causes a person to act (*Seventh New Collegiate Dictionary*, 1983). An action, however, is influenced by intention. In this sense it is the will of the individual, or purpose or design, or similar terms.

(ii) There is a direction of the motive/purpose and therefore it is essential to know the direction towards which motivation is channelised. In other words a motive is directed towards an objective that when achieved satisfies the individual who is experiencing the intention or motive. In this schema of concepts, the will has to be driven or there is a drive or force towards which the individual is directed by others or directs himself.

(iii) Motivation is an unfolding process of energy as emphasised by Freud (1936), Lewin (1935) and Tolman (1936). The major emphasis is that motivation is distinct from the learning process, and is a prerequisite force. Directional behaviour is emphasised by Freud, Lewin and Tolman.

(iv) Motivation is therefore an inherent drive embedded in the evolutionary theory of needs. Need is the difference between what is existent within the individual, as contrasted to what the individual wants/desires in order to experience satisfaction. We refer here to the theory of needs postulated by Murray, who dealt with the conceptualisation of personality where his primary premise was the existence of psychogenic needs (Murray, 1938). A need is a construct which stands for force in the brain region, a force which organises perception, apperception, intellect, conation and action in such a way as to transform thinking in a different direction to that which is existing.

(v) Motivation is based on needs which are placed in a relative hierarchy; the major ones are dominance, affiliation, achievement, autonomy, defence, aggression and abasement. They could be stimulated by visceral processes from within the individual by affecting a change in the immediate situation called need-press. A need may be manifested by various means, such as a typical behavioural trend, a mode of action, a movement towards selection or avoidance. It is accompanied by an expression of a characteristic, a notion and, finally, manifestation of satisfaction (achievement of an affect). At this point we need to differentiate between McDougall's conceptualisation of instincts (which has now been discarded as it has overtones of spontaneity of thought and action peculiar to primates) (McDougall, 1923) and the present emphasis on need-press (Murray, 1951: 266–92), energy and need-fulfilment, and more especially the other demands made by society and the environment to delay, postpone or move towards gratification. So that while one might view need for hunger as primitive, one must also underscore that in the human being hunger can be controlled by reasoning or internal evaluation and that hunger can be appeased at certain times, namely, socially approved times and places of eating (Hull, 1952).

(vi) Primary to the understanding of motivation is the idea that it can be considered as a synonym for the phrase 'an innate force', which impels the human being towards a perceived goal. In understanding the concept, it is essential to accept the fact that drive or force is not a consequence of any singular past experience, but of a combination or recombination of several dispositions. For instance, academic achievement is not simply the impelling force to want to gain more knowledge, it is also propelled, more clearly seen in the Indian culture, by the anxiety stimuli of parents and by the world of media which offers many attractive opportunities for those who achieve academically. It is common in the Indian culture that parents (especially the achieving middle class) are anxious that their children do well, urge them to put in long hours of study, get better report cards and even go to the extent of hiring tutors which they can ill afford. Motivation, per se, is essentially covert while stimuli, past and current, may operate simultaneously to impel an overt action.

(vii) The process of motivation within the individual can only be inferred from his action. If, for instance, one were to ask a group of people watching a cricket match what motivates them to sit day after day watching test series, it will be difficult to pinpoint which singular motive is responsible. There may be a host of secondary motives, such as going with friends to be seen as 'a cool guy' interested in the national sport, to want to be a part of the gang, and so on. But the intrinsic motive can only be explained as an inner interest, namely, liking for the sport.

Motivation is a consciously or deliberately acted out thought process. It may or may not be implemented in action. For instance, the child may desire, want or wish to possess an attractive toy in a shop. He is motivated or driven to find strategies to gain possession of the toy. He may express his desire as most children do: 'I want that train.' His mother might say that it is too expensive. His motivation to acquire the first toy is thwarted. However he constructs the social experiences, using pros and cons, and is able to gauge that once his mother has said 'no' he cannot pursue the motivated direction. Instead he either has to deflect the motive to accept his mother's offer of another toy, or he goes into a tantrum, sulks, does not comply and may even, if very young, cry to get his wish. Thus we see that motivation is also linked with the process, the strategy and the opportunity of the situation. It might well happen that this desire being thwarted is frustrated and therefore covertly leads the child, on returning home, to refuse to eat, thus punishing his mother in return for her non-compliance. Therefore inherent in the understanding of the concept of motivation are degrees of forces attached to the motive. A child may be motivated to take an exam because he wants to achieve and satisfy his ego, because he wants to please his parents, and so on. However, besides this attribute of motivation another accompanying attribute is the covertness or overtness of motivation. A young male teenager, for instance, may tell his group of friends as a group of girls pass by: 'Arre yaar woh beech wali ladki se mujh ko dosti karni hai' ('I want to be friends with the girl in the centre'). This is an overt expression of his motive. On the other hand, his friend standing next to him may also have exactly the same desire secretly but does not express it for fear of competition from a dear friend to whom he is loyal. Again, inherent in this dimension of covert and overt attributes is a situation of conflict.

Conflict in competing motives implies the interaction of different forces with different rates of energy: some may be weak and some may be strong and the strongest force overcomes the others. We refer here to the approach-avoidance conflict behaviour model, related to motivation. The assumptions of this model are: the tendency to approach a goal is stronger, the nearer the individual is to it (gradient of approach); the tendency to avoid an object or event or person or thing is stronger, the nearer the individual approaches the goal (gradient of avoidance). The latter may be a stronger gradient than the former, and lastly, the increase in drive increases the gradient and when two drives are incompatible the stronger prevails. Drive or motivation is the basic force leading to accomplishment or achievement (Brown, 1948).

To give an illustration, if the child is asked to pick from a range of toys the one he likes most he will select that which is more attractive, or which is something unfamiliar and exciting, or one which his friend has but he does not, and so on. If he has a recent experience stored in memory of having seen the toy with his friend he carries over the covert perception of need; it surges up as the most dominant motive of the moment. Therefore, there is not only a motivation to want the object but also the want to lessen the need. This ambivalence leads to a state of mind deemed 'conflict'.

(viii) Motivation is accompanied by other emotions, mainly conflict and anxiety, till the achievement is complete or the emotion dissipates. Sometimes, the individual will keep trying repeatedly in spite of failure, and during this process of repetition, his anxiety and conflict levels increase, whether he analyses himself as being capable, loses self-esteem or whether he gives up as unattainable the pursuit he has undertaken and thereby resolves the conflict.

(ix) These reflexive actions and reactions over a period of time, and with repetition, get embedded into what is known as habit. Such habits form patterns and often one habit leads to another without any precondition or conscious effort to enact the habit, thus forming the linkage, like the ablutionary movements every morning become a habit without conscious motivation. 'The nervous system which ingrains this habit formation is a pathway between a sensory terminus *a quo* and a muscular, glandular or other terminus *ad quem*' (James, 1890).

How does habit associate or disassociate itself from the conscious self since apparently it is an impulsive behaviour? It is like the motion of driving away a pestering fly. The movement is done with the knowledge of the individual (inner self-movement) consciously to ward off the fly. When the individual repeatedly performs the same actions, the response of warding off the fly becomes automatic or habitual (without conscious effort). Therefore in order to understand what this inner drive of inner force is, we need to explore the dimensions of the unconscious automated self and the conscious or deliberately willed self. James (1902) said, 'Introspection reveals consciousness to be present when nerve processes are hesitant.' Consciousness is neither instinctive action nor rapid automatic habitual action. It is primarily a selective agency. Consciousness is evident when there is purposeful movement of either thought or action to further the ends of the individual. However the conscious self or, in Freudian terms, the ego is that part of knowledge of the self as a human being in the world of other human beings. It is the monitor of what can be done between the impulse and the voice of conscience or that which tells the human being what is good or bad (super ego). From the conscious self there are other related factors, primary among which is emotional content, the height of interest and the purpose to satisfy oneself immediately or to defer the satisfaction. All these aspects connote the concept of motivation. To put these constructs into more comprehensive terms, motivation is the deliberate act of consciousness to satisfy a need immediately or to defer the satisfaction over a period of time to achieve a goal. Motivation is therefore purposeful direction or force or energy within the individual. To will, or to volitionaly achieve, a goal so as to diminish or eradicate the gap between need and its fulfilment is the aim of being motivated.

(x) Motivation is also correlative with the concept of need reduction, which is related to goal-directed behaviour (Miller, 1951: 435–72). Let us illustrate it with some examples:

In the early years of child upbringing, a child moves impulsively towards a bright object. As a toddler the child attempts to put it into his mouth. Here the movement is the directional force and, if it is the first time, there is volition or conscious effort on the part of the child to fulfil the need, and when the object is in his mouth it leads to a further need to bite, or the need to tear it apart, or the need to bang it. All these are attempts to fulfil the child's curiosity in a conscious way. Repeatedly, these acts become automatic or without volition, till a newer dimension of the object is presented. As the child matures, the object, which perhaps was a rattle and therefore stimulated more than one sense, now becomes a moving object and therefore has an added dimension of attraction to explore and fulfil curiosity. If we move from this simplistic stage to that stage of a college student studying science, we see a more complicated form of conscious effort. Here there are two sets of needs. The first is the self-satisfaction need to immediately complete the course successfully. This is an immediate goal. The second is that by such activities, he might be a successful researcher/teacher. This is a deferred goal. It is expected that the immediate goal has a direct-line relationship to the deferred goal. But since there is a period of time and many intervening variables may occur, this goal may be modified, limited or disappear, and it may be supplanted by some other priority goal like changing over to business school, which has achieved a greater attraction in the meanwhile. There should be a difference made between immediate fulfilment which brings about gratification. Motivation to attain a goal is not only because of the need for solving a problem but also because solutions of increasing complexity test intelligence levels and therefore stimulate risk taking and decision making to reach a goal. The goal itself as consciously visualised is an attainment of status for the individual in the emotional context, in that if he gets a first class in the school board examination, it not only satisfies him as an individual, but also brings him parental and peer approval, fulfilling his need for recognition. These are secondary motives related to the conditioning by the environment. If he were living in a primitive society then it would be his hunting skills which would bring him recognition.

We need to underscore the socio-ecological influences on motivation. The effect of the environment on individual behaviour has many variations. The reinforcement history of the person and cultural context jointly shape the motivational orientation of the individual.

One's motivational orientation is affected by poverty conditions which leads to low need for achievement, low extension need and high need for dependency (Pareek, 1970: 300–17). Thus the motive to act is based on the motive to want to fulfil a need (whether primary or secondary). This is basically an innate tendency. It is fostered or minimised by the effect of the environment on the individual.

Language Development

Without language there would be no knowledge of culture and history (both religious and social), and man would be handicapped in the furtherance of knowledge. The formation of constructs like thought and ideas in human beings is greatly dependent upon man's ability to translate the constructs into written or spoken language that is comprehensible. There is a structure of rules which relate to the formation of expressions of these thoughts (Greenberg, 1966). The precise replication of the thought, whether newly constructed or recalled from memory, gives clarity to thinking and therefore to reasoning and logical deduction.

The Beginnings of Language Formation

The ordered hierarchy of language development begins with pre-linguistic forms of expression in the infant who, like the primeval animal, through sounds and body language expresses behaviour. Many of these non-verbal but expressive forms carry over into adult life where they imply much more meaning than the conventional grammatical language. Sounds of pain and exclamations of joy are some such expressions carried over into adulthood.

Simplistic conceptualisations have been developed about the origin of language. One such conceptualisation is that sounds of objects were mimicked by man, such as the whirr of a windmill, the sound of a bell and the clack-clack of wheels, which led to depicting with gestures the activity indicated (Thompson, 1952: 338). Thus, naïve conceptualisation in the prehistoric years had a relation to the mystical sound of inanimate objects giving them a mythical existence. Another conceptualisation had to do with the sounds of nature, air, water, thunder, and so on, and the natural sounds made by animals. A further conceptualisation about the origins of speech related to the incidental relation of early spontaneous sounds elicited by a child in relation to stimuli in the environment, much as a baby prattles while playing. A further metaphysical conceptualisation relates to the idea that the tongue was in a sense tied to bodily movements which stimulated sounds spontaneously expressed by clicking. Thorndike speculated that mimetic sounds uttered and exchanged by human beings became the origin of primitive language (Thorndike, 1943: 1–6). While these are naïve conceptualisations of folk psychology, we need to know how the child acquires basic phonemes (speech sounds). For understanding this we turn to intergenerational patterns of exchange of sounds. The child has to acquire a certain level of maturation moving from unrehearsed sounds to developing an expansion of phonemes and then pruning them to a limited set of phonemes influenced by the culture in which a particular language exists (Lewis, 1936). In this way, there is a gradual development of the use of vowels, consonants, diphthongs and aspirates (Bean, 1932: 181–202). A child, for instance, babbles nonsense, while an adult tries to teach him the correct utterances by exaggerated or expanded use of words. This he does through exaggerated movements of the lips, facial contractions or expansions to say, for example, 'Krishna'. The child tries to imitate the sound and using his observations and maturational powers limited to his chronological age will say 'kwiswa' or some such utterance till by repetition he says Krishna. Lisping and mispronunciation occur several times before the model is perfectly imitated. Thus the development of speech phonemes depends upon verbal interaction initially, gradually expanding into group interaction.

Man is the major species of mammals who has a highly developed form of communicative behaviour through structured forms of interactive, verbal and non-verbal actions. Certainly other mammals like chimpanzees, dolphins and whales are said to have some form of speech which we humans have been able to identify, the ramifications of which still remains a dark area. As far as human beings go, the attempts to define language are straightforward. Language is the formed structure of the development of sounds following a grammatical style and syntax. This is achieved either through formal instruction or by imitation. For instance, the child of four or five years will tend to use the subject, the verb and the object in a sentence and very infrequently the adverb or the conjunction like 'mother is going shopping'. An older child will tend to conjugate sentences like my (possessive noun) mother (subject) had gone (past tense) shopping (verb) and (conjunction) has not (verb again) brought home any biscuits (object). It is no exaggeration to say that this form of communication is perhaps the greatest intellectual usage for man's thoughts and ideas, philosophical and scientific. Language is necessary for human beings to attain technical, social and conceptual competence (Munroe and Munroe, 1975: 81). Language is culturally conditioned (Gardner, 1984). Vygotsky has been the great progenitor of the theory that cognitive competence is a part of cultural conditioning (Vygotsky, 1978). Language in its original state relates to the early form of oral expressions (phonemes), growth of vocabulary, signs and symbols, understanding and comprehension of language. In the prehistoric stages, the function of language was elementary, mainly related to tasks and simple pronouns and the environment of sustenance. Thus, the beginnings of language are to be found in the social and interactional context (Mohanty, 1991). However this social imagery of language acquisition was not sufficient grounds for understanding how a language acquired roots and how, so to speak, these roots grew branches. Any literature proves that language is not only used for practical communication but for imagery fantasy and, most of all, for creativity. Chomsky's thesis that rules are conventional in the acquisition of language so that the structure is well rooted has now been well accepted as the scientific basis of grammatical language development (Chomsky, 1965b). For, from this base, the individual mind on the basis of motivation, interest and creativity in intellect can innovate, construct and reconstruct not only logically but also idiomatically, the latter being the channel for social language.

Creativity therefore is also a part of the construct of motivation. Because of social rules of group organisation the child learns to internalise specific relative descriptions, for example, the relational network. He cognitively constructs and stores in his memory bank the concept of relationships. Similarly, there is the concept of task obligation in relation to task expectation. Therefore, relational strands are set in a structural manner as a child chronologically stores such relational attributes of the outside world and internalises them. Linguistics depends on various factors for its optimum development.

One is internalisation of rules of speech, especially grammar (Chomsky, 1959: 26–58). The second is the individual child's intellectual ability to have a command and mastery over the language/languages in which he is guided and which is/are reinforced. The third is the ability of an individual child to make the switch in language (written or spoken) between the idiomatic, colloquial and the classical format of the given language. The fourth is the ability to intonate so as to use the same sentence implying different types of intent. There are two characteristics in the development of language as a skill. One is internalisation of the cognitive aspects of the auditory or written symbol of the object identified. This ability is developed into an ontogenetic trait, although its roots of origin are phylogenetic. The child learns to put sounds together to recognise the word as implying the abstract and concrete object. The pre-school child, for instance, identifies a round red edible object as an apple. This is internalisation and we have such phrases as 'apples are red', 'pomegranates are red' and 'red is a colour'. Such internalisation implies recognition, demonstration and repetition like 'A is for Apple', and so on.

The second relates to the ability to learn and use the grammar of a language and the amount of stimulation from the environment. It is known that in deprived ecologies in India communication in the form of spoken language is not strongly profiled. Hence sentences are short, idiomatic and related to the objective ecology surrounding the child. On the other hand, in urban elitist family settings where parents are educated, stimulation is stronger. However, if the child has a mental disability or is dyslexic or has lessened attention span, the probability is that speaking or writing a strictly grammatical language will present a challenge.

Children are known to have a flexible capacity to understand and use language. Their plasticity in quick cue grasp of sequential and successive sentences is phenomenal. They also acquire fine nuances of transacting between the affirmative and negative; between the simple unilinear and the additional; between expansion and contraction of the sentence; and between the realistic and the fantastic of any given sentence. For example, children's stories which are spontaneously related, can change from a positive to a negative tone. For example: 'He did not like the food' (Negative); 'He would have liked some other food' (Positive).

Then again, 'he did not like the food' can be expanded to 'he did not like the food because he was not hungry'. Here children learn to use the adverbial or conjunctional form of sentences easily. There is also the movement from expansionist to contractionist: 'he did not like the food/it looked greasy/it had peas/He doesn't like peas'. Contraction is simply 'the food was not good' or even 'bad food'. The realistic is the description of the food as it is: 'he did not like the food, it looked bad'. 'He did not like the food, he was thinking of the food that would be brought to him from the restaurant to which he went yesterday and where he ate the chocolate dessert.' In such strategy of language usage, the growing child is able to transform a structured sentence implying various meanings. Then, there is also the sophisticated individual who has mastered the language enough to use it with great facility as an interjection, as sarcasm, as emphasis and as implying the opposite. There are fine nuances of tonal inflection which are implicit. For instance, a person who wants to be sarcastic and comments on a person gorging himself says 'he really is eating very little, isn't he?' Such inflections are used in witty repertoire and in limericks, and are most often observed in Shakespearian language.

There are several principles stated in the acquisition of language. These principles state that there is evidence of a genetic programme. If we analyse this carefully, it refers to the inherent tendencies, namely, the inherent motivation level, the inherent cognitive level and the perceptual abilities. The environment is supported to the extent that it allows the programming to operate or disallows/reduces its operationalism. This is explained when we analyse the activating supports or deactivating behaviour that allows the intrinsic values to operate. We see the relationship between environment and genetic propensities. The environment allows the channelising of the culture to be interpreted. If the environment is physically poor, the genetic programme of intrinsic ability is inhibited for children from deprived ecologies, who may have the propensity, if stimulated, to become geniuses through innovation and inventions, which can be recorded and repeated in successive trials. We have seen such geniuses emerging in the Indian context from poor environments. For example, we have articulate political orators and business magnates originating from poor environments. Yet, on the other hand, given an enriched environment like all the facilities for tutorship in education and high-quality stimulating environment, many frequently are unable to make use of their opportunities to hone their skills. Therefore, a poor genetic programme cannot operate successfully.

Some languages are very well understood in short direct sentences while others have many additives which distort or elongate the interpretation; for instance, the English language can have a very elaborate grammatically correct set of sentences as also the Amharic language of the Ethiopians, while a language like German is brusque, with short to-the-point sentences. In other words, some languages are ornate and convey the same impression that very short sentences in other languages will convey. Chomsky calls this the parameters of speech, that is, the language sets the limits of interpretation and communication.

There is a sense of universal grammar in language to which cognition is related. Individually each child uses his intuitive knowledge and intimate knowledge of one language. Its grammar gives him a better hold on interpreting similarly linked languages. For instance, if he knows one south Indian language, his mother tongue Telugu, it is not difficult to understand the import or meaning of Tamil, Kannada or Malayalam. Similarly if Hindi is the mother tongue it is not difficult to bridge the gap between it and Bhojpuri, Urdu and some of the dialects of Rajasthan. Chomsky also proposed the principle of structure dependence. In essence this refers to an innate capacity in language acquisition where the child automatically, perhaps through some phylogenetic transformation, speaks the language in its grammatical form. In other words even though formal learning may not take place in learning grammatical syntax or the positioning of noun and verbs, structure dependence sets the limits of the rules that are to be followed in the acquisition of the language.

Chomsky's conceptualisation about language development has genetic biological bases which give rise to the concept of critical imprinting, that is, the ability to assimilate, categorise, differentiate speech forms during a certain chronological period (Chomsky, 1965a). Although not much research is available in this area it is commonly observed that children learn more languages than adults. It is essential that a developmental conditionality be added to Chomsky's theorising, which assumes that there is an automatic genetic potential for grammar from the onset of the time a child speaks a language.

There is some concern that even though language may be structure dependent it may not be automatically spontaneous. Phylogenetic tendency for children to straightaway use the grammatical rules is highly debatable for a child has to have experiences in the learning of grammatical rules, sentence construction and spoken language to understand and to be understood. In general this theory is of utility in understanding the 'universals' of language in the Indian culture. More especially we need to state a further proposition that stimulating micro-, meso-, and ecosystems increase opportunities and therefore make for better performance in language development. We need also to state that in language acquisition the place of motivation is fundamental and therefore there are individual differences in language acquisition. Even when language is taught formally and is well understood, all children, even though they may be intellectually similar, may not use the structural system of language in the same manner. In the Indian situation, environment is a much more limiting factor in language acquisition, where the mother tongue is different from the official language. This heterogeneity creates barriers between geo-ecological areas where there are different languages.

Therefore the tendency in the Indian situation is not only to know the mother tongue but also to acquire some knowledge of other language(s). What is more important is that the major official language is generally utilised in almost all other Indian languages as a substitute to a greater or lesser extent. Further, with global intercommunication and mobility, and the growing tendency for multinationals to set up businesses and industry in India and the increasing outsourcing of services from the West to India, the use of many English words in Indian languages has become common. The development of the spoken and written word spans generations, starting from symbolic writings on stones and leaves, and aided by the ability of man to store, remember and repeat information.

In studying the development of phoneme sounds into an intelligible and understood speech, Irwin in 1941 was one of the first experts in the field in the West to demonstrate development trends in language acquisition. He found that a newborn's vocabulary consisted of about 1,000 sounds (Irwin, 1941: 277–85). He also found that vowel sounds were developed in the first year but the trend was reversed in the second year when consonants took over, and by two and a half or three years, a child developed almost the full complement of vowel sounds as an adult but only two-thirds of the consonants. The ordering was as follows: labial and labial dental, lingual dental, post-dental velar and then glottal (Irwin, 1947: 397–401). Correlative with age maturation and the accumulation of repetitive articulation, the preschool child of three in the western culture has the full complement of sounds necessary for learning a structured form of a particular language.

Given the enormous complexity of Indian socio-linguistic realities, analysis of language is limited without the cultural context. India has been conceptualised as a socio-linguistic giant (Pandit, 1972). Unlike English, Indian languages have a relatively free word order. Indian languages are SOV (subject–object–verb) languages (Mohanty, 2000: 211). Indian research on language processing has dwelt on a traditional verbal learning system rather than holistic psycholinguistic approaches and in fact studies have concentrated more on the structure of Indian languages.

Studies on language acquisition by children have been done in the West, as stated by A.K. Mohanty (2000), where there is a great deal of empirical data to understand language acquisition. In the Indian context it is all the more essential given the myriads of official languages and their optional dialects (Slobin, 1992). In Slobin's vast accumulation and analyses of data from a group of other societies, the major exceptions are the grouping together of languages according to their syntax.

Studies which are available also emphasise the traditional rules of grammar (form and syntax) and have only just ventured into the area of phonology. Contemporary studies on psycholinguistic approaches have been done in the West (Vasanta and Sailaja, 1993). However, given the multilingual character of the Indian society, the types of socialisation in different mother tongues is an area that needs further exploration. Jacobson's theoretical analysis that there is a universal sequence of acquisition from common phonemes to those of particular languages has been applied by Baig (1991) in the Indian context, but not on the status of other regional languages on the dominant language. However, a few state languages have been studied; for instance, medial consonants were found in clusters in the study of Telugu (Nirmala, 1983/1984: 1–20), similar to those by Sharma (1969) in Hindi and Sridevi (1976) in Kannada. Most of the available studies are on bilingualism.

Studies by linguists on morphology indicate that the Indian children by and large exhibit some awareness of rules in the use of vowels and consonants (Raghavendra and Leonard, 1989: 313–22). There is no doubt that there is a certain ordering of sentences in most Indian languages. For instance, subjects speaking different languages used similarly the subject and then the verb in ordering in their own state languages for grammatical structure (Mishra, 1994; Vasanta and Sailaja, 1993).

This diversity of language forms is compounded by the facts that school children not only have to learn in their own state language but are required simultaneously to know the national language. This is further exacerbated by the current trend of inclusion of English words scattered at random in the native language. Most school-going and literate adults use words as 'problem', 'tension' and even phrases like 'but *yaar*' and '*kitna* spend *karenge*?'

Influences on Language Development

There is sparse information on the influences on language development in the Indian context due to inadequate findings obtained from small scattered samples. The upper classes seem to have better verbal fluency as compared to the lower classes (Kumar, 1986: 99–106). Sahu and

Jena (1983) found that socially disadvantaged children performed poorly as compared to the socially privileged.

Growth and physical development and health status have been found to have a significant influence on language development. Bhargava et al. (1982: 123–29) found that the small-for-dates low birthweight children had a slower rate of acquisition of language compared to the normal birthweight, full-term born children. Another category is the effect of training. Sahu and Swain (1985: 1–8) reported the positive effects of language training imparted in school. Again, ecology seems to be an influencing factor. Economically deprived ecologies have been found to affect the language ability of children (Shukla and Mohanty, 1986: 44–50). Styles of language expression have been differentiated by what are called referential and expressive styles (Nelson, 1973). In the referential style, children use a large number of common nouns in their language and a large number of personal, social and proper names, action words and routine social phrases.

These few studies in the Indian context add to the well-known thesis that language acquisition does not occur in a vacuum and that several factors, especially culture, influence its development. Among the major ones is the level of intelligence. It was found in one study by Irwin that the development of speech of four-year-old, mentally challenged children resembled that of normal one-year-olds (Irwin, 1942: 29–39). Further, the occurrence of superior forms of speech in children from the upper socio-economic status is the function of the family environment which stimulates and enriches the child's vocabulary. This has been found also in studies of Indian children (Muralidharan, 1970) and also in families where the mother is educated and deliberately reinforces the child's speech (Urwin, 1985). In deprived ecologies in India, the use of speech for communication, even from early infancy, is relegated to the background as much of the daily events are known and repetitive, and there is more emphasis on activity rather than on the discussive part of it (Lamb et al., 2002). Due to lack of a stimulating environment there is less opportunity to converse on an individual basis, and group interactive speech through dance and song is generally encouraged in Indian rural communities (Peter et al., 1987).

It is also possible that the earlier the stimulation is given in the use of language, the more accelerated would be the language development. In this respect, however, it is necessary to stress that language development is a uniform inherited, genetic pattern unless speech is otherwise impaired by malformation of the vocal cords and brain damage disabilities such as hairlip and cleft palate. Speech can also be impaired by malformed dental lines or jawbones. However, accelerated development of speech and language or its retardation is perhaps due to the differential capacities among individuals. There are varied explanations such as neuro-maturation, genetics, social class, home stimulation and an innate tendency or trait to be motivated to learn.

Therefore in terms of a hybrid model, Schuel has proposed a tentative correlative picture of hypotheses. He identifies several factors affecting language development: (*a*) gender: females are more highly cue-grasp-oriented or referential while males are more expressive; (*b*) birth order:

primarily first born are referential, learning different and quantitatively more elaborate codes (c) socio-economic status: the middle class is more responsive with a higher reinforcing human environment than lower class families (Sheil, 1995: 73).

In the normal context there is little doubt that formal learning of the language accelerates speech through practice and training (Williams and Matteson, 1942: 233–45), home (Van Alstyne, 1929), play and social interaction (Smith, 1935: 182) which offer formal learning have a significant influence on the development of language plasticity. Further language development is also stimulated by the human environment, where language development is found to be related to other positive factors, especially mother's education (Mathew and Sireesha, 1973: 81–89). In a stimulating and reinforcing environment vis-à-vis a non-stimulating one, children tend to use a more elaborate vocabulary and words with intense meaning as they are stimulated by the human environment around them (Muralidharan and Bannerji, 1974: 10–15). In the Indian situation, R. Muralidharan also found that home stimulation significantly increased children's vocabulary and verbal expression of intricate thoughts (Muralidharan, 1970: 45–51). Saraswathi et al. (ibid.) have reviewed a set of developmental norms of children aged 2–5 years from seven cities, where the major finding as to be expected was that the urban children perform better than the rural ones (Bevli, 1983). This however begs the question that variables are neither urban or rural, standing by themselves as environments, but they connote a cluster of variables related to urban and rural habitats. These clusters are composed of sub-variables like income, occupation, caste, regionality, access to technology and related facilities. The test was adapted from Gesellian norms standardised in the West.

It is also the nurturants in close communication with a child in multi-dyad relations who influence the child's pattern of speech who learns through repetition and imitation of the nurturant's speech style (Lewis, 1951). This, however, is dependent on the individual inherent capacities of the child to copy and demonstrate domains, to code and encode the differential patterns in the multilingual environment in India.

Bilingualism and Multilingualism

An important aspect of language relates to the influence of bilingualism and multilingualism on children. Children who grow up in an environment where there are two languages suffer word–concept confusion, with the tendency to intersperse words that have greater meaning in one language rather than another in their speech production. The child will invariably use expressions relating to his mother tongue or articulate using the phonetics of his mother tongue. In most of the ethnic groups of India, where two or more languages compete for the child's expression of his concepts, word–concept retardation in each is likely to appear than in monolingualism (Arsenian, 1945: 65–86). Bilingualism handicaps speech growth as well as inhibits clear concept formation.

Some studies have even indicated in western cultures that singletons in a family have better speech development as compared to twins in a family, since the former have either adults or older siblings as speech models (Day, 1932: 179–99). On the other hand, we have conflicting results of a study by Mohanty and Patnaik where the results showed that bilinguals have better scores than monolinguals when tested for metalinguistic ability (Patnaik and Mohanty, 1984: 63–70). The result was interpreted as indicating the positive effects of second language on the individual's thought processes. In another comparative study of a large sample of Indian children by Southworth, the results indicated that there was no difference in the performance of monolinguals and bilinguals (Southworth, 1980: 121–46). It has been found in his longitudinal study that children of parental bilingualism vis-à-vis monolingualism eventually caught up in their expressions of vocabulary and were as competent as the latter in expression. We need, therefore, to deduce what exactly influences a child's competence in language interaction in a multilingual country such as India. In the few available studies in the Indian context, we found an interesting development in Mohanty's attempt to provide a context specific conceptual-isation on language development. In his study of observations of verbal interaction of four to seven year old children in a multilingual environment, he has suggested that children pass through several stages of development of communicative awareness for the competent use of language in a socially appropriate manner. The progressive stages are:

    (i) the period of language differentiation: (*a*) emergence of language differentiation, (*b*) knowledge of language differentiation;
   (ii) the period of awareness of languages: (*a*) emergence of social awareness of language in use, (*b*) development of social understanding of the role of languages, preferences and hierarchy;
  (iii) the period of multilingual functioning: (*a*) assignment of functional roles to language, (*b*) multilingual functioning in communication (Mohanty, 1994).

These conceptualised stages have arisen from an extensive analysis of the data. While they are still hypothetical in nature, the author expresses concern that there is still insufficient data to move from the hypothetical to the empirical. However, we might speculate that the challenge of living in multicultural and multilingual India today is greater in the face of the social changes taking place. In the last two decades, the source of technology, globalisation, geographical mobility and the growing desire of parents that their children should achieve academic and professional competence have given rise to two challenging phenomena. First, the average middle class child is exposed to computerised knowledge, to recent information, and to the electronic media such as the TV available in almost all Indian homes, rich or poor. The second phenomenon is the increased volume of information specific to one or two major languages, mainly Hindi followed by English. The child is exposed to science and technology through an enormous school curriculum. For motivated parents the latter implies assisting the child in homework and/or employing tutors. Thus, there is a momentum towards better competence in language acquisition and in its functional use, especially among the rising middle class. In a monolinguistic society, homogeneity prevails, as in the western world. For example, in America, everyone irrespective of their country of origin speaks English, whereas in a diverse country like India, English, Hindi and often the mother tongue are used in combination. This is truly observable even amongst the educated, who revert to their mother tongue when it comes to counting in numbers, yet at the same time they will interpret information in English or Hindi. We see this occurrence on a larger geographical area of India. Because of their extensive knowledge of Hindi and their fluency in it, UP-ites are comfortable in any place in north India, whereas a person from the south or from the North-East states may not feel as comfortable. Therefore, various factors—home, school, social and political—together interact to make for progressive language development, which if encouraged from the early stages of childhood create language competence.

It is also well known that maturation and resilience support a child's ability to acquire proficiency in multilingualism. We do know, for instance, that the earlier a child is inducted into multilingualism the more consistent and well grounded is the ability. The learning of other languages in later years is more difficult because of the growing chronological rigidity towards change. Thus the phenomenon of social change over time and place contribute to human proficiency in language development and use of several languages in a pluralistic society. The base of this is an informed socialisation process, which again is aided by better parenting by better educated and achievement-oriented families. Mohanty emphasises that children become socially competent in a multilingual environment by developing a notion of language hierarchy, using implicit norms and switching from one to another through consistent rule-based code mixing (Mohanty and Perregaux, 1977).

As such the question of bilingualism or monolingualism has its roots perhaps in the broad canvas of articulations, gesticulations and body languages in pre-linguistic period of the child's development. A child who ontogenetically is vocal as compared to a less vocal sibling, relative or peer has increased opportunities for expansion of vocabulary. Further, the development of linguistic ability has a language potential and a child who is innately and intuitively curious, creative and motivated will tend to look for expressions even in the tangential languages. What we find is that a child with a higher IQ is more likely to be attentive to expressions of his thought processes in oral behaviour. This does not mean that all intelligent children are highly vocal but that there is a tendency of vocal children to ask questions of themselves or their environment and to use answers to develop higher orders of conceptualisations, namely, increased logical thinking and therefore higher orders of cognitively expressed systems.

Mohanty, Panda and Misra have commented on this controversy by citing several related studies. They cited models like social interaction, cognitive and linguistic models. The authors comment that the models have not yet been able to answer what is actually learned, how it is utilised and how learning proceeds (Mohanty et al., 1999: 125). They cite Goldfield and Snow's discussion stressing individual variations in language acquisition (Goldfield and

Snow, 1993), in which there are continuing processes of modification of experiences, where using syllables, phonemes and the joining of articulated sounds is aligned with conceptual thought processes. In the continual usage of these attributes of speech, the human being simultaneously processes thought and word together in the expression of logical thinking. This ability is obtained through the continuous practice of these processes. When this ability is exhibited we tend to say that the person has attained fluency in oration or is an excellent writer. Chatterjee in her discussion highlights the functional aspects of lullabies, relating to folklore, sung by mothers as an illustration of reinforcing social history through song and rhyme. These lullabies expose the child initially to fantasy and then to reality even though in a complex manner. We find that in the subcultural systems almost all ethnic groups expose the child to imagination and then to gradual understanding of the range of cultural heritage and its language correlates (Chatterjee, 1999: 62–84).

It is generally said that language socialisation is a process in the general socialisation techniques for the child. Also, the concept of early language learning functioning is a successful 'negotiation process' in understanding cultural patterns. Singh in her study of speech patterns has highlighted the crucial role of the major nurturer—the mother mostly—as the shaper of language styles and that the home environment is the major 'developmental stimulus' for receptive and expressed skills in the child's acquisition of language skills (Singh, 1987: 134).

The Indian society, as is well known, is pluralistic in a secular domain. The exposure to varied oral and written communication is a challenge to the young child. Take the illustration of children attending state schools. They come from various types of families (joint/nuclear, Hindu/Muslim and others) and at the same time have to cope with different language styles/ patterns between the home and the school. The acquisition of language requires a process of adjusting the sound to the understanding of the child, and the child's refining of the sound, finding equivalence to the home language in order to comprehend the formal language in school. A little child, for instance, would tend to say 'Mona wants milk', implying herself, as she is in the egocentric stage of perception where things are directly related to her in action and reaction. Gradually she perceives that Mona is a name which identifies her, and then proceeds to learn prepositions like 'me', 'mine', 'they' and 'theirs'.

This joining and fissioning occurs as experiences test the understanding of the word in relationship between oneself and another individual. That is why developmental specialists consider interaction in the human context as vital to the learning of one or more languages. The problem envisaged is that there are unique variables which interact in multiple ways so that while group tendencies in a particular ethnic group are discernible, each individual in that particular ethnic group has an individually unique way of acquiring a language and functionalising it.

Take for instance the usage of a particular phrase to indicate acceptance of a situation. In the Hindi language to confirm an idea presented by the other, the tendency is to say 'Woh toh hai' which in English literally means: 'That is there', which is not grammatically correct when translated into English. Thus, there are ways of converting thoughts into literal translations from one language to another overruling grammatical rules. For instance a child would say: 'He is *maaroing* the sweet.' *Maaro* means 'to steal' but the suffix attached is the English present participle '–ing', and so there occurs a mixing of two languages to make up another enriched third language which is neither one or the other. Chaudhary in her study shows clearly the impact of fine nuances of the environment on speech patterns of the mother–child dyad (Chaudhary, 1999).

These nuances are detailed in Chaudhary's observational study of such interactive patterns. In her study of mothers who are homemakers and where several languages were spoken, the observed data on analysis showed elaborated and restricted codes where the younger the child, the more restrictive was the code and as the child grew, utterances increased (ibid.). This case study approach has in fact amplified the conceptualisation that in-depth case studies of individuals reveal more individual differences than studies of groups as several unique patterns were revealed. The major normative variable was socio-economic class, given the educational background of the mother.

What we are saying in this discussion on language development is that there is no one-to-one relationship between classificatory variables and the development of language. Inferences may be gathered from Indian studies about the following influencing aspects:

- the geo-ecological context (the remote tribal village vis-à-vis urban conglomerate);
- the rate of social interaction (joint versus nuclear family systems);
- the levels of motivation and education of the family, especially the major nurturant;
- the relevance of familial norms (authoritarian vis-à-vis egalitarian relations in the family);
- the exposure to information systems.

The Environment of Language Development

The acquisition of language depends greatly on the positive or negative stimulation of the environment. In economically deprived ecologies, a more limited vocabularly is used as compared to urban areas where the spoken word is more frequent and is expanded through advertisements and media. Cognitive functioning which is a major aspect of intelligence is also one which can be limited or encouraged by the environmental stimuli. The richness of a language flourishes when it is expanded in a functional manner and when speech and grammar are integrated. The learning of grammatical language is an important aspect of self-expression and self-esteem and schools pay a great deal of importance to these aspects. Multilingualism enhances the cognitive functions, and therefore the cultural expressions of a people. The ability to think in more than one language enhances the ability to be resilient to change. On the other hand, lack of knowledge of a language of another state or tribe can limit the ability to understand and accept the ways of others.

Intelligence and its Functionality

The operation of intelligence can be observed in overt behaviour. The levels of intelligence are related to expressed behaviour. It enables man to think and perform to his maximum, and to create and contribute to science and technology. But intelligence can lie dormant if the human endeavour to utilise it does not exist, either due to genetic disorders, birth trauma, brain damage, temporary withdrawal symptoms due to depression or the deliberate restraint of its use by the individual. The will to achieve, even if it is to fulfil a primary need like assuaging hunger, indicates primeval intelligence, in that the individual exhibits food-seeking behaviour. How does the human being think and perform well? Does this depend upon his innate ability to recognise, to differentiate, to logically order his thoughts, to act upon them, to reason, to rationalise, to make decisions and more than that to innovate, to imagine and to create? For these very reasons of possessing these attributes, man as of now seems to have the highest form of intellectual behaviour. The major drawback in assessing intelligence levels is that in the Indian culture there is a continued use of western-oriented tests which contaminate culturality. Their operational definitions originate in the West, to which they are indigenous and deflect the reality in the Indian context. In the Indian culture, much of the assessment is, for the most part, geared to adopting or adapting the contextual meanings of tests, sometimes using items unfamiliar to the Indian context. For instance, using knives and forks is relatively unfamiliar to the average Indian who tends to eat with his hand and only with the right hand. Therefore using assessments of dexterity in the use of these implements transposed to the Indian situation is irrelevant, and therefore not valid. What is more important is how the strategies used for processing the information we derive are relevantly used. For instance, given the hypothesis that in the Indian culture there are differential norms for upbringing of the sexes, we tend to use tests (adopted or adapted) for differentiating between attributes of the sexes, borrowing concepts from a culture where there is more homogeneity or egalitarianism as compared to Indian differential sex upbringing patterns. When we test universal human traits such as cognitive development, in assessing, for instance, differences between attitudes towards male and female upbringing, we know that there is more restrictiveness towards females. Again, in assessing sex-related behaviour, the Indian female tends to be reluctant to talk freely about it, which may be misconstrued as 'introversion'.

The bridge between one human being and another is communication. Stability of the thinking process together with emotional control are contributory factors towards stable performance. The motive to achieve is the spurt to think and act intelligently. The major hindrance here is that we cannot decipher thought processes simultaneously with their occurrence to determine whether the individual is thinking intelligently or not. The only way we can assess its quality is through articulated, reported or acted-out behaviour, whose major vehicle is language. The use of intelligence operates in an unstable fashion, for while man can control his mind, he cannot control the forces of environment and thus there is a constant confrontation between man and his environment. This control is obtained through coping mechanisms adapted to solving problems in a given situation. A man, for instance, marooned on an island, will use his intelligence to eat from the produce of the island, to light a fire with stones, to fish, and to find ways and means to clothe himself. This taxes his intelligence in the same manner but to a lesser degree than a scientist's in an atomic energy laboratory. What we are saying here is that the level of intelligence is genetically obtained and ontogenetically processed. Thus it is for the human being to hone his basic intelligence to cope with and control the environment.

The earliest documented evidence of interest in man's intelligence, which distinguished him from the primate, dates back to Plato and Aristotle who used to hold forth discourses in public places on the philosophy of life and on the place of man in the process of development (Sternberg, 1990). Plato described three aspects of divinity within the human being, which distinguish him from the lower order of mammals. The three attributes are intellectual, emotional and moral. He placed the first in the highest position of driving the other two towards their fulfilment. These three concepts are also labelled as cognition, affection and connation (Burt, 1955: 158–77). Cicero was the first to use the word 'intelligentsia', to mean a quickness and high cue grasp of the ideation processes, orally communicated. Intelligence is therefore a combination of perception and interpretation, both in terms of the sequential timing of ideations (maturation), and their expression in art and science. With the advent of scientific enquiries in the West and movement to find scientific premises for thought and behaviour, Spearman in his book *The Abilities of Man* (1927) investigated a 'g' or general factor of mental ability including its offshoot, the 's' category of specific factors. In Galton's days, this general factor was accepted as a definition of intelligence (Galton, 1869/1962). Thus, we see a gradual process of defining intellectual ability as something innate and inherent, which can be modified (enhanced or depressed) by environmental stimuli and has several sub-categories of intelligence. The 'g' factor was conceptualised on a statistical derivation from large sample surveys. On the other hand, the biological aspect constructed by Spencer (Das and Thapa, 2000: 152) regards intelligence as being both a differentiator between ideas and objects, and a collator of similar objects. We see here a similarity to the concepts of differentiation and integration mooted by deterministic experimentalists (Marek, 1988: 75–115). In fact, events in life while assumed to be strictly 'cause and effect' deterministic postulates do not indicate how far the ramifications of intelligence can overcome a straight-line relationship between cause and effect. There are many other variables which deepen the understanding of the effect. For instance, a genius does not stop with understanding a simple relationship such as 'something thrown up will fall'. There are other variables intervening: barriers to break the fall, and gas-filled balloons and aeroplanes which do not necessarily fall when up in the air. How did this understanding come about? It is through the painstaking efforts of persistent geniuses.

The factor of intelligence may therefore be described as cognition, comprising sensory, perceptual, associative and relational processes of the mind's activities. These send out receptors and bring in preceptors, which encode, code and decode ideas. Weschler defined intelligence as similar to acting in a general manner with a purpose to arrive at solutions of problems through logical premises (Weschler, 1994: 3). Intelligence is the functional system that analyses responses (using conventional methodology, sampling and statistics), which gives information about a particular statistic, like an average, for instance, but when identifying individuals, it reduces them to inanimate statistical figures. What seems to be more important is the way the schema which the individual uses to interpret information he receives is categorised and reduced to premises applicable to daily living. For instance, questioning a child about the difference between a straight line and the same length of line converted into another object only gives information about the similarity of length in differential perceptual configurations. These, observed in the concrete operational stage of cognition (three to four years), form the foundation for later abstraction and mathematical solutions.

In the initial stages, using western tests and then tailoring them to Indian realities was like fitting a square peg into a round hole. With the introduction of western education, an alien system of thinking was imposed upon Indian children through the learning of English and English-related information, especially in missionary schools. For instance, alien English nursery rhymes were taught routinely, such as 'Mary had a little lamb whose fleece was white as snow' or 'Ring a ring a roses, pocket full of posies'. There was a dissonance between the far-removed system and the ground realities of living in deprived situations of poverty and meagre facilities where there were no roses made into posies, no fleece, and so on. Thus the imposition of an alien culture introduced rote learning of rhyming words. To this day this system still exists in many elite nursery schools which attempt to ape the West. They do not equip the pliable mind to be attuned to the realities and to learn coping mechanisms within their settings.

However, since systematic education began earlier in the West than in the East, when it arrived in India there was a hiatus between the elite who had access to this education and the masses who were illiterate. Over time, there was a gradual realisation, following independence, that there was a mismatch between the system of British education and the learning needs of the general population. This prompted academicians to attempt to derive indigenous conceptualisations of learning through cognition of the environment, communicated in the indigenous languages (Whorf, 1939).

We will discuss in Volume II the role of perception, learning, memory, storage and retrieval in cognitive processes. These make up the inferential knowledge based upon similarity/dissimilarity of concepts, of synonyms and antonyms, cumulated into experiential knowledge (Luria, 1976). If this is the composite base of inferential behaviour, indicating a high or low intellectual grasp, how does it apply to the strategies used by the Indian in his thought processes?

Indian Philosophical Discussions on Intelligence and Intelligent Behaviour

Wisdom or *buddhi* grows out of experiential learning accumulated over time and is related to chronological age. The older one gets, the wiser one is expected to become. For these reasons the early years are treated as a maturing process, where children are not looked upon as adults, for the mind is still forming. The laws of Manu, the *Bhagwad Gita* and Samkhya Yoga are the basis of intellectual thoughts. The Samkhya Yoga is stated as operating through five sense organs and five motor organs. These represent concepts of seeing, smelling, hearing, taste and touch, and are parallelled by the statements on the senses in western writing. In eastern ideation these senses relate to speech, grasping, locomotion, expelling waste from the body, and inhaling and exhaling to cleanse the systems (Das and Thapa, 2000: 154).

In contrast to them are the internal organs: mind, ego and intelligence (*manas*, *ahamkara* and *buddhi*). The sensors, which operate these processes, monitor them. The activities arising from the mind, the ego and intelligence are distinct from the organs as they are abstract processes. These abstract processes collect experiences from the external faculties, are sensed by the self and are again monitored, sifted and censored in the intelligence domain. The abstract mind, the *manas*, is expected to indicate some activity in the perceptive and sensory processes taking place or avoid them as painful processes (Das and Thapa, 2000: 154). Let us take an example. The mind (also allied to the soul of the individual) takes in experiences from the sensors transmitted by the ego, the ahamkara. It then decides on the basis of emotional intelligence whether an experience is pleasurable or painful, and if painful, such as a confirmed vegetarian being forced to eat meat, he will reject the appeal of the id (the unconscious, uninhibited self, which is routinely pleasure-seeking) and calculate through intelligence that meat eating is in contrast to socio-religious norms. These norms are instilled from birth, and the vegetarian therefore finally avoids or rejects non-vegetarian food. It is of course a moot point whether the act is intelligently processed or vetted by a faculty of wisdom. The act can still be by passed by the ego. Often this is how guilt and its accompanying anxiety are built up in those who non-intelligently function against social norms for their own pleasure. The Hindu scriptures explain intelligence through the Samkhya Yoga philosophy, identifying five attitudes. These are knowledge, conduct, detachment, manifestation and renunciation (ibid.). This same philosophy has eight *bhava*s or states. These are *dharma* or virtue, *jnana* or knowledge, *viraga* or non-attachment and *aisvarya* or power, together with their opposite states *adharma* or non-virtue, *ajnana* or ignorance, *raga* or attachment and *anaisvarya* or weakness. It is to be remembered that these are philosophies arising from the high thinking of religious treatises. These are major beliefs and therefore not amenable to empiricism, except to indicate the positiveness and the negativeness of the attributes. It would be intriguing to hypothesise how these are processed into bipolar dimensions. It is possible that it is due to the passing down of values from one generation to another, through appropriate behaviour, on the assumption that these can have the potential of being imitated by the young. In the traditional family set-up, authority was accepted, and rules and regulations were followed, with rewards for compliance, and punishment for negligence. In the current era of social change, these norms are not strictly enjoined because of greater individual freedom due to socio-political approval of the democratic values. At this point, we see clear linkages to the psychological concept of self-image and self-identity, indicating the inner workings of the mind.

The other viewpoint of Samkhya Yoga slants towards the development of the consciousness or the self. Also, closely related to the self is the conscious or the ego and the unconscious or the libido of Freudian psychology. This view is supported by Sri Aurobindo's work emphasising that intelligence must be a purifying process which differentiates man from animal. Man must be in control of his senses by meditating on his actions and reactions, using his higher consciousness or the superego, in Freudian terminology. This super-consciousness of man causes him to reflect on the value of actions and reactions. This analytical thinking or buddhi compels man to think and rethink and to refine his thought processes, as is apparent in the writings of philosophers. Buddhi is understanding, following the Samkhya Yoga tradition (Sri Aurobindo, 1922). According to this view, that which is moral is that, which 'does not think or cause harm to others irrespective of what they have done' (Shastri, 1985). This is very much like the Christian notion of 'turn the other cheek', and the biblical saying 'do good to them that harm you and love those who hate you' implying that the highest form of humanity consists of entertaining good thoughts. In English we have the phrase 'what is your problem' (implying 'the problem rests with you not with me'). We find the phrase used in conversation even in the Indian society *'aap ko kya* problem *hai?'* The difference between the thought expressed in the West is an unconditional 'It is your problem' but in the Indian context it extends to empathic emotion 'I can help you'. We see this behaviour even in common-day occurrences when we lose our route/direction and ask a passer-by. Invariably even though the passer-by does not have a clue he will try to direct you, or politely say *'aagay ja kay poocho'* ('Ask ahead'). The central theme of this philosophy is that intelligence must be purified by discriminating thought processes, which perceive the objective of moral principles as different from personal judgement of the activity. If somebody makes a mistake it is common to respond with, 'this happens sometimes' or *'kabhi, kabhi yeh ho jaata hai'*. The human mind is such that there are constant thought processes whether negative or positive. When there are no such active processes occuring, the mind becomes regressive, since the very process of thinking moves from the simple to the complicated. If the mind is not progressively thinking it is said to be 'the devil's workshop' or *'khalee dimaag shaitan ka ghar hai'*. Comments on buddhi system are furthered by concepts such as *'nyaya vaisesika'* and *'prajna'* in the Patanjali yoga system in which a term *pratibha* is used, which means flash of light (akin to intuition) (Das and Thapa, 2000: 155). Shastri's concepts imply achieving wisdom through good deeds, and a realistic concept of the finiteness of life and the function of the self during the span of finiteness. If the mind consistently and continuously is proactive and creative then it is exercising its functions at higher levels. *Jnana* is acquired through the learning transferred from a teacher, termed as learning from an educated and informed teacher. Srivastava, Tripathi and Misra comment that intelligence in the Indian philosophical treatises has been viewed as a state, a process and an entity (Srivastava et al., 1995: 30–45). Its capacity to function is dependent upon the motivation to use it in a proactive manner. We see this in the behaviour of an adult towards a child. Among educated parents, the child is consciously encouraged to be curious and inquisitive so that he develops his discriminatory abilities and forms judgments about cause and effect among events critical to reality and objectivity. If emotionality tinges this objectivity, like revenge and hate or self-indulgence or inactivity occur, these distort objectivity. Hence the defensive mind finds mechanisms, which obscure the functioning of realistic intelligence. Similar intervening variables prejudice the reasoning process. The Indian view emphasises the understanding of space and time as crucial components of intelligence. In the western conceptualisation of intelligence, Piaget has emphasised the discriminatory ability to understand concepts of space (*'desh'* or geographical area) and time (*'kaal'*), and the recognition of time, which are the operational stages in the preschool development years. Indians are very susceptible to the idea of 'good' and 'bad' time. For instance, we have auspicious times and inauspicious times in relation to socio-religious events like marriage; *rahu kalam* is inauspicious time and is usually related to the appearance or disappearance of the sun.

In the Indian frame, intelligence is closely allied with the themes of religious thought: purity, higher-order thinking and morality. These concepts are comparable to the biblical themes of the eight Beatitudes in the New Testament of Christianity. This relationship to religious and philosophical thinking is less evident in the western explanation of intelligence. It is very much a part of morality and ethics in India. In fact, intelligence is not thought of as static or influenced by heredity, as in western thinking, but is taken as a part of the creation of man, as being a continuity with past incarnations, where a man is given the material to work with for a future incarnation, whether he will ascend to higher forms or descend to lower forms of a future existence. In western thought it is said to be nurture or the environment, which acts and reacts on the native or inherited intelligence levels. In Indian thought, this is a carry-over of basic materials shared by all individuals alike at birth. It is the response of the human being to evil that sharpens or dulls the human intellect. The more related meaningful concepts then keep on adding dynamically to his intelligence. This reflects on intelligent behaviour till he reaches the stage of purification of thought and action: the stage of a *sanyasi* (attaining *sanyas* or completed understanding of his self in relation to god and the world). Social and individual history of human beings (phylogeny) is repeated by the faculty of ontogenics (or the individual capacity to adapt to higher levels).

Neurological Interpretations of the Origin and Function of Intelligence

Besides the above scientific and spiritual interpretations of intelligence, there is a neurological aspect. Much of the knowledge about neurology of intelligence is gained through interlinking the brain processes of ideation, processed by the level of intelligence. The processes are extrapolated mainly from studies of brain damage (Sabhesan and Natrajan, 1988: 29–32), tumours (Gupta and Jain, 1995: 97–102) and intake of alcohol and drugs (Gupta et al., 1994: 185–88; Nirmala and Swaminathan, 1985: 73–78). Also, the part played by drugs in inducing hypnosis must not be discounted, for it tells about the workings of the unconscious. About a 100 years ago it was discovered that the left frontal lobe of the brain is responsible for speech and expressive language. Further, language becomes distorted when injury to the temporal lobes occur. These deficits are called expressive aphasia and receptive aphasia (Damasio, 1992). Thus various damaged parts of the brain were identified as affecting cognitive structures (Luria, 1966).

Luria also demonstrated that the expression of thoughts in writing could exist side by side with expressed speech, thus indicating the relationship between the spoken word and the written word. Specific dysfunctions discovered were seen in neurologically impaired patients in their ability to recognise and understand small objects, but the ability to recognise and understand large objects was not dysfunctional because of such impairment (McCarthy and Warrington, 1990). Language, in terms of parts of speech, was also found to be varied in such cases of brain damage (Broca, 1960: 49–72). Neuroscientists in examining memory discovered a distinction or different systems in memory between recall and recognition of items and a learned skill (Polster et al., 1991: 95–116). Delayed retention and recall are also areas of further investigation. Das and Thapa (2000) state that there is a growing system of empirical knowledge of the intervention of neuropsychology or epistemology in understanding knowledge, its representation in memory and related intelligence levels in cognition and its intelligent functioning. Distortions of various types occur when various parts of the brain are damaged, such as face recognition and spatial perception (Farah, 1995). As assumed by most psychologists, cognitive processes are a part of the function of intelligence levels, and if cognitive functions are affected by loss of memory, amnesia occurs. The use of sophisticated advances in molecular energy and technical devices have improved the expansion of EEG functions, and the understanding between neural and cognitive functions, through investigation of the images of the mind, and its representations (Posner and Raichle, 1994). In trying to arrive at scientific data, neurophysical and psychological processes are investigated by studying damaged functions of the brain through overt expressions. They have not achieved the status of psychometrics precisely because of the clinical approach used in studying the relatively few cases available.

The conceptualisations, therefore, offer only tentative approaches to hypotheses, as they require validity and reliability measures. The current use of intelligence tests like the Weschler and the Halstead–Reitan Battery intelligence tests (Benton, 1994: 1–23) and other such adult intelligence testing do not offer a diagnosis directly related to neurological impairment as they only elicit overt behaviour. This description of the state of neurological preceptors and inter-receptors in intellectual functioning describe only neurological impairments in the brain, which relate to cognition. It is generally accepted that neurological findings are affiliates of conceptualisation as they play a large part in the function of intelligent thought and behaviour. According to the western and Indian views of intelligence, it operates on the basis of experiential knowledge and is accumulated, stored and retrieved in an organised manner. But here the similarities end. Intelligence in the Indian way of thinking has to be specific, not a generalised ability as viewed by Spearman and his associates (Spearman, 1927). Also, perception and action articulate the senses. These are controlled by the rules of conduct, renunciation and attachment (Kaviraj, 1966: 1–44).

In summation therefore, we need to assess the critical innate skills from the viewpoint of their utility in the Indian context. Stating a unilateral assessment would be unrealistic. It has been reported that the assessment of intelligence as a general ability has been superseded by a new concept that intelligence can be operationalised by a single idea. Currently, it is the speed of time or reaction time to tasks as advocated by Jensen and Eysenck. However speed is only amenable to measurement. The actual intelligence package is composed of dormant cognitive processes. When these are comprehended and activated by the growing individual as in the early stages of language development, they are the indicators of cognitive development as expressed from one chronological stage to another. For example, the package of cognitive processes is limited in expression in a two-year-old as compared to that of a 10-year-old. It may be considered as the unfolding process of dormant intellectual ability (Jensen, 1982: 255–310). Indians live in different geo-ecological areas, many of them uneducated or educated in one-room or poorly run schools where teachers are indifferent, frequently absent and where facilities are meagre. In such environments there is very little stimulation to evoke intelligent activities. Intelligence remains dormant unless awakened by opportunity and it is evident that when opportunity occurs children educated in rural and district towns turn out to be as intelligent in their behaviour as an educated, well-cushioned, urban child.

For the very reason that we do not know the intelligence level of a particular person, behaviourists have come into their own. They have produced standardised tests on large normal populations whose profiles are considered normative and can be comparable to other such samples derived from other such populations (see Chapter 6, 'Research Concerns'). The purpose is to find out how intelligent a person is in relation to others of his type. The equation developed is called the intelligence quotient. This quotient is a number which assumes that there is a normal distribution of intelligence in any population and the average is assumed to be 100. Using a normal curve distribution, a standard deviation is computed from the test. Scores above and below 100 describe whether a scorer is above average or below average in intelligence. For the most part, however, scores are handles for monitoring future progress in academic or intellectual work. Intelligence tests are based on items orally or reportedly responded to. It is said to measure individual intelligence levels against a normative standard set of values. We will mention here a test of intelligence called Stanford–Binet test of intelligence (Terman, 1916). Alfred Binet developed a test in 1896 to measure intelligence for the specific purpose of identifying intellectually deficit children. This was further refined by Binet and Simon employing questions of increasing difficulty to measure memory, attention and verbal skills. Futher revisions took place and the Stanford Binet Test 5 is currently used. It took into account various variables such as gender, ethnicity, regionality and other socio-economic indices, after it was standardised on 4,800 individuals derived randomly from the US census. Its adaptation has proved to be useful in the Indian context as it has relevance to the major parameters that are universal. In a test of intelligence such as described earlier, the behaviourists use a standard reference to identify the position of the respondent along a dimension of continuous scores. The theoretical construct thus hypothesised is that the test items evoke responses which indicate differential abilities when taken together, as specific abilities compose the package measuring an abstract construct called intelligence. This test therefore infers the level of intelligence, and gives a handle for further empirical data and a progression in the understanding of what is intelligence. Such tests have been given in Appendix I. Some examples of tests of intelligence adapted to Indian conditions are Raven's coloured progressive Matrices

(Ghuman, 1978: 281–94) which is used for non-verbal reasoning ability, especially for those who have limited command over the English language and in a sense is a culturally related test based on reasoning arising from assessing figures in relation to their meaning; Wechsler's test, was developed in the 1950s based on Binet's concepts to operationalise separately verbal and performance IQ attributes. This was further combined to give a total score of mental ability. It has however not completely eradicated 'error variance' as it is not a culture-free test, but has been found useful in schools to distinguish between verbal and performance intelligence skills. Over the years the factorial approach is becoming more popular since intelligence can be disaggregated into many components besides the '*g*' or generic factor. There are many more '*s*' or specific factors which operationalise the '*g*' factor. Thurstone, in the 1930s, developed seven separate primary skill tests. These were perceptual speed, numerical ability, word fluency, verbal comprehension, space visualisation, associative memory and reasoning (Thurstone, 1938).

The evolutionary theory derived by Darwin, and furthered by other experts states the survival of the fittest. This includes those with the highest intelligence level. This attribute differentiates between the abilities of animals and the human. It is also a theory closely allied to the theory of inherent or inherited abilities where chromosomes of the genes of the parents or the lineage are transferred to the progeny, through the operation of dominant and recessive genes. Further, there are several small group studies or studies of ethnicity which substantiate these conceptualisations. For example, children reared in institutions with little stimuli were compared to those raised in foster homes. The latter showed more intelligent behaviour, indicating the relationship between nature and nurture on intelligent behaviour (Thompson, 1952).

In defence of the normative method of identifying intelligence, Wechsler popularised the '*g*' factor (the generic factor) of intelligence. This '*g*' factor, as said before, was identified by Spearman (1927). The '*g*' factor subsumed trait factors such as verbal intelligence, mechanical intelligence, and such like. Spearman had also identified a variety of emotional factors such as anxiety and conflict. Further factors identified were correlative such as intensity and extensity of these factors. Thus, test of intelligence used qualifying adjectives like 'extensity of trauma' and 'intensity of empathy' to further clarify these correlative factors, thus expanding the meaning of intelligence, one of the most popular being social intelligence. Stoddard's definition of intelligence is that 'intelligence is the ability to undertake activities that are characterised by (*a*) difficulty, (*b*) complexity, (*c*) abstractness, (*d*) economy, (*e*) adaptiveness, (*f*) social value and (*g*) originality.' He also stressed that intelligence further implied the conditions under which they should operate, namely, concentration of energy and a resistance to emotional forces and maintaining objectivity (Stoddard, 1943).

Among some formal definitions of intelligence there are those which say that intelligence is what the intelligence test measures, which means little, for it circumvents the real issue of what intelligence is (Sternberg, 2000: 117). Binet and Terman were the first who in the initial stages studied intelligence through finding some operational definitions which are reliable and valid. Binet's definition of intelligence was the ability of the individual to direct his behaviour towards a goal, to modify his strategies to obtain the goals and to identify the achievement made towards the goals. His conceptualisation was 'that intelligence comprised comprehension, invention, direction and censorship' (Forest, 1954). This implied that the goal direction must always be focussed. Also, the goal must always be in sight and reason; its deductive and inductive inferences should be used rationally and objectively. His definition was the quality of one's experiences for the solution of immediate problems and anticipatory alertness towards the future, both similar and dissimilar. Terman defines intelligence as an individual's ability to carry on abstract thinking and use abstract symbols in all kinds of problems' (Terman, 1916). In this definition he identified the size of vocabulary as the single, most strong variable to indicate intelligence. Spearman gave the concept of general intelligence but Terman delinked the excessive faith in mathematical reasoning (Terman, 1930). A culture-free test was first conceived of by Jensen (1980). Since speed is considered as the major indicator of intelligence, it is reasonable to assume that every individual can learn, memorise and respond, but the ability to quickly assess and react is now gaining in popularity as the single most important factor, namely, the ability to cue-grasp. Jensen revived the concept of 'g' factor as a measure of performance. Though he based his rationale on the cognitive ability required to accomplish the task, a factor analysis showed that the 1937 Stafford revision of the Binet scale does measure to a large extent the general factor or 'g' factor of intelligence. Warner, Havighurst and Loeb however suggest that there is a social class bias to the so-called 'culture free tests' as they cannot entirely divest themselves of the cultural connotations of the society in which they are formulated (Warner et al., 1944). On the other hand Terman found several interpretations to the concept of intelligence. This, however, did not deter other experts from formulating their own operational definitions of intelligence. The problem arises because individuals have many types/levels of intelligence. This gave rise to the preparation of tests of intelligence which are multi-factoral. (Wechsler, 1944). The use of abstract thinking is basically the foundation of human intelligence, and for this reason the development of cognition has had a very important place in the context of intelligence. Thorndike concurred with this thinking (Thorndike et al., 1928). He abstracted three independent variables from Binet's scale: altitude (the harder the task, the greater the intelligence); breadth (the greater the number of tasks of equal difficulty, the greater the intelligence); and speed (the more quickly a correct response is given, the greater is intelligence displayed). The last characteristic has come to be accepted by most current experts as the most important factor indicating intelligence. Predictiveness, therefore, is also exemplified as the usefulness of this type of test, though Thorndike identified altitude or that the harder or more challenging the task, the greater is the intelligence displayed. Thurstone's test has an eclectic frame as he used most of the processes expressed by the previous workers, through factor analysis (Thurstone, 1924).

The merit of intelligence, in view of the lack of any other alternative, is the major measure for assessing the spectrum of cognitive competencies, which are based on native or inherent structures. Simple, unambiguous multiple-answer tests are compiled for establishing reliability, and where the stimulus questions are explicitly valid. Most tests are based upon accuracy of perception in discriminant functions of similarity/dissimilarity. Mental tests are becoming most useful in psychoneurological diagnosis and in reading disabilities such as dyslexia. However since progress is scientifically engendered, mechanical and technical gadgetry are progressing with increase in speed and communications. There is general interest in knowing how cognitive functions process information in test measures.

This brings us to the issue of the third view on intelligence, namely, the Hindu philosophical view of intelligence, as related to the ego and the individual potential to gain knowledge. In this view, the individual's energy is part of the cosmic energy. In his search for more knowledge, the individual introspects or meditates by internalising a scrutiny of his self. He looks inwards. He relates his actions or dharma and adharma to what is true knowledge. This view is a moral and ethical introspection of the self and differs from assessing intelligence through neurological examination of brain-damaged individuals by the neuro-scientific approach. It also differs from the assessment of conceptual cognitive processes expressed in the concepts of behaviour. In the spiritual frame of Hindu philosophy, the use of intelligence is to seek the truth as based on moral and ethical injunctions of the scriptures. In this respect, it therefore relates to individual differences in the powers of thinking and reasoning, and cannot be tested empirically on a large population to acquire standardisation, as the assessment is subjective unlike the tests of intelligence administered in the psychological situation.

In the Hindu view, the search for the truth by an individual is what he perceives it to be, through a regimen of introspective search. This need not necessarily be compatible with the objective results of psychological tests. On the other hand, group tests indicate average intelligence or deviation from the average. Some may be super and some may be less intelligent. The neurological viewpoint has much to contribute to the psychological concept of intelligence, for brain damage is a good indicator of lessened intelligent ability. Suffice it to say that all these viewpoints described are complementary. The major shortcoming is that no one can cover or uncover the meaning of intelligence in its totality except through reliable observation of behaviour. All that these tests do is to elicit behaviour which at some level indicates a corresponding level of intelligence 'within the limits of the said test'.

This takes us back to the conceptualisation of Jensen to find a test that is culture- and context-free. However, even his test of intelligence among various ethnic groups in America across a large geographical sample evoked criticism, for it indicated that African Americans performed more poorly than the Anglo-Saxons, leading to notions indicating the superiority of the latter vis-à-vis former. Some new information on the processing phenomenon indicates further advances.

Information Processing

We have talked so far about the meaning, structure, functions and measurement of intelligence. There is also a reference to culture-free tests in the previous section. However, we need to discuss some concepts as to how information is processed, and how a question stimulates a response. The processing of information is of interest to psychologists as more sophisticated and stimulating devices for diagnosis have become available. The criteria related to performance are (*a*) speed and (*b*) accuracy of the strategy used to arrive at the performance, (*c*) the techniques used by the processor, (*d*) the mental representation of the strategy and (*e*) the utilisation of the related knowledge at the time of testing or eliciting of a response.

The new age is an enquiry into mental functions. Here we see a movement into enquiring about the source of knowledge and not the product (the behaviour). Let us take an example. A respondent to a test may be well prepared, may indicate a high IQ, may have within his repertoire several strategies and may be a very speedy respondent. But at the time of responding to the test he may be sick, have a lowered volition, be distracted, may have had a quarrel with his mother just before leaving, be preoccupied about host of other things of which there is no observed symptomatic behaviour; these may all be intervening variables. Therefore they may deflect the true response. Sperry (1973: 209–29) examined the mental functions of the left and right hemispheres of the brain following a surgical separation of the two halves, which created a barrier. Added to this was the innovation of creating computer models to investigate the processes of mental activity in-depth. Newell for instance experimented with stimulating brain functions to test the corresponding mental activity (Newell, 1981: 203–26). The efforts of Guilford in psychometrics (Guilford, 1956: 267–93) have been complemented by such approaches which led to greater information about the working of cognitively related functions exercised by brain reactions. The theories of Jensen (1982: 255–310) and Eysenck (1986: 1–34) are based on the biological substratum of intelligent behaviour, using the biological approach. However their tests were not culture-free.

The theoretical concepts of Thorndike (1913) which use associations as the base for eliciting intelligent behaviour rest on the assumed relation between sensory information and neural impulses. For example, the law of cause and effect assumes connectionism between two events. Connectionism explains cognitive activities in terms of the interaction between neurons (Schneider, 1987: 73–83). The basic processes are made through nodes and links termed 'units of connections'. The former are assumed to be processing devices (taking in messages and sending them to the brain areas where the various cognitive functions reside and link the necessary connections). They transmit action over the links that lie between nodes. One might assume that the links are chains between the different nodes. The foci on which the messages arrive after transmission are activated through the relevant links to return the message. We might go further on to say that what the author means is simply that there are brain foci for various cognitive reactions. The modular mechanisms are the repositories of these cognitive reactions. The individual using the principles of connectionism stimulates the relevant nodes which are activated through the related links (links attuned to the cognitive information). He processes the response and sends them back through the nerves to the individual's mind (abstract concept of self). The links have their own strengths: the more they connect through the nodes, the stronger the linkages. The linkages however have both positive and negative actions and connectivity (similar to Lewin's concept of valences). The Indian, for instance, is used to *roti, dal* and *chawal* (unleavened bread, lentils and rice). He may enjoy, for some time, European cuisine, but after the novelty has worn off he will long for his own ethnic food since the links between the nodes established in childhood in relation to food are stronger for satisfying the need. We therefore see a relationship to another theory, the need theory of Maslow (1966), where higher-valued behaviour has a greater instantaneous connection for satisfaction than the less-valued. The major difference here is that the proponents of the newer biological forms of intelligence concentrate on a biological connectivity rather than on the stimulus response theory of behaviourists like Thorndike and Guilford.

These new proponents go a little further than behaviourists in their attempts to find out the functioning of the mind, namely, the biological components in the brain and the processing of information. The given network of the nodes and their linkages exhibit a level of performance depending upon the 'weights' for positivity and negativity. Accumulation of experiences forms a repository of concepts which can be elicited by appropriate stimuli. This accumulation of cognitive experiences forms the storehouse of our intelligent behaviour. Connectionism as a biological cognitive explanation of the working of cognitive associations is within this network of nodes and their linkages. Its overt explanations are still to be empirically demonstrated by adequate validity. Shastri and Ajjanagadde (1993: 417–94) have discussed this theorem to have existed in their book *SHRUTI*, or 'Knowledge', in which they attempt to advance a theory of intelligence based on non-cultural bound and non-contextual tests of intelligence. Based upon models of artificial intelligence, Sternberg (1990: 146) states: 'Considering all aspects of even a moderately complex problem takes too much time. Instead intelligence systems know what aspects to consider and what aspects not to consider.'

Testing Intelligence in the Indian Situation

The development of testing intelligence in the psychological sphere has not taken off as expected. Experts comment that academicians are driven by knowledge quest rather than by testing situations which are of applicability to the Indian psyche. Drawn from the West, a model of the Indian is a result of researchers unwittingly using the western measures of intelligence testing. The concentration has been on programmes for development which would automatically lead to descriptions of behaviour of contact between policy makers and researchers (Sinha and Mishra, 1993: 139–50). One of the major limitations is the lack of theoretical models that are applicable to the Indian situation. The same applies to research on cognition, intellectual constructs and concepts. As said before, the types of intelligence tests used show little relevance to the Indian culture. Several intelligence tests show defects affecting the validity, reliability and the effectivity of normative data (Srivastav et al., 1996: 1–11). The documentation of tests is done by National Library of Educational and Psychological Tests (NLEPT) at NCERT, Delhi. K. Kumar did a review of over a decade of intelligence tests used in India (Kumar, 1991: 546–67). Most of these were verbal, 234 were non-verbal and none was performance-based.

Evolutionary theory states that the processes are phylogenetically acquired behaviour—the inherent natural potentials of individuals which by genetic inheritance are existent from birth. The environmental view observes that the ontogenetic behaviour is influenced by the social structure, the ecology and, most of all, the micro system, the family (Bronfenbrenner, 1979). It may make for differences in behaviours among different nationalities, like the eating of raw beef and fish by some societies. The people of the Middle East eat from one platter because it demonstrates kinship, as distinct from Indians who do not eat from one platter to avoid pollution and preserve purity. Indians use the right hand for eating and the left for ablution and thus keep them separate. On the other hand, a westerner eats with cutlery and uses either hand, as ablution is accomplished by the use of special paper. This behavioural difference does not connote lack of intelligence but the use of different norms. For the reason of differences in cultural norms, the use of western oriented tests have been much criticised for their utility in India. Even adaptations are so literal that they measure different cultural norms than differences within the culture. If, for instance, a tribal living in the hills is asked to draw a man, he will draw a background of the hills and trees. In Africa it may be a man climbing a tree. In desert areas, it might be just sand dunes. For the same reason, the word 'pear' when pronounced in a test might be recognised as 'pair'. A criticism of the use of tests measuring many factors with a common denominator is that there is the dilemma of homogeneity. If a sample shows high scores on some items and low on others, then which are heterogeneous and which are homogeneous? The problem still remains very distinct: If a test is standardised for one society in one country, how valid is it for another society in another country, where experiential knowledge is different? For this reason, there is a great demand for the development of indigenised normative tests which can account for different habitats, ecologies, kinship, norms and ethnic/religious groups. In recent years, there has been an attempt to develop such context-specific tests. But there is another impediment, that of lack of theoretical models which have assumptions credible for the Indian society. Indian experts, by and large, use western conceptualisations. For this reason, the Indian Hindu philosophical conceptualisations on the raising of thought to the level of spiritualism merit some consideration. Again if intelligence is to know, then knowledge is the ultimate. We are not talking here of scientific knowledge but of cognitive knowledge which uses the trait of reasoning logical precepts (the tool which is intelligence) to solve the problems in the test as constructed.

Adaptive Resilience in Skill Performance

Adjustment implies adjusting to a particular set of behaviour and related values. These values differ from one culture to another. One culture tolerates competition, another lauds it and yet another downplays it (Munroe and Munroe, 1977: 145–46). In the Indian culture, assertive and aggressive competition is deplored; while competing with oneself, namely doing better than the last time, is extolled. There is also the much debated concept of dependency. In the western culture, dependency is considered self-abnegation and in others, it is considered sharing of oneself and being altruistic (Diaz-Guerrero, 2003).

Therefore, cultural relativity which identifies whether behaviour is well adjusted or maladjusted is evaluated against a set of cultural norms. Again, bias in perception distorts judgement. A family member is usually forgiven a violation. If the individual is a child, the usual response is 'he is young and immature'. However, if the individual is older, he is expected to be knowledgeable as to what is right and what is wrong. But if the person happens to be of a different caste or class, he is valued and judged as an outsider. If he consciously and deliberately opposes the existing norms, he is judged as maladjusted.

The development process, besides having other effects, also promotes resilience and flexibility in adapting to the circumstances, and may even foster the change process. An Indian lives in an environment where behaviour has a relation to the ethics and the ethos of the dominant culture. Abiding by the norms of the society transmitted by the family is said to be normal, violation is considered abnormal (Mowrer, 1948).

While we have different stages of development delineated by the *samskaras* we have little large-scale homogeneous data regarding the other culturally approved attributes of the Indian psyche, except in discursive terms of sharing, cooperation, putting the other before self, moral values, respect, obedience and working towards righteous living enjoined by the scriptures. It is difficult to say whether these are indeed validated, as only small scale studies are available relating to these attributes.

There are six principles of adjustment which we offer here. These are

  (i) a complex process of the self's maturation through the ability to learn right and wrong values in family, kinship and society;
 (ii) the ability to satisfy needs from the environment or obtain fulfilment from the environment;
(iii) the support given to the individual to be secure with his identity within his group;
 (iv) the tendency to abide or not to abide by civic rights and the law and order mandates of the country;
  (v) the capacity to accept differences, be tolerant of differences—in other words to be non-judgemental;
 (vi) society's acceptance of an individual as a member of society.

These principles of adjustment are crucial given the fact that the world is becoming competitive and individuals are expected to have the motivation to succeed; exercise intellectual functions to the fullest, academically and professionally; develop language proficiency and, finally, possess interpersonal competence. These acquisitions are besides the acquisition of manual and cognitive skills. No doubt there are other traits in the Indian context which are considered critical. We have detailed some for discussion. In the Indian context, the child from birth is exposed to multiple mothering and to his kin group members. In his environment, the child interacts with other children at annual festivals, marriages, pujas and other social events. The child has several authority figures, his father, grandfathers and uncles from both sides, all of whom freely and automatically guide, chastise and praise him (Khatri, 1970: 394). The child grows up into a familial male or female role and learns what is expected in terms of role performance. The child also observes adults around him/her, and imitates them (Bandura, 1977). The behaviour he observes is the way in which a particular individual plays different roles at different times. In the presence of older people, for instance, his father, he acts deferentially. For children, the father is an authority figure, He expects his wife, no matter what the social class is, to undertake the dual job of childcare and household management. The child constructs reality the way he perceives it (James and Prout, 1990). Adults behave differently in different situations with no confusion as to which role to play at what time. In a sense, adjustment takes place so that it is not a question of whether an individual is dependent or not but with whom he shows dependency. Most husbands depend upon their wives to run the home. Most children depend upon their mother to nurture them and maintain the family systems. Emotional dependence is a strong bond (Narain, 1964) in Indian families. It does not however preclude in the individuals from exhibiting individual, independent initiative when required. Altruism and generosity are inculcated early so that a child learns to share and cooperate, but if required can be competitive and competes with others, but non-aggressively. Given the fact that most Indian children live in harsh ecologies (urban slums, rural areas, tribal jungles and hills) they experience material deprivation of one kind or another, while also perceiving that the rich have plenty and to spare. This makes them adaptive to their situation.

Adjustment is the process of finding a compatibility between the needs of the self and the needs of others (Murray, 1938). The self composed of the id, the ego and the superego has an energy, a drive towards the fulfilment of such needs. There is a constant push and pull among the three identities. The ego tries to act as a policeman, aware of the pros and cons of the situation, while the id is a rash and impulsive libidinal energy espousing the cause of self-pleasure and avoidance of pain. The superego is the voice of conscience that is constantly telling the ego what is moral and just.

It is necessary to state that skills intertwine dynamically with each other, either in pairs or in multiples. For instance, to use intelligence is an essential skill. However, without the motivation, the drive for need-fulfilment is stymied. On the other hand, if the level of motivation is low there is indifference and lack of will to hone these skills. Language is an essential vehicle to communicate one's needs, to be successful in the direction of one's motivation. On the other hand, even with the honing of skills in language and the use of one's intelligence, if there is little effort to adapt to the needs of the situation there is a low level of performance and achievement. Underlying all these skills is the essential inner drive to want to experience and be successful in each situation, whether it is in relationships, or the accomplishment of a task or even in experiencing a level of equilibrium. Therefore, skills are interlinked so that the lower levels of skills are related to the higher levels. It is obvious, therefore, that competence is the key word in the maximum utilisation of these skills, to attain one's goals. In the Indian context, the question of competence needs further exploration. This is: How does an individual increase the speed of response in problem solving, which is the acme of the use of intelligence? To utilise one's intelligence, how essential is language? In a multilingual environment, as in India, does level of intelligence influence the optimum functions of language? If science and technology speed up information processing, how dependent are we upon the mechanisation of language with the growing takeover by computer technology so that eventually we communicate through cellphones and e-mails and forget the use of spoken language? Is the increasing role of robots taking over the functions of intelligence and the use of language? Will humans become eventually push-button robots? Are social psychologists aware of the takeover by the computer age, and to what extent are they reinforcing the use of verbal language and mental functions, so that they do not become obsolete? What will happen when the technological systems fail? What alternatives exist? How prepared is the world for crises as the interactive net is becoming closer and more tight-knit? Thus, these critical skills form the bedrock of strategies that the individual uses as coping mechanisms for an equilibrium between his and societal needs. The Indian's resilience to adapt his strategies as related to each different situation depends on three major components: (*a*) his will to act, (*b*) his overt ability to express himself and understand others, (*c*) his ability to assess needs and use of his intelligent cue-grasping ability to perform competently.

References

Agarwal, K.N., D.K. Agarwal and S.K. Upadhyaya, 1987, 'Malnutrition and Mental Functions in School Children', in K.N. Agarwal and B. Bhatia (eds), *Update Growth*. Varanasi: Department of Paediatrics, Banaras Hindu University Publications.

Agarwal, S.K., 1977, 'A Psychosocial Study of Academic Underachievement', *Indian Educational Review*, 12(2): 105–10.

Allport, G.W., 1966, 'Traits Revisited', *American Psychologist*, 21: 1–10.

Anderson, C., 1995, *The Stages of Life: A Groundbreaking Discovery: The Steps to Psychological Maturity*. New York: Atlantic Monthly Press.

Annamalai, E., 1986, 'Bilingualism through Schooling in India', in A. Abbi (ed.), *Studies in Bilingualism*. New Delhi: Bahri Publications.

Arsenian, S., 1945, 'Bilinguism in the Post-war World', *Psychological Bulletin*, 42: 65–86.

Atkinson, J.W., 1953, 'The Achievement Motive and Recall of Interrupted and Completed Tasks', *Journal of Experimental Psychology*, 46: 381–90.

———, 1964a, 'A Theory of Motivation', in J.W. Atkinson, (ed.), *An Introduction to Motivation*. Princeton, NJ: D. Van Nostrand Company.

———, 1964b, 'Introduction: The Viewpoint of Common Sense', in J.W. Atkinson (ed.), *An Introduction to Motivation*, p. 1. Princeton, NJ: D. Van Nostrand Company.

Badami, M.D. and B. Tripathi, 1973, Group Acceptance–Rejection as a Function of Intelligence and Scholastic Achievement', *Indian Journal of Psychology*, 48(1): 69–74.

Baig, M.A.K., 1991, *Psycholinguistic and Language Acquisition*. New Delhi: Bahri Publications.

Bandura, A., 1977, *Social Learning Theory*. Englewood Cliffs, NJ: Prentice-Hall.

Bardhan, P., 1970, 'On the Minimum Level of Living and the Rural Poor', *Indian Economic Review*, 5(1): 129–36.

Bean, C.H., 1932, 'An Unusual Opportunity to Investigate the Psychology of Language', *Journal of Genetic Psychology*, (40): 181–202.

Belfer, M.L., 2003, 'Epidemiology of Child and Adolescent Mental Disorders: A Cross Cultural Perspective', in J.G. Young, P. Ferrari, S. Malhotra, S. Tyano and E. Caffo (eds), *Brain, Culture and Development*. New Delhi: Macmillan.

Benton, A.L., 1994, 'Neuropsychological Assessment', *Annual Review of Psychology*, 45: 1–23.

Bettelhiem, B., 1958, 'Individual and Mass Behaviour in Extreme Situation', in E.E. Maccoby, T.M. Newcomb and E.L. Hartley (eds), *Readings in Social Psychology*. New York: Henry Holt.

Bevli, U.K., 1983, *Developmental Norms of Indian Children 2½ to 5 years, Part IV: Language Development*. New Delhi. National Council of Educational Research and Training.

Bhaduri, A., 1971, 'A Comparative Study of Certain Psychological Characteristics of the Over and Under Achievers in Higher Secondary Schools', D.Phil. (unpublished), Calcutta University.

Bharathi, V.V. and S.R. Venkataramaiah, 1976, 'Birth Order, Family Size and Anxiety', *Child Quarterly*, 9(3): 11–17.

Bhargava, S.K., I. Datta and S. Kumari, 1982, 'A Longitudinal Study of Language Development in Small-for-Dates Children from Birth to Five Years', *Indian Pediatrics*, 19(2): 123–29.

Bisht, G.S., 1972, 'A Study of the Level of Educational Aspirations in Relation to Socio-economic Conditions and Educational Attainment', Ph.D. thesis (unpublished). Agra: Agra University.

Bowlby, J. 1958, 'The Nature of the Child's Tie to his Mother', *International Journal of Psychoanalysis*, 39: 350–73.

Broca, P., 1960, 'Remarks on the Faculty of Articulate Language, followed by an Observation of Aphemia', in G. Von Bonin (ed.), *Some Papers on the Cerebral Cortex*. Springfield, IL: Charles C. Thomas. (original work published 1861).

Bronfenbrenner, U., 1979, *The Ecology of Human Development*. Cambridge, MA: Harvard University Press.

Broota, A., H. Kaur, and U. Priyadarshini, 1985, 'Effect of Praise and Blame on the Work Achievement of Introverts and Extraverts', *Indian Journal of Clinical Psychology*, 12(2): 1–5.

Brown, J.S., 1948, 'Gradients of Approach and Avoidance Responses, and their Relation to Level of Motivation', *Journal of Comparative Physiological Psychology*, 41: 450–65.

Burt, C., 1955, 'The Evidence for the Concept of Intelligence', *British Journal of Educational Psychology*, 25: 158–77.

Chatterjee, G., 1999, 'Nursery Rhymes and Socialisation', in T.S. Saraswathi (ed.), *Culture, Socialisation and Human Development: Theory, Research and Application in India*. New Delhi: Sage.

Chaudhary, N., 1999, 'Language Socialisation: Patterns of Caregiver Speech to Young Children', in T.S. Saraswathi (ed.), *Culture, Socialisation and Human Development: Theory, Research and Application in India*. New Delhi: Sage.

Chomsky, N., 1959, 'A Review of Verbal Behaviour by BF Skinner', *Language*, 35(1): 26–58.

———, 1965a 'Formal Properties of Grammar' in R. Lewis, R. Bush and E. Galanter (eds), *Handbook* of *Mathematical Psychology, Vol. 2*. New York: John Wiley.

———, 1965b, *Aspects of the Theory of Syntax*. Cambridge, MA: The MIT Press.

Conel, J.L., 1939, *The Postnatal Development of Human Cerebral Cortex: The Cortex of the New Born*. Cambridge, MA: Harvard University Press.

Conklin, G.E., 1922, *Heredity and Environment in the Development of Men*. New Jersey: Princeton University Press.

Damasio, A.R. 1992, 'Aphasia', *New England Journal of Medicine*, 326: 531–39.

Das, J.P. and K. Thapa, 2000, 'Intelligence and Cognitive Processes', in J. Pandey (ed.) *Psychology in India Revisited— Development in the Discipline, Vol. 1: Physiological Foundation and Human Cognition*. New Delhi: Sage

Day, E.J., 1932, 'The Development of Language in Twins: I. A Comparison of Twins and Single Children', *Child Development*, 3: 179–99.

Dewsbury, D.A., 1991, 'Psychobiology', *American Psychologist*, 46(3): 198–205.

Diaz-Guerrero, R., 2003, 'Is Abnegation a Basic Experiential Trait in Traditional Societies?', in J.W. Berry, R.C. Mishra and R.C. Tripathi (eds) *Psychology in Human and Social Development*. New Delhi: Sage.

Dolan, Frances E., 2000, 'Introduction', in William Shakespeare, *As You Like It*. New York: Penguin Books.

Eysenck, H.J., 1986, 'The Theory of Intelligence and the Psychophysiology of Cognition', in R.L. Sternberg (ed.), *Advances in the Psychology of Human Intelligence, Vol. 3*. Hillsdale, NJ: Erlbaum.

Farah, M.J., 1995, *Visual Agnosia*. Cambridge, MA: MIT Press.

Festinger, L.A., 1942, 'Theoretical Interpretations of Shifts in Levels of Aspirations', *Psychological Review*, 49: 235–50.

Filipek, P.A., 1999, 'Neuro Imaging in the Developmental Disorders: The State of Science', *Journal of Child Psychology and of Psychiatry*, 40(1): 113–28.

Forest, I., 1954, *Child Development*. New York: McGraw-Hill.

Freud, S., 1936, 'The Problem of Anxiety'. New York: Psychoanalytic Quarterly Press.

Frisch, R.E. and R. Revell, 1970, 'Height and Weight at Menarche and a Hypothesis of Critical Body Weights and Adolescent Events', *Science*, 169: 397–98.

Galton, F., 1869/1962, *Heredity: Genius*. Cleveland, OH: World Publishing Co.

Gangopadhyay, P.K., 1973, 'Anxiety Persistence and Performance on Programme', *Indian Educational Review*, 8(2): 21–31.

Ganguly, S.R., 1988, 'On Measuring Communicative Competence', *Psycho Lingua*, 18: 23–32.

Gardner, H., 1984, 'The Development of Competence in Culturally Defined Domains: A Preliminary Framework', in R.A. Shweder and R.Z. LeVine (eds), *Culture Theory: Essays on Mind, Self and Emotion*. Cambridge, MA: Cambridge University Press.

Gesell, A., 1929, 'Maturation and Behaviour Pattern', *Psychological Review*, 36: 307–19.

———, 1946, 'The Ontogenesis of Infant Behaviour', in L. Carmichael (ed.), *Manual of Child Psychology*. New York: John Wiley.

Ghuman, P.A., 1978, 'Nature of Intellectual Development among Punjabi Children', *International Journal of Psychology* 13(4): 281–94.

Goldfield, B. and C.E. Snow, 1993, 'Individual Differences in Language Acquisiton', in J. Berko Gleason (ed.), *The Development of Language*, 3rd edn. New York: Macmillan.

Goldstein, K., 1940, *Human Nature*. Cambridge, MA: Harvard University Press.

Greenberg, J.H. (ed.), 1966, *Universals of Language*, 2nd edn. Cambridge, MA: MIT Press.

Guilford, J.P., 1956, 'The Structure of Intellect', *Psychological Bulletin*, 53: 267–93.

Gupta, A. and L.A. Jain, 1995, 'Study of the Cognitive Performance of Brain Tumour Patients', *Journal of Personality and Clinical Studies*, 6: 97–102.

Gupta, U., G.P. Dubey and B.S. Gupta, 1994, 'Effects of Caffeine on Perceptual Judgement,' *Neuropsychobiology*, 30: 185–88.

Hamblin, R.L., C. Hathaway and J.S. Wodarski, 1971, 'Group Contingencies, Peer Tutoring and Accelerating Academic Achievement', in E. Ramp and W. Hopkins (eds), *A New Direction for Education: Behaviour Analysis*. Lawrence: University of Kansas.

Havighurst, R.J., 1972, *Developmental Tasks and Education*, 3rd edn. New York: David McKay.

Hull, C.L., 1952, *A Behaviour System*. New Haven, CT: Yale University Press.

Irwin, O.C., 1941, 'Research on Speech Sound for the First Six Month of the Life', *Psychological Bulletin*, 38: 277–85.

———, 1942, 'The Developmental Status of Speech Sounds of Ten Feeble-minded Children, *Child Development*, 13: 29–39.

———, 1947, 'Infant Speech: Consonant Sounds According to Place of Articulation, *Journal of Speech Disorders*, 12: 397–401.

James, A. and A. Prout, 1990, *Constructing and Reconstructing Childhood: Contemporary Issues in the Sociological Study of Childhood*. London: Falmer Press.

James, W., 1890, *The Principles of Psychology, Vols 1 and 2*. New York: Henry Holt.

———, 1902, *The Principles of Psychology, Vol. 1*. New York: Holt.

Jensen, A.R., 1980, *Bias in Mental Testing*. New York: Free Press.

———, 1982, 'The Chronometry of Intelligence', in R.J. Sternberg (ed.), *Advances in the Psychology of Human Intelligence, Vol. 1*. Hillsdale, NJ: Erlbaum.

Johnson, M.H., 1991, *Developmental Cognitive Neuroscience*. Cambridge: Blackwell.

———, 1993, *Brain Development and Cognition: A Reader*. Cambridge: Blackwell.

Kapur, M., 2001, 'Childcare in Ancient India', in J.G. Young, P. Ferrari, S. Malhotra, S. Tyano, E. Caffo (eds), *Brain Culture and Development*. New Delhi: Macmillan.

Kaviraj, M.M., 1966, 'The Doctrine of Pratibha in Indian Philosophy', in G. Kaviraj (ed.) *Aspects of Indian Thought*. Burdwan: University of Burdwan.

Khalakdina, M., 1979, *Early Child Care in India*. London: Gordon and Breach.

Khatri, A.A., 1970, 'Personality and Mental Health of Indians (Hindus) in the Context of their Changing Family Organization', in E.J. Anthony and C. Koupernik (eds), *The Child in his Family, Vol. 1*. New York: John Wiley.

Kohli, T.K., 1976, 'Characteristic Behavioural and Environmental Correlates of Academic Achievement of Over and Under-achievers of Different Levels of Intelligence', Ph.D. Thesis (unpublished), Punjab University.

Kornadt, H.J., L.H. Eckensberger and W.B. Emminghaus, 1980, 'Cross Cultural Research on Motivation and its Contribution to a General Theory of Motivation', in H.C. Triandis and W. Lowner (eds), *Handbook of Cross-cultural Psychology, Vol. 3*. Boston: Allyn & Bacon.

Kuhl, J. and H. Heckhausen, 1985, 'From Wishes to Action: The Dead Ends and Shortcuts on the Long Way to Action', in M. Frese and J. Sabini (eds), *Goal-directed Behaviour: The Concept of Action in Psychology*. Hillsdale, NJ: Erlbaum.

Kumar, D., 1986, 'Influence of Caste and Class on the Fluency of Speech', *Psycho Lingua*, 16(2): 99–106.

Kumar, K., 1991, 'Research in Test and Measurement: A Trend Report', in M.B. Busch (ed.), *Fourth Survey of Research in Education*. New Delhi: NCERT.

Lamb, M.E., D.M. Teti and M.H. Bornstein, 2002, *Development in Infancy: An Introduction*. New York: Lawrence Erlbaum.

Lenneberg, E.H., 1967, *Biological Foundations of Language*. New York: Wiley.

Lewin, K., 1935, *A Dynamic Theory of Personality*. New York: McGraw-Hill.

Lewis, M.M., 1936, *Infant Speech: The Beginnings of Language*. New York: Harcourt Brace.

———, 1951, *Infant Speech: A Study of the Beginnings of Language*, 2nd edn. New York: Harcourt Brace.

Luria, A.R., 1966, *Human Brain and Psychological Processes*. New York: Harper and Row.

———, 1976, *Cognitive Development: Its Cultural and Social Foundations*. Cambridge, MA: Harvard University Press.

Marek, J.C., 1988, 'A Buddhist Theory of Human Development', in R.M. Thomas (ed.), *Oriental Theories of Human Development*. New York: Peter Lang.

Maslow, A.H., 1966, *The Psychology of Science*. New York: Harper and Row.

———, 1970, *Motivation and Personality*, 2nd edn. New York: Harper and Row.

———, 1987, *Motivation and Personality*, 3rd edn. New York: Harper and Row.

Mathew, A. and V. Sireesha, 1973, 'Vocabulary of Preschool Children', *Indian Educational Review*, 8(2): 81–89.

McCarthy, R.A., and E.K. Warrington, 1990, *Cognitive Neuro-psychology: A Clinical Introduction*. San Diego, CA: Academic Press.

McClelland, D., 1958, 'Risk Taking in Children with High or Low Need for Achievement', in J.W. Atkinson (ed.), *Motive in Fantasy: Action* and *Society*. Princeton, NJ: D. Van Nostrand Company.

———, 1961, *The Achieving Society*. Princeton, NJ: Van Nostrand Company.

———, 1984, *Human Motivation*. Glenview, IL: Scott, Foresman.

McDougall W., 1923, *An Outline of Psychology*. New York: Scribners.

———, 1945, *Social Psychology*, 23rd edn. London: Methuen.

Megeoch, J.A., 1942, *The Psychology of Human Learning*. New York: Longman.

Menon, S.K., 1973, 'A Comparative Study of the Personality Characteristics of Overachievers and Underachievers of High Ability', Ph.D. thesis (unpublished), Kerala University.

Miller, D.T., 1976, 'Ego Involvement and Attribution for Success and Failure', *Journal of Personality and Social Psychology*, 34: 901–06.

Miller, G.A., E. Galanter and K.H. Pribram, 1960, *Plans and the Structure of Behaviour*. New York: Holt Rinehart and Winston.

Miller, N.E., 1951, 'Learnable Drives and Rewards', in S. Stevens (ed.), *Handbook of Experimental Psychology*. New York: Wiley.

Mishra, B., 1994, 'Word Order in Expression of Bitransitive Verbs in Hindi: Impact of Deprivation', Paper presented at the International Conference on Early Childhood Communication. Bhubaneswar: Utkal University.

Mohan, V. and A. Bhanot, 1976, 'Qualitative Differences in the Performance of Introvert and Extrovert Children on Continuous Tasks', *Asian Journal of Psychology and Education*, 1(2): 23–29.

Mohanty, A.K., 1991, 'Social Psychological Aspects of Languages in Contact in Multilingual Societies', in G. Misra (ed.), *Applied Social Psychology in India*. New Delhi: Sage.

———, 1994, *Bilingualism in a Multilingual Society*. Mysore: Central Institute of Indian Languages.

———, 2000, 'Language Behaviour and Processes', in J. Pandey (ed.), *Psychology in India Revisited: Developments in the Discipline, Vol. 1: Physiological Foundation and Human Cognition*. New Delhi: Sage.

Mohanty, A.K., S. Panda and B. Misra, 1999, 'Language Socialisation in a Multilingual Society', in T.S. Saraswathi (ed.) *Culture, Socialisation and Human Development: Theory, Research and Application in India*. New Delhi: Sage.

Mohanty, A.K. and C. Perregaux, 1977, 'Language Acquisition and Bilingualism', in J.W. Berry P.R. Dasen and T.S. Saraswathi (eds), *Handbook of Cross-cultural Psychology, Vol. 2: Basic Processes and Human Development*, 2nd edn. Boston, MA: Allyn & Bacon.

Moulton, R.W., A.C. Raphelson, A.B. Kristoferson and J.W. Atkinson, 1958, 'The Achievement Motive and Perceptual Sensitivity under Two Conditions of Motive Arousal', in J.W. Atkinson (ed.), *Motive in Fantasy: Action and Society*. Princeton: D. Van Nostrand Company.

Mowrer, O.H., 1948, 'What is Normal Behaviour?', in L.A. Pennington and I.A. Berg (eds), *An Introduction to Clinical Psychology*. New York: Ronald Press.

Munroe, R.L. and R.H. Munroe, 1975, *Cross-Cultural Human Development*. Monterey, CA: Brooks/Cole Publishing Co.

———, 1977, 'Cooperation and Competition among East African and American Children', *Journal of Social Psychology*, 101: 145–46.

Muralidharan R., 1970, 'Home Stimulation and Child Development', *Indian Education Review*, 5(2): 45–51.

Muralidharan, R. and U. Bannerji, 1974, 'Effect of Preschool Education on the Language and Intellectual Development of Underprivileged Children', *Journal of Education and Psychology*, 32(1): 10–15.

Murphy, G. and L.B. Murphy, 1968, *Asian Psychology*. New York: Basic Books.

Murray, H.A., 1938, *Explorations in Personality*. New York: OUP.

———, 1951, 'Some Basic Psychological Assumptions and Conceptions', *Dialectica*, 5: 266–92.

Naidu, U.S. and V.S. Nakhate (eds), 1985, *Child Development Studies in India*, Tata Institute of Social Science Series, 56. Mumbai: TISS.

Narain, D., 1964, 'Growing Up in India', *Family Process*, 3: 127–54.

Nelson, K., 1973, Structure and Strategy in Learning to Talk, *Monograph of the Society for Research in Child Development*, 38, (1–2, Serial No. 149).

Newell, K.M., 1981, 'Skill Learning', in D. Holding (ed.), *Human Skills*. New York: John Wiley.

Nirmala, C., 1983/1984, 'Development of Plural in Telugu Children', *Osmania Papers in Linguistics*, 9 and 10: 1–20.

Nirmala, M.L. and V.D. Swaminathan, 1985, 'Effects of Cigarette Smoking on Learning and Retention', *Journal of Psychological Researches*, 29: 73–78.

Panda, K.C. and M.D. Panda, 1978, 'Intellectual Achievement Responsibility: Effects of Organismic Variables, Cultural Differences, and Relationships with School Achievement', *Indian Educational Review*, 13(1): 88–100.

Pandey, R.P., 1981, 'Academic Achievement as a Function of Neuroticism and Extraversion', *Indian Psychological Review*, 20(1): 1–4.

Pandit, P.B., 1972, *India as a Socio-linguistic Area*. Pune: University of Pune.

Paranis, H.N., 1978, 'Investigation into the Causes of Backwardness in Mathematics of Students from Standards V–VIII', *Jnana Prabodhini*, Pune.

Pareek, U., 1970, 'Poverty and Motivation: Figure and Ground', in V. Allen (ed.), *Psychological Factors in Poverty*. Chicago: Mackhan.

Patel, A.S. and R.J. Joshi, 1977, 'A Study of Adjustment Processes of High and Low Achievers', *Journal of Psychological Researches*, 21: 178–84.

Patnaik, K. and A.K. Mohanty, 1984, 'Relationship between Meta-linguistics and Cognitive Development of Bilingual and Unilingual Tribal Children', *Psycholingua*, 14(1): 63–70.

Pavlov, I.P., 1928, *Lectures on Conditioned Reflexes: Twenty Five Years of Objective Study on the Higher Nervous Activity* (translation). New York: International Publishers.

Peter, C.J., J. Handoo and D.P. Pattnayak (eds), 1987, *Indian Folklore II*. Mysore. Central Institute of Indian Languages Press.

Piaget, J., 1947, *The Psychology of Intelligence*, Vol. 20. Paris: Armand Colin.

———, 1954, *The Construction of Reality on the Child*. New York: Basic Books.

Polster, R.M., L. Nadel and D.L. Schacter, 1991, 'Cognitive Neuroscience Analyses of Memory: A Historical Perspective', *Journal of Cognitive Neuroscience*, 3(2): 95–116.

Posner, M.I. and E. Raichle, 1994, *Images of Mind: Exploring the Brains Activity*. New York: W.H. Freeman and Co. (New York: Scientific American Library).

Prasad, B., 1977, 'A Study of Impact of Social Reinforcement on Academic Achievement', Ph.D. thesis (unpublished), Patna University.

Pylyshyn, Z.W., 1991, 'Computing in Cognitive Science', in M.I. Posner (ed.), *Foundations of Cognitive Science*. Cambridge, MA: The MIT Press.

Raghavendra, P. and L.B. Leonard, 1989, 'The Acquisition of Agglunating Languages: Converging Evidence from Tamil', *Journal of Child Language*, 16(2): 313–22.

Rapport, D. and J.M. Gill, 1959, 'The Points of View and Assumptions of Metapsychology', *International Journal of Psychoanalysis*, 40: 153–62.

Rosenfels, Paul, 1978, *The Nature of Psychological Maturity* (Ninth Street Centre Monograph). New York: Ninth Street Centre.

Rosenzwieg, S., 1944, 'Converging Approaches to Personality: Murray, Allport, Lewin', *Psychological Review*, 51(4): 248–56.

Sabhesan, S. and M. Natrajan, 1988, 'Fantastic Confabulations after Head Injury', *Indian Journal of Psychological Medicine*, 11: 29–32.

Sahu, S. and A. Jena, 1983, 'Psycholinguistic Abilities of Socially Disadvantaged Children', *Psycho Lingua*, 13(1): 25–30.

Sahu, S. and J.B. Swain, 1985, Effect of Language Training Programme on Low Language Achievers', *Perspectives in Psychological Researches*, 8(2): 1–8.

Saraswathi, T.S. (ed.), 1999, *Culture, Socialisation and Human Development: Theory, Research and Application in India*. New Delhi: Sage.

Schneider, W., 1987, 'Connectionism: Is it a Paradigm Shift for Psychology?', *Behaviour Research Methods, Instruments and Computers*, 19(2): 73–83.

Schroeder, C.S. and B.N. Gordon, 2002, *Assessment and Treatment of Childhood Problems: A Clinicians Guide*. New York: Guilford Press.

Seth, P., 1978, 'Low Academic Achievement and Emotionality—A Study', *Indian Educational Review*, 13(2): 97–102.

Seventh New Collegiate Dictionary, 1983. Springfield, MA: Merriam-Webster Inc.

Sharma, V., 1969, 'A Linguistic Study of Speech Development in Early Childhood', Ph.D. thesis (unpublished). Agra: Agra University.

Shastri, L. and V. Ajjanagadde, 1993, 'From Simple Associations to Systematic Reasoning: A Connectionist Representation of Rules, Variables and Dynamic Bindings using Temporal Synchrony', *Behavioural and Brain Sciences*, 16(3): 417–94.

Shastri, V., 1985, *Sanskrit Sukti Ratnakar*. Sarvabhoma Sanskrit Prachar Sansthanam.

Sheil, C.M., 1995, *Explanations for Individual Differences in Language Development*, Individual and Developmental Series, Vol. 7. New Delhi: Sage.

Shukla, S. and A.K. Mohanty, 1986, 'Development of Syntactic Ability among Hindi Speaking Children', *Social Science International*, 2: 44–50.

Sidana, U.R. and S.K. Saluja, 1978, 'Effect of Academic Achievement History, Immediate Performance and Magnitude of Reinforcement on Child's Self Confidence', *Psychological Studies*, 23(2): 83–86.

Singh, A., 1987, 'Certain Deprivational Factors in Language Development in Children', Ph.D. thesis (unpublished). Allahabad: University of Allahabad.

Singh, B. and P. Kumar, 1977, 'Anxiety and Educational Achievement', *Journal of Psychological Researches*, 21(1): 56–60.

Sinha, D. and R.C. Mishra, 1993, 'Some Methodological Issues Related to Research in Developmental Psychology in the Context of Policy and Intervention Programmes', in T.S. Saraswathi and B. Kaur (eds), *Human Development and Family Studies in India*. New Delhi: Sage.

Slobin, D.I., 1992, 'Introduction', in D.I. Slobin (ed.), *The Cross-linguistic Study of Language Acquisition*, Vol. 3. Hillsdale, NJ: Lawrence Erlbaum.

Smith, M.E., 1935, A Study of Some Factors Influencing Development of the Sentence in Preschool Children, *Journal of Genetic Psychology*, 46: 152–212.

Southworth, P.C., 1980, 'Indian Bilingualism: Some Educational and Linguistic Implications', *Annals of the New York Academy of Sciences*, 345: 121–46.

Spearman, C., 1927, *The Abilities of Man*. New York, Macmillan.

Sperry, R.W., 1973, 'Lateral Specialisation of Cerebral Function in the Surgically Separated Hemispheres', in F.J. McGuigan and R.A. Schoonover (eds), *The Psychophysiology of Thinking*. New York: Academic Press.

Sri Aurobindo, 1922, *Essays on Gita*. Pondicherry: Sri Aurobindo Ashram.

Sridevi, S.V., 1976, 'The Aspects of Acquisition of Kannada by 2+ Year old Children', M.phil. dissertation (unpublished), All India Institute of Speech and Hearing, Mysore.

Srivastava, A.K., A.M. Tripathi and G. Misra, 1995, 'Western and Indian Perspectives on Intelligence: Some Reflections', *Indian Educational Review*, 30: 30–45.

———, 1996, 'The Status of Intelligence Testing in India: A Preliminary Analysis', *Indian Educational Review*, 31: 1–11.

Sternberg, R.J., 1990, *Metaphors of Mind: Conceptions of Nature of Intelligence*. Cambridge, MA: Cambridge University Press.

———, 2000, *Handbook of Intelligence*. New York: Cambridge University Press.

Stoddard, G.D., 1943, *The Meaning of Intelligence*. New York: Macmillan.

Terman, L.M., 1916, *The Measurement of Intelligence*. Boston: Houghton-Mifflin.

———, 1930, *The Promise of Youth, Follow-up Studies of a Thousand Gifted Children: Genetic Studies of Genius, III*. Stanford, CA: Stanford University Press.

Thomas, R.M., 1997, *Theories of Moral Development. Secular and Religious*. Westport, CT: Greenwood.

Thompson, G.C., 1952, *Child Psychology*. New York: Houghton Mifflin.

Thorndike, E.L., 1913, *Educational Psychology, Vol. 2: The Psychology of Learning*. New York: Teachers College, Columbia University.

———, 1943, 'The Origin of Language', *Science*, 98(2531): 1–6.

Thorndike E.L., E.D. Bregman, M.V. Cobb and E.I. Woodyard, 1928, *The Measurement of Intelligence*. New York: Teachers College, Columbia University.

Thorpe, L. and A. Schmuller, 1958, *The Biological Basis of Personality: a Interdisciplinary Approach*. Princeton, NJ: OUP.

Thorpe, L.P., 1950, *The Psychology of Mental Health*. New York: Roland Press Co.

Thurstone, L.L., 1924, *The Nature of Intelligence*. London: Kegan Paul, Trench, Trubnor and Co.

———, 1938, *Primary Mental Abilities*. Chicago: Chicago University Press.

Tiwari, G., R. Kumar and K.K. Morbhatt, 1980,' Level of Aspiration as a Function of Anxiety and Sex among High and Low Academic Achievers', *Indian Psychological Review* 19(4): 46–51.

Tolman, E., 1936, 'Cooperational Behaviourism and Current Trends in Psychology', Proceedings of 25th Anniversary Inaguration Graduate Studies, LA: University of South California.

Urwin, C., 1985, 'Constructing Motherhood: The Persuasion of Normal Development' in C. Steedman, C. Urwin and V. Walkerdine (eds), *Language, Gender and Childhood*. London: Routledge and Kegan Paul.

Van Alstyne, D., 1929, 'The Environment of Three-year-old Children; Factors Related to Intelligence and Vocabulary Tests', in Teachers College Contributions to Education, No. 366. New York: Columbia University.

Vasanta, D. and Sailaja, 1993, 'Phonolinguistic Evidence for Word Order Variation within Dative Constructions in Telugu', Paper presented at the National Seminar on Word Order in Indian Languages. Hyderabad: Osmania University Press.

Verma, P., L. Saini and S. Gupta, 1976, 'Nutritional Status of Children in a Welfare Home', *Indian Pediatrics*, 13(7): 499–506.

Vernoy, M.W. and K. Huffman, 1991, *Psychology in Action*. New York: John Wiley.

Veroff, J., J. Atkinson, S. Feld and G. Gurin, 1960, 'The Use of Thematic Apperception to Access Motivation in a Nationwide Interview Study', *Psychological Monographs*, 74(499).

Vijayalakshmi, J., 1980, 'Academic Achievement and Socio-economic Status as Predictors of Creative Talent', *Journal of Psychological Researches*, 24(1&2): 43–47.

Vygotsky, L., 1978, *Mind in Society*. Cambridge, MA: Harvard University Press.

Warner, W.L., R.J. Havinghurst and M.B. Loeb, 1944, *Who shall be Educated?*, 3rd edn. New York: Harper and Bros.

Weschler, D., 1994, *The Measurement of Adult Intelligence*, 3rd edn. Baltimore: Williams and Wilkins.

Whorf, B.L., 1939, 'The Relation of Habitual Thought and Behaviour to Language', Reprinted in J.B. Carroll (ed.), *Language, Thought and Reality: Selected Writings of Benjamin Lee Whorf*. New York: John Wiley.

Williams, R.M. and M.I. Matteson, 1942, 'The Effects of Social Groupings upon the Language of Preschool Children', *Child Development*, 13: 233–45.

Woodfield, A., 1976, *Theology*. Cambridge: Cambridge University Press.

Young, G.J., P. Ferrari, S. Malhotra, S. Tyano and E. Caffo (eds), 2003, *Brain Culture and Development*. New Delhi: Macmillan.

9

Societal Mores: Their Implications for Human Development

Introduction

SOCIETAL MORES arise out of continued and inter-generationally transmitted sets of behavioural experiences. This heritage of experiences is carefully nurtured and imbibed, mainly through the process of socialisation. The experiences are further continuously modified and adapted according to the changing times and needs of the society, as it progresses towards modernisation (Dube, 1988). For instance, even in the 21st century, traditional business families conduct expensive *puja*s as thanksgiving to the benignity of gods and goddesses, especially Goddess Lakshmi, invoking further prosperity. Such societal mores are mainly attitudes and beliefs, operationalised into behaviour as customs and practices according to certain abiding and understood rules, usually arising from socio-religious sources (Dutt, 1979). Since the dominant religion is Hinduism, many of its social experiences have been accepted by people of other religions, and, in a sense, have become indigenous. Most Indians celebrate Diwali and Holi. For instance, in the *mohalla*s of Delhi, Hyderabad and Lucknow, many non-Hindus take part in the festivities of their Hindu friends in a spontaneous manner, typifying the spirit of camaraderie. In the walled areas of old cities, Hindus and Muslims have been living together for decades, respecting each other's norms and customs. Therefore, secularism, enunciated in the Constitution of independent India, is no new idea. Secularism thus arises out of the spiritual philosophy of both Muslims and Hindus from ancient times. It continues to be a strong ethos in the modern world (Cox, 1984).

The culture of the Indian society, with its ethical tenets of religious tolerance, of different social classes and castes living together, tends towards a unique pattern of heterogeneity within the Indian society. Louis Murphy in her description of childhood has emphasised the ingrained sense of tolerance of differences in the Indian psyche (Murphy, 1953). Though it is also true that in several traditional village communities the Harijans live on the outskirts of the village and do not inter-dine with the higher castes. These attitudes, however, are becoming eroded in the cities. It happens when other factors override the caste factor. For instance, a Harijan bureaucrat may have a retinue of higher caste employees, which is accepted as a normal pattern. Several psychosocial factors enter into these dynamics, for instance the factors of occupational competence, rules of official hierarchy in government offices and the fact that socio-religious privacy and territory are not crossed. Such examples of mutual respect for each other's statuses in interdependence can be multiplied.

Again, psychologically speaking, it has not been firmly established that the deprived or lower castes are genetically less intelligent than the higher castes, though Jensen's study of the Western world sought to unsuccessfully establish that African Americans were inherently less intelligent than the Anglo-Saxon Americans. This is a significant factor for it affects societal mores in deliberately differentiating the 'less' from the 'more' in the population. Over time, and given the opportunity, the less privileged can perform as well or better than the more privileged. It is becoming increasingly evident through research that opportunity and self-achievement orientation are also significant factors for human development. We have only to consider the example of industrial magnates who have come up from the lower economic rungs to give evidence to this fact. Thus, when economic status is in higher profile than the social, a period of dissonance occurs. For instance, a disadvantaged Dalit, who suddenly through his own genius makes a great deal of money, is initially not able to cope with the economic prosperity into which he has suddenly been catapulted. Such suddenly rich people are called 'nouveau riche'. They are confronted with the ways of the stabilised wealthy.

When a community is static, living the same life continuously, then mores become static, so that this stability gives a sense of unchanging security. This sense of security is based on the tenets of religious philosophy that act as an anchor (Griffin, 1988). Unfortunately, while rationalism and logic are the bases of religious ideology, as far as scientific research on these are concerned, there has not been much empiricism about the philosophies expounded through the ages. Such ideologies tend to remain on the socio-religious plane, which, nevertheless, are internalised and become a core part of the behaviour of the average Indian. In India, such socio-religious norms become consolidated into cultural beliefs, which then become the springboard for cultural behaviour of the Indian who attempts to find his identity (Giddens, 1991). The core cultural behaviour patterns of the dominant religious group have been accepted by other religious groups who form the minorities. For generations, their shared social and political history, from which social norms and customs evolved, have been a cementing factor (Bandyopadhyaya, 1982). Several years ago, the renowned sociologist Hiller in describing norms stated that, 'the concept mores refers to the attributes of obligations of norms based upon ideas of rightness and welfare. Like all norms, these denote rules or standards and therefore are a means by which to judge conduct' (Hiller, 1947: 46). We will analyse the influences, both positive and negative, that affect the cultural behaviour of the Indian given the pluralistic nature of the Indian society (Friedman, 1990). Additively, the underpinnings of economic development affecting societal mores also act as variables in the social framework (Cyper and Deutz, 2004).

We have stated in Chapter 1 that the human being through experiences imbibes, stores, recalls and adapts to situations which grow in gradual complexity. Through the process of recognising cues in his environment, the growing individual perceives the roles he has to play in differing situations. For instance, the same cranky husband who grumbles that everything is not right in his home, is the smiling boss in his office, or vice versa. Some calm personalities remain so even in the face of crises, while others become hysterical in such situations. In spite of differences in practising religion, the minority Christian or Muslim participates in the festivities of Diwali and Dussehra, and generally accepts the forms of Hindu festivities. The dominant ethos pervades the Indian way of viewing the world. Whatever his class, caste or religion, the individual also adapts his thinking towards acceptance of differences in others' behaviour, especially regarding rituals and superstitions like the evil eye and auspicious times. This merging with the dominant ethos in a secular society has existed over time and space, and, except for some politically motivated influences, for the most part the differing religions have co-existed. Thus we see that the individual develops coping mechanisms to know what is the accepted social performance and what is the accepted private performance in behaviour (Lazarus, 1974). For instance, it is common for family members to hold back when there is little food on the table and guests are at the table, just as it is hospitable to pile food continuously on the guests' plates. Initiating greetings towards elders is an accepted norm, as is avoidance of eating with the left hand and the removal of shoes before entering a place of worship. Thus, demonstrative of the interface between traditionality and modernity, a Brahmin will perform his *puja* in the morning before leaving for work, then get into his Mercedes and use his cellphone to call his broker, while on his way to office.

Socio-cultural Beliefs

It has been stated by Klaus that the individual is a productive processor of reality (Huerrelmann, 1988). One conceptualisation is that development (and, therefore, learning of new experiences) does not stop with physical growth, but continues by accumulating psychological and sociological experiences throughout the lifespan. Personality is the individual's reference point in the network of social relations (Burkitt, 1992). Another conceptualisation of the human being is the separation of man from his environment into two different forms. They are nothing more than two different processes which interact with each other, similar to the Freudian concept of the ego and the superego (Freud, 1923: 13–59).

Further, it is stated that the human personality is continuously producing and is continuously produced, resulting in a network of socialised products, and material and ecological living conditions (Elias, 1991). George Mead states that the individual is a personality, insofar as he is a member of the society, actively involved in the social experience of reality, and thereby controlled in his conduct (Mead, 1934: 255). What do we make of these several perspectives? First, that there is a socialised personality, set in ways and forms of behaviour (Allport, 1961). Second, he thinks, feels and acts as influenced by his genetic make-up and in relation to his interaction with the environment. What, therefore, is this environment? While geo-ecological and sociological aspects make the environment appear similar for those within its perimeters, how each individual perceives the same environment is different. It is differentially perceived because of the combination of the unique genetic factors of the particular individual (Danziger, 1990). The environment of the social group to which he belongs, however, does not change, except over long periods of time, due to extraneous variables, such as civil disorganisation or changes in the country's economic situation. What remains fundamentally the same and unchanged are the ways of the people, in order to hold the organisation of the social group together. In India, the caste system came into being because of the need for organised categories of professions and related tasks. It were the groups which usurped for themselves the positions of higher authority in relation to others, by virtue of birth, who commandeered the arena of socio-cultural beliefs, like the Brahmins (Bougle, 1992). So far we have indicated that the institutional framework of society and caste are intrinsic to the occurrence of mores as they set the stage for expected and performed role behaviour in the societal network. However, both caste and society are being affected by changes, due mainly to science and technology, which have changed the face of socio-economic and political frames (Srinivas, 1972). Exposed to the latter phenomena, the individual and society are on shifting planes. In reality, even these are peripheral to the culturally rooted personality. The deep-rooted attitudes and values that make up the mentality and behaviour of the Indian do not change much in terms of social reality (Arbib and Hesse, 1986). The social reality of the individual is that on whatever rung of the socio-economic ladder one may be, there is a motivation to improve one's quality of life. It is rare that an individual is immune to the attractiveness of possessions and of status, for, in a sense, he is an achieving individual in an achieving society (Agarwal and Misra, 1986: 217–31). At the same time, the essence of the Indian society prompts the individual to consider himself as an integral part of his community and caste, and thus his self-image is cohesive with the society. In a study across two cultures (Indian and American), the concept of self was found to be socially constructed and existing in a cultural context. Indians were found to describe self more in terms of group, caste and gender identities (Gergen, 1971). Roland also found similar attributes and categorised the Indian as being family-oriented (familialism) with values and norms emphasising social obligations, filial duties and normative pressure to fulfil gender role demands, whereas Americans were found to be independent and autonomous (Roland, 1987). The Indian remained in the orbit of rules and regulations set by his society in terms of the beliefs subscribed to by forces of the cultural milieu.

The cultural milieu consists of the patterns, the attitudes, the behaviours and the practices that mark the individual as an Indian, a member of a particular community, whose norms he abides by. What, therefore, are these norms? We might categorise them in relation to the roles:

(i) The roles to be performed, which are that of the patriarch, the householder, the male as the major income earner of the household. In lineage terms, he is the patriarch and, therefore, is a locus of control and power. As regards the female, her role is that of a nurturant, a caretaker, a socialiser transmitting goals and values.

(ii) The rites and rituals which devolve upon the individual as being a member of a certain community, for instance a Khatri or a Nair from north and south India, respectively. The individual is to behave like one of his caste/community and is expected to bring up his children with the same norms (Freed, 1982: 189–202).

(iii) The individual inevitably uses the upper caste/class as a model to imitate. He must send his children to better schools than he went to himself, to have access to better leisure/cultural activities, which would mark him out to be of a higher rank (which he attempts to imitate).

(iv) The individual abides by the proscriptions and prohibitions of his community so as to remain within his caste/community structure.

The above points notwithstanding, the picture is never static. With growing internationalism and the inter-community interactions, these lines are being crossed and categories are becoming diffused. Rituals, customs and socio-religious events are, by virtue of the nature of progress, becoming eroded, diluted and diffused in the upper echelons of society, and especially among the younger generation. There is now inter-caste marriage, inter-religious marriage and in the upper elite group, inter-racial marriage, creating a situation of flux. What seems to remain undisturbed are the major religious practices which identify the Indian as being either Hindu Indian, Muslim Indian, Christian Indian, Zoroastrian Indian and, in some places like Kerala, Maharashtra and West Bengal, Jewish Indian. It is thus obvious that modernisation, while it brings with it certain peripheral changes, does not destabilise the roots of socio-religious identity (Bharati, 1985: 185–230).

A holistic view of the individual is pertinent, bringing together the essential elements of social structure, action theory and personality development from a three-dimensional point of view. These include concepts of socialisation, of individuation as a personality and interactive modes in a system of reciprocity. Thus, experiences relating to the self which are imbibed by the individual tend to correlate with the common experiences in the community in which the individual lives, so that there is a cohesion between the values of the self and the community (Markus and Kitayama, 1991: 224–53). It directs the moulding of the image of one's self, creating more or less a stable identity through different phases of the lifespan (Anandalakshmy, 1998: 278; Erikson, 1950).

Given the bases described earlier, the inextricable linkage between individuation and the culture's socialisation constructs are operationalised as patterns of behaviour (Shek, 1995: 175–90). In a study on the perception of Chinese adolescents of parenting styles exhibited by parents, the children said that these styles related to the teachings of Confucius, thus indicating the bond with religion (Ho, 1986).

In the world of today, although different political ideologies prevail, similar socio-religious norms are also prevalent. For example, Indians practise Buddhist principles in a democratic structure while the Chinese practise the same within a communistic structure.

Cross-cultural research views cultural beliefs, social mores, customs and conventions of societies in a comparative manner (Whiting and Whiting, 1975). These comparisons only tell us about the differences in patterns of living and behaviour in relation to oral and historical beliefs. The Indian culture is pluralistic, multi-religious and even multiracial. It does not bear comparison but contrasts with others. It is unique in its patterns of cultural norms and behaviour, with its own set of societal norms. These norms create a collation of long-standing beliefs, such as belief in rebirth, belief in *karma* and *dharma*, belief in patriarchy and hierarchical lineage. These, in essence, make an Indian different from a Chinese or Japanese, or, more so, a Westerner, whose societal mores are entirely different. For instance, the Chinese culture as contrasted with the Indian gives evidence that even though it has adopted and adapted sophisticated technology, family and social values are still traditional. On the other hand, there is a tendency in India, having been exposed to a colonial democracy, to adopt western modes, perceived to be freer and more attractive (Yue and Yang, 1987: 51–98).

In contrast to that of the West and within the general structure, there are varied compositions of beliefs and behaviours. The basic behaviour patterns, reinforced and expected of the growing adult are: impulse control and motivation for meeting one's goals (Maslow, 1943: 370–96). The control of impulse is considered a necessary precondition for achievement; in other words, the instilling of a disciplinary attitude towards accomplishment of goals. This is achieved mainly through role learning as a high priority. While in the early years, parental behaviour is towards indulgence, protection and gratification with minimum frustration of the child's needs; in the later years of pre-adolescence and adolescence, there is demand for conformity to societally approved norms of behaviour. These norms are mainly in the areas of responsibility, deference to elders and occupational choices (Saraswathi and Pai, 1997: 77–78). These areas are similar to that of the Eriksonian concept of mastery over the environment (Erikson, 1959). The disposition that children acquire as a consequence is low anxiety and a sense of accomplishment.

Later on, these dispositions are subsumed under parental guidance. When the child is learning independence the techniques used are generally to guide the child in controlling negative behaviour towards others and towards initiating him into responsibility taking. These processes reinforce the child's dependency on others' responses which in early childhood is said to reinforce inter-dependency. Over a period of time, these traits continue into adulthood and become a part of the cultural framework of the individual (Malhotra, 2003: 7). Cognitive capacities are, therefore, carefully moulded through various types of reinforcement, especially during the socialisation process. Studies on achievement indicate that two independent variables affecting task accomplishment are containment of thought to the task at hand and the immediacy of focus. This is combined with parental encouragement through verbal reinforcement as parents are the channels of change for their young (Ostor, 1993). Thus, obedience and respect towards the locus of authority assumes a high profile. These are in contrast to the western models of encouraging independence and allowing for the expression of curiosity and verbal skills. The culturally valued forms of behaviour have their repercussions on positive mental development processes in the Indian. These valued forms of moral behaviour are similar to the principles enjoined by Confucius, the Chinese philosopher who expounded a major religious philosophy in the Far East (Sinha and Kao, 1997). Extreme internal control can repress anxiety and lead to behavioural disorders. It is, therefore, important to examine the contextual reference system of the family, and its growing children. Adults' perceptions reveal the true functionality of parenting styles, as they are internalised into value systems of autocratic expectations of control and achievement in their children. Family dynamics reflect the positivity or negativity of authority and control (Sharma, 2003: 13–47). It is the vehicle which gives the child the ability to perceive and understand the experiences in the world around him. The negative/positive vibes and events communicated non-verbally to the child are internalised and lead to positive or negative mental health in childhood. We observe that these modes of behaviour, encultured in the repertoire of parenting, have their effect on the type of personality of the child that emerges in adulthood (Benedict, 1934). At this point, it is necessary to indicate that the parenting process is a reflection of the cultural norm; namely that which is most prized in the ethos of a society is usually the most practised in parenting. However, new conceptualisations emphasise that the child is not a passive receiver of the parenting processes, but himself rearranges such instructions, demands and injunctions, to suit the cognitive image of his own needs (Prout and Prout, 1997).

In contrast, in the Chinese parenting/acculturation processes, it is necessary to emphasise that the Chinese have been enveloped in the communist ideology, which also encourages collectivism and groupism versus individualism. In the Indian culture, however, it is religious tradition which is the driving force of the motivation to achieve and to realise perceived goals. In the culture of Dakar, Senegal, a study of children under two years of age was based on genetic evolution and differences in the means the child used in adapting to his environment (Simone, 1973: 276–89). The relationship between the child's hereditary endowment and equipment, and the child's cultural inheritance was examined. It was commented in this study that there is a pervasive interaction between the biological individual and the norms and representations of the group in which the child lived. The pre-language communications were studied, such as gestures and expressions, and primordial utterances. They were affected by the maternal factors of interaction and were thereby connected with the family and social system. The mother absorbed the group norms before interpreting them to the child; in other words she was found to be a transmitter of the cultural norms of behaviour. Therefore, the underlying organisation of the group was intermediary, interpersonal and spatially related. The child was studied in the family environment, acting spontaneously. The observations led to the following conclusions: (a) the cultural system of the African child favoured human relations and references to the mother; (b) the group had access to cultural practices which were both modern and traditional. We have given examples of two such completely different developing societies above, namely Chinese and African. Although so dissimilar, some of their values and traditions were found to be similar. The mother/parent bond was strong, frequently continuing into adulthood (Khaleque, 2003). While the Chinese instructed, modelled and reinforced the kinds of behaviour demanded by the communist society, the Africans utilised an approach that was a combination of tribal tradition and the urbanised culture (Dallymar and Devi, 1998). What is remarkable is that like in the Indian subcontinent, traditional roots were similar. One might say, in the Chinese we see a form of the achieving easterner, while in the African we see a form of transitional movement from eastern to western modes of behaviour. India is more similar to the African ethos in its socio-religious beliefs, and curiously more similar to the Chinese in its trend towards science and technology. This example brings to light the fact that there is a social historicity in the development of societal mores, customs and conventions in the Indian context.

The Varying Communities

The knowledge of the human being's development is embedded in the varieties of ecologies of the country. It is also encased in myriad lifestyles, which defy homogeneity, except in the basic principles of growth and development. There are various examples of lifestyles in interior tribal areas which are still elementary. For instance, the Katkarias were a small, self-contained community in the erstwhile Bombay Presidency, whose major occupation was fishing (Weling, 1934). To this day, there are many small, self-contained village communities which still live off fishing produce. There are several such communities scattered all over India which to this day live by their art and craft. The social structures of small societies in India are varied and criss-crossed by a variety of rituals, mores, family ties, marriage rituals and childcare systems. This rich variation is a tapestry of habits, attitudes and values, which makes up the Indian in his unique locale. Yogender Singh (1980: 9) in his analysis of social structures in India states that 'structural properties of caste have direct implications for the system of social stratification and the level at which the structure of caste tends to be relevant for social stratification is important.' Caste is, thus, a potent example of stratification and divisibility. These factors tinge the type and pattern of mores practised within each caste system. This pattern is repeated for the class structure and its divisions. Many communities are bifurcated along caste lines. Although caste structures are still fairly well adhered to in social interaction, like marriage, family rituals and the like, there tends to be a blurring in caste (occupational) spheres, especially in cosmopolitan areas. Subramanyam (1975) has cited this point in her study where she says that white collar jobs is one avenue where there is upward mobility and where caste distinctions become blurred. Khalakdina (1979: 51) described the differences in living patterns in four ecological areas, the traditional tribal, the interior rural, the villages which are part of urban complexes and mid-city middle class neighbourhoods. Kuppuswamy (1974) clearly indicated that child rearing was more or less traditional in most families, in respect of socio-religious rituals. Thus, it is apparent that societal mores may be divided into two categories. One category exemplifies homogeneity, irrespective of any social stratification, in the dominant culture of Hinduism. The behavioural characteristics are: deference to elders, overt behaviour indicating obedience to instructions and commands by the older generation, marriage ritualism including dowry giving (covert or overt) and differing status of the female as compared to the male (where more restriction is imposed on the female and more liberty is given to the male). The other category highlights the existence of differences in the ritualistic performance at funerals, births and deaths. Even today, in the business community, new books of accounts, (*khata*s) are opened on Diwali, and Goddess Lakshmi is offered special obeisance. In this community, Tuesdays are avoided for business transactions, as it is considered inauspicious. Horoscopes are important in marriage transactions; the belief in evil eye (*nazar*) is present in some communities who are superstitious (Bhowmick 1963: 147–83; Godwin, 1972: 135–76; Mathur, 1964: 88; Naik, 1972: 252). Further, these practices are not homogeneous across castes/communities. As one moves from the modern to the very traditional communities, practices become more and more conservative, and less and less scientific-oriented. It is well known that Indian society is closely dictated by the scriptures emanating from the pantheology of the godheads. God in his various *avtar*s becomes a special deity in different ethnic households, for instance, Krishna (god of love) is the deity in most of the north Indian communities, Ganesh (lord of auspicious events) is most revered amongst the families of Gujarat and Mahrashtra and Shiva (lord of fertility) is most revered in south India. If we compare these godheads to similar representations of god in Greek mythology, we observe a similarity between the two mythologies. It is our observation that the eastern pattern of parenting seems to have a common trend in countries of the Far East, Middle East and African cultures. Children in traditional families are discouraged from expressing their views, exhibiting curiosity or interfering in adult conversation. There is both a continuity and discontinuity between modes of childcare from early childhood to adolescence. In the former, the child, especially the male, is indulged in, and at primary school stage, there is a discontinuity when he is expected to become responsible, and to imitate adult behaviour. Therefore, continuity is observed in expecting the norms of society to be adhered to as soon as the growing child is able to perceive right from wrong (Mencher, 1963: 54–65). By and large, dependency is expected during early childhood, communication is discouraged and very few nurturers, especially from the underprivileged classes, encourage creativity. Some studies in Japan indicate lack of parent–child verbal communication, but increase in parent–child interaction (Khalakdina, 1979: 199–219). The mother–child relationship is conceptualised in terms of the quality of physical healthcare and security provided by the mother, rather than mental stimulation (Kazuo et al., 1986: 249; Stroufe, 1977: 1184–99).

We have to understand that traditional patterns are resistant even in the face of modernisation. We refer to the data on vital statistics in the latest report of the UNDP (2004). India is now in the 21st century, with an economic growth comparable to global trends. In 2001–02, its GDP grew at 4 per cent (Brett, 2003), and is expected to reach 8–9 per cent by 2007. It is now self-reliant in terms of food, major industries, transport systems and consumer items. However, the burgeoning population exceeds the limits of available basic facilities like water and electricity. With the increase in pollution levels and the increase in tenement/slum dwellings in urban areas, children are still at risk. Although longevity has increased, it has done so at poor status levels. Even though science and technology have increased, the status of illiteracy and poverty deflect the usage of their products for improvement in these statuses. Current statistics indicate that IMR and MMR are still high in larger states like UP, Bihar and Madhya Pradesh which are economically poorer as compared to smaller ones, namely, Kerala and Punjab. Parliament has still to reserve seats for women representatives although there are women chief ministers.

If we examine the government programmes, the emphasis on human development is mainly in the ministries of Health, Education and Human Resource Development. The general focus is on the educationally deprived, the health deprived and those in need of charity and welfare supplements. In the international forum, there are conventions on education for all, development with a human face, policies for the child in need, labour welfare, amenities and subsidies for health and women-specific activities. These are mainly oriented towards physical welfare and better living conditions, and are lopsided in terms of holistic development. There is little awareness of mental or emotional development of the human being and even less in several programmatic concerns. The numbers of those who are educationally poor and under the poverty line are still proportionally large. There is an inadequate number of institutions of higher learning for a population of one billion, and fewer have access to higher opportunities. Education at higher levels is highly competitive and is becoming more expensive, especially in professional fields. Frequently, political power accrues to the less advantaged; ironically there is also less in terms of a better quality of life (education, health and welfare). In fact, the government's budgetary allocations for these sectors are dismally poor. The fact that these facilities are poor tends to compress traditional behaviour into more conforming modes. While exposure to modernisation is becoming greater, the cognitive, mental and physical capacity of the social human being is not commensurate with such techno-economic increases.

These facts portend that the face of the community and its participation in development are not adequately reflected in the scientific and technological milieu. Families are becoming nuclear. Children are left to fend for themselves, while parents are at work. The joint family ethic which prevailed since ancient times is gradually splintering into nucleated families (Gore quoted in Singh, 1977) and there is increasingly growing neglect of the older generation of grandparents.

While it must be said that the quality of human interaction is still very high in India vis-à-vis the West, technology and modernisation are slowly creating destabilising inroads into family systems. Since the family is the crux of providing the child with care and access to facilities, its lessened abilities in terms of physical care have its repercussions on mental stability of the members. There is growing occurrence of pre-marital cohabitation and extramarital affairs ending often in divorce and destabilising living patterns of children, especially in the upper elite classes (Leeder, 2003). However, Sharma and Sharma (1999) have raised an interesting speculation, namely, that where families are catapulted into difficult circumstances such as economic loss, emotional deprivation and family disorganization there is a tendency to accept the circumstances and make the most out of the given situation for the sake of survival. For instance, where there are calamities like flood and famines, the family members tend to come closer emotionally in trying to bear the burden of deprivation. As the country moves forward in its technological pacing, there is increasing concern about the Indian psyche becoming diffused into a westernised prototype, divested of its cultural heritage (Beteille, 1971). There is a growing concern about the hiatus between the rich and the poor, the political inroads in societal matters, the unrest of youngsters in their impatience to westernise and increasing signs of family disorganisation (Madan, 1966).

This is to be expected given the plurality of cultures, the multi-ethnicity and several fissionings of the caste/class structure. As such, the modernising influences create a cultural dissonance in the life of the Indian in relation to his mores and customs. As the country accelerates its modernising trends, the westernising Indian tends to blend with the rest of the global world.

The attempt to preserve one's cultural heritage is obvious in the private and public motivation to enhance art, music and literature, and to preserve Indian architectural heritage. The former colonial attitude has almost died out. Indian contextual principles are being quoted more often and the study of the Indian in his habitat is assuming greater importance. But the task is enormous and the trickle-down effect is slow. Basic amenities for the sustenance of the health and well-being is still not commensurate with demand. Empirical work at the habitat or field level is still far behind in its aim to develop conceptualisations for theory building. There are still children disadvantaged and uncared for and little is known about their problems and much less about care facilities.

We still have to unearth those research measurements which are validly applicable to the Indian situation and are not adopted or adapted from the West. We still have a long way to go in eradicating the divisiveness amongst the castes. Although tomes have been written about the caste structure and its implications in a democratic country, the pervasiveness of the system continues to dominate the historical and political structure, especially at the grassroots level (Basu, 2003: 153). In sum, there is a hiatus between knowledge and action, between abstract concepts of human development and their implementation (Saraswathi, 1993: 27–29).

The question which is puzzling is how can academic information on development of the human in the discipline of the social sciences be transformed into social action (Dube, 1976: 27–38).

We are then faced with two issues: the unrelenting change of socio-economic patterns of living, and the catch-up effect of academicians researching these changes. Coupled with these are the varying interpretations of planners and programmers in understanding the social reality of such changes. Relentless also is the pace of change, whichever the strata in the Indian society. Understanding the complexity of changing mores as the culture is bombarded by technological stimuli is changing. What traditions and their mores will remain intact and what will change partially, completely or assume other forms—the future will tell.

Transmitters of Societal Mores

From its ivory tower in the departments of sociology, anthropology and psychology of universities, the concept of human development originated from child development, taught mainly in colleges of home science as a full-fledged study course, as a partial course in some women's colleges and in some IITs. Large national institutions like ICSSR (Indian Council for Social Science Research), ICAR (Indian Council of Agriculture Research), NIPCCD (National Institute of Public Cooperation and Child Development), NCERT (National Council for Educational Research and Training) and NIPA (National Institute of Public Administration) and some at the state levels have emphasised research and training in child/human development. It is only recently that some of these institutions have begun to enlarge their scope of study to cover the lifespan and have moved from labelling this area of study from child development and family relations to human development. In spite of a hesitancy towards full support for human development as a composite area of study, there is a growing movement towards considering holistic concepts of human development. Such concepts in the development process include two generic areas as discussed in Chapter 2. These are inherent traits that all human beings share and traits perceivable during the normal developmental process. Such traits, as we have said before, are phylogenetic, emerging from the genetic material which all human beings share. These traits enable the human being to walk, talk, feel and see. Living in a particular habitat, being born in a certain race and a certain ethnic group, a particular human being from a particular society develops specific skills. These are ontogenetic in nature. These skills enable him to adapt his individual needs (Sriram et al., 2002) to be balanced with the needs of his society. Such skills give him the ontogenetic ability to fine-tune his skills to adapt in such a way that he becomes proficient in his task/profession. For instance, a doctor develops skills in surgery, a pilot in flying an aircraft, a dancer in learning the techniques and so on. In the early years of conceptualisation of these ontogenetic skills, concepts tended to be based on universals transferred from one culture to another. In the Indian context, historically, dependency upon western-oriented conceptualisation held sway. Consequently, sociologists tended to depend heavily upon western concepts as the base to develop specifics about the Indian society (Singh, 1977: 267).

In the early years of documentation of the social sciences, concepts, mainly western-oriented, formed the basis of academic discussions. The academia dealt mainly with social issues like poverty, caste, community and religious differences and also psychological experimentation. Very few expanded on the profoundness of the Indian philosophy which reflected the Indian psyche and its identity. There was an unhappy cognitive dissonance between academic documentation and the stark reality of the lives of the majority of Indians who were rural. (Kakar, 1979a). It was only in the later 1950s that vigorous attempts were made to understand and document the conditions of the vast majority of the Indians in the countryside. From then onwards began a spate of documentation which did not exist before, from scholars like Singer (1955), Marriot (1961: 22), Vidyarthi (1961), Srinivas (1962: 42), Dube (1965: 421–23), Singh (1977: 267), Kakar (1979a) and Paranjpe (1998: 416), who with others examined the validity of 'universals' (generic concepts) propounded by western scholars. The late entry into the indigenous field of Indian sociology also delayed practical implementation. Psychology, like sociology, has followed the same pattern of evolving its themes from western conceptualisations.

Also, there are different interpretations for the same phenomena depending upon which discipline is propounding it. For instance, psychology tells us that the child is reinforced positively or negatively (psychological theory of behaviour modification), anthropology, that he lives in a particular cultural setting which is either rural, urban or tribal (the concept of ecology), and sociology, that he lives in a group with societal norms of behaviour (the sociological interpretations). These parameters set the Indian psyche in its idiomatic context. If we examine this network of interrelated concepts, we may not be able to present a totally holistic picture of the development of the Indian individual in terms of his self-concept and the concept of others, as the more individualised is the description, the greater the variations (Heider, 1959).

We see a growing trend to enlarge the profile of ethnographic and idiographic studies as they tell us more about the individual self (Choudhury, 1999: 144–66; Seymour, 1999: 323). The idiographic methodology is increasing in popularity for it gives an insight into the world of the child/individual in a particular setting (Kumar, 1999: 45–61). The complexity of the variables affecting individual development probably increases in geometric progression.

However, the use of sample methodology gives us very little information about the individual per se. It is a Catch-22 situation. The more we describe through idiographic means the specific individual, the less we know of the generic group from which he comes; and the more generalised our description (as in statistics), the more vague are the descriptions as applied to any one of the individuals. We are attempting to point out here that through the process of empiricism the most that we can understand about the make-up of the individual in relation to the variable studied is in relation to an average or a percentile. However, with little choice, we know with whatever knowledge we possess that the Indian child is nurtured in a very protected environment, where harmony is highlighted during the early years. But when he reaches the age of six or seven he is tonsured and is said to acquire *buddhi*, given responsibility, however small, within the socio-religious normative values instilled in him. Thus, there is discontinuity in the sense that he is now nurtured to be a responsible part of the family in its work ethics (Cowell, 1970). In any case, all children are made aware of the hierarchy of elders, to understand where the locus of authority is, to put the collective before self, to hold back aggression, to share and cooperate, and so on. The bonding between the adult and the child continues, but on different planes, throughout the growing years (Ainsworth, 1973; Kakar, 1978).

Ideologically, the nurtured Indian learns to operationalise the tasks related to role expectations. The major one is to make himself economically viable. These days moving out of their family-centered roles, women also on their own initiative as well as due to economic needs are becoming financially independent. To this end, the country in its professed ideology has embarked, in a socio-political sense, on modernisation, through democratic strategies (Constitution of India, 1952). The latter, imposed upon a society that is mainly traditional, illiterate and poverty-stricken, create an imbalance.

An integrated holistic view of the Indian people points towards the belief in harmony and recognition of the relationship between man and his physical ecology. The attitudes of an Indian may be hypothesised as being relatively less materialistic or less competitive, as contrasted with the West. Given this ideological umbrella, and a population of over 1.3 billion, with approximately two-thirds living in rural areas, and about one-third under the poverty line, there is an inevitable struggle to motivate and educate people who are beset with problems of day to day survival. Progress, however slow, is inevitable. The elite rich are more easily able to adapt to change. In fact, their type of adaptation is overly apparent. The middle class is struggling to reach levels of common comfort and services. The rest are beyond the pale economically and are acutely aware of their lowly economic status, but unable to do much because of lack of resources. Over time, this creates a sense of resentment, frustration and aggression. However, this negativity is tempered by the still feudalistic attitude of the 'have-nots' towards the 'haves'. The perception of the differences in norms of behaviour and customs becomes vividly apparent among the groups. In this milieu, there is need for the average Indian, brought up with traditional values, to find a congruence and harmony between traditionality and modernity (Dube, 1988) in internalising and exhibiting a pattern of lifestyle that is moving towards betterment.

At the same time, the proponents of modernisation indicate that if the Indian does not swim with the stream of modernisation that has swept over Singapore, Thailand and Indonesia in South Asia and the Far East, the Indian will be left huddling behind his traditions. Perhaps, it is inevitable that he is faced with the challenges of science and technology to modernise his lifestyles (Hall, 1990).

In the early 11th century when Albiruni visited India, he documented that there was less emphasis on empiricism and greater importance given to theorism (Beteille, 1998). We must underscore that the inheritance of knowledge in the Indian situation was, in the colonial days, filtered through the elitist Brahmins, who considered themselves, as Carstairs (1968: 63–76) states, the 'twice born'. Today, however, this modernising trend is accelerating appreciably in some states like Punjab, Haryana, Gujarat and Kerala. In the villages of Haryana, for instance, it was the custom to give a glass of *lassi* (buttermilk) to the Harijans, who swept the street. Nowadays, it is not so. In the slum areas of metropolitan cities it is common to see almost every household possessing a television set.

These are some modernising signs, though few and far between for a vast and diverse ecology like India, often compared to being a subcontinent. Thus, we find, in summarising the above, that the fundamentals of beliefs and practices relating to sociological and psychological processes have not moved much from the original framework. Rituals at each chronological/ biological age even reinforce intergenerationally communicated patterns of acceptable social behaviour (Chowdhary, 1979). They are internalised and where matters of privacy are concerned are strictly adhered to. The performance of rituals during certain periods of the lifespan is still maintained. The stage of *brahmacharya* or being single and the subsequent stages of *grihastha*, *vanprastha* and *sanyasa* are still maintained as mores. Celebrating religious festivals and other events like the birth of children, especially males, and other socio-religious events like *karvachauth*, Janmashtami, the *mundan* ceremony of a boy and the fulfillment of vows for *mannat*s made to specific deities are all part of the life of an Indian.

Just as in the economic sphere, there are fluctuations between demand and supply, as well as swings in share market index, so also are there fluctuations in the psycho-social sphere relating to societal conventions. There is fluctuation:

(i) between idealism and realism: for example the individual believes in doing charity, and yet at the same time does not have much concern about the conditions of poverty around him.

(ii) between myth and fact: for example there is veneration of goddesses, yet at the same time, a blind eye is turned towards the incidence of wife battering.

(iii) between orthodoxy and the acceptance of modern ways outside the network of the family and household: for instance, the practice of removing one's shoes before entering the kitchen or prayer room is still adhered to. Yet the very same practitioner will not think twice about drinking and smoking in pubs and restaurants, even when forbidden by societal norms/religion.

(iv) between the state of scarcity and the state of plenty: for instance, during famines or floods, a situation of scarcity of goods/commodities occurs, which an individual accepts as a matter of course. Yet, this very same individual will incur lifelong debts in order to spend lavishly on socio-religious events, especially the marriage of his daughters, the birth of a son, or the celebration of a business deal.

Importance of Male Progeny in the Patriarchal Ethos

In most developing societies the importance of male progeny is highly valued. Several studies (Meade, 1973: 89–100, Meade, 1972: 93–99 and Elson, 1996: 1–28) indicate that when asked for preference of sex of the child, samples from India as compared to samples from the West indicate a greater preference for male children. This is understandable given the ethos that in India male children are necessary for the performance of important ritualistic ceremonies like carrying on the ancestral lineage, the expectation of care of parents, the performance of *kanyadan* for a marriageable sister and the rituals at the death of a relative. Value for progeny is significant and is culture engendered as found in a study of Muslims and Hindus (Meade, 1973). Meade (1972) studied Indians and Americans on their future time perspectives, and in a follow-up study using the same projective technique, Meade (1973) studied the motives for childbearing. Elson (1996) also found that irrespective of the culture, there was a preference for greater number of boys, more so in the Indian Muslims.

When comparisons were made between American and Indian parents, Indian mothers expressed a greater sense of security in male progeny while Indian fathers expressed a heavier burden in the care and upbringing of female progeny. Child rearing in these studies was more casually viewed by Indian parents vis-à-vis American parents (Meade, 1973). Further, male progeny in the Indian context was said to add to the status of the family (Paranjpe, 1970).

We often hear the saying that 'he has many sons to take care of his affairs as daughters are merely guests in their parents' home till they get married.'

Between Traditionalism and Scientism

We have so far focussed on the individual in his setting. We will now touch upon the social realities to understand the forces that impinge on him: (*a*) the first and the foremost is his relationship to his families of procreation and orientation; (*b*) the second is to his family network, the extended family; (*c*) the third is his caste/*gotra* and the religious orientation of his family; (*d*) and, finally, social privileges conferred on him and the prohibitions which his society expects him to comply with.

For this information, we turn to the knowledge of tradition and science, mainly in the philosophical sense rather than the empirical. However, it is a positive sign that we are looking more intensively and sensitively towards our roots which offer many hypotheses to help us understand better the two-fold axis of the Indian psyche: the roots of 'Indianism' and the expanding world of science. The latter need not be anathema to the Indian perspective, for the Indian has the flexibility by and large to respond to dynamic changes. Witness the fact that in most cosmopolitan cities, the illiterate or the neo-literate carries with him a cellphone, even though he may not be able to read or write fluently.

The relationship of tradition to knowledge is what links the past with the present. It is the past in the present. Ideas, beliefs and values are modified by every new generation. Linkages are transmitted often in an automatic fashion—accepted for their credence as a link before and after. In the process of acculturation to the modified versions, the new is related to the old. For example, the rituals of the Arya Samaj are less elaborate than the usual typical Hindu rituals at marriages. Even in the world of today there is a movement towards retention of ethnic art within the modern compass, for instance, in fashion and design. These movements of acculturation go back and forth creating an admixture that is unique to the Indian. Again we only have to observe the tourist trends in India where agencies offer packages remade to recreate the old within the new, in a fluid manner. Also, the trend towards mixed marriages is accelerating. India is less of an interest as to its scientific and technical know how, but more a matter of interest in its mysticism and myth (Paranjpe, 2003: 18–30).

Since its inception and knowledge of its contents, the tradition inherited by Indians showed no distinction between psychology, philosophy and religion in analysing social behaviour which was holistic (Dalal and Misra, 2002: 19–49). According to the Rig Veda and Gautam's Dharmashastras around 600 BC, dharma was the duty of a human being on this earth towards his fellow men and himself. It has shaped the psychological and social behaviour of man through the ages (Kakar, 1979b). Inclusive in this precept is the concept of life stages and the life cycle. Even to this day the concept of dharma interweaves itself intricately in all walks of life. It is one's dharma to feed the poor, to respect the elderly, to take care of the destitute in the kin group, to give alms at the temple and to give *daan*. This concept euphemistically interpreted by some as 'ritualism' has an inner sense of linkage with the past, the present and the future of one's life.

If we examine this concept dispassionately it is not far from the philosophical thinking of the West from the days of Aristotle and Plato: that man is responsible for his fellow men. Just as the Bible is a treatise of Jesus' messages when he says through the apostles, 'I say unto you ... go out and do good'. Similarly, the treatises of the Ramayana and the Mahabharata contain concise and clear instructions on the how of behaviour of man to man, man to nature and man to the supreme being who lives in everything animate—that lives and breathes. For this reason, the Jain priests cover their mouths so that they might not breathe in germs which are said to be living. Profoundly also they serve a scientific basis that germs which infect are not breathed in, very much like the modern-day medical masks. There are various other examples not so extreme but relevant to the thinking of how human beings are guided into developmental processes essential for their adaptation to the environment (Barry and Bacon, 1959: 51–63). For instance, the use of sunlight for antiseptic purposes or roots and herbs of the ayurvedic system to cure diseases indicate the close alignment between *manas* and *dharti mata* and the cosmic energy. The word *shanti* has more meaning than peace. It also indicates being in harmony with god and nature, an interdependence and inter-relatedness. In the birth of the child we see his symbiosis in the bonding relationship between the dyad. It is then interlinked further with siblings and relatives with a strong habit en-cultured of abstract bonding of different types of different plateaux. The father has a strong patriarchal authoritarian relationship of obedience and deference directed towards him (Kakar, 2001: 132–40). The mother is the nurturant and the emotional tie for the child's 'storm and stress' during the growing up years. He expects and gets indulgence and sympathy from her. In this way structures and systems have their own supportive linkages, which rewarded and punished, subtly creating a gender differentiation in the process of growing up.

The concept of development has also its flip side. Much research has indicated the relevance of poverty as an inhibiting factor to development, cognitively and even physically (Misra, 2001: 280–300; Pareek, 2001: 262–79). Misra, as a leading authority on the relationship of deprivation to the Indian, states that the independent variable has been in operation from short-term to long-term variation (Misra, 1990: 119–40). Classificatory variables have been used more popularly (socio-economic status, cultural and other distal variables), with little knowledge of the underlying cognitive dependent-factors. He has made a plea for examining variations in a holistic manner when discussing the probabilities of occurrence and conse-quences of deprivation. The major conclusion he has arrived at are that deprivation, both economic and social, of a prolonged nature depresses cognitive functions. Elsewhere we have analysed this phenomenon and suggested that the deprivation indicating poor performance may also be due to the factor of less or no opportunity (experience) to exhibit the skills to indicate high or low cognitive performance on tasks. Acquisition, storage and retrieval capacities are subject to enhancement through intensive experiences, especially if they are related to the individual in his social context (Tiwari, 1986: 31–35). It is however not clear what the components of deprivation are, as a test only serves to give a total package effect and no specificity, with which we are concerned in development. For instance, a child deprived of food may, when he has access either to his mother or to the food, choose to go to his mother as a source of security rather than the food (Harlow, 1961). This gives some indication of the strength of the need-deprivation complex in the individual's repertoire (Rath, 1973).

It is often stressed that if there was comparable economic development between India and Japan, it would then give the Indian the opportunities which are equal to the West. Granted that this assumption might work, but then we have to ask ourselves if economic development automatically means social development. True, the joint family is disappearing under the stress of economic changes (married children and parents live separately), the fact remains however, that in spite of separate residences, the spirit of the joint family ethos still prevails. There are some studies which have attempted to examine central beliefs and values of Hinduism. These are a belief in rebirth, belief in cosmic causation, tendency to fatalistic helplessness and the belief that human experience is transitory and illusionary. It was felt that Hinduism which placed emphasis on myth and astrology limited man's need to achieve in social and economic pursuit. It was stated that the rigidity of fatalism precluded the endeavours of man to achieve further and better his position (Kapp, 1963; Mishra, 1962). Opponents have stressed, on the other hand, that these conclusions are based on the superficial aspects of Hinduism when compared with the values of capitalism propounded by the Protestant ethics of the West.

Individualism is based on equally highly regarded but different values. For example the values of the Vaishya community are likely to be more favourable to economic betterment than that of Brahmins. Different codes are prescribed for different *varna*s in the Hindu texts, which are themselves flexible in the changing milieu, for they are moral injunctions for all times. For instance, those who have big business houses have their own godheads and their own temples in their courtyards and are subservient to all rituals of the household deity Ganesha, as observed in western India (Ghurye, 1962). There are, for instance, six systems of Indian philosophy beside three non-Vedic schools, and the meaning of the terms used in the Vedas differs from one system to another (Rao, 2004).

Buddhist and Vedantic philosophies have since their inception bonded the mind and body in unison, a phenomenon acquiesced by western thought but not fully discussed in developmental processes except to acknowledge the biological aspects of cognition and the brain (Patel and Arocha, 1998: 280–99). Vedic thought also discusses its operation in the occurrence of psychiatric disorders (Malhotra, 2002: 2–7). '*Mann*' and '*roop*' are the terms used for the conjunction of the mind and body, which are ever changing but normally in tandem. The vedantic view of the *jiva* or the living being is a multi-layered entity. Consciousness is nested in the jiva (Paranjpe, 1986) and is the major focus of psychological thinking. It goes beyond the conscious state to other frames such as sleep, dreams and astral body which link these frames to personality. These are believed to be mysticism and superstition by the West but which in some respects give credence to these events as paranormal psychology. As said by Rao (2004: 33) many of these traditional aspects are also located in Japanese thought, and thoughts like emancipation, enlightenment and sartori are notions similar to nirvana in Chinese Buddhism. There is an interchange between external and internal stimuli in the western psychology. As Kakar (1996) puts it (as in Indian Vedic, Japanese Zen and Chinese Buddhism), thought in the Asian tradition comparises *chetna* or consciousness, conditions of *sukh* and *dukh*, dharma, karma, *samskara*, jiva, *atmatant, nirvana* are the concepts which occupy an important role in traditional social thought. These combine to make a broader spectrum of religious thought.

However, it must be admitted that while these are socially relevant to understanding the Indian psyche, not much attention has been paid to their empiricism. There are few models or hypotheses or even theoretical frames based on the traditional belief systems, to develop concepts and therefore theories based on the Indian experience. Even if projective methods are required to elicit data (Roland, 1980: 73–87), at least such data can then form the bases of development of hypotheses and therefore conceptualisations. For as yet Indian thought is still in the preliminary stages of formulation and needs to be subjected to rigorous empiricism. A beginning can be made through ethnographic/anthropological/case-study approaches to evolve concepts, though we do need to take cognisance of western-originating ideas, like the newly emerging idea that the child is a socially constructed individual (Prout and Prout, 1997). Our perception is to look at human development objectively and dispassionately bearing in mind the following points:

(i) First, we have leapfrogged into the western conceptualisation of human development.

(ii) Second, we need to take into consideration the universal basis of human growth and development as evolved from the West.

(iii) Third, we need to separate these basic facts from their re-interpretation in the Indian context.

(iv) Fourth, it is essential in this age and stage to divest ourselves of thinking of the growing human as an empty slate or an entity to be subordinated to adult manoeuvres.

(v) Fifth, we ought to think in a forward manner the contributions that the human himself makes to the emerging content of development as a process, where he/she creates and recreates his/her own societal frame.

The Interactions between the Self and Societal Norms

We have said that the emergence of Indian thinking on socio-psychological aspects of development were concepts transported from the colonial era. This occurred even though the traditions of India were rich with developmental concepts, not only in terms of the physical but also socio-emotional knowledge (Broughton, 1989: 128–64). This knowledge was combined with an abiding religiousness that was secular in nature, in that many religions existed side by side fairly harmoniously (Cobb and Griffin, 1977). There were relatively few occurrences of 'communal incidents', especially after the dust of the partition had settled down in India. The incidents which did occur were mainly provoked by socio-political interests of the powers that be.

There was a gap between the availability of Indian philosophical knowledge and its utilisation in the explanation of human thinking, behaviour and its usage in the realm of social realities (Gergen, 1989: 51–62). Current-day trends indicate that the umbrella of modernisation overarching the Indian psyche has compelled academicians to look back at their own social history and to evolve a context-specific framework (Sinha, 1965: 6–17). The top segment of the Indian society is almost, if not more, westernised than the western world, adopting western values and patterns of living in an indiscriminate fashion. India, by demographic standards, is still largely rural and will be so for many decades to come as the wheels of change, although set in motion, are slow. Already, major changes are evident, like the geographical disjointedness of the family, intergenerational conflict and the difficulty of the young to adapt to changing pressures, and so on (Kaura and Chaudhary, 2003). These are transitory plateaux which appear and disappear in quick succession, as one level of adaptation is quickly superimposed by another, very much like the evolutionary process advocated by biologists. Thus, this process is transferred to the socio-psychological area. Eventually in the Indian context as in the context of any other culture, the specifics of its culture are interspersed with different mixes of societal and ecological variables with their own interactive influences. But individuals are not passive recipients; they also interact volitionally, and perhaps with deliberate plans and policies, on the environment (science and technology) and on each other (education and societal norms in behaviour) to form a cohesion at any one time. Disruption of their juxtapositioning causes war, poverty, terrorism, and the worst afflicted are the powerless, mainly women and children.

We have emphasised the development of thinking and action as processed by the brain which is the neurological base of human development. But how does the human being think and act? What evidence do we have? For responses to these questions, we turn to the social sciences. It has been recognised for sometime now that human development draws heavily from biology, paediatrics, education, social work, psychiatry, anthropology, sociology and other life sciences to provide information and empirical data on the growing individual (Naidu and Nakhate, 1985). Knowledge of man's development is embedded in the varieties of ecologies of the country and the myriad representations of lifestyles in the various caste structures which defy homogeneity, except in the basic principles of physical growth, development and religious thinking.

Beteille (1971) highlights from an illustration of the Brahmins of Sripuram that a caste may subsume many other categories. He also shows the multipolarity in the functioning of caste in the Indian social structure. The many caste and sub-caste formulations are examples of such distinctions in the varied geo-ecological areas (Chauhan, 1960; Karve, 1961; Mayer, 1960; Yogesh, 1969).

Indigenous Mores and their Ethos

Sinha and Mishra (1993: 139–50), in their comments on the status of policy and research, state that there is still a need for a fraternity of common conceptualisation among the various experts in their cocooned disciplines to give a holistic picture to the study of human development.

The picture for all disciplines is that they still remain in their ivory towers. It can be further demonstrated that movement towards holistic development is hampered by the types of research currently conducted in institutions of higher education. More concerning is that many of these remain on shelves, since several of them do not contain practical information for implementation at the field level. The field level is one of social reality, far removed from the sophisticated conceptualisations stated in western academia. India is still a country where in the social psychological sphere, socio-religious philosophy dominates social customs. Irrespective of its march towards a better economic scenario, there are several counterbalancing factors that detract from the utilisation of this growth phenomenon. These are (a) the struggle to maintain age-old structures and systems; (b) the national identity which individuals and groups try to preserve; and (c) the counteracting interface between the traditional ethos and the attempts of the democratic government to modify them (such as the dowry act, the age of marriage act and reservation of educational seats and jobs for the deprived).

Notwithstanding this, the government at the same time is trying to keep pace with global economic trends against social realities such as the rural migrant urban slum dwellers and their burgeoning populations in urban slums which by force affect participatory interaction in each other's socio-religious customs. For instance, a rural migrant Rajasthani exposed to the overt performance of the pujas of a south Indian becomes a familiar part of their scenario. However, increasingly, because of the rise in real wages, more of the lower class are coming into higher profile. This is evidenced in the fact that in political constituencies, political representatives are now also from people who were hitherto marginalised. Many of these political representatives bring with them their own 'desi' culture to public and parliamentary scenarios and, at many times, the highly educated, lowly occupied Brahmin is beholden to these less educated, less statured political figures. Thus, there is an increasing pot-pourri of societal mores that are criss-crossing hitherto rigid boundaries of interaction.

Further, in conjunction with conceptual frames of sociology and to some extent anthropology, psychologists have also tried similar conceptualisations. Many of the conceptualisations of the Indian reality interact in a homogeneous manner with those of sociology of the individual in his community, in his society and his socio-religious network. The nexus of them, of you and I, of self and others, and an accurate perception of each others' roles in the organisational structure gives the individual his perception of his role in the practice of the mores (Laing, 1961). These parameters radiate in various combinations and permutations affecting the growing individual. For this reason, it is often seen that when describing a group, there is frequently a tendency for authors to illustrate their results by use of examples from the group, as any one individual is not totally representative of the entire group, nor is there any feasible explanatory channel to know everything about any individual. As such when describing the adherence to societal mores, there are always variations. Some individuals adhere much more than the others; some perform more socio-religious rites and rituals than others, and some are more orthodox than others. For instance, if one were to ask a modern day urbanite who is a vegetarian, whether he ever does eat non-vegetarian food, many a time one hears such remarks as 'no, but I eat eggs sometimes', or 'I do not eat mutton, because it is like human flesh, but I eat chicken'. Such variations in adherence to societal norms are often mere statistics. In this milieu, there is need for the average Indian, brought up with traditional values, to find a congruence/harmony between traditionality and scienticism in internalising and exhibiting a pattern of lifestyle that is moving towards economic betterment, however uncertain the socio-psychological betterment may be.

The major issues which face the Indian today are varied. If we stop midstream and look back at the socio-political history of India, it is apparent that we have inherited a distinct culture, ancient and rooted in socio-religious norms. India is, as is well known, composed of many races, divided into many castes and ethnic groups. How does one begin to talk in truth of a system of societal mores with these heterogeneous groups? To come to terms with this paradox of heterogeneity, we must accept the fact that while generic practices for all are similar, the specifics vary in subtle ways so as to differentiate between individuated identities (Stern, 2003).

It is well understood that mores are deeply ingrained. The problem is that the Indian society is in a flux; it is not static. This is true of any other culture which is exposed to the global changes which are occurring. However, not all strata of a caste or class, or an ethnic or religious group, are changing at the same pace. India is a civilisation in transition, from the age-old forms of the pastoral times to a technologically driven economy. It is an exposed society and no longer a sheltered one. It is also impacted by other exposures such as that of media, technological improvements, advances in the medical arena, the microchip society and the modernised fashion-oriented society. However, this is true of only half of the people of India. The other 50 per cent of India is still immersed almost rigidly in various stages of traditional living and thinking.

This vast panorama has hardly been viewed by social scientists in a holistic manner. We admit that no one prescription of any one discipline is sufficient. We should also admit that when we talk about a conceptual framework of various psychosocial traits, we also have to consider the implications of the milieu in which the Indian lives. In a generic sense, while being Indian, he is also a Punjabi, or Keralite, or one of the myriad sub-groups in the country. The individual tends, therefore, to move in his own orbit, adjusting, aspiring and coping with the changes. It is a universal theme that all societies socialise their children, during which times fundamental values are inculcated and internalised in the early years. This segment is viewed as priority in most societies, and therefore investment in policies and programmes which work at the ground level are important (Boyden, 1990: 184–216).

It is obvious from the above scenario that the tapestry of societal mores in relation to the individual is complex and dynamic. The individual, sociologically speaking, has to juggle his roles between being a conformist and an independent entity in his own right. As a totally unconditional conformist, he loses a part of his creativity and innovativeness, in doing what his neighbour does. On the other hand, if he is a deviant, he suffers from a sense of isolation, from a sense of being a 'social *anomie*'. He adapts by separating his public role from his private, and for the former he puts on a social face. If he persists in deviancy, he becomes a non-conformist, and eventually a deviant. Thus, he straddles two worlds: the world of traditionality and the world of modernity, into which he is inexorably being channelled. Given this shifting base, there is a need to view the Indian psyche in a paradigm that accommodates these shifts.

As often happens in a society transitioning from one domain to another, the temporality (or the time factor) and the multidimensionality needs to be viewed simultaneously (Dube, 1988).

The Changing Structures and Systems of Societal Mores

We have mentioned in the aforesaid pages the major conditioning determinants which influence the ways in which the Indian behaves in his milieu. These are the classificatory variables of caste, class, ethnicity, religion and region. But because of the dynamism of the Indian's environment, there are many other intervening variables. For instance, an Indian may not only be a Muslim, but also a Christian or a Hindu. He may or may not be in a joint family. He may be moving from one geographical area to another, or remain static. These are the fissioned variables that arise from the major ones mentioned above. We need to be clear at this point to have a summarised perspective on the dynamism of the particular society and the changing structure of the mores to which he ascribes his behaviour. Mores are therefore valued systems of unitary behaviour based on systems communicated from one generation to another and practices as customary behaviour regulated by rules of interaction and the regulatory mechanism of ethics, law and order. They act and interact in various combinations. Thus, a more is assmilitated as a belief system which is acted out, accepted as such and which often may not have scientific reasoning. For instance, when we ask a village woman why she practises traditional childbirth methods, a usual reply will be *'humaare buzurgon ne humein ye sikhaya hai, aur aise aadtein zamane se chali aa rahi hain'* ('We have learned this from our elders and we continue to practise since they have come down from generations ago'). If we translate this in terms of the psychological state of mind of the village woman, what she is actually saying is that 'these have been traditionally tried out methods, and we feel safe and secure with them'. Also built in the psychological make-up is the probablity that she knows no other secure alternative measures. This is not to say that this system of behaviour valued as an unchanging belief is continuous with time. As the country moves forward, and as more scientific facilities are being provided, especially in districts and outlying villages where there are maternal and child health clinics and where many are exposed to health messages through televised media, more tend to go to pre-natal clinics and have medically attended childbirths.

In the psyche of the Indian, we may note six tendencies of changing mores, which are modulated by the changing environment:

    (i) The continuum of social centricism to ego-self involvement. In the days of the old, for instance, the family was joint and intensely interactive. Now, there is a tendency for families to be scattered and in fact the family is viewed through global lenses (Gupta, 1971).

(ii) The value given to a traditional more is being modified along the continuum towards logical and scientific reasoning. For instance, as education increases, adolescents are being taught sex education in schools, which in many families is usually a taboo subject.

(iii) Widening spheres of upward mobility have their influence on those in the surrounding ecology and imitative behaviour of the upper strata now clashes with traditional mores.

(iv) With the range of consumerism widening and the perceived lessened ability of the poorer to have the same as those who are rich widens the chasm, especially among the young who suffer from greater frustration than did those of the previous generation. For instance, street children are a common figure in most market and public places who leave school in order to earn a daily wage to procure what the children of upper strata have. Thus, there is a boomerang effect and school dropouts are a problem that governance has contended with even though primary school education is free and compulsory.

(v) There is, therefore, a significant chasm between the values and mores of the parent generation vis-à-vis the child. We see this happening in everyday life. Parents have aspirations for their children which clash with those of their children, whose mores about life and occupation are more influenced by peers and media.

(vi) Finally, society as such is an abstract term, but when operationalised we know that the individual lives in several simultaneous sub-societies: the social group of his family, the social group of his workplace and the social group of his peers/friends.

References

Agarwal, R. and G. Misra, 1986, 'A Factor Analysis of Achievement Goals and Means: An Indian View', *International Journal of Psychology*, 21: 217–31.

Ainsworth, M.D.S., 1973, 'The Development of Infant Mother Attachment', in B. Caldvell and H. Ricciuti (eds), *Review of Child Development Research, Vol. 3*. Chicago: University of Chicago Press.

Allport, G.W., 1961, *Pattern and Growth in Personality*. New York: Holt, Rinehart & Winston.

Anandalakshmy, S., 1998, 'The Cultural Context', in M. Swaminathan (ed.), *The First Five Years: A Critical Perspective on Early Childhood Care and Education in India*. New Delhi: Sage.

Appadurai, A., 1997, *Modernity at Large: Cultural Dimensions of Globalisation*, New Delhi: OUP.

Arbib, M.A. and M.B. Hesse, 1986, *The Construction of Reality*. Cambridge: Cambridge University Press.

Bandyopadhyaya, N.C., 1982, *Kautilya, or An Exposition of His Social Ideal and Political Theory*. Varanasi: Endological Bookhouse (originally published in 1927).

Barry, H.J. and M.K. Bacon, 1959, 'The Relations of Child Training to Subsistence Economy', *American Anthropologist*, 61: 51–63.

Basu, S., 2003, *Caste and Class: Differential Response to the Rajbansi Movement*. New Delhi: Manohar.

Benedict, R., 1934, *Patterns of Culture*. New York: Hougton Mifflin.

Beteille, A., 1971, *Caste, Class and Power: Changing Patterns of Social Stratification in a Tanjore Village*. Berkeley, CA: University of California Press.

———, 1998, 'The Indian Heritage—A Sociological Perspective', in D. Balasubramaniam and N. Appaji Rao (eds), *The Indian Human Heritage*. Hyderabad: Oxford University Press.

Bharati, A., 1985, 'The Self in Hindu Thought and Action', in A.J. Marselles, G. De Vos and F.L.K. Hsu (eds), *Culture and Self: Asian and Western Perspectives*. New York: Tavistock Publications.

Bhowmick, P.K., 1963, *The Lodhas of West Bengal*. Calcutta: Punthi Pustak.

Bougle, C., 1992, 'The Essence and Reality of the Caste System', in Dipankar Gupta (ed.), *Social Stratification*. New Delhi: OUP.

Boyden, J., 1990, 'Childhood and the Policy Makers: A Comparative Perspective on the Globilasation of Childhood', in A. James and A. Prout (eds), *Constructing and Reconstructing Childhood*. London: The Falmer Press.

Brett, D., 2003, *Asia & Pacific Review 2003/2004: Economic and Business Report*. Saffron Walden, UK: Walden Publishing.

Broughton, J.M., 1989, 'The Psychology, History and Ideology of the Self', in K.D. Larsen (ed.), *Dialectics and Ideology in Psychology*. Norwood, NJ: Ablex.

Burkitt, I., 1992, *Social Selves: Theories of the Social Formation of Personality*. London: Sage.

Carstairs, G.M., 1968, *The Twice Born*. London: The Hogarth Press.

Chauhan, B.R., 1960, *A Rajasthan Village*. New Delhi: Vir Publishers.

Choudhury, N., 1999, 'Language Socialisation: Patterns of Care Giver Speech to Young Children', in T.S. Saraswathi (ed.), *Culture, Socialisation and Human Development: Theory, Research and Application in India*. New Delhi: Sage.

Chowdhary, K., 1979, 'Industrialisation and Changing Values', in R. Mukherjee (ed.), *Sociology of Indian Sociology*. New Delhi: Allied Publishers.

Constitution of India, 1952.

Cobb, J.B., Jr and David R. Griffin, 1977, *Mind and Nature: The Interface of Science and Philosophy*. Washington, DC: University Press of America.

Cowell, F.R., 1970, *Values in Human Society: The Contribution of P.A. Sorokin to Sociology*. Boston: Porter Sargent.

Cox, Harvey, 1984, *Religion in the Secular City: Towards a Postmodern Theology*. New York: Simon and Schuster.

Cyper, J.M. and J.L. Deutz, 2004, *The Process of Economic Development*. London: Routledge.

Dalal, A.K. and G. Misra, 2002, 'Social Psychology in India: Evolution and Emerging Trends', in A.K. Dalal and G. Misra, *New Directions in Indian Psychology, Vol. 1*. New Delhi: Sage.

Dallymar, R. and G.N. Devi, 1998, *Between Tradition and Modernity: India's Search for Identity*. New Delhi: Sage.

Danziger, I.K., 1990, *Constructing the Subject*. Cambridge: Cambridge University Press.

Dube, S.C., 1965, 'The Study of Complex Cultures', in T.K.N. Unnithan, Indiradeva and Yogendra Singh (eds), *Towards a Sociology of Culture in India*. New Delhi: Prentice-Hall.

———, 1976, 'Role of the Social Science', in S.C. Dube (ed.), *Social Sciences and Social Realities, Role of the Social Sciences in Contemporary India* (Seminar Papers). Shimla: Indian Institute of Advanced Study.

———, 1988, *Modernisation and Development: The Search for Alternative Paradigms*. Tokyo: The United Nations University Press.

Dutt, M.N., 1979, *The Dharmashastras: Hindu Religious Codes, Vols I and IV*. Delhi: Cosmos Publications.

Elias, N., 1991, *The Society of Individuals*. Blackwell: OUP.

Elson, D., 1996, 'Male Bias in the Developing Process: An Overview of Diane', in D. Elson (ed.), *Male Bias in the Development Process*, 2nd edn. Manchester: Manchester University Press.

Erikson, E.H., 1950, *Childhood and Society*. New York: Norton.

———, 1959, *Identity and the Life Cycle*. New York: International University Press.

Freed, S.A., 1982, 'Changing Family Types in India', *Ethnology*, 21(3): 189–202.

Freud, S., 1923, *The Ego and the Id, Vol. 18*, pp. 13–59, Standard edn. London: Hogarth Press.

Friedman, Jonathan, 1990, 'Being in the World: Globalisation and Localisation', in M. Featherstone (ed.), *Global Culture: Nationalism, Globalisation and Modernity*. New Delhi: Sage.

Gergen, K.J., 1971, *The Concept of Self*. New York: Holt Rinehart & Winston.

———, 1989, 'Realities and their Relationships' in W.J. Baker, M.E. Hyland, R. van Hezewijk and S. Terwee (eds), *Recent Trends in Theoretical Psychology*. New York: Springer-Verlag.

Ghurye, G., 1962, *Gods and Men*. Bombay: Popular Prakashan.

Giddens, Anthony, 1991, *Modernity and Self-identity: Self and Society in the Late Modern Age*. Cambridge: Polity Press.

Godwin, C.J., 1972, *Change and Continuity*. Bombay: Tata McGraw-Hill.

Gore, M.S., 1961, 'The Impact of Industrialisation and Urbanisation on the Agarwal Family in the Delhi Area', Ph.D. dissertation (Unpublished), Columbia University, p. 207.

Griffin, David, 1988, *God and Religion in the Postmodern World*. Albany: State University of New York Press.

Gupta, G.R. (ed.), 1971, *Family and Social Change in Modern India*. New Delhi/Durham (NC): Carolina Academic Press.

Hall, S., 1990, 'Cultural Identity and Diaspora', in J. Rutherford (ed.), *Identity: Community, Culture, Difference*. London: Lawrence and Wishar.

Harlow, H.F., 1961, The Development of Affectional Patterns in Infant Monkeys', in Foss B.M. Metheun (ed.), *Determinants of Infant Behaviour, Vol. 1*. London: John Wiley.

Heider, F., 1959, *The Psychology of Interpersonal Relations*. New York: John Wiley.

Hiller, E.T., 1947, *Social Relations and Structures: A Study in Principles of Sociology*. New York and London: Harper and Bros.

Ho, David Y., 1986, 'Chinese Patterns of Socialisation: A Critical Review', in Michael Harris Bond (ed.), *The Psychology of Chinese People*. New York: OUP.

Huerrelmann, Klaus, 1988, *Social Structure and Personality Development*. New York: Cambridge University Press.

Jensen, A.R., 1969, 'How Much Can We Boost IQ and Scholastic Achievement', *Harvard Educational Review*, 39(1): 1–123.

Kakar, S., 1978, 'Images of the Life Cycle and Adulthood in Hindu India', in E.J. Anthony and C.L. Chiland (eds), *The Child in his Family: Children and their Parents in a Changing World, Vol. 5*. New York: John Wiley.

———, 1979a, 'Childhood in India: Traditional Ideals and Contemporary Reality', *International Social Science Journal*, 31(3): 444–56.

———, 1979b, *Identity and Adulthood*. New Delhi: OUP.

———, 1996, *The Indian Psyche*. New Delhi: OUP.

———, 2001, 'The Themes of Authority in Social Relations in India', in A. Dalal and G. Misra (eds), *New Directions in Indian Psychology*. New Delhi: Sage.

Kapp, K.W., 1963, *Hindu Culture, Economic Development and Economic Planning in India*. Bombay: Asia Publishing House.

Karve, I., 1961, *Hindu Society: An Interpretation*. Poona: Deccan College.

Kaura, I. and N. Chaudhary, 2003, 'Continuity and Change: Narratives of Conflict from the Lives of Indian Adolescents', Paper presented at the conference of the International Association for Cross-cultural Psychology, Budapest, July.

Kazuo, M., J. Campos, J. Kagan and D.L. Bradshaw, 1986, 'Issues in Socio-emotional Development', in Harold Stevenson, H. Azuma and K. Hakuta (eds), *Child Development and Education in Japan*. New York: W.H. Freeman and Company.

Khalakdina, M., 1979, *Early Child Care in India*. London: Gordon and Breach.

———, 1998, 'Insight on Site: A Study of Mobile Crèches', M. Swaminathan (ed.), *The First Five Years: A Critical Perspective on Early Childhood Care and Education in India*. New Delhi: Sage.

Khaleque, A., 2003, 'Attachment and Life Span Development: A Review of the Adult Attachment Literature', *Psychological Studies*, 48(1): 28–35.

Kumar, K., 1999, 'Children and Adults: Reading an Autobiography', in T.S. Saraswathi (ed.), *Culture, Socialisation and Human Development: Theory, Research and Application in India*. New Delhi: Sage.

Kuppuswamy, B., 1974, *A Textbook of Child Behaviour and Development*. Delhi: Vikas Publishing House.

Laing, R.D., 1961, *The Self and Others*. London: Tavistock Publications.

Lazarus, R.S., 1974 , 'The Psychology of Coping: Issues of Research and Assessment', in G.V. Coelho, D.A. Hamburg and J.E. Adams (eds), *Coping and Adaptation*. New York: Basic Books.

Leeder, E.J., 2003, *The Family in Global Perspective: A Gendered Journey*. Thousand Oaks, CA: Sage.

Madan, G.R., 1966, *Indian Social Problems: Social Disorganisation and Reconstruction*. New Delhi: Allied Publications.

Malhotra, S., 2002, *Child Psychiatry in India*. New Delhi: Macmillan.

———, 2003, 'Socio-cultural Diversity and Ethnocentrism in Child Mental Health', in J.G. Young, P. Ferrari, S. Malhotra, S. Tyano and E. Caffo (eds), *Brain, Culture and Development*. New Delhi: Macmillan.

Markus, H. and S. Kitayama, 1991, 'Culture and Self: Implications for Cognition, Emotion and Motivation', *Psychological Review*, 98: 224–53.

Marriot, McKim, 1961, 'Changing Channels of Cultural Transmission in Indian Civilisation', *Journal of Social Research*, 4(1–2): 13–25.

Maslow, A.N.A., 1943, 'Theory of Human Motivation', *Psychological Review*, 50: 370–96.

Mathur, K.S., 1964, *Caste and Ritual in a Malwa Village*. Delhi: Asia Publishing House.

Mayer, A.C., 1960, *Caste and Kinship in Central India*. Berkeley, CA: University of California Press.

Mead, G., 1934, *Mind, Self and Society*. Chicago: University of Chicago Press.

Meade, R., 1972, 'Future Time Perspectives of Americans and Subcultures in India', *Journal of Cross-cultural Psychology*, 3: 93–99.

———, 1973, 'Motives for Child-bearing in America and in India', *Journal of Cross-cultural Psychology*, 4: 89–110.

Mencher, J., 1963, 'Growing up in South Malabar', *Human Organisation*, 22: 54–65.

Mishra, G., 1990, 'Psychology of Deprivation', in G. Misra (ed.), *Applied Social Psychology in India*. New Delhi: Sage.

———, 2001, 'Deprivation and Cognitive Competence', in A.K. Dalal and G. Misra, *New Directions in Indian Psychology*. New Delhi: Sage.

Mishra, V., 1962, *Hinduism and Economic Growth*. Bombay: OUP.

Murphy, Louis B., 1953, 'Roots of Tolerance and Tension in Indian Child Development', in G. Murphy (ed.), *In the Minds of Men*. New York: Basic Books.

Naidu, U. and V.S. Nakhate, 1985, *Child Development Studies in India—An Overview*, Tata Institute of Social Sciences Series 56. Mumbai: TISS.

Naik, T.B., 1972, *Applied Anthropology in India: A Survey of Research in Sociology and Social Anthropology*. New Delhi: Indian Council of Social Science Research.

Ostor, A., 1993, *Vessels of Time: An Essay on Temporal Change and Social Transformation*. New Delhi: OUP.

Paranjpe, A.C., 1970, *Caste, Prejudice and the Individual*. New Delhi: Lalvani.

———, 1986, 'The Self beyond Cognition, Action, Pain and Pleasure: An Eastern Perspective', in K. Yardley and T. Honess (eds), *Self and Identity: Psychosocial Perspectives*. New York: Praeger.

———, 1998, *Self and Identity in Modern Psychology and Indian Thought*. New York: Plenum Press.

———, 2003, 'Contemporary Psychology and a Mutual Understanding of Europe and India', in J.W. Berry, R.C. Mishra and R.C. Tripathi (eds), *Psychology in Human and Social Development*. New Delhi: Sage.

Pareek, U., 2001, 'Poverty and Motivation: Figure and Ground', in A.K. Dalal and G. Misra, *New Directions in Indian Psychology*. New Delhi: Sage.

Patel, V. and J. Arocha, 1998, 'Expertise and Reasoning in Medicine: Evidence from Cognitive Psychological Studies, in Indramani Singh and Raja Parasuraman', *Human Cognition: A Multidisciplinary Perspecitive*. New Delhi: Sage.

Prout, A. and A. Prout, 1997, *New Paradigm for the Sociology of Childhood—Constructing and Reconstructing Childhood*. London: The Falmer Press.

Rao, M.S., 2004, 'Religion and Economic Development', in R. Robinson (ed.), *Sociology of Religion in India*. New Delhi: Sage.

Rath, R., 1973, *Psycho-social Problems of Social Change,* Monograph No. 6 of A.K. Sinha Institute of Social Studies. Patna: Allied Publishers.

Rath, R., A.S. Dash and U.N. Dash, 1979, *Cognitive Abilities and School Achievement of the Socially Disadvantaged Children in Primary Schools*. Bombay: Allied Publishers.

Roland, A., 1980, 'Psychoanalytic Perspectives on Personality Development in India', *International Review of Psycho-analysis*, 7: 73–87.

———, 1987, 'The Familial Self, the Individualised Self, and the Transcendent Self: Psychoanalytic Reflections on India and America', *Journal of Psychoanalytic Review*, 74: 237–50.

Saraswathi, T.S., 1993, 'Need for Interface between Child Development Research and Policy Planning in India', in T.S. Saraswathi and B. Kaur (eds), *Child Development Research and Policy Linkage in Human Development and Family Studies in India*. New Delhi: Sage.

Seymour, S.C., 1999, *Women Family and Child Care in India*. Cambridge University Press.

Sharma, D., 2003, 'Infancy and Childhood in India', in D. Sharma (ed.), *Childhood, Family and Socio-cultural Change in India: Reinterpreting the Inner World*. New Delhi: OUP.

Sharma, N. and B. Sharma, 1999, 'Children in Difficult Circumstances: Familial Correlates of Advantage While at Risk', in T.S. Saraswathi (ed.), *Culture, Socialisation and Human Development: Theory, Research and Application in India*. New Delhi: Sage.

Shek, D.T.L., 1995, 'Chinese Adolescents' Perception of Parenting Styles of Fathers and Mothers', *Journal of Genetic Psychology*, 156(2): 175–90.

Simone, Valantine, 1973, 'Problems in Observation of Children Raised in Various Cultural Environments', *Journal of Early Child Development and Care*, 2 (Handbook 3a): 276–89.

Singer, Milton, 1955, 'Cultural Pattern of Indian Civilisation: A Preliminary Report of Methodological Field Study', *Far Eastern Quarterly*, l(15): 23–26.

Singh, Y., 1977, *Modernisation of Indian Tradition*, p. 178. Faridabad: Thomson Press Ltd.

———, 1980, *Social Stratification and Change in India*. New Delhi: Manohar.

Sinha, D., 1965, 'The Integration of Modern Psychology with Indian Thought', *Journal of Humanistic Psychology*, 5: 6–17.

Sinha, D. and H.S.R. Kao, 1997, 'The Journey to the East', in H.S.R. Kao and D. Sinha (eds), *Asian Perspectives on Psychology*. New Delhi: Sage.

Sinha, D. and R.C. Mishra, 1993, 'Some Methodological Issues Related to Research in Developmental Psychology in the Context of Policy and Intervention Programs', in T.S. Saraswathi and B. Kaur (eds), *Human Development and Family Studies in India*. New Delhi: Sage.

Srinivas, M.N., 1962, 'A Note on Sanskritisation and Westernisation', in M.N. Srinivas, *Caste in Modern India and Other Essays*. London: Asia Publishing House.

———, 1972, *Social Change in Modern India*. Bombay: Orient Longman.

Sriram, S., P. Ralhan and N. Chaudhary, 2002, 'The Family and Self in Dialogue', Paper presented at the Conference of the Dialogical Self, Ghent, October.

Stern, R.W., 2003, *Changing India: Bourgeois Revolution in the Subcontinent*, 2nd edn. Cambridge: Cambridge University Press.

Stroufe, L.A., 1977, 'Attachment as an Organized Construct', *Child Development*, 48: 1184–99.

Subramanyam, Y. S., 1975, *Social Changes in Village India—An Andhra Case Study*. Delhi: Prithvi Raj Publishers.

Tiwari, B.D., 1986, 'Development of Memory in Relation to Some Socio-cultural Factors', *Psycho Lingua*, 16: 31–35.

UNDP, 2004, *Human Development Report: 'Cultural Liberty in Today's Diverse World'*. New York: Hoechestwater Printing Co.

Vidyarthi, L.P., 1961, *The Sacred Complex in Hindu Gaya*. Bombay: Asia Publishing House.

Weling, A.N., 1934, *The Katkarias: A Sociological Study of an Aboriginal Tribe of the Bombay Presidency*. Bombay: The Bombay Book Depot.

Whiting, B.B. and J.W.M. Whiting (in collaboration with R. Longabaugh), 1975, *Children of Six Cultures: A Psycho-cultural Analysis*. Cambridge, MA: Harvard University Press.

Yogesh, A., 1969, 'The Changing Frontiers of Caste', in Andre Beteille (ed.), *Social Inequality*. Harmondsworth, UK: Penguin Books.

Yue, A.B. and K.S. Yang, 1987, 'Social and Individual Oriented Achievement Motivation—A Conceptual Analysis', *Bulletin of the Institute of Ethnology Academy of Sinica (Taiwan)*, 64: 51–98 (in Chinese).

A Concluding View

Holistic Perspective

SO HOW do the foregoing discussions lead to a holistic perspective on development of the Indian? Unlike the West, where the background of research and study is relatively homogeneous (Shuster and Aburn, 1992: 958), we cannot assume a similar homogeneity about India's people. We have stressed right through the chapters about the intervening variable of the environment alongside the genetic make-up. Orthogenetically, the same human formula exists in all human beings except that the environment moulds its shaping. However, the collectivity of environmental factors has a great role to play during the continual process of development. These factors cement that process into a mould that is holistically speaking an 'Indian mould'. One cannot mistake a Japanese or a Chinese, unless he is influenced by other cultures, such as in the case of an American Japanese who would have cultivated habits that are western but is rooted in 'easternism'.

The totality of the Indian should be viewed against this backdrop of holism. This holism is a package of characteristics towards which the individual in the Indian culture has been distinctively acculturated. The Indian is affected by his proximate surroundings. For the Indian holism is a package which comprises traditionalism, regionalism, ethnocentricity, collectivism, familialism, interdependency and a deep-rooted belief in his socio-religious norms. Therefore, the focus in this volume is on his social and cultural developmental process. This focus is arrived at by using wherever possible available data from the fields of psychology, sociology, anthropology and their derivatives and, therefore, stresses foundational systems. These foundational systems are bases of the processes within the individual and those processes outside which influence the individual in his ontogenetic development. The Indian is accustomed to be in his kinship network, and is brought up in close proximity to the older members of his family. This happens on a generic basis, irrespective of what ethnic, religious, regional or ecological group to which he belongs. Therefore, if we observe only his physiological behaviour, for instance, he is no different from any other individual of the same age. As he grows he behaves differently from individuals in other countries. He cannot be mistaken for an Italian or an Australian as he is a product of his Indian environment.

The Indian identity is particularly related to socio-political history, to changing economic systems and to the effects of governance. If today there is a hue and cry about power prices, it is because the average family is relating it to its budget as it affects everyone in the family. There is an immediate repercussion arising out of family interaction processes, such as when a family crisis occurs. Such critical events are affected by the radiating intervening variable of economic stress. For instance, if a family crisis such as the sudden death of a patriarch occurs, there is a rippling effect not only on the immediate biological family, but its circles of kinship groups where other elders of the family help make decisions about the restructuring of relationships and responsibilities. This is the heuristic ecological model of the spiralling effects of the immediate wave before the next in the rippling effect. Therefore, when we talk about an individual in his society we, in fact, are looking at him in a prismatic manner, as the intervening variables influence a particular form of behaviour.

It is said that there can be as many interpretations, as there are onlookers, of a phenomenon. This is so of a hybrid field of analyses, such as human development. All theories and concepts of disciplines, namely, sociology, psychology, anthropology, economics and political sciences influence this development. These social sciences are upheld by the socio-political history and the socio-religious philosophy of the Indian. If we examine, for instance, the stages of infant growth cognitively, Piaget (1952) would be correct in describing the stages of cognitive development; McGraw (1943) would be correct in describing physical growth; Erikson (1950) would be correct in describing his psycho-dynamic concepts of the progression of development. The fact remains that all studies relate to the human individual, and, as it is said, all roads lead to Rome, so do all social science disciplines/theories attempt to explain the human individual.

India has a long social history, interwoven with its myths and mythologies, with its remnants of feudalism, and the turmoil of adjusting to an eco-politically changing scenario. It has been said that the psychology of the eastern mind is based on dissociation and detachment, unlike the western psychological model based on logical interpretation of the functions of the personality. Thus, we find that the psyche of the Indian is atypically of its own making. This point cannot be overemphasised; as cross-cultural studies are increasing, there is greater knowledge on the differentiation in the psychological make-up of various nationalities. Indians are both homogeneous and heterogeneous in behaviour depending upon the situations and their stimuli (Pederson, 1979). Using the widening ecological compasses of linking contexts, Bronfenbrenner (1970; 1989: 185–246) views the inextricable proactive and reactive processes of the environment and the human being to explain the individual in a culture-specific environment. In this flux and vortex of so many different sources of influences, how do we make sense in terms of a paradigm? We cannot do so precisely or in any detailed sense. Time is inexorable, and what is true today is displaced by another perspective or truth on the morrow. To understand change and fluctuations and their effects on the individual, it is important to keep a 'resilient perspective' while stating current facts and while detailing differences from one country-specific society to another. This statement emphasises therefore the need for accuracy of information, which can be obtained by an understanding of how to research and to cull out the facts from fiction, as the saying goes 'to sift the wheat from the chaff'. We have, therefore, given great importance to the specific nature of researching in human development.

A radical and proactive perspective is essential. In other words, the total spectrum of all possible cited influences and, what is more important, the strength of these influences, or as Lewin puts it, the strength of valences in affect and effect are significant variables (Lewin, 1936). Therefore, while still a challenge, it is essential to keep an open-door perspective in varied disciplinary conceptualisations about the Indian in his society.

The Relevance of the Earlier Chapters in Understanding Human Development

Looking back over the chapters, it is essential that we state some concluding comments. What has been said in them reflects the present stage of scientific and technological progress. The pace and the intensity of these developments are unpredictable, given the state of the political and economic volatility in the world of today. These are affecting socio-psychological values of identity, and this is especially true of the developing world of which India is a part. When we look around we can identify tribes who have lived their lives comparatively unchanged over the past centuries. At the same time the urban youth is changing, sometimes more rapidly than his western counterpart. From the illiterate migrant who can use a cellphone competently to the young female CEO of a large corporate house, identities are undergoing change and reflect on the competencies required in interrelationships, which are being dynamically juxtapositioned. These have been discussed in the chapters on identity and interpersonal competence. Traditionally the female is the second sex, but professionally she is beginning to command males working under her supervision. There is consequently a chain reaction, affecting the observance of societal mores within the family system. To identify such socio-economic changes in the Indian psyche, we have only to look at the changing societal mores, habits and attitudes of the Japanese and Chinese. Japan and China are now fast-paced, economically developed countries. These countries are still, however, rooted in their socio-religious norms, which gives them their unique identities of being both modern and traditional. Communism has a new meaning in Russia and is little talked about in China where consumerism is spurting to greater heights, with India close on its heels. Youngsters in India are earning more and earlier than did their parents. The hiatus, especially in urban areas, is growing wider between parent and child generations. Social change lags behind economic and technological change, and perhaps this is the main reason why the Indian still stays within his traditional mores while he adapts to a modernising economy.

The sources of information will continue to become more scientific and sophisticated as information on genomes and genetic engineering catches up. Industrialisation and globalisation surreptitiously affect the ecological parameters of living, and perhaps pollution and epidemiology will contend for the first place in the growing concerns of nations. This new information will affect the study of human beings, especially in the physiological and biochemical sphere, where, for instance, in India today, needy urban women are not averse to becoming birthing surrogates for infertile parents for monetary compensation. More females work outside the homes and grandparents are becoming babysitters. The latter's familial status is precarious as they become liabilities with increasing fragility and declining health as they age. These events lead to a rise in family dissonance and will probably change our concepts of human development in the domains of traditionality and modernity.

It therefore becomes all the more important that the critical skills of language, information processing and increasing one's intellectual skills become more significant. Language is increasing in significance as computer technology takes over face-to-face communication. Given the opportunity, the lowly educated technician is a whiz at fixing mechanical items better than the highly educated engineer, perhaps because he is innately more intelligent. He learns through sheer necessity the right English words although it is only the phonetic sound that he knows. Having been exposed to economic deprivation of one kind or the other most rural people, when they come to urban conglomerates, have an amazing ability to acclimatise to conditions around them, indicating that they have a high potential for resilience in adapting to their changing surroundings.

But how does one have the acumen to know what is valid and reliable about human nature and processes? Growing in stature and in strategy the ability to search for the truth is an important skill for understanding human skills and for performance. Hence, the need for research acumen. These chapters are therefore essential for understanding human development in a fast evolving development scenario. What is fact and what is fiction, what is wheat and what is chaff? The development of research skills or critical skills, and knowledge of identity will equip the reader to critically examine the information in Volume 2 which deals with the context and content of human development as it is known today. Information and its processing are prolific, given the various tools and channels of communication and therefore demand a heightened awareness of its use and impact.

This volume confines itself to the relevance of the social and psychological parameters of the developing human. Much of the discussion rests on available and reliable information referred to in this volume. Several stalwart professionals have devoted their writings to the need to understand the Indian in his milieu. Given the paucity of empirical data, much of the content of the author's presentation has moved into newer hypotheses in the discussion. The challenge is to continue to test them and to add to available information. For instance, what happens to domestic relations when women in the family earn more than men? How does one cling on to societal mores in the face of runaway technology which threatens to commercialise socio-religious events like karvachauth, and 'western' observances like St. Valentine's Day?

At this point in time we honestly do not know, but the challenge is to search out and research new data to expand our knowledge of indigeneity in the Indian context. The only permanent constant is change. What is said in this book for this generation will change through increased knowledge giving readers a wider perspective on human development.

References

Bronfenbrenner, U., 1970, *Two Worlds of Childhood*. New York: Russell Sage Foundation.

———, 1989, 'Ecological Systems Theory', *Annals of Child Development*, 6: 185–246.

Erikson, E.H., 1950, *Childhood and Society*. New York: Norton.

Lewin, K., 1936, *Principles of Topological Psychology*. New York: McGraw-Hill.

McGraw, M.B., 1943, *Growth: The Neuro-muscular Maturation of the Human Infant*. New York: Columbia University Press.

Pederson, P., 1979, 'Non-western Psychology: The Search for Alternatives', in A.J. Marsell, R.G. Tharp and T.J. Cibordwski (eds), *Perspectives on Cross-cultural Psychology*. New York: Academic Press.

Piaget, J., 1952, *The Origins of Intelligence in Children*. New York: International University Press.

Shuster, C.S. and S. Aburn, 1992, *The Process of Human Development: A Holistic Lifespan*. Philadelphia: Lippincott Williams and Wilkins.

Appendix I

Selected Measures Used in the Indian Context

1. *Differential Aptitude Tests (DAT)*. Authors: G.K Bennett, H.G. Seashore and A.G. Wesman. New York: Psychological Corporation, 1973.
2. *Picture Frustration Study*. Author: S. Rosenzweig. Distributed by author, 1948; Indian adaptation by Uday Pareekh. Delhi: Mansayn, 1959.
3. *Children's Apperception Test (CAT)*. Authors: L. Bellack and S. Bellack. Distributed by authors; Indian adaption by Uma Chowdhury. Delhi: Mansayn, 1988.
4. *Thematic Apperception Test (TAT)*. Authors: C.D. Morgan and M.D. Murray. Cambridge, MA: Harvard University Press, 1943. Indian adaptation by Uma Chaudhury. Delhi: Mansayn.
5. *Make a Picture Story*. Author: E.S. Schneidman. New York: The Psychological Corporation, 1948.
6. *Rotter's Incomplete Sentences Blank*. Authors: J.B. Rotter and J.E. Rafferty. New York: The Psychological Corporation, 1950.
7. *Rorschach Ink Blot Test*. Author: H. Rorschach. Bern: Hans Huber Publication, 1951.
8. *Weschler's Preschool and Primary Scale of Intelligence (WPPSI)*. Author: D. Weschler. New York: The Psychological Corporation, 1963.
9. *Rorschach Psycho-diagnostic Test*. Author: Dr. Oberhulzere. Bern: Hans Huber Publication, 1942.
10. *Bhatia's Battery of Performance Tests of Intelligence under Indian Conditions*. Author: C.M. Bhatia. London: Oxford University Press, 1955.
11. *Early School Personality Questionnaire (ESPQ)*. Authors: R.W. Coan and R.B. Cattell. Champaign, IL: Institute for Personality and Ability Testing, 1966.
12. *Maudsley's Personality Inventory (MPI)*. Author: H.J. Eysenck. London: University of London Press, 1959.
13. *Culture Fair Intelligence Test*. Authors: R.B. Cattell and A.K.S Cattell. Champaign, IL: Institute for Personality and Ability Testing, 1969.
14. *Raven's Progressive Matrices*. Author: J.C. Raven. London: HK Lewis and Co. Ltd., 1958.
15. *Weschler's Intelligence Scale for Children (WISC)*. Author: D. Weschler. New York: The Psychological Corporation, 1949.
16. *Group Intelligence Test*. Author: P. Mehta. Delhi: Mansayn, 1962.
17. *Bayley's Scale of Infant Development*. Author: N. Bayley. New York: The Psychological Corporation, 1969.
18. *Kent Rosenoff Word Association Test*. Author: K. Rosenoff. Indian adaptation by B. Swami and L.N. Powar. Delhi: Mansayn, 1967.
19. *High School Personality Questionnaire (HSPQ)*. Campaign, IL: Institute for Personality and Ability Testing, 1968.
20. *Jung's Word Association Test (WAT)*. Author: C.G. Jung. Studies in World Association, Original from the University of Michigan, 1918.
21. *Pictorial Monograph of Motor and Mental Development of Indian Infants*. Auhtor: P. Pathak. Pune: Parasuram Process, 1977.

22. *16 Personality Factor Questionnaire.* Author: R.B. Cattell. Champaign, IL: Institute for Personality and Ability Testing, 1976.
23. *Draw-a-Man Test.* Author: P. Pathak. Pune: Parasuram Process, 1966.
24. *Senguin Form Board.* Authors: S.K. Goel and M. Bhargava. Agra: National Psychological Corporation, 1990.
25. *Passi Test of Creativity.* Author: V.K. Passi. Agra: National Psychological Corporation, 1978.
26. *Multidimensional Parenting Scale.* Authors: N.S. Chauhan and C.P. Khokhar. Meerut: Maapa Publications, 1985.
27. *Mohite Home Inventory.* Author: P. Mohite. Agra: National Psychological Corporation, 1989.
28. *Malin's Vineland Social Maturity Scale.* Author: A.J. Malin. *Manual for Vineland Social Maturity Scale,* Indian adaptation. Nagpur: Child Guidance Clinic, 1961.
29. *Children's Personality Questionnaire (CPQ).* Authors: B.P. Rutherford and R.B. Cattell. Champaign, IL: Institute for Personality and Ability Testing, 1968.
30. *Neuroticism and Introversion–Extroversion Inventory.* Authors: I.S. Muhar, P. Bhatia and G. Kapoor. Indian adaptation, Agra: National Psychological Corporation, 1992.
31. *Locus of Control Scale.* Authors: N. Hasnain and D.D. Joshi. Lucknow: Ankur Psychological Agency, 1992.
32. *Chadha and Ganeshan Social Intelligence Test.* Authors: N.K. Chadha and U. Ganeshan. Agra: National Psychological Corporation, 1986.
33. *Binet Simon Scale (Indian).* Author: S.K. Kulshreshtha. Allahabad: Nagri Press, 1960.
34. *Sex Behaviour Attitude Inventory.* Author: Y. Singh. Agra: National Psychological Corporation, 1977.
35. *Emotional Maturity Scale.* Authors: Y. Singh and M. Bhardwaj. Agra: National Psychological Corporation, 1984.
36. *Emotional Competence Scale.* Authors: H.C. Sharma and R. Bhardwaj. Agra: Mapal, 1995.
37. *Self-concept Questionnaire.* Author: R.K. Saraswath. Agra: National Psychological Corporation, 1994.
38. *Children's Self Concept Scale.* Author: S.P. Ahluwalia. Agra: National Psychological Corporation.
39. *Finger Dexterity Board.* Authors: Dr Jagdish and V. Bhargava. Agra: National Psychological Corporation, 1997.
40. *Developmental Assessment Scale for Indian Infants Questionnaire.* Author: P. Pathak. Baroda, 1997.

Appendix II

Samskaras	Assessment of Development	Ayurvedic Assessment	Appropriate Age	Area of Development
Jatakarma	Bio-physical development	Sensory faculties	At birth	Physical
Namkarna	Socio-psychological	Social identity	11 days to 1 year	Sociological
Nishkarmana	Sensory development	Early auditory and perceptual development	3 to 4 months	Physical
Annaprashana	Nutritional development	Initiated into supplementary weaning	5 to 6 months	Physiological
Karnavedhana	Psychological development	Release of antigens	6, 7 or 8 months	Psycho-biological
Chudakarana	Educational development	Introduction to hygienic awareness	1 to 3 years	Socio-educational
Vidyarambha	Educational development	Marking the ability to formal education	3 to 5 years	Psycho-educational
Upnayana	Socio-religious development	Formal induction as a member of the religious group	5 years	Socio-religious
Brahamcharya	Psycho-biological development	Moral restraint	5 to 21 years	Psycho-biological
Grihastha	Socio-emotional development	Procreation	21 to 50 years	Social
Vanprastha	Spiritual-emotional development	Retreat from worldly pleasures	50 to 75 years	Spiritual
Sanyasa	Spiritual development	Attainment of moksha	75+ years	Spiritual

The Meaning of Samskaras

The stages of development, as documented by Western scholars through their research, are different from the ancient Indian conceptualisation of the life cycle. The empirical data on the Indian life cycle has not been adequately documented. They, however, are very pertinent to the life situation of the Indian, especially the Hindu, as the life cycle or their stages (ashramas) are practised by most in the Hindu culture. The major exception noted is the philosophical cum behavioural characteristic of development based mainly on Ayurveda as commented upon by scholars like T.S. Saraswathi and S. Pai ('Socialisation in the Indian Context' in H.S.R. Kao and D. Sinha (eds), *Asian Perspectives on Psychology*, New Delhi: Sage Publications, 1997, pp. 74–92); S. Anandalakshmy ('The Cultural Context' in M. Swaminathan (ed.), *The First Five Years*, New Delhi: Sage Publications, 1998, pp. 272–84); M. Kapur ('Child Care in Ancient India', in J.G. Young, P. Ferrari, S. Malhotra, S. Tyano and E. Caffo (eds), *Brain, Culture and Development: Tradition and Innovation in Child and Adolescent Mental Health*, New Delhi: Macmillan, 2003); A.C. Paranjpe (*Self and Identity in Modern Psychology and Indian Thought*, New York and London: Plenum, 1998); and others. The chronological events were indexed by physical changes during the early years and related behaviour, and their accompanying rituals. Samskaras are rites implying movement from one stage of development to another.

1. The first stage is *Jatakarma*, when, at birth, the child is given a small quantity of ghee and honey mixed with gold dust. At this point the sucking reflex is observed. The event is observed for ensuring good physical development and mental health.

2. The second stage is *Namkarna* between 11 days and one year. The child is given a name after his ancestors or according to stars, or according to symbols in the horoscope. At this point, a general assessment of his physical activities is made.

3. The third stage is *Nishkarmana*. This occurs at about the third or fourth month when the child is taken outdoors to see the sun, and to the temple where temple bells are rung and chanting takes place. His visual and auditory responses are observed at these events.

4. The fourth stage is *Annaprashana*. When it is thought that the child's digestive system is strong enough, semi-solids are introduced into its diet. This event is accompanied by social religious rituals occurring between fifth and sixth months and is said to indicate that a nutritious supplement is added to the diet of the child and to wean the child from the breast.

5. The fifth stage is *Karnavedhana*. This ceremony of piercing the ears occurs at the sixth, seventh or eighth months where the child's tolerance to pain is assessed, and where, it is believed, according to Ayurvedic theory, antibodies are released into the system. This is similar to the concepts in Chinese accupunture.

6. The sixth stage is *Chudakarana*. This is a stage at which the child's head is tonsured, done between one to three years in order to assess the closure and hardening of the fontella.

7. The seventh stage is the *Vidyarambha*. A ceremony is performed between the ages of five to seven years, when the child is said to be ready for formal education.

8. The eighth stage is *Upnayana*. By about the seventh year, the sacred thread ceremony is performed indicating that the child is ready for being initiated into responsibility taking and given the status of being a member of his social group. This event is similar to the concept of formal operations of the Piagetian theory. The father performs the ceremony symbolising that the child is ready for tutelage.

9. The ninth stage is that of *Brahamcharya*, where the young boy is expected to grow into a young man through a process of induction into philosophy of life by a guru. This generally occurs among Brahmins as the child is expected to get an intensive education in the scriptures. The male child is sent to a gurukul and is expected to live a celibate life concentrating on his studies.

   The Vedas however do not emphasise the tutelage of the girl child. She is expected to be under the care and protection of the family and inducted into preparation for marriage and family responsibilities by the female members of the family.

10. The tenth stage is *Grihastha*. At this stage the young man is inducted into marriage and its related responsibilities. He becomes a 'householder'.

11. The eleventh stage is *Vanprastha*. This is the stage of gradual withdrawal from earthly pleasures and after fulfilling responsibility of a spouse and parenthood when children are married and settled. This stage is the preparation for the next and the last stage, namely, *Sanyasa*.

12. The twelfth and the last stage is that of *Sanyasa*. In this stage, the adult male, in preparation for the next incarnation, is expected to withdraw from earthly activities and devote himself to prayer, fasting, meditation and charity.

    The closest that the concept of these ashramas comes to western thinking is in the stages of life cycle as explained by Erik H. Erikson (*The Life Cycle Completed*, New York: Norton, 1982).

Glossary

Aap	respectful form of addressing a person, especially the elders
Aasmani	sky-blue colour
Abhidhamma	key Sanskrit text of Mahayana Buddhism, written by Vasubandhu
Achara	moral conduct
Adharma	improper conduct, inappropriate way of living
Adheems	schools for education, especially in the religious scriptures
Afghani	person from Afghanistan of whom quite a few reside in north India
Aga	passion
Aggarwal	a business community of north India
Agla janam	next incarnation (birth)
Ahamkara	egotism, belief of self-consciousness or 'I-ness'
Aisvarya	prosperity
Ajnana	ignorance
Akbar	one of the kings of the Mughal dynasty known for his charitable and secular vision and deeds
Almora	place in the hill state of Uttarakhand, north India
Anaisvarya	incapacities, non-prosperity
Andhrite	person of Andhra Pradesh, a state in south India (pradesh means state)
Annamaya kosa	in the Vedic philosophy, the jiva or the living being is considered to be enclosed within five sheaths (kosas), which are like the sheaths of an onion. The five sheaths are food sheath (Annamaya Kosa), vital sheath (Pranamaya Kosa), mental sheath (Manomaya Kosa), intellectual sheath (Vijnanamaya Kosa) and the bliss sheath (Anandamaya Kosa)
Ant	end

Arjun	the third among the five Pandava brothers depicted in the ancient Hindu epic, the Mahabharata; the Peerless Archer
Artha	wealth, one of the four goals of life
Arthashastra	Indian treatise on statecraft, economic policy and military strategy written by Kautilya, also known as Chanakya
Aryabhatta	ancient Indian astronomer
Arya Samaj	Hindu reform movement founded by Swami Dayananda in 1875
Ashramas	states or stage of life (in the Hindu life)
Ashtottara	offering prayers 108 times
Atma/Atman	the soul; one's 'true self' beyond identification with the phenomenal reality of worldly existence
Atmatant	the divine self
Avtaras	incarnations of God
Awas	residence
Ayahs	maids
Ayurveda	Vedic medicine, the ancient Indian medicinal system
Babu	term used for a clerical worker, mostly scribes
Bahu	daughter-in-law
Baigani	purple colour of the vegetable called eggplant
Bakra	goat; implying gullibility
Balsevika	term used for pre-school workers in rural areas
Balwadi	nursery school in rural India
Bania	class of shopkeepers, merchants belonging to the Vaishya varna (caste)
Banswara	tribal district in Rajasthan
Baudhayana	Indian mathematician-added appendices to the Vedas giving rules for the construction of altars
Bechara woh	helpless person
Bengali	native of the state of Bengal
Bhagwad Gita	scriptures, according to Lord Krishna, one of the reincarnations of the godhead in the Hindu pantheology
Bhajan mandals	prayer meetings
Bhajans	devotional songs
Bhavas	state of being or becoming
Bhil	tribe in Rajasthan
Bhokta	reaping the benefits of life as a result of experiences, positive or negative
Biradari	family kinship network
Birbal	one of members of the court of the Mughal emperor Akbar, known for his wisdom and witticisms

Brahminic	of or belonging to the Brahmin or the Brahmin varna
Brahma	godhead of the Hindu trinity governing creation
Brahmachari	male who is pursuing control of sexual energy
Brahmacharya	stage in the life cycle, usually the youth, where the male is expected to learn to control his passions especially his sexual desires
Brahmaputra	river in India
Brahmin	the priestly class among Hindus; the highest of the four varnas of Hindus
Brahmo Samaj	Hindu social reform movement founded by Raja Ram Mohan Roy
Buddhi	intellect
Chalta hai	'it is alright', a euphemism or 'life goes on' or 'life is like that'
Chappals	flip flops (slippers)
Chawal	rice
Chetna	consciousness
Chhandas	metres (poetry) for chanting Vedic hymns
Chipko movement	movement for the protection of trees, started by a group of villagers in the Uttarakhand region of India. The movement was well-known for its tactic of hugging (*chipak*) trees. 'Ecology is permanent economy' is a Chipko slogan
Chitta	mind
Cochin	commercial and port city in the state of Kerala
Coorg (now Kodagu)	hilly region in the Indian state of Karnataka
Daan	alms given in charity
Dal	lentil
Dalit movement	socio-political movement of the Dalits against various forms of exploitation, social and political discrimination
Dalits	members of the Scheduled Castes
Darsana	philosophy
Desh	native place country, geographical area
Desi	person, indigenous to his country of residence
Devis	Hindu goddesses
Dharma	right way of living or proper conduct; dharmas are codes of conduct in the Hindu way
Dharmashastras	ancient law books of Hindus, which form the basis for the social and religious values, codes of conduct for them
Dharti Mata	Mother Earth
Didi	elder sister
Diwali	Hindu religious festival where lamps are lit, firecrackers are burnt signifying joy and happiness

Dukh	sorrow
Dussehra	Hindu religious festival, celebrated to signify the victory of good over evil
Dvesa	hatred
Ganesh Chaturthi	Hindu religious festival on the birthday of Lord Ganesha
Ganesh	Hindu god venerated for prosperity
Gautam	ancient Hindu sage
Gautam's Dharmashastras	dharmashastras ascribed to Gautam, an ancient Hindu sage
Ghotuls	tribal system of education for the young
Gilli danda	Indian street game played with sticks and stones
Gita	Bhagavad Gita
Gotra	kinship groups related by endogamy
Gram sevikas	female village workers
Grama	village
Grihashastras	books for living the life of a householder
Grihastha ashrama	stage of householder
Grihastha	householder
Grihasutras	Hindu texts on domestic sacrifices and rites
Gujarat	state in west India
Gujaratis	natives of the Indian state of Gujarat
Guna	quality, positive attribute or virtue
Guru Granth Sahib	sacred book of the Sikh religion
Gurukul	residential school in which the students live in a guru's residence. The students learn from the guru and also assist him in his day-to-day life
Harijan	literally meaning 'children of god', the term was coined by Mahatma Gandhi to refer to the members of 'untouchable' castes
Harijan Sevak Samaj	social organisation founded by Mahatma Gandhi for the welfare of Harijans (lower castes)
Havan	religious ceremony where devotees pray around sacrificial fire
Hidayaat	commandments in the Quran
Himachal Pradesh	northern state in the Himalayas
Hindu dharma	tenets of the Hindu religion
Hindu	person following the Hindu religion
Hisaab kitaab	books of accounts of business people
Holi	Hindu festival celebrated with colours
Idli	rice-based south Indian food preparation

Jagirdars	landlords in pre-independent India
Jaisalmer	place/district in Rajasthan
Jajmani	reciprocal social and economic arrangement among members of a community
Jamuni	colour of a fruit called 'jamun' which is purple in colour
Janamashtami	Hindu festival celebrated on the birthday of the Hindu god Krishna
Janampatri	horoscope
Jati	caste
Jharas	people who cast away the evil spirit from those suspected of being bewitched
Jhuggis	collection of huts inhabited by the urban poor
Ji	suffix which connotes a deferential respect
Jiva	the individual self
Jnana	ultimate wisdom leading to divinity
Jyotish	astrology
Kaal	time
Kalidasa	author of many Sanskrit plays and also a poet
Kali Mata	alternate name of Goddess Durga
Kalyug	Hindu concept of the Dark Ages
Kama	pursuit of sensual pleasures—one of the Purush
Kanyadaan	ceremonial handing over of a bride in marriage by the father or the closest male relative
Kapha	one of the three doshas (energy forces) of the human body mentioned in Ayurveda
Karma	behaviour governing one's destiny
Karta	author
Karva chauth	day of full fasting by the wife done for the health and well-being of her husband
Kashmiri	native of the Indian state of Kashmir
Katha Upanishad	Hindu text describing the spiritual journey of a human being
Katkarias	small self-contained community in the erstwhile Bombay Presidency
Kauravas	group of brothers mentioned in the ancient Indian epic of Mahabharata, who wage war against another group, the Pandavas
Kautilya	author of Arthashastra, also known as Chanakya. He was prime minister to the Maurya emperor Chandragupta (340–293 BC)
Kerala	state in south India
Keralite	belonging to Kerala

Khatas	accounts
Khatri	person belonging to the Khatri community of the Kshatriya varna
Khwaja Moin-ud-din Chisti	revered Sufi saint
Kirtans	devotional songs
Kleshas	defilements of the mind
Kosas	sheaths covering the self
Kotyarchana	offering 1 crore flowers
Krishna	Hindu god, considered to be one of the avatars of Lord Vishnu
Kshatriya	belonging to the Kshatriya varna, renowned for being warriors
Kshatriya dharma	righteous acts and duties prescribed in the Vedas for the people belonging to Kshatriya varna
Kutumb	family network
Lagadha	author of *Vedanga Jyotisha*, the text on Vedic astronomy that has been ascribed to have been written in 1350 BC
Lakshman rekha	circular line drawn by Lakshmana, brother of Rama, a Hindu god so as to keep Rama's wife, Sita, protected within its parameters
Lakshmi Puja	prayers to Lakshmi, Goddess of Wealth
Lassi	Indian drink of liquefied yogurt
Lok sangraha	solidarity of the world; uplift of the world
Maan	respect
Maaro	to steal
Maaroing	stealing (*slang*)
Madhukaris	an ancient system of imparting elementary education
Madrasas	Muslim religious schools
Mahabharata	one of the two major Sanskrit epics of ancient India, the other being Ramayana
Maharishi	a great sage
Mahila mandals	women's gatherings for meetings and other developmental purposes
Manas	mind
Mannat	vow made to a particular deity asking for a favour and promising to do charity in the name of that deity when the favour is fulfilled
Manomaya kosa	one of the kosas—the mental sheath
Mantras	hymns
Manu	ancient Indian scholar cum philosopher known to have written the laws of moral conduct
Manusmriti	ancient Hindu treatise on moral laws and ethics
Marwari	class of business people of northern India

Mauryas	ancient Indian dynasty of 3rd and 4th centuries BC
Maya	concept of illusion in Hindu philosophy
Moha	infatuation or delusion
Mohallas	localities, usually in large cities
Moksha	emancipation of the soul from rebirth
Mughal	Muslim dynasty which ruled most of India from 12th century AD until the British rule
Mukhiya sevikas	female supervisor of women's and children's programmes, especially in ICDS
Naga	tribe in northeastern India living in the state of Nagaland
Naidu	Naidu is a Kshatriya sub-caste usually found in the state of Andhra Pradesh
Nair	caste/community from Kerala
Narmada Bachao Andolan	people's movement against the construction of big dams across the river Narmada which was expected to be detrimental to the communities around it
Narmada	river in central India
Naukars	servants
Navratri	Hindu festival of worship and dance comprising of nine nights of celebration as a part of Dussehra
Nawabs	noblemen emanating from the days of the Mughal period who were given these titles in recognition of their status
Naxalite	member of an extremist political group which began in the Naxalbari village in the present-day West Bengal state of India. It started as splinter group from the Communist Party of India, professing elimination of 'class enemies' to achieve its political objectives
Nazar	evil eye
Neeti	justice
NEFA	abbreviation for North East Frontier Agency, now the state of Arunachal Pradesh
Nirukta	etymological interpretation, particularly of obscure words occurring in the Vedas
Nirvana	ultimate liberation of the soul from from earthly reincarnations
Nitishastras	class of ancient Hindu texts on politics and statecraft. The most important text of this group is the Arthashastra by Kautilya
Nyaya Vaisesika	school of ancient Indian philosophy
Nyaya	name given to one of the six orthodox or astika schools of Hindu philosophy, specifically the school of logic

Pahari	hill tribesmen, a term usually used in northern India
Pali	ancient Indian language
Panchatantra	text of moral stories
Panchayat	village council
Pandal	decorated and enclosed place for conducting public functions/ ceremonies
Parivar	family
Patanjali yoga	yoga as prescribed by Patanjali, a Hindu philosopher
Patwari	village officer in charge of collecting taxes and levies
Peedas	stools
Pitta	one of the three doshas (energy forces) of the human body mentioned in Ayurveda
Pradhan	head of a village council
Prajana	consciousness
Prana	life
Pranamaya kosa	vital sheath—one of the kosas
Pratibha	flash of light (intuition)
Puja	Hindu religious ceremony
Pundits	learned people , especially relating to Brahmins
Punerjanam	reincarnation
Punjab	state in India
Punjabi	person belonging to the state of Punjab
Puranas	Hindu texts of an epic nature like Mahabharata and Ramayana
Purushartha	prescribed goals of a Hindu male
Purushastra	four goals prescribed for a Hindu
Purvamimamsa	one of the six systems of philosophy of ancient India
Quran	religious text of Islam
Raga	attachment
Ragi	type of millets, used mostly in south India
Rahukaal	inauspicious time
Raja	king
Rajas	one of the three energy forces mentioned in the scriptures
Rakshas	demon
Ramayana	famous Hindu epic, on the life of Lord Rama
Reiki	technique for healing through touch
Renas	debts
Rig Veda	first of the four Vedas
Rta	harmony

Roop	form
Roti	type of unleavened bread
Sabhyata	cultured behaviour, civilisation
Sadhu	religious mendicant
Sahibs	respectful terms used for employers
Sai Baba of Shirdi	'holy' person venerated as a saint, said to possess spiritual and healing qualities
Samajik gahayita	meta-identity (one's own perception through the eyes of the society)
Sambhar	south Indian food preparation
Samjhota	compromise, agreement
Samkhya yoga	system of yoga
Samkhya	one of the six schools of classic Indian philosophy
Samskaras	rituals and sacrifices appropriate to each life stages
Sanatana	eternal
Sanskriti	culture, refinement
Sanyasa (or sanyas)	spiritual renouncement
Sanyasa Ashrama	life stage of renunciation
Sanyasi	one who renounces worldly possessions
Satsangs	prayer gathering where devotional songs are sung and religious discourses are held
Sattva	essence
Shastras	various Hindu treatises on different subjects
Shiksha	learning, education
Shiva	one of the holy trinity of Hindu deities, god of destruction
Shivratri	Hindu religious festival, associated with Lord Shiva
Shrama	hard work or labour
Shudra	lowest of the four Hindu varnas
Siddhanta	view of a school of Indian philosophy
Smritis	ancient, sacred law codes of the Hindus
Sri Aurobindo	Indian nationalist and philosopher
Sruti	canon of Hindu sacred texts
Sukh	happiness
Suktis	good words
Sulbha Sutra	texts of rules for the construction of altars
Susral	residence of one's in-laws
Sutra	thread
Swami	spiritual guru

Tamas	quality of inertia
Tamil Nadu	state in south India
Tamilian	person belonging to the state of Tamil Nadu
Tattva-jnana	philosophical knowledge
Teej	Hindu festival
Tenali Raman	Telugu courtier known for his witticism (17th century saint poet of India)
Thanda	cool drink
Tibetan	of or belonging to Tibet
Travancore	erstwhile princely state in south India
Tulsidas	Hindi devotional poet (1532–1623)
Tum	you—informal usage
Upanishad	Hindu scriptures that form parts of the Vedas. They primarily deal with philosophy, meditation and the nature of God
Upnayana	sacred thread ceremony for male children of the Hindus
Uttaramimamsa	one of the six systems of philosophy of ancient India
Vaisheshika	ancient Hindu school of philosophy
Vaishnavite	a person of the Vaishnavite sect, worshipping Vishnu as the supreme god
Vaishya	business class/community
Vanprastha	one of the stages in the Hindu life cycle where the man detaches himself from worldly pleasures
Varahamihir	renowned astrologer and astronomer during the time of Chandragupta, the first Mauryan emperor
Varna	category of classification of Hindu people, mainly according to their occupations
Vashishtha	sage portrayed in Hindu epics
Vatta	air, one of the three doshas (energy forces) of the Ayurveda system of medicine
Vedanga	six *anga*s or parts of the Vedas
Vedanta	one of the six orthodox philosophies of Hinduism, chiefly concerned with knowledge of Brahman, the universal supreme pure being
Vedantic	of or related to the Vedanta system of philosophy
Vedic	of or belonging to the Vedas, prescribed in the Vedas
Vijnanamaya kosa	sheath of intelligence in the mental make-up of the self
Vyayvhara	behaviour, social etiquette and activities

Yaar	friend (*slang*)
Yagyavalkya	ancient Hindu sage known for his deep knowledge of the Vedas and wisdom
Yatras	religious pilgrimage
Yelamanchilli	forest where tribals eke their living from their environment
Yoga	ancient Indian spiritual practices based on Vedic science
Yogadarshana	philosophy of yoga
Yudhishtir	eldest among the Pandava brothers depicted in Mahabharata
Zamindari	landholding and tenancy system that prevailed in pre-independent India

Index

About the Author

Margaret Khalakdina has had a long and distinguished professional career as a teacher of postgraduate students and as an independent consultant. She did her doctorate from the Cornell University, and is a recipient of fellowships from Syracuse University, Altrusa International and Ford Foundation. She has been Dean of the College of Home Science at Haryana Agricultural University, and has worked on various assignments for UNICEF and WHO throughout the world.

Dr Khalakdina is the author of *Early Child Care in India*, one of the 'Early Child Care in Various Countries' series, sponsored by Russell-Sage Foundation. She has contributed to various publications such as *The First Five Years* and other related journals like *Indian Journal of Social Work* and *Journal of Human Ecology*. She is also the Founder-President of the Society for Home Scientists and Agricultural and Rural Institutions.